theoretical models and processes of reading second edition

Editors

Harry Singer, University of California at Riverside
Robert B. Ruddell, University of California at Berkeley

With a Foreword by James F. Kavanagh, Growth and Development Branch, National Institute of Child Health and Human Development, Bethesda, Maryland

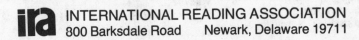

ira INTERNATIONAL READING ASSOCIATION
800 Barksdale Road   Newark, Delaware 19711

INTERNATIONAL READING ASSOCIATION

Copyright 1976 by the
International Reading Association, Inc.
Library of Congress Cataloging in Publication Data
Main entry under title:
Theoretical models and processes of reading.
   Includes bibliographies and index.
   1. Reading—Congresses.   I. Singer, Harry.
II. Ruddell, Robert B.
LB1049.95.T43   1976   428'.4   76-2732
ISBN 0-87207-432-3
Second printing, November 1976

Contents

Perception

Word Recognition

Cognition

Affect

Cultural Interaction

Section Three   MODELS

Psycholinguistic Models

v

The preparation of this monograph was supported in part by the
National Institute of Child Health and Human Development, NIH.

Foreword

In the Foreword to the first edition of *Theoretical Models and Processes of Reading* there appeared a brief historical discussion of the national interest in the health problems of children which provided the impetus for the establishment of the National Institute of Child Health and Human Development (NICHD) in 1963. At that time President John F. Kennedy assigned to the Institute, as a part of the National Institutes of Health, the important task of encouraging and supporting both biomedical and behavioral research concerning the nature of human development across the life span and upon certain complex health problems affecting children and their parents.

The Foreword to that edition also reported that in 1965 the members of the first National Advisory Child Health and Human Development Council singled out the area of reading for special attention and urged the Institute to accelerate its support of research in this area. These senior non-Federal advisors to the Institute expressed deep concern for the large number of otherwise normal children who were unable to take full advantage of the opportunities provided by United States schools because of inadequate reading ability. The Council recommended that the Institute aggressively search for appropriate ways to encourage and support fundamental research in reading. The Council was convinced that an understanding of what may interfere with normal reading might be achieved through a better understanding of the basic processes involved and by determining how this complex language-related skill is normally acquired.

Since the establishment of the Institute, the Growth and Development Branch, an extramural program area responsible for the support of research related to the growth and development of humans from infancy to maturity, has been the focal point for all NICHD activities related to reading.

In addition to a variety of other "programing" activities designed to stimulate reading research, the Growth and Development Branch sponsored an informal conference in New Orleans in 1968 on the Reading Process. This meeting and subsequent publication (*The Reading Process*, Ed. J. F. Kavanagh, GPO, 1968) surfaced a number of theories and models of the reading process and thus led to G&D Branch involvement with the 1969 symposium on "Theoretical Models and Processes of Reading" and the IRA monograph which followed.

The "no-papers" New Orleans conference also prompted several participants to discuss the differences between language learned through the eye and through the ear. Their discussions continued after the meeting and encouraged NICHD to hold a formal conference in 1971 to examine the contrast between the ease with which most children acquire speech and the difficulty many have with reading. (*Language by Ear and by Eye*, Ed. J. F. Kavanagh and I. G. Mattingly, The MIT Press, Cambridge, Mass., 1972).

With continuing interest in language through several modalities, late in 1973 the G&D Branch brought another group of specialists together to talk about the function of speech in language. The conferees attempted to determine how and within what limits the acoustic signal, the articulation that produces it, and the phonetic message it conveys are related to the rest of the language system. The edited proceedings of this meeting, the fifth book in our Communicating by Language series, appear in *The Role of Speech in Language* (J. F. Kavanagh and J. E. Cutting, The MIT Press, 1975).

In 1975 the NICHD reorganized its total extramural effort into two divisions, the well-established Center for Population Research and a new Center for Research for Mothers and Children. The CRMC consists of three program areas concerned with child development: the Mental Retardation Branch, the Perinatal Biology and Infant Mortality Branch, and the Growth and Development Branch.

The Growth and Development Branch, while continuing to support fundamental research related to normal growth and development, has identified and assigned high priority to several research problem areas. One is related to the unanswered, researchable questions dealing with specific learning disabilities including reading disorders. The Institute currently provides more than 15 million dollars in support of projects related to reading.

The Growth and Development Branch welcomes this opportunity to participate in the publication of a book which is designed primarily to reveal what is now known about the reading process and, by raising important questions, to stimulate useful research.

JAMES F. KAVANAGH

Preface

> And so to completely analyze what we do when we read would almost be the acme of a psychologist's achievements, for it would be to describe very many of the most intricate workings of the human mind, as well as to unravel the tangled story of the most remarkable specific performance that civilization has learned in all its history.
>
> Edmund Burke Huey

This quotation, taken from Huey's classic book on the psychology and pedagogy of reading, was written over sixty years ago.[1] It appeared in the first edition of this volume and still provides a pertinent introduction to the second edition which includes current theories, models, and processes involved in the reading act.

The first edition of *Theoretical Models and Processes of Reading*, which began as a memorial symposium to Professor Jack A. Holmes, has served a useful function as a textbook in many graduate courses in education and psychology. Consequently, we have purposefully attempted to make the second edition more useful as a textbook.

Altogether, we made a number of significant changes in this edition: We invited Dr. Constance M. McCullough, Past President of the International Reading Association and a reading theorist herself, to lead off with an introductory overview.[2,3] Approximately 75 percent of the selections are new to this revision. Articles have been organized and grouped into three sections: processes, models, and issues in research and teaching. At least one current research article illustrates a mode of inquiry and a heuristic procedure in each process area. Models are now grouped into

---

[1] Edmund Burke Huey. *The Psychology and Pedagogy of Reading.* Cambridge, Massachusetts: M.I.T. Press, 1968. First published by Macmillan in 1908.

[2] Constance M. McCullough. Balanced reading development. In Helen M. Robinson (Ed.), *Innovation and Change in Reading Instruction*, Sixty-Seventh Yearbook of the National Society for the Study of Education, Part II. Chicago, Illinois: University of Chicago Press, 1968, 320-356.

[3] Constance M. McCullough. What teachers should know about language and thought. In R. Hodges and R. Rudorf (Eds.), *Learning to Read.* New York: Houghton Mifflin, 1971, 202-215.

ix

psycholinguistic, information processing, developmental, and affective categories. A new section has been added on "Teaching and Research Issues." This section concludes with a critique of inferences derived from theories of development and applied to processes of reading. A set of focusing questions has been placed at the beginning of each of the three major sections. Finally, an author and subject index completes the volume.

Over the past decade, theories have been formulated and research has been conducted at a rapid pace in the psychology and pedagogy of reading. If this volume provides further stimulation to theory formulation and serves to augment research productivity, it will have satisfied our immediate purpose: to improve understanding of the nature of reading. Moreover, further development of good theory and stimulation of research will contribute to our more practical purposes: to improve instruction in reading and to increase the level of literacy in the United States.[4] For we agree with Professor Holmes' frequent quotation of the eminent social psychologist, Professor Kurt Lewin, that what is most practical is a good theory.

We wish to thank our contributors for their theoretical and research contributions. We also express our appreciation to the publishers who granted permission to reprint articles, often without any fee. Mrs. Faye R. Branca, IRA Professional Publications Editor, was instrumental in securing this cooperation. She worked on this revision, as she did on the original edition, from the manuscript stage of development to the completed publication. We also appreciate the enormous and onerous task of indexing done by Hilda Stauffer, Patricia Connolly, and Prudence Blades. Last, we wish to thank our wives and children, Terri, Deborah, and Abraham Singer and Annette, Amy, and Bobby Ruddell for their patience and consideration as we worked on this revision.

HARRY SINGER and ROBERT B. RUDDELL

---

[4]John Downing. *Comparative Reading.* New York: Macmillan, 1973.

Section One

INTRODUCTION

Pioneers of Research in Reading

CONSTANCE M. MCCULLOUGH
Professor Emeritus
California State University at San Francisco

The first edition of *Theoretical Models and Processes of Reading,* which appeared in 1970, was dedicated to Jack Alroy Holmes (1911-1967), Professor of Education and Research Psychologist in the Institute of Human Development at the University of California at Berkeley. The dedication described him as "a theorist, researcher, and teacher."

One of his distinguished contributions to the psychology of reading was his Substrata Factor Theory (1953), which made headlines throughout the United States when he reported it at the St. Louis Convention of IRA in 1961. One of its effects was to spur research scholars to generate additional research-based theories of the components of reading and the process of engaging in it.

That first edition of the present book filled a need. In many institutions it became the major textbook for a new course of the same title. Stocks of the volume were quickly depleted. In the United States, a relatively affluent society, there still were children and adults who were unsuccessful in learning how to read; yet there were elaborate curriculum guides and an abundance of books to read and instructional materials from which to choose. All of the attractiveness which money could buy beckoned the reader. Researchers were in abundance and more studies of reading instruction and reading materials appeared every year. But something was missing.

Existing concepts of reading, upon which materials and choices of aspects to be researched were based, were inheritances from established practices from many cultures. (According to the latest archeological evidence, the first invention of notation and the consequent need to transmit its meaning to another generation could have occurred at least 300,000 years ago.) Many conflicting opinions existed on reading, but the theoretical basis for many practices lacked the support of a body of sound research evidence. There was not even a good inventory of existing theories with research which could be thought to corroborate each one.

If the field of reading was ever to make firm progress in perfecting the transmission of literacy, it would have to proceed from theories backed by substantial evidence and tailored to the code and the society. This implies that researchers must turn from random choices of areas of investigation toward participation in research ventures converging on the validation of a given theory. The relationships of one theory to another must also be determined, for one theory is not enough to account for "the most remarkable specific performance that civilization has learned in all its history."[1]

The Second Edition

In the long history of literate man, there were many pioneer teachers and philosophers. G. D. Sharma, our Indian correspondent in Mauritius and a Sanskrit scholar, quotes Manu, the Code Giver, as having written in his *Manusmriti,* Chapter 12, Verse 103: "Literates are better than illiterates, retainers [who can recollect] are better than literates, thinkers [who understand, interpret, and judge] are better than the retainers, and those who use [the learning] are better than the thinkers—and decidedly best of all."

Sharma writes: "This defines reading so well that it seems to be almost corresponding to Dr. Russell's formula."[2] Manu lived before 5,000 B.C., and thus about 7,000 years before modern research could assess this wisdom.

The second edition of *Theoretical Models and Processes of Reading* is dedicated to pioneers in research on reading and in theories about reading, upon whose shoulders current researchers (and their teachers' teachers' teachers) stand. Throughout this book, reference is made to a few of their many studies. It is an embarrassment to this writer to write so little after the name of each of these giants, but this is only an introduction, not an encyclopaedia. The names are listed here roughly in order of the dates of the studies cited:

Emile Javal, whose study of the saccadic movements of the reading eye was published in 1878.

James McKeen Cattell, whose discovery (1885) that it takes longer to read letters than to read words gave status to the whole-word approach.

---

[1] Edmund Burke Huey. *The Psychology and Pedagogy of Reading.* Cambridge, Massachusetts: M.I.T. Press, 1968. First published by Macmillan in 1908.

[2] David H. Russell. *Children Learn to Read.* Boston: Ginn, 1961.

Edmund B. Huey, who observed (1908) that "we read by phrases, words, or letters as may serve our purpose best. But . . . the reader's acquirement of ease and power in reading comes through increasing ability to read in larger units" (p. 116).

Edward L. Thorndike, whose zest in exploding clichés (practice makes perfect) influenced learning theory, whose vocabulary studies (1944) were landmarks, and whose observations and insights into readers' comprehension errors (1917) are receiving renewed appreciation.

Guy T. Buswell, who studied the eye-voice span in reading (1920) and discovered that difficulties in the recognition of meaning are reflected in the character of eye movements.

Charles H. Judd, who, with Buswell (1922), studied various types of silent reading and found that readers change their patterns of eye movement behavior according to their purposes and the demands of the task, that numerous irregular eye movements indicate that the reader is having trouble in mentally parsing the sentence. (If linguistic science had reached a helpful stage at that time, Judd, Buswell, and Gray could have advanced the field by fifty years.)

James M. McCallister, whose study of content area reading in the secondary schools (1930) led to the publication of the first book on reading at that level (*Remedial and Corrective Instruction in Reading.* New York: Appleton, 1936).

Miles A. Tinker, author of more than one hundred laboratory studies of reading eye movements under various conditions, whose summary of research (1958) contained the conclusion that training readers to be more rhythmical in their eye movements did not lead to increased reading efficiency and/or comprehension.

Ernest Horn, whose valuable insights[3] include the following statement: "[The author] does not really convey ideas to the reader; he merely stimulates him to construct them out of his own experience. If the concept is . . . new to the reader, its construction more nearly approaches problem solving than simple association."

Ruth M. Strang, whose many trail-blazing contributions in reading interests, diagnosis, and evaluation included interview techniques as a mode of investigation, and whose *Explorations in Reading Patterns* (1942) was a clinical equivalent to substrata theory.

William S. Gray, who did research in such areas as readability (with B. Leary, 1935), vocabulary (with E. Holmes, 1938), and adult reading patterns (with B. Rogers, 1956) and who crowned decades of

[3] Ernest Horn. *Methods of Instruction in the Social Studies.* New York: Scribners, 1937, 154.

reporting and evaluating research studies related to reading with a theory and model on process.

Arthur I. Gates, whose numerous research studies in reading, spelling, and evaluation set a standard of quality in behavioral science research in design, execution, and interpretation.

Luther C. Gilbert, whose many studies of the eye movements of readers of all ages produced theories which influenced research and instruction such as the meaning of saccadic movements (1959), the persistence of characteristic eye movements in a given individual (longitudinal study), and the effect of listening to oral reading while looking at the page (1940).

David H. Russell, whose research studies in spelling (with A. I. Gates, 1937), vocabulary (1954), and children's thinking (1956) were among many original contributions.

Nila Banton Smith, whose classic *American Reading Instruction* (now published by IRA) follows the effects of theories in the classroom and who also conducted pioneer research in reading in the content areas.

Jack A. Holmes, whose teaching and substrata factor theory (1953) generated renewed and broad interest in the development and testing of theories of reading.

The above comments on each of these pioneers are meager tokens of their astounding productivity over lifetimes of dedication and ingenuity. Awesome is the word for their perception of the groundwork which had to be laid by someone before the field could function with any confidence in the wisdom of its choices. Very versatile people, they could and did make contributions to fields other than reading. It is fortunate for the world that they were so generous to this field in practice, in theory, and in the transmission of their skills, insights, and zeal to future researchers. But for them, this volume would not now exist.

The Reader

This book is a growing experience for readers, teachers of reading, researchers, writers, diagnosticians, and those who plan or administer reading programs. Every act, every thought which we employ in dealing with human beings as readers—teaching them, diagnosing them, prescribing for them, evaluating them, choosing for them or letting them choose for themselves—is expressive of a theory about what reading is, of what it is composed, what supports its being, how it can be engaged in successfully, and how its cultivation can be fostered. Some of us think that theory is one thing and practice is another. Not so. Every practice is expressive of one or more theories. The reading of this book will help all of us, whatever our sophistication, to grow a little more circumspect and discerning as readers and contributors to the literacy of others.

As we read the articles, there will be the temptation to wax inordinately fond of one point of view or another and to confine our allegiance to it. It is a temptation to be resisted for, among other things, reading is a universe of dynamic relationships. (It is not in a universe of galaxies and comets for nothing.) It is not even so simple as a hen's egg, which may be mistaken for a circle when viewed from one position.

Neither, however, should we decide that a point of view is completely worthless. These ideas are to be reflected upon and held up to our own experience, so that we can add dimensions to our own conceptions. Our oversights (inadvertent omissions) about the nature of reading continue to obstruct our progress.

In the First Grade Studies a few years ago, which compared different ways to teach beginning reading, greater variability was found among *teachers* in the results obtained, whatever the approach, than among *approaches*. A prevalent interpretation of this finding is that, since teachers (not approaches) make the greater difference, a teacher should choose and use a variety of approaches. This decision presupposes that if one approach which did not make so great a difference was somehow insufficient, several such insufficient approaches—end to end, simultaneous, stirred and served, or presented separately in an inviting smorgasbord—would create a sufficiency.

But *suppose* the truth is that all of the approaches contain many of the same kinds of insufficiency. Suppose none of the materials, procedures, strategies, nor recommended teaching techniques contain essentials yet to be discovered in a still-developing field. Even psychology, upon which teachers of reading and producers of materials have greatly depended, is a relatively young science. Linguistics as applied to reading is about fifteen years old. Neurologists are still making basic discoveries. Sociologists are still debating and researching the effects of reading materials.

What if the "better" reading teachers have insights they have never been taught—insights which result in behaviors which supplement the insufficient, established offerings of the present time? What if the concerned reader, reading this book, begins to be aware of what some of those insights are? What if he sees ways of making room for their use in a curriculum crowded with insufficiencies? What if he learns that he has been operating as though all was known that was needed to be known in the field of reading; that actually he may never have been impressed by the discoveries by pioneers before his time; and that discoveries have been made during his teaching career which, had he known them promptly, would have been reason to experiment and explore with his students rather than to follow customary patterns? What if the producer of materials begins to see the wisdom in altering practices which previously have appeared to be right and fixed for all time? What if the researcher sees the importance of joining others to converge on critical truths about reading behavior, given certain linguistic constraints?

The power of this book to release and direct the power of the readers it attracts (or snares in courses) may well eject us out of the slow spiral of repeated returns to old solutions of old problems into a more direct course of progress. Researchers may consult teachers and teachers may consult researchers.[4] The more the teachers understand the frontier thinking, the more creative and helpful they can be in exploring practical solutions to problems. The more the researchers talk directly with teachers and study their classroom situations, the more they will understand about the realities of learning and teaching reading and the more they will learn to make themselves understood. Teachers will not find themselves ten to a hundred years behind the times for want of communication. Researchers will not expend their precious energies on overworked areas.

Some of the research cited in the articles shows differences between the behaviors of children and those of adults in reading. The thoughtful reader will be given to wonder whether there is a relationship between how and what we have taught the child and what he is unable to do. Undoubtedly, some of these differences are created by adult imposed emphases and adult inspired misconceptions of the reading task.

Certainly, no thoughtful reader can leave this book without wondering how a child can learn to read as a skillful reader reads, when instruction focuses on letter-sound correspondences, word form, word meaning, and questions on the meaning of what was read. If the child is led to believe that sounds and meanings of words are all that is needed to produce comprehension of natural reading material, he does not realize what else he must do, and what he must do instead of stringing words together. The successful teacher has been doing something which has failed to occur to most of us. The presentation in this book of a hundred years of research pointing to neglected features in the reading process is suggestive of reforms long overdue.

Editors Harry Singer and Robert Ruddell are to be commended for a masterful job in selecting articles for this volume. The early pioneers would approve.

---

[4] Jeanne Chall. Keynote Speech: Reading and Development. Twentieth Annual Convention, International Reading Association, New York City, 1975.

The Nature of the Reading Process*

JOHN B. CARROLL**
Educational Testing Service
Princeton, New Jersey

As you silently read this very paragraph, what are you doing? If you are a skilled reader and are attending carefully to what this paragraph is trying to say, you will notice the following. First, what are your eyes doing? Moving together in a swift and well-coordinated way, your eyes are making a series of fixations, jumping from place to place on the page of print. The jumps are exceedingly rapid; you see little while your eyes are jumping. What is important are the fixations, when your eyes come to rest. Most of these fixations are actually on or close to the line of print, but unless you are reading quite slowly you cannot easily predict or control where your eyes will fixate. The fixations are usually quite short in duration; each one will last about one-quarter of a second on the average.

Usually the fixations progress from left to right along the first line of print, then back to the beginning of the next line and again from left to right across the line, and so on. For the average adult reader there will be about two fixations per inch of ordinary type like this. Some of these fixations may be very brief, amounting to minor adjustments in order to bring the print better into view. During most of the fixations, you receive an impression of a certain amount of printed material; that is, you instantaneously perceive and recognize one or more words, perhaps up to four or five in some cases. You are more likely to recognize the words that are in the immediate area of fixation; words outside this immediate area may be less well recognized, but some of them have been recognized in a previous fixation, and others may be more clearly recognized in a future fixation. Some of the words may never be clearly recognized, but you apprehend enough of the stimulus to fill them in from the general drift of what you are reading.

---

*Prepared by the author for the Advisory Committee on Dyslexia and Related Reading Disorders.

**Now Kenan Professor of Psychology and Director of the L. L. Thurstone Psychometric Laboratory, University of North Carolina at Chapel Hill.

Let us just think about this process of instantaneous word recognition. Most of the words you see are words you have seen many times before; even though in actuality they may be relatively rare, they are familiar enough to you to permit "instantaneous" recognition. Of course recognition is not really instantaneous; it takes a certain amount of time. Experiments in which words are exposed very briefly show that common words can be recognized quite accurately in less than 1/10 of a second; even words that are quite rare can be recognized with at least 50 percent accuracy in exposures of about 1/5 of a second. During the average fixation lasting 1/4 of a second it is often possible to take in several words. The point is that most words are recognized extremely rapidly. If you are a skilled reader you do not have to stop to figure out the pronunciation of a familiar word from its spelling; you are hardly conscious of the spelling at all. Still less do you attend to the particular phonetic values of the letters; in reading the word *women* it would scarcely occur to you to note that the "o" in the first syllable stands for a sound that rhymes with /i/ in *whim.* The printed word *women* is a gestalt-like total stimulus that immediately calls to mind the spoken word that corresponds to it—or if not the spoken word itself, some underlying response which is also made when the word is spoken. As a skilled reader, you can consider yourself lucky to have a large "sight" vocabulary.

The actual process by which we recognize words is not well understood, simply because the whole process of "pattern perception," as it is called, is one of the most mysterious problems in psychology. How, for example, do we recognize a table, a goblet, or a flagpole for what it is, regardless of the angle of regard? Nevertheless, it is a simple fact that we *can* learn to recognize words even though the words may be printed in different typefaces or written in different cursive styles, and in different sizes. Now even though word recognition is rapid, it obviously depends to a large extent on cues from the letters composing the word. There is little confusion among such highly similar items as *cob, rob, mob,* and *nob* even in fast single exposures. We do know that in recognizing longer words, the letters standing at the beginning and end are more critical than letters in the middle, for in fast exposures these middle letters can sometimes be altered or replaced without this being noticed by the reader. In ordinary reading we frequently fail to notice words that contain printer's errors. But there is little evidence to support the idea that a mature reader recognizes words merely by their outlines or general shape. It is unlikely that if you see the shape ⌐⊃ you will recognize the word *dog*; you might just as well think it to be *day* or *dug.* Beginning readers sometimes use mere shape cues in trying to recognize words, but they will be overwhelmed with confusion if they depend solely on such cues apart from the recognition of the letters themselves. In the mature reader the process of rapid word recognition seems to depend upon his ability to integrate the information provided by the separate letters composing the word, some letters being more critical as cues than others. Because the recognizability of a word is apparently correlated rather highly with its frequency of use, word perception seems to be a skill that depends upon large amounts of practice and exposure.

Suppose, however, that the skilled reader comes to a word that he has never seen before, like *dossal, cunctation,* or *latescent,* or an unfamiliar proper name like *Vukmanovich* or *Sbarra.* Though the skilled reader can hardly be said to "recognize" a word he has never seen before, he nevertheless recognizes elements of it—letters and patterns of letters that give him reasonably good cues as to how the word should be pronounced. *Dossal* may be recognized as similar to *fossil* and pronounced to rhyme with it, the first letter cuing the /f/ sound. *Cunctation* may give a little more difficulty but be recognized as somewhat similar to *punctuation* and at the same time to *mutation*; by following the total pattern of cues the reader may be able to infer the correct pronunciation. *Latescent* will probably be recognized not as a compound of *late* and *scent,* but as a member of a family of words like *quiescent, fluorescent,* etc. Somewhat the same principles apply to the reading of foreign proper names; even if he is not familiar with the foreign language involved, the skilled reader will be sensitive to the possible values of the letters and letter-combinations in the name, and come up with a reasonable pronunciation.

It should be noted that thus far we have been speaking of the recognition of words as particular combinations of letters. Actually, in English there are numerous instances of homographs—words that are pronounced in different ways depending on their use. The word "read" is an interesting example: in the context *to read* it rhymes with *bead*, but in the context *to have read,* it rhymes with *bed*. The skilled reader instantaneously interprets the word in its proper "reading" or pronunciation depending upon the context—i.e., the surrounding words and their meanings.

This takes us, in fact, to the next stage of our analysis of the reading process. As you take in material recognized in the succession of rapid fixations that is characteristic of skilled reading, it somehow merges together in such a way as to build up in your mind an impression of a meaningful message—a message that is in many ways analogous to the message you would apprehend if someone read the paragraph aloud to you, with all its proper inflections and accents. Some people report that as they read they can "hear" (in the form of internal auditory images) the message as it might be spoken; at least they report that they "hear" snatches of such a message. Other readers feel that they apprehend a meaning from the printed message directly—that is, without the intervention of any auditory images. In slow readers, or even in skilled readers reading very difficult material, one may notice slight articulatory movements that suggest that the reader is trying to pronounce the words subvocally.

The process of scanning a paragraph for a meaningful message does not, of course, always run smoothly. As one reads, there may be momentary lapses of attention (which can be due to lack of interest, distractions, or even stimulation from the content itself), or of comprehension (which can be due to the difficulty of the material, poor writing, or other conditions). The process of comprehension seems to have some influence on the movements of the eyes: when the reader fails to attend or comprehend, his eyes may "regress," moving back to fixate on a portion of the material already scanned. Difficulties in recognizing particular words may cause the eyes to dwell on or around a particular point in the text longer than the usual amount of time. There are large differences among individuals in all the reading processes we have mentioned. Some readers can read with markedly fewer fixations per line; some read with an abnormally high number of fixations per line and exhibit many more regressions than normal. Few individuals have the same pattern of eye movements, even when they read at approximately the same speed. Obviously, there are wide individual differences in rate and accuracy of comprehension.

The *essential* skill in reading is getting meaning from a printed or written message. In many ways this is similar to getting meaning from a *spoken* message, but there are differences, because the cues are different. Spoken messages contain cues that are not evident in printed messages, and conversely. In either case, understanding language is itself a tremendous feat, when one thinks about it. When you get the meaning of a verbal message, you have not only recognized the words themselves; you have interpreted the words in their particular grammatical functions, and you have somehow apprehended the general grammatical patterning of each sentence. You have unconsciously recognized what words or phrases constitute the subjects and predicates of the sentence, what words or phrases modify those subjects or predicates, and so on. In addition, you have given a "semantic" interpretation of the sentence, assigning meanings to the key words in the sentence. For example, in reading the sentence "He understood that he was coming tonight" you would know to whom each "he" refers, and you would interpret the word *understood* as meaning "had been caused to believe" rather than "comprehended." Somehow you put all these things together in order to understand the "plain sense" of what the message says.

Even beyond getting the simple meaning of the material you are reading, you are probably reacting to it in numerous ways. You may be trying to evaluate it for its truth, validity, significance, or importance. You may be checking it against your own experience or knowledge. You may find that it is reminding you of previous thoughts or experiences, or you may be starting to think about its implications for your future actions. You may be making inferences or drawing conclusions from what you read that go far beyond what is explicitly stated in the text. In doing any or all of these things, you are "reasoning" or "thinking." Nobody can tell you exactly what to think; much of your thinking will be dependent upon your particular background and experience. At the same time, some thinking is logical and justified by the facts and ideas one reads, while other kinds of thinking are illogical and not adequately justified by the facts and ideas one reads. One aspect of a mature reader's skill consists in his being able to think about what he reads in a logical and well-informed way. This aspect of reading skill sometimes takes years to attain.

We have described the process of reading in the skilled reader—a process that is obviously very complex. How is this process learned or attained?

As in the case of any skill, reading skill is not learned all at once. It takes a considerable amount of time. Furthermore, the process of learning to read is *not* simply a slow motion imitation of the mature reading process. It has numerous components, and each component has to be learned and practiced.

There are probably a great many ways to attain reading skill, depending upon the order in which the various components are learned and mastered. It may be the case that some ways are always better than others. On the other hand, children differ in their aptitudes, talents, and inclinations so much that it may also be the case that a particular way of learning is better for one child while another way is better for another child. It all depends upon which components of reading skill a given child finds easier to learn at a given stage of his development. In referring to different orders in which component skills would be learned, we do not mean to imply a lock-step procedure in which the child first learns and masters one skill, then goes on to learn and master another skill, and so on. Actually, a child can be learning a number of skills simultaneously, but will reach mastery of them at different periods in his development. From the standpoint of the teacher, this means that different skills may need to be emphasized at different periods, depending upon the characteristics of the individual child. This is particularly true in the case of the child who is having difficulty in learning to read.

Let us try to specify the components of reading skill. Some of these components come out of our analysis of the mature reading process; others out of a further analysis of *those* components.

1. *The child must know the language that he is going to learn to read.* Normally, this means that the child can speak and understand the language at least to a certain level of skill before he starts to learn to read, because the purpose of reading is to help him get messages from print that are similar to the messages he can already understand if they are spoken. But language learning is a lifelong process, and normally there are many aspects of language that the individual learns solely or mainly through reading. And speaking and understanding the language is not an absolute prerequisite for beginning to learn to read; there are cases on record of children who learn to read before they can speak, and of course many deaf children learn the language only through learning to read. Foreign-born children sometimes learn English mainly through reading. Children who, before they begin to read, do not know the language, or who only understand but do not speak, will very likely require a mode of instruction specially adapted to them.

2. *The child must learn to dissect spoken words into component sounds.* In order to be able to use the alphabetic principle by which English words are spelled, he must be able to recognize the separate sounds composing a word and the temporal order in which they are spoken—the consonants and vowels that compose spoken words. This does not mean that he must acquire a precise knowledge of phonetics, but it does mean that he must recognize those aspects of speech sound that are likely to be represented in spelling. For example, in hearing the word *straight,* the child must be able to decompose the sounds into the sequence /s, t, r, ey, t/.

3. *The child must learn to recognize and discriminate the letters of the alphabet in their various forms (capitals, lower case letters, printed, and cursive).* (He should also know the names and alphabetic ordering of the letters.) This skill is required if the child is to make progress in finding correspondences between letters and sounds.

4. *The child must learn the left-to-right principle by which words are spelled and put in order in continuous text.* This is, as we have noted, a very general principle, although there are certain aspects of letter-sound correspondences that violate the principle—e.g., the reverse order of *wh* in representing the sound cluster /hw/.

5. *The child must learn that there are patterns of highly probable correspondence between letters and sounds, and he must learn those patterns of correspondence that will help him recognize words that he already knows in his spoken language or that will help him determine the pronunciation of unfamiliar words.* There are few if any letters in English orthography that always have the same sound values; nevertheless, spellings tend to give good clues to the pronunciation of words. Often a letter will have highly predictable sound values if it is considered in conjunction with surrounding letters. Partly through direct instruction and partly through a little-understood process of inference, the normal child can fairly readily acquire the ability to respond to these complex patterns of letter-sound correspondences.

6. *The child must learn to recognize printed words from whatever cues he can use—their total configuration, the letters composing them, the sounds represented by those letters, and/or the meanings suggested by the context.* By "recognition" we mean not only becoming aware that he has seen the word before, but also knowing the pronunciation of the word. This skill is one of the most essential in the reading process, because it yields for the reader the equivalent of a speech signal.

7. *The child must learn that printed words are signals for spoken words and that they have meanings analogous to those of spoken words. While decoding a printed message into its spoken equivalent, the child must be able to apprehend the meaning of the total message in the same way that he would apprehend the meaning of the corresponding spoken message.* As in the case of adult reading, the spoken equivalent may be apprehended solely internally, although it is usual, in early reading efforts, to expect the child to be able to read aloud, at first with much hesitation, but later with fluency and expression.

8. *The child must learn to reason and think about what he reads, within the limits of his talent and experience.*
It will be noticed that each of these eight components of learning to read is somehow involved in the adult reading process—knowing the language, dissecting spoken words into component sounds, and so forth. Adult reading is skilled only because all the eight components are so highly practiced that they merge together, as it were, into one unified performance. The well-coordinated, swift eye movements of the adult reader are a result, not a cause, of good reading; the child does not have to be *taught* eye movements and therefore we have not listed eye-coordination as a component skill. Rather, skilled eye movements represent the highest form of the skill we have listed as 4—the learning of the left-to-right principle. The instantaneous word recognition ability of the mature reader is the highest form of the skill we have listed as

6—recognition of printed words from whatever cues are available, and usually this skill in turn depends upon the mastery of some of the other skills, in particular 5—learning patterns of correspondence between letters and sounds. The ability of the adult reader to apprehend meaning quickly is an advanced form of skill 7, and his ability to think about what he reads is an advanced form of skill 8.

The "great debate" about how reading should be taught is really a debate about the *order* in which the child should be started on the road toward learning each of the skills. Few will question that mature reading involves all eight skills; the only question is which skills should be introduced and mastered first. Many points of view are possible. On the one hand there are those who believe that the skills should be *introduced* in approximately the order in which they have been listed; this is the view of those who believe that there should be an early emphasis on the decoding of print into sound via letter-sound relations. On the other hand, there are those who believe that the skills should be introduced approximately in the following order:

1. The child should learn the language he is going to read.
6. The child should learn to recognize printed words from whatever cues he can use, but initially only from total configurations.
7. The child should learn that printed words are signals for spoken words, and that meanings can be apprehended from these printed words.
8. The child must learn to reason and think about what he reads.
4. The child should learn the left-to-right principle, but initially only as it applies to complete words in continuous text.
3. The child should learn to recognize and discriminate the letters of the alphabet.
2. The child should learn to dissect spoken words into component sounds.
5. The child should learn patterns of correspondence between letters and sounds, to help him in the advanced phases of skill 6.

This latter view is held by those who argue that there should be an early emphasis on getting the meaning from print, and that the child should advance as quickly as possible toward the word-recognition and meaning-apprehension capacities of the mature reader. Skills 2, 3, and 5 are introduced only after the child has achieved considerable progress towards mastery of skills 4, 6, 7, and 8.

These are the two main views about the process of teaching reading. If each one is taken quite strictly and seriously, there can be very clear differences in the kinds of instructional materials and procedures that are used. It is beyond our scope to discuss whether the two methods differ in effectiveness. We would emphasize, rather, that methods may differ in effectiveness from child to child. Furthermore, it is possible to construct other reasonable orders in which the various components of reading skill can be introduced to the child. There is currently a tendency to interlace the approaches distinguished above in such a way that the child can attain rapid sight recognition of words at the same time that he is learning letter-sound correspondences that will help him "attack" words that he does not already know.

For the child who is having difficulty in learning to read, it may be necessary to determine exactly which skills are causing most difficulty. The dyslexic child may be hung up on the acquisition of just one or two skills. For example, he may be having particular trouble with skill 3—the recognition and discrimination of the letters of the alphabet, or with skill 2—the dissection of spoken words into component sounds. On determining what skills pose obstacles for a particular child, it is usually necessary to give special attention to those skills while capitalizing on those skills which are easier for the child to master.

Uncertainties and Research Problems

The above description of the nature of the reading process is based on the findings of nearly three-quarters of a century of research. A good deal is known about reading behavior, yet there are many questions that have not been answered with precision and certainty. We shall list the most important of these.

Questions about the Mature Reading Process

1. How does the individual's ability to recognize words instantaneously develop? What cues for word recognition are most important? How and when does awareness of spelling clues and inner speech representation recede, if at all? What is the extent of the sight vocabulary of the mature reader? (It should be noted that most studies of word recognition processes have been conducted with adults; there is need for developmental studies in which word recognition processes would be investigated over different chronological age levels.)

2. How do skilled readers process unfamiliar words? To what extent, and how, do they use patterns of letter-sound correspondences?

3. How do skilled readers find the proper readings of homographs and other types of ambiguous words?

4. What are the detailed psychological processes by which skilled readers comprehend the simple meaning of what they read? In what way do lexico-semantic, syntactical, and typographical factors interact to yield this comprehension?

5. How are eye movements controlled by comprehension processes, and how does the individual develop skill in scanning print?

6. How does the mature reader acquire skill in reasoning and inferential processes?

7. What are the major sources of individual differences in rate and accuracy of comprehension in mature readers?

Questions about Certain Components of Reading Skill
as They Affect Learning

1. In what way does knowledge of the spoken language interact with learning to read? What kinds and amounts of competence are desirable before the child undertakes any given task in learning to read?

2. What is the nature of the ability to discriminate sounds in the spoken language and to dissect words in terms of these sounds? How does it develop, and what role does it play in the beginning reader's learning of letter-sound correspondences? How can this ability be taught?

3. How do children learn to recognize and discriminate alphabetic letters in their various forms? When children have difficulty with letter recognition, how can these difficulties be overcome?

4. How do children learn the left-to-right principle in orthography, both as applied to individual words and to the order of words in continuous text? Are there children with special difficulties in learning this component of reading skill?

5. Exactly what are the most useful and functional patterns of letter-sound correspondence in English orthography, and in what order should they be learned? How, indeed, *are* they learned? Is it better to give direct instruction in them, or is it better to rely upon the child's capacity to infer these patterns from the experience he acquires as he learns to read? Should the characteristics of particular children be taken into account in deciding this?

6. When a child has acquired the ability to recognize words and read them in order, yet does not appear to comprehend the message as he would if it were spoken to him, what is the nature of the difficulty?

Questions about the Ordering of the Components of
Reading Skill in the Teaching Process

1. In what way are the various skills prerequisite for each other? What aspects of each skill are necessary to facilitate progress in another skill?

2. Is there one best order in which to introduce the components of reading skill in the learning process, or are there different orders depending upon characteristics of individual children or groups of children? If so, how can these individual or group characteristics be determined?

3. On the assumption that there is an optimal ordering of skills for any given child, how much mastery of a given skill is desirable before another skill is introduced?

Section Two

PROCESSES OF READING

Introduction to Processes of Reading

The reader is encouraged to examine Carroll's article, "The Nature of the Reading Process," to identify focusing questions which will be of value in the study of the various articles included in the Processes of Reading section. A critical synthesis of the information contained in these articles should greatly facilitate an understanding of the nature of the reading process. The reader, however, should probe each selection in this collection for areas of the process which require further research. In this manner, active participation by the reader should be encouraged as new research hypotheses are formulated to expand our frontiers of knowledge in this area.

The coauthors have designed the following questions to assist the reader in the search for synthesis and hypothesis generation:

Language

What is the relation between language acquisition and the reading process?

How does this relationship vary relative to the maturity of the reader?

What linguistic variables appear to be common to the language and reading acquisition process? Different?

What additional information is needed to better understand the relationship between the acquisition of language and reading?

Visual Processing

How are syntactic and semantic variables related to visual processing of printed material?

What linguistic and cognitive variables affect length of fixation? Regressions? Forward scanning?

What linguistic and cognitive variables affect speed of processing visual stimuli?

What syntactic variables affect visual attention and processing in silent reading? Oral reading?

Perception and Word Recognition

How does recognition of distinctive features vary with maturity of the reader?

How does "set for variability" aid decoding transfer?

What graphic units possess psychological reality support for the decoding process?

How would reliance on these units be expected to vary developmentally?

What decoding strategies are used in the reading process?

How do these decoding strategies vary developmentally?

Cognition

What role does conceptualization play in acquiring decoding and comprehension abilities?

What cognitive prerequisites are critical to successful beginning reading? Advanced reading?

Affect

What affective variables are involved in the reading process?

How are affective factors related to the acquisition of reading skills? To advanced reading skills?

Cultural Interaction

How is the cultural context of the classroom related to acquisition of reading skills?

What communication conflicts might be expected to interfere with reading acquisition? Advanced reading development?

How is dialect related to reading achievement? To teacher evaluation?

The reader will undoubtedly wish to formulate new focusing questions or expand the above questions to incorporate special areas of personal interests. This should certainly be encouraged to assist in better understanding the selections presented in this collection and to formulate additional research hypotheses for investigation.

Language

Language Acquisition and the Reading Process

ROBERT B. RUDDELL
University of California at Berkeley

The acquisition of one's native language is indeed a complex process. In fact, little is known about the exact nature of the development of this miraculous phenomenon. Two language acquisition theories which have received greatest acclaim in recent years hold, first, that in a more traditional sense language is acquired through an elaborate association and mediational learning process (*51, 54*), and, second, that language as the species specific characteristic develops as latent structures are "triggered" physiologically and influenced by the model language available to the child (*9, 27*). Convincing arguments have been posited for both points of view; however, it would seem plausible that both theories contribute in some sense to an understanding of language acquisition. Assuming that latent language structures are present and basic to the development of grammatical competency and language performance (*21*), it is also logical to assume that value stems from consistent social reinforcement and sentence expansion opportunities in refining and extending child grammar (*8*) as well as lexicon (*24*). The purpose of this paper, however, is not to review various theories on preschool language acquisition but instead to examine continued language acquisition in the early school years and explore its relationship to the reading process.

As one reads various language research summaries, it is not uncommon to find conclusions which suggest that, upon entrance to the first grade, the child's language development is for the most part mature and that he is sufficiently equipped to handle most forms of discourse which embody highly complex structures and vocabulary. Comparatively speaking, the child has made fantastic progress during his six years of life. He can recognize and produce novel sentences; discriminate between grammatical and nongrammatical sentences (e.g., The bike hit the tree. vs. The hit bike the tree.); utilize context and prosodic clues to disambiguate

22

sentences possessing the same surface structure (e.g., They are *visiting* children. vs. They are *visiting children*.); comprehend sentences which possess different surface structures but have identical underlying meaning (e.g., The boy ate the apple. vs. The apple was eaten by the boy.); and also comprehend sentences which possess identical constituent structure but different deep structure (e.g., Miss Rufkin is easy to please. vs. Miss Rufkin is eager to please.).

By the time the child enters the first grade, he has made great strides in language maturation, but it must be recognized that substantial growth in structural and lexical language components must occur in the elementary school years. In this regard it is important that a discussion of language development account for language maturity not only in standard but in nonstandard dialects as well. It is also important that the relationship between language experience and the reading process be accounted for. The following discussion will thus be mainly devoted to the acquisition and control of structural and lexical dimensions of the language of standard and nonstandard speakers during the elementary school years, with special concern for the relationship between language production and the reading process.

Control of Structural Components

Phonological and morphological development. Various status studies have consistently shown that by the time the child enters the first grade he has a high degree of control over his phonological system (*32, 56*). In fact by the time the child is four to five years of age he has mastered the great majority of English sounds (*13*). Likewise, his morphological development is well along upon entrance to the primary school (*2, 47*). Only on occasion will he utilize an inflectional form (e.g., drinked) which deviates from the adult norm (*29*).

This language progress, however, assumes that the child has been provided with a "standard English" model and that opportunity has been present for language interaction in a wide variety of language environments. If these assumptions cannot be met then the language maturity criteria for the phonological and morphological systems will need to account for nonstandard forms and performance levels in limited language environments.

Recent work on nonstandard dialects provides evidence of highly regular systems which in past years were considered to be degenerate forms of "good English." This regular nature is evident in the l-lessness common to the nonstandard Black dialect and results in consistent production of homonyms so that *toll* becomes *toe,* and *fault* becomes *fought.* The simplification of consonant clusters in final positions such as /st/⟶ /s/ and the loss of /t/ and /d/ results in homonyms so that *past* becomes *pass, meant* becomes *men,* and *hold* becomes *hole.* The English speaking youngster from a Spanish speaking background may have difficulty with vowel contrasts which distinguish the words b*i*t /i/ and b*eat* /iy/, b*e*t /e/ and b*ai*t /ey/; and initial consonant contrasts such as *s*ue /s/ and *z*oo /z/. The Navajo child has difficulty with initial consonant distinctions in words like *v*ote /v/ and *b*oat /b/; and *ch*ip /c/ and *g*yp /j/.

These variations in the phonological system may result in meaning confusion between nonstandard and standard English speakers in situations where sentence context is not sufficient to clarify the intended meaning. If we are to understand the relationship between the phonological system and the graphological system, it becomes clear that dialectal variation must be accounted for. Otherwise, the operationalized reading program makes false assumptions about the language performance of the nonstandard speaker and the teacher may attempt to develop sound-letter correspondences which are not possible for the child.

Reading-decoding. Linguists such as Venezky (*59*), Wardhaugh (*61*), and Reed (*41*) have strongly recommended that it is necessary to consider letter patterns beyond the simple sound-letter correspondence level if a more consistent relationship between oral and written language forms is to be realized. This recommendation is based on the linguistic unit known as the morphophoneme, or the intermediate (between phoneme and morpheme) sound-spelling unit. The importance of this unit is obvious at once in the examination of the words supr*e*me and supr*e*mity. On the first consideration the second *e* grapheme would appear to possess little regularity in its representation of a given sound. However, when the large spelling pattern is considered, a highly regular pattern becomes evident. In the alterations—supr*e*me, supr*e*m*ity*; extr*e*me, extr*e*m*ity*; obsc*e*ne, obsc*e*n*ity*—we observe a consistent shift in the sound value (/iy/ to /i/) in adding the suffix *ity.* The same principle is present in the letter pattern using the final *e* marker (e.g., s*i*t /i/, s*i*te /ay/).

Consideration also needs to be given to the possible value of utilizing phonological or sound segmentation rather than morphological or word-affix segmentation in teaching decoding skills. An experiment by Rodgers (*42*) asked children to repeat words containing two syllables (e.g., toas-ter) and the same words divided between the two morphemes (e.g., toast-er). He found that the children were more successful in redividing words along syllabic or phonological breaks than along the morphological breaks, thus supporting phonological segmentation.

The work by Gibson and her colleagues (18) has indicated that children develop higher-order generalizations in the early stages of reading and that these generalizations follow English spelling patterns. The children in the experiment appeared to perceive regularities in sound and spelling patterns and transfer these to decoding unfamiliar trigrams even though taught by what the researchers refer to as the "whole word" approach. The above research thus suggests the possible value and need to consider decoding units which extend beyond sound-letter correspondences and account for more complete regularity in the English spelling system.

As the classroom teacher and the theoretician view the relationship between language acquisition and the reading process, both must not only be aware of the previously discussed cultural levels (25, 40), such as standard and nonstandard dialects, but also cognizant of functional varieties of language such as informal, formal, and literary. These varieties may exist within a given cultural level. Additional variation in language performance may be expected to result from the child's limited experience with language forms unique to a particular social environment. As a result one child may be able to function on only an informal functional variety level while a second child from a highly enriched language environment may shift with ease from the informal to the formal level.

By placing oral expression and written language forms on a functional variety continuum ranging from informal through formal to literacy (40), we can examine the "fit" between these forms of communication for the beginning reader. Figure 1 indicates what we might expect to find.

Functional Variety Level	Oral Language	Written Language
Informal	Home and school language.	Personal notes, letters to friends, unedited language experience stories.
Formal	Classroom lectures, public speeches.	School textbooks, edited language experience stories.
Literary	Formal papers, speech as an art form.	Literature as an art form, aesthetic dimensions of written language.

Figure 1.   Levels of functional variety in oral and written expression

Two problems are immediately obvious. First, the written language material which the child intially encounters in the instructional setting will in most cases be at least one level above his informal and familiar oral language style. Second, the child from a limited language environment, which has provided little opportunity for the development of shift in a functional variety is at a decided handicap in approaching the printed page which is written for the most part at the formal level. For example, *hafta, gonna, hadda, oughta, hasta,* and *wanna* are quite appropriate in informal conversational settings for oral language, but in written language are realized as *have to, going to, had to, ought to, has to,* and *want to (29).* The contractions *I'll, she'll, he'll,* and *they'll* are most appropriate in informal oral language situations; however, the written equivalents *I will, she will, he will,* and *they will* appear in many children's textbooks at the formal level from the child's earliest encounter with printed matter.

The problem, then, for the nonstandard speaker is striking when we consider that he must not only account for dialectal deviations but also levels of functional variety in the second dialect. Speakers of standard and nonstandard forms, however, must accommodate the functional variety shift from informal to formal or literary styles. As Goodman *(20)* has emphasized, certain oral language sequences, which result from morphophonemic rules cutting across morpheme boundaries in the flow of speech, are so common that the young speaker does not differentiate the individual components in the sequence as in *going to* (gonna), *with them* (with'm), *with him* (with'm), *must have* (must'v) and *should have* (should'v). Thus, oral language at the informal level may use one unit, while the early encounter with printed forms at the formal level may require two units. This variation must be taken into account in both the instructional program and abstract explanations of the reading process. More will be said about the problem of stylistic shift in the following discussion which considers syntactical and lexical aspects of language acquisition.

Syntactical development. The control of syntactical patterning by the preschool primary grade child has been demonstrated in various studies including those by Fraser, Bellugi, and Brown *(16)*; Brown and Fraser *(6)*; Strickland *(55)*; Loban *(30)*; Ruddell and Graves *(47)*; and O'Donnell, Griffin, and Norris *(38)*. These studies indicate that, by kindergarten and first grade, the child is able to comprehend sentences and produce expanded and elaborated sentences through the use of movables (words, phrases or clauses with no fixed position in the sentence) and transformed subordinating elements.

The research evidence also suggests that the developmental sequence in syntactical control extends well into and perhaps through the elementary grades. Menyuk's work *(33)* has identified some sequential components in children's syntax extending from nursery school into the first grade. She noted that even in the first grade some patterns such as "if" and "so" clauses, perfects, and nominalizations were still in the process of development. Lenneberg (28) has discussed the difficulty presented by transformations in the passive voice for the mentally retarded child. The work of Strickland (55) shows a definite relationship between sentence complexity and grade level. Loban's research (30) revealed that throughout the elementary grades the average communication unit length increased indicating a developmental sequence of complexity in sentence structure.

The detailed study by Harrell (22) compared selected language variables in the speech and writing of children aged nine, eleven, thirteen, and fifteen using a short movie as the speech and writing stimulus. The investigator found that the length of the compositions and clauses used in oral and written expression increased with age, with a large percentage of subordinate clauses being used by the older children in both written and spoken composition. The children were found to use a larger percentage of subordinate clauses in writing than in speaking. More adverb and adjective clauses were used in written compositions, while a larger number of noun clauses were used in speaking. A larger percentage of adverbial clauses, excepting those of time and cause, were used in the children's speech. The developmental increase of each language variable in relation to age was found to be greater for written compositions than for oral.

The work of O'Donnell, Griffin, and Norris (38) at kindergarten and grades one, two, three, four, and seven also lends support to the general notion of a developmental sequence of syntax acquisition in the elementary grades. These researchers have observed that some transformations (e.g., relative clause, "The man who was wearing a coat . . .") were used much more frequently in kindergarten than in later grades while other items (e.g., noun modification by a participle, "The man wearing a coat . . .") were more frequent in later grades. The researchers observed that such a developmental sequence would appear to be a logical one from the standpoint of transformational grammar in that many of the later constructions are derived from more complex deletion rules.

Also of interest in the O'Donnell, Griffin, and Norris research was the finding of distinct variation in the syntax of speech and writing in grades three, five, and seven. At third grade, oral expression was deemed superior to written expression in transformational complexity, while at grades five and seven the reverse was true. These findings are similar to those of the previously mentioned Harrell study and suggest that by the intermediate grades the child has some production control over stylistic variations which require more complex constructions in written expression.

By examining research which contrasts the language development of children possessing hearing deficiency with that of normal children, the relationship between oral language experiences and written language production is brought into sharper focus. Heider and Heider (23) secured written compositions based on a motion picture from a large number of deaf and hearing children ranging in age from eleven to seventeen years and eight to fourteen years, respectively. Although the deaf children were three years older, their compositions were found to resemble the less mature hearing children. The deaf children were found to use fewer numbers of words and clauses than the hearing children, while the hearing children used more compound and complex sentences with a larger number of words in coordinate and subordinate clauses, thus indicating a more advanced development in language production.

The written language of normal and defective hearing children has been examined in Templin's research (57). Children having hearing deficiencies were found to use more words in their explanations of natural phenomena than hearing children of the same age, grade, and intelligence. This finding was interpreted to reflect less adequate control over vocabulary, and perhaps syntax, rather than representing a more complex type of expression. The children with defective hearing apparently needed more words to express a concept due to low efficiency in expressing their ideas through elaborated sentences and more abstract vocabulary.

Both the Heider and Heider and the Templin studies point to a significant relationship between oral and written language development. The opportunity for oral language experience through hearing would appear to directly influence performance in written language.

The language deviations of the nonstandard speaker also result in significant grammatical variations. The previously discussed 1-lessness, for example, may affect future forms where *you'll* becomes *you,* *he'll* becomes *he,* and *they'll* becomes *they.* Thus, when the child reads the sentence "He will go." as "He go.", he is consistently translating the sentence in his dialect. An example used by Shuy (49) states that the written sentence "John asked if Mary wore a coat." is frequently read by the ghetto child as "John asked did Mary wear a coat." In this instance the substitution of *did* for *if* and *wear* for *wore* does not represent an error in reading in terms of the child's dialect. If, however, the child read "John asked Mary if did she wear a coat." or "John asked Mary if she wear a coat.", the alterations do vary from the consistent nonstandard forms and would represent a reading difficulty. The child's consistent performance may thus be interpreted to indicate that he possesses a high degree of language competence in the same manner as the standard speaker of English.

An understanding of the relationship between the communication process and the standard and nonstandard syntactical forms is of importance to both the classroom practitioner and the theorist. Bernstein's research (3, 4) supports the viewpoint that the "restricted" code associated with lower socioeconomic status and related language experiences is characterized by limited subordination and is syntactically redundant. In contrast, the "elaborated" code uses more complex forms of subordination which can account for logical relationships and great causality. The "elaborated" code makes provision for meaningful explication of specific topics with strangers or new group members. The contribution of syntactical factors to the "elaborated" code would appear to be in terms of subordination and expression of complex relationships. Although these dimensions can be handled in the "restricted" code, a definite economy is present in the utilization of the "elaborated" code with a majority population that does not possess the competency necessary to comprehend the unique features of the "restricted" code.

The "elaborated" code would also be expected to make provision for easier transition from oral to written language comprehension and production particularly in terms of greater subordination control required in the stylistic shift from an informal to a formal functional variety level.

Reading comprehension. The close relationship between comprehension ability and language production receives support from a variety of studies. The research of Fraser, Bellugi, and Brown (16) supports the view that children must comprehend grammatical contrasts before they are able to produce these contrasts. The previously cited research of Strickland (55) and Loban (30) report significant relationships between children's reading and listening comprehension achievement and their demonstrated use of movables and subordination in oral language.

From the early study of mistakes in paragraph reading of sixth grade children, Thorndike (58) noted that understanding a paragraph is dependent upon the reader's selection of the right elements and synthesizing them in the right relations. The child's ability to comprehend material whether written or spoken would seem to be a function of his ability to see the relationships between key elements in the sentence. Thus, relating various subordinating elements to the central idea of the sentence is of basic importance for comprehending the discourse.

Using a "disarranged phrase test," Gibbons (17) studied the relationship between third grade children's ability to understand the structure of sentences and their reading achievement. She found a high correlation (.89) between the ability to see relationships between parts of a sentence and the ability to understand the sentence, when intelligence was partialled out. A significant correlation (.72) was also found between the ability to see relationships between parts of sentences and total reading achievement.

The importance of familiarity with syntactic patterning to reading achievement is evident in MacKinnon's research (31). In a detailed study of beginning readers he observed that children attempted to substitute syntactic patterns which they had previously read and were familiar with in place of unfamiliar patterns in their attempt to decode unfamiliar reading materials.

A study of Ruddell (43), at the fourth grade level, examined the effect on reading comprehension of written patterns of language structure which occur with high and low frequency in children's oral language. By controlling the vocabulary difficulty, sentence length and subject matter content in a series of reading passages, the relationship between reading comprehension and pattern complexity was examined. Reading comprehension scores on passages written with high frequency patterns of language structure were found to be significantly superior to comprehension scores on passages written with low frequency patterns of language structure.

The child's understanding of the sentence structure would be expected to enhance his ability to narrow alternate word meanings and thus contribute to comprehension. For example, the word *that* not only cues a noun which follows but may also clarify or emphasize the semantic nature of the noun (e.g., *That* yellow canary ate the cat. vs. *Some* yellow canary ate the cat.). Miller (35) and Miller, et al. (36) have demonstrated that words in context following a similar grammatical pattern are perceived more accurately than when in isolation. Additional support for the importance of context in narrowing semantic possibilities is found in the research of Goodman (19). He has shown that although children may be unable to decode words in isolation, they deal successfully with the same words in a running context. These findings support the importance of contextual association which provides sufficient delimiting information to enable the child to determine the semantic role of a word and, further, to recognize and comprehend it in a sentence.

A longitudinal study by Ruddell (45, 46) has demonstrated that the sentence and paragraph meaning comprehension of first and second grade children can be significantly enhanced by emphasizing the meaning relationships between key structural elements within and between sentences. Additionally, the doctoral dissertation research of Baele (1), which was part of the longitudinal study described above, indicated that by the end of third grade the children who had participated in the treatment stressing the relationship between key structure elements were expressing themselves in written form with longer communication units and with greater clausal depth, thus indicating control over more complex constructions and subordination in the written language performance. This research parallels in some respects the preschool oral language research of Cazden (*8*). Her work with two- and three-year-old children indicated that the use of full grammatical sentences in response to the children's verbal expression and the expansion of their telegraphic speech to full adult grammatical sentences resulted in an increased level of performance on several measures of grammatical development when contrasted with a control group. The "richness of verbal stimulation" appeared to be of great import in extending grammatical control. These findings indicate that language comprehension and production can be enhanced in the preschool and early grades by placing emphasis on structural relationships which influence meaning within and between sentences.

Control of Lexical Components

Concept development. The child's conceptual development makes rapid progress during the preschool years, and he will recognize and possess control over many hundreds of words by his first year of school (*52, 53*). During this time a variety of concepts are formulated as the youngster associates common properties of an object with the object label. As Vygotsky (*60*) has pointed out, the preschooler calls a *cow* a *cow* because it has horns, and a *calf* a *calf* because its horns are still small, while a *dog* is called a *dog* because it is small and has no horns. Eventually the child comes to conceptualize the arbitrary nature of language itself as he understands that word labels are assigned to concepts and that a particular label may represent several concepts, depending upon its contextual use.

There is ample evidence to support the view that concepts develop along a continuum from concrete through the semiconcrete or functional to the abstract levels as illustrated in the research of Fiefel and Lorge (*15*). The work of Russell and Saadeh (*48*) is also illustrative of research supporting such a continuum. These researchers contrasted student conceptual responses at grades three, six, and nine on multiple-choice questions designed to measure various levels of abstracton. They concluded that third grade children favored "concrete" responses while sixth grade and ninth grade children favored "functional" and "abstract" responses. As Ervin-Tripp (*14*) has emphasized in her extensive research summary of child language, conceptual maturation moves from concrete referents to "hierarchies of superordinates which may have rather vague features (e.g., mammal, vertebrate) and they [adults] speak of nonvisible referents such as politics and energy."

Various background variables have been credited with enhancement of language performance. John and Goldstein's verbal mediation research (24) reveals that a child's verbal interaction with a mature speaker is of importance in making provision for testing tentative notions about word meanings. Such opportunity would appear to produce greater verbal control and enable the child to rely on words as mediators facilitating thought. Vygotsky (60) has suggested that the availability of adults for dialogue with the child is of great import to language acquisition. This consideration also receives support from Davis' early research (10), which revealed that in families of only children language facility was found to develop more rapidly than in families of children with siblings; and children with siblings were found to develop language facility faster than twins.

The effect of factors in the home environment on language achievement is evidenced in Milner's investigation (37). Following the selection of high and low achievers in first grade reading, a depth interview was carried out exploring the children's use of language in the home. Milner found that the high achieving children had an enriched verbal environment with more books available and were read to more often by highly esteemed adults than the low achieving children. The high scoring children also engaged in conversation with their parents more often than the low scoring children. She noted further that in many of the home environments of low scoring children a positive family atmosphere was not evident nor did the children have an adult relationship pattern established. There appeared to be little opportunity for these children to interact verbally with adults possessing adequate speech patterns and who were of high personal value to the children.

In classroom instruction the child is frequently required to provide requested information at the formal functional variety level. As Bernstein (3, 4) has emphasized, the child from the low socioeconomic environment using the "restricted" code is required to use language in situations which he is neither equipped nor oriented to handle. This may be due not only to the past discussion of syntactical factors but also to his limited lexical control and ability to shift from an informal and intimate style developed in situations oriented toward immediate and concrete needs to a formal style characterized by abstractions which carry highly efficient explanatory power. Certainly a limited vocabulary represents a most critical factor in reading comprehension. This problem is highlighted in Metfessel's findings (34) that second grade children from concept deprived backgrounds possessed a comprehension vocabulary only one-third the magnitude of the average of their age-equivalent peers. Again, the classroom teacher and the theoretician must account for the child's lexical control if the wide range of conceptual variation is to be accounted for in practice and theory, respectively.

Comprehension strategies and objectives. The importance of a cognitive strategy to the conceptualization process has been clearly demonstrated in the research literature (7). If the language user is to participate actively in the process of communication, he must evolve a symbol-processing system which will provide for the conceptualization of his experience. This is basic to his success in examining alternate approaches to decoding a new word and in comprehending written material which requires high level inference skill. From his concept formation study with elementary school children, Kress (26) concluded that achieving readers were superior to nonachievers in their versatility and flexibility, their ability to draw inferences from relevant clues, and their ability to shift set when new standards were introduced. There is considerable research to support the relationship between language comprehension and an individual's ability to change, modify, and reorganize previously formed concepts (50).

The child's communicative objectives must also be viewed as critical to the development of his communication skills. These objectives must be of a real and meaningful nature to the child if they are to be operationalized as the individual confronts the reading material. The reading objectives should provide immediate self-direction for the child and will be of value in developing high motivation as revealed in his persistence and drive. This view also obtains support from the previously mentioned study of Kress. He has reported that achieving readers demonstrated more initiative in exhausting solutions and were found to persist in problem solving under changing conditions in contrast to the non-achieving readers. Durkin's extensive work (11, 12) with the preschool child suggests that the early reader is an individual who is serious and persistent, is curious in nature, and possesses the ability to concentrate. The research of Piekarz (39) has identified the high level reader as an individual who provides significantly more responses in interpreting a reading passage, a trait indicating greater involvement and participation. The high level reader was also found to be more objective and impersonal in synthesizing the information sought which may be interpreted to support the importance of establishing reading objectives.

Thus, an individual's cognitive strategy is seen as a method of organizing and assimilating data as well as making provision for hypothesis formulation and testing. Provision for self-directing behavior through formulation of personal and immediate communication objectives would be expected to enhance the child's participation, persistence, and drive leading to more effective language control.

Summary and Recommendations

In conclusion, upon the child's entry to formal education he displays language performance which reflects a high degree of competence. Even so, however, four significant factors must be recognized and accounted for in any operational and theoretical formulation of the reading process. First, the child's ability to comprehend language precedes and exceeds his ability to produce language. Second, his language comprehension appears to be a direct function of his control over the grammatical and lexical components of the discourse. Third, his language competence and performance appear to move through a developmental sequence during the elementary school years which in some respects parallels the competency model proposed by the transformational grammarian. And, fourth, his language performance is directly related to his language environment, including the available language model and opportunity for language interaction, his comprehension strategies and objectives, and possibly maturation of his latent language structures.

Many essential informational areas which are required to explain the multitude of interactions which occur during the reading process are blank. The reading-language researcher and theoretician must carefully include the following dimensions in future research exploration:

1. A detailed mapping of the child's developmental performance in gaining control over his grammar during the elementary school years.

2. A parallel longitudinal study which examines the relationship between the child's grammatical performance and his lexical control.

3. A parallel longitudinal study which examines the relationship between his comprehension ability and his grammatical and lexical performance.

4. An intensive investigation designed to explore meaning interference which may be caused by variation in standard and nonstandard and functional varieties in language—including phonological, morphological, morphophonemic, syntactical and lexical items.

5. A study of the unique characteristics of "language enrichment" approaches and the relationship between these characteristics and the grammatical and lexical development of standard and nonstandard speakers during the preschool and elementary school years.

6. A study of various decoding units (e.g., grapheme-phoneme, morphographeme-morphophoneme) and the relationship between these units and early reading success.

7. A parallel study which will examine the relationship between various decoding units and reading success of children speaking standard and nonstandard dialects.

These problem areas are illustrative of the types of information required in order to formulate a theory of reading which will have explanatory power. Until such information is available, our theoretical formulations of the reading process will remain extremely weak. It is obvious that we have far to go.

REFERENCES

1. Baele, Ernest R. "The Effect of Primary Reading Programs Emphasizing Language Structure as Related to Meaning Upon Children's Written Language Achievement at the Third Grade Level," unpublished doctoral dissertation, University of California at Berkeley, 1968.

2. Berko, Jean. "The Child's Learning of English Morphology," *Word,* 14 (1958), 140-177.

3. Bernstein, Basil. "Elaborated and Resricted Codes: Their Social Origins and Some Consequences," *American Anthropologist,* Volume 66, Part 2 (1964), 55-69.

4. Bernstein, Basil. "Social Structure, Language, and Learning," *Educational Research,* 3 (1961), 163-176.

5. Brearley, Molly, and Elizabeth Hitchfield. *A Teacher's Guide to Reading Piaget.* London: Routledge and Kegan Paul, Broadway House, 1966.

6. Brown, Roger, and Colin Fraser. "The Acquisition of Syntax," in U. Bellugi and R. W. Brown (Eds.), *The Acquisition of Language,* Monographs of the Society for Research in Child Development, 29 (1964), 43-79.

7. Bruner, J., J. Goodnow, and G. Austin. *A Study of Thinking.* New York: Wiley, 1956.

8. Cazden, Courtney B. "Environmental Assistance to the Child's Acquisition of Grammar," unpublished doctoral dissertation, Harvard University, 1965.

9. Chomsky, Noam. "Review of Skinner's Verbal Behavior," *Language,* 35 (1959), 26-58.

10. Davis, Edith A. *The Development of Linguistic Skill in Twins, Singletons with Siblings, and Only Children From Ages Five to Ten Years.* Minneapolis: University of Minnesota Press, 1937.

11. Durkin, Dolores. "Children Who Learn to Read before Grade One," *Reading Teacher,* 14 (January 1961), 163-166.

12. Durkin, Dolores. "The Achievement of Preschool Readers: Two Longitudinal Studies," *Reading Research Quarterly,* 1 (Summer 1966), 5-36.

13. Ervin, Susan M., and W. R. Miller. "Language Development," in H. Stevenson (Ed.), *Child Psychology,* The 62nd Yearbook of the National Society for the Study of Education. Chicago: University of Chicago Press, 1963, 108-143.

14. Ervin-Tripp, Susan. "Language Development," *Review of Child Development Research.* New York: Russell Sage Foundation, 1967, 55-105.

15. Feifel, H., and I. B. Lorge. "Qualitative Differences in the Vocabulary Responses of Children," *Journal of Educational Psychology,* 43 (1962), 170-174.

16. Fraser, Colin, Ursula Bellugi, and Roger Brown. "Control of Grammar in Imitation, Comprehension, and Production," *Journal of Verbal Learning and Verbal Behavior,* 2 (August 1963), 121-135.

17. Gibbons, Helen D. "Reading and Sentence Elements," *Elementary English Review,* 18 (February 1941), 42-46.

18. Gibson, Eleanor J., et al. "The Role of Grapheme-Phoneme Correspondences in the Perception of Words," *American Journal of Psychology,* 75 (1962), 554-570.

19. Goodman, K. S. "A Linguistic Study of Cues and Miscues in Reading," *Elementary English,* 42 (1965), 639-643.

20. Goodman, K. S. "Words and Morphemes in Reading," in K. Goodman and J. Fleming (Eds.),*Psycholinguistics and the Teaching of Reading.* Newark, Del.: International Reading Association, 1969, 25-33.

21. Gough, Philip B. "The Limitations of Imitation: The Problem of Language Acquisition," in Alexander Frazier (Ed.), *New Directions in Elementary English.* Champaign, Ill.: National Council of Teachers of English, 1967.

22. Harrell, Lester E., Jr. "An Inter-Comparison of the Quality and Rate of the Development of the Oral and Written Language in Children," *Monographs of the Society for Research in Child Development,* 22 (1957).

23. Heider, F. K., and Grace M. Heider. "A Comparison of Sentence Structure of Deaf and Hearing Children," *Psychological Monographs,* 52 (1940), 42-103.

24. John, Vera P., and Leo S. Goldstein. "The Social Context of Language Acquisition," *Merrill-Palmer Quarterly of Behavior and Development,* 10 (1964), 265-274.

25. Kenyon, John S. "Cultural Levels and Functional Varieties of English," *College English,* 10 (October 1948), 31-36.

26. Kress, R. A. "An Investigation of the Relationship Between Concept Formation and Achievement in Reading," unpublished doctoral dissertation, Temple University, 1955.

27. Lenneberg, Eric. *Biological Foundations of Language.* New York: Wiley, 1967.

28. Lenneberg, Eric. "Speech as a Motor Skill with Special Reference to Nonaphasic Disorders," *Monographs of the Society for Research in Child Development,* 29 (1964), 115-127.

29. Lindsay, Marie R. "A Descriptive Exploration of the Growth and Development of Spontaneous Oral Vocabulary of Elementary School Children," unpublished doctoral dissertation, University of California, 1969.

30. Loban, Walter D. *The Language of Elementary School Children.* Champaign, Ill.: National Council of Teachers of English, 1963.

31. MacKinnon, A. R. *How Do Children Learn to Read.* Vancouver: Clopp Clark, 1959.

32. McCarthy, Dorothea A. "Language Development in Children," in L. Carmichael (Ed.), *Manual of Child Psychology.* New York: Wiley, 1954, 492-630.

33. Menyuk, Paula. "Syntactic Structures in the Language of Children," *Child Development,* 34 (June 1963), 407-422.

34. Metfessel, Newton S. In J. L. Frost and G. R. Hawkes (Eds.), *The Disadvantaged Child.* New York: Houghton-Mifflin, 1966.

35. Miller, G. A. "Some Psychological Studies of Grammar," *American Psychologist,* 17 (1962), 748-762.

36. Miller, G. A., G. A. Heise, and W. Lichten. "The Intelligibility of Speech as a Function of the Context of the Test Material," *Journal of Experimental Psychology,* 41 (1951), 329-335.

37. Milner, Esther. "A Study of the Relationship between Reading Readiness in Grade One School Children and Patterns of Parent-Child Interaction," The 62nd Yearbook of the

National Society for Study of Education. Chicago: University of Chicago Press, 1963, 108-143.

38. O'Donnell, Roy C., William J. Griffin, and Raymond C. Norris. *Syntax of Kindergarten and Elementary School Children: A Transformational Analysis.* Campaign, Ill.: National Council of Teachers of English, 1967.

39. Piekarz, Josephine A. "Getting Meaning from Reading," *Elementary School Journal,* 56 (1956), 303-309.

40. Pooley, Robert C. *Teaching English Usage.* New York: Appleton-Century, 1946.

41. Reed, D. W. "A Theory of Language, Speech and Writing," in Priscilla Tyler (Ed.), *Linguistics and Reading.* Highlights of the 1965 Preconvention Institutes. Newark, Del.: International Reading Association, 1966, 4-25.

42. Rodgers, T. S. "Linguistic Considerations in the Design of the Stanford Computer Based Curriculum in Initial Reading," Institute for Mathematical Studies in the Social Sciences, Technical Report No. 111, USOE Grant Number OE5-10-050, 1967.

43. Ruddell, Robert B. "Effect of the Similarity of Oral and Written Patterns of Language Structure on Reading Comprehension," *Elementary English,* 42 (April 1965), 403-410.

44. Ruddell, Robert B. "Psycholinguistic Implications for a Systems of Communication Model," in K. Goodman and J. Fleming (Eds.), *Psycholinguistics and the Teaching of Reading.* Newark, Del.: International Reading Association, 1969, 61-78.

45. Ruddell, Robert B. "Reading Instruction in First Grade with Varying Emphasis on the Regularity of Grapheme-Phoneme Correspondences and the Relation of Language Structure to Meaning," *Reading Teacher,* 19 (May 1966), 653-660.

46. Ruddell, Robert B. *Second and Third Year of a Longitudinal Study of Four Programs of Reading Instruction with Varying Emphasis on the Regularity of Grapheme-Phoneme Correspondences and the Relation of Language Structure to Meaning,* U. S. Department of Health, Education and Welfare, Office of Education Cooperative Research Projects No. 3099 and 78085, 1968.

47. Ruddell, Robert B., and Barbara W. Graves. "Socioethnic Status and the Language Achievement of First Grade Children," *Elementary English,* May 1967, 730-739.

48. Russell, David H., and I. Q. Saadeh. "Qualitative Levels in Children's Vocabularies," *Journal of Educational Psychology,* 43 (1962), 170-174.

49. Shuy, Roger W. "Some Language and Cultural Differences in a Theory of Reading," in K. Goodman and J. Fleming (Eds.), *Psycholinguistics and the Teaching of Reading.* Newark, Del.: International Reading Association, 1969, 34-47.

50. Singer, Harry, "Conceptualization in Learning to Read: New Frontiers in College-Adult Reading," in G. B. Schick and M. M. May (Eds.), *The 15th Yearbook of the National Reading Conference.* Milwaukee: 1966, 116-132.

51. Skinner, B. F. *Verbal Behavior.* New York: Appleton-Century-Crofts, 1957.

52. Smith, Mary K. "Measurement of the Size of General English Vocabulary through the Elementary Grades and High School," *Genetic Psychology Monographs,* 24 (1941), 311-345.

53. Smith, Medorah E. "An Investigation of the Development of the Sentence and the Extent of Vocabulary in Young Children," *Studies in Child Welfare,* 5 (1926). Iowa City: State University of Iowa, 28-71.

54. Staats, Arthur W., and Carolyn K. Staats. *Complex Human Behavior.* New York: Holt, Rinehart and Winston, 1964.

55. Strickland, Ruth G. *The Language of Elementary School Children: Its Relationship to the Language of Reading Textbooks and the Qualtiy of Reading of Selected Children,* Bulletin of the School of Education, 38 (July 1962). Bloomington, Ind.: Indiana University.

56. Templin, Mildred. *Certain Language Skills in Children,* University of Minnesota Institute of Child Welfare Monographs. Minneapolis: University of Minnesota Press, 1957.

57. Templin, Mildred C. *The Development of Reasoning in Children with Normal and Defective Hearing.* Minneapolis: University of Minnesota Press, 1950.

58. Thorndike, E. L., "Reading and Reasoning: A Study of Mistakes in Paragraph Reading," *Journal of Educational Psychology,* 8 (1917), 323-332.

59. Venezky, R. F. "English Orthography: Its Graphical Structure and Its Relation to Sound," *Reading Research Quarterly,* 2 (Spring 1967), 75-106.

60. Vygotsky, Lev. S. *Thought and Language.* Cambridge and New York: MIT Press, 1962.

61. Wardaugh, R. "Linguistics-Reading Dialogue," *Reading Teacher,* 21 (February 1968), 432-441.

Reactions to Language Acquisition and the Reading Process

RICHARD E. HODGES*
University of Chicago

Robert Ruddell has lucidly pointed out that significant relationships exist between a child's functional language abilities and the acquisition of the reading process. Although the inferences for reading which Ruddell draws from selected child language studies may be subject to discussion, the fact that he has attempted to translate these research findings into possible implications to be considered in respect to the reading process should be acknowledged. As can quickly be surmised from scanning current reading periodicals, current views of language and its acquisition in relation to reading have generated considerable interest. The tendency of some educationists to translate theory and research directly into practice—to seek instructional panaceas—can be a disservice when unconsidered, even irrational, instructional applications are made, thereby demeaning otherwise promising contributions. Ruddell's reasoned and cautious discussion provides a standard which might profitably be followed by others.

A few specific comments seem in order. A most pertinent aspect of Ruddell's discussion is his reminder that, contrary to some popular misconceptions, language continues to develop beyond school entrance age. This point is important because a model of reading instruction that embodies the premise that children have achieved basic linguistic mastery must attend primarily to the refinement and application of those linguistic skills which pertain specifically to reading. On the other hand, a model of reading instruction which posits that linguistic skills are developmental should also take into account that *both* reading materials and instructional strategies ought to lead toward the mastery of skills not yet acquired.

Ruddell also reminds us that a developmental approach to the study of language acquisition has fostered numerous research investigations

---

*Now at the University of Puget Sound.

into the language production of the elementary school child, an area which has had until recently relatively little study in contrast to the language of the preschool child. The relative dearth of research of elementary school children's language habits, of course, has partly been a consequence of the view that linguistic mastery has been regarded as functionally complete by school entrance age. His summary of language development studies during the elementary school years provides a useful overview of the kinds of investigations which contemporary language theory has fostered. It should be pointed out, however, that interpretations of these studies ought to take into account the stimulus mode employed in eliciting language samples, since the stimulus situation can have a fundamental effect on the kind of language elicited. Nonetheless, emerging from contemporary language studies is the observation that language appears to be acquired in a rather fixed order, although the *rate* of acquisition may vary considerably due to individual and environmental factors.

In conjunction with this point, it is well to keep in mind that many findings reported from child language research are expressed in terms of normative data, with the consequence that mean scores on tests or mean chronological ages in linguistic development obscure ranges in individual scores or ages that comprise the mean. Language norms provide important measures for use by the researcher and the practitioner; but language *variation* ultimately must be taken into account. Normative data ought not be used to obscure the fact that ranges around a mean often are far more informative, particularly in regard to a developmental view of language acquisition. As Ruddell has implied, each individual's biological endowments, in combination with the consequences of his particular linguistic environment, can lead to a substantial variation among elementary school children's language performances.

Distinguishing among *causes* of language variation is another implication brought out in Ruddell's presentation. Causal factors of language variation might be distinguished in at least three ways: developmentally, dialectally, and pathologically. Each factor raises the possibility that a model of reading instruction should take into consideration how modes of instruction may differ because of possibly different language inputs into the reading process.

For example, developmental variation suggests that many so-called reading difficulties may represent a mismatch between the level of a child's developing linguistic sophistication and that of the reading material with which he is confronted. Dialectal variation, on the other hand, may pose another kind of possible mismatch, that which results from differences between the formal features of the language of instruction and the formal features of language which the child has learned in his particular linguistic community. The instructional resolution of such a mismatch is currently a topic of considerable debate specifically regarding whether or not focus should be placed on altering the language of instruction to match the language of the child or vice versa. Pathological variation, in turn, poses the possibility that, in addition to whatever developmental and dialectal differences might exist, special instructional techniques may be needed that are not ordinarily encompassed in a reading program; as, for example, the techniques that may be used in working with the visually or auditorily handicapped child.

These three factors—developmental, dialectal, and pathological—are not intended as inclusive forms of linguistic variation. Nonetheless, they do call attention to the need for a model of reading instruction to outline instructional interventions which are cued by the kinds of linguistic variations which can and do occur in the language of the elementary school child.

A concluding remark: despite the growing data about language acquisition, Ruddell's admonition that substantial work in other dimensions of language in relation to reading is needed is fully warranted. His presentation clearly indicates that, despite some significant theoretical formulations and equally significant research, there is still a good distance to go in developing a theory of reading and, from such a theory, a model of reading instruction. Ruddell's own contributions, and his comprehensive summary of the contributions of other researchers, are welcome additions to the accumulating data about the reading process and its language base.

Theories of Language Acquisition in Relation to Beginning Reading Instruction[*]

RONALD WARDHAUGH[**]
University of Michigan

Introduction

Numerous summaries of research in language acquisition exist: McCarthy (1954) summarizes work completed prior to 1950; Elkonin (1958), Brown and Berko (1960), Carroll (1960), Brown (1965), Ervin-Tripp (1966), Ervin-Tripp and Slobin (1966), McNeill (1966, 1970a, 1970b), and Slobin (1971) summarize parts, or the whole, of more recent work; and Kelley (1967) provides one of the most interesting discussions of many of the major issues. The purpose of this paper is to isolate and assess major theories of language acquisition and to relate these theories to beginning reading instruction. The particular focus is the acquisition of syntax. The theories are also reviewed from the perspective of the linguistic knowledge available today; consequently, certain cognitive and affective factors are minimized. These factors are not to be considered unimportant in beginning reading instruction; rather, they are to be considered beyond the scope of this paper.

Language Acquisition

Atheoretical Studies

A reading of McCarthy's summary article (1954) induces mixed feelings in anyone trained in linguistics. She reports on a wide variety of descriptive and normative studies, but all seem unrevealing insofar as

[*]Reprinted from *Reading Research Quarterly,* 7 (Fall 1971), 168-194. Preparation of this paper was supported by Office of Education Contract OEC-0-70-4790 (508) to Rutgers, The State University. The paper was initially edited at Rutgers by Dr. Fred B. Davis. The author is grateful to Patricia Dishuck and Mary Ann Gatten for their assistance.

[**]Now at the University of Toronto.

current interests in language acquisition are concerned. The studies reported appear atheoretical today because the investigators made little attempt to formulate and test fruitful hypotheses and to handle data other than quantitatively. Consequently, no coherent account of language acquisition emerges from the studies reviewed by McCarthy. Instead, child language appears to drift somehow from a prevocalic stage, through various stages replete with errors and deficiencies, toward the clearly articulated speech of an ideal speaker of Standard English. As a result, sounds "emerge" in ways that are never specified, "first words" are uttered at a characteristic time, grammatical distinctions are "acquired," often through the elimination of various "errors," and vocabularies "expand" as the child's dictionary gains more entries. Gradually, by some process of making successive approximations, the child's language becomes more and more like the language ascribed in traditional grammars to those who speak the language "properly."

Working in such a way, investigators may try to discover when the child learns to distinguish *pin* from *pen* and *witch* from *which*, all the while ignoring the fact that in certain dialects such distinctions are not made at all. Or they may try to count various sentence types using formulae for sentence description that derive from analyses of writing and studies of rhetorical devices rather than from any close observation of spoken language. Or they may calculate word frequencies and compute type-token ratios without defining the concept of "a word" or devising the most appropriate elicitation procedures. Such investigators often collect considerable quantities of data which can be neatly inventoried and displayed in tables and figures (for example, tables of errors in articulation which show a gradual reduction in frequency as age increases). However, the data are essentially unrevealing because the investigators do not ask why it is that one linguistic skill is acquired before another, or what is the nature of the linguistic ability of the child at various stages in his linguistic development.

Only in recent years have such questions been asked by psychologists and linguists engaged in the study of language acquisition. They have realized that inventories are unrevealing unless they show which items contrast with each other within the inventories. They no longer disregard regional and social variations in speech and developments in modern linguistics. They insist that is is impossible to describe language acquisition without first spelling out either a specific theory of language or a general theory of learning. Recent work on language acquisition, therefore, confronts these theoretical issues. It does so at the expense of large-scale data collection, investigators preferring to test out hypotheses on as few as two or three children, as Brown and Bellugi (1964) did with Adam and Eve, or on a single phonological, grammatical, or semantic distinction, as Klima and Bellugi (1966) did with negation.

One issue that has never been dealt with satisfactorily, even in recent work, is the specification of the ultimate linguistic knowledge or ability that is being acquired. Obviously, more is involved than knowledge of a dictionary or of an inventory of sentence patterns, or the ability to combine words and patterns. N. Chomsky (1965) has proposed the term *competence,* as distinguished from *performance,* to describe this knowledge. However, this term has become more of a slogan than a well-defined concept in linguistics. Since research in language acquisition must focus on such issues as "increasing complexity" and "developing competence," a certain vagueness results when the end point toward which the child is assumed to be progressing still remains largely hidden from view. Menyuk (1969) discusses some of the problems that result in attempts to interpret data in such circumstances. Fortunately, many of the data are not in dispute among those who study language acquisition, for all agree that certain stages or trends can be observed: babbling ends around 18 months; holophrastic utterances precede two- and three-word utterances; early speech is "telegraphic"; control of word order antedates control of inflections; and comprehension outstrips production. The interpretation of the data is the crucial issue.

Behavioristic Theories

In his book *Verbal Behavior,* Skinner (1957) proposes a comprehensive theory of language acquisition and language behavior in which specific linguistic behaviors are acquired through operant conditioning and then extended through response generalization. The devastating review of the book by N. Chomsky (1959) demonstrates the inappropriateness of Skinner's proposal. His criticisms reiterate earlier arguments from *Syntactic Structures* (1957) that existing theories of language are inadequate for almost any purpose and that the kind of theory he himself proposes is needed. The review also attacks the adequacy of reinforcement theory and the notion of generalization, as formulated by Skinner, in explaining either language acquisition or language behavior. Chomsky claims that the theory is illusionary, that most of its concepts are irrelevant in explaining linguistic behavior, and that the real issues are never confronted. Chomsky (1959) is particularly critical of Skinner's failure to recognize the contribution that the child makes to language acquisition, declaring that

. . . a refusal to study the contribution of the child to language learning permits only a superficial account of language acquisition, with a vast and unanalyzed contribution attributed to a step called "generalization" which in fact includes just about everything of interest in this process. If the study of language is limited in these ways, it seems inevitable that major aspects of verbal behavior will remain a mystery (p. 58).

However, in spite of Chomsky's criticisms of the inadequacy of conditioning or reinforcement theories to explain language acquisition, such theories are still proposed. Staats and Staats (1962, 1963, 1968), for example, use such terms as *operant learning, reinforcing stimuli, time and scheduling of reinforcement, successive approximation, chaining, extinction,* and *discrimination and generalization* to explain how language is acquired. Such concepts can only weakly explain why all children exhibit much the same pattern of development, how they construct novel utterances even in the earliest days of language use, and in what ways they master the abstract relationships that are not readily apparent in the utterances they hear. This last point is extremely important because, as Garrett and Fodor (1968) argue, the facts of language are abstractions which children must acquire from masses of highly variable data. Language is a mentalistic phenomenon, and S-R theories are unable to account for either its acquisition or use. The theory proposed by Staats and Staats involves the learning of a finite set of responses according to certain probabilities of occurrence. On the other hand, the current view is that a language is an infinite set of responses that are available to a speaker, and that language use is essentially creative. Probability has little to do with language use, although, of course, certain linguistic usages can be conditioned to events in the world *once such usages have been acquired.*

Jenkins and Palermo (1964) propose a theory of language acquisition that recognizes some recent linguistic advances. The basic problem they see in language acquisition is that of explaining how the child acquires the frames of a phrase-structure grammar and the ability to substitute items within these frames. They propose that the child learns the stimulus-and-response equivalences that can occur in the frames. They heavily emphasize imitation, either overt or covert, as a force in establishing bonds between stimuli and responses, and they claim that the child generalizes to form classes of responses. However, they do not explain how control of such classes allows the child to construct longer sentences. Their theory does not attempt to analyze complex issues; it merely hints at them. The linguistic theory that Jenkins and Palermo propose is one N. Chomsky (1957) criticizes for being inadequate in that it does not account for the abstract nature of linguistic knowledge. Weksel (1965) is also critical of their proposal, claiming that it is linguistically inadequate and nowhere comes to grips with its central concept of generalization.

Another theory of language acquisition cast in the behavioristic mold comes from Braine (1963a, 1963b, 1965). This theory involves the principle of "contextual generalization," according to which the child observes that certain sets of items occur in certain positions. He makes generalizations about positions rather than about the sets of items that occupy them. The positions themselves are not simply linear, but may be hierarchical. Consequently, the theory attempts to explain how the child acquires the hierarchical grammatical structures of sentences. Braine claims that transformations can be learned through contextual generalization. If they cannot, he declares that the failure argues as much for a reshaping of linguistic theory as it does for a reshaping of the principle of contextual generalization:

> If there is a possiblility that the simpler of two possible grammatical solutions might require the more complex acquisition theory, then the domain over which simplicity is taken cannot be restricted to grammar alone and must include acquisition theory—otherwise the grammarian merely purchases simplicity at the psychologist's expense (1965, p. 491).

Slobin (1970a) objects to Braine's proposal, citing evidence from a variety of languages. Bever, Fodor, and Weksel (1965a, 1965b) argue that no dominant patterns of word order exist for the child to generalize from, even in a language such as English, and that word ordering also occurs during language acquisition when the language has free word order. They say that the child must learn abstract structures for which no word-order patterns exist in the data to which he is exposed. Answering this last criticism, Braine (1965) points out that data do exist and that closer attention must be paid to how the child uses these data in the process of acquiring language.

Nativist Theories

Lenneberg (1967) proposes a theory of language acquisition heavily buttressed by biological evidence from studies of normal language development in children and of abnormal language development brought about congenitally, as in nanocephalic dwarfism, or environmentally, as in brain damage or aphasia. He emphasizes the development of the organism's capacities and shows how these mature along a fairly fixed schedule. Language emerges during this maturational process when anatomical, physiological, motor, neural, and cognitive developments allow it to emerge. Every child must learn the specific details of the language of his community, but the ability to learn language is innate and part of the biological endowment of the organism. The learning mechanisms, such as certain modes of perception, abilities in categorization, and capacities for transformation, are biologically given. According to Lenneberg, the child "resonates" to the language of his environment during the acquisition process; however, he never clearly specifies exactly what resonance is. One of Lenneberg's most interesting observations is that there is a critical, biologically determined period for language acquisition between the ages of two and twelve.

Since Lenneberg is interested in the biological bases of language acquisition, he has almost nothing to say about how particular linguistic items are learned, except to deny that statistical probability and imitation are important in the process. He claims that language acquisition is a natural activity, much as learning to walk is a natural activity. Both activities occur universally unless a pathological condition exists. Learning, as this term is traditionally defined, is not involved. Instead, Lenneberg carefully locks language acquisition into the general biological development of the organism.

McNeill (1966, 1968, 1970a, 1970b) takes a rather different nativist position toward language acquisition. He says that anyone who wishes to study the problem of language acquisition must begin with a knowledge of what it is that the child must acquire:

> A major requirement for any theory of language acquisition is that it explain a known phenomenon, which means that theories of development must be related to particular grammatical analyses, to particular theories about language itself (1968, p. 406).

McNeill claims that the child must acquire a generative-transformational grammar. Following N. Chomsky (1957, 1965), he asks what intrinsic properties must a device, a Language Acquisition Device (LAD), possess to acquire such a grammar from the corpus of utterances to which it is exposed:

> LAD is, of course, a fiction. The purpose in considering it is to discuss real children, not abstract ones. We can accomplish this because LAD and children present the same problem. LAD is faced with a corpus of utterances from which it develops a grammar on the basis of some kind of internal structure. So do children. We can readily posit that children and LAD arrive at the same grammar from the same corpus, and stipulate that children and LAD therefore have the same internal structure, at least within the limits that different children may be said to have the same internal structure. Accordingly, a theory about LAD is *ipso facto* a theory about children (1970a, p. 71).

The child must possess certain innate abilities; otherwise it is impossible to explain how the random, finite linguistic input into the child results in the output of linguistic competence.

According to McNeill, one innate property of the LAD is the ability to distinguish speech sounds from other sounds in the environment. A second property is the ability to organize linguistic events into various classes which can later be refined. This ability allows for the development of both the phonological and syntactic systems. One of the innate organizing principles is the concept of the "sentence." A third innate property is knowledge that only a certain kind of linguistic system is possible and that other kinds are not. McNeill claims that the child is born with an innate knowledge of linguistic universals. He distinguishes (1970a) between what he calls "weak" linguistic universals (reflections in language of universal cognitive abilities) and "strong" linguistic universals (reflections in language of specific linguistic abilities). He is more interested in the latter and seems skeptical of any claims advanced by cognitive theorists about the former. A fourth property is the ability to engage in constant evaluation of the developing linguistic system so as to construct the simplest possible system out of the linguistic data that are encountered.

In an attempt to justify his position, McNeill attacks S-R theory on the grounds that language acquisition is beyond its domain:

> Because S-R theory is so limited, the problem of language acquisition simply falls beyond its domain. This in itself is not a serious matter. Not all psychological theories need account for language acquisition. More serious, however, is the fact that the application of S-R principles causes theorists to redefine language in such a way as to make the phenomenon fit the theory. There is perhaps some irony in this outcome of modern empiricism (1968, p. 412).

McNeill also argues against the importance of the frequency of stimuli in language acquisition, using examples from Japanese, and against the importance of imitation. He claims that theories requiring imitation fail to explain why only certain responses occur. He criticizes Braine for ignoring the essential transformational nature of grammatical structure. Moreover, to Lenneberg's notion of a biological foundation for language, he adds a strong cognitive "content" component in the form of a structure for the mind that allows only certain kinds of language learning to occur. The organism has the capacity to learn and to generalize, but must realize this capacity within certain innate constraints that are suggested by a particular linguistic theory.

McNeill actually says very little about the mechanisms of acquisition. In addition, his claim that in the earliest stages the child speaks in the universal base structures of a generative-transformational grammar may not be linguistically sound. His further claim that the child "honors" grammatical distinctions before actually making them has been attacked as invalid by Bloom (in press).

Cognitive Theories

Like Fodor (1966), Slobin (1966a, 1966b) does not subscribe to nativistic theories of language acquisition. He says:

> It seems to me that the child is born not with a set of linguistic categories but with some sort of process mechanism—a set of procedures and inference rules, if you will—that he uses to process linguistic data (1966b, pp. 87-88).

Slobin regards language acquisition as an active process in which certain abilities of the child develop. One is the cognitive ability to deal with the world; a second is the mental ability to retain items in short-term memory, to store items in long-term memory, and to process information increasingly with age. The developments control the pace of language acquisition. Others are important, too, such as the ability to segment utterances into sounds and meanings, and then to combine and recombine these segments, the ability to isolate meaning units, and the ability to make wide generalizations before attempting to accommodate exceptions. However, according to Slobin, general cognitive and mental development is the critical determinant of language acquisition.

Slobin marshals evidence from a variety of languages to support his position that language acquisition is one kind of general development, and that the general principles involved in the latter must be recognized. He differs from McNeill in the way he uses linguistic data. McNeill uses such data to postulate the presence of innate linguistic principles; Slobin uses the same data to support innate principles of cognition. For example, in discussing McNeill's proposal concerning the child's innate knowledge of substantive linguistic universals, Slobin says:

> Perhaps all that is needed is an ability to learn certain types of semantic or conceptual categories, the knowledge that learnable semantic criteria can be the basis for grammatical categories, and, along with this substantive knowledge, the formal knowledge that such categories can be expressed by such morphological devices as affixing, sound alternation, and so on. The child's "preprogramming" for substantive universals is probably not for specific categories like past, animate, plural, and the like, but consists rather of the ability to learn categories of a certain as-yet-unspecified type (1966b, p. 89)

Slobin differs from the behaviorist theorists in that he is a cognitive-learning theorist who regards the human learner as an active participant in learning rather than as a relatively passive reactor to external stimuli:

> The important advances in language development thus seem to be tied to such variables as increasing ability to perform a number of operations in a short time, increasing short-term memory span, and increasing cognition of the categories and processes of human experience. In fact, it may be that strictly *linguistic* acquisition is completed by age three or so. Further development may reflect lifting of performance restrictions and general cognitive growth, without adding anything basically new to the fundamental structures of syntactic competence. We have begun to gather data on the earliest stages of language development. We have very little data on later stages. And our understanding of the mental processes underlying the course of this development is extremely rudimentary indeed. At this point I believe we are in need of much more data on children's acquisition of various native languages . . . (1970b, p. 184).

Cromer (1968) provides further evidence of the role of cognitive abilities in determining the language the child can use. From a study of the development of temporal reference in two children over a four-year period, he notes that several new types of reference to points in time begin to occur regularly at about the age of four to four and one-half for each child. Viewed together, these new forms indicate that the child has greatly expanded his range of temporal reference and increased his sense of the possible relations between times. Cromer notes that the ability develops to express events out of chronological order, to make statements about possibility, and to relate one time to another time. He hypothesizes that a single factor alone accounts for the observed linguistic changes: the child suddenly finds that he can free himself from the immediate situation and the actual order of events and can imagine himself at other points in time and view events from that perspective. This increase in his cognitive ability enables him to express new meanings, and he immediately masters the necessary syntactic apparatus to do so.

There are even stronger claims for a cognitive basis to language acquisition than those made by Slobin. Schlesinger (1971) claims that linguistic structures are ". . . determined by the innate *cognitive* power of the child," and Sinclair-de Zwart (1968) claims that "linguistic universals exist precisely because thought structures are universal." However, no empirical evidence apparently exists to confirm either claim.

Linguistically-Oriented Theories Versus
Learning-Oriented Theories

In trying to develop a theory of language acquisition, an investigator is faced with a fundamental decision concerning a starting point. Should he begin by accepting certain principles from linguistics or certain principles from psychology? In other words, should he begin by saying, as McNeill does, that what must be explained is how the child acquires a generative-transformational grammar, or by saying, as Staats and Staats do, that a behavioristic theory employing such principles as association-formation and stimulus and response generalization should be able to account for language acquisition? McNeill proceeds to dismiss current learning theories as inadequate to explain the special behavior or knowledge which he claims comprises linguistic competence, and Staats and Staats proceed to ignore certain kinds of linguistic data.

Braine attempts to fasten on to the best in both linguistic theory and learning theory. He claims that each must, if necessary, be changed to accommodate the other. The two extremes of the general positions taken by McNeill and by Staats and Staats are probably equally untenable, for at one extreme the interest is basically in the linguistic description of child language with very little concern for learning principles, and at the other extreme the interest is in applying learning principles derived from experiments with animals to the one behavior that no animal exhibits, linguistic behavior. Neither McNeill nor Staats and Staats take these extreme positions, but sometimes they seem to be approaching them. In the circumstances, Braine's middle ground may appear to be more attractive; however, both linguists and learning theorists find his proposed compromises unacceptable.

Fodor acknowledges the necessity for postulating some innate structure without committing himself as to whether this structure derives from innate linguistic principles or innate learning principles:

> . . . the child must bring to the language learning situation some amount of intrinsic structure. This structure may take the form of general learning principles or it may take the form of relatively detailed and language-specific information about the kind of grammatical system that underlies natural languages. But what cannot be denied is that any organism that extrapolates from its experience does so on the basis of principles that are not themselves supplied by the experience (1966, p. 106).

Slobin's position is less equivocal. He considers the child to be endowed with the cognitive capacity to perform extremely complicated tasks. The child accomplishes the complicated task of language acquisition according to general laws of development, learning, and perception. Consequently, he brings a particular capacity to the task rather than knowledge of a set of innate linguistic principles.

Four Controversial Issues

It is of interest to examine how various theories deal with the problems of the frequency of stimuli, the place of imitation, the role of expansion, and the function of meaning in language acquisition. In this way the theories can be shown to differ in certain important respects, and some preliminary assessment can be made of their relevance to beginning reading instruction.

The relative frequency of stimuli must be important in any behavioristic theory of learning. The most frequently occurring words and structures in the language should be acquired first by the child. However, the empirical evidence for language acquisition contradicts this expectation. Telegraphic speech, for example, omits the most frequently occurring words in the language, and investigators agree that every child goes through a "telegraphic" stage. There must be some reason for the existence of such speech, but it appears to have little to do with the frequency of stimuli in the environment.

McNeill (1966, 1968) also argues that Japanese children acquire a less frequent grammatical marker *ga* before a more frequent marker *wa* because *ga* is important as a deep subject marker whereas *wa* is not. He later (1970a, pp. 30-31) offers a rather different interpretation of the same data in accordance with the kinds of predicates (intrinsic with *wa* and extrinsic with *ga*) that the child is capable of forming at the age when *wa* and *ga* first appear in speech. Slobin (1970a) cites similar examples from other languages. If frequency is not important and certain kinds of learning occur in a definite progression, then the crucial issue is to account for this learning and the progression. McNeill argues that the structure of language and of the child's mind controls the learning, whereas Slobin argues that the child's cognitive and mental capacities at each stage regulate his ability to learn. However, each agrees with the other that the relative frequency of stimuli is of little importance in language acquisition.

Imitation in the sense of modeling also holds an important place in behavioristic theories of learning in which some kind of modeling of behavior must occur. While there is evidence that children do practice language (Weir, 1962) and do repeat some of the utterances of persons around them, they do not imitate indiscriminately. For example, Weir's child produced certain imitations but also made many variations on the imitated utterances. Babies do not imitate sounds in general, but they do respond quickly to human sounds. Lenneberg, Rebelsky, and Nichols (1965) also report that the prelinguistic vocalization behavior of deaf infants is no different from that of hearing infants. Therefore, imitation is not a critical factor in this very early stage of development, as it is, for example, in Jenkins and Palermo's (1964) theory. Menyuk (1963b) notes that the ability to imitate depends on the acquisition of some prior ability since children give evidence of various difficulties in imitating utterances. Utterances such as *allgone shoe, allgone lettuce,* and *allgone vitamins* reported by Braine (1963b) also argue against imitation and for some other ability, for no such sentences occurred in the environment of the child who produced them. Similar evidence is reported by Brown and Bellugi (1964) and by Miller and Ervin (1964).

One obvious constraint upon the child's ability to imitate is the limitation imposed by his short-term memory span. It is also very difficult to explain how simple imitation leads to development. Obviously, some issue has been skirted. Young children are actually rather poor imitators, as McNeill (1966) shows in the following sample:

> The signs are that sometimes a child's tendency to assimilate adult models into his current grammar is so strong that even when he makes a deliberate effort to copy adult speech, the effort may at first fail. One child, in the phase of producing double negatives while developing the negative transformation, had the following exchange with his mother:
>
>   Child: Nobody don't like me.
>   Mother: No, say "nobody likes me."
>   Child: Nobody don't like me.
>   [eight repetitions of this dialogue]
>   Mother: No, now listen carefully; say *"nobody likes me."*
>   Child: Oh! Nobody don't likes me.
>
> The exchange is interesting because it demonstrates the relative impenetrability of the child's grammar to adult models, even under the instruction (given by the mother's "no") to change. The child behaves at first as if he did not perceive the difference between his mother's sentence and his own, though later, when the mother supplied great emphasis, the child recognized a distinction. With this much delay in introducing changes, spontaneous imitations are bound not to be grammatically progressive because they consist only of a single exchange. The fact that a change ultimately was made, however, illustrates that children can profit from adult models. (p. 69).

McNeill does not deny the importance of models to the child in his learning, but does show that simple imitation of such models provides an inadequate explanation of linguistic development. Ervin (1964) demonstrates that imitations by children are not grammatically progressive, for they are less complicated syntactically than concurrent free utterances. Menyuk (1963a), Lenneberg, Nichols, and Rosenberger (1964), and Slobin and Welsh (1967) all report that children produce in imitation only what they produce in spontaneous speech even to the extent of reducing adult-given sentences to the forms they are currently producing.

Still another difficulty with relying heavily on imitation in any theory of language acquisition is the fact that much of the speech to which the child is exposed is considerably fragmented. Yet he learns to filter out poor examples in forming his grammar. This accomplishment is at least as difficult to explain as is the accomplishment of being able to react to more complex utterances than he can produce. Some factor other than imitaton must be involved in each case. Lenneberg (1962) points out one specific case in which imitation could not have been involved in language acquisition, that of a boy with a congenital motor disability that prevented him from speaking. However, since the same boy could understand complicated instructions, neither imitation nor reinforcement could be used to explain his abilities. The language of the environment in which the child finds himself is vitally important to him in his acquisition of language. But direct imitation of that language seems not to occur except in rather small amounts.

The role of expansion in language acquisition is a still more complicated issue. Parents do correct and expand the speech of their children. However, there is evidence that children are not particularly receptive to direct instruction in language, as is obvious in the quotation cited above from McNeill. Although corrections might be expected to extinguish certain undesirable linguistic behaviors, they are unlikely to promote desirable ones. Expansions might be helpful in stimulating linguistic development, and some agreement exists that middle-class mothers expand their children's speech about 30% of the time and that such use of expansion forms a part of the normal mother-child relationship. Cazden (1965) tested the hypothesis that expansions of children's utterances would aid language acquisition more than would comments on their utterances, which she called models, and that both would produce better results than no expansion or modeling responses. She divided twelve 2½-year-old children into three groups: the first group received intensive and deliberate expansions; the second group received qualitatively equal exposure to well-formed sentences that were models, not expansions; and the third group received no special treatment at all. Her experiment lasted twelve weeks. The results do not show quite the expected differences; modeling, not expansion, was more effective. That is, semantically enriched responses were more effective than syntactically enriched responses. However, a more recent study by Feldman and Rodgon (1970) reports results at variance with those of Cazden. In a further study, Brown, Cazden, and Bellugi (1968) analyzed the conversations of mothers and children aged one to four years to determine what happens during such conversations. They report that the syntactic correctness or incorrectness of a child's speech does not control the mother's approval or disapproval. Rather the truth or falsity of the utterance does. They conclude that parents tend to reward true statements and punish false ones; however, somewhat surprisingly, the result is the eventual production of syntactically correct sentences.

Deliberate expansion of children's language by adults would seem to be one of the most important possible influences on language development. However, the evidence does not confirm this hypothesis. Having considered the evidence from research in the use of both imitation and expansion, Slobin (1968) concludes that there is little evidence to support imitation. However, he takes a more positive attitude toward expansion:

> It has been suggested that frequency of parental expansion of child speech may be related to such variables as social class and education, and, in turn, be partly responsible for differences in language acquisition and ability in children of different socioeconomic backgrounds. The issue is certainly complex, and we are far from being able to determine the function—if any—of expansion and imitation in the human child's remarkable acquisition of language. Until the necessary data are amassed, I would still like to believe that when a child hears an adult expansion of his own speech he learns something important about the structure of his language (1968, p. 443).

The results as a whole argue more for the acceptance of language-acquisition theories like those of Lenneberg, McNeill, and Slobin than they do for those of Braine and Staats and Staats, and more for the importance of some kind of innate linguistic or cognitive structure than of the actual stimuli encountered in the environment.

Studies of language acquisition tend to focus on the acquisition of phonology or syntax. The place and function of meaning in language acquisition have largely been ignored. However, meaning is today assuming greater importance in studies of language acquisition.

Following a comprehensive review of Russian data on language development in children, Slobin (1966a) suggests that the order of emergence of various syntactic categories depends on their relative semantic difficulty rather than on their grammatical complexity. The first grammatical distinctions to appear are those like the singular-plural distinction that make some concrete reference to the outside world. Later to emerge are the diminutive suffixes of nouns, imperatives, and categories based on relational criteria, such as the case, tense, and person markings of verbs. Conditional forms of the *if-then* variety are not learned until near the end of the third year. Still other abstract categories of quality and action continue to be added until the age of seven. Slobin argues that semantic complexity rather than grammatical difficulty determines the developmental sequence. Grammatical gender in Russian is the most difficult of all the categories for the child to master since it has almost no semantic correlates. No rules exist that the child can discover to make the learning easier, so the acquisition of gender is a long, drawn-out process. Slobin (1966a) concludes: "The semantic and conceptual aspects of grammatical classes thus clearly play an important role in determining the order of their development and subdivision" (p. 142).

Telegraphic speech is full of "contentive" words. Slobin (1971, pp. 44-46) shows some of the semantic range of telegraphic speech in various languages (English, German, Russian, Finnish, Luo, and Samoan). Following an analysis of such speech, a reexamination of the data from the pivot grammars of investigators such as Braine, and some work of her own, Bloom (1970, in press) argues that the evidence indicates that semantic competence outstrips syntactic competence. Her own research showed that noun-noun combinations in the speech of very young English children expressed at least the following five relations: conjunction (*block dolly*), attribution (*party hat*), genitive (*daddy hat*), subject-locative (*sweater chair*), and subject-object (*mommy book*). She also found that an utterance such as *no truck* could have various meanings, which themselves showed an order of emergence: "nonexistence" (*There's no truck here*) preceding "rejection" (*I don't want a truck*), which in turn precedes "denial" (*It's not a truck; it's something else*). She concludes that the child's underlying semantic competence is more differentiated than the surface forms of his utterances, because he is aware of more types of meaning relationships than he can reveal through the linguistic devices he controls. Before he develops these devices, his two-word utterances can only be properly interpreted through the use of the nonlinguistic context. Quite often a young child must produce a series of short utterances in order to convey information that an adult or an older child expresses in a single utterance. For example, he might say *raisin there / buy more grocery store / raisins / raisins / buy more grocery store / grocery store / raisin a grocery store* instead of one sentence about buying more raisins at the grocery store. Consequently, Bloom (1970) claims that three components operate in the development of language competence: cognitive-perceptual development, linguistic experience, and nonlinguistic experience. She notes that these components converge during the child's development.

An Assessment of the Theories

The studies reported by McCarthy encompass massive quantities of data but lack clearly defined theories of language acquisition. A concern for such theories is a fairly recent development in studies of language acquisition. However, all such theories have at least the weaknesses of lack of detail and lack of empirical validation. They are all very general, often being little more than series of claims about what must be, the claims being supported by reference to carefully selected data often acquired from no more than a few children. Consequently, they are often hardly any more convincing than former presentations of large quantities of data that really make no claims at all.

Recently proposed theories make either a language or learning component central. Making a language component central requires postulation of a strong innate predisposition toward the acquisition of very specific kinds of linguistic facts, for the child is assumed to "know" much about language in general before any learning of specific details begins. Environmental factors are relatively unimportant in such theories. On the other hand, older behavioristic learning theories hold the environment to be extremely important in providing language stimuli and controlling the learning that occurs. According to such theories, language acquisition is achieved through such processes as association and response generalization. The child makes little or no active contribution to the total process and learns language in much the same way as he learns anything else.

A less extreme position is that language acquisition is unique because language is different from anything else that is learned, but that the learning requires use of many of the same principles as other kinds of learning. In this case, the theory may have a large biological component that emphasizes the importance of certain kinds of universal neurological and physiological developments. Or it may assume the availability of this component and emphasize the kinds of meaningful situations that stimulate language acquisition and the cognitive limitations that human development places on the acquisition process. Unfortunately, since meaning has long been a stepchild in linguistics and cognitive theory a poor relation in psychology, it is difficult at present to fill out the details of any such theory.

An evaluation of the importance of such factors as frequency, imitation, and expansion in language acquisition leads to the rejection of any kind of monolithic behavioristic theory. However, it does not eliminate linguistically based theories nor does it contradict cognitively based ones. The evaluation reveals how unimportant each of the factors is in language acquisition, and indicates the necessity of crediting the child with some kind of innate knowledge or capacity. The difficulty with the innate-knowledge hypothesis is that investigators like McNeill have very little to say about the mechanisms through which that knowledge reveals itself, nor do they try to relate language learning to other kinds of learning. The result is something less than a parsimonious view of total human development. The advantage of the innate-capacity hypothesis is that general laws of learning, but not exclusively behavioristic ones, can be used to explain both language acquisition and other kinds of learning. Sachs (1971) summarizes this problem as follows:

> Theories of language acquisition that consider only the linguistic aspect will not be able to explain why the child learns new forms when he does, or in fact why he ever changes his form of expression. It is only through more research on the complex relationship between cognitive development and language acquisition that we will have a full understanding of either. Hopefully in the future we will find more studies of this type, and a closer communication between psycholinguists and psychologists studying other aspects of child development (p. 394).

The linguistically based theories all have one serious drawback in that they are concerned with the ideal child. Theories recognizing individual and group differences are ignored in favor of theories that try to account for the development of abstract linguistic competence. Social, motivational, and cultural variables are all ignored. The child is said to have acquired his basic linguistic competence by the age of five or six. While performance is acknowledged to vary from child to child, such variability, whatever its cause, is ignored, often under the guise of "performance" differences, which are at best of peripheral interest. The result is a deliberate biasing of the theories toward accommodating one set of factors in language acquisition and ignoring almost all others.

Language Acquisition and Beginning Reading

Language Acquisition after Age Six

Although many linguists claim that the major part of language acquisition takes place in the years between the ages of one and four, children who enter school do not have the linguistic abilities of adults. Furthermore, the linguistic abilities of adults change, and sometimes develop, during their lives. It is of interest to know the precise differences between the linguistic abilities of children entering school and of adults. Numerous investigators have shown that significant language development still occurs in all children after the age of five or six, among them Harrell (1957), Strickland (1962), Loban (1963), Menyuk (1963b), and O'Donnell, Griffin, and Norris (1967).

In a recent study, C. S. Chomsky (1969) points out several grammatical developments that occur during the years that follow six: a grasp of the difference between the *eager to see* and *easy to see* constructions; a realization that *ask* and *tell* require different syntactic constructions; the ability to handle relationship requiring *and* and *although;* and a control of pronominalizations. Kessell (1970) used a Piaget-type interview technique similar to that used by C. S. Chomsky in further work on some of the same problems. His study confirms her results but also reports evidence of a somewhat earlier mastery of the complex constructions. Menyuk (1969) points out other examples in which a more complicated structure is learned later than a less complicated one. However, in every case it is possible to argue that the linguistic development has not occurred because the cognitive capacities of the child did not allow it rather than because the structure which is learned second is more complicated than the one which is learned first. Of course, since it is also possible to argue that the structure learned second is grammatically more complicated, the temptation is to postulate a linguistic rather than a cognitive constraint on development, particularly when the investigator is linguistically oriented.

Two linguistic abilities that children of about age six appear to have are those to overdiscriminate and to overgeneralize. N. Chomsky (1964) points out that they have very sharp abilities to discriminate among phonetically close stimuli. Ervin (1964) and Miller and Ervin (1964) say that they tend to eliminate from their language irregular but correct inflections in favor of regular but incorrect ones for a while. Slobin (1970a), citing evidence mainly from Russian, discusses this same phenomenon, which he calls "inflectional imperialism." Bever, Mehler, and Valian (1968) report that children aged two to four temporarily overgeneralize newly acquired semantic strategies. There is also some agreement that children do not interpret "same" and "different" in the way that mature adults do, nor are they able to work in a conscious analytic fashion with language, as many adults can. Slobin (1970a) points out that the Russian data he analyzed provide evidence that any kind of direct instruction in the analysis of language is rather ineffective with children.

In one crucial area for any kind of reading instruction that relies on the relationship of individual sounds to symbols, the acquisition of phonology, six-year-olds have not mastered the system that educated literate adults appear to have mastered (Chomsky & Halle, 1968; C. S. Chomsky, 1970). The abilities of the two groups appear to be quite different. *Indeed language acquisition in this area appears to depend on the acquisition of the ability to read, but this is the only place where this particular dependency occurs.*

Some Important Differences between Language Acquisition and Beginning Reading

Whatever theory of language acquisition an investigator subscribes to, behavioristic, nativistic, or cognitive, he must readily admit that important differences exist between the acquisition of language and the acquisition of beginning reading skills. Staats and Staats (1962), Carroll (1966), and Natchez (1967) are among those who point out some of the specific differences.

Language is acquired gradually and the acquisition process is probably never completed, for something always remains to be learned. The process is also one that had no conscious beginning point for the child. On the other hand, learning to read often has a sudden onset for children, although some are fortunate to avoid this kind of introduction. Even though some of the cognitive and motor skills necessary for reading have been developed for other activities, the child is often required to put them all together rather abruptly in learning to read in a formal school setting.

The level of anxiety in the context in which learning to read takes place may also be quite high: the anxiety of the parent, teacher, and the child. Little such anxiety is manifested during the process of learning to talk. Certainly, it is the rare child who exhibits anxiety, and, if the occasional parent is anxious about a particular child's speech, this anxiety seems to have little influence on the child's language development. There is also often a concomitant assignment of blame for any "failure" that occurs in beginning reading instruction. Children are not "blamed" when they fail to acquire language; rather, they are given special help.

Reading instruction is very formal and deliberate. Language, however, is learned informally and unconsciously from a wide range of stimuli. No deliberate instruction is necessary. Language is not learned from programmed stimuli, from making conscious distinctions among stimuli, from learning "about" language, and from acquiring control of a variety of analytic and synthetic techniques. While controversy does exist as to the function of linguistic stimuli in language acquisition, there is agreement that such stimuli vary in both form and content in ways that are not well understood, but which the child is well able to handle.

The usual reinforcements experienced by literate adults for reading may be irrelevant for many children in the beginning reading stages: the benefits are often too abstract, distant, and meaningless, and the effort to be expended for such remote ends may seem to be quite wasteful and unpleasant to the child. On the other hand, the benefits of learning to speak are too obvious to mention.

The two activities are also different in certain other ways. Learning to read depends on the acquisition of special skills in visual discrimination. The redundancies in the two language systems that are involved are also different, as is quite often the content, that is, the meanings that are conveyed. Writing is not simply speech written down: it is more abstract than speech in content; it usually employs carefully edited and controlled language for reasons different from speaking; and it functions rather differently in the lives of the recipients of the message. Vygotsky (1962) writes as follows on these very points, but in connection with writing rather than reading:

> Written speech is a separate linguistic function, differing from oral speech in both structure and mode of functioning. Even its minimal development requires a high level of abstraction. . . . Our studies show that it is the abstract quality of written language that is the main stumbling block, not the underdevelopment of small muscles or any other mechanical obstacles.
>
> Writing is also speech without an interlocutor, addressed to an absent or an imaginary person or to no one in particular—a situation new and strange to the child. Our studies show that he has little motivation to learn writing when we begin to teach it. He feels no need for it and has only a vague idea of its usefulness. In conversation, every sentence is prompted by a motive. Desire or need lead to request, question to answer, bewilderment to explanation. The changing motives of the interlocutors determine at every moment the turn oral speech will take. It does not have to be consciously directed—the dynamic situation takes care of that. The motives for writing are more abstract, more intellectualized, further removed from immediate needs. In written speech, we are obliged to create the situation, to represent it to ourselves. This demands detachment from the actual situation.
>
> Writing also requires deliberate analytical action on the part of the child. In speaking, he is hardly conscious of the sounds he pronounces and quite unconscious of the mental operations he performs. In writing, he must take cognizance of the sound structure of each word, dissect it, and reproduce it in alphabetical symbols which he must have studied and memorized before (pp. 98-99).

Reid (1966), Meltzer and Herse (1969), and Downing (1970) all point to the confusion that children often experience in learning to read. Evidently, many children do not understand what reading is, or what they are supposed to be doing, or what the terms mean that are used in the instructional process.

The usual methods of reading instruction employ imitation, repetition, control of stimuli, correction, and expansion—exactly those factors examined earlier in relation to the acquisition of language. These factors were found not to be very important in language acquisition; however, they are very important in reading instruction. Of course, instruction implies some kind of methodology, so the reason for their existence is obvious. Yet, it would be well to subject that methodology to periodic critical assessment in the light of the latest findings from relevant disciplines. Of course, one can also argue that since language acquisition and learning to read are quite different tasks, these factors may still be important in the teaching of beginning reading.

Finally, language acquisition does not cease at age six. Consequently, some kinds of acquisition overlap with learning to read. However, little is known about the extent of this overlap, for the later stages of language acquisition are even more of a mystery than are the earlier stages. It may be that more than one of these stages depends on the child's acquiring certain reading abilities just as beginning reading ability quite definitely depends on the acquisition of considerable linguistic competence. However, this acquisition has occurred in six-year-olds except in rare pathological cases.

Conclusion

The theories of language acquisition that are available to us today are largely irrelevant in deciding issues in beginning reading instruction or even in devising models of the reading process. Moreover, reading failure cannot easily be linked to deficiencies in language acquisition, for children who are asked to learn to read are almost invariably well on the way to linguistic maturity.

Reading methods themselves are almost unrelated to theories of language acquisition. Both phonics and whole-word methods depend on the possession of certain language abilities which all children of six apparently have: What they might not have are some of the cognitive abilities that the methods require: abilities to make certain kinds of discriminations, to form generalizations, and to verbalize knowledge. Furthermore, much of what is taught "about" language in such methods is antiquated and not very useful to anyone, particularly to six-year-olds.

Reading is often taught to improve language. Research has long demonstrated that such teaching is generally ineffective. Some linguistic skills apparently derive from the acquisition of the skills of literacy, but these skills appear to be few and certainly do not seem to be acquired during the critical period of beginning reading instruction.

REFERENCES

Bever, T. G., Fodor, J. A., & Weksel, W. Is linguistics empirical? *Psychological Review,* 1965a, 72, 492-500.

Bever, T. G., Fodor, J. A., & Weksel, W. On the acquisition of syntax: A critique of "Contextual generalization." *Psychological Review,* 1965b, 72, 467-482.

Bever, T. G., Mehler, J. R., & Valian, V. V. Linguistic capacity of very young children. Unpublished manuscript, ERIC ED 018-796, 1968.

Bloom, L. *Language development: Form and function in emerging grammars.* Cambridge, Mass.: M.I.T. Press, 1970.

Bloom, L. Why not pivot grammar? *The Journal of Speech and Hearing Disorders,* in press.

Braine, M. D. S. On learning the grammatical order of words. *Psychological Review,* 1963a, 70, 323-348.

Braine, M. D. S. The ontogeny of English phrase structure: The first phase. *Language,* 1963b, 39, 1-13.

Braine, M. D. S. On the basis of phrase structure: A reply to Bever, Fodor, and Weksel. *Psychological Review,* 1965, 72, 483-492.

Brown, R. *Social psychology.* New York: Free Press, 1965.

Brown, R., & Bellugi, U. Three processes in the child's acquisition of syntax. *Harvard Educational Review,* 1964, 34, 133-151.

Brown, R., & Berko, J. Psycholinguistic research methods. In P. H. Mussen (Ed.), *Handbook of research methods in child development.* New York: Wiley, 1960.

Brown, R., Cazden, C. B., Bellugi, U. The child's grammar from I to III. In J. P. Hill (Ed.), *The 1967 Minnesota symposium on child psychology.* Minneapolis: University of Minnesota Press, 1968.

Carroll, J. B. Language development in children. In *Encyclopedia of educational research.* New York: Macmillan, 1960. Pp. 744-750.

Carroll, J. B. Some neglected relationships in reading and language learning. *Elementary English,* 1966, 43, 577-582.

Cazden, C. B. Environmental assistance to the child's acquisition of grammar. Unpublished doctoral dissertation, Harvard University, 1965.

Chomsky, C. S. *The acquisition of syntax in children from 5 to 10.* Cambridge, Mass.: M.I.T. Press, 1969.

Chomsky, C. S. Reading, writing, and phonology. *Harvard Educational Review,* 1970, 40, 287-309.

Chomsky, N. *Syntactic structures.* The Hague: Mouton, 1957.

Chomsky, N. Review of B. F. Skinner, *Verbal behavior. Language,* 1959, 35, 26-58.

Chomsky, N. Comments for project literacy meeting. *Project Literacy Reports,* 1964, 2, 1-8.

Chomsky, N. *Aspects of the theory of syntax.* Cambridge, Mass.: M.I.T. Press, 1965.

Chomsky, N., & Halle, M. *The sound pattern of English.* New York: Harper & Row, 1968.

Cromer, R. The development of temporal references during the acquisition of language. Unpublished doctoral dissertation, Harvard University, 1968.

Downing, J. The development of linguistic concepts in children's thinking. *Research in the Teaching of English,* 1970, 4, 5-19.

Elkonin, D. B. *Razvitie rechi v doshkol'nom vozraste* (The development of speech in preschool age). Moscow: Akad. Pedag, Nauk RSFSR, 1958.

Ervin, S. M. Imitation and the structural change in children's language. In E. H. Lenneberg (Ed.), *New directions in the study of language.* Cambridge, Mass.: M.I.T. Press, 1964.

Ervin-Tripp, S. M. Language development. In M. Hoffman & L. Holman (Eds.), *Review of child development research, 2.* Ann Arbor: University of Michigan Press, 1966.

Ervin-Tripp, S. M., & Slobin, D. I. Psycholinguistics. *Annual Review of Psychology,* 1966, 17, 435-474.

Feldman, C. F., & Rodgon, M. The effects of various types of adult responses in the syntactic acquisition of two- to three-year-olds. Unpublished paper. Department of Psychology. University of Chicago, 1970.

Fodor, J. A. How to learn to talk: Some simple ways. In F. Smith & G. A. Miller (Eds.), *The genesis of language: A psycholinguistic approach.* Cambridge, Mass.: M.I.T. Press, 1966.

Garrett, M., & Fodor, J. A. Psychological theories and linguistic constructs. In T. R. Dixon & D. L. Horton (Eds.),*Verbal behavior and general behavior theory.* Englewood Cliffs, N. J.: Prentice-Hall, 1968.

Harrell, L. E., Jr. An inter-comparison of the quality and rate of the development of the oral and written language in children. *Monographs of the Society for Research in Child Development,* 1957, 22.

Jenkins, J., & Palermo, D. Mediation processes and the acquisition of linguistic structure. In U. Bellugi & R. W. Brown (Eds.), The acquisition of language. *Monographs of the Society for Research in Child Development,* 1964, 29 (1, Serial No. 92).

Kelley, K. L. *Early syntactic acquisition.* Santa Monica, Calif.: Rand Corporation, 1967.

Kessell, F. S. The role of syntax in children's comprehension from ages six to twelve. *Monographs of the Society for Research in Child Development,* 1970, 35, No. 6 (Whole No. 139).

Klima, E. S., & Bellugi, U. Syntactic regularities in the speech of children. In J. Lyons & R. Wales (Eds.), *Psycholinguistic papers.* Edinburgh: Edinburgh University Press, 1966.

Lenneberg, E. H. Understanding language without the ability to speak: A case report. *Journal of Abnormal Social Psychology,* 1962, 65, 419-425.

Lenneberg, E. H. *Biological foundations of language.* New York: Wiley, 1967.

Lenneberg, E. H., Nichols, I. A., & Rosenberger, E. F. Primitive stages of language development in mongolism. *Proceedings of the Association for Research on Nervous and Mental Disease,* 1964, 42, 119-137.

Lenneberg, E. H., Rebelsky, F. G., & Nichols, I. A. The vocalization of infants born to deaf and to hearing parents. *Vita Humana,* 1965, 8, 23-27.

Loban, W. D. *The language of elementary school children.* Champaign, Ill.: National Council of Teachers of English, 1963.

McCarthy, D. Language development in children. In L. Carmichael (Ed.), *Manual of child psychology.* New York: Wiley, 1954.

McNeil, D. Developmental psycholinguistics. In F. Smith & G. A Miller (Eds.), *The genesis of language: A psycholinguistic approach.* Cambridge, Mass.: M.I.T. Press, 1966.

McNeill, D. On the theories of language acquisition. In T. R. Dixon & D. L. Horton (Eds.), *Verbal behavior and general behavior theory.* Englewood Cliffs, N. J.: Prentice-Hall, 1968.

McNeill, D. *The acquisition of language: The study of developmental psycholinguistics.* New York: Harper & Row, 1970a.

McNeill, D. The development of language. In P. A. Mussen (Ed.), *Carmichael's manual of child psychology.* New York: Wiley, 1970b.

Meltzer, N. S., & Herse, R. The boundaries of written words as seen by first graders. *Journal of Reading Behavior,* 1969, 1, 3-13.

Menyuk, P. A preliminary evaluation of grammatical capacity in children. *Journal of Verbal Learning and Verbal Behavior,* 1963a, 2, 429-439.

Menyuk, P. Syntactic structures in the language of children. *Child Development,* 1963b, 34, 407-422.

Menyuk, P. *Sentences children use.* Cambridge, Mass.: M.I.T. Press, 1969.

Miller, W., & Ervin, S. M. The development of grammar in child language. In U. Bellugi & R. Brown (Eds.), The acquisition of language, *Monographs of the Society for Research in Child Development,* 1964, 29 (1, Serial No. 92).

Natchez, G. From talking to reading without really trying. *The Reading Teacher,* 1967, 20, 339-342.

O'Donnell, R. C., Griffin, W. J., & Norris, R. C. *Syntax of kindergarten and elementary school children: A transformational analysis.* Champaign, Ill.: National Council of Teachers of English, 1967.

Reid, J. F. Learning to think about reading. *Educational Research,* 1966, 9, 56-62.

Sachs, J. The status of developmental studies of language. In J. Eliot (Ed.), *Human development and cognitive processes.* New York: Hold, Rinehart, & Winston, 1971.

Schlesinger, I. M. Production of utterance and language acquisition. In D. I. Slobin (Ed.), *The ontogenesis of grammar: Facts and theories.* New York: Academic Press, 1971.

Sinclair-De Zwart, H. Sensorimotor action schemes as a condition of the acquisition of syntax. Unpublished paper, University of Geneva, 1968.

Slobin, D. I. The acquisition of Russian as a native language. In F. Smith & G. A. Miller (Eds.), *The genesis of language: A psycholinguistic approach.* Cambridge, Mass.: M.I.T. Press, 1966a.

Slobin, D. I. Comments on "Developmental psycholinguistics." In F. Smith & G. A. Miller (Eds.), *The genesis of language: A psycholinguistic approach.* Cambridge, Mass.: M.I.T. Press, 1966b.

Slobin, D. I. Imitation and grammatical development. In N. S. Endler, L. R. Boulter, & H. Osser (Eds.), *Contemporary issues in developmental psychology.* New York: Holt, Rinehart, & Winston, 1968.

Slobin, D. I. Early grammatical development in several languages, with special attention to Soviet research. In T. G. Bever and W. Weksel (Eds.), *The structure and psychology of language.* New York: Holt, Rinehart, & Winston, 1970a.

Slobin, D. I. Universals of grammatical development in children. In G. B. Flores d'Arcais & W. J. M. Levelt (Eds.), *Advances in psycholinguistics.* Amsterdam: North Holland Publishing Company, 1970b.

Slobin, D. I. *Psycholinguistics.* Glenview, Ill.: Scott, Foresman, 1971.

Slobin, D. I., & Welsh, C. A. Elicited imitation as a research tool in developmental psycholinguistics. Unpublished paper, Department of Psychology, University of California, Berkeley, 1967.

Staats, A. W., & Staats, C. K. A comparison of the development of speech and reading behavior with implications for research. *Child Development,* 1962, 33, 831-846.

Staats, A. W., & Staats, C. K. *Complex human behavior: A systematic extension of learning principles.* New York: Holt, Rinehart, & Winston, 1963.

Staats, A. W. *Language, learning, and cognition.* New York: Holt, Rinehart, & Wintston, 1968.

Strickland, R. G. The language of elementary school children: Its relationship to the language of reading textbooks and the quality of reading of selected children. *Bulletin of the School of Education,* 1962, 38, Bloomington: Indiana University.

Vygotsky, L. S. *Thought and language.* Cambridge, Mass.: M.I.T. Press, 1962.

Weir, R. *Language in the crib.* The Hague: Moulton, 1962.

Weksel, W. Review of U. Bellugi and R. Brown (Eds.), *The acquisition of language. Language,* 1965, 41, 692-709.

The Effects of Grammatical Complexity on Children's Comprehension, Recall, and Conception of Certain Semantic Relations*

P. DAVID PEARSON
University of Minnesota

This study consists of 3 separate experiments, 2 of which have several parts. Experiment 1 examined, through the use of wh-type questions, the effects of syntactic complexity on children's comprehension of causal relations and of modifying (adjective-noun) relations. Experiments 2 and 3 were conducted subsequent to Experiment 1 in order to shed some light on some of the ambiguous results emanating from Experiment 1.

Experiment 2 examined children's preferences among several syntactically different ways of expressing a common idea. Children were given a question to answer, followed by a set of statements, each of which contained the answer to the question. They were asked to rank the statements according to the degree of helpfulness each provided in answering the question.

Experiment 3 examined differences between the syntactic form in which statements were read by subjects and the syntactic form in which the same statements were later recalled.

Purpose of the Study

Considering the 3 experiments as a group, this study was designed to provide an assessment of linguistic variables which might conceivably affect the way in which children comprehend verbal data when they read. It was simultaneously designed to investigate certain explicit claims and implicit assumptions emerging from research and theoretical positions in the field of transformational-generative grammar.

---

*Reprinted from *Reading Research Quarterly*, 10, 2, 1974-1975, 155-192.

Theoretical Positions under Consideration

Three theoretical positions are considered as possible candidates in explaining the data obtained in this study as well as that in related studies.

The first theoretical position is referred to as the *readability hypothesis* because it emanates from assumptions and conclusions stemming from readability research. Broadly speaking, this hypothesis claims that sentence length and sentence complexity contribute to comprehension difficulty.

The second theoretical position is the *deep structure model.* It arises from psycholinguistic research which has been based upon transformational-generative grammars (*e.g.,* Miller and McKean, 1964; Mehler, 1963). It attempts to establish correlates between operations used in transformational-generative grammar and operations used by people in processing verbal data. In short, it attempts to use a grammatical model as a psychological model. The relevant claim of such a model, as it relates to the 3 experiments in this study, is that as surface structure form (the way we see and hear language) approaches deep structure form (the state in which we consciously or unconsciously process and understand language in the mind), comprehension is facilitated. This facilitation occurs because the listener or reader must undergo fewer operations (transformations) in order to analyze, or break down, the surface structure form into deep structure form.

The third theoretical position is referred to as the *chunk model.* It is called the chunk model because it claims that comprehension consists of synthesizing atomistic propositions into larger conceptual or semantic units rather than analyzing complex units into atomistic propositions. If the surface form of a statement is already highly synthesized, comprehension is facilitated. If, on the other hand, the surface form is broken down somewhat (is closer to its deep structure form), comprehension is impeded.

The chunk model and the deep structure model represent diametrically opposed theoretical positions. That which the chunk model predicts will be difficult, the deep structure model predicts will be simple, and vice-versa. The readability hypothesis represents a theoretical position near, but not identical to, the deep structure model. As will be explicated later, sentence length and grammatical complexity tend to co-vary with transformational complexity. That is, longer sentences and sentences with more subordinate clauses and phrases also tend to have more transformations.

Discussion of Related Readability Research

Classic Readability Procedures

Since the readability hypothesis is one of the 3 theoretical positions tested by the data from this study, it is useful to review the procedures used to construct a readability formula.

The classic mode for constructing a readability formula includes these steps:

1) A series of passages known to be graded with respect to difficulty is selected. The basis for grading the passages is usually the number of correct responses made by students judged to have the ability to read at various grade levels to a variety of multiple choice comprehension items accompanying the passages. However, more recently cloze test procedures have been used (*e.g.*, Bormuth, 1966).

2) All potential factors in the passages which might prove to be predictive of passage difficulty are enumerated. They may be formal factors: the number of words per sentence, the number of subordinate clauses, the number of prepositional phrases. Or they may be conceptual factors: the number of words with concrete referents, the number of "vivid" words, the number of abstract words. Usually formula writers have resorted to formal factors because they can be more reliably and objectively measured. Also, since they appear at the surface level, they do not require expert judgment concerning their occurrence. Gray and Leary (1935), who performed the "classic" study in this mode, began with 82 potential formal factors when they set out to develop a formula. The concluded that 44 of the factors were significantly related to reading difficulty. Bormuth (1966), in a more recent attempt, found over 60 formal (or structural) factors that were useful in predicting comprehension difficulty.

3) A multiple regression analysis is performed to determine which factors are most highly related to the criterion measure and at what point the inclusion of another factor in the regression equation ceases to yield a significant increase in the predictive power of the equation.

4) Mathematical transformations are used to translate the formula into grade level equivalents (*e.g.*, 3.2, 4.5, etc.)

Factors Commonly Found in Readability Formulas

While a variety of factors have appeared in different readability formulas, 3 types of factors consistently appear (Klare, 1963). First, almost all formulas have some measure of word difficulty. These usually turn out to be a direct or, more commonly, an indirect measure of word frequency. Second, about 60 per cent of the available formulas use some measure of sentence length. Third, about 30 per cent use some measure of sentence complexity (*e.g.*, number of prepositional phrases or the number of subordinate clauses).

Uses of Readability Formulas

After the regression equations are built, the formula is ready to use as an instrument to measure the difficulty of existing material or as an aid to use in constructing new material. Flesch (1945, 1946a, 1946b, 1951), for example, has prepared several handbooks and sets of recommendations to guide a writer in constructing new materials. While some of his recommendations relate to conceptual elements (abstractness/concreteness), most are methods for reducing sentence length. For example, he recommends using as few adjectives and adverbs as possible and avoiding prepositions and replacing coordinating and subordinating conjunctions with periods.

Such recommendations reveal a common error in interpreting correlational data by assuming that correlation means causality. The fact that sentence length, sentence complexity, or any other factor correlates with the difficulty people experience in answering questions does not imply that altering those correlates will reduce difficulty. It may be that length and complexity are simply indices of complex semantic content; that is, a long or complex sentence is long or complex because it represents a concept or principle that could not be communicated in simpler language.

Experimental Studies Based on Readability Formulas

An interesting question to ask is: If you have a concept that you want to communicate, what syntactic form should you select in order to maximize comprehension? Such a question cannot be answered by using correlational analysis. Its answer demands that semantic content be held constant, while syntactic form is varied, between versions of a passage.

Several studies appear to have been designed to answer this question or similar questions. They fall out into 3 groups distinguishable by their independent variables (see Table 1). All the studies in group 1 used sentence length as the independent variable; those in group 2, word frequency; those in group 3, total readability score (an independent variable which included both sentence length and word frequency). The

Table 1. **Studies using reading comprehension criteria**

Group	Author(s)	Date	Independent Variable	Findings
1	1. Orndorff	1925	Long vs. short sentences	No difference
	2. Gibbons	1931	Long vs. short sentences	Indeterminate
	3. Holland	1933	Long vs. short sentences	Indeterminate
	4. Hites	1950	Long vs. short sentences	No difference
2	5. Nolte	1937	Low vs. high vocabulary scores	No difference
	6. Kueneman	1931	Low vs. high vocabulary scores	No difference
3	7. Marshall	1957	Low vs. high readability scores	No difference
	8. Brown	1952	Low vs. high readability scores	Low scores yielded better comprehension
	9. Klare, Shuford and Nichols	1957	Low vs. high readability scores	Low scores yielded better comprehension

studies are summarized in Table 1. The dependent variable in each was total score on a comprehension test.

An interesting pattern develops. There were no differences between versions when either sentence length or word frequency was the independent variable. The simultaneous application of both, however, appeared to do what neither could do alone.

Unfortunately, there exists no single study which employed a design that permits one to measure the effects of either factor as well as the unique effects due to their interaction.

It is highly unlikely that the studies in group 1 or 3 were adequate measures of the influence of sentence length. Adequacy depends on the kinds of questions that were asked in the comprehension tests. For example, if one rewrites sentence (1) as sentence (2) (which, incidentally, takes Flesch's recommendations), he is manipulating sentence length as a variable. If he uses question (3) to determine the influence of sentence length, he has provided an adequate test of its effect.

(1) Because the dog barked a lot, the boy kicked the dog.

(2) The dog barked a lot. The boy kicked the dog.[1]

(3) Why did the boy kick the dog?

(4) Who kicked the dog?

If, however, he uses question (4), he has tested a relation whose syntactic form is constant across sentences (1) and (2). Question (4) is not relevant to the causal relation whose form is varied between (1) and (2).

---

[1] It can be argued that no causality occurs here. However, causality is often implied in written text rather than made explicit. Hence, this statement represents a real rather than a hypothetical alternative. (Cf., Flesch, 1945, 1946a, 1946b, 1951).

Because so many of the classic readability formulas were constructed so long ago, the investigator was unable to uncover any of the tests that were used to grade the passages. Nevertheless, given the general kinds of criteria historically used to build comprehension tests, it seems reasonable to infer that the tests included a variety of types of comprehension questions (e.g., literal comprehension of facts, word meaning, main idea, inferential reasoning, critical reading). If this is a fair inference, then it follows that at least some of the questions would have tested relations whose form was constant across versions (such as question (4)), while some questions would have been so global in nature (e.g., main idea question) that the alterations in form were irrelevant.

In short, it appears unlikely that any of the correlational or experimental studies in readability has provided a fair test of the variables traditionally assumed to influence comprehension difficulty. The question that must be asked to generate an adequate criterion is, "If I have an *idea* I want to communicate, what's the best *way* to communicate it?"

More Recent Readability Research

The most exhaustive readability study in recent years was conducted by Bormuth (1966). He used correlational and multiple regression analyses to determine the predictive power of over 100 structural variables. His study is of special interest because he analyzed a number of variables not used in the classical research and because he used a new criterion to measure passage difficulty: the subjects' ability to fill in cloze tests over the passage.

In general, the same variables that have traditionally shown high correlations with passage difficulty maintained their status. In addition, he found a number of new variables that exhibited high correlations. Several parts of speech ratios were highly related to passage difficulty (e.g., pronoun/conjunction: $r = .81$; interjection/pronoun: $r = .62$; verb/conjunction: $r = .73$). A new measure of sentence complexity based on Yngve's (1960, 1962) word depth analysis was also significantly related to passage difficulty ($r = -.55$).

Coleman (1965), working with adults, found that relative clauses written in highly embedded forms like (5) were harder to recall than those written in less highly embedded forms, such as (6).

(5) The rat that the cat killed ate the malt.

(6) The cat killed the rat that ate the malt.

He also found that the nominalizations of active verbs (example (7)) were harder to recall than sentences using the active verbs themselves (example (8)).

(7) The boys' planning of the party was a lot of work.

(8) The boys planned the party, and it was a lot of work.

It is difficult to assess the relevance of Coleman's findings to the present study because of his response measure. He had his subjects write down as much as they could remember from passages written in less versus more highly embedded forms and active verb versus nominalization forms. If one tests comprehension with wh-type questions, Coleman's findings might be reversed. For example, given the question,

(9) Which rat ate the malt?

form (5) might well prove to yield better comprehension than form (6).

Hypotheses emanating from readability research

A number of plausible hypotheses concerning the influence of structural factors on comprehension emerge from the classical and recent readability research. If conceptual equivalence is maintained, then a) one longer sentence should prove more difficult than 2 or more shorter sentences; b) the inclusion of subordinating and coordinating conjunctions should increase comprehension difficulty; c) highly embedded forms should be more difficult than low-embedded forms. It is interesting to note that hypothesis b (and to a lesser degree, hypothesis (c) also tests hypothesis (a). Conjunction almost always increases sentence length; embedding usually does.

Recent psycholinguistic research

With the advent of transformational-generative grammars (Chomsky, 1957), many psychologists interested in verbal behavior began to look to this new approach to linguistics as a model for explaining language comprehension and production. Beginning with the work of Miller (1960), there have been a host of studies that have attempted in one way or another to make a direct correspondence between the psychological model of the speaker, hearer, or reader and the units and operations of transformational-generative grammars.

Several studies found that transforming kernel sentences (simple active voice declarative statements) into passive, or negative, or interrogative form increases the difficulty that subjects experience in processing the sentences (Miller, 1962; Miller and McKean, 1964; Mehler, 1963). There was a fair relationship obtained between the amount of time taken to process a sentence and the number of transformations involved in getting from the kernel form to the other forms. Gough (1965) tested subjects' ability to verify statements made about pictures placed in front of them. He found that as the number of transformations for a form increased, subjects took longer to verify the statement.

Savin and Perchonok (1965) investigated this issue by using a short term memory task. A sentence was presented along with a string of unrelated words. The subject was instructed to remember the sentence as well as the additional words. Fewer unrelated words were recalled in the case of passive, negative, or interrogative forms than in the case of simple active forms, even though some of the transformed versions were, in fact, shorter than the active versions. In a follow-up study Savin (1966) found that subjects were able to recall more words following right branching forms (10) than following self-embedding forms (11).

(10) The contractor built a house that had three bedrooms.

(11) The house that the contractor built had three bedrooms.

He concluded that the forms involving more transformations or more complex transformations interfered more with memory because they required additional psychological processing in order to get to a deep structure representation.

The relevant point about these studies is that the investigators have explicitly claimed or implicitly assumed a correspondence between grammatical and psychological models. While there is by no means unanimity of opinion regarding these claims (Fodor and Garrett, 1966), much current research operates under the same assumptions. In addition, researchers concerned with the technology of written instruction (e.g., Bormuth, Manning, Carr, and Pearson, 1970; Coleman, 1964, 1965) have conducted experiments that have assumed such a correspondence. It seems useful, therefore, to describe the grammatical bases upon which the corresponding psychological model is founded.

A Sample Transformational Grammar

One of the major distinctions within a transformational generative grammar is between deep structure and surface structure. The meaning of a sentence is represented by its deep structure; the form in which a sentence emerges as speech or writing is represented by its surface structure. The distinction is not trivial because a single surface structure may have more than one possible deep structure, in which case the sentence is ambiguous. Consider the classic example:

(12) Flying planes can be dangerous.

It can mean either that you had better stay out of airplanes or that you had better hide when you hear a plane flying overhead. Surface structure ambiguities are resolved at the deep structure level.

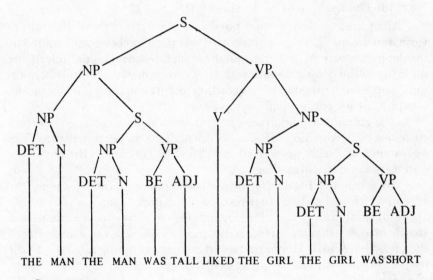

S = sentence
NP = noun phrase
VP = verb phrase
N = noun
V = verb
DET = determiner
BE = form of *to be*
ADJ = adjective

Figure 1. Deep structure representation of a sentence with 2 embedded adjectives

A single deep structure may have several possible surface structure representations. Consider the deep structure given in Figure 1. Such a deep structure has several possible surface structure forms. By simply disembedding the 2 sentences under noun phrases, for example, we could get

(13) The man liked the girl. The man was tall. The girl was short.

By embedding *short* as an adjective, we get

(14) The man liked the short girl. The man was tall.

By embedding *the man was tall* as a relative clause, we get

(15) The man who was tall liked the short girl.

By embedding *tall* as an adjective, we get

(16) The tall man liked the short girl.

All of these as well as other possible surface structures differ only in form, not meaning. The semantic interpretation has been determined by the deep structure. Whether or not these surface forms communicate the meaning of the deep structure with equal efficiency is an empirical question. The point is that they are, according to a grammatical interpretation, semantically (or conceptually) equivalent.

In a grammatical analysis, one gets from deep structure to surface structure by performing certain transformations on deep structure. The operations by which we arrived at (13), (14), (15), and (16) are crude statements of transformations.

If one believes that deep structure corresponds in some fashion to the state in which verbal data are processed in the mind, then it is plausible to argue that the number of transformations necessary to get from deep structure to a particular surface structure is an index of the complexity of the surface structure. Hence surface structures exhibiting relatively fewer transformations should be processed with greater speed and accuracy, and vice-versa.

In the set examples (13)—(16), (13) requires the fewest transformations, (14) the second fewest, (15) the third fewest, and (16) the most. If one believes that the grammatical model is a one-to-one mapping of a psychological model (that is, that is describes how data are processed mentally), then it is reasonable to argue that if one tested the efficiency of these forms, they would rank (13) > (14) > (15) > (16). These are exactly the kinds of claims made by the deep structure model.

Recent Research in Conceptual Abstraction
(the Chunk Model)

Within the past 5 years, there has been an attempt by some psycholinguists to offer an alternative view of verbal processing (e.g., Bransford

and Franks, 1971). This view hypothesizes that conceptual representational structures or "semantic chunks," rather than atomistic deep
structure components, constitute the verbal data which are processed in
the mind. Hypothetical storage units might be "tall man," "short girl," or
"the tall man hit the short girl." The hearer or reader has to go through
some sort of synthesizing process to cement them together (or else he fails
to do so and never comprehends the relation.)

Bransford and Franks (1971) have completed several studies supporting the chunk model. They presented adult subjects with larger and
smaller components of sentences like (17).

(17) The rock which rolled down the mountain crushed the tiny hut
     on the edge of the forest.

Later they asked the subjects to state whether or not they had actually
heard certain components, and to rate the confidence they had in their
judgments. Larger components were given higher recognition scores and
confidence ratings than smaller components, irrespective of whether or
not they had actually been heard. In other words, the subjects felt more
confident about having heard (18) than (19), even though they might have
actually heard both of them or neither of them.

(18) The rock which rolled down the mountain crushed the hut.

(19) The hut was tiny.

Bransford and Franks concluded that the findings supported a
psychological model that gives primacy to semantic rather than syntactic
relations.

In the set of examples (13)—(16), the chunk model would predict that
the ranking for comprehension efficiency of the forms would be the exact
reverse of the ranking predicted by the deep structure model. Whereas
the deep structure would predict (13) >(14) > (15) > (16), the chunk
model would predict (16) > (15) > (14) > (13).

Review of Theoretical Positions and
Purposes of the Study

It is clear that the deep structure model and the chunk model stand in
opposition to one another. What the one predicts will be simple, the other
predicts will be difficult. The third theoretical position, the readability
hypothesis, co-varies to a great extent with the deep structure model. For
example, when embedded elements are removed from one sentence and
expressed as a separate sentence, average sentence length, and, many
times, grammatical complexity are reduced.

It should be pointed out that this study has a practical purpose which is relatively independent of its theoretical purpose. That is, it may be possible, using a methodology which holds constant the semantic—or conceptual—nature of a statement while it allows syntactic form to vary, to determine the relative efficiency of various syntactic forms in communicating a given idea. Such a scaling of communication efficiency could prove useful to persons who prepare materials for children, quite independently of whether or not the scaling supported any particular theoretical position.

The Experiments

The data from the 3 separate experiments are reported in this section. Experiment 1 examined children's comprehension of causal and adjectival relations. Experiments 2 and 3 were conducted subsequent to experiment 1 for the purpose of clarifying ambiguity found in the first experiment. Experiment 2 examined children's preference for various syntactical representations of a common idea. Experiment 3 examined children's recall of causal relations.

The situation is further complicated by the fact that experiments 1 and 2 each had 3 parts. In the sections of this report for experiments 1 and 2, the methodology is described for all of experiment 1 and all of experiment 2; however, the results for each of the 3 parts of experiment 1 are reported and discussed separately.

Experiment 1: Comprehension

Subjects

The subjects were 64 third and fourth grade students attending elementary school in a middle class suburb of Minneapolis. The subjects were selected by participating teachers who were instructed to choose the 5 ablest students from each of their high and middle reading groups. Low ability students were eliminated in order to reduce the likelihood that word recognition problems would complicate measures of comprehension. Initially, 80 subjects were selected. Because of absences, failures to understand the task, and random deletion, the group was reduced from 80 to 64 subjects. The resulting sample was subdivided into 4 groups: 16 medium-achieving third graders (3M), 16 high-achieving third graders (3H), 16 medium-achieving fourth graders (4M), and 16 high-achieving fourth graders (4H). Most of the data were analyzed using grade and achievement level as factors distinguishing between subjects.

Materials

The materials were relatively simple sentences or groups of sentences constructed by the experimenter. They were typed on plain white 4″ x 6″ index cards in heavy black type. One general criterion was used in generating the materials: that they be as similar as possible to "real" written discourse that children encounter in textbooks and tradebooks. In order to meet this criterion, the experimenter reviewed children's trade books and basal reading texts to make certain that the sentence types he had chosen for the study represented real alternatives in commonly used materials.

Items for the 3 parts of the comprehension experiment were generated using 4 steps.

Step 1. For each part, decide on the surface structure forms that are of interest as well as the type(s) of wh-questions which provide a fair test of the relation whose surface structure is varied across forms.

For experiment 1.1, eight different surface structure forms were generated by crossing all the combinations—2 levels of each of 3 factors: cue, order and sentence.[2] Table 2 lists these factors in a Form Code, explains the levels of each factor, and gives an example of each of the surface structure forms generated by crossing all levels of all factors. In addition, it shows the particular wh-question used to test the relations.

Table 2. Structural variations in causal relations

Form Code*	Example of Form
000	Because John was lazy, he slept all day.
001	John was lazy. So he slept all day.
010	John slept all day because he was lazy.
011	John slept all day. This was because he was lazy.
100	John was lazy and he slept all day.
101	John was lazy. He slept all day.
110	John slept all day, and he was lazy.
111	John slept all day. He was lazy.
—*wh*	Why did John sleep all day?

*The 3 columns of the form code denote the 2 levels of each factor. The left hand column refers to cuing condition. A cue can either be *present* (O) *or absent* (1). The second column denotes level of order; it can be either *cause-effect* (O) or *effect-cause* (1). The last column denotes sentence level. It can be a *one-sentence* construction (O) or a *2-sentence* construction (1).

[2] The experimenter was unable to locate any transformational-generative grammatical analysis of causal relations as specific and detailed as those available for modifying relations. Hence these operations were generated by the experimenter as a quasi-substitute.

For experiments 1.2, and 1.3, four surface structure forms were generated by applying successive transformations on the deep structure representation of a sentence containing 2 embedded sentences which dealt with adjectival relations. Table 3 gives examples of the surface structure forms generated by applying these transformations. It also lists the test questions generated by applying wh-transformations to the deep structure. The *which* question was used in experiment 1.2; the *who* question in experiment 1.3.

Table 3.   Sample forms for adjectival experiments (1.2, 1.3, 2.2, and 2.3)

Form Code	Example of Form
1	The tall man liked the short woman.
2	The man who was tall liked the short woman.
3	The man liked the short woman. He was tall.
4	The man liked the woman. He was tall. She was short.
Which	Which man liked the short woman?
Who	Who liked the short woman?

Step 2. Select as many sentence contents (sentences which contain the relation of interest) as there are surface structure forms. For experiment 1.1 it was necessary to select 8 sentences; for 1.2, four sentences; for 1.3, four sentences.

Step 3. Build a sentence by form matrix by applying each operation outlined in Step 1 to each of the sentences selected in Step 2.

Step 4. To build a test item, select a particular sentence x form combination (a cell in the matrix) and the appropriate test question to go with it. (Note that the test question is the same for all surface structure forms of the same sentence.) Notice that 64 test items are generated in the 8 x 8 causal matrix for experiment 1.1, while 16 test items are generated in each of the 4 x 4 matrices for experiments 1.2 and 1.3.

A test for a given subject was built by assigning test items so that he was exposed to each surface structure form and each sentence once and only once. In experiment 1.1, then, each subject received 8 unique sentence x form combinations (8 unique cells in the matrix). This meant that 8 subjects were needed to gather data on each cell in the matrix—that is, for one complete replication of the matrix. Similarly, 4 subjects were needed to complete a replication of the 4 x 4 matrix in either experiment 1.2 or 1.3.

To control for practice effects and "experimental set," 2 precautions were taken. First, for a given matrix, each surface structure form and each sentence were tested equally often in each serial position within a test.

Second, the test items from a given matrix were separated from one another by 7 intervening "dummy" items.

Since the data for each of the 3 comprehension experiments were collected in the same testing situation, items from experiment 1.2 and 1.3 could serve as a portion of the "dummy" items for experiment 1.1, and vice-versa.

Testing Procedures

Each subject was individually tested in an unused classroom relatively free of disturbances. The experimenter told the subject that he was interested in how well children answer questions about what they read. The subject's task was to pick up a card from the tray, read it aloud and hand it to the experimenter. The experimenter than asked the subject a question testing the relation of interest. The experimenter recorded the subject's response on a preconstructed answer sheet. In addition, the entire session was tape recorded so that the experimenter could subsequently verify his response classifications. The subject was tested on 6 practice items before he began the test. Any subject who could not understand the task or who seemed unduly anxious was dismissed from the session.

Treatment of the Data

All of the data from the 3 comprehension experiments were analyzed by using between-subject, within-subject analyses of variance for dichotomous data (Winer, 1962). Two between factors, grade level (3 or 4) and achievement level (medium or high), were common to analyses from experiments 1.1, 1.2, and 1.3. The within-subjects factors (operations used to generate surface forms) as well as the scoring procedures for experiment 1.1 (causal relations) differed from those used in experiments 1.2 and 1.3

For experiment 1.1 and 3 within-subjects factors were cue, order, and sentence level (c.f., Table 2). Two dependent variables were used: number of correct responses and number of subordinate responses. A response was scored correct if it contained the major lexical elements in the dependent clause of form 000. Reasonable paraphrases were also scored correct. Using the example in Table 2, (20), (21), and (22) would have been scored correct.

(20) because John (or he) was lazy.

(21) John (or he) was lazy.

(22) Lazy people sleep all day.

A response was scored as subordinate if it began with the word *because* or a reasonable semantic substitute for *because* (since, as, for). Subordinated responses were examined in order to assess the stability of response outputs as a function of the varying stimulus inputs.

For the experiments 1.2 and 1.3, surface structure form (the 4 forms shown in Table 3) served as the within-subjects independent variable. In each case, form 1 was always the form representing the greatest number of transformations (from deep to surface structure), while form 4 represented the fewest. The overall statistical test for *form* was omitted, allowing these orthogonal contrasts:

$$\Gamma_1 = F_1 + F_2 - F_3 - F_4$$
$$\Gamma_2 = F_1 - F_2$$
$$\Gamma_3 = F_3 - F_4$$

For experiment 1.2, the adjective experiment which used a *which* question to test the effect of structural changes, there were 3 dependent variables: a) number of *errors,* b) number of *adjectival* responses, and c) number of *clausal* responses. The 3 dependent variables constituted mutually exclusive categories. A response was scored as *adjectival* if it was of the form, "the *tall* boy," or "the *tall* one." A response was scored as *clausal* if it was of the form, "the boy *who was tall*," or "the one *who was tall*." The following kinds of responses were scored as *errors*: a) incorrect adjectives or clauses assigned to the nominal, b) no response, c) any otherwise unclassified response.

For experiment 1.3—the adjective experiment which used a *who* question—the dependent variables were slightly different from those used in experiment 1.2. They included number of *errors,* number of *adjective-noun* responses (like the *adjective* responses in 1.2), number of *noun-clause* responses (akin to the *clausal* responses in 1.2), and number of *noun* responses. The classification procedures were identical to the adjective-*which* study, except for *noun* responses. A response was classified as a *noun* if the correct noun was used without either an adjectival or a clausal modifier.

Results and Discussion

Experiment 1.1—causal relations. When the number of correct responses is analyzed, the surprising finding is that differences between groups, among forms, or among cells are so small. The largest difference between groups is 2; the largest between forms, also 2. In short, virtually every subject responded correctly to every form. Out of a total of 512 responses, there were only 11 errors. No analysis of variance was computed.

A different picture results when the dependent variable is number of subordinated responses. Cell totals are reported in Table 4.

Table 4. Cell totals: experiment 1.1—number of subordinated responses

				Form					
Group	*000*	*001*	*010*	*011*	*100*	*101*	*110*	*111*	T_{Group}
3M	11	8	14	13	7	7	10	8	78
3H	13	9	15	14	10	11	9	7	88
4M	11	8	13	13	9	9	10	7	80
4H	16	10	12	13	12	7	10	4	84
T_{Form}	51	35	54	53	38	34	39	26	330

There was a significantly higher total for the *cue-present* $(0++)^3$ condition (T = 193) than for *cue-absent* $(1++)$ condition (T = 137), $F_{(1, 60)} = 26.3750$, p < .01. The difference between *one-sentence* $(++0)$ forms (T = 182) and *2-sentence* $(++1)$ forms (T = 148) was also significant $F_{(1, 60)} = 16.5034$, p < .01. Differences for other main effects were not significant.

Of the 26 interactions, only 2 were significant: a) cue x order, $F_{(1, 60)} = 17.6667$, p < .01; and b) cue x order x sentence $F_{(1, 60)} = 8.2640$, p < .01. The cue x order interaction graph indicates that when a cue was present, the *effect-cause* order produced more subordinated responses, but that when no cue word was present, the *cause-effect* order produced more. This interaction was really due to the unique influences of forms 001 and 111. Form 001, the *so* form was the only form within the *cue-present* condition that was different from the others. It did not contain the subordinating conjunction *because*. Form 111 likewise depressed the totals for the *effect-cause* order within the *no-cue* condition. An examination of the cue x order x sentence interaction revealed that these same 2 forms, 001 and 111, are mainly responsible for the interaction.

It is clear that, in terms of number of correct responses, no support for the readability hypothesis or the chunk model is possible. The surprising finding is how well, not how poorly, all groups did on all forms. Perhaps the semantic content of the sentences was so simple that it masked possible differences due to form.

In terms of the number of subordinated responses (those that begin

---

[3] Numbers refer back to Table 2. The + signs indicate that we are summing over levels of these variables. The first of the 3 numeral positions indicates cuing variable; the second, order; the third, sentence.

with *because* or one of its synonyms), there are clear effects due to conditions of cuing and sentence; the cuing effect is even more striking if one compares form 001, the *so* form, with the other *cue-present* forms. The other 3 all contained the word *because;* and they all elicited a higher number of *because* responses than the *so* form. This difference is not surprising because, given a *why* question about a causal relationship, there is no reason to begin the response with *so*. It is syntactically and logically unnecessary. The more interesting fact is that there were as many subordinated responses as there were to the *so* stimulus condition and to the various *cue-absent* stimulus conditions.

Despite the cue x order x sentence interaction, the sentence effect is in the same direction across cue x order conditions. If one regards each successive pair of forms as minimal pairs differing only with respect to sentence condition, the difference between members within each pair favor the *one-sentence* condition. (See Table 5.) It is true, however, that the differences between members of a pair vary widely between pairs.

Table 5.   Differences due to sentence condition within and between pairs classified by cue and order conditions: experiment 1.1

				Pair				
		1		*2*		*3*		*4*
Code	Cue × Order	00__	00__	01__	01__	10__	10__	11__	11__
	Sentence	__0	__1	__0	__1	__0	__1	__0	__1
Totals		51	35	54	53	38	34	39	26
Differences		16		1		4		13	

Differences obtained by subtracting (__1) from (__0).

It is somewhat difficult to evaluate what it is that the dependent variable of number of subordinated responses means. It is clear that (23) is just as correct an answer as (24); perhaps the insertion of *because* indicates a more *unified* conception of the causal relation.

(23) John was lazy.

(24) Because John was lazy.

If that is a reasonable view, it follows that both cuing and sentence conditions have an effect on children's ability to unify a causal relation, but that the effects do vary across levels of order (that is, the cue x order x sentence interaction). At best, however, this is a speculative explanation. However, data from experiments 2.1 and 3 do shed light on this explanation.

Table 6.   Cell totals: experiment 1.2—number of responses by form and group

		Form				
Response Type	Group	1	2	3	4	T_{Group}
Errors	3M	5	1	4	3	13
	3H	2	1	4	4	11
	4M	3	3	6	5	17
	4H	2	0	4	6	12
	T_{Form}	12	5	18	18	53
Adjective Responses	3M	11	7	7	9	34
	3H	14	2	7	5	28
	4M	13	6	8	10	37
	4H	14	2	7	7	30
	T_{Form}	52	17	29	31	129
Clausal Responses	3M	0	8	5	4	17
	3H	0	13	5	7	25
	4M	0	7	2	2	11
	4H	0	14	5	3	22
	T_{Form}	0	42	17	16	75

Experiment 1.2—adjective relations (using a which question). The cell totals for the 3 dependent variables are reported in Table 6. The ANOVA for the number of *errors* revealed that none of the between-subject effects and none of the interaction effects were significant. The only significant comparison within subjects was the contrast:

Γ_1 : $F_1 + F_2 - F_3 - F_4$
      $12 + 5 - 18 - 18$
$F_{(1, 180)} = 8.2904, p < .01.$

F_1 and F_2, the highly cohesive forms, yielded significantly fewer errors than the less cohesive forms, F_3 and F_4. The comparison between the adjective form (Form 1) and the clausal form (Form 2) favored the clausal, but the difference was not significant.

The ANOVA for the number of *adjectival responses* indicated that none of the between-subject comparisons was significant.

Of the 3 specific orthogonal contrasts between levels of form, only the contrast Γ_2 was significant:

Γ_2 : $F_1 - F_2$
      : $52 - 17$
$F_{(1, 180)} = 46.6113, p < .01.$

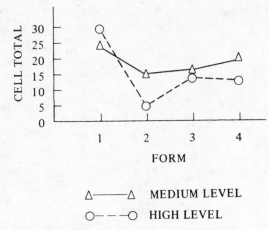

△————△   MEDIUM LEVEL

○— — —○   HIGH LEVEL

Figure 2.   Graph of level X form interaction: Experiment 1.2: number of *adjectival* responses

There was a high incidence of *adjectival* responses to both F₃ and F₄ stimuli. One interaction was significant: level x form, $F_{(3, 180)} = 2.1705$, $.01 < p < .05$. The interaction graph, Figure 2, indicates that high achievers gave more *adjectival* responses to adjective (F₁) stimuli, but that medium achievers gave more *adjectival* responses to other stimulus forms.

The results for the dependent variable, number of *clausal* responses, revealed a significant effect due to level ($T_M = 28$, $T_H = 47$), $F_{(1, 60)} = 6.0368$, $.01 < p < .05$. The contrast between the adjective and clausal stimulus forms was also significant:

$\Gamma_2 : F_1 - F_2$

$: 0 - 42$

$F_{(1, 180)} = 69.7667$, $p < .01$.

Only one of 6 between-subject comparisons was significant. There are few data to indicate any important developmental trends in the response outputs made by the different groups of subjects. There is a tendency, however, for high achievers to give relatively more *clausal* responses, while medium achievers seem to give more *adjectival* responses.

All 3 dependent variables were sensitive to differences between forms, but none of them matched the predictions outlined by the transformational model. The error data lend partial support to the chunk model, but they separate the forms into 2 rather than 4 categories. Comprehension of the *which* question is better when the relationship is stated more cohesively (F₁ or F₂) than when it is stated less cohesively (F₃ or F₄), but there are no significant distinctions within these categories.

The lack of a distinction between F_3 and F_4 is reasonable because the relationship tested by the *which* question was constant across these forms. A relative clause structure (F_2) appears, however, to provide as much, if not more, cohesiveness for the nominal-modifier relationship than does an adjective structure (F_1).

The other dependent variables, number of *adjectival responses* and number of *clausal responses,* provide predictable results. Within the 2 highly cohesive forms (F_1 and F_2), there is a strong tendency for responses to match the stimulus input. While there is a small amount of crossover from a clause input to an *adjectival* output (response), there is no crossover in the opposite direction. The crossover from less cohesive inputs (F_3 and F_4) was proportional for both *adjectival* and *clausal* responses. If the 4 forms are placed on a continuum from the theoretically most cohesive to the theoretically least cohesive (Figure 3), then output flow is unidirectional; that is, it goes only from less cohesive inputs to more cohesive outputs. Thus both the error data and the correct response data lend some support to the chunk model. Responses move toward a more cohesive form because the subjects' perception of the relationships involved converges on the more cohesive forms.

Experiment 1.3—adjective relations (using a who *question).* The unidirectional flow in Figure 3 presents an interesting, but biased, picture. It is interesting because the flow is unidirectional, indicating that increasingly cohesive forms are more stable in terms of output. But it is biased because there is no crossover possible from F_1 or F_2 to F_3 or F_4; that is, the *which* question preempts a *noun* response.

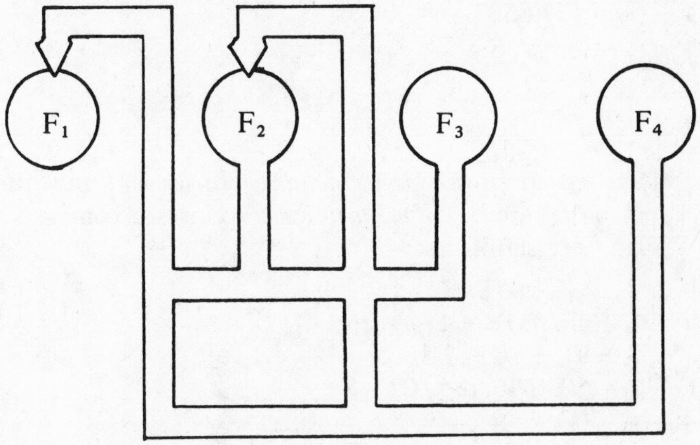

Figure 3.   Diagram of response output flow from stimulus inputs: Experiment 1.2

When a set of materials identical in form to those in experiment 1.2 are constructed, and when the relationship tested is the *nominal-rest of the sentence* relationship, the data provide a more reasonable test of the flow model in Figure 4. This results from the fact that, given a *who* question, a single *noun* ("the *boy*") is equally as reasonable a response as an *adjectival* ("the *tall boy*") response or a *clausal* ("the boy *who was tall*") response. Note, however, that a price is paid for this test: the *who* question does not test the nominal-modifier relationship, according to the criteria established earlier (c.f. examples 1-4, p. 71). Even so, it is a useful study because it allows one to look at the stability of different forms as measured by the crossover tendencies of responses elicited from stimulus inputs.

The results from experiment 1.3 are reported in Table 7. In general, there were no significant effects due to either grade or level; nor were there any significant interactions. The cell totals for number of *errors* are notable for their infrequency rather than their frequency. Of the 256 responses classified, only 5 were classified as *errors*.

The ANOVA for number of *adjective-noun* responses revealed 2 significant contrasts between levels of form.

a) $\Gamma_1 : F_1 + F_2 - F_3 - F_4$
     $: 61 + 8 - 16 - 13$
    $F_{(1, 180)} = 50.6483, p < .01.$
b) $\Gamma_2 : F_1 - F_2$
     $: 61 - 8$
    $F_{(1, 180)} = 177.8387, p < .01.$

Clearly, F_1 elicited far more *adjective-noun* responses than any other form. With respect to the number of *noun-clause* responses, 2 contrasts between levels of form were significant:

a) $\Gamma_1 : F_1 + F_2 - F_3 - F_4$
     $: 0 + 51 - 16 - 11$
    $F_{(1, 180)} = 19.4546, p < .01$
b) $\Gamma_2 : F_1 - F_2$
     $: 0 - 51$
    $F_{(1, 180)} = 175.7811, p < .01$

Table 7. Cell totals: experiment 1.3—number of responses by form and group

Response Type	Group	Form 1	Form 2	Form 3	Form 4	T_{Group}
Errors	3M	0	0	0	3	3
	3H	0	0	0	0	0
	4M	1	0	0	1	2
	4H	0	0	0	0	0
	T_{Form}	1	0	0	4	5
Adjective-Noun Responses	3M	16	0	5	1	22
	3H	15	1	3	4	23
	4M	15	3	3	3	24
	4H	15	4	5	5	29
	T_{Form}	61	8	16	13	98
Noun-Clause Responses	3M	0	13	4	4	21
	3H	0	15	5	3	23
	4M	0	11	4	2	17
	4H	0	12	3	2	17
	T_{Form}	0	51	16	11	78
Noun Responses	3M	0	3	7	8	18
	3H	1	0	8	9	18
	4M	0	2	9	10	21
	4H	1	0	8	9	18
	T_{Form}	2	5	32	36	75

The results obtained when the dependent variable was number of *noun-clause* responses were nearly the perfect inverse of the results obtained when the dependent variable was number of *adjective-noun* responses.

The ANOVA for the number of *noun* responses indicated that one contrast was significant.

$$\Gamma_1 : F_1 + F_2 - F_3 - F_4$$
$$: 2 + 5 - 32 - 36$$
$$F_{(1, 180)} = 99.1480, p < .01.$$

The least cohesive forms elicited far more *noun* responses than the more cohesive forms. The differences between the 2 less cohesive forms or between the 2 more cohesive forms were small and insignificant.

The error data provide no basis for distinguishing between any factors. There are too few errors on which to make any judgments. The

data from the other 3 dependent variables are consonant with the data
from experiment 1.2, and the crossover patterns from stimulus input to
response output provide support for the model diagrammed in Figure 3.
Some modifications are necessary, however, because there is at least some
crossover from more cohesive inputs to less cohesive outputs. Table 8
provides a useful format for scrutinizing the data. Stimulus inputs are
listed in the rows; response outputs are listed in the columns.

Table 8.   Input-output matrix: experiment 1.3

		Form of the Response			
		Adj-Noun	Noun Clause	Noun	Error
Form of the Stimulus	F_1 Adj-Noun	61	0	2	1
	F_2 Noun Clause	8	51	5	0
	F_3 Noun$_1$	16	16	32	0
	F_4 Noun$_2$	13	11	36	4
Total		98	78	75	5

First of all, the data do not discriminate very well between F_3 and F_4
inputs. Apparently once the modifier is formally removed from the nominal, no further psychological separation occurs. If F_3 and F_4 are considered as a single state, then it appears that as input forms become less
cohesive, stability (the incidence of matches between input and outputs)
decreases.

The general trend of response flow convergence is toward more
cohesive forms for those responses that do not match stimulus inputs. The
crossover toward less cohesive forms is minimal.

Taken as a unit, experiments 1.2 and 1.3 indicate that more cohesive
forms yield better comprehension and more stable comprehension. Furthermore, subjects' preception of the stimulus inputs for adjectival relationship move toward the more cohesive response outputs. The chunk
model can accommodate these findings more easily than the deep structure model. In fact, they are not predictable at all under the deep structure model. The only question about the chunk model is whether or not
there are really 4 levels of cohesiveness. The data would seem to indicate
that 2, possibly 3, levels are more reasonable.

Experiment 2: Preference Studies

Because of the failure of the comprehension experiments to yield an
unambiguous interpretation of the models and in order to determine

whether or not important effects in the comprehension experiments were generalizable across response modes, a follow-up preference study was conducted.

Subjects for Experiment 2

The subjects were 24 fourth grade students randomly selected from 2 fourth grade classrooms not involved in the comprehension study. All readers in these classrooms were reading materials at grade level. Hence it is unlikely that word recognition problems interfered with reading the comparatively easy test items.

Materials for Experiment 2

The materials were developed in essentially the same manner as in the comprehension study; that is N x N sentence x form matrices were constructed. However, the method for extracting an item was quite different. The subjects' task was to choose which form, from among N forms, he preferred when all forms were represented within an item. Therefore, items were distinguished only by sentence content. In the comprehension study, a 4 x 4 matrix generated 16 items; but in the preference study, a 4 x 4 matrix generated only 4 items.

The factor of order (C-E or E-C) was eliminated from the causal comprehension matrix, yielding a 4 x 4 rather than an 8 x 8 matrix. The experimenter felt that the subjects would not be able to rank 8 forms reliably. Besides the items generated for the adjective studies and the causal study, buffer items were generated by including 5 other 4 x 4 sentence x form matrices. Each subject received a test booklet containing 36 items. The 4 items from a particular matrix were separated from one another by 8 intervening items. The serial position for a given form was rotated between items so that every form appeared in every position.

A sample item for the experiment 2.1 (causal relations) was

Why did John sleep all day?
____1. Because John was lazy, he slept all day.
____2. John was lazy. So he slept all day.
____3. John was lazy, and he slept all day.
____4. John was lazy. He slept all day.

A sample item for experiment 2.2 (adjective relations which) was

Which man thanked the young woman?
____ 1. The tall man thanked the young woman.
____ 2. The man who was tall thanked the young woman.
____ 3. The man thanked the young woman. He was tall.
____ 4. The man thanked the woman. He was tall. She was young.

A sample item for experiment 2.3 (adjective relations who) was

Who thanked the young woman?
____ 1. The tall man thanked the young woman.
____ 2. The man who was tall thanked the young woman.
____ 3. The man thanked the young woman. He was tall.
____ 4. The man thanked the woman. He was tall. She was young.

Testing Procedures for Experiment 2

The preference testing was carried out in a group situation. The experimenter told the subjects that their task was to rank the forms in terms of their perceptions about the relative clarity and simplicity of the forms; that is, how much help they thought each form would provide in answering the question listed at the beginning of each item. To the form the subjects considered the best, easiest, and clearest, they assigned a rank of 1; to the second best, easiest, and clearest, a rank of 2; for the third, a rank of 3; for the worst, hardest, and least clear, a rank of 4. The experimenter explained the task to the subjects, conducted 4 examples with the entire group, and circulated among the subjects to make certain that each one understood the task.

Treatment of the Data

Ranks for each form summed across the 4 items within a matrix for each subject. The resulting sum was used to rerank the forms. When ties occurred, average ranks were assigned. For example:

If the summed ranks for a subject were:	Then the assigned ranks for that subject were:
Form 1—8	1
Form 2—10	2.5
Form 3—10	2.5
Form 4—12	4

The assigned ranks were subjected to a Friedman χ^2 analysis of ranks (Winer, 1962) to determine differences due to form.

Results and Discussion of Experiment 2

The sums of ranks and the mean ranks for each of the forms are reported in Table 9. The differences attributable to form are significant for each of the 3 sets of ranks:

Causal—$\chi^2_{(3)} = 8.6266$, $.025 < p < .05$
Adjective which—$\chi^2_{(3)} = 29.5107$, $p < .001$
Who—$\chi^2_{(3)} = 34.7125$, $p < .001$

The magnitude of the test statistics for the adjective data indicate a clear trend on the part of subjects to select the more cohesive, more heavily embedded forms as preferable to the less cohesive, less heavily embedded forms.

Table 9.   Sums of ranks between forms: experiments 2.1, 2.2, 2.3

	Experiment 2.1 Causal		
Code	Form	Σ ranks	M rank
000	because	49.0	2.04
001	so	54.5	2.27
100	and	64.0	2.67
101	no cue	72.5	3.02

	Experiment 2.2		Experiment 2.3	
	Which Study		Who Study	
Form	Σ ranks	M rank	Σ ranks	M rank
1	36.0	1.50	35.5	1.49
2	56.0	2.33	51.5	2.15
3	65.0	2.70	71.5	2.98
4	83.0	3.46	81.5	3.39

The trend is not nearly as impressive for the data in the causal study; however *one sentence* forms are preferred to *two sentence* forms in either cuing conditions, and *cue-present* forms are preferred to *cue-absent* forms in either sentence condition.

A revealing picture results when the frequency of ranks between forms for the causal is graphed. The data in Figure 4 are even more striking than the summed ranks in Table 9. Ranks #1, #2, and #3 each predict the "closeness" of the 4 forms as measured by the sums of ranks.

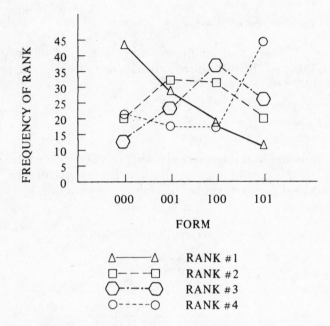

Figure 4. Frequencies of ranks between forms for the causal relation: Experiment 2.1

Only rank #4 does not discriminate along a scale. It appears to classify the 4 forms into 2 rather than 4 categories. This probably happens because the subjects rank from best (#1) through worst (#4). Hence, they may have run out of discriminating power by the time they get to #4.

Clearly, the data indicate a marked preference for the more cohesive, more grammatically complex forms. These findings can be accommodated quite easily by the chunk model. They lend no support to either the readability hypothesis or the deep structure model.

Experiment 3: Aided Recall of Causal Relations

In order to shed light on some of the ambiguous results obtained in experiment 1.1, a modest follow-up experiment was conducted. It was felt that an examination of the relationship between stimulus input and recall output might help to explain how subjects deal with relations of causality.

Method for Experiment 3

The subjects were 8 fourth grade students who had not been used in the comprehension study. All were judged by their teachers to be average or high achievers; however, achievement level was not used as a blocking variable.

The materials were exactly the same as those used in the causal-comprehension set. In addition, 16 buffer items were included to separate the causal forms. They were selected from among the other sets in the comprehension study.

Each subject was tested individually. The experimenter told him to read each sentence and to try to remember it as best he could, because later on he would be asked to recall it. After the subject had read all 24 sentences, the experimenter began the aided recall procedure. It proceeded in this fashion: Assume that the recall item was

(25) John was lazy, and he slept all day.

The first cue was always the first lexical item in the sentence, in this case, *John*. The experimenter asked, "Do you remember the sentence about *John*?" If the subject did, the experimenter recorded the form in which he recalled it. If he did not, the experimenter gave the second lexical item as a cue; in this example, *lazy*. The third cue was the third lexical item, *slept*. If the subject did not recall the sentence after 3 cues, the experimenter went on to a new item. The form of the response was recorded by the experimenter.

Results and Discussion of Experiment 3

The results from the aided recall study indicate very strong influences due to cuing condition and sentence condition. Because of the small number of subjects and because the results were so clear cut, the data were not subjected to inferential statistical analysis. Instead they are summarized in Table 10 in the form of an input-output matrix. The input denotes the form in which the subjects read the statement; the output denotes the form in which they recalled it. The notation for forms are the same as those used in experiment 1.1 and shown in Table 2.

A measure of input-output stability is indicated by the diagonal from upper left to lower right. Numbers in the diagonal indicate a direct match between input and output. Only forms 000, 001, 010 were stable. All other inputs, for the most part, were very unstable.

The influence of cuing condition is overwhelming. For *cue-present* inputs there were 29 *cue-present* outputs and no *cue-absent* outputs. Of the 3

Table 10.   Aided recall of causal relations: experiment 3—input-output matrix

	Code				Form of the Response					
		000	001	010	011	100	101	110	111	Error
Because	000	6	2	—	—	—	—	—	—	—
So	001	2	6	—	—	—	—	—	—	—
Because	010	1	—	6	—	—	—	—	—	1
This was because	011	1	—	5	—	—	—	—	—	2
and	100	2	2	—	—	1	1	—	—	2
- - - -	101	4	2	—	—	1	1	—	—	—
and	110	2	1	3	—	—	—	1	—	1
- - - -	111	1	1	3	—	—	—	—	—	3
Total		19	14	17	0	2	2	1	0	9

(Left margin label: Form of the Stimulus)

errors, 2 resulted from a form 011 input, an extremely unstable form. As a matter of fact, there were no outputs in form 011 regardless of input form.

On the other hand, for *cue-absent* inputs, there were 21 *cue-present* outputs. Furthermore, more errors (T = 6) than *cue-absent* outputs (T = 5) resulted from *cue-absent* inputs.

The effect or order is also quite striking. No *cause-effect* input was recalled as an *effect-cause* output, but 7 *effect-cause* inputs resulted in *cause-effect* outputs. In addition, the *effect-cause* order yielded 7 errors as opposed to only 2 for the *cause-effect* order.

The sentence factor also proved to be striking. There were no differences in number of errors. However, there was stability for *one-sentence* inputs (22 out of 32) than for *2-sentence* inputs (10 out of 32). With respect to *2-sentence* outputs, 14 out of 16 were form 001 (*so*) outputs.

The results of the recall study must be tempered by the fact that a small sample (N = 8) was used. Even so, the findings shed considerable light on the ambiguous results of the comprehension experiment on causal relations (1.1).

First of all, it is clear that if there was a *cued* input, a *cued* output resulted. More importantly, if there was an *uncued* input, chances are there was still a *cued* output. It is possible that children store these relations in long term memory in a *cued* form regardless of the input they get. Furthermore, if they don't recall them in a *cued* form, the chances are at least 50-50 that they won't recall them at all. Given an *uncued* input, the frequency of errors was greater than the frequency of *uncued* outputs (6 vs. 5).

This helps to explain the fact that in the comprehension study there were no differences between forms in the number of correct responses made. The subjects apparently provided the necessary cues even when they were not there.

Another important finding in the recall study relates to the effect of the *so* cue. In the comprehension study, the nature of the *why* question pre-empted a response beginning with *so;* there was a consequent reduction in the number of subordinated responses. The recall study provides a fairer test of the influence of this cue. The nature of the recall task does not stack the cards against the *so* cue by pre-empting a *so* response; it is reasonable to assume that a *so* response is equally as likely as a *because* response or an *uncued* response. The fact that other *cued* and *uncued* inputs were recalled as *so* inputs, indicates that it is a useful device for storing and recalling causal relations. In fact, it acted more like a subordinating form than a nonsubordinating form. Perhaps the view of traditional grammar (that *so* is a coordinating rather than a subordinating conjunction) is merely a grammatical convention. Psychologically it appears to be a subordinating conjunction.

One comment is necessary about the form 011 (*this was because*). The fact that there were no 011 outputs, not even from 011 inputs, indicates that the *this was* portion of the cue is superfluous. In fact, five of the eight 011 inputs were recalled as 010 outputs. The only difference between 010 and 011 is the insertion of a period and the inclusion of *this was*. Apparently that portion of the cue serves no function in memory and recall of causal relations.

The main conclusion to be drawn from the recall study is that, in order to store a causal relation, a subject virtually cannot help but store it in a unified, subordinated chunk. If he doesn't, he is just as likely to forget as he is to remember it. This finding provides strong evidence supporting the chunk model as a model of the psychology involved in processing verbal data. At least with respect to causality, people store data in unified rather than discrete units.

The small number of subjects used in the causal-recall experiment demands that it be replicated before too much credence is given to the results. It does, however, suggest an interesting hypothesis concerning children's strategies for storing semantic relations.

As an aside, one of the interesting outcomes from the aided recall study stemmed from the "dummy" items. "Dummy" statements (26) and (27) were often recalled in a form like (28), whereas "dummy" sentence (29) was seldom, if ever, recalled by any of the subjects. It is almost as if adjectival relations could be scaled on a compellingness-arbitrariness continuum. Arbitrary relations seem to serve an identification function, as in (29). Compelling relations seem to signal a more significant relation between the adjective and the noun, as in (27). The tallness of the man in (29) has little to do with the activity in the sentence; however, the anger of the bear in (27) is related to the activity.

(26) The bear chased the man. The bear was angry. The man was frightened.

(27) The angry bear chased the frightened man.

(28) The bear chased the man because he (or it) was angry.

(29) The tall man met the short woman.

In this connection, a study conducted by Myers (1967) provides confirming evidence. Myers asked subjects to choose paraphrases for sentences like:

(30) The slavegirl loved the kind master.

(31) The slavegirl loved the old master.

(32) The slavegirl loved the master. The master was kind.

(33) The slavegirl loved the master. The master was old.

When the elements within a sentence were highly related as they are in (30) and (32), subjects tended to choose a paraphrase written in subordinated form, as in (34).

(34) The slavegirl loved the master because the master (he) was kind.

However, when the elements were not highly related, as in (31) and (33), subjects tended to choose adjective or coordinated paraphrases (*and*), like (31) or (35).

(35) The slavegirl loved the master, and the master was old.

All the causal sentences used in this study represented highly related units; all the effects were reasonable outcomes of the causes. Hence the tendency for nonsubordinated forms to be recalled in subordinated forms might well have been predicted from Myers' findings.

General Discussion

With respect to the 3 theoretical positions outlined earlier—the readability hypothesis, the deep structure model, and the chunk model—the evidence favors the chunk model. Most of the data in the various experiments can be explained by the chunk model, while virtually none can be explained by the deep structure model or the readability hypothesis. This does not mean that the latter 2 positions are totally invalid, nor does it mean that the chunk model is a fully articulated psychological theory. The most reasonable conclusion is that, in general, any psychological model which attempts to explain the way in which verbal data are processed must begin with a semantic representation of the total relations involved rather than a syntactic description of the units which make up the relations. In short, some content must be put into the head before syntactic processing can occur. In this light, it will be interesting to examine the follow-up work of Bransford and Franks (1971) who seem to be attempting to develop a complete theory, accounting for perceptual as well as verbal phenomena.

The failure of the deep structure model to explain the present data says nothing at all about the validity of transformational-generative grammars as devices for representing the grammatical relations which occur in the language. There is no need whatever for a competence model (a model of an idealized speaker-hearer) to make any claims about a performance model (a model of real speakers, hearers, or readers). While it has been the hope of linguists and psychologists that a competence model would provide insight into the actual performance of language users, its failure to provide that insight does not, in principle, reduce its validity as a competence model. In short, a transformational grammar can serve as a powerful tool for generating all of the grammatical, but none of the ungrammatical, sentences of the language without making any claims about performance.

Implications

Pedagogically, the data lend no support to the recommendation that the difficulty of written discourse can be reduced by eliminating subordinating constructions or reducing sentence length. When the semantic relation is held constant and when the test question is relevant to the relation whose form is varied, either comprehension is equally efficient across forms or else the more subordinated and longer sentence forms elicit better comprehension. The well documented correlation between sentence length and comprehension difficulty should be viewed in one of 2 ways: a) the relationship exists because longer sentences are communicating more complex semantic relations than shorter sentences, or b) the relationship is an artifact of test questions which have measured semantic relations whose form is constant across longer and shorter versions of a unit of discourse.

While any recommendations concerning the most efficient surface structure forms for presenting various semantic relations must be tempered by the limitations of the present sample and testing procedures, the present findings certainly support an easing of concern for sentence length and complexity in the middle grades. However, before more specific recommendations can be made regarding structural efficiency, research is needed to assess the influences of the variables used in this study when sentences occur in naturalistic passage contexts. But the fact remains that, at least in this study, children seem not only to be able to handle complexity, but actually to prefer it.

The fact that grammatically more complex or longer statements equal or out-perform their simpler or shorter counterparts is not surprising. What happens can be explained as a trade-off relationship between explicitness on one hand and simplicity on the other. The causal relationship in (36) is explicit. If one rewrites (36) as (37), he has reduced grammatical complexity and average sentence length, but he has placed a new inferential burden on the reader.

(36) Because the chain broke, the machine stopped.

(37) The chain broke. The machine stopped.

What was previously complex but explicit becomes simple but implicit. A similar analysis accounts for the subjects' performance on adjectival relations. One limitation of the present study in this regard is that the statements selected for inclusion in the causal experiments all represented quite natural and predictable causal relations within a child's experience. One wonders whether or not children would be able to infer any causal relation from statements like (38), where their experience would be less helpful in making the inference.

(38) The new king clamped down on public meetings. Many residents
       emigrated to a new land.

The possible implications for social science and science content, where the intent is often to present *new* causal relations, are quite serious.

Further Research

There are several follow-up studies suggested by findings in this study. It would be enlightening, for example, to see what happens to comprehension when statements similar to those selected for the present study are placed in paragraph or passage contexts. It may well be that when a subject is confronted with a search task in addition to a comprehension task, errors due to form are accentuated. The preliminary evidence from the Bormuth *et al.* study (Bormuth, Manning, Carr, and Pearson, 1970) would suggest that errors increase in contextual settings.

Second, the methodology used in this study could be applied to other classes of semantic relations, e.g., relations of adverseness (*however, although, in spite of*), time (*before, after, during,* etc.), purposiveness (*so that, in order to*), and conditionality (*if, once, provided that, unless*). This needs to be done to determine whether or not the conclusions regarding semantic cohesiveness are generalizable across a variety of verbal stimuli.

Third, traditional notions about readability should be reexamined. While the present study in no way suggests that readability formulas ought not to be used to predict the difficulty readers may encounter with particular passages, chapters, or books, it does suggest a new direction in research on readability. Studies need to be conducted in which different versions of a passage are constructed according to some rule-governed procedures, rather than according to the intuitions of the investigators. Furthermore, the questions used must be relevant to the structural changes which have been effected. In short, readability studies must begin with the question: What is the best way to communicate a given idea?

REFERENCES

Bormuth, John R. Readability: a new approach. *Reading Research Quarterly,* Spring 1966, *1,* 79-132.

Bormuth, John R.; Manning, John C.; Carr, Julian W.; & Pearson, P. David. Children's comprehension of between- and within-sentence syntactic structures. *Journal of Educational Psychology,* October 1970, *61,* 349-357.

Bransford, John, & Franks, Jeffrey. The abstraction of linguistic ideas. *Cognitive Psychology,* October 1971, *2,* 331-350.

Brown, James I. The Flesch formula. *Through the looking glass. College English,* April 1952, *7,* 393-394.

Chomsky, Noam. *Syntactic structures.* The Hague: Mouton, 1957.

Coleman, E. B. The comprehensibility of several grammatical transformations. *Journal of Applied Psychology,* June 1964, *48,* 186-190.

Coleman, E. B. Learning of prose written in four grammatical transformations. *Journal of Applied Psychology,* October 1965, *49,* 332-341.

Flesch, Rudolf F. The science of making sense. *American Mercury,* 1945, *60,* 194-197.

Flesch, Rudolf F. *The art of plain talk.* New York: Harper and Brothers, 1946. (a)

Flesch, Rudolf F. How to say what you mean. *Science Digest,* 1946, *20,* 37-39. (b)

Flesch, Rudolf F. *The AP writing handbook.* 1951.

Fodor, J., & Garrett, M. Some reflections on competence and performance. In J. Lyons & R. J. Wales (Eds.) *Psycholinguistic papers.* Edinburgh: Edinburgh University Press, 1966.

Gibbons, Helen D. Reading and sentence elements. *Elementary English Review,* February 1941, *18,* 42-46.

Gough, Phillip B. Grammatical transformations and speed of understanding. *Journal of Verbal Learning and Verbal Behavior,* 1965, *4,* 107-111.

Gray, W. S., & Leary, Bernice. What makes a book readable. Chicago: University of Chicago Press, 1935.

Hites, R. W. The relation of readability and format to retention in communication. Unpublished doctoral dissertation, Ohio State University, 1950. Cited by G. R. Klare, *The measurement of readability.* Ames, Iowa: The Iowa State University Press, 1963.

Holland, B. F. The effect of length and structure of sentences on the silent reading process. Paper delivered at American Psychological Association annual meeting. Chicago, 1933.

Klare, George R.; Shuford, Emir H.; & Nichols, William H. The relationship of style difficulty, practice, and ability to efficiency of reading and to retention. *Journal of Applied Psychology*, August 1957, *41*, 222-226.

Klare, George R. *The measurement of readability*. Ames, Iowa: The Iowa State University Press, 1963.

Kueneman, H. A study of the effect of vocabulary changes on reading comprehension in a single field. Unpublished master's thesis. State University of Iowa, 1931. Cited by G. R. Klare, *The measurement of readability*. Ames, Iowa: The Iowa State University Press, 1963.

Marshall, J. S. The relationship between readability and comprehension of high school physics textbooks. *Dissertation Abstracts*, 1957, *17*, 64. (Abstract)

Mehler, Jacques. Some effects of grammatical transformations on the recall of English sentences. *Journal of Verbal Learning and Verbal Behavior*, November 1963, *4*, 748-762.

Miller, George A. Some psychological studies of grammar. *American Psychologist*, November 1962, *11*, 748-762.

Miller, George A.; Galanter, E.; & Pribram, K. *Plans and the structure of behavior*. New York: Holt, 1960.

Miller, George A., & McKean, Kathryn. A chronometric study of some relations between sentences. *Quarterly Journal of Experimental Psychology*, November 1964, *16*, Part 4, 297-308.

Myers, William A. An experimental study of syntactic and semantic interaction. Unpublished doctoral dissertation, University of Minnesota, 1967.

Nolte, Karl F. Simplification of vocabulary and comprehension in reading. *Elementary English Review*, April 1937, *4*, 119-124.

Orndorff, B. A. An experiment to show the effect of sentence length upon comprehension. Unpublished master's thesis, State University of Iowa, 1925. Cited by G. R. Klare, *The measurement of readability*. Ames, Iowa: The Iowa State University Press, 1963.

Savin, Harris B. Grammatical structure and the immediate recall of English sentences: 2. Embedded clauses. Cited in J. Lyons & R. J. Wales (Eds.) *Psycholinguistics papers*. Edinburgh: Edinburgh University Press, 1966.

Savin, Harris B., & Perchonock, Ellen. Grammatical structure and the immediate recall of English sentences. *Journal of Verbal Learning and Verbal Behavior*, October 1965, *5*, 348-353.

Winer, B. J. *Statistical principles in experimental design*. New York: McGraw Hill, 1962.

Yngve, Victor H. Computer programs for translation. *Scientific American*, June 1962, *206*, 68-76.

Yngve, Victor H. A model and hypothesis for language structure. Proceedings of the American Philosophical Association, 1960, *404*, 444-446.

Memory for Syntactic Form as a Function of Semantic Context[*]

JEFFERY J. FRANKS AND JOHN D. BRANSFORD
Vanderbilt University

Psycholinguistic researchers have begun to emphasize the effects of context on language processing. For example, while early research stressed that active sentences were easier to comprehend than passives, affirmatives easier than negatives, etc. (e.g., Gough, 1965, 1966), subsequent research has shown that under appropriate contextual conditions such comprehension differences may diminish or disappear. Thus Wason (1961) has discussed the contexts of plausible denial, Slobin (1966) and Olson and Filby (1972) have investigated situations that are conducive to the processing of passive sentences, and Huttenlocher, Eisenberg, and Strauss (1968) have shown that the same sentences may differ in ease of comprehensibility depending on the contextual situations to which they refer. Such studies are important because they lead one away from asking solely about "intrinsic" differences in sentence processing and orient one toward specifying the conditions under which various grammatical constructions may be used.

Contextual considerations are important for research on sentence memory as well as comprehension. Rather than ask how well a particular sentence or sentence type is recalled or recognized, one might inquire into the conditions under which memory will be good or poor. Consider, for example, Slobin's (1968) study comparing recall for full vs. short ("truncated") passive sentences. The latter form deletes any mention of the actor; e.g., *The floor was washed* rather than *The floor was washed by the janitor*. Slobin found that the Ss showed a very high percentage of verbatim recall for short passive (SP), but not for full passive (FP), sentences. One might conclude that there is something especially distinctive about the "transmission code" (cf. Bregman & Strasberg, 1968) of SP sentences that

*Reprinted from *Journal of Experimental Psychology, 103*, 1974, 1037-1039. Copyright 1974 by the American Psychological Association. Reprinted by permission. This research was supported in part by National Institute of Mental Health Grant 22366 to Jeffery J. Franks and Grant NE-6-00-3-0026 to John D. Bransford and Jeffery J. Franks.

accounts for their high degree of verbatim recall. On the other hand, there may exist contextual conditions under which SP sentences do not result in such high degrees of verbatim memory. For example, Slobin's findings may depend very little on uniquely remembered *syntactic* properties of SP sentences, but instead depend on the fact that *semantic* information about underlying actors was never supplied. The present study seeks to determine whether verbatim memory for a set of SP sentences can be manipulated by varying semantic context. In this study identical target sentences are embedded in two different contexts: one that supplies information about the underlying actor (in a subsequent sentence) and one that does not. The degree of verbatim memory for the SP targets is then assessed. If Slobin's results are due mainly to unique syntactic properties of SP sentences, then semantic context should have little effect on verbatim memory. However, if semantic factors are important, the contextual manipulation may lead to memory differences. The present experiment was also designed to allow assessment of the replicability of Slobin's original results.

Method. The Ss were 18 students enrolled in an introductory psychology course who received course credit for participation in the experiment. Two groups of 9 Ss each were read three unrelated paragraphs and were asked to listen to them carefully because they would later be asked questions about them. The three paragraphs were different for the two groups but were similar in themes. Each paragraph contained approximately 12 sentences including short passives, full passives, full actives, and 1 sentence with a generalized actor (i.e., someone). For one of the short passives in each paragraph (SP-alone) the underlying actor of the sentence was not supplied by the remainder of the paragraph. For a second short passive (SP-semantics), the actor was supplied by the immediately succeeding sentence. Examples of the latter are as follows: *After the harvest a huge feast was served. Mrs. Brown, who did it, was a very good cook. Bob was asked how he liked school. His teacher said that she was very glad to hear such news.* The two groups of Ss received slightly different versions of each paragraph in order to counterbalance sentence materials. For example, if a particular SP sentence occurred as an SP-alone for one group of Ss, it occurred as an SP-semantics for the other group (and vice versa).

After exposure to the three paragraphs, Ss were given a 3-min. break and then were given a recognition test for sentences that occurred in the paragraphs. The Ss received sheets with nine blocks of sentences typed on them. Each block of sentences contained five syntactic versions of a particular semantic idea: a full passive (FP), full active (FA), short passive (SP), passive with generalized actor (GP), active with generalized actor

(GA). One of the sentences in each block actually occurred in one of the paragraphs. An example of a block of test sentences is as follows:

FP: After the harvest a huge feast was served by Mrs. Brown.
FA: After the harvest Mrs. Brown served a huge feast.
SP: After the harvest a huge feast was served.
GP: After the harvest a huge feast was served by someone.
GA: After the harvest someone served a huge feast.

The recognition foils always used actors and actions that Ss had actually heard at some point during acquisition. Since each of the nine blocks contained one sentence that had actually occurred in a paragraph, the total recognition list contained nine sentences Ss had just heard. Of these nine, three were FP, three were SP-alone, and three were SP-semantics. The Ss' task was to check the sentence in each block that they had actually heard.

Results. For each type of acquisition sentence tested in recognition, i.e., FP, SP-alone, and SP-semantic, the proportion of responses to each of the sentence forms in a recognition sentence block was computed. These values are presented in Table 1. The GA and GP responses have been combined. The proportion of verbatim recognition responses for FP, SP-alone, and SP-semantic sentences are .48, .74, and .39, respectively. An ANOVA indicated significant differences among these three sentence types, $F (2, 34) = 9.36, p < .001$.

First compare the verbatim recall of FP sentences and SP-alone sentences. This comparison corresponds to the one investigated by Slobin (1968). Note that Slobin's SP sentences were equivalent to the present SP-alone sentences. He found better verbatim recall for FP than FP sentences, and the same pattern of results are revealed in the present recognition experiment. A S by S analysis of verbatim recognition scores for the SP-alone vs. FP sentences revealed that these two sentence types were remembered with reliably different verbatim accuracies. Thirteen Ss exhibited a higher proportion of verbatim recognition for SP-alone than for FP sentences and there were four ties ($p < .01$) by a sign test. Thus these results replicate those of Slobin.

Next compare verbatim memory for SP-alone vs. SP-semantic sentences. Since these two sentence types are the same sentences counterbalanced across groups, there are no within-sentence differences between them. Only extrasentential (i.e., contextual) information differentiates the two. The data indicated that this semantic context had a marked effect on recognition ratings. The S were able to identify SP-alone sentences

Table 1.   Proportion of Recognition Responses for Four Sentence Categories
Identified at Recognition

Acquisition sentence	Recognition sentence block			
	Full passive (FP)	Full active	Short passive (SP)	Generalized active or passive
FP	.48	.46	.06	.00
SP-alone	.07	.09	.74	.10
SP-semantics	.34	.27	.39	.00

with 74% accuracy, but the corresponding score for SP-semantics sentences dropped to 39%. Thirteen Ss exhibited higher verbatim recognition for SP-alone sentences than for SP-semantic sentences and there were four ties ($p < .01$) by a sign test.

Discussion.   The results of the present experiment shed some light on the reasons behind the precise verbatim memory for SP sentences demonstrated by Slobin (1968). If the syntactic form of SP sentences was the determining factor, one would expect no difference in verbatim memory for SP-alone vs. SP-semantic sentences. The syntactic properties of both types of SP sentences are identical. It is only the extrasentential contextual factors in this study that differentiate SP-alone from SP-semantic forms. Thus the basis for the verbatim recall of SP-alone sentences must lie in the nature of the semantic information expressed by them, as Slobin suggested. Lack of semantic information about an actor apparently restricts the syntactic form into which sentences might be recorded. When such information is supplied by the semantic context, as in the SP-semantic sentences, there is a greater tendency to recode the information into alternative syntactic forms. These data appear related to the results of Bregman and Strasberg (1968) indicating that Ss often reconstruct information about syntax from semantic information. For example, one might remember whether a sentence was expressed in an affirmative or negative form by remembering that he agreed with what that particular sentence expressed. In the present experiments it is the lack of semantic information, i.e., the lack of the actor, that appears to lead to reconstruction of the SP style of expression. When such information is supplied by the linguistic context, Ss tend to think they heard other syntactic forms.

The present study also provides evidence for the more general question of whether the individual sentence should be considered *the* unit of memory. These experiments support a view of linguistic memory that emphasizes integrated semantic representations (see also Barclay 1973;

Bransford & Franks, 1973). They do not support the assumption of the sentence as the basic unit of memory. In many cases the information in memory seems to be an integration of the information contained in a number of sentences, as was evidenced by the fact that SP-semantic inputs used in the present study often resulted in outputs where the originally deleted actors were supplied. An adequate theory of paragraph memory will have to take into account this semantic integration. Rather than simply storing representations of individual sentences, Ss frequently appear to use information communicated by various sentences to construct wholistic descriptions of semantic events. And if Ss simply stored representations of individual sentences, one would frequently want to say that they did not adequately understand the passage. Note, for example, the performance of Barclay's Ss in the explicit memorization groups. Although the necessity for some construct of integration seems intuitively obvious, it is nevertheless theoretically important. Like the considerations of context discussed in the introduction, it affects the nature of the questions one asks. Rather than ask about the comprehensibility or memorability of certain isolated sentence types, one might ask about sentence effectiveness relative to the goal of communicating a certain integrated semantic description. In short, one might explore the contextual conditions under which certain forms of input result in greater understanding and recall.

REFERENCES

Barclay, J. R. The role of comprehension in remembering sentences. *Cognitive Psychology*, 1973, *4*, 229-254.

Bransford, J. D., & Franks, J. J. The abstraction of linguistic ideas: A review. *Cognition*, 1973, *1*, 211-249.

Bregman, A. S., & Strasberg, R. Memory for the syntactic form of sentences. *Journal of Verbal Learning and Verbal Behavior*, 1968, *7*, 396-403.

Gough, P. B. Grammatical transformations and speed of understanding. *Journal of Verbal Learning and Verbal Behavior*, 1965, *4*, 107-111.

Gough, P. B. The verification of sentences: The effects of delay of evidence and sentence length. *Journal of Verbal Learning and Verbal Behavior*, 1966, *5*, 492-496.

Huttenlocher, J., Eisenberg, K., & Strauss, S. Comprehension: Relation between perceived actor and logical subject. *Journal of Verbal Learning and Verbal Behavior*, 1968, *7*, 527-530.

Olson, D. R., & Filby, N. On the comprehension of active and passive sentences. *Cognitive Psychology*, 1972, *3*, 361-381.

Slobin, D. I. Grammatical transformations in childhood and adulthood. *Journal of Verbal Learning and Verbal Behavior*, 1966, *5*, 219-227.

Slobin, D. I. Recall of full and truncated passive sentences in connected discourse. *Journal of Verbal Learning and Verbal Behavior*, 1968, *7*, 876-881.

Wason, P. C. The contexts of plausible denial. *Journal of Verbal Learning and Verbal Behavior*, 1961, *4*, 7-11.

Visual Processing

Relations between Language and Visual Processing

STANLEY F. WANAT
State University of New York at Stony Brook

Research in language and linguistics deals with one of four language functions—listening, speaking, reading, and writing—or with similarities and differences among these functions. Kavanagh and Mattingly's (1972) collection of articles on language deals with similarities and differences in the two receptive language functions—listening and reading.

Sticht, Beck, Hauke, Kleiman, and James (1974) present a related approach to the study of these higher mental processes. They provide a synthesis of studies dealing with the relations between speech comprehension skills and reading comprehension skills. Their developmental model of reading defines reading as a special kind of looking. For them, reading is "Looking at script in order to language."

We now have two approaches to the study of these higher mental processes: identifying similarities and differences in the two receptive language functions of *listening* and *reading* (see Kavanagh & Mattingly, 1972) and identifying similarities and differences between *reading* and *other looking* (or *visual processing*) *skills* (see Sticht et al., 1974).

In a fascinating study of visual information processing, Mackworth and Morandi (1967) showed that perceivers attend to the more informative areas of the picture being shown to them. Would one expect to find the same selective looking in the visual processing of linguistic displays? If we were to adopt the Sticht et al., position that reading is a special kind of looking behavior, we would expect this to be the case. Also, Smith's (1971) analysis provides three principles about reading: 1) The reader has to be fast; 2) the reader has to be selective; and 3) the reader has to be able to use prior knowledge. If the reader has to be selective, then one might expect this selectivity to show itself at the stage of information input.

Consider the following data about visual processing: 1) The eye only stops for about a quarter of a second (Geyer & Kolers, 1974) to process an area of text; and 2) Simon (1974) points out that "Fixation of information in long-term memory has been shown to take about five or ten seconds per chunk." Since it takes 20 to 40 times as long to fix something in long-term memory as it does for the eye to pick up information from text, then there are vital transformations and combinations of information occurring between the input and comprehension (or storage) stages in reading. One viewpoint that has been expressed is that the eye photographs parts of the text, next the brain develops and arranges these photographs into a meaningful unit, and then the brain files the meaning in its long-term memory album.

Another position is that the reader *acts as if* he were reasoning about the linguistic structure of the text he is looking at. Anyone who has observed the oral reading behavior of children who are learning to read is forced to the conclusion that the child's reading errors are systematic. The child's learning-to-read behavior shows a systematic pattern of errors, just as the child's learning-to-speak behavior shows a systematic pattern of errors. In reading acquisition, there is a pervasive logic that links the child's incorrect verbal responses to the visual stimulus.

In such slow and labored attempts at making sense out of what he is looking at, the child behaves almost like a "junior archaeologist" (to use Neisser's [1967] reader-as-archaeologist metaphor), constructing meaning from bits and pieces of information. One source of information that both beginning and accomplished readers use is their knowledge of language structure. For example, even though the reader might not know a particular word, he knows that it must be a noun because of the words surrounding it. The kinds of errors made by adult, fully proficient readers are systematic—they adhere to the grammatical rules of the reader's language. There is a constant interplay between looking and thinking— and one of the things the reader thinks or reasons about is the structure of language.

Ruddell's (1965) research suggests that reading comprehension is enhanced by a closer match between the child's oral language patterns and the language patterns in the materials to be read. Perhaps the mismatch between the language structure rules that the linguistically different, poor reader has stored in his long-term memory, and the linguistic structure of the materials he has to read, prevents him from effectively and efficiently allocating his attention to the most informative parts of the text. Eye movement technology may become a highly valuable aid in diagnosing reading difficulties.

While there is general agreement among reading researchers that language plays a central role in the reader's information processing, the extent to which language guides the eye in reading needs to be systematically investigated. The research to be discussed here explores the role that language plays in guiding the reader's eye. The two major issues to be considered here are: 1) Does the reader selectively allocate his visual attention in extracting meaning from written language? 2) If so, are areas of relatively greater or lesser visual attention predictable from the linguistic structure of the material being read? The research to be presented here was designed to examine the eye-fixation patterning of proficient readers while they read materials that contained specific kinds of linguistic features considered central to comprehension. Prior to the presentation of these findings, a brief review of related research literature will be presented. The review will center on three aspects of reading: 1) Reading as text sampling, 2) the role of grammatical structure in visual sampling, and 3) eye movement studies of reading that emphasize linguistic variables.

Text Sampling

In a 1974 review of research bearing on reading as information processing, Geyer and Kolers note that "visual processes are more active and intentional than was long believed." A clear indication that proficient readers attend to less than the total available information in word recognition and in the reading of sentences is the phenomenon of "proofreader's errors." Very proficient readers can read materials without detecting errors such as letter substitutions, transpositions, omissions, or additions (Neisser, 1967; Pillsbury, 1897). Function words can be repeated (e.g., "the the") or omitted entirely without the reader noticing the error. If the total available information were being processed, such proofreader's errors would not be so easy to demonstrate. In his review of the literature, Fleming (1969) concluded that the research evidence shows that foveal attention is highly selective. Yarbus (1967) concluded that "The human eyes voluntarily and involuntarily fixate on those elements of an object which carry or may carry essential and useful information." Kolers (1970) found that if the reader were forced to adopt a letter-by-letter strategy, his rate would drop to one-tenth of his normal reading speed. Gould and Schaffer (1967) showed that viewers look longer at those objects they are searching for. Nodine and Steuerle (1973) showed that older children are more likely to fixate more informative areas of the visual display than kindergartners. Vurpillot's (1968) research shows that young children tend to see similarities and to ignore small differences in detail when they are asked to decide whether two complex pictures are exactly alike or different. Nodine and Lang (1971) noted the same phenomenon when children were asked to judge whether two words were identical. As children mature, their eye movements reflect more appropriate and efficient ways of coping with the task at hand (N. H. Mackworth & Bruner, 1970).

Feinberg (1949) notes that at one-half inch from the fixation point, two-thirds of visual acuity is lost. N. H. Mackworth (1968) and Rayner and McConkie (1974) have demonstrated that at about seven to twelve letter spaces past the point being fixated, even such gross visual characteristics as overall word shape and initial letters cannot be detected. Research described in McConkie and Rayner (1973, 1974), Rayner (1975), and Rayner and McConkie (1974) shows that the reader can get useful information from only an extremely limited area around the point he is fixating: "the word—non-word distinction appears to be made for the letter strings beginning no further than about four character positions from the fixation point" (McConkie & Rayner, 1974). A serious limitation of McConkie and Rayner's work is the highly unnatural constraints put on the reader by their apparatus. McConkie and Rayner (1973) describe part of their data-gathering procedure as follows: "When a subject arrived for the experiment, a bite bar [a dental wax bite bar that the subject had to rigidly clench with his teeth while he read] was prepared for him which served to reduce head movements during the experiment. Then the eye tracking sensors, mounted on glasses frames and held more securely with a head band, were placed on him and adjusted." Whether or not the reader's eye-movement behavior when he is strapped into an apparatus such as McConkie and Rayner's differs dramatically from his eye-movement behavior when he reads in a natural setting is a serious question. (There are currently available and in use systems to unobtrusively record a subject's eye-movement behavior. With such a system, the subject is not even aware that his eye movements are being monitored.) Also, the bite bar necessitated by apparatus such as that used by McConkie and Rayner rules out the possibility of assessing the subject's oral reading, since the subject cannot read aloud if he is rigidly clenching the bite bar with his teeth.

Cooper (1974) has shown that viewers "tend to spontaneously direct their line of sight to those elements which are most closely related to the meaning of the language concurrently heard." Cooper refers to this scanning as an "active anticipative process." Coffing (1971) demonstrated "significant relationship between stimulus selection [visually] and success [in a visual processing task]."

Buswell (1922) and Hoffman (1927) have shown that poor readers identify fewer letters or words per fixation. Smith (1971) has argued that "the reader must be selective—it doesn't matter how much information enters the visual system, he can get only four or five items through the processing bottleneck into short-term memory. So, in addition to being fast, he must choose the four or five items that will best meet his information needs." Gough (1972) states that "If the words in a sentence are to be integrated into a semantic reading, they must be deployed in the PM [Primary Memory] together. . . . If it takes too long to read a given word, the content of the immediately preceding words will have been lost from the PM, and comprehension will be prevented." Biemiller (1974) cites a study by Robinson (1934) which demonstrated that a training procedure increasing speed of letter and word perception had the effect of increasing fixation width 62 percent. Smith and Holmes (1971) point out that unless a reader can read 200 words per minute or more, he will not be able to comprehend because of memory limitations. One way to move more quickly is to stop less often—to sample the text.

Willows (1974), in a study of intrusion errors in a selective-attention-in-reading task, suggests that the poorer reader is more stimulus-bound than the better reader. Willows, using a procedure reported on by Neisser (1969), found that "poor readers were unable to ignore the adjacent irrelevant lines." Marchbanks and Levin (1965) found that the first letter of a word was the cue most used by children in a word-matching experiment. Weber (1970) analyzed the oral reading errors of children learning how to read and found that in some cases the subjects depended more on context cues while in other cases they depended more on stimulus cues. The preference for one kind of cue over another, shown in the Marchbanks and Levin study and in the Weber study, indicates that beginning readers do not process all of the available information. This phenomenon can be observed in the many beginning readers who occasionally fail to attend to the medial letters in a word. (Samuels [1973] comments on some possible relations between instructional emphasis and the kinds of cues attended to by children as they learn to read.) Thus, there is ample evidence of selectivity in visual processing.

Role of Grammatical Structure in Visual Sampling

The studies mentioned above show that all of the available information is not processed by the reader. This section of the literature review will consider the role that grammatical structure may play in determining which parts of the text are sampled. Kolers (1970), in studies of how subjects read optically transformed text, found that subjects made word substitutions that preserved the part-of-speech of the stimulus word. The sentence verb was most likely to preserve its part of speech: 82 percent of the words substituted for verbs were themselves verbs. Kolers' research was with adults. Weber (1970) studied the oral reading errors of first graders and found that the word-substitutions made by poorer readers did not differ from the substitutions made by better readers when one assessed their grammatical acceptability to the *preceding* context. However, when a substitution made the *rest* of the sentence ungrammatical, better readers corrected such substitutions six times as often as they ignored them, while poorer readers ignored such substitutions more often than they corrected them. Thus, for Weber's subjects, poor readers as well as good readers can predict items that are grammatically appropriate, but poor readers are not able to monitor what their predictions do to the following sentence context.

The effect of context on word perception has been explored in the homograph studies of Cornell's Project Literacy group. See Gibson and Levin (1975), Levin, Gibson, and Gibson (1968), and Levin and Williams (1970). Ford and Levin (1968), Levin and Ford (1968), and Levin, Ford, and Beckwith (1968), in their research on the perception of homographs presented either with or without semantic or syntactic frames, showed that context facilitated perception. It appears that the context served as an additional source of partial information which the reader used to identify the stimulus item.

The literature supports the view that there is an inverse relationship between context information and stimulus information (Brown, 1970; Morton, 1964a; Tulving & Gold, 1963; Weber, 1970). Morton (1964b) found that "fast readers use contextual cues more effectively than slow readers and presumably use more context." When Miller, Bruner, and Postman (1954) varied the amount of redundancy in the visual information presented to the perceiver, they found that the amount of information picked up by the perceiver was generally constant. This same result was found by Wanat and Levin (1975) in their eye-voice span analyses of subjects reading sentence structures containing varying amounts of information. Where more information had to be processed, the eye-voice span was smaller.

Mackworth, Grandstaff, and Pribram (1973) found a relationship between language difficulties and less efficient visual scanning strategies.

Buswell (1920) and Fairbanks (1937) found that good readers had a higher material span than poor readers. Anderson and Swanson (1937) and Morton (1964b) found that better readers make fewer eye movements in oral reading than poorer readers. Factors in the interaction between reader and text affect visual selectivity, since Fairbanks' 1937 study showed that the material span's size does not remain constant during reading.

Shiffrin and Gardner (1972) found that "the initial stages of visual processing, up to at least the level of letter recognition, take place . . . without attentional control." Biemiller (1974) argues that the reader's proficiency in processing individual letters may be directly related to higher levels of reading skills.

Geyer and Kolers (1974) conclude that "context . . . has its main effects through feedback processes which reduce alternatives and structure expectancies." See also Gibson and Levin's (1975) discussion of this issue. Geyer and Kolers (1974), like Wanat (1971), follow Giuliano's (1969) model to suggest that, in reading, samples of text are continuously processed for testing against what the reader expects.

The eye-voice span (EVS) studies of the Project Literacy group also shed light on the relationship between reading and grammatical structure. See Levin's forthcoming monograph on the eye-voice span, and also Gibson and Levin (1975), Levin, Gibson, and Gibson (1968), and Levin and Williams (1970). The eye-voice span is the distance, usually measured in words, separating the eye and the voice in oral reading. The EVS measure is obtained by obscuring the text from the subject's view when the subject's voice reaches a predetermined word in his oral reading. The subject is then asked to report all the words he saw but did not yet have a chance to say aloud. The number of words correctly reported is his eye-voice span for that particular instance. The procedure just described is one way of obtaining an eye-voice span measure. Another procedure is described by Geyer (1966). The "lights-out" procedure used by the Project Literacy group to obtain measures of the reader's eye-voice span should actually be referred to as an eye-voice *store* measure, according to N. H. Mackworth (1970). His position is that the lights-out procedure provides a measure of the information being held at that instant in the reader's short-term memory system. The Project Literacy group's eye-voice span studies do not provide direct information on where the reader's eye is in relation to where his voice is, since they do not monitor the reader's eye movement behavior. These studies do, however, provide interesting information about the reader's linguistic and visual processes.

Levin and Turner (1968) found that the reader's EVS is not a fixed number of words, but rather that it is elastic, tending to expand and contract so as to coincide with phrase boundaries. Their results parallel Schlesinger's (1969) finding that readers pick up and process phrase units. This tendency for the reader to "chunk" the sentence into phrase units is characteristic of mature readers, but not of beginning readers.

Thus, the grammatical structure of the sentence determines the nature of the unit processed by the mature reader.

Levin and Kaplan (1968) devised another study in which the EVS was the dependent variable, while the predictability of a particular kind of phrase within a particular kind of context was the independent variable. In this study, Levin and Kaplan found that the reader had a longer EVS in the area following the verb in passive sentences than in active sentences. Clark (1965) had found the passive form to be more constrained or predictable in this area. Levin and Kaplan's study demonstrated that greater constraints (or predictability) between sentence parts resulted in a larger amount of information being processed in a "chunk." Here, differences in the grammatical relations between sentence parts affected the reader's information processing.

Another EVS study (Levin, Grossman, Kaplan, & Yang, 1972) in this series measured the reader's EVS in left-embedded and right-embedded sentences. A left-embedded sentence is one in which there is a relative clause which modifies the subject. In a right-embedded sentence, a relative clause modifies the object of the main verb. An analysis of left- and right-embedded sentences by Levin et al. had determined that the right embedding is much more predictable. Their EVS experiment showed that the more predictable or expected form resulted in a larger eye-voice span.

Also utilizing the EVS technique, Wanat and Levin (1975) presented two different words within identical sentence contexts. The context led the reader to expect a word with a particular kind of structural feature (i.e., an underlying agent in a passive sentence type) but did not lead him to expect a particular word. For example, given the sentence context "The boat was piloted by the _____," the word "helper" is more predictable as a completion than is "harbor." This is so because the sentence context leads the reader to expect to find *who* piloted the boat—the underlying agent of the verb. The difference between the size of the EVS for the more predictable form and the less predictable form again showed that the structural relations between the sentence parts affect the reader's information processing. The effect of context on the size of the eye-voice span has also been demonstrated by Lawson (1961) and Morton (1964b). They found the distance between the eye and the voice to increase as a function of increasing contextual constraint.

Wanat and Levin (1975) theorized that the reader assigns priority to certain kinds of tentative structural descriptions in reading. With reading materials in which this initial hypothesis is confirmed, processing is facilitated. Therefore, the reader is able to process more information, as shown by a larger eye-voice span. Given Levin's (1968) finding that the agent-included form is more expected by the reader, Wanat and Levin (1975) theorized that when the reader encountered the beginning of a passive sentence, he would expect to find an agent after the verb. If such were the case in the sentence, then processing would be more efficient. The results of their experiment support this interpretation, since the reader's EVS following the passive sentence verb was greater when the agent was present than when the agent was missing. In two related studies, Blumenthal (1967) and Blumenthal and Boakes (1967) found that the underlying agent in a passive sentence served as a more effective prompt to help the subject recall the sentence than did a nonagentive noun substituted for the agent.

The view that perceiver expectations based on grammatical structure operate in reading was discussed by Huey in 1901. He stated that it was the operation of reader expectations which permitted the more fluent processing of connected versus unconnected materials. The contingencies between items in the connected materials enable the perceiver to anticipate what is coming. Thus, there is ample evidence that grammatical structure is an important factor in the reader's information extraction.

Eye-Movement Studies Emphasizing Linguistic Variables

The studies mentioned above show that the reader's linguistic knowledge is reflected in his visual information processing. This section of the literature review will consider eye-movement studies of reading that emphasize linguistic variables. The studies in this section involve as dependent variables aspects of the reader's overt scanning behavior. To generalize, earlier eye-movement studies of reading presented a number of differentiated measures of the reader's overt scanning, with little systematic attention to the different kinds of structural variables operating in language. For example, in a 1922 study, Judd and Buswell maintained that numerous irregular eye movements indicate that the reader is trying to break the material up into units. However, in their experimental procedure, they did not systematically vary the nature of the linguistic elements to measure their effect on eye movements. Judd and Buswell's statement fits with Buswell's more general statement (1920) that difficulties in the recognition of meaning are reflected in the character of the reader's eye movements.

Also, Woodworth's (1938) analysis of the available research (which he described as being "indeed rather scanty") indicated that the reader's difficulty might be traced to factors such as "an unfamiliar word; a word used in some other than its common conversational meaning; an ambiguous word not sufficiently prepared for by the context; a superfluous word from the reader's point of view." Woodworth's analysis of eye-fixation differences related to "particular sorts of words" does not consider words—let alone higher-order linguistic units—in terms of any linguistically defined frame of reference. When Tinker reviewed the eye-movement research in 1958, none of the studies cited dealt with variables involving linguistic structure. The same holds for Bower's 1964 review. Since that time, there have been a number of eye-fixation studies of reading that directly address the question of linguistic determinants of attention.

Morton's (1964b) study of the relationship between eye movements and the nature of the textual materials was mentioned in the preceding section. He found that greater contextual constraint decreased the number of both forward and regressive eye movements. He also showed that better readers are able to utilize more contextual constraint than poorer readers. The major limitation in his study is that varying statistical approximations to normal, connected English text were used. The results show that the reader's sampling of the text becomes less dense as the materials approach the contextual constraints found in normal, connected English prose. However, since most reading situations involve the processing of connected text, Morton's results do not shed much light on the nature of the reader's eye movements in normal reading situations. His results do not specify which characteristics of the text (other than the general characteristic of contextual constraint) let the reader sample connected text more efficiently.

The way in which linguistic units are reflected in the reader's eye movements was studied by Mehler, Bever, and Carey (1967). On the basis of a study of the reader's overt scanning behaviors, they formulated the general eye-fixation rule that the reader fixates on the first half of each immediate constituent. Thus, the linguistically defined immediate constituent determines the unit of fixation. Mehler et al.'s concern (1967) with the effect of specific linguistic variables on eye-fixation patterning in reading was an important step beyond the instrumentally refined but linguistically naive studies of earlier researchers in the field. There are, however, some major difficulties with the Mehler et al. (1967) study:

First, they discarded approximately half of their data. One of their criteria for discarding records of eye fixations was the presence of many fixation points on the record. A case in which the reader had to fixate many points suggests the presence of factors in the sentence which made it difficult to process visually; yet, this served as a basis for discarding the record.

Second, their technique only took into account whether or not an area was fixated. They did not differentiate between forward fixations and regressions. Thus, there was no way to determine if a particular area was regressed to, or whether a regressive movement originated at a particular area. Their procedures also failed to take into account the duration of a fixation. It is impossible to determine from their data if some areas took more time to process than others.

Finally, Mehler et al. (1967) used sentences that were ambiguous. Since relatively few sentences encountered in natural reading situations are ambiguous, it is possible that this characteristic of their test materials limits the generalizability of their findings. In summary, although the Mehler et al. (1967) study attempts to examine the effect of specific linguistic variables, limitations in the type of eye-fixation measure used, the types of records retained for analysis, and the nature of the reading materials, all raise questions about the validity of the study.

In another examination of the relationship between eye movements and the nature of the textual materials, Kennedy (1967) found that regressive eye movements in reading tend to take place within, rather than across, major constituent boundaries. Kennedy reexamined some of Buswell's data (1920) and found that the probability of a regression occurring across a constituent boundary was inversely related to the strength or primacy of that boundary. For example, a regressive eye movement was more likely to occur across a relatively weak constituent boundary such as that between an adjective and the following noun, and much less likely to occur across a relatively strong constituent boundary such as the major sentence break between the subject phrase and the predicate phrase. Thus, the linguistically defined primacy or importance of a constituent structure boundary is an index to the likelihood that a regression will cross it.

There are two limitations in Kennedy's study. First, the characteristics of the readers are not known. It is therefore difficult to know the extent to which his results are generalizable. Second, his findings are restricted to one aspect of the reader's overt scanning behaviors—whether or not a regressive movement crossed a particular kind of constituent boundary.

Comunale's (1973) eye-movement study involved the presence or absence of prepositional phrases to separate sentence components. His research was limited to only one measure of the reader's overt scanning behaviors. Zargar's thesis (1973) suggests that nouns are attended to far more than verbs. However, in his inquiry into possible relations between grammatical features and eye-fixation patterning, Rayner (1975) found that "there were not perceptual span differences as a function of the part of speech."

To generalize, then, earlier studies presented a number of differentiated measures of the reader's overt scanning behaviors, with little systematic attention to the different kinds of structural variables operating in language. Some more recent studies, on the other hand, have taken into account linguistic variables, but without regard to different components of the reader's overt scanning behaviors. Different components of the reader's eye-fixation patterning should be considered since each may have a function in reading. This is suggested by Anderson's (1937) finding that nearly every component measure clearly differentiated between good and poor readers.

Coffing (1971), Cooper (1974), Loftus (1972), N. Mackworth and Bruner (1970), Noton and Stark (1971), Simon and Barenfeld (1969), and others have shown that the perceiver's eye-fixation patterning reflects his internalized cognitive structures, maps, and strategies for processing *pictorial* information. The present study investigates the question of whether the reader's eye-fixation patterning reflects his internalized *linguistic* rules. The research to be described here deals with measures of the reader's allocation of attention to different linguistic structures. Its purpose is to study the effects that manipulation of different kinds of linguistic variables has on different components of the reader's overt scanning behaviors. Also considered in the present study is mode of reading; that is, whether the material was read silently or orally. One of the reasons for including mode of reading as an experimental variable was the study of Anderson and Swanson in 1937. They found that the correlations between each of their measures of eye movements in silent reading and the same measure in oral reading were positive and high, and that there were significant differences between the oral and silent scores. The present research is an attempt to build upon earlier studies of reading as a sampling process.

Five measures of the reader's overt scanning behaviors were used. These dependent variables were:

1. Time spent on forward fixations.
2. Number of forward fixations.
3. Time spent on regressive fixations.
4. Number of regressive fixations to areas in the sentence.
5. Number of regressions from areas in the sentence.

These measures were obtained for the sentence as a whole, and for each area of the sentence.

One of the independent variables was mode of reading; that is, whether the sentence was read aloud or silently. Other independent variables involved differences in sentence structure:

Some sentence manipulations affected the immediate constituent analysis (the surface constituent phrase structure) of the sentence, as in the case of left-embedded sentences versus right-embedded sentences.

Other structural manipulations changed the grammatical relations between parts of a sentence while keeping the immediate constituent analysis the same, as in the case of active sentences and different passive sentence types.

In some of the manipulations, the predictability of a particular kind of phrase within a given sentence context was the independent variable, as in the case of agent-included constituents versus agent-deleted constituents in passive sentences.

Word category was also an independent variable. Eye-fixation scores on test sentences in which a content word was used to signal a particular kind of grammatical relation were compared to the scores on test sentences in which a function word was used to signal the same grammatical relation. This was done to see if differences in word category were reflected in the reader's line of sight.

In the present study, the eye movements of 12 mature readers were recorded while each read 80 sentences. The subjects were professional staff members at the Stanford University Medical Center. The equipment used to photograph the reader's eye-fixation patterning was a wide-angle reflection eye camera (N. H. Mackworth, 1968). This camera provides a motion picture record of the test display as it is reflected on the subject's eye. When the motion picture film is developed and examined, the outline of the pupil is seen to encircle the area of the stimulus being fixated by the reader.

On the film, different areas of the visual display are shown to be successively encircled by the pupil as the reader successively fixates different areas along the line of print. N. H. Mackworth (1968) has demonstrated that the center of the pupil marks the position of the display being fixated. For each frame of the motion picture film, the procedure was to locate the center of the pupil, and then to determine what part of the sentence was being fixated.

Each subject was tested separately. He read 40 sentences at each of two test sessions. Half of the test items were read silently and half were read aloud. For every comparison made of contrasting linguistic features, each subject read eight examples of the first linguistic type and eight examples of the contrasting linguistic type. Thus, for every structural comparison, 192 sentence readings were analyzed—2 linguistic features X 8 sentences per linguistic feature per subject X 12 subjects.

Each subject read one member of each test pair at each of two test sessions, so that if he read the left-embedded (subject-modifying) form "On the picnic the girls that Bill teased saw the child" at the first test session, he would get the corresponding right-embedded (object-modifying) form "The girls saw the child that Bill teased on the picnic" at the second test session one week later. The subjects were instructed to read the sentences naturally and to attend to their meaning. To insure that the subject attended to the meaning of the sentence, he was told that after he read a sentence, he might be asked to paraphrase it. There were 18 such requests for paraphrase on randomly selected sentences for each subject.

Selective Attention to Sentence Areas

Is there significant variability in the amount of visual attention allotted to different areas of the sentence? Rayner (1975) presents the view that it is essential to find out what guides the eye. The three possibilities he notes are constant pattern, stimulus control, and internal control. It seems likely that the determining factor is some combination of stimulus control and internal control, but there are these three possible guides, and various combinations of these three.

In the present study, analyses of variance of the scores for each of the five measures of eye-fixation patterning showed significant variability in the scores for individual areas. On three of the five measures, the level of significance was .001; for one measure, at the .005 level of significance; and for one measure, at the .01 level of significance. Thus, the hypothesis that the reader selectively allocates his visual attention to different areas of the sentence is supported by the scores on each of the five measures of eye-fixation patterning.

Differences Between Left-Embedded and Right-Embedded Sentences

Are there differences in the amount of visual attention allotted to left-embedded (LE) versus right-embedded (RE) sentences. (See Table 1.)

Table 1.   List of left embedded (LE) and right embedded (RE) sentences.

LE$_1$ On the picnic the girls that Bill teased saw the child.

RE$_1$ The girls saw the child that Bill teased on the picnic.

LE$_2$ In our building the man that John caught scolded the lad.

RE$_2$ The man scolded the lad that John caught in our building.

LE$_3$ In the kitchen the chef that Pete tested hired the crew.

RE$_3$ The chef hired the crew that Pete tested in the kitchen.

LE$_4$ At the office the clerk that Mary phoned fired the boy.

RE$_4$ The clerk fired the boy that Mary phoned at the office.

LE$_5$ At the airport the gang that Mike called beat the guard.

RE$_5$ The gang beat the guard that Mike called at the airport.

LE$_6$ At the clinic the nurse that Joan taught liked the kid.

RE$_6$ The nurse liked the kid that Joan taught at the clinic.

LE$_7$ In the scuffle the kids that Jack seized aided the lady.

RE$_7$ The kids aided the lady that Jack seized in the scuffle.

LE$_8$ At the contest the gang that Jean backed liked the team.

RE$_8$ The gang liked the team that Jean backed at the contest.

LE sentences contain a relative clause that follows and modifies the sentence subject. RE sentences contain a relative clause that follows and modifies the sentence object. The LE and RE sentence types were used because Levin et al. (1972) found that these sentence types differ in their structural predictability. When Levin et al. (1972) presented sentence frames to subjects with just the embedded phrase omitted, subjects completed 78 percent of the RE frames with embeddings, but only 33 percent of the LE frames with embeddings. When subjects were presented with a sentence frame in which either a right embedding or a left embedding could occur, an RE occurred three times as often as an LE. Thus, the RE sentence structure is more predictable than the LE sentence structure.

In terms of the structure of English, there are a number of factors that might explain the difference in predictability. For example, there is a greater range of structures that can follow the subject of the sentence than can follow the object: After the subject, either a main verb or a left embedding can occur. The main verb cannot occur after the object in place of a right embedding.

Levin et al. (1972) conducted a constraint analysis of these two forms. They used a modified cloze procedure to measure the constraint (the inverse of the information uncertainty) in the LE and RE forms. They found the RE form to be more constrained. Levin et al. (1972) also showed that the reader's eye-voice span was different in these two forms, with the reader's EVS being greater in the sentence area where the RE form is more highly constrained than in the corresponding area in the LE form. It would be expected that differences in structural predictability would affect the reader's pickup and processing of information.

In the present study, a sentence-construction procedure was devised to insure that any differences in eye-fixation scores were attributable to differences in sentence structure, and not to differences in constituent phrases, or to differences in individual words. A single set of phrases was used to construct both the LE and RE members of a test pair. The phrases were combined one way to form an LE sentence, and the same phrases were combined another way to form an RE sentence. Thus, 8 sets of phrases were used to construct the 8 LE-RE test pairs. The 12 subjects each read 8 LE and 8 RE sentences. Consequently, eye-fixation scores on 96 LE and 96 RE sentence readings were analyzed.

The total time spent on forward fixational pauses in reading the less predictable left-embedded sentences was significantly greater than the total time spent on forward fixational pauses in reading the more predictable right-embedded sentences ($p < .005$). The average number of forward fixational pauses for the LE form was equal to the number for the RE form. None of the three measures of regressive eye movements showed any significant differences between the two types. Thus, differences in the structural predictability of the two sentence forms significantly affected the amount of time spent on forward fixational pauses. These results are complementary to the Levin et al. findings, since the form shown to be more constrained in the modified cloze procedure is the form shown to be easier to process, since it has been shown to permit a larger eye-voice span and to require a smaller amount of visual attention. Thus, a sentence type which is less structurally predictable requires more visual attention.

Differences Within Left-Embedded and Right-Embedded Sentences

Does a sentence's immediate constituent analysis (surface constituent phrase structure—the way we would parse a sentence) affect the way that

the reader's visual attention is distributed across the sentence? This inquiry was based upon Kennedy's (1967) reexamination of some of Buswell's (1920) data, suggesting that regressions are more likely to take place
within, rather than across, phrase boundaries. Both the Kennedy and the
Mehler et al. (1967) studies provide provocative (but inconclusive) data
about the sensitivity of the reader's visual scanning to a sentence's immediate constituent analysis.

Let us briefly look at the immediate constituent analyses of LE and RE
sentences. It has already been pointed out that LE sentences contain a
relative clause following and modifying the subject, and that RE sentences
contain a relative clause following and modifying the object. Thus:

LE = SUBJECT + REL CLAUSE + VERB + OBJECT.
RE = SUBJECT + VERB + OBJECT + REL CLAUSE.

In the sentences used in this study, a "filler" prepositional phrase has been
added to each LE and to each RE sentence, so that the relative clauses
would all line up letter-for-letter. (See Table 1.) Examination of the test
materials in Table 1 will show that the LE and RE member in each test pair
is made up of the same set of phrases. The phrases are combined one way
to yield an LE sentence, and the same phrases are combined another way
to yield a matched RE sentence.

To answer the question posed in the paragraph immediately above,
the following reasoning was used: From the discussion in the section
headed Differences *Between* Left-Embedded and Right-Embedded Sentences, it is known that both LE and RE sentences each have, on the
average, the same number of forward fixations per sentence. It is also
known that the LE and RE sentences have different immediate constituent
analyses. Therefore, if the analysis of variance of the eye-fixation scores
indicated a significant Sentence Area X Sentence Type interaction, this
would indicate that there is significant variability in the way that the same
amount of visual attention is distributed across these Sentence Types
differing in their immediate constituent analysis. This was shown to be the
case, since there was a significant Sentence Area X Sentence Type interaction ($p < .01$). Since differences in the structural predictability of the two
types have been shown not to affect the number of forward fixations in
each sentence, it can be concluded that differences in the sentences'
immediate constituent analysis affect the distribution of forward fixational pauses.

Active and Passive Sentences

Will the reader's allocation of visual attention be affected by changing the grammatical relations that hold between parts of a sentence while holding the immediate constituent analysis the same? In this section, data will be presented on comparisons between sentence types differing in the structural predictability of corresponding constituents, but which all have the same surface constituent phrase structure.

Comparison A: Differences between active and passive sentences. In this section of the study, active and passive sentences were constructed so that they all had the same surface constituent phrase structure. (See Table 2.)

Table 2.   List of active (ACT) and passive (+AGC) sentences.

ACTIVE (ACT) SENTENCES

The maid was washing in the alcove of her room.

The poet was writing in the studio of his home.

The serf was working in the market of our town.

The bird was romping in the branch of the tree.

The lady was reading in the meadow of the park.

The calf was running in the shrubs of the farm.

The star was dancing in the ballet of the show.

The boat was sailing in the marina of the lake.

PASSIVE (+AGC) SENTENCES

The ship was beached by the helper in the storm.

The boat was piloted by the leader to the pier.

The pack was guarded by the deputy in the afternoon.

The wife was injured by the beggar on the farm.

The gang was stopped by the police in the morning.

The lady was brought by the escort at the theater.

The auto was damaged by the driver in the rushhour.

The babe was carried by the doctor to his bedroom.

Comparison B: Differences between agent-included and agent-deleted passive sentences using a content word to signal this contrast. This section also involved a comparison between two different passive sentence types. For this comparison, passive sentences that included the underlying agent of the sentence were paired with passive sentences that were identical in all respects except that the agent phrase was replaced by a nonagent phrase. (See Table 3.)

Table 3.   List of agent-included ($+$AGC) and agent-deleted ($-$AGC) sentences.

```
+AGC₁   The ship was beached by the helper in the storm.

-AGC₁   The ship was beached by the harbor in the storm.

+AGC₂   The boat was piloted by the leader to the pier.

-AGC₂   The boat was piloted by the shoals to the pier.

+AGC₃   The pack was guarded by the deputy in the afternoon.

-AGC₃   The pack was guarded by the forest in the afternoon.

+AGC₄   The wife was injured by the beggar on the farm.

-AGC₄   The wife was injured by the stable on the farm.

+AGC₅   The gang was stopped by the police in the morning.

-AGC₅   The gang was stopped by the garden in the morning.

+AGC₆   The lady was brought by the escort at the theater.

-AGC₆   The lady was brought by the pillar at the theater.

+AGC₇   The auto was damaged by the driver in the rushhour.

-AGC₇   The auto was damaged by the avenue in the rushhour.

+AGC₈   The babe was carried by the doctor to his bedroom.

-AGC₈   The babe was carried by the parlor to his bedroom.
```

Thus, the first sentence in Table 3 is an agent-included passive sentence. The phrase "by the helper" specifies who performed the action described by the verb. The second sentence in Table 3 is paired with the first. In this second sentence, the agent phrase is deleted and replaced by a nonagent phrase, such as "by the harbor." Each of the sentences in Table 3 is paired with another sentence in Table 3 in the manner described above.

Note that the nonagent versus agent difference in the sentences in Table 3 is signalled using a content word (e.g., *harbor* versus *helper*).

Comparison C: Differences between agent-included and agent-deleted passive sentences, using a function word to signal this contrast. This section also involved another comparison between two different passive sentence types. Like the comparison described in the preceding paragraph, passive sentences that included the underlying agent of the sentence were paired with passive sentences that were identical in all respects except that the agent phrase was replaced by a nonagent phrase. (See Table 4.)

Table 4. List of agent-included ($+$AGF) and agent-deleted ($-$AGF) sentences (using function word cues to differences in underlying structure).

$+$AGF$_1$ The note was brought by the leader of the forces.

$-$AGF$_1$ The note was brought to the leader of the forces.

$+$AGF$_2$ The gift was awarded by the victor at the tourney.

$-$AGF$_2$ The gift was awarded to the victor at the tourney.

$+$AGF$_3$ The book was shipped by the market on the highway.

$-$AGF$_3$ The book was shipped to the market on the highway.

$+$AGF$_4$ The bill was offered by the dealer at the store.

$-$AGF$_4$ The bill was offered to the dealer at the store.

$+$AGF$_5$ The pass was granted by the sentry at the gateway.

$-$AGF$_5$ The pass was granted to the sentry at the gateway.

$+$AGF$_6$ The toll was charged by the holder of the lease.

$-$AGF$_6$ The toll was charged to the holder of the lease.

$+$AGF$_7$ The club was opposed by the others in the union.

$-$AGF$_7$ The club was opposed to the others in the union.

$+$AGF$_8$ The cost was allowed by the victim of the accident.

$-$AGF$_8$ The cost was allowed to the victim of the accident.

Thus, the first sentence in Table 4 is an agent-included passive sentence. The phrase "by the leader" specifies who performed the action described by the verb. The second sentence in Table 4 is paired with the first. In this second sentence, the agent phrase is deleted and replaced by a nonagent phrase, such as "to the helper." Each of the sentences in Table 4 is paired with another sentence in Table 4 in the manner described above. Note that the nonagent versus agent difference in Table 4 is signalled using a function word (e.g., *to* versus *by*).

Let us now turn to the results of these comparisons involving the active sentences and the various passive sentence types. Analysis of variance of the data on the amount of time spent on forward fixations showed no significant variation in the scores. Similarly, analysis of variance of the data on the number of forward fixations showed no significant variation. Analysis of variance of the data on the amount of time spent on regressive fixations shows that there is significant variation among the scores ($p < .025$). When the scores for the active and the various passive sentence types are compared, some of the differences are quite pronounced. For example, the time spent on regressive fixations for the agent-deleted passive sentence type in which a content word signals the agent-deletion (see Table 3) is 2¼ times as large as the corresponding score for the active sentence type (see Table 2). This is so even though the surface constituent structure of these two sets of sentences is identical, with the words in each sentence lining up letter-for-letter.

Analysis of variance of the data on the number of regressive fixations *to* areas of these sentences shows that there is significant variation among the scores ($p < .05$). As with the preceding measure, differences are pronounced. Looking again at the agent-deleted passive sentence type with the content-word cue to agent deletion, and at the active sentence type, the score for this passive is 1¾ times as large as the score for the active.

Analysis of variance of the data on the number of regressions *from* areas in these sentences shows that there is significant variation among the scores ($p < .05$). As with the two preceding cases, differences are pronounced. Considering again the agent-deleted passive sentence type with the content-word cue to agent deletion, and the active sentence type, the score for this passive is again 1¾ times as large as the score for the active.

To conclude our discussion of the results obtained in these comparisons of active sentences and the various passive sentence types, it is clear that the reader's visual attention is affected by changing the grammatical relations that obtain between parts of a sentence while holding the immediate constituent analysis the same.

Word Category Differences

Do different surface structure cues to the same kinds of underlying sentence relations require different amounts of visual attention? Rayner

(1975) found that "there were not perceptual span differences as a function of the part of speech." Rather than Rayner's perceptual span measure, the present study used different measures of the reader's allocation of visual attention. In this exploration of whether or not different surface structure cues require different amounts of visual attention, the following strategy was used: The test sentences in Table 3 were constructed so that one member in each pair differs from the other member by only one word—a content word. The sentences in Table 3 are either agent-included or agent-deleted passive sentences, and in each case, this difference is signalled by a content word. The sentences in Table 3 can be looked upon as sentence frames into which a content word can be inserted.

The sentences in Table 4 can be similarly characterized. There are eight agent-included passives matched with eight agent-deleted passives. Within each of the eight pairs of test sentences, the two sentences are identical except that in the agent-included form, the preposition *by* follows the main verb, while in the agent-deleted form, the preposition *to* follows the main verb. The sentences in Table 4 were constructed so that one member in each pair differs from the other member by only one word—a function word. The sentences in Table 4 can be looked upon as sentence frames into which a function word can be inserted. Inserting the word *by* after the verb makes the sentences in Table 4 into agent-included passives, while inserting the word *to* in that position makes the sentences into agent-deleted passives.

Identical sentence frames were provided for the *by* versus *to* manipulation in Table 4 (as well as for the content-word manipulation in Table 3), so as to eliminate any possible effects attributable to differences between individual words comprising the sentence frames in which the *by* and *to* occurred.

If different surface structure cues do *not* require different amounts of visual attention, then we would expect that the agent-included ($+$AGC) versus agent-deleted ($-$AGC) difference when a content word cue is used will *not* differ from the agent-included ($+$AGF) versus agent-deleted ($-$AGF) difference when a function word is used. Or, to use the abbreviations for the sentence types being compared, we would expect that ($-$AGC) $-$ ($+$AGC) $=$ ($-$AGF) $-$ ($+$AGF).

If, however, different surface structure cues do require different amounts of visual attention, then we would expect that ($-$AGC) $-$ ($+$AGC) $\neq$ ($-$AGF) $-$ ($+$AGF).

Let us now examine the data. It has already been pointed out that there is no significant variability among the forward fixation scores when the data for the active and various passive sentence types are analyzed. When we consider the data on the amount of time spent on regressive fixations, it has already been noted that there is significant variability among the scores ($p < .01$). The scores for the two sets of agent-included passives ($+$AGC and $+$AGF) were identical. However, the difference between the $-$AGC form and the $+$AGC form was four times as large as the difference between the $-$AGF form and the $+$AGF form. This indicates that different word catagory cues to the same underlying sentence relations require different amounts of visual attention. In the case of the amount of time spent on regressive fixations (as well as in the case of the number of regressive fixations to areas in the sentence, and in the case of the number of regressive fixations from areas in the sentence), differences in the allocation of visual attention to the two sentence types (agent-included versus agent-deleted) were much more pronounced with content word cues than with function word cues. It must be concluded that the reader's allocation of visual attention is affected differently when a content word is used to indicate particular underlying sentence relations than when a function word is used to indicate the same set of underlying sentence relations. The results here demonstrate that the grammatical features characterizing an individual word may affect the reader's eye-fixation patterning differently from the grammatical features characterizing another individual word, even when those two words signal equivalent grammatical relations.

Linguistic Control Mechanisms for Forward Versus Regressive Scanning

Do some kinds of linguistic manipulations affect some aspects of the reader's allocation of visual attention, while other kinds of linguistic manipulations affect other aspects of the reader's allocation of visual attention? This section of the study deals with possible differences in the linguistic control mechanisms for the reader's forward visual scanning behavior, and for his regressive visual scanning behavior. This question relates to Hochberg's constructs (1970) of Peripheral Search Guidance and Cognitive Search Guidance and his discussion of how they might operate to guide the reader's information extraction. This question also relates to Goldman-Eisler's finding (1969) that there are two kinds of pauses in spontaneous speech, one reflecting conventional parsing, and the other reflecting cognitive planning, searching, and testing. If there are these two functionally distinct types of pauses in language production processes, perhaps there would be two parallel types of pauses in language reception processes. Also, Weber's analysis (1970) of the kinds of oral reading errors made by young children learning how to read indicates that the skill of going back and correcting linguistically inappropriate guesses marks an important stage in reaching maturity in reading. Thus, strands in linguistic research suggest that somewhat different kinds of attentional guidance factors, performing somewhat different kinds of meaning-extraction tasks, might be at work in reading.

Examination of the data in the present research indicates that forward eye-fixation patterning tends to be related to the sentence's immediate constituent analysis, whereas regressive eye-fixation patterning tends to be related to the structural predictability of constituents within the sentence frame. Recall that the left-embedded and right-embedded sentences (see Table 1) differ in their immediate constituent analysis and that there was significant variability in the way that the same amount of visual attention (the number of forward fixations) was distributed across the sentence areas of these two sentence types. Note that although the immediate constituent analysis differences between left-embedded and right-embedded sentences affected forward eye-fixation patterning, they did not affect regressive eye-fixation patterning. Note also that the active/passive structural differences involved manipulating the structural predictability of constituents within a single sentence frame. This manipulation of items within a given immediate constituent framework affected regressive eye-fixation patterning, but not forward eye-fixation patterning. There was not a single instance where manipulating the structural predictability of items within a given immediate constituent framework resulted in significant variability in forward eye-fixation patterning measures. Thus, the data presented here indicate that some kinds of linguistic manipulations affect some aspects of the reader's allocation of visual attention, while other kinds of linguistic manipulations affect other aspects of the reader's allocation of visual attention. Specifically, differences in the immediate constituent analysis of left-embedded and right-embedded sentences affected the placement of forward fixational pauses across the areas of the sentence, while differences in the structural predictability of items placed within a given immediate constituent framework, in the case of the active and the various passive sentence types, affected components of the reader's regressive eye-fixation patterning.

Oral and Silent Reading

Are there differences in the amount of visual attention required by the oral and silent reading of textual materials? Recall that one-half of the sentences in each test category were read silently and one-half were read orally so as to permit investigation of the possible effects of reading mode on the reader's allocation of visual attention. Analysis of variance of the data on oral versus silent reading performance, on the measure of time spent on forward fixations, showed a significant difference ($\rho < .001$). Oral reading required the reader to spend 25 percent more time on forward fixational pauses than silent reading of the same kinds of sentences. The data on the number of forward fixational pauses also showed that oral reading required significantly more visual attention than silent reading ($\rho < .01$). Analysis of the data did not indicate that the amount of visual attention required by oral reading differed from the amount of visual attention required by silent reading in the case of regressive eye-fixation patterning.

It should be noted that, with respect to the linguistic features discussed in preceding sections of this study, the effects of differences in linguistic features on visual attention were generally more pronounced in oral reading than in silent reading. There were two significant Reading Mode (oral versus silent) × Sentence Type interactions, indicating that the relationship between oral and silent reading scores was not consistent across the active and the various passive sentence types. There was one significant Reading Mode (oral versus silent) × Sentence Type × Sentence Area interaction. This finding points to the usefulness of including mode of reading as a factor in studying the reader's eye-fixation patterning. For that reason, research conducted with apparatus that confines the reader to only the silent mode (such as the apparatus used by Comunale; McConkie; Mehler et al.; Rayner; etc.) has serious limitations (in addition to the limitations mentioned at the beginning of this paper). Linguistic factors affecting the reader's allocation of visual attention may behave differently in oral reading than they do in silent reading.

Conclusions

Earlier research on eye-fixation patterning in reading dealt with a number of differentiated measures of overt scanning behaviors, but incorporated little analysis of linguistic variables. More recent line-of-sight research, on the other hand, has been based upon explicit consideration of linguistic variables, but without regard to different components of overt scanning behaviors.

The research reported here investigated the effects that manipulations of different kinds of linguistic variables would have on different components of overt scanning behaviors. Eye-fixation patterning was analyzed into the following components: Time spent on forward fixations; number of forward fixations; time spent on regressive fixations; number of regressive fixations to areas in the sentence; and number of regressions from areas in the sentence.

A wide-angle reflection eye camera recorded reader eye-fixation patterning. Analysis of 960 sentence readings by 12 mature readers indicated that: The reader selectively allocates his visual attention to different sentence areas. A sentence type which is less structurally predictable requires more visual attention. A sentence's immediate constituent analysis affects the way the reader's visual attention is distributed across the sentence. Varying the structural predictability of items inserted into the same immediate constituent framework affects the amount of visual attention required. Differences in the kinds of linguistic cues (i.e., content words versus function words) to the same underlying sentence relations affect the reader's allocation of visual attention. Differences in the immediate constituent analysis of sentences affect forward scanning, while differences in the structural predictability of items within a given immediate constituent framework affect regressive scanning. Oral reading requires more visual attention than the silent reading of the same types of materials, and linguistic factors affecting the reader's allocation of visual attention may behave differently in oral reading than they do in silent reading.

REFERENCES

Anderson, I. H. Eye-movements of good and poor readers. *Psychological Monographs*, 1937, *48*, 1-35.

Anderson, I. H., & Swanson, P. E. Common factors in silent and oral reading. *Psychological Monographs*, 1937, *48*, 61-69.

Biemiller, A. *Relationships between oral reading rates for letters, words, and simple text, and the development of reading ability.* Manuscript, Institute of Child Study, University of Toronto, 1974.

Blumenthal, A. L. Prompted recall of sentences. *Journal of Verbal Learning and Verbal Behavior*, 1967, *6*, 203-206.

Blumenthal, A. L., & Boakes, R. Supplementary report: Prompted recall of sentences. *Journal of Verbal Learning and Verbal Behavior*, 1967, *6*, 674-676.

Bower, T. *Bibliography of work in eye movement techniques* (Project Literacy). Unpublished manuscript, Cornell University, 1964.

Brown, R. Psychology and reading. In H. Levin & J. P. Williams (Eds.), *Basic studies on reading*. New York: Basic Books, 1970.

Buswell, G. T. An experimental study of eye-voice span in reading. *Supplementary Educational Monographs*, 1920, *17*.

Buswell, G. T. Fundamental reading habits: A study of their development. *Supplementary Educational Monographs*, 1922, *21*.

Clark, H. H. Some structural properties of simple active and passive sentences. *Journal of Verbal Learning and Verbal Behavior*, 1965, *4*, 365-370.

Coffing, D. G. *Eye-movement preferences as individual differences in learning.* Unpublished doctoral dissertation, School of Education, Stanford University, 1971.

Comunale, A. S. *Visual selectivity in reading: A study of the relationship between eye movements and linguistic structure.* Unpublished doctoral dissertation, School of Education, University of Massachusetts, 1973.

Cooper, R. M. The control of eye fixation by the meaning of spoken language. *Cognitive Psychology*, 1974, *6*, 84-107.

Fairbanks, G. The relationship between eye movements and voice in oral reading of good and bad silent readers. *Psychological Monographs*, 1937, *48*, 78-107.

Feinberg, R. A study of some aspects of peripheral visual acuity. *American Journal of Optometry and Archives of the American Academy of Optometry*, 1949, *26*, 49-56.

Fleming, M. Eye-movement indices of cognitive behavior. *A-V Communication Review*, 1969, *17*(4), 383-398.

Ford, B. L., & Levin, H. Homographs in a semantic context. In H. Levin, E. J. Gibson, & J. J. Gibson (Eds.), *The analysis of reading skill: A program of basic and applied research.* U. S. Office of Education Final Report, Project #5-1213. Ithaca: Cornell, 1968.

Geyer, J. J. *Perceptual systems in reading: A temporal eye-voice span constant.* Unpublished doctoral dissertation, University of California, Berkeley, California, 1966.

Geyer, J. J., & Kolers, P. A. Reading as information processing. In *Advances in librarianship.* New York: Academic Press, 1974.

Gibson, E. J., & Levin, H. *The psychology of reading.* Cambridge: The M. I. T. Press, 1975.

Goldman-Eisler, F. *Psycholinguistics: Experiments in spontaneous speech.* New York: Academic Press, 1969.

Giuliano, V. E. Analog networks for word association. In D. A. Norman (Ed.), *Memory and attention.* New York: Wiley, 1969.

Gough, P. B. One second of reading. In J. F. Kavanagh & I. G. Mattingly (Eds.), *Language by ear and by eye.* Cambridge, Massachusetts: The M. I. T. Press, 1972.

Gould, J. D., & Schaffer, A. Eye-movement parameters in pattern recognition. *Journal of Experimental Psychology*, 1967, *74*(2), 225-235.

Hochberg, J. Components of literacy. In H. Levin & J. P. Williams (Eds.), *Basic studies on reading.* New York: Basic Books, 1970.

Hoffman, J. Experimentelle-psychologische Untersuchungen ueber Leseleistungen von Schulkindern. *Archiv Gesammte Psychologie*, 1927, *58*, 325-388.

Huey, E. B. On the psychology and physiology of reading. *American Journal of Psychology*, 1901, *12*, 292-313.

Judd, C. H., & Buswell, G. T. Silent reading: A study of the various types. *Supplementary Educational Monographs*, 1922, *23*.

Kavanagh, J. F., & Mattingly, I. G. (Eds.). *Language by ear and by eye.* Cambridge, Massachusetts: The M. I. T. Press, 1972.

Kennedy, J. M. *Regressive eye movements may depend on syntax.* Unpublished manuscript, Department of Psychology, Cornell University, 1967.

Kolers, P. A. Three stages of reading. In H. Levin & J. P. Williams (Eds.), *Basic studies on reading.* New York: Basic Books, 1970.

Lawson, E. A note on the influence of different orders of approximation to English language upon eye-voice span. *Quarterly Journal of Experimental Psychology*, 1961, *13*, 53-55.

Levin, H. Personal communication. Department of Psychology, Cornell University, 1968.

Levin, H., & Ford, B. L. Homographs vs. non-homographs. In H. Levin, E. J. Gibson, & J. J. Gibson (Eds.), *The analysis of reading skill: A program of basic and applied research.* U. S. Office of Education Final Report, Project #5-1213. Ithaca: Cornell, 1968.

Levin, H., Ford, B. L., & Beckwith, M. Homographs in grammatical frames. In H. Levin, E. J. Gibson, & J. J. Gibson (Eds.), *The analysis of reading skill: A program of basic and applied research.* U. S. Office of Education Final Report, Project #5-1213. Ithaca: Cornell, 1968.

Levin, H., Gibson, E. J., & Gibson, J. J. (Eds.). *The analysis of reading skill: A program of basic and applied research.* U. S. Office of Education Final Report, Project #5-1213. Ithaca: Cornell, 1968.

Levin, H., Grossman, J., Kaplan, E., & Yang, R. Constraints and the eye-voice span in right and left embedded sentences. *Language and Speech,* 1972, *15*(1), 30-39.

Levin, H., & Kaplan, E. Eye-voice span within active and passive sentences. *Language and Speech,* 1968, *11*(2), 251-258.

Levin, H., & Turner, E. A. Sentence structure and the eye-voice span. In H. Levin, E. J. Gibson, & J. J. Gibson (Eds.), *The analysis of reading skill: A program of basic and applied research.* U. S. Office of Education Final Report, Project #5-1213. Ithaca: Cornell, 1968.

Levin, H., & Williams, J. P. *Basic studies on reading.* New York: Basic Books, 1970.

Loftus, G. R. Eye fixations and recognition memory for pictures. *Cognitive Psychology,* 1972, *3,* 525-551.

Mackworth, N. H. A wide-angle reflection eye camera for visual choice and pupil size. *Perception and Psychophysics,* 1968, *3,* 32-34.

Mackworth, N. H. Personal communication. Department of Psychology, Stanford University, 1970.

Mackworth, N. H., & Bruner, J. S. How adults and children search and recognize pictures. *Human Development,* 1970, *13,* 149-177.

Mackworth, N. H., Grandstaff, N. W., & Pribram, K. H. Orientation to pictorial novelty by speech-disordered children. *Neuropsychologia,* 1973.

Mackworth, N. H., & Morandi, A. J. The gaze selects informative details within pictures. *Perception and Psychophysics,* 1967, *2,* 547-552.

Marchbanks, G., & Levin, H. Cues by which children recognize words. *Journal of Educational Psychology,* 1965, *56,* 57-61.

McConkie, G. W., & Rayner, K. *The span of the effective stimulus during fixations in reading.* Paper presented at the annual meeting of the American Educational Research Association, New Orleans, 1973.

McConkie, G. W., & Rayner, K. An on-line computer technique for studying reading: Identifying the perceptual span. *Twenty-second yearbook of the National Reading Conference,* 1974. Pp. 119-130. (Also reprinted in this volume, pages 163-175.)

Mehler, J., Bever, T. G., & Carey, P. What we look at when we read. *Perception and Psychophysics,* 1967, *2,* 213-218.

Miller, G. A., Bruner, J. S., & Postman, L. Familiarity of letter sequences and tachistoscopic identification. *Journal of General Psychology,* 1954, *50,* 129-139.

Morton, J. The effect of context on the visual duration threshold for words. *British Journal of Psychology,* 1964, *55,* 165-180.(a)

Morton, J. The effects of context upon speed of reading, eye movements, and eye-voice span. *Quarterly Journal of Experimental Psychology,* 1964, *16*(4), 340-354.(b)

Neisser, U. *Cognitive psychology.* New York: Appleton-Century-Crofts, 1967.

Neisser, U. *Selective reading: A method for the study of visual attention.* Paper presented at the Eleventh International Congress of Psychology, London, 1969.

Nodine, C. F., & Lang, N. J. Development of visual scanning strategies for differentiating words. *Developmental Psychology,* 1971, *5*(2), 221-232.

Nodine, C. F., & Steuerle, N. L. Development of perceptual and cognitive strategies for differentiating graphemes. *Journal of Experimental Psychology,* 1973, *97*(2), 158-166.

Noton, D., & Stark, L. Eye movements and visual perception. *Scientific American,* 1971, *224*(6), 34-43.

Pillsbury, W. B. A study in apperception. *American Journal of Psychology,* 1897, *8,* 315-393.

Rayner, K. The perceptual span and peripheral cues in reading. Research Report No. 2, Reading and Learning Series, Department of Education, Cornell University, 1974.

Rayner, K. The perceptual span and peripheral cues in reading. *Cognitive Psychology,* 1975, *7,* 65-81.

Rayner, K., & McConkie, G. W. *The perceptual span and peripheral cues in reading.* Paper presented at the annual meeting of the American Educational Research Association, Chicago, 1974.

Robinson, F. P. An aid for improving reading rate. *Journal of Educational Research,* 1934, *27,* 453-555.

Ruddell, R. B. The effect of oral and written patterns of language structure on reading comprehension. *The Reading Teacher,* 1965, *18,* 270-275.

Samuels, S. J. Success and failure in learning to read: A critique of the research. *Reading Research Quarterly,* 1973, *8*(Winter), 200-239.

Schlesinger, I. M. *Sentence structure and the reading process.* The Hague: Mouton, 1969.

Shiffrin, R. M., & Gardner, G. T. Visual processing capacity and attentional control. *Journal of Experimental Psychology,* 1972, *93*(1), 72-82.

Simon, H. A. How big is a chunk? *Science,* 1974, *183*(February 8), 482-488.

Simon, H. A., & Barenfeld, M. Information-processing analysis of perceptual processes in problem-solving. *Psychological Review,* 1969, *76*(5), 473-483.

Smith, F. *Understanding reading.* New York: Holt, Rinehart, and Winston, 1971.

Smith, F., & Holmes, D. L. The independence of letter, word, and meaning identification in reading. *Reading Research Quarterly,* 1971, *6,* 394-415.

Sticht, T. G., Beck, L. J., Hauke, R. N., Kleiman, G. M., & James, J. H. *Auding and reading: A developmental model.* Monterey: Human Resources Research Organization, 1974.

Tinker, M. A. Recent studies of eye movements in reading. *Psychological Bulletin.* 1958, *55*(4), 215-231.

Tulving, E., & Gold, C. Stimulus information and contextual information as determinants of tachistoscopic recognition of words. *Journal of Experimental Psychology,* 1963, *66,* 319-327.

Vurpillot, E. The development of scanning strategies and their relation to visual differentiation. *Experimental Child Psychology,* 1968, *6*(4), 632-640.

Wanat, S. F. Linguistic structure in reading. In F. B. Davis (Ed.), *The literature of research on reading with emphasis on models.* New Brunswick, New Jersey: Rutgers, 1971.

Wanat, S. F., & Levin, H. *The eye-voice span in sentences containing different amounts of information.* Unpublished manuscript, Department of Psychology, State University of New York at Stony Brook, 1975.

Weber, R.-M. First graders' use of grammatical context in reading. In H. Levin & J. P. Williams (Eds.), *Basic studies on reading.* New York: Basic Books, 1970, Pp. 147-163.

Willows, D. M. Reading between the lines: Selective attention in good and poor readers. *Child Development,* 1974.

Woodworth, R. S. *Experimental psychology.* New York: Holt, Rinehart, and Winston, 1938.

Yarbus, A. L. *Eye movements and vision.* New York: Plenum Press, 1967.

Zargar, A. M. *Planning in human performance: Grammatical expectancies during reading.* Unpublished doctoral dissertation, Department of Industrial Engineering, Stanford University, 1973.

Identifying the Span of the Effective Stimulus in Reading: Literature Review and Theories of Reading*

GEORGE W. MCCONKIE AND KEITH RAYNER**
Cornell University

The experimental study of reading in psychology has a rich history dating back to Javal's observation that the eyes execute a series of saccadic movements as a person reads a line of print (Huey, 1908). Much of the basic knowledge that we have concerning skilled reading was discovered around the turn of the century and was reviewed by Huey (1908) and Woodworth (1938). Since that time, relatively little has been added to understanding the processes involved. Research on reading among psychologists began to dwindle in the 1920s. Undoubtedly, the difficulty of studying a process as rapid and as private as skilled reading, coupled with the rise of Behaviorism and the focus on observable behavior, led to this disinterest. Also, researchers in the field of reading began to separate from the main stream of psychology and to form their own professional organizations and journals in the 1920s (Blumenthal, 1970). Soon, reading laboratories began to be centered in schools of education. Since education is mainly concerned with the improvement of learning, many people interested in reading directed their research to comparing the effectiveness of different methods of reading instruction. It was also during this time that much emphasis was placed on the development of reading tests and of materials and techniques which could be used to improve reading.

The net result of this shift from psychology to education, together with the rise of Behaviorism, was that the research on the basic cognitive processes underlying reading virtually ceased. Recently, there has been an upsurge of interest in this area once again, stimulated by the

*Reprinted from Final Report, Project No. OEG 2-71-0531, U.S. Office of Educaton, 1974.

**Keith Rayner is now at the University of Rochester.

emergence of cognitive psychology and psycholinguistics. Despite renewed activity in basic reading research, it is still the case that few of these
studies involve subjects in the highest form of skilled reading: rapid, silent
reading. Of those studies which focus on skilled reading, the vast majority
involve reading aloud, experimenter paced reading, or tasks quite unlike
normal reading. From these types of studies, several theories have recently been proposed to account for skilled reading (Smith, 1971;
Mackworth, 1972; Hochberg, 1970; Levin & Kaplan, 1970).

Within these theories, a number of old research questions have been
revived once again. These include: 1) What is the size of the area from
which the reader acquires visual information during a fixation? 2) What
guides the reader's eyes as he reads? 3) What part do cues from peripheral
vision play in reading? The research which will be described in later
chapters was concerned with these interrelated questions. Some new
techniques for investigating these questions will be described which involve computerized eye tracking and text display changes during reading.

The remainder of the present chapter will be devoted to a review of
the research literature related to the three questions listed above.

The Perceptual Span in Reading

Determining the size of the area from which a person picks up
information during a fixation in reading has long intrigued psychologists.
If a reader fixates on a certain letter on a page of text, he finds that he can
recognize words two or three lines above and below that being fixated. In
addition, he can recognize words some distance to the left and right of his
fixation. Beyond these areas, punctuation marks, capital letters, word
boundaries, and the beginnings and ends of paragraphs are visible
(Woodworth, 1938). On the other hand, if a string of letters is presented
visually for a few milliseconds, the reader is able to identify only 4 to 6 of
the letters (Sperling, 1960). Somewhere between these two extremes must
lie the size of the perceptual span in reading.

Four general types of research have been used to identify the perceptual span in reading. The first and simplest type of research has been to
divide the number of letters per line by the number of fixations per line
(Taylor, 1957; Taylor, 1965). Observations such as these have generally
found that skilled readers make fewer fixations per line, suggesting that
they have a wider perceptual span. However, Hochberg (1970) has argued that this difference in number of fixations is not the result of
differences in what the readers can actually see, but it reflects differences
in cognitive activities during each fixation. This method of estimating the

perceptual span is also based on the assumption that on successive fixations the perceptual spans do not overlap or that they overlap the same amount. This assumption is likely false.

The second, and oldest, type of research has utilized the tachistoscopic presentation of letters and words. Since the material is generally presented for very brief exposures to exclude the possibility of an eye movement during the presentation this method has often been thought of as being analogous to a single fixation in reading. The earliest studies by Cattell and by Erdmann and Dodge (described by Huey, 1908 and Woodworth, 1938), found that the perceptual span for letters combined in words is much greater than for non-word strings. With an exposure of 10 milliseconds, it was found that a subject could read 3-4 unconnected letters, 2 unconnected short words, or 4 connected short words. Recent research (Wheeler, 1970; Reicher, 1969; Baron & Thurston, 1973) has found that it is easier to decide which of two letters was presented tachistoscopically if the critical letter was in a word rather than a non-word letter string or in isolation. Tulving and Gold (1963) and Morton (1964) have reported that increased contextual information increases the amount that can be reported from a tachistoscopic presentation. All of these recent studies have shown that the number of letters or words that can be reported depends on the redundancy of the stimulus.

A limitation of this method of determining the perceptual span was mentioned by Woodworth (1938) and later verified by Sperling (1960). Sperling found that subjects are able to see much more than they can retain and later report. Thus, what subjects report from a brief presentation cannot be taken as a complete specification of what they actually saw. Geyer (1970) has pointed out that even if the verbal report coincided with what the person actually saw, there is no particular reason to believe that the perceptual span obtained in a tachistoscopic presentation actually coincides with that of a fixation during reading. One conclusion that recent research in cognitive psychology is forcing upon us is that subjects are able to adapt their strategies to the task in which they are engaged. It is very likely that normal reading and tachistoscopic report vary enough to induce different strategies in readers. The tachistoscopic studies generally involve the isolated presentation of some stimulus material, whereas reading involves fixations at the rate of four per second, with a very complex stimulus pattern having a great deal of redundancy. Due to these differences, the perceptual span in reading could be either larger or smaller than that found with tachistoscopic presentations. It could be larger because the contextual constraint allows a reader to identify words with less visual information, or it could be smaller because of the rapid sequence of fixations and the complexity of the surrounding stimulus pattern which may lead to what Mackworth (1965) has referred to as tunnel vision.

The third method of investigating the perceptual span is to have a subject fixate some point and then have him identify stimuli presented at various distances from his fixation point (Huey, 1908; Woodworth, 1938; Feinberg, 1949; Bouma, 1973). Research of this type has generally found that only four or five letters around the fixation point are identified with near 100 percent accuracy and that from the point of clearest vision outward, in either direction, words and letters are seen with decreasing clarity. Although this information regarding the area of visual acuity is valuable for setting the upper bounds of the perceptual span, it cannot be taken as evidence for what information a person actually uses during a fixation in reading.

The fourth technique is to manipulate the amount of text which is visible to a subject at a given moment. Poulton (1962) had subjects read aloud from text over which a mask containing a window was passed. The speed and size of the window varied systematically on different trials, and the subjects' eye movements were recorded electronically. In this research, the text was immobile, and the window passed over it, allowing only a certain amount to be seen at once. Newman (1966), on the other hand, kept the window stable and passed the text beneath it. He presented text on a screen, with the letters moving from right to left, and varied the number of letters on the screen at any moment, the number of new letters that were added at once, and the rate at which they were added. Both investigators found that smaller windows create greater disruption in reading. These techniques, however, disrupt normal reading because the person's natural eye movements are disrupted.

None of these techniques appear to provide a very definite answer to the original question. The last three techniques involve tasks rather unlike normal, silent reading; and it is possible that the demands of these various tasks induce strategies in the subjects that are quite different from those normally used in reading. It may well be that the perceptual span varies with the task structure. The first technique is based on questionable assumptions. Thus, the differences in the estimates of the size of the perceptual span which have come from these studies is likely the result of different strategies on the part of the subjects, different amounts of context in the stimulus materials, etc.

The ideal situation for answering the perceptual span question would be one in which the subject is involved in the act of reading normal text to understand its meaning. Then a means would be used to obtain data from the subject concerning the perceptual span as he is engaged in this, the normal reading task. Once this is achieved, the answer to the question of how far into the periphery he acquires visual information is likely to be quite complex. First, we must recognize that it is likely that different aspects of the visual stimulus are probably acquired at different distances into the periphery. Thus, there is probably not a single perceptual span, but a number of perceptual spans for information of different types: full featural detail of letters may be obtained only a certain distance from central vision, with information about general external word shape, word length patterns, location of such irregularities as punctuation, italicization, etc., and location of ends of lines being obtained farther and farther into the periphery. The investigation must then explore how far into the periphery each of these, and other, types of visual information is obtained by the reader. Second, we must make a distinction between information registered by the visual system and information actually used in reading. It may be that during a fixation the visual information from a rather large area is actually registered at some level in the visual system, and thus could be used for some purpose, but that in the act of reading the person processes and uses the information from a much more restricted area. In the investigation of reading, we are most interested in defining this latter area, the region from which the reader obtains information which is actually used in the reading act. Finally, it must be recognized that the size of the regions from which different types of visual information are acquired and used in reading may vary from fixation to fixation. It is conceivable that the reading span may vary with such factors as syntactic structure of the sentence, amount of redundancy of the text, etc.

What Determines the Reader's Eye Movements?

During reading there are two important eye movement components called fixations and saccades. Fixations, which take up over 90 percent of the time, are periods when the eye is relatively still. It is during these periods when visual information is extracted from the text. The remaining 10 percent of the time is spent in saccades, where the eye moves from one position to another. Thus, there are two questions which must be asked about eye movement behavior. What determines how long the eye will remain in a fixation? And what determines where the eye will be sent in the next saccade?

Prior to discussing these questions, two characteristics of the saccadic movement need to be considered: visual input during the saccade and the nature of the saccadic movement itself.

Although there is a great deal of controversy on the topic, it is generally believed that there is a period of visual suppression during a saccade. The controversy centers around which of two possible mechanisms, central inhibition or retinal blurring is responsible for the suppression. The first position, central inhibition, assumes that visual input is blanked out or suppressed to some degree by some central inhibitory process during this period. The retinal blur position also assumes that little or no useful visual information is acquired during the saccade, but that this is due to the optical blurring or smearing of the visual image across the retina as the eye moves at a high rate during the saccadic movement. The majority of the research (Volkman, 1962; Volkman, Schick, & Riggs, 1968; Uttal & Smith, 1968) confirms the retinal blur position. That is, the evidence indicates that visual input is not totally suppressed during a saccadic movement. However, there is also evidence that visual sensitivity is reduced substantially, not only during the movement itself, but also shortly before and after the eye has settled on a new position (Haber & Hershenson, 1973). Thus, it appears that the lack of useful visual input during the saccade is not totally accounted for by the notion of retinal blur.

While little is known about the central inhibitory mechanism that causes the visual suppression found during and immediately after a saccade, Haber and Hershenson (1973) indicate that it is functional in that it minimizes the perception of blur which might occur during the saccadic movement. Volkman (1962) has shown that there is a rise in visual thresholds during movement. Although the change is not great considering the total range of sensitivity of the visual system, it is probably enough to reduce the blur below annoyance levels. This change in threshold is probably also enough to reduce the sensitivity of details that pass across the retina and the chances of noticing new information or fine detail during saccadic movement is thus greatly reduced (Haber & Hershenson, 1973).

Another accepted characteristic of the saccadic movement is that it may be regarded as a ballistic movement whose trajectory, once begun, cannot be influenced. Voluntary effort or practice, for example, will not alter saccadic velocity (Becker & Fuchs, 1969; Komoda, Festinger, Phillips, Duckman, & Young, 1973; Westheimer, 1954). The velocity of the eye in a saccade has been carefully studied. The velocity rapidly rises during the saccade to a maximum which occurs shortly before the midpoint of the movement, then drops at a slightly slower rate until reaching its target region. The peak velocity reached is a monotonic function of the saccade length. If the target, say a spot of light, is shifted to a new position while the eye is in motion, no compensatory change occurs in the trajectory. Rather corrective movements are made once the eye finishes the initial saccade. (Westheimer, 1954).

The studies just described support the notions that visual input during reading occurs primarily, and perhaps entirely, during the fixation, and that the saccade is directed by a flight plan established prior to its launching rather than by any visual input during its tenure. Thus, the only visual information which might influence the saccade is that acquired on prior fixations.

Turning now to the questions initially stated in this section, it is safe to say that there is less evidence available on the nature of eye movement control during reading than there is on the size of the perceptual span. Still there is some evidence and much speculation about this. In the following discussion, we will deal first with the control of fixation locations, and then with fixation durations.

The explanations of control of fixation locations appear to fall into three categories, with some explanations involving more than one of these categories. These categories will be referred to as the constant pattern explanation, the stimulus control explanation, and the internal control explanation.

The *constant pattern explanation* asserts that the reader simply moves his eyes across the page in a uniform manner, sometimes overshooting or undershooting the average distance, on each saccade. A number of people have emphasized the importance of rhythmical eye movements, i.e., regular forward movements along a line of print with about the same number of fixations from line to line (Taylor, 1966; see the reviews by Tinker, 1946, 1958). These people seem to have accepted a constant pattern position. They emphasize the notions that a good reader is efficient because he is able to establish rhythmical eye movement habits and that favorable typography fosters rhythmical movements. According to this position, the eye is simply under physiological and oculomotor control, and it is the task of the reader to process the text as the eye makes its mechanical movements across the page. The poor reader is distinguished from the good reader because he has not developed good oculomotor control. The only specific control assumed might be an adjustment of saccade length for reading materials of different difficulty level.

The original version of this position suffered a substantial blow when it was found that training people to be more regular and rhythmical in their eye movements did not lead to increased reading efficiency and/or comprehension (Tinker, 1958). Without assuming that regularity in eye movements produces good reading, several recent researchers have argued once again for a constant pattern of eye movement control. Carver (1974) dubbed this "apping," taking letters from the phrase "*a*utomatic *p*ilot for *p*rose." Bouma and deVoogd (1974) showed that subjects could read when the visual stimulus was presented in a manner simulating rhythmical eye movements.

A closely related position is one which assumes a great deal of randomness in eye control. This might be thought of as a constant pattern explanation with a random oscillatory component as part of the eye control mechanism. This position has been explicitly stated by Bouma and deVoogd (1974) who argue that it matters little just how far along the line the eye is sent on a saccade during reading; thus the only requirement is that the eye is advanced at proper intervals.

The constant pattern explanation is easy to accept as one reviews the many summaries of eye movement data which have been reported, describing the average saccade length and fixation duration of readers of different types and ages. However, an examination of the raw data of even good readers shows such great variability in eye movement behavior that the present authors find this position difficult to accept. Though the mean saccade length may be 8 or 9 character positions, the data values frequently range from 2 to 18 character positions or more. Though the mean duration of fixations may be ¼ second, the data values actually range from 1/6 to ½ second, with occasional fixations as long as a full second or more. It seems to us difficult to conceive of this great variability in saccade lengths and fixation durations as being the product of inaccuracy of the oculomotor system as it attempts to generate a standard, rhythmical eye movement pattern. Whether this variability can be accounted for purely on the basis of random variability in saccade length will have to be tested in further research. Any findings of predictable patterns in saccade lengths will challenge this position.

The second explanation of eye position guidance in reading is that the eye is under *stimulus control*. According to this position, the movements of the eye are determined by visual characteristics of the text. Information acquired in the peripheral areas of vision cause the eye to be sent to a particular location on the next saccadic movement.

A considerable amount of data collected on eye movements in non-reading tasks is generally supportive of the stimulus control position. Studies dealing with the free viewing of pictures indicate that viewers tend to fixate on the most informative (non-redundant or unpredictable) areas (for instance, Mackworth & Morandi, 1967). According to workers in this area, peripheral vision serves the function of processing and editing out the redundant stimulus. It is generally thought that foveal vision is reserved for those elements containing information needed by the observer during perception, while the peripheral retina screens out the predictable aspects and guides the eye to the unpredictable and unusual stimuli (Mackworth & Morandi, 1967; Mackworth & Bruner, 1970; Yarbus, 1967; Buswell, 1935).

Further data from other types of studies also point out the functional utility of the peripheral retina. Gould and Schaffer (1965) utilized a scanning task with numeric displays and concluded that the more easily seen aspects of a stimulus field are detected with equal accuracy either in the fovea or in the periphery. They also concluded from the data that when more difficult items are initially detected in the periphery, the eyes are then directed to produce a foveal fixation of them. In a later study, Gould (1967) recorded eye movements while subjects scanned for target patterns. He found that some patterns were correctly recognized without foveal fixation; they were discriminated peripherally. From his findings Gould concluded that a function of peripheral detection is not only to indicate the locus of the next fixation but also to signal whether or not a particular pattern requires foveal fixation.

Hence, studies involving visual tasks other than reading give credibility to the notion of stimulus control in reading. It should be pointed out, however, that although these tasks are like reading in some ways, they differ in others. In viewing pictures, the eye is guided to areas of greater visual complexity. In reading, however, the stimulus pattern is of very similar complexity within the region where text is present. Thus, there is no simple correlation between the visual complexity of the stimulus and its potential informativeness, as there is with pictures. With the scanning task, where the specific target stimulus is known, purely visual characteristics of the stimulus pattern can again be a guide to the potentially informative regions; that is, letter strings having certain gross visual characteristics are more likely candidates as the target than are other letter strings. As one reads, however, the important aspects of the stimulus are the syntactic and semantic characteristics encoded by the physical stimulus. Thus, a decoding is required to obtain the important information. This being the case, either some decoding of the perhipheral stimulus for syntactic and/or semantic information must occur, thus yielding an indication of where the more important information is likely to reside, or else some basis for a correlation between aspects of the physical form and the potential informativeness of areas of text must be described. Kolers and Lewis (1972) have argued against the first of these possibilities, that of decoding of peripheral information. They pointed out that such a position would seem to require parallel decoding of information from two regions of the visual field, the normal decoding for meaning of foveal information, and the decoding of peripheral information for the semantic or syntactic information necessary to determine where to send the eye. Their experiments test the notion that the reader could render a semantic decoding of letter sequences arriving at two locations on the retina at the same time. Their subjects were unable to do this. Though these experiments were sufficiently unlike normal reading that they cannot be taken as providing a final evaluation of this position, they do provide some evidence against it. Another experiment might be seen as providing some evidence for this position. Mehler, Bever and Carey (1967) report that the skilled readers who served as their subjects tended to fixate the first half of phrase structure constituents more than the second half. Problems with the experiment itself suggest that this finding needs to be replicated before it is accepted as reliable. However, if reliable, it might be suggested that eye guidance follows some syntactic analysis of peripheral information. An alternative explanation will be offered later, however.

If it is to be assumed that purely visual aspects of the text in the periphery might be used for eye guidance, without the assumption of semantic or syntactic decoding, it is necessary to find some existing correlation between these visual stimulus characteristics and characteristics important in the processing of the text for meaning. The most simple possibility would be that longer words tend to be more informative, assuming that articles and function words tend to carry little of the information in the text. The hypothesis that the reader might tend to fixate longer words more than shorter was investigated by Woodworth (1938), who reported a slight relationship in the opposite direction: short words received more fixations. Another possibility is that the word length pattern provides strong cues to the location of phrase structure groupings in the text, since phrases frequently begin with shorter words (prepositions and articles, primarily). The present authors have explored this possibility to some extent, and found that college students are able to mark the boundaries between phrases quite successfully in text in which all letters have been replaced by X's. Thus, from the word length and punctuation patterns alone, much syntactic information is given. It may be that the word length pattern is obtained from peripheral vision, which yields some likely syntactic information of coming text, and that this in turn is used to guide the eye.

The distinction between presence and absence of text in an area is undoubtedly acquired from peripheral vision and used to determine whether the next saccade should be to the left or right, and to send the eye past areas which may be blank (Abrams & Zuber, 1972). Thus, to this extent stimulus control is undoubtedly correct. The extent to which the entire eye movement pattern can be accounted for on this basis remains to be seen.

The final type of explanation of eye position guidance in reading is that the eye is under some form of *internal control,* rather than strictly stimulus control. This position is differentiated from the constant pattern positions in that the movement of the eye is thought of as being determined by momentary internal states, rather than being a simple rhythmical pattern. Thus, irregularities in fixation durations and saccade lengths are the product of internal state differences, rather than just random deviations. Geyer (1968), for instance, has suggested that the eye-voice span (the distance that the voice trails the eye in oral reading) is a constant such that the eye is always ahead of the voice by a certain amount of time. By extension it could be suggested that in silent reading the eye strives to stay ahead of the semantic interpretation of the sentence by a certain amount. Thus when semantic decoding difficulty is encountered fixations are lengthened and/or saccade lengths are reduced in order to keep the eye from getting too far ahead. One data pattern which would support this position would be a strong relationship between the duration of a fixation and the length of the saccade prior to or following it, assuming that when difficulty is encountered both longer fixations and shorter saccades are used to slow the eye's progress. Reder (personal communication) has analyzed a number of eye movement records to determine these correlations, and has found them to be very low. This does not, of course, disprove this particular theoretical position, but it does complicate it in that fixation durations and saccade lengths do not appear to be determined by the same mechanisms. Thus, the separate adjustment of fixation duration and saccade length must now be explained.

A number of writers have emphasized the part which expectancy or prediction plays in reading (Hochberg, 1970; Levin & Kaplan, 1970; Goodman, 1970). Some of these have suggested another possibility of internal control of eye movements. The notion is that the reader, on the basis of the text he has already read and his knowledge of language rules and common usage, is able to predict what is likely to come next. His next task is to acquire that visual information which can most effectively be used to test the accuracy of his prediction. Presumably, on the basis of his prediction his eye is sent to the region of text which is expected to be most informative in acquiring visual information necessary to make this test. If the prediction is inaccurate, the eye is likely to be sent leftward in a regressive movement to determine if an incorrect interpretation of earlier-encountered text was made. This position will be discussed more fully in a later section. At this point it is sufficient to indicate that there is no conclusive evidence to support this mechanism as being the basis of eye guidance, and that the required experimental research necessary to provide an adequate test will be extremely difficult.

Various combinations of these three sources of eye guidance are also possible within a single theory. Hochberg (1970) proposed that eye movement control involves both peripheral search guidance (PSG) and cognitive search guidance (CSG). In agreement with many others, he argues that due to language redundancy the reader need not see every word in order to understand the text. Because of his knowledge of the spelling, grammar and idiom of the text he can anticipate the message. Thus visually he needs only to sample the text to confirm his guess. This is the cognitive search guidance (internal control). In addition, peripheral visual input can be the basis for informed guesses about where the important words can be found, and thus can also be used to direct the eye to those regions which will be most informative in testing his expectations. This is the peripheral search guidance (stimulus control). Hochberg suggests that the main peripheral cues are the initial letter of a word, word length, and spacing between words. Of greatest importance is word length. Shorter words are usually functors like *on, in, to,* etc. He suggests that the reader is able to detect that a functor lies at some distance out along the line of text in the periphery and then decides either to look at the word or, if it is likely to be redundant, to look at the word after it. He cites a study by Hochberg, Levin and Frail (1966) as support for the importance of word length and interword spaces in guiding the eye. They had beginning readers (1st and 2nd grade) and more advanced readers (5th and 6th grade) as subjects, and had them read stories typed normally or with all spaces filled in. Having spaces filled had only a slight effect on beginning readers, who were still presumably looking letter by letter and had little knowledge of orthographic and syntactic redundancies. Better readers, who are able to direct their gaze more selectively on the basis of their knowledge of the redundancy of text, showed a substantial reduction in reading rate when spaces were filled. It should be pointed out, however, that the study just cited does not indicate where the locus of the problem is when spaces between words are filled; whether this is disruptive to the eye movement mechanisms, for instance, or whether added processing is required to identify the location of words. Of course, the answer may be that both types of interference are occurring.

While there is little conclusive information on the nature of eye position control in reading, even less consideration has been given to the control of fixation durations. It has been noted that average fixation duration tends to increase with more difficult reading material, and also that the data frequently reveal particularly long fixations on unusual words, proper names, numbers, etc. (Woodworth, 1938).

As with eye position control, it is possible that the control of fixation durations might be either an attempt to follow a rhythmic pattern, with deviations around the average duration being simply due to inaccuracy in the control system, or the length of each duration may be determined in some way by the cognitive processes taking place at that time. The great amount of variance in fixation durations of a single subject reading a single passage argues against the rhythmic pattern position, as does the finding of long fixations on particular types of content in the passage, as mentioned above.

The alternative position, that fixation duration is determined by the perceptual and cognitive processes occurring at the moment, introduces the requirement of very rapid processing of the text being fixated during a fixation. Certainly, some time lapses between the time a saccade is called for and the time it is actually initiated. Sufficient processing of the input must occur early in the fixation period to provide the basis on which to decide when to terminate the fixation (as well as, perhaps, where to send the eye next). Thus, this position would not allow much lag between input and processing of that input for syntactic and semantic information. Different theories of reading assume different types of activities during the fixation, and hence would provide different bases on which the decision might be made to terminate a fixation. At present there is little evidence to select among these. However, if further evidence indicates that fixation durations are under the momentary control of cognitive processing activities, these data will be valuable in discriminating among the different theories of cognitive processes involved in reading.

Peripheral Cues in Reading

As seen in the last section, considerable interest has focused on the possible role of peripheral visual information in guiding the eye in reading. It is possible that this peripheral information may be useful to the reader in other ways as well. This section will explore this possibility.

In order to see a stationary stimulus with the highest degree of acuity, a viewer must move his eyes so as to place the image on each fovea (Schiffman, 1971). The fovea is a very small region, subtending an angle of only about 2° as compared to the retina as a whole which cover a visual angle of 240° (Llewellyn-Thomas, 1968). The foveal retina contains a large quantity of cones. Anatomically and functionally, the distribution of cones has been linked with acuity so that maximal resolving power occurs at the fovea, where the distribution of cones is greatest, and diminishes toward the periphery (Schiffman, 1971). The peripheral retina is very effective in conditions of poor illumination and is very good at detecting movement. Most authorities hold that visual detail is not possible with peripheral vision. However, a number of studies reviewed in the preceding section have indicated that the peripheral retina is utilized in scanning tasks and viewing pictures.

Recently, Kerr (1971) has challenged the notion that visual acuity in the peripheral retina drops rapidly within 5° of the center of the fovea and then continues to drop at a slower rate out to the far periphery. He obtained results indicating that previous findings had underestimated the acuity of the periphery; that is, the person seems to be able to obtain more visual detail in the near periphery than previously believed. Schiffman (1971) attributes these high acuities to improvements in the control of experimental conditions of assessing acuity. Thus, although there is a definite loss of detail in peripheral vision, still certain characteristics of the stimulus are represented in some detail which are useful in examining pictures and in scanning, and which might be of use to readers.

Besides its use in directing eye movements, peripheral visual information might be of use to the reader in two ways. First, in the near periphery there may be sufficient detail to permit the identification of words and meaning. Second, the information acquired may be of use in reducing or directing processing on future fixations.

As a stimulus is moved into the periphery, the first information to be lost is the detailed features of internal letters in a word; that is, those letters not bounded by spaces. Still, extreme letters may be identifiable, as well as such aspects of the text as the location of letters having ascending and descending parts, general word shape, word length patterns, and such irregularities as punctuation marks, italicization, underlining, etc. Some of this information can be the basis for word identification, especially in a situation where there is a good deal of redundancy.

Neisser (1967) has pointed out that in the tachistoscopic identification of words, overall word shape is a useful cue. Woodworth (1938) also gave detailed consideration to this notion. Words like *lint* and *list* have the same general word shape, while *line* and *lift* do not. When words are printed in capital letters, thus having the same rectangular shape, they are harder to identify than when presented in lower case type (Neisser, 1967). Studies by Havens and Foote (1963, 1964; also Foote & Havens, 1965) found words like *lint,* whose distinctive shape is shared by many other common words in the language, have higher recognition thresholds than words like *drab* that do not have as many shapemates. They concluded that subjects first identify the shape of a word presented tachistoscopically, and then produce the most common word which is compatible with that shape.

Initial and final letters of words, because they are partially free from masking by adjacent letters, are thought to stand out clearly from the other letters and hence be a valuable cue for both tachistoscopic word identification and normal reading. Marchbanks and Levin (1965) presented pseudoword trigrams and quingrams to beginning readers. They found that the first letter of a word was the most important cue to word recognition, the last letter was the second most informative cue, and word shape was the last used cue. Williams, Blumberg, and Williams (1970) have replicated Marchbanks and Levins' finding with beginning readers, but fount that adults used complex strategies including the use of word shape as a basis for word recognition. Levin, Watson, and Feldman (1964) have also argued that the initial and final letters of a word provide the most important cues for recognition of a word. A number of tachistoscopic letter string identification studies (Bruner & O'Dowd, 1958; Harcum & Jones, 1962; Crovitz & Schiffman, 1965) have reported a bowed serial-position effect when letter strings were presented left or right of the central point of fixation indicating the greater identifiability of initial and final letters. In addition to the initial and terminal letters, dominant letters (letters that extend above and below the line and capitals) have often been thought to be important in word recognition (Woodworth, 1938).

Thus, it appears quite possible that enough visual detail is available from words falling in the near peripheral areas of vision to permit normal reading to occur, even when full visual detail is not available. Those characteristics of the visual pattern which are avaiiable may be sufficient to test hypotheses or identify words or meanings under conditions of high textual redundancy. How far into the periphery the reader can identify words or meaning likely depends on the nature of the language constraints at that point, and the particular words involved (such as whether there are several alternative words having the same general shape or extreme letters which would fit the syntactic and semantic context, or only one).

A second way in which peripheral cues may facilitate reading concerns the interaction of perceptual representations of the text from one fixation to the next in reading. Much has been made, recently, of the effects of masking a visual stimulus, and the destructive effects which this has on its perception (Haber & Hershenson, 1973). And it is certainly true that when the eye moves and fixates a new location, the new stimulus pattern overrides the retinal activity pattern produced by the prior fixation. However, we would suggest, with J. Mackworth (1972), that at a higher level in the perceptual processing system the visual information from the two fixations are brought together into a single representation of the stimulus. That is, the visual information from at least two, and perhaps more, fixations is integrated into a single representation. This will be referred to as the Integrative Visual Buffer. Thus, while at one level of perceptual processing masking may occur as the input from one fixation overrides the image from the prior fixation, we assume that at a higher level the information from the two fixations are integrated. This is possible, of course, only because the input from the two fixations is capable of being integrated; i.e., there is sufficient commonality of pattern that they can be justified with one another. This justification of the two patterns may be based strictly on their commonality, or it may be that the eye movement is critical, particularly knowing about how far the eye has been cast. If the visual patterns from the two fixations are entirely different, then masking would be expected to occur at this higher level as well as at the lower perceptual level. It should be stressed that the integrated image is a highly complex one, providing visual information about a number of full lines of text, the book or paper on which the text is printed, the stimuli around the book, etc. A great deal of detail is available concerning some of the region, much less about other areas. Probably sufficient detail is available from several lines of print, and for some distance on each, to permit reading if so desired. Thus, the integrated image should not be regarded as a representation of only a few words on the line being read.

The visual input from each fixation will have its own region of greatest visual detail. Thus, when the pattern from fixation n − 1 is integrated with that of fixation n, in some areas of the representation added detail will be provided over that previously available. However, in these areas, some detail was available before, but just not as much.

It is further supposed that in the Integrative Visual Buffer the representation of the stimulus is still entirely a visual one. Essentially this representation provides a very large set of visual features which serve as a source of information for further cognitive processes involved in reading. Thus, by an attention type mechanism, the reader selects visual detail from a specific region of the total representation which will be used for his reading purposes, whether to identify words or meaning or to check hypotheses. The detail available in the region being attended depends, of course, on the distance of the corresponding region of text from central vision on the last one or two (or few) fixations. If that region was centrally fixated on the last fixation, full visual detail is available.

As reading occurs during a fixation, it would seem reasonable that the reader might not know how far from the point of present reading the available visual detail will support accurate reading. This can be determined only by attempting to read. It is likely that many attempts to read, and perhaps the attempt made on every fixation, extend far enough into the area of peripheral vision that reading fails for lack of visual detail. This means that some processing has been carried out involving the visual features of the text from a given region, but that with the lack of visual detail available ambiguity still remains. Presumably the eye would, on the next fixation, be cast further along the line, thus providing added visual detail from that region, and further processing could proceed. This raises a question: When the reader moves his eye, and the same region is still within the range of his perceptual span, but this time more centrally fixated, must the reader reprocess the text from that region, or is he able to begin the new processing at the point where processing was previously forced to terminate due to insufficient visual data? If the latter is the case, the information obtained from the periphery on the prior fixation(s) will facilitate processing on the present fixation because some of the work has already been done.

Thus, it is suggested that visual information about text falling in the near periphery may facilitate the further processing of that same text when it is later centrally fixated. Some of the visual information about the text needed for its word or meaning identification has already previously been obtained, and on the next fixation, the reader need only obtain the added detail required for its specification, or for testing the hypothesis.

As mentioned above, we do not know how long the information from a fixation remains present in the Integrative Visual Buffer; that the visual data deteriorates fairly rapidly is suggested by the existence of regressions. If full data from the last five or six fixations were present in this buffer, the reader would not have to physically cast his eye backward to gain added visual detail concerning a part of the text recently read. Thus it may be that the visual detail remains in this Buffer for less than a second; that is, that the buffer contains data from only the last one or two fixations, in addition to the present one.

At present there is little data available concerning perception in reading that is specific enough to provide a test of these notions.

Theories of Reading

As the resurgence of cognitive psychology has inspired interest in reading during recent years, so it has stimulated a number of theories about the nature of the cognitive processes involved in reading. Most of the recent theories which attempt a detailed description of cognitive processes involved in reading can be separated into two categories, based on the nature of the cognitive activities which are assumed to be carried out during the fixation. These will be termed the Hypothesis Position and the Direct Perception Position.

A number of people engaged in experimental studies of reading have recently advocated models of reading patterned to some degree after the analysis-by-synthesis theory of speech perception (Jakobson & Halle, 1956; also see Neisser, 1967). This approach, the *Hypothesis Position*, assumes that reading is primarily an activity of generating hypotheses or guesses about the text yet to be encountered, and then using a small part of the visual detail available to check the accuracy of these hypotheses. (For example, see Goodman, 1968, 1970; Hochberg, 1970; Kolers, 1970; Levin & Kaplan, 1970; Wanat, 1971). On the basis of the information the reader has from reading a passage up to a given point, plus the knowledge he has about 1) the redundancy and rules of language, 2) common language usage, and 3) the topic being discussed in the passage, he generates a hypothesis of what will be encountered next. He then obtains some featural information from the visual display and checks his hypothesis against this information. If the visual information agrees with his hypothesis, as it is assumed usually occurs, he then repeats the cycle. If it is not in agreement, further processing is required, the nature of which varies with different theories. The reader may be thought of as then generating additional hypotheses which are also tested (a pure analysis-by-synthesis approach) or he may be thought at some point to use the stimuli available to directly determine the interpretation of the text. This last process is thought to be much less efficient than the generation and testing of hypotheses, though at some points it must certainly be required, such as at the beginning of a new passage, or when reading words or sentences in isolation. If disagreement between the interpretation of present and past text occurs, the eye is then sent backward in a regressive movement to find the source of the inconsistency.

The popularity of this model of reading has probably risen from its ability to account for several important aspects of reading behavior. It provides a means for explaining how one can read at rapid rates. Assuming that the bottleneck in reading is the input of visual information and that hypothesis generation occurs very rapidly and accurately, this model accounts for rapid reading by permitting the person to obtain the meaning of the passage with the input of a minimal amount of visual information. This model can also account for reading speed changes with different types of text. The critical variable is the redundancy and predictability of the text; less predictable text results in more incorrect hypotheses and requires the acquisition of more visual detail. Finally the model can account for the fact that when misreadings occur they tend to be syntactically and semantically appropriate to the context (Weber, 1970; Kolers, 1968).

In theories taking the Hypothesis Position, then, the reader is thought to spend his time during a fixation, first, in obtaining a small amount of visual detail needed to confirm his hypothesis, and then in generating a new hypothesis concerning what he will encounter in the next region of text which he has not yet encountered. Added activities also might include determining just which aspects of the visual display should be acquired to permit an efficient test of the hypothesis, and perhaps determining how far to send the eye on the next saccade to place it at the region where the visual detail lies which is most important to the testing of his hypothesis. Thus, a relatively small amount of the cognitive activity is involved in perception of the fixated region; more is involved in predicting what lies in the as-yet-unfixated region to be encountered next.

The second category of theories, those taking the *Direct Perception Position,* assumes that the fixation period is spent primarily in determining the nature of the text within the fixated region, rather than in hypothesizing what is to come. Although those taking the Hypothesis Position have done so primarily in opposition to this position, it appears that the Direct Perception Position can account for the same facts about reading which have been cited as providing evidence for the Hypothesis Position. Consider the following possibility. We know that it is possible for a person to access his memory strictly on the basis of prior information and his knowledge of the language; he is able to take part of a sentence and readily emit words which could reasonably continue the sentence. This is the task he is asked to perform in certain forms of the cloze task and in the sentence-completion task. We also know that he can access memory strictly on the basis of visual patterns; he is able to read a word in isolation. It is reasonable, therefore, to believe that the person can also access memory on the basis of some combination of these two types of information. Thus, as the person reads, he has context information (which alone is not usually sufficient to specify the word or word group to appear next), and he begins, during the fixation, to add to it visual featural information until the combination is successful in specifying a reading for the next segment of the text. At that point, processing terminates for that portion of the text. Of course an incorrect identification may have resulted, but a single interpretation has emerged to which the reader is committed.

This view of processing during a fixation is consistent with the same facts and assumptions which have given credence to theories taking the Hypothesis Position. It provides for rapid reading on the basis of less than complete examination of the visual input. It permits reading to vary according to the redundancy of the text; if the text is less predictable, the contextual information will be less powerful in specifying the words being encountered, and the reader will have to depend upon a more complete visual analysis to acquire sufficient information to specify the text. Since words are being selected on the basis of both contextual and visual information, it would be expected that misreadings would be consistent with one or both of these sources of information depending upon the situation. Thus the model predicts context appropriate misreadings without resorting to the notion of generating of hypotheses or guesses, unless these terms are used in a trivial sense. Finally, the model would allow for regressions during reading. If a wrong identification is made, this leads to incorrect contextual information for making the next identification. Thus, with more and more visual information, it is likely that no identification will be made because of the incorrect context until finally the visual information is sufficient to complete the identification on this basis alone. At this point, the inconsistency between the prior and the new information is detected, and the eye is sent back in a regressive movement to seek the nature of the inconsistency.

The two positions just described differ most greatly in terms of what the reader is assumed to be doing during a fixation. The Hypothesis Position has the reader testing his hypothesis and then generating another. The Direct Perception Position suggests that the reader spends this time in the direct analysis of the visual input available on that fixation, using it together with contextual information to identify the text being fixated. The Hypothesis Position seems to assume that a majority of the fixation time is spent considering text not yet encountered, whereas the Direct Perception Position assumes that most time is spent analyzing the text in central vision.

As this alternative model of a Direct Perception Position type has shown, the Hypothesis Position is not required by the available data about reading; other positions are able to deal with the same facts concerning rapid reading. In addition there are some reasonable arguments against the Hypothesis Position as a model of the reading process. For one thing, the proponents of this position have not actually specified what it is the reader makes guesses about. If this model is to account for the fact that misreadings are syntactically appropriate, it would appear that the reader must be making hypotheses about the specific words to be encountered. The technique used by Levin and Kaplan (1970) to assess the redundancy of different parts of sentences, on the other hand, investigated the degree to which people anticipated the grammatical form of the sentence. This might suggest that readers form a hypothesis about the grammatical form. Another possibility might be that the reader, from his prior knowledge of the topic being discussed, anticipates the general argument or description which is to follow, without necessarily knowing the specific words in which it will be communicated.

The last two possibilities, anticipation of grammatical form or of the general meaning, seem to lose some of the characteristics of the Hypothesis Position. Since the hypothesis of syntactic form does not lead to predictions of the specific words to be encountered, it is difficult to see how it could account for the syntactic and semantic appropriateness of misreadings. The words which are emitted must be selected on some other basis than the hypothesis itself, if the hypothesis is not assumed to be an anticipation of the words to be encountered. Thus, the model would seem to resort to the direct perception of visual features to select words. At this point, the distinction between the Hypothesis Position and the Direct Perception Position becomes fuzzy. Both assume the use of a combination of contextual and visual information to specify the words to be read. Just what part a hypothesis might play in the process is not clear unless it simply permits the words to be identified with fewer visual cues. If this is so, the Hypothesis Position and the Direct Perception Position become indistinguishable. Once this has occurred, it leaves one wondering what is gained by proposing a hypothesis-generating mechanism in the reading act; it seems sufficient to assume that words are accessed on the basis of both contextual and visual information.

On the other hand, if the hypothesis is assumed to be an anticipation of the meaning of the message, one might suppose that it is possible to go from text to meaning directly, without the necessity of individual word identification. This position would suppose that the reader anticipates the meaning of the passage, and then is able to check the accuracy of that meaning against the input of a relatively few visual features. Again this seems to present some serious problems. As the linguists have stressed and particularly Chomsky (1965) with his transformational grammar, a given meaning can be expressed in a large number of word combinations and arrangements. Thus, it seems unlikely that any meaning which requires a combination of words to be expressed, other than such common combinations as "alarm clock" or "Holy Bible," has any invariant set of visual features in the text associated with it. There would seem to be no small set of visual features which could be tested to determine whether a given meaning matches that expressed in the text, without consideration for the words and their arrangement in the text. If this is so, the testing of the accuracy of a hypothesis of meaning must necessarily be mediated through some amount of word identification; either the hypothesis must indicate what words to expect so the reader can use visual features to test the hypothesis directly, or the reader must use visual features to determine what words are present in the text, and their order, so he knows what particular word string was used to express the meaning he anticipated. In the first instance, the hypothesis returns to that of word anticipation. In the second, the position is subject to the same problems as the syntax-hypothesis position and becomes indistinguishable from the Direct Perception Position.

It appears, then, that for the Hypothesis Position to be effectively based on a hypothesis-then-confirmation cycle as a mechanism for reading, and to be distinguishable from the Direct Perception Position, it must be assumed that the reader anticipates the actual words of the text to some degree. Only then is the expected visual form sufficiently concrete that it would be possible to sample a small set of visual features and on that basis determine that the hypothesis was accurate or not without using the visual information for word identification in the process. However, this encounters another problem. Although much has been written about the great amount of redundancy of language, it is still true that if a person reads a passage up to a given point and then attempts to guess the next word, he will be wrong far more often than he is correct, for most text. Normal English prose, though quite redundant, is not sufficiently redundant that the next word can usually be anticipated. This suggests that it is not sufficiently redundant to allow a hypothesis model of reading, based on anticipating words and then simply sampling the visual input to confirm the hypothesis, to work. It is interesting in this regard that the computer programs that have been at all successful in understanding language have not used an analysis-by-synthesis approach (Winogard, 1972).

Finally, the Hypothesis Position makes some very strong assumptions that are seldom expressed. It assumes that the bottleneck in reading is the visual input process. The generation of hypotheses must be much faster than the act of taking in visual information and using it to identify the words or meanings of the text, else why not simply look to see what the stimulus is rather than hypothesize about it. This assumption does not seem to be obviously correct. Another assumption already mentioned concerns the degree of redundancy in the language.

In summary, then, the model which we find most useful is based on the Direct Perception Position. It assumes that the reader, at the beginning of a fixation, has contextual (syntactic and semantic) information which can be used to access his memory store. Visual detail is acquired at the beginning of the fixation, and is integrated with similar detail from prior fixations in the Integrative Visual Buffer. Visual featural data is taken from that buffer, according to where the reader is in his reading, and is used for the cognitive processing operations involved in identifying the meaning of the text.[1] As these data are selected they are added to the contextual information already available. At some point, this combination of information is sufficient to specify the words and/or meaning of the text in this region. Thus, the amount of visual information required depends on the amount of redundancy in the language at this point. If an error is made in identification, this may lead to a regressive movement on some later fixation, if the error provides a context in which later words are inappropriate.

This model further assumes that the reader has available to him different degrees of specificity of the visual pattern at different distances into the periphery. Since only some visual information is needed to identify the text, the reader is able to make this identification further into the periphery than he is able to obtain full featural detail; how far depends on the language redundancy at that point and on the visual similarity of alternative approrpiate words. This leads to the suggestion that saccade lengths may be governed to some degree by the distance into the periphery in which text identification was possible. Other information from peripheral visual areas, such as word length patterns, may also have an influence. It is further assumed that a new fixation adds visual detail to the Integrative Visual Buffer which allows the processing of the text to continue from the point reached on the prior fixation. Finally, it is assumed that the duration of a fixation is determined by the cognitive activities the reader is engaged in. Thus, points where added activities such as meaning integration processes are required, or where text redundancy is low and added visual detail is required in identifying the text, result in longer fixations. Points where text is highly redundant, where meaning integration cannot be carried out, or where little visual information resides produce short fixations.

[1] Brown (1970) has suggested a "noticing order" of cues for a word which may represent the order in which visual data is taken from the Integrative Visual Buffer: first word length and possibly general shape, then first letter, next final letter, and finally visual detail of internal parts of the word.

REFERENCES

Abrams, S. G., and Zuber, B. L. Some temporal characteristics of information processing during reading. *Reading Research Quarterly,* 1972, *8,* 42-51.

Baron, J., and Thurston, I. An analysis of the word superiority effect. *Cognitive Psychology,* 1973, *4,* 207-228.

Becker, W., and Fuchs, A. F. Further properties of the human saccadic system: eye movements and correction saccades with and without visual fixation points. *Vision Research,* 1969, *9,* 1247-1258.

Blumenthal, A. L. *Language and Psychology.* New York: John Wiley & Sons, 1970.

Bouma, H. Visual interference in the parafoveal recognition of initial and final letters of words. *Vision Research,* 1973, *13,* 767-782.

Bouma, H., and DeVoogd, A. H. On the control of eye saccades in reading. *Vision Research,* 1974, *14,* 273-284.

Bruner, J. S., and O'Dowd, D. A note on the informativeness of words. *Language and Speech,* 1958, *1,* 98-101.

Buswell, G. T. *How People Look at Pictures.* Chicago: University of Chicago Press, 1935.

Carver, R. P. Toward a comprehensive theory of reading and prose rauding. Paper presented at the American Educational Research Association meetings, Chicago, 1974.

Chomsky, N. *Aspects of the Theory of Syntax.* Cambridge, Mass.: MIT Press, 1965.

Crovitz, H. F., and Schiffman, H. R. Visual field and the letter span. *Journal of Experimental Psychology,* 1965, *70,* 218-223.

Feinberg, R. A study of some aspects of peripheral visual acuity. *American Journal of Optometry and Archives of the American Academy of Optometry,* 1949, *26,* 49-56 and 105-119.

Foote, W. E., and Havens, L. L. Stimulus frequency: determinant of perception or response. *Psychonomic Science,* 1965, *2,* 153-154.

Geyer, J. J. Perceptual systems in reading: The prediction of a temporal eye-voice span constant. In H. K. Smith (Ed.), *Perception and Reading.* Newark, Delaware: International Reading Association, 1968.

Geyer, J. J. Models of perceptual processes in reading. In H. Singer, and R. B. Ruddell (Eds.), *Theoretical Models and Processes of Reading.* Newark, Delaware: International Reading Association, 1970.

Goodman, K. S. The psycholinguistic nature of the reading process. In K. S. Goodman (Ed.), *The Psycholinguistic Nature of the Reading Process.* Detroit: Wayne University Press, 1968.

Goodman, K. S. Reading: a psycholinguistic guessing game. In H. Singer and R. B. Ruddell (Eds.), *Theoretical Models and Processes of Reading.* Newark, Delaware: International Reading Association, 1970.

Gould, J. D. Pattern recognition and eye movement parameters. *Perception and Psychophysics,* 1967, *2,* 399-407.

Gould, J. D., and Schaffer, A. Eye movement patterns in scanning numeric displays. *Perceptual and Motor Skills,* 1965, *20,* 521-535.

Haber, R. N., and Hershenson, M. *The Psychology of Visual Perception.* New York: Holt, Rinehart, and Winston, Inc., 1973.

Harcum, E. R., and Jones, M. L. Letter recognition within words flashed left and right of fixation. *Science,* 1962, *138,* 444-445.

Havens, L. L., and Foote, W. E. The effect of competition on visual duration threshold and its independence of stimulus frequency. *Journal of Experimental Psychology,* 1963, *65,* 6-11.

Havens, L. L., and Foote, W. E. Structural features of competitive responses. *Perceptual and Motor Skills,* 1964, *19,* 75-80.

Hochberg, J. Components of literacy: speculations and exploratory research. In H. Levin and J. P. Williams (Eds.), *Basic Studies on Reading*. New York: Basic Books, 1970.

Hochberg, J., Levin, H., and Frail, C. Studies of oral reading: VII. How interword spaces affect reading. Mimeographed, Cornell University, 1966.

Huey, E. B. *The Psychology and Pedagogy of Reading*. First published in 1908 by The Macmillan Company. Republished: Cambridge, Mass.: MIT Press, 1968.

Jakobson, R., and Halle, M. *Fundamentals of Language*. Gravenhage: Mouton, 1956.

Kerr, J. L. Visual resolution in the periphery. *Perception and Psychophysics*, 1971, *9*, 375-378.

Kolers, P. A. The recognition of geometrically transformed text. *Perception and Psychophysics*, 1968, *3*, 57-64.

Kolers, P. A. Three stages of reading. In H. Levin and J. P. Williams (Eds.), *Basic Studies on Reading*. New York: Basic Books, 1970.

Kolers, P. A., and Lewis, C. L. Bounding of letter sequences and the integration of visually presented words. *Acta Psychologica*, 1972, *36*, 112-124.

Komoda, M. K., Festinger, L., Phillips, L. J., Duckman, R. H., and Young, R. A. Some observations concerning saccadic eye movements. *Vision Research*, 1973, *13*, 1009-1020.

Levin, H., and Kaplan, E. L. Grammatical structure and reading. In H. Levin and J. P. Williams (Eds.), *Basic Studies on Reading*. New York: Basic Books, 1970.

Levin, H., Watson, J., and Feldman, M. Writing as pretraining for association learning. *Journal of Educational Psychology*, 1964, *55*, 181-184.

Llewellyn-Thomas, E. Movements of the eye. *Scientific American*, 1968, *219*, 88-95.

Mackworth, J. F. Some models of the reading process: learners and skilled readers. *Reading Research Quarterly*, 1972, *7*, 701-733.

Mackworth, N. H. Visual noise causes tunnel vision. *Psychonomic Science*, 1965, *3*, 67-68.

Mackworth, N. H., and Bruner, J. S. How adults and children search and recognize pictures. *Human Development*, 1970, *13*, 149-177.

Mackworth, N. H., and Morandi, A. J. The gaze selects informative details within pictures. *Perception and Psychophysics*, 1967, *2*, 547-552.

Marchbanks, G., and Levin, H. Cues by which children recognize words. *Journal of Educational Psychology*, 1965, *56*, 57-61.

Mehler, J., Bever, T. G., and Carey, P. What we look at when we read. *Perception and Psychophysics*, 1967, *2*, 213-218.

Morton, J. The effects of context upon the visual duration thresholds for words. *British Journal of Psychology*, 1964, *55*, 165-180.

Neisser, U. *Cognitive Psychology*. New York: Appleton-Century-Crofts, 1967.

Newman, E. B. Speed of reading when the span of letters is restricted. *American Journal of Psychology*, 1966, *79*, 272-278.

Poulton, E. C. Peripheral vision, refractoriness and eye movements in fast oral reading. *British Journal of Psychology*, 1962, *53*, 409-419.

Reicher, G. M. Perceptual recognition as a function of meaningfulness of stimulus material. *Journal of Experimental Psychology*, 1969, *81*, 275-310.

Schiffman, H. R. Sensory and perceptual aspects of the reading process. In F. B. Davis (Ed.), *The Literature of Research in Reading with Emphasis on Models*. New Brunswick, New Jersey: Graduate School of Education, 1971.

Smith, F. *Understanding Reading*. New York: Holt, Rinehart, & Winston, 1971.

Sperling, G. The information available in brief visual presentations. *Psychological Monographs*, 1960, *74*, No. 11.

Taylor, E. A. The spans: perception, apprehension, and recognition. *American Journal of Ophthalmology*, 1957, *44*, 501-507.

Taylor, E. A. *The Fundamental Reading Skill.* Springfield, Illinois: Charles C. Thomas, 1966.

Taylor, S. E. Eye movements in reading: facts and fallacies. *American Educational Research Journal,* 1965, *2,* 187-202.

Tinker, M. Recent studies of eye movements in reading. *Psychological Bulletin,* 1958, *55,* 215-231.

Tinker, M. The study of eye movements in reading. *Psychological Bulletin,* 1946, *43,* 93-120.

Tulving, E., and Gold, C. Stimulus information and contextual information as determinants of tachistoscopic recognition of words. *Journal of Experimental Psychology,* 1963, *66,* 319-327.

Uttal, W. R., and Smith, P. Recognition of alphabetic characters during voluntary eye movements. *Perception and Psychophysics,* 1968, *3,* 257-264.

Volkman, F. C. Vision during voluntary saccadic eye movements. *Journal of the Optical Society of America,* 1962, *52,* 571-578.

Volkman, F. C., Schick, A. M. L., and Riggs, L. A. Time course of visual inhibition during voluntary saccades. *Journal of the Optical Society of America,* 1968, *58,* 362-369.

Wanat, S. *Linguistic Structure and Visual Attention in Reading.* Newark, Delaware: International Reading Association, 1971.

Weber, R. M. First-graders use of grammatical context in reading. In H. Levin and J. P. Williams (Eds.), *Basic Studies on Reading.* New York: Basic Books, 1970.

Westheimer, G. H. Eye movement responses to a horizontally moving visual stimulus. *Archives of Ophthalmology,* 1954, *52,* 932-943.

Wheeler, D. D. Processing in word recognition. *Cognitive Psychology,* 1970, *1,* 59-85.

Williams, J. P., Blumberg, E. L., and Williams, D. V. Cues used in visual word recognition. *Journal of Educational Psychology,* 1970, *61,* 310-315.

Winogard, T. Understanding natural language. *Cognitive Psychology,* 1972, *3,* whole issue.

Woodworth, R. S. *Experimental Psychology.* New York: Henry Holt, 1938.

Yarbus, A. L. *Eye Movements and Vision.* New York: Plenum Press, 1967.

An On-Line Computer Technique For Studying Reading: Identifying the Perceptual Span[*]

GEORGE W. MCCONKIE
Cornell University

KEITH RAYNER[**]
Cornell University

In the psychological study of reading, as in the study of many other aspects of human functioning, it is useful to distinguish between process and product. We can think of the mental acts involved in reading as a set of processes which result in a product, the changes made in the memory store. In the study of skilled reading, most research has dealt with the product resulting from reading. The primary data of most studies is in the form of test scores, indicating the degree to which the reader can remember various aspects of the information communicated in the passage. From these data, attempts are sometimes made to infer something about the processes involved in reading. But the direct study of the processes involved in skilled, silent reading is difficult due to their rapid and private nature.

When specific questions about reading processes have been investigated (for instance, such questions as: What cues are used to identify words? From what size area is the reader acquiring visual information during a fixation? What cues are used to guide the eye? How is ambiguity in the language handled during reading? How are lexical units mapped

[*]Reprinted from Phil L. Nacke (Ed.), *Diversity in Mature Reading: Theory and Research.* Twenty-Second Yearbook of the National Reading Conference, Vol. 1, 1973, 119-130. Reprinted by permission of the authors and the National Reading Conference, Inc. This research was supported by Grant No. OEG 2-71-0531 from the U.S. Office of Education, and was carried out while the senior author was on a National Institutes of Health Special Fellowship at Massachusetts Institute of Technology. Special thanks are extended to Dr. Marvin Minsky, who made it possible to conduct the research at the Artificial Intelligence Laboratory at M.I.T., and to David Silver, staff programmer there, who did much of the programming involved.

[**]Keith Rayner is now at the University of Rochester.

onto meaning? How long does it take to identify the meanings of words in reading? Must lexical items be encoded in a form which contains sound or pronunciation information in order to be understood?) the researchers have typically been forced to set up experimental tasks that departed from normal silent reading. These tasks have involved tachistoscopic presentation, oral reading, presentation of single words or sentences, etc. In most instances, these tasks have not been characterized by certain features which typify the normal reading task: namely, freedom of the reader to pace the input of information, the reading of rather large segments of integrated text, and the attempt to remember the gist of the message rather than all the detail or the particular words in which the message was expressed. An important goal for reading research is to develop techniques for studying the processes involved in reading as the person is engaged in the normal reading task, reading a passage for meaning, rather than having to depend so completely on other tasks which are thought to be similar to normal reading in certain ways.

In our own search for methods of studying reading behavior as it is in progress, we have turned to on-line computer techniques for stimulus manipulation and data gathering. A small computer with a cathode-ray tube (CRT) provides the researcher with a type of stimulus control never before possible in the study of reading. The computer can display on the CRT the text which the subject is to read. This text can then be changed very rapidly, within 1/60th second at most, in almost any way the experimenter desires, while the subject is engaged in the act of reading from it. The computer can also receive input from an eye-tracking device, so it can record complete data on the reader's eye movements: the location and duration of each fixation, the length of each saccade, the time required for each saccade, etc. Thus, it is possible to examine the effect of specific display changes on the person's eye-movement behavior. Finally, since the computer has information about the person's direction of gaze (sampling eye position at a rate of 60 times per second or more), it is possible to program the computer to make display changes at specific locations with reference to the reader's point of fixation, and at specific times with reference to whether the eye is moving or still. Even velocity, direction, or distance of movement can be taken into account in determining when to make a display change or what type of change is to be made. This type of stimulus control and detailed data collection holds great promise for the investigation of a number of basic issues about reading which previously could not be studied in a normal reading task. This includes many of the research questions listed earlier.

So far, our own studies have focused on one issue, the size of the perceptual span during a fixation in reading. More specifically, the question is, from what regions around the point of fixation does the reader acquire various useful types of information during a fixation in reading. The rest of this paper consists of a brief description of two experiments which have investigated this question. These experiments involved quite different approaches to the same basic question and thus serve as illustrations of how on-line computer techniques can be employed to study reading. Since both experiments are quite complex and have generated a great deal of data which are presently being analyzed in several ways, this paper will not attempt a complete report of either study. More complete reports will be published later in other sources. Instead, a brief presentation is made of certain of the more straight-forward aspects of the data. This illustrates both the nature of this type of research and provides data on the perceptual span question.

Experiment I

The first experiment involved manipulating the visual information which was available to the reader at different distances from his point of fixation, with each fixation he made in reading, and observing the effects these manipulations produced on his reading behavior. The technique for accomplishing this and the rationale behind it will be explained after first describing the materials used.

Materials

Passages were selected from a high school psychology text, each about 500 words long. Mutilated versions of each of these passages were prepared by replacing each letter in the original with some other letter. This was done in such a way that, though the text was rendered unreadable, certain gross visual characteristics of the original text were maintained. Three basic algorithms were used to accomplish this mutilation. The first replaced each letter with an X, called (X) substitution. The second replaced each letter with a letter visually confusible with it (Buoma, 1973), called compatible (C) substitution. The third replaced each letter with a letter not visually confused with it. In fact, letters having ascenders and descenders were replaced with letters not having these characteristics, and vice versa. This was called noncompatible (NC) substitution. Each substitution was applied in two ways. In one, the Spaces (S) application, spaces and punctuation marks were left in the text. In the other, the Filled (F) application, spaces and punctuation marks were replaced by appropriate letters ("X" in the X substitution, other letters in the C and NC substitutions). This produced six mutilated versions of the original text. The *CS version*, though destroying the readability of the text, still maintained such visual aspects of the original as word length patterns, external word shape of individual words, and even some of the more salient featural characteristics of the individual letters themselves. The *CF version* was similar except that word length pattern information was removed. The *NCS version* provided inappropriate word shape and letter information, but did maintain the word length patterns from the original, while the *NCF version* destroyed this as well. The *XS version* provided a homogeneous pattern which maintained only the word length pattern from the original text, whereas, the *XF version* eliminated the word length information. All versions maintained visual information about length of lines, paragraph indentations, etc.

The original version and one of the mutilated versions of a passage were stored in the computer at once. The computer originally displayed the mutilated version on the CRT. However, when the reader looked at the first line of the text, as soon as the eye was detected as having fixated, the letters within a certain number of character positions to left and right of the fixation point were replaced by the corresponding letters from the original passage. Thus, on the fixation there was normal text for him to see within a certain region around the point of central vision, and beyond that region was a stimulus pattern which maintained certain visual aspects of the original passage, but which did not maintain others. The region within which normal text was displayed will be referred to as the *window*, and the area outside the window in which the mutilated text was displayed will be referred to as the *background*.

When the reader moved his eye to make his next fixation, the letters in the initial window area were converted once again to background characters and the letters in the window area around his new fixation point were replaced by corresponding letters from the original passage. Thus, the person was able to read the passage quite normally; wherever he looked in the visual display he saw the appropriate text for that region. He was free to make normal eye movements in reading, except that he could not return to a prior line or make long regressions (more than about 45 characters), and he was required to read each line in succession. An example of the appearance of the display during a particular fixation is given in Figure 1.

Variables

Two variables were manipulated in this experiment: the visual pattern (type of text mutilation) present in the area outside the window, and

```
XXXXX XXXXXXX. XXX XXXXXX XXX XXXXXX
XXXXXX XXX XXXXXXXXX XXXXXX XX XX XXXXX
XXX XX XX XX XXd has the patiencX. XXXXX XX XX
XXXXXXXXXX XXXXX XXXXXXXX. XX XXXXXX,
XXXX X XXXXXX XXXX X XXXXXXXX XXXXXXXXX
XX XXXXXXXXX
```

Figure 1.   An example of a display with window size of 17, with the X version of
              mutilated text in the background. This display would be seen by a
              subject during a fixation if he fixated the letter *e* in the word *the*. The
              original display actually had 7 lines; this figure is reduced to conserve
              space.

the size of the window within which normal text was displayed. The six
visual patterns used in the background have already been described.
Eight window sizes were used: 13 character positions (the character the
computer identified as being directly fixated, and 6 characters to right and
left of it), 17, 21, 25, 31, 37, 45, and 100 character positions.

Six high school students, all juniors or seniors, identified as being
among the best readers in their school (Cambridge High and Latin,
Cambridge, Mass.) by the teacher responsible for reading instruction,
served as subjects. Each read sixteen passages, six pages each, with window size remaining constant throughout a given passage, but background
stimulus pattern changing from page to page. Each subject read 2 pages
under each of the 48 conditions (6 background types by 8 window sizes) in
the experiment.

Rationale

It is frequently assumed that good readers acquire different types of
visual information at different distances into their peripheral vision during a fixation. For instance, it may be that within a certain area of greatest
acuity readers have full access to the complete detail of the visual pattern
of the letters, and can obtain any aspects of those patterns for identifying
the stimulus. There may also be areas further into the periphery from
which they obtain only less detailed information, such as general word
shape or word length patterns, etc. The data from Experiment I can
reveal how far into the periphery these different types of information are
acquired. As an example, suppose that the subjects studied typically have
access to complete detail in the stimulus within an area of 8-character
positions left and right of the fixation point, and beyond that use only
word shape and word length information. If this were the case, then
reading with a window of size 17, with the CS version of the text in the

background (periphery), would provide them with all the visual information they normally use in reading: full detail within 8-character positions of the fixation point, and word shape and word length beyond that. However, either the NCS or CF background would remove from the display certain information which they normally use from the periphery in their reading (word shape information with NCS; word length patterns with CF). Since they no longer have access to certain stimulus information they normally use, this should interfere with their reading to some extent. This interference should be reflected in their eye movement patterns, producing shorter saccades, longer fixations, or more regressive movements, as compared with reading when the CS version is in the background. On the other hand, if the window were large enough that the subjects did not obtain useful information beyond its boundaries, then the type of visual pattern displayed in the background area would have no effect on reading. The general research and data analysis strategy, then, was to have subjects read under conditions of different window sizes, and to see if, at each window size, the type of visual pattern in the periphery had an effect on the indices of reading behavior. If the type of visual pattern did have an effect, the data were analyzed further to see what aspect of the visual pattern was producing the effect; that is, what aspect of the visual pattern was being acquired by readers in the area outside the window.

Results

Some of the data will now be briefly summarized. For each page of text read by each subject, summary statistics were obtained for a number of indicies of eye movement behavior. For most of these variables there was a clear effect due to window size, as can be seen in Figures 2 and 3 which present data on saccade length and fixation duration. Reducing the window to 13 character positions increased the fixation durations by 30 percent, decreased the median length of forward saccades by 26 percent, and increased reading time by 60 percent, as compared to a window size of 100 character positions. Interestingly enough, window size had no effect on retention test scores.

For each dependent variable, the data were subjected to a series of analyses of variance, one for each window size. Each was a 3 x 2 x 6 design: X, C or NC substitution, S or F application of the substitution and subjects. The subjects factor was almost always significant for all dependent variables and window sizes, but seldom interacted with the other variables.

The type of substitution used to produce the mutilations had their effect primarily on fixation duration, and the presence or absence of spaces primarily affected saccade length. Both of these variables had an effect on the frequency of regressive movements.

Figure 2 shows the effect of presence vs. absence of word spaces on saccade length. The data plotted are means of the third quartiles for the distributions of saccade lengths. As can be seen in Figure 2, the presence of spaces and punctuation results in longer saccades at least up to a window size of 25; the curves are still separate beyond that, but the differences are not large enough to be statistically significant. These data suggest that during fixations the readers picked up and used word space information at least as far as thirteen or fourteen character positions from the fixation point, and that this information had its effect on how far the readers sent their eyes on a saccade. First and second quartile data show the same pattern, but differences are significant only at smaller window sizes.

Figure 3 presents the effects of X, C and NC background patterns on fixation durations. Presence or absence of spaces had no effect on this measure. Maintaining the word shape (C condition) facilitated reading in comparison with the NC condition at the smallest window sizes, but this effect disappeared at window size 21. Apparently external word shape information was not utilized further than about 10 character positions away from the point of fixation. Having X's outside the window area produced shorter durations through window size 21, as compared to the C and NC conditions, but not at 25.

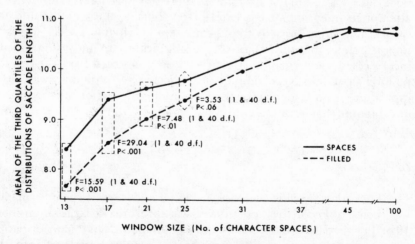

Figure 2.   Means of the third quartiles of the distributions of saccade lengths plotted by window size. Space and filled conditions are plotted separately. Significant differences are indicated.

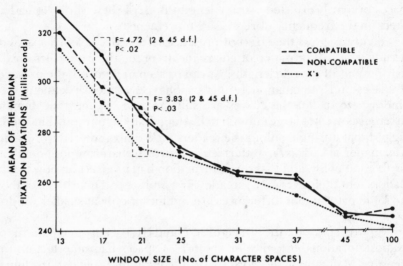

Figure 3.   Means of the median fixation durations, plotted against window size.
Different curves are for different background text mutilation conditions. Significant effects are indicated.

A likely explanation of this difference is as follows. With X's in the
periphery, it was very obvious to the readers where the boundary of the
window was, whereas, with the other two conditions, the boundary was
not evident. Thus, in the X condition there was probably less tendency to
attempt to integrate wrong letters from outside the window into the
words. The superiority of the X condition at window size 21 seems to
indicate, then, that the subjects were still picking up and using specific
incorrect letter information 10 character positions away from the fixation
point in the C and NC conditions. At 12 character-positions away, however, there is no evidence for the pickup of either letter or word shape
information, that is, the X, C, and NC conditions did not differ from one
another.

Discussion

These data provide evidence that letter and word-shape information
were being picked up by these subjects within an area no larger than about
10 or 11 character positions from the fixation point, but that information
about word length patterns was being acquired further into the
periphery, at least 13 character-positions from the fixation point, and was
being used to guide the eye.

Though the results from Experiment I appear quite clear, the fact that such substantial changes in the display were being produced on each fixation raises the possibility that the readers' normal perceptual processes were being disrupted, and that this was influencing the results obtained in the experiment. Evidence against this possibility exists in the form of subjects' reports that they were able to read quite normally in the experimental situation except for encountering some difficulty at the smallest window sizes, and that they seldom noticed display changes taking place on the screen. Apparently the computer was able to change the display fast enough after the eye stopped that the change was not seen by the subjects.

Still, it was thought wise to use a different technique to investigate the same basic question, the size of the perceptual span, but one which did not involve the massive and frequent display changes involved in Experiment I. This was the basis for undertaking the next experiment.

Experiment II

Rationale

Two basic assumptions underlie the second experiment. First, it is assumed that if a reader encounters a string of letters which does not make a word, this produces a difficulty for the cognitive processing system which reveals itself in the form of a lengthened fixation duration. Second, it is assumed that subjects attempt to integrate visual and semantic information acquired on successive fixations. If a subject acquires certain information from a particular word location on one fixation, that information is integrated with the information he acquires from the same area of the page on the next fixation. However, if the stimulus in that location has actually been changed between the fixations, then it is possible for the information acquired on the two fixations to be incompatible. If so, this should produce some irregularity in the reading pattern, which would be expected to be revealed by a lengthened fixation duration on the fixation immediately following the stimulus change. If the type of change in the stimulus pattern is such that the information acquired on fixations prior to the change is compatible with the new stimulus, of course no disruption in reading would occur.

Method

In the experiment, ten Massachusetts Institute of Technology undergraduates were presented with 15 blocks of 15 short paragraphs each to read. In each paragraph one word position was identified as the critical word location (CWL) in which a stimulus change would take place during reading. The paragraphs were displayed one at a time on the CRT, and the subjects' eyes were tracked as they read. When a subject began reading a paragraph, one of five alternative stimulus patterns was present in the CWL. When his eye reached a certain location, called the boundary, on the line containing the CWL, the stimulus in the CWL was replaced by the word originally contained in the paragraph, called the *original word*. The change took place while the reader's eye was moving. After reading each block of passages, the subject was given a recognition test of retention.

The five stimulus alternatives initially displayed in the CWL will now be described. Each bore a particular relation to the original word. As an example, suppose the sentence were

The robbers guarded the _____ with their guns.

where the blank indicates the CWL. The stimulus alternatives were: (1) the original word from the paragraph (palace) which occupied that location. This was called *W-Ident* since the stimulus in the CWL was a word (W), and it was identical (Ident) with the original word. (2) A word (police) which fit semantically and syntactically into the paragraph, and which began and ended with the same letters and maintained the basic external word shape of the original word. This condition was called *W-SL*, since it was a word, and both the word shape (S) and extreme letters (L) were identical to the original. The remaining alternatives were all non-word (N) letter strings. (3) A letter string (pcluce) which was similar to the original word in both word shape and extreme letters, called the *N-SL* condition. (4) A letter string (pfltce) which had the same extreme letters as the original word, but not the same word shape, called the *N-L* condition. (5) A letter string (ycluec) which had the same word shape as the original word, but which had different extreme letters, and was called the *N-S* condition. Thus specific alternative stimuli differed from the original along several dimensions: meaning, whether it was a word or not, initial and final letters, and external word shape.

All original words, and hence all alternative stimuli, contained five, six, or seven letters.

Variables

The first independent variable in the experiment was type of stimulus alternative initially displayed in the CWL. The second variable was the location of the boundary which triggered the display change. It was either at the fourth or first character-position in the CWL, or it was 3, 6, or 9 character-positions left of the CWL.

Results

Two preliminary analyses have been completed on these data. The first investigated how far into the periphery the reader detects the difference between words and non-word letter strings. Mean fixation durations were calculated for each subject for fixations made immediately prior to crossing the boundary, and at different locations with respect to the first letter of the CWL, when either word (W) or non-word letter strings (N) appeared in the CWL. These data were plotted according to the location of the fixation. Fixation durations for fixations directly on the CWL showed much longer fixations when N stimuli were displayed than when W were, and this difference was significant when tested by a t-test. There was also a significant difference for fixations made as far as 3 or 4 character-positions to the left of the CWL. However, for fixations farther to the left of the CWL than that, the curves for N and W conditions came together and were not significantly different. Thus, the data provided no evidence that the readers were detecting a difference between words and non-words for letter strings beginning further than about 4 character-positions to the right of the fixation point.

The second analysis investigated how far from the fixation point readers pick up certain visual characteristics of words, or identify the meanings of words. This analysis only considered data on the fixation durations of fixations made directly on the CWL itself, and which were the first fixation after crossing the boundary; that is, the fixation on which the changed stimulus pattern first appeared. These data were classified according to the location of the prior fixation (how far it was to the left of the CWL) and according to the stimulus alternative which was initially in the CWL. Five prior fixation locations (each contained three character-positions) and five stimulus alternatives resulted in 25 conditions: a mean was calculated for each subject for each condition. These data were then combined and the resulting graph is shown in Figure 4.

When the subjects' fixations prior to the display change were more than 12 character-positions to the left of the CWL, fixation durations on the CWL itself for the different conditions were almost identical. Thus, there is no evidence that the subjects were picking up either specific letter or word shape information from words 13 or more character-positions to the right of their fixation points. However, the curves do separate in the 10-12 character-position range. Using the W-Ident condition as a baseline to judge the others against it appears that even the small visual differences between the Ident and the SL conditions were noticed this far into the periphery, but the effects of changes in either the word shape or the first

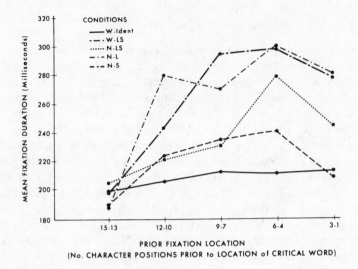

Figure 4. Mean fixation durations of fixations on the critical word location, plotted as a function of location of the prior fixation. Different curves are for different types of words or letter strings displayed in the critical word location at the time of the prior fixation.

and last letters were particularly noted. Word shape, and specific detail about both extreme and internal letters all appear to be acquired from words beginning 10-12 character positions to the right of the fixation point. In addition, the W-SL and N-SL curves are almost identical at the more distant locations, and separate only when the prior fixation was 6 character-positions or less from the CWL. Since these conditions had very similar visual patterns, the difference was produced by the fact that the W-SL condition involved a word whereas the N-SL condition involved only a letter-string. Thus, it appears that although the readers were picking up visual information about words farther into the periphery, they were not discriminating between words and non-words, nor identifying the meanings of words, for stimulus patterns beginning more than about 4-6 character positions to the right of the fixation point.

Discussion

The two experiments described, though involving quite different approaches to the investigation of the perceptual span in skilled, silent reading, yield data which are consistent with one another, thus increasing our confidence in the conclusions drawn from these studies. It appears that different types of information are acquired different distances into the periphery, and are used for different purposes. Word length pattern information is acquired furthest into the periphery, at least 13 or 14 character positions from the fixation point and possibly more. This information is probably used primarily for eye guidance. Visual shape of words and letters is picked up less far into the periphery: the first experiment suggests a maximum of about 10 character-positions, and the second indicates that this can be acquired for words beginning as far as 10-12 character-positions to the right of the fixation point. No evidence was found in either study to indicate that word shape is identified further into the periphery than is specific letter shape. Finally, the actual identification of word meanings seems to occur only for words beginning no further than 4-6 character-positions to the right of the fixation point. The reader appears not to make the distinction between words and non-words further into the periphery than that.

Although additional research is needed to establish further the validity of the results of these studies, the data do seem to fall into a clear and comprehensible pattern, providing answers to basic questions about reading which have been the subject of speculation and experiment since the 1800's. The method used in this research is made possible through the stimulus-control capabilities of modern computer techniques. These research methods hold promise for the investigation of other aspects of stimulus acquisition during a fixation and of individual differences in this aspect of reading. They also have possible diagnostic applications.

REFERENCE

Buoma, H. Visual interference in the parafoveal recognition of initial and final letters of words. *Vision Research,* 1973, *13,* 767-782.

Speed of Processing Visual Stimuli and Its Relation to Reading*

LUTHER C. GILBERT
University of California at Berkeley

Tachistoscopic records have demonstrated repeatedly that both good and poor readers at the college level can identify the visual stimuli of phrases of sense material after exposure for a period which is only a fraction of the time required for the fixation pause in reading easy prose. A possible explanation of the phenomenon appears to lie in the use of the *after image* and the *memory after image* in the tachistoscopic tests. It appears possible that the use of these images tends to give a false measure of the speed and span of visual perception. It also appears possible that maximum use of such images may compensate for certain processing deficiencies.

It has occurred to the writer that the experimental interruption of the use of the retinal images is possible and that this technique can be employed to give a better understanding of the discrepancy between the speed and span of visual perception as measured by the tachistoscopic tests and the speed of reading easy prose.

Purpose of the Investigation

The purpose of this study was to investigate the influence of varying the processing times for the first stimulus before the Ss were permitted to encounter an interfering stimulus. The data were analyzed a) to determine something of the nature of individual differences in speed of processing visual stimuli and b) to determine relationship between the accuracy of perception and reading ability.

Studies relating to the broad topic of speed and span of visual perception are too numerous to review here in detail. Many of these studies are

*Reprinted from *Journal of Educational Psychology*, 50, 1, 1959, 8-14. With permission of the author and American Psychological Association, Inc.

summarized critically in the reports of Arnoult and Tinker (1939), Huey (1912), Vernon (1931), and Woodworth and Schlosberg (1954).

These earlier studies presented evidence to show that adult *S*s could see four or five short familiar words in 1/10 or even 1/100 of a second, provided the words formed a simple phrase or sentence and the *S*s were not required to make a saccadic movement or encounter interfering visual stimuli immediately before or after the flashed material.

These earlier studies presented evidence to show that adult *S*s could see four or five short familiar words in 1/10 or even 1/100 of a second, provided the words formed a simple phrase or sentence and the *S*s were not required to make a saccadic movement or encounter interfering visual stimuli immediately before or after the flashed material.

In attempting to measure speed or visual perception some investigators had the *S*s press a key as quickly as the words were recognized. The most commonly used method was to expose the words for a short period and the *S*s were requested to report the words they recognized after the stimuli were removed from the screen. This method seems to be more a measure of speed of vision than speed of perception, since the procedure permits the *S*s to continue the processing of the material after the flashed words are removed from the screen. The method fails to identify and evaluate the processing time, and consequently yields inexact measures of speed of visual perception.

In a preliminary study (Gilbert, 1957) using 68 *S*s, it was found that when two words were flashed on the screen for 1/24 of a second and followed immediately by nonsense letters[1] on the same place on the screen, only 3.68 percent of the words were correctly reported. Only one *S* reported correctly as many as 20 percent of the words. Since the writer was interested in measuring the speed with which the readers could avoid the influence of interfering stimuli on perception of sense material, these nonsense letters seemed to constitute a good test of interference.

Subjects

The *S*s included 64 college juniors, seniors, and graduates, who were members of classes in educational psychology. Of the 64, 41 were women and 23 men. For all of them, the native language was English.

The rate of reading on a standard level, nonfiction article of approximately 2,300 words ranged from 143 words per minute to 464 words per minute. The average for the group was 262 with a standard deviation of 74.14.

---

[1] Letters typed in a random order and in a manner to avoid this formation of sense material.

Materials

Reading tests. For measuring the speed and comprehension of reading, a 2,307-word test-adapted from one of the University of California weekly broadcasts was used.[2] This test and a second broadcast test,[3] similar in character to the first, were given to 110 Ss. The correlation between the two tests was .85 ± .02, which indicates a reliability sufficiently high to justify using it as a group test.

Span of perception tests. The six tests used to measure span of perception were all similar in every way. All the words were short and thoroughly familiar. The phrases gradually increased from one word to five words and from one letter to 25 letter spaces. Each test was composed of five spans, increasing from a one-word span to a five-word span. There were five test items for each span. The material was all typed in lower case on the same IBM executive typewriter using Warren High Gloss paper and black carbon ribbon. The material was then photographed with a Cine-Kodak Special II camera at a distance of nine inches to give a large clear type on the screen. A Bell and Howell projector set at 24 frames per second was used for flashing the material on the screen. Plus-X Reversal Safety film was used in the negative form in order to get black words on soft eggshell-color background. A blank page of the Warren High Gloss paper was photographed using enough film to permit the projector to run for three seconds before the words appeared and two seconds after they had disappeared. This allowed ample time for starting and stopping the projector and at the same time for controlling the illumination on the screen.

The material was projected on a Da-lite screen in a room with the lights turned down to where the Ss were just able to see to write their answers, but not dark enough to produce full dark adaptation. Each S was asked if he could see clearly the material as it appeared on the screen. The Ss who reported that the words blurred were eliminated from the study. Only six Ss were lost for this reason. A further check on vision was made by flashing two words on the screen for 2/24 of a second without an interfering stimulus following. The 64 Ss reported correctly 98.43 percent of these words. It seems reasonably certain that defective vision was not an important factor in the findings.

The nonsense letters used as interfering stimuli were typed in lower case on the same typewriter used for typing the words. The letters were

---

[2] Broadcast Number 2573, U. E. Number 868, University of California Radio Service, October 29, 1944.
[3] Broadcast Number 1254, U. E. Number 3049, University of California Radio Servive, February 24, 1952.

typed in a random order and in a manner to avoid the formation of sense material. In each case a sufficient number of nonsense letters was used to extend at least two letter spaces beyond the beginnings and ends of the words.

The three examples of test items which follow show a) the sense material and b) the nonsense letters used as interfering stimuli:

Item 1

(a)   words
(b) lupytkoie

Item 2

(a)   his best shoes
(b) bnvcrmxztghjfedksl

Item 3

(a)   they will come home early
(b) zaqwsxcderfvbgtyhjshuiklopzxc

The first test in this group was used to measure the span of perception when the *S*s were allowed unlimited time for use of the images after the words left the screen. This span is designated the "basic" span. This is the kind of tachistoscopic span commonly reported in the literature and the kind commonly used when training for speed of visual perception. The percentage of words correctly reported on each test as a whole is designated "accuracy" of perception. The other five tests used to measure span and accuracy of perception were all designed in a manner to control the time allowed for processing the words being flashed on the screen. This was accomplished by increasing the time the words were left on the screen before superimposing nonsense letters on the same spot on the screen where the words had been presented. For example, the designation 2-0-2 for the first test means that the words were photographed on two successive frames and were followed without a blank frame by nonsense letters on two successive frames. In other words, the words were left on the screen for 2/24 of a second and were followed immediately by nonsense letters. In each case the nonsense letters were left on the screen for 2/24 of a second. Each control test increased by 1/24 of a second the length of time the material was left on the screen. Thus in the fifth test in the series the words were left on the screen for 6/24 of a second before nonsense letters were superimposed. The exposure time for the nonsense letters was held constant at 2/24 of a second in each test.

Preliminary instructions requested each *S* to fixate at the point on the screen where three small dots appeared and to try to see the words which appeared on the screen. The center dot was placed at exactly the mid-point for the sense material. A number of examples familiarized the Ss with the procedure. In each case the dots were left on the screen for exactly the same length of time, i.e. 8/24 of a second and were followed by two blank frames, i.e. 2/24 of a second. This made it possible for the Ss to anticipate the words. After each phrase was flashed, time was allowed for the S to write the words. The Ss were tested in small groups of not more than 25 and no S was more than 25 feet from the screen and not more than three chairs from the center of the screen. Further evidence that the words on the screen could be seen was the fact that the group as a whole reported accurately more than 98 percent of the words up to and including the two-word level on the uncontrolled span.

The same procedure (used for the basic span of perception) was followed with the tests for the controlled spans, with the exception that the instant the sense material left the screen there appeared at the same spot on the screen nonsense letters. The Ss were instructed to ignore as far as possible the nonsense letters and to remember the phrases of sense material.

Comparison of the Basic and Control Spans of Perception

Table 1 presents data showing the percentage of the words correctly reported on the basic span and on the various controlled spans for each word level and the test as a whole. It is interesting to note that when the Ss used a very narrow span of one and two words nearly all the Ss were able to arrive at a very high level of efficiency even when allowed only 3/24 of a second before the interfering stimulus was superimposed. Also of interest is the fact that, as the span of perception the Ss were required to use became greater, the longer the sense material had to be left on the screen before superimposing the nonsense letters in order for the Ss to achieve the level of the basic span. The data presented in Table 1 bring into sharp focus the fact that in visual perception such as used in reading sense material, *the fixation pause must be long enough in duration to allow time not only to see but also time to process the visual stimuli.* It may well be that the individual differences in speed of processing visual materials is an influential factor in both the span of perception and the length of the fixation pauses used in reading easy prose. If the data in Table 1 were presented graphically they would show the group curves of the controlled spans crossing the lines for the basic spans at various time levels. The group curve for the controlled test of accuracy of perception crosses the line for the basic test between the levels of 5/24 and 6/24 of a second. It is interesting to note that this point of crossing is close to the average length of the fixation pauses commonly found for mature readers reading simple prose.

The data in Table 1 show a marked increase in the percentage of words reported from the 2/24 to 6/24 of a second, with the greatest gain taking place between the 2/24 and the 3/24 time units. At the level of 4/24 of a second the group had reached a level of efficiency on the control span which was slightly above the basic spans of the three words or less. By the level of 5/24 of a second the control span of four words had equaled or exceeded the four-word basic span. By the level of 6/24 of a second the imposed stimuli had no measured detrimental influence on the groups' five word span of perception. However, some of the very slow readers were still experiencing some interference.

Table 1.   Mean percentage of words correctly reported on the various spans

Length of Span in Words	Time Units—Percentage Correct in Each Unit					
	2-0-2	3-0-2	4-0-2	5-0-2	6-0-2	2-0-0 (Basic Span)
One Word	81.25	97.81	98.75	100.00	99.68	99.37
Two Words	86.71	97.81	99.06	99.53	99.68	98.43
Three Words	64.44	93.74	96.24	98.22	96.56	95.94
Four Words	56.14	83.82	85.54	93.04	92.65	91.63
Five Words	36.06	64.06	66.50	71.93	81.32	75.56
Percentage of total	58.38	82.01	84.01	88.36	91.14	88.56
SD	17.76	12.94	10.54	9.50	9.64	10.82

These data also indicate that the noninterference times of 4/24 or 5/24 of a second following the flashing of the words on the screen constitute a very important factor in the span of perception. Furthermore they indicate that the time words are left on the screen is not the only factor which should concern us in studying speed and span of perception. Note that words left on the screen for 2/24 of a second and not followed by other visual stimuli were as accurately reported as words left on the screen for 5/24 of a second and followed by interfering visual stimuli. Both the length of time the words are left on the screen *and* the length of the period free from interfering stimuli are important factors. These data suggest the possibility that some readers may use part of their fixation time to avoid interference from a new stimulus during the period they need free for processing the visual stimulus. In other words, part of the fixation time may be preventive in nature.

Comparison of Rate of Reading and Speed and Accuracy of Perception

For the purpose of showing the differences in rate of processing the sense material for readers of different levels of ability the group of 64 Ss was ranked from the best to the poorest on the gross reading rate and then divided into fourths. The best 25 percent are designated as S_1 and the poorest 25 percent are designated as S_4. (S_2 and S_3 constitute the middle 50 percent). Table 2 shows the difference between the slow reading group (S_4) and the fast readers (S_1) in speed of processing sense materials. When the sense material was left on the screen for 3/24 of a second, then followed by an interfering stimulus, the S_1 group got a considerably higher percentage of the material than the S_4 group did when the sense material was left on the screen for 6/24 of a second, then followed by an interfering stimulus. Another point of interest in these data is the fact that the S_4 subjects experienced greater difficulty in avoiding interference from the interrupting stimuli than was true for the S_1 students.

Table 2.   Mean percentage of words correctly reported in the various time units by S_1 and S_4 groups

Subjects	Time Units					Basic Span
	2-0-2	3-0-2	4-0-2	5-0-2	6-0-2	2-0-0
S_1 Best 25% of the Readers	78.49	93.07	92.41	96.08	97.17	94.56
SD	14.14	4.66	5.07	3.14	3.02	5.53
S_4 Poorest 25%	39.74	71.74	77.60	81.20	86.91	83.41
SD	19.15	13.28	11.81	8.12	6.96	8.50
Main Difference	38.75	21.34	14.75	14.84	10.26	11.15
t*	6.4	5.9	4.5	5.8	5.2	4.3

[a] Ranked on gross reading rate.

*All the t ratios are significant at better than the .01 level.

Correlation Between Speed and Accuracy of Perception and Rate of Reading

This positive association between rate of processing simple phrase material and the gross reading rate of simple prose material is brought out a little more clearly in Table 3 which shows the coefficients of correlation for the percentage of words processed on each test of perception and the gross reading rate. The magnitude of these correlations with the gross reading rate decreases in an irregular pattern from the 2-0-2 time unit to the 6-0-2 time unit level. It should be remembered that the average accuracy for the 6-0-2 time unit test is similar in magnitude to that on the basic span test and at this time level there seemed to be very little influence resulting from the nonsense letters as reflected in the group average. (However, a few of the poor readers were still experiencing some interference.) Therefore it is not surprising that this correlation between scores on the 6-0-2 test and gross reading rate is of a similar magnitude as that found between the basic span test and gross reading rate.

Table 3 also reveals that the magnitude of the correlations between the speed and accuracy of processing the phrases and the effective reading rate[4] are slightly larger but similar in magnitude to those reported for the gross reading rate. The effective reading rate seems to reflect a little better than the gross reading rate the speed with which the Ss can process the stimuli which they receive from each fixation pause. If this assumption is true, it would seem logical that the correlations between effective reading rate and speed and accuracy of processing the phrases would be a little higher than for the gross rate and speed and accuracy of processing the stimuli. However, since the correlation between the gross and effective rates for this group of Ss was .86 ± .012, no great differences in the magnitude of the correlations between gross rate and processing of phrases and effective rate and processing of phrases should be anticipated.

Table 3.   Relation of percentage of words correctly perceived to gross reading rate and effective reading rate

	Time Units					Basic Span
	2-0-2	3-0-2	4-0-2	5-0-2	6-0-2	2-0-0
Gross Reading Rate						
r	.63	.58	.48	.55	.22	.32
SE	.076	.083	.097	.087	.019	.080
Effective Reading Rate						
r	.68	.63	.57	.58	.30	.23
SE	.067	.075	.085	.084	.114	.120

Eye Movements

The evidence presented in the literature on visual perception in reading establishes quite clearly the tendency for slow readers, in reading

---

[4]The effective reading rate is computed by multiplying the gross number of words read by the percentage of correct answers on the test of comprehension.

simple prose, to use a smaller span of visual perception and a longer fixation pause than do faster readers. There are, however, many exceptions to this tendency. These exceptions are doubtless, in many instances, due to the interaction of certain of the major factors involved. For example, the evidence on speed and accuracy of processing visual stimuli of simple phrases of sense material shows that short phrases can be processed faster and with fewer errors than longer phrases. Consequently certain slow readers may, by keeping their units of visual perception very small, be able to read simple prose with shorter than average fixation pauses. The record of Subject R is a good illustration of this type of reading pattern. She read simple prose at the rate of 186 words per minute, with good comprehension. Her eye movement records show that she used 80 fixations per 100 words with average fixation pauses of 6.4 thirtieths of a second. Her fixation pauses were much shorter than the average for slow readers. On the speed of perception tests she demonstrated a high degree of speed and accuracy of processing short phrases of sense material, but was very slow and inaccurate in processing long phrases. The record of Subject P reveals a very different pattern. This S read simple prose at 176 words per minute. Her eye movement records show that she used 53 fixations per 100 words, but with an average fixation pause of 9.4 thirtieths of a second. Her wide span of perception and unusually long fixation pauses reveal a very different pattern from that of R. The speed of perception tests reveal that P needs a considerably longer interval of time free from interfering stimuli than the average college student in order to make use of her larger than average span of visual perception.

The fixation pauses in reading serve three purposes. First, the eyes are much more efficient in transmitting the visual stimuli to the cortex when at rest than when in motion. Therefore, the eyes are stopped along the line of print in order to achieve maximum functional efficiency. Second, in order to achieve maximum efficiency in processing the visual stimuli, the retina or cortex needs an interval of time free from interfering visual stimuli. The length of this uninterrupted period is determined by the length of the fixation pause. Individual differences in the length of time needed for retinal or central processing of the visual stimuli no doubt account in part for individual differences in the length of the fixation pauses in reading simple prose. The first two purposes are prerequisites to the third, namely, providing time needed to comprehend the ideas and relationships involved. The substantial correlation .50 ± .14 between the speed and accuracy of visual perception as measured by Test 2-0-2 and the length of the fixation pauses in reading simple prose seems to support this theory.

Summary of Findings

The findings of the investigation may be summarized as follows:

1. Among college students the span of visual perception is unequally influenced by an increased restriction in the period of freedom from interfering visual stimuli following the presentation of simple phrase material.

2. For the average college student, if the phrases are left on the screen for 1/5 or 1/4 of a second before the extraneous visual material is presented, the extraneous visual material has little influence on the span of visual perception.

3. In exceptional cases, Ss needed more than 1/4 of a second to be able to avoid the interference of the extraneous material.

4. The narrower the span of perception the easier it is to avoid the influence of the extraneous visual material.

5. Interfering stimuli have a greater influence on the span of visual perception for the slow readers than they do for the fast readers.

6. The greater the degree of freedom from interfering stimuli the lower the correlation between span of visual perception and rate of reading.

7. There is a substantial correlation between the length of the fixation pauses Ss use in reading simple prose material and the speed with which the Ss can process tachistoscopically-presented stimuli resulting from simple phrases.

REFERENCES

Arnoult, D. C., & Tinker, M. A. The fixational pause of the eyes. *J. exp. Psychol.,* 1939, *25,* 271-280.

Gilbert, L. C. Influence of interfering stimuli on perception of meaningful material. *Calif. J. educ. Res.,* 1959, *10,* 15-23.

Huey, E. B. *The psychology and pedagogy of reading.* Macmillan, 1912.

Vernon, M. D. *The experimental study of reading.* Cambridge Univer. Press, 1931.

Woodworth, R. S., & Schlosberg, H. *Experimental psychology.* Henry Holt, 1954.

Perception

Trends in Perceptual Development:
Implications for the Reading Process[*]

ELEANOR J. GIBSON
Cornell University

Just about 13 years ago I was spending a year at the Institute for Advanced Study in Princeton, New Jersey, working with great determination, but not as great confidence, on a book on perceptual learning and development. I had planned this book, struggled with problems of theory construction and pursued relevant research (not only my own but other people's) ever since my arrival at Cornell in 1949. I had thought of it much earlier when I was a graduate student. Still, it wasn't going as smoothly as I had hoped. One day two of my Cornell colleagues telephoned and said they wanted to come to Princeton and talk about a new joint research proposal to study basic psychological processes involved in reading. I said no, this was the year of the book. But they came anyhow and argued that perceptual development was undoubtedly a major factor in the acquisition of reading skill and that reading was an appropriate as well as a useful area in which to apply the theory I had been developing.

A few weeks of thought convinced me that they were right, and I began planning experiments that were under way less than a year later. For the most part the book lay fallow as far as writing went until 1964, when I started it all over again at the Center for Advanced Study in the

*Reprinted from Anne D. Pick (Ed.), *Minnesota Symposia on Child Psychology, 8,* 1974, 24-54. Copyright 1974 by the University of Minnesota, University of Minnesota Press, Minneapolis. Reprinted with permission.

NOTE: The writer wishes to acknowledge support from the National Institute of Mental Health and from the United States Office of Education during the period of work covered in this paper. Acknowledgement and deepest appreciation are due to the many (onetime) students who contributed so heavily to the research described. Some of the research was done in collaboration with the author but much of it was done independently as theses and research reports.

Behavioral Sciences. This time I knew where I was going and it pretty much wrote itself. Since 1960 I have had twin projects that seem to dovetail very neatly—seeking to understand the principles of perceptual learning and development and trying to apply them to the reading process.

The purpose of this paper is to explain how the theory and the experiments are related. Since I cannot describe the theory in detail in a brief paper, I have decided to try to show how the experiments are related to the three trends in perceptual development that I discussed in the last chapter of my book. They were generated by a long foregrounding in theoretical concepts and factual descriptions of the development of perception of objects, the spatial layout, events, pictures, and symbols, and so these trends serve as a summary that I find exceedingly useful. The three trends were identified as: 1) increasing specificity of correspondence between information in stimulation and the differentiation of perception; 2) increasing optimization of attention; 3) increasing economy in the perceptual process of information pickup.

Other trends in cognitive development, in a wider sense, could be pointed out, and they might be equally or nearly as relevant for understanding the process of learning to read. One that seems to me especially important is the increasing ability to be *aware* of one's own cognitive processes, from the segmentation of the phonetic stream all the way up to the understanding of strategies of learning and problem solving. There seems to be a kind of consciousness-raising that goes along with many aspects of cognitive development, and it turns out, I think, to be associated with attaining mature reading skills. But I shall confine myself to the three trends I mentioned and to some of the research associated with them.

Increasing Specificity

Perceptual learning, as I see it, is characterized by an increased specificity of correspondence between stimulation and the precision of the responding organism's discrimination. My husband and I argued many years ago that the essence of perceptual learning was differentiation rather than enrichment and this kind of learning was not adding something like a response or an image to sensations but rather was a change in *what* was responded *to* uniquely and specifically (Gibson & Gibson, 1955). Early experiments with Dr. Anne Pick and Dr. Harry Osser (Gibson, Gibson, Pick, & Osser, 1962) pursued this trend and demonstrated the progress of the discrimination of letter-like forms and the way in which confusions decreased and unique identifications increased with age. In later research (Gibson, Osser, Schiff, & Smith, 1963; Gibson, Schapiro, & Yonas, 1968) I sought to specify the distinctive features that are used in letter discrimination and to compare them for several age groups. All of this work was at the perceptual level, and I would of course acknowledge that reading, although based on perception, is a very complex cognitive process.

For this reason I have been speculating further, perhaps overboldly, about the role of differentiation in reading. I am inclined to think that the problem of perceptual differentiation is accompanied by the growth of meaning, first at a perceptual level and later at a more abstract semantic level. The process of differentiating things and events in the world requires the abstraction of contrastive distinctive features and invariants. Objects, events, and their functional relations in the world are differentiated so that perceptions of them come to correspond with information in stimulation at a pretty early age. But the symbolic notations for these objects, events, and relations (*words* both spoken and written) come into more specific correspondence with their referents only later and more gradually. I propose the hypothesis that the meanings of words, like the meanings of things and events, are gradually differentiated and *converge*, eventually, with the meanings of things (and pictures of things, which are also differentiated very early [Hochberg & Brooks, 1962; Ryle, 1966]).

The meaning itself, I think, is *abstract*—neither imagistic nor linguistic. Semantic meaning may in its origins be an abstraction from the distinctive features (themselves abstracted) that permit perceptual differentiation (cf. Clark, 1973). Lexical features of words must in some sense correspond with distinctive features of things and of the events in which they are constituents, but the lexical features presumably are arrived at later. I believe that only much later are they *accessed* as immediately as are distinctive features of perceived objects, especially when the word is written. These arguments are consistent with and may help to explain the observation that immediacy of access to meaning from written verbal input is a characteristic of developmental progress in reading.

An experiment was designed on the basis of the argument just presented (Gibson, Barron, & Garber, 1972). The method was to compare over a wide range of ages the judgments of sameness or difference of a pair of pictures, a pair of words, and a pair consisting of a word and a picture. We predicted that the reaction time of the younger subjects especially would be faster when the items they were judging were presented in the same mode than when the modes were mixed (picture with word). We further predicted a developmental decline in the difference between single mode and mixed mode latencies, with the mixed mode latency converging toward the single mode conditions. The reasoning was that if matching can only be done on the basis of meaning and if the meanings of the word and the thing gradually come to have the same abstract representation with the same access time, then the difference between single mode and dual mode comparisons should progressively decline with age.

Since we wished our subjects to make a comparison on the level of meaning rather than on physical match, sets of words were prepared in two kinds of type (upper and lower case), a condition that has been found to discourage the processing of only graphic features (Posner & Mitchell, 1967), although processing could still stop at a naming stage. Two versions of each picture were also prepared representing similar, but not physically identical, objects—for instance two fish pictured from different angles or differing in a few noncritical details. Simple outline drawings of 12 objects (fish, bird, dog, cup, sock, boat, frog, lamb, cat, key, iron, plane), each in two versions, were prepared on slides, and the names of the objects were set in two kinds of type. The slides were combined appropriately in three conditions: PP, in which pairs of pictures of the same object or two different objects were to be compared; WW, in which pairs of words, either the same word or two different words, were to be compared; and WP, in which a picture and a word indicating the same object or two different ones were to be compared.

The experiment thus had three display conditions, with types of display presented in random order. Half of the displays required a same judgment and half required a different judgment. Each S saw all three types of display, prepared on slides and projected simultaneously with position (right or left) counterbalanced. Subjects were drawn from the second, fourth, and sixth grades and from a college group of summer school students.

Median latencies for each display condition and for each type of response (same or different) were computed for each subject. Means of these medians for the different age groups are presented in Table 1. An analysis of variance showed that the main effects of age and display conditions were significant, but there was not a significant difference overall between same and different responses. It should be noted, however, that *same* responses are shorter in seven out of eight cases for the *unimodal* displays. This trend is in accord with the typical finding in many previous experiments (cf. for example, Gibson, Schapiro, & Yonas, 1968).

The interaction between grade and display, the result of particular interest to us, was significant (p<.025). There was a relative decline with age in the difference between the dual mode (WP) condition and the other two. A difference score was calculated by the formula WP - $\frac{WW + PP}{2}$ and is plotted for the three age groups in Figure 1. The rationale of this formula was that bimodal comparison would take longer than unimodal in either mode but that as meaning of a word and its pictured counterpart converged toward the same abstract semantic features the difference would decrease. From the second to the sixth grade the predicted downward trend is evident in the responses of different. The trend is absent, however, for the responses of same.

MINNESOTA SYMPOSIA ON CHILD PSYCHOLOGY

Table 1.   Mean latencies for each grade as a function of display condition and type of response (in msec)

Grade	Picture-Picture Display		Word-Word Display		Word-Picture Display	
	Same	Different	Same	Different	Same	Different
Two	1,957	1,987	2,044	2,133	2,141	2,281
Four	1,364	1,343	1,318	1,330	1,479	1,418
Six	1,114	1,194	1,132	1,162	1,224	1,221
College	821	856	783	842	939	893

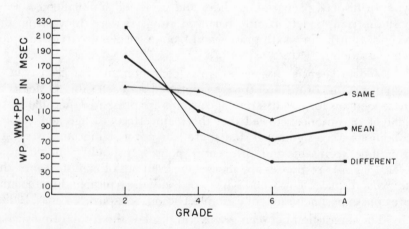

Figure 1.   Difference in latency between the WP condition and the mean of the PP and WW conditions across grades.

A second interaction, a triple interaction of grade, display, and type of response (same or different), was also significant (p<.001). An interpretation of this interaction was suggested in a comparison of some first-order effects at different grade levels. For the second-grade subjects the PP condition had a shorter latency than the WW condition. Fourth and sixth graders did not differ in latency for the PP and WW conditions; but the adults had a longer latency on the PP comparison than on the WW comparison. When same responses and different responses were compared for the WP condition, an age difference again appeared. The responses of same were shorter for second graders but the responses of different were shorter for college students. (The apparent difference for fourth graders was not significant.) There appears to be a radical difference in the processing of WP displays by second graders, and by adults.

What can we say about these differences that might throw light on the development of processing the meaning of written words? The speculation is as follows. Perhaps for the second grader the WW condition elicits the naming of words. When the second grader is faced with a WP display, he looks at the picture first, since pictures are salient and highly meaningful for him but written words are less so. He names the picture to himself in order to compare the name with the word. If the word coincides with the name, his reading will be facilitated and thus the same judgments will be faster (as they were, by 140 msec.).[1] But for adults words have become highly salient; they arouse a meaning before the word is spoken. The abstract meaning of the word can be compared directly with the abstract meaning of the picture. If they are different, no further processing is necessary. The picture need not be named because the meaning was accessed before the name (Moore, 1919).

What sort of process might the hypothesized comparison entail for the adult? The meaning of a word, I assume, is a set of abstract lexical features, such as animate, nonhuman, house pet, furry, etc., derived from earlier comparisons of real things. These features for the word could be compared with semantic features for the picture. In the WP condition of the present experiment, this comparison might take place serially. Template or "wholistic" processing seems implausible, if not impossible, with two modes of presentation. Thus a mismatch would be identified earlier than a match, and the judgments of different would be faster than the judgments of same. The other features need not be checked out, nor need the *name* of the picture even be processed for a judgment of different. Why should same judgments, on the other hand, be faster in the

---

[1] A recent experiment by Garber (personal communication) confirms the fact that reading a word at this age is facilitated if it is preceded by a picture identifiable by the same word.

unimodal comparisons? We can only speculate that unimodal same comparisons can be made on a more wholistic or superficial basis, especially when the set of items has become known, because some physical features, like the tails of the fish or the similarity of two letters (e.g., C and c, S and S) might suffice for the making of a match.

This view of the picture-word comparison of the adult predicts that a different pair would require a greater amount of time for a decision, the more features the members of the pair share (e.g., deciding that *cat* and *dog* are different should take longer than *cat* and *iron*). Insofar as our data afford a comparison, the results are in accord with the prediction, but the data are too few to provide a convincing test. Dr. R. W. Barron is at present replicating the experiment with a proper test of the hypothesis. We should not expect to find this result for children at the second-grade level, for we suspect that they would do an entirely different kind of processing (naming the picture and comparing it with the word) before they have attained a well-developed set of abstract lexical features that is easily accessed by the printed word.

Some of the assumptions we are making are shared by other psychologists. That meaning is abstract, neither imagistic nor linguistic, has been defended not only by the Wurzburg school (cf. Moore, 1919) but more recently as well. Chase and Clark (1972) say for instance: "Our results suggest that the comprehension of both pictures and sentences must ultimately be represented in the same mental symbolic system. We do not mean by this that the ultimate representation of pictures and sentences is identical to linguistic descriptions of deep structure, but rather that there is a deep or conceptual structure that is common to both sentences and pictures. . . . Our conception is that meaning is to be found in a modality-free symbolic memory, but can be converted into modality-specific images when this is wanted" [p. 225].

The assumption that denotative meaning can be analyzed as a set of lexical features or abstract "semantic markers" was proposed by Katz and Fodor (1963). The notion of abstract semantic features is thus not new, nor is the notion that there is a correspondence between distinctive features of objects and the set of semantic features that comprise lexical meanings. That idea was suggested by Rubenstein (1971) as follows: "If they are the same, we would have a single set of features which would serve as locators for lexical entries both when the input is conceptual as well as when it is perceptual. To play both these roles these features would have to be abstract, that is, not lexical entries themselves . . ." [p. 50]. A similar view has been proposed by Clark (1973), who was particularly interested in the development in children of the semantic features of words.

Now we have come full circle to the hypothesis with which I started: that meanings of words converge developmentally toward a more specific correspondence with the meanings of things and events. I conceive of the meanings of both as sets of abstract features, but they are abstracted for objects early in life, while the development of abstract meanings for words progresses later as language and then reading skills are acquired. The immature reader does not access the abstract meanings directly from the word as he reads it. He probably decodes it to a phonetic representation and matches words (the name of this object and the word he has decoded), in contrast to the adult who has become capable of matching word and picture meanings directly via comparison of amodal, abstract features that have progressed to a high degree of correspondence. These ideas as presently formulated are doubtless more provocative than convincing, but I think the time has come to grope with the problem of how the printed word elicits meaning.

Optimization of Attention

One of the most striking aspects of perceptual development is the improvement of strategies for extracting the relevant and wanted information. Selection of critical features improves progressively, as does the apparent ability to ignore noisy, irrelevant information. The descriptive applicability of this trend to the acquisition of reading skill is so obvious that I hardly need argue it. But I would like to be more explicit. To do so it is necessary to talk a little first about what's in a word—what kinds of information it provides. That a written word has *graphic* information is an essential characteristic of a writing system. A written word has potential *acoustic* information too. We can read it aloud or *sotto voce* to ourselves or we can imagine how it sounds. It can carry *syntactic* and *morphological* information: it is a part of speech like a noun or a verb and it may be inflected to indicate that it is a modifier or a particular tense or plural rather than singular. Most important, a word carries *semantic* information. Our interest in communication is to get across our meaning to someone else or to discover the meaning of what the other one is saying or writing.

Optimization of attention in reading is uniquely characterized, I think, by the reader's ability to extract that aspect of the information that is most useful to him and to ignore or give secondary priority to the rest. I do not think the other information is often completely ignored; an example in point would be Rothkopf's (1971) finding that subjects who were instructed to read to learn facts from a text and who knew they were to be tested on their reading, retained some information about where a reference to a given fact had appeared in the text. Nevertheless, an optimal reading strategy usually assigns some priorities to certain aspects of the information which results in selective reading.[2]

The aspect of the information that should be selectively attended to depends on the reader's task—the purpose he has assigned himself or the instructions given him by his teacher or perhaps his boss. He may want to get the closing prices at the end of the day for 10 Wall Street stocks, which will result in a scan-and-pause strategy; he may be reading to learn his lines for a play, which will result in alternation of reading and rehearsal, with rather strong attention to phonetic aspects of the material so that he can try out intonations.

One can think of reading tasks which give priority to every one of the aspects of written text that I have mentioned. I have done experiments on only a few of them, but one task I have investigated in detail with the help of my colleagues and students is the task of scanning down a list to find a target such as a letter or a word. The experiments considered as a whole illustrate quite well the highly selective attention of the scanner to one kind of information so as to optimize the efficiency of the scan.

The first of these experiments was carried out in collaboration with Dr. A. Yonas (Gibson & Yonas, 1966a). We used a scan-and-search task modeled on that of Neisser (1963), with a few alterations to make it more feasible for children. Second-grade children and college students scanned down a list for a single letter target randomly inserted in different list positions to cover all positions equally over a series of trials. Although the children had much slower scan rates than the college students, the children did scan quite systematically, as is shown by the correlation between list position and time for scan. The correlation increases for college students, however, so attention in the scanning does become more systematic with age. Scanning rate, as well, becomes enormously faster with development.

There is strong evidence that in this task the subjects attend with high priority to graphic information. Gibson and Yonas (1966a) compared the effect of high and low graphic similarity of context letters to a target letter. Embedding a target letter in a context of letters containing many of the same distinctive features slows the scanning rate greatly, compared to the

---

[2] Compare this idea with a statement by Luria: "The characteristic feature of the adult's verbal meanings is that *the word preserves in itself all systems of connections inherent in it,* beginning with the very elementary and visual and ending with the very complex and abstract. Depending on the task, any of the systems of connections can become dominant. Without this ability, flexible thinking is impossible" (Luria, 1969, p. 137).

rate for finding the same letter embedded in a set with different features. This effect holds for both seven-year-old children and adults, but the interference in one experiment was relatively greater for the children, suggesting that adults may have developed greater efficiency in attending to minimal, optimal distinctive features in this task. Given an opportunity for practice, subjects learn to scan for a single very economical graphic feature as Yonas (1969) and Schapiro (1970) showed in appropriate transfer experiments.

Gibson and Yonas (1966b) also investigated the effect of extra-modal auditory interference on the scanning task. While scanning the list visually, the subject heard over earphones a voice pronouncing letters with names similar in sound to the target letter. Somewhat to our surprise there was no effect at all on the scanning rate of adults or even of seven-year-old children. Acoustic features of letters, or the sound of their names at least, appeared to be virtually ignored in this task. Obviously pronouncing all the letters subvocally while scanning for the target would slow the scanning rate, so this attentive strategy is highly economical. Kaplan, Yonas, and Shurcliff (1966) provided confirmation for this conclusion in a different experiment in which they compared the effect of high and low acoustic similarity of context letter names to the name of the target letter. The target was embedded in a context of letters that rhymed with it (e.g., B, V, D, T) or in a context of nonrhyming letters. Unlike graphic similarity of context, there was no effect on rate of scan of rhyming similarity. Acoustic similarity can, however, produce confusion and interference in another task, notably short-term memory, in which the subject attends particularly to the acoustic information, presumably as an aid to rehearsal.

The lack of interference from competing auditory stimulation in the second-grade children might seem to argue against developing optimization of attentional strategies. But in another thesis experiment, performed by Shepela (1971), improvement of attentional strategies with bimodal input was found when somewhat younger age groups were compared. She performed a detection experiment, a developmental study of "bimodal vigilance," with kindergarten and second-grade children. They detected a given target presented at intervals within a rapid succession of other items under both unimodal and bimodal conditions. The unimodal condition consisted of either a succession of pictures accompanied by the instruction to press a key whenever a picture of a bird appeared or a succession of spoken words presented over earphones with the instruction to press the key whenever the word "bird" was heard. The bimodal condition combined the two types of presentation but target occurrence for the two modes was not redundant. For the kindergarten children, target detection was significantly impaired under the bimodal condition, but for the second-grade children there was no impairment at all compared to unimodal presentation at the same rates. These children were able to attend successfully to both modes of input when the task required it.

It is interesting to ask whether semantic information is picked up in a scanning task. That it *can* be is suggested by findings from experiments in which the subject is required to search for a target *word* which is embedded in a list of other words. Neisser and Beller (1965) asked Ss to search for a word naming a member of a category, such as an animal (e.g., cat, dog, tiger). They were not given a specific target and the target item shifted from trial to trial. The scanning rate was fast, even though the S presumably had to examine each word individually for meaning. The rate, about 300 words per minute, is almost identical to the speed of scan found in a comparable experiment by Gibson, Tenney, and Zaslow (1971) and compares very favorably with the rate of scanning for a single letter. The rate of scan for a single letter tends, in fact, to be considerably slower, depending of course on the type of context, whether the target is repeated or changed, and on practice. Does this comparison imply that in scanning meaning is picked up faster than graphic information? Probably not. A word can be picked up as a whole, but random strings of letters must be scanned letter by letter. In a thesis by Clare (1969) it was shown that pronounceability (orthographic acceptability) of a target item significantly facilitated the search for the item as compared to a random string of letters; so the strategy of searching for a "whole" item, a string of letters that can be picked up as a unit, appears to be the important factor. The fact that context words were poorly remembered perhaps bears this out, but context letters in letter search are poorly remembered too. Unfortunately we have no data at present on children's rate of scan for words as compared with letters, so we do not know how early this attentive strategy develops.

Gibson, Tenney, and Zaslow (1971) investigated the effect on search rate of common categorical meaning in context items (e.g., all items are names of fruit) as opposed to a different category of meaning for target items (e.g., all targets are names of animals). The question was whether semantic structure would facilitate the rate of search for a target word. The target word was embedded in a set of categorically related words. In a preliminary experiment, the S was presented with the specific target word before each scan began, but this procedure resulted in S's resorting to graphic information (scanning for the first two letters of the target, for instance), which was (or was considered to be by the *S*s) more economical than processing meaning. The procedure was changed to Neisser and Beller's, and the subject was instructed to look for a target belonging to a category, either a name of an aminal or a part of the body. (Only one category was used for a subject.) We hoped that this procedure would force *S* to process for meaning and would allow the categorical structure of the context, when present, to influence the search rate. It did not, however. Categorical structure among context words afforded no faster rate of scan than did randomly selected words carefully matched for word length, initial letters, word frequency, and so on. We were forced to conclude that meaning plays a minor role in a scanning task. "Wholeness" of the items results in fewer units for *S* to process, but apparently the presence of meaning is not the source of facilitation.

Other tasks, in contrast to search and scanning, are characterized by high utility for meaning, especially categorical meaning. A well-known example of such a task is relatively long-term, as opposed to short-term, memory. Findings from numerous experiments attest to the utility of a common category or categories in a list of words to be remembered. Subjects remember more and tend to cluster by category. In a number of experiments the development with age of attention to common categories and the utilization of them for improved recall has been investigated. Children are not as adept at using categories for this purpose as are adults, but findings about age and categorizing vary with a number of parameters in the experiments.

I would like to summarize one study concerning the development of the use of categories, a very recent Ph.D. thesis by Tenney (1973). Tenney's problem, specifically, was to study the development of strategies of cognitive organization. She wanted to relate the development of the awareness of categories to the spontaneous adaptive use of them. She employed a task designed for this purpose, asking her subjects to tell her words that would be easy to remember along with one (a "key word") that she would give them. She told them that she would write down the words and that she would ask them to remember the words later. Therefore the child could choose what material he would recall, even making use of idiosyncratic strategies if he appreciated the importance of organizational principles and could select and attend to them.

There were three experimental conditions but the subjects took part in only one. One was the *category* condition in which subjects were given a key word such as "blue" by the *E* and were told to give three words belonging to the same category, which was defined for them. There were 12 categories (such as colors, days of the week, names), all of which had previously been shown to be known by young children. The second condition was the self-directed condition in which the Ss freely generated lists specifically for the purpose of easy recall, again having been given the same 12 key words by E but without any suggestion of a category or strategy. In the third condition, the *incidental* condition, the Ss were never informed of the purpose of the task; instead they generated the lists by free-associating to the 12 key words. The subjects were drawn from kindergarten and from the third and sixth grades. They participated in two sessions scheduled a week apart. During the first session they generated their lists of words (36 words in all for each S, including the key words). In the second session they were tested for recall. The S was read a list of 12 words drawn from the lists he had generated before being asked to recall this selected list. Half of the Ss were asked to recall a clusterable list and the other half a nonclusterable list.

Tenney's experiment was so rich in results that I can only present the gist of them. When the *self-directed* condition was compared with the *incidental* condition, there was a significant age interaction. The older children used deliberate strategies for selecting words for recall, but the younger children settled for the first three words that occurred to them. Sound relationships were very apparent in the lists they generated in both conditions. The use of sound relationships declined significantly with age. The older children made greater use of categories than did the younger children no matter what the condition, although there was category structure in the younger children's lists in the *category* condition.

As for recall, the effect of age on clustering was especially interesting in light of its interaction with condition. There was no significant difference with age in clustering in the category condition. The kindergarten children were helped by the instruction to categorize and were able to make use of it. Nor was there a significant difference among children of different ages in the incidental condition. Clustering by incidental free associations was insignificant at all ages. But in the *self-directed* condition, organization by structural principle—some kind of spontaneous categorizing—increased steadily with age. The kindergarteners showed no more clustering in this condition than in the *incidental* condition, but the older children clustered well above chance. The sixth graders clustered significantly more in this condition than when they were instructed to categorize. There was a strong developmental trend from ease of organization by category structure in response to E's suggestion to ease of organization by a self-directed structure. This seems to me to be a prime example of optimization of attentional strategies with increasing age. The younger children had little insight into how things could be remembered

easily, although they could use categorical structure when it was presented to them. But the older subjects deliberately selected words according to a plan of their own, in this case one based on meaningful categorical
relationships.

Tenney's results not only illustrate the optimization of attentional
strategies with development, they also illustrate the third developmental
trend, the trend in perceptual development that I called the increasing
economy of information pickup. In the present case, the wording might
be broadened to read the increasing economy of cognitive processing.
The experiments to be discussed in the following section range, again,
from what would ordinarily be termed perceptual tasks to cognitive tasks
of presumably greater complexity such as problem solving.

Increasing Economy of Information Pickup
and Cognitive Processing

There are two important and contrasting ways of increasing the
economy of extracting information. The way that has the greatest utility
depends on the task. One is the detection and use of the *smallest possible
distinctive feature* that will permit a decision. This strategy is particularly
efficient in a scanning task or in a task requiring perceptual categorizing
of the Sternberg type. For instance, if there is a positive and a negative set
to be distinguished in a reaction time experiment, an S will learn with
practice to make his decision on the basis of the *minimal* feature difference
that separates the two sets into unique categories. This type of learning
has been documented in Ph.D. theses by Yonas (1969) and by Barron
(1971). Evidence that the tendency to find the minimal most economical
feature for perceptual categorizing increases with development is
nonexistent, so far as I know. One reason for this lack may be that the
tendency to make decisions on the basis of minimal useful information is
present as early as we can make reliable observations of the behavior.
Yonas (1969) observed children as well as adults in his experiment and
found an enormous quantitative difference in reaction time for categorizing letters but found no interaction between age and the reduction of
time with a minimal feature distinction. When the condition permitted
greater economy of processing, the children exhibited the trend. One is
tempted to conclude that cognitive processing tends toward the "least
cost" at any age. What develops, I think, is S's ability to select minimal
distinctive features that are of increasing validity and subtlety; but the
research remains to be done.

The second way of increasing economy is the use of superordinate structure and rule systems to create increasingly larger units. The detection of higher-order structure in the stimulus array is the essence of efficient cognitive processing, and a skilled reader makes use of the rule systems available in written language at many levels—the orthographic level, the syntactic and morphological levels, and the semantic level. Redundancy and constraints within words and between words provide the rules for unit formation, and a reader learns to process textual information in the *largest possible units that are appropriate for his task*. I am not the first to say this, although I believe I have worked longer than most trying to document the trend and find out how it works. Huey remarked on it in 1908 as follows: "We are brought back to the conclusion of Goldscheider and Müller that we read by phrases, words, or letters as may serve our purpose best. But we see, too, that the reader's acquirement of ease and power in reading comes through increasing ability to read in larger units" [p. 116].

Huey might have mentioned Cattell as well. Although Cattell did not note that the reader chooses the unit that serves his purpose best, he showed (Cattell, 1885) that it takes longer to read a letter than to read a word and that a word is recognized in at least as short an exposure interval as is a letter. Since then it has been demonstrated that a letter embedded in a word can be identified at shorter exposure durations than a letter exposed alone (Baron & Thurston, 1973; Reicher, 1969; Wheeler, 1970). Words can be recognized at a distance in type too small to permit the recognition of an individual letter (Erdmann & Dodge, 1898). And detection of a word target in a search-and-scanning task is faster than detection of a letter target (Gibson, Tenney, & Zaslow, 1971; Neisser & Beller, 1965).

It is the principle of extracting and processing higher-order structure that is particularly applicable to the reading process. I would like to show how work of mine and my students relates to this principle and how we have tried to locate the relevant structural variables. What are the structural principles for unit formation? Cattell thought that the "word-superiority effect," as it is often referred to, was the result of the word's familiarity and meaning. But there are other possibilities that, as it turns out, deserve even more serious consideration. There are rules or predictable relations within words and there are relations, syntactical rules, and meaningful relations between words in phrases, sentences and passages of discourse. It is these relations with which I am concerned in this section.

Use of Orthographic Regularities within the Word

English has conditional rule systems for spelling that are morpho-phonemic in nature. Syllables may be morphemic units, but whether a syllable is a morpheme or not, it is a unit with some describable rules. It must have a vocalic center, which may or may not be preceded or followed by a consonant or a consonant cluster. The consonants, and especially the consonant clusters, are often constrained as to whether they can appear in initial or final position. English, compared to many other languages, makes wide use of consonant clusters, and these are nearly always constrained. According to Fries (1963) of the more than 150 consonant clusters in frequent use in English, all but three are constrained to initial or final position. Consider such examples as *script, strict, cling, twelfth.* Other vowels can be inserted in the center of the monosyllable and it retains legal English orthography as long as a vowel is present. But in no case can the final and initial consonant cluster be exchanged without violating English spelling patterns. This feature of English spelling provides enormous redundancy of a useful nature in the sense that there is more than one source of information (beyond the single letter) for what the word can be.

There is also redundancy of a different kind in sets of English spelling patterns that are easily classified and contrasted, thus yielding useful rule-like systems. Fries (1963) has categorized these and the following are examples:

bat→ bate	bit→ bite	cot→ cote
cat→ cate	fit→ fite	dot→ dote
fat→ fate	kit→ kite	got→ gote
mat→ mate	mit→ mite	mot→ mote

There are many such repetitive patterns in English and they provide for easy generalization in reading new English words, once the youthful reader has learned the principle. According to Garner (1962), there is more redundancy within words than between them, so it is not a waste of time to study the development of pickup of higher-order structure at the word level, even though we ordinarily read in larger units like phrases and clauses. I will describe research from our laboratory on intraword redundancy which is grouped by four experimental paradigms that supplement one another.

Tachistoscopic word recognition. The first of these experiments was performed by Gibson, Pick, Osser, and Hammond in 1962. Nonwords, termed pseudowords, were generated using constrained initial and terminal consonant clusters with a vowel between to provide two contrasting lists called (at that time) pronounceable and unpronounceable, respectively. The pronounceable items were monosyllabic (e.g., SLAND) and orthographically legal but they did not have referential meaning. The unpronounceable items were constructed by exchanging the initial and final consonant clusters (e.g., NDASL). The items, 25 of each, were presented to Ss tachistoscopically in a mixed order. Numerous replications of the experiment in which parameters such as exposure time, repetition, type of judgment (e.g., identification, recognition in a multiple choice set), and method of scoring were varied have yielded the same result as did the original experiment. The legal pseudowords are perceived better than the illegal ones.

The original experiment was performed on adults. We followed it up with an experiment on children who had just finished first or third grade (Gibson, Osser, & Pick, 1963). Sets of three-letter words and nonsense syllables were constructed to yield a real word in the first grader's reading vocabulary, a legal nonword made by permuting the letters of the word, and an illegal nonword (e.g., *ran, nar, rna*). The words and legal nonwords were all of the CVC pattern. Twenty four- and five-letter nonwords, ten of them legal ones and ten their illegal counterparts, were added. The items were presented tachistoscopically in a randomized sequence and the children spelled out what they saw (an undesirable way of getting the response, since it could encourage letter-by-letter looking, but seemingly unavoidable). For the three-letter items, words were read best overall, legal pseudowords next best, and illegal pseudowords least well. The two types of longer pseudowords were not differentiated from each other by first graders. All of them, whether legal or illegal, were read poorly. But the third graders read the legal combinations of longer pseudowords better than illegal ones. Accuracy did not approach that of adult Ss, but the difference between the two types was discriminated by some of the third graders.

We began by calling the legal pseudowords "pronounceable," implying thereby that ease of pronunciation had something to do with their superiority. Later when we recast our thinking in terms of an orthographic rule system, with all of its potential constraints and regularities, the pronounceability of the items became a less appealing choice and it certainly was not the only possible facilitator. An experiment was therefore run comparing deaf and hearing Ss of college age (Gibson, Shurcliff,

& Yonas, 1970). The subjects were given instructions in sign language and wrote down what they saw. A new comparison group of hearing Ss of similar age was run. The deaf Ss, chosen for maximal and congenital or extremely early hearing loss, perceived fewer words correctly overall than did the hearing Ss, but the difference between the two sets of words was just as significant and just as striking for the deaf as for the hearing, suggesting that orthographic rules, rather than ease of pronouncing, accounted for the difference.

Each deaf S wrote a paragraph about how he had learned to read. We gained little from the factual content of these paragraphs, but the almost total absence of spelling errors was notable, although there were frequent grammatical and morphological errors. Evidently generalized spelling patterns and rules can be learned without the benefit of hearing accompanying sound mappings.

In an attempt to compare the roles of meaning and of pronounceability (as we were still calling it) on recognition and on recall, Gibson, Bishop, Schiff, and Smith (1964) prepared sets of nonword trigrams that varied in both meaningfulness and pronounceability. There were three types: one had referential meaning and formed a set of well-known initials (e.g., IBM); the second was a reordering of the initials in a CVC pronounceable arrangement (e.g., BIM); and the third was a reordering of the initials in a non-CVC unpronounceable arrangement (e.g., MBI). Recognition thresholds for the three types of items were obtained by increasing the brightness contrast of an item until it was read correctly. The lowest threshold was obtained for the pronounceable items. The difference was highly significant compared to both of the other types. The meaningful items did have an advantage, however, over the unpronounceable meaningless items; therefore meaningfulness of an item was apparently effective, even though its utility for this method of reading was not as great as was the unit structure of the spelling pattern. When the same items were tested for recall, the utility of the two features (meaningfulness and structure) was reversed; meaningfulness was more effective for enhancing recall.

Morphological features of a word such as classes of morpheme provide another system that might assist in forming structural units. I thought at first, naively it now seems, that adding a well-known inflectional ending to a base word would create a subordinate unit and thus make it easier to read and afford a longer letter span than a noninflected word of equal total length. Gibson and Guinet (1971) investigated the effect of adding a verb inflection (present tense s, past tense ed, or progressive ing) to monosyllabic base words of three kinds—real verbs such as *rain,* legal permutations such as *nair,* and illegal ones such as *nrai.* The bases varied in length from three to six letters. The words were presented tachistoscopically to third- and fifth-grade children and to adults. The extension of word length by inflection did not increase the length of the word that could be read (e.g., when an inflected word like *trying* was compared with a noninflected word like *listen,* the inflected word had no advantage). The results for nonwords indicated that an inflected ending, per se, was perceived as an intact unit when compared with a segment of the word of equivalent length without morphological significance. Older children noticed and commented on inflections more often than did younger children.

A base morpheme would seem to have priority for the reader; but an inflection also has integrity. These two features of a word, we concluded, provide different kinds of information, and the information is probably extracted independently. That the meaning of the base morpheme is processed separately from that of the tense marker was suggested by the tendency for *S*s to confuse inflected endings and sometimes to substitute one for another. With a fast exposure the *S* in such a case perceived the base morpheme and noted that it was inflected but did not have time to process the inflection accurately. Thus there may be two kinds of meaning within the word, each with its own rules.

Scanning experiments. Scanning experiments—searching for a word or letter target—have provided a small amount of evidence for the use of intraword structural constraints. As we remarked earlier, word-search is faster than letter-search and a pronounceable legal nonword is a better target than an illegal one (Clare, 1969). Gibson, Tenney, Barron, and Zaslow (1972) sought to determine whether or not context letter strings that were well structured orthographically would permit a faster search rate than poorly structured strings of context letters. The *S*s scanned for a single-letter target embedded in lists with or without good orthographic structure in the context items (e.g., *sland* versus *ndasl; clept* versus *ptecl*). The identical target letter was assigned to all lists. Subjects were fifth-grade children and adults. In neither age group did orthographically well-structured context facilitate the discovery of the target letter. Apparently any advantage of a structured background that could be processed in units larger than a letter was cancelled by the necessity of further processing for a specific target letter. The pickup of orthographic structure was apparently not the most economical strategy in this high-speed scanning task and was not used; the *S*s settled for graphic features.

If built-in structure were made economical for a search task, it should, according to our view, be used. Zaslow (1972), in a senior honors thesis, designed a search task in which a structural feature of orthography had potential utility. She selected consonant clusters constrained as to position within the word (e.g., *CL* would be a possible initial cluster only, whereas *PT* would be a possible final cluster only) and assigned such clusters (half initial and half final) as targets for search, using a different target for each list. In one condition the target was in its legal constrained position in a pronounceable five-letter string (e.g., *CLEPT*); the target assigned might be either CL or PT. The 29 context items were also five-letter pronounceable strings, all different but formed in the same way (e.g., *GLINK, FRAND,* etc.). In the other condition unpronounceable target and context items were constructed by reversing the consonant clusters (e.g., *PTECL*) and the same targets were assigned. Thus in one condition a given target item was located in a legal position in a string embedded in similarly formed strings. In the other condition the identical target was located in the reverse, illegal position in a string embedded in similar orthographically illegal strings. The subjects were unaware of the method of list construction.

The *S*s (college students) located the targets faster when they were in their properly constrained positions. They thus generalized this knowledge of consonant constraint to advantage, even though the letter strings were not words. The experiment bears out the previous findings that good orthographic structure is a critical factor in the word-superiority effect, and it also confirms the notion that consonant constraint is an important feature of orthographic structure.

Judging word-likeness. Word recognition under enforced, very brief exposure is not a usual condition of reading, so it is interesting to ask whether other types of judgment will reveal the generalizability of the word-superiority effect. A method employed by several of my students has proved successful in extending some of the conclusions stated above. The *S* is presented with a pair of nonwords, one orthographically regular and one not, and asked to judge "which is more like a real word." Rosinski and Wheeler (1972) presented pairs of nonwords taken from the lists of Gibson et al. (1962, 1963) to children from the first, third, and fifth grade. The words varied in length from three to six letters. The first graders performed at chance level, but the third and fifth graders ranged from 69 to 80 percent correct in their choices. Word length in this experiment did not have a significant effect. Nine of the 16 first graders were located the following year and retested. They still did not discriminate between the word types.

Golinkoff (1972) repeated this experiment with several changes. The pairs of nonwords used by Rosinski and Wheeler had not been matched in the sense of being counterparts of one another; for instance a pair might be CLATS versus SPIGR. We thought that contrasting arrangements of the same letters would provide better control and would also be more likely to elicit a discrimination. Pairs of nonsense words ranged from three to six letters each in length. The poorly structured item in the four- to six-letter pairs had a consonant cluster illegally placed in either initial or final position (e.g., TARB - RBAT; GRET - TEGR). There were three conditions of the experiment, two of them adding redundant auditory information to the visually presented items. In one of them, the S heard the word pronounced over a tape recorder as he looked at the printed item. In the other he was asked to read the words aloud as he looked at them. All the Ss were drawn from second grade, toward the end of the school year. The children, over all conditions, discriminated the two types of nonword better than chance (74 percent correct), but neither of the auditory conditions differed from the nonauditory condition. Redundant sound did not facilitate judgment, either because the children pronounced the word subvocally when they were told only to look at it or because judgment of orthographic legality is based on purely visual information. Word length, as in the Rosinski and Wheeler experiment, made no difference, but there was some tendency to make more accurate judgments when the misplaced cluster appeared at the beginning of the word rather than at the end.

Golinkoff (1973) repeated her experiment, with modifications, with Ss from first and second grade (late in the school year). There were three conditions of word presentation: visual, auditory, and redundant visual and auditory. The results revealed an interaction of age with condition. First-grade children performed only slightly better than chance with visual or auditory presentation alone, but they performed significantly better (72 percent correct) when the presentation was bimodal. But the second graders were significantly better with visual presentation alone (82.5 percent correct, as compared to 65 percent for auditory presentation and 70 percent for bimodal presentation). Thus combining auditory and visual presentation appeared to help in the beginning stages of learning to read, but toward the end of second grade, visual information for word-likeness had become of predominant importance. Golinkoff correlated performance on the word-likeness test with reading scores on the Metropolitan Achievement Test (given at the end of the year) and found a significant relationship ($r = .50$). We infer that ability to generalize knowledge of English orthography does reflect reading ability measured in other ways.

Learning experiments. Taken together, the preceding experiments suggest that normally children are learning and generalizing at least some aspects of the orthographic rule system in the second grade. How are they doing it? The research strategy by which I attempted to answer this question was a combination of training with a series of small problems requiring abstraction of a common spelling pattern and a learning set procedure. A typical problem consisted of eight words or word-like letter strings, each printed on a card, which the child was to sort into two piles. Half of the words had two letters in common in a given position; the other four contained the two letters but they were never arranged in the same way. When the common pattern was present, the other letters always differed. A typical sorting problem might be:

mean	name
beat	belt
leap	laep
read	road

The words were presented in random order and E corrected sorting errors, but the child made the abstraction for himself as in a concept learning experiment. He was not required to proceed for more than a specified number of trials (four trials in the first experiment) if he did not succeed in sorting correctly, but he was given a new problem. One problem followed another, six a day over five days of training in the first experiment (Gibson, Farber, & Shepela, 1968). The first children tested were in kindergarten and the experiment was not only grueling both for experimenters and for children, but it was a monumental failure. Only one child developed a learning set, showing gradually increasing success over problems. The next year we tried a slightly modified procedure with first-grade children with only a little more success. The patterns that stood out maddeningly to the experimenter seemed to have no salience at all for the children.

An answer frequently suggested by kindly critics was "why don't you just tell them?" So we did. Lowenstein (1969) ran a sorting experiment with the same problems over three days with children nearing the completion of first grade. There were three groups of children, and each group was given different instructions. The control group was run like the earlier experiments; the only instructions given were to "sort the mail, and put all yours here." A card for each pile was laid out for him and the procedure went on as before. The full-information group was told by the experimenter, "You will always know your mail because it will have these two letters in it, in this place." The common feature (constrained letter pair) was pointed out for each problem for the first two days. The third group was told, "You will know your mail because it will have the same two letters in the same place," but they were never shown the letter pair. The full-information group performed significantly better than the other two groups for the first two days, nearly everyone doing perfect sorts on the second day. On the third day, no further instructions were given. The group given the partial hint continued to improve, greatly exceeding the control group. But the full-information group deteriorated to the level of the control group. They had learned nothing from "being told." Apparently, S had to search actively and think for himself in order to learn something generalizable. Other psychologists, including Vygotsky and Piaget have emphasized that concepts are not "the sum of certain associative bonds formed by memory" and that they cannot be taught by drilling. To quote Vygotsky: "Practical experience also shows that direct teaching of concepts is impossible and fruitless. A teacher who tries to do this usually accomplishes nothing but empty verbalism, a parrotlike repetition of words by the child, simulating a knowledge of the corresponding concepts but actually covering up a vacuum" (Vygotsky, 1962, p. 83).

It occurred to me at this point that the sorting task might not make clear enough the economy of using a common feature or "collative principle." I decided to try another learning task, a simple one in which the economy of using a common feature is very obvious. We (Gibson, Poag, & Rader, 1972) set up a two-stage verbal discrimination task, comparing discrimination learning and generalization when there was or was *not* a common feature useful for learning the task in stage 1. All Ss were to learn which of two buttons to press for each of four words when the words were presented one at a time. They were given feedback on each trial. They were run to a criterion of 10 perfect trials or stopped after 60 trials. One group of Ss was presented with two rhyming pairs of words (king and ring; yarn and barn). The members of a rhyming pair were assigned the same button by E, so S had only two associations to learn if he noticed and used the rhyme or common spelling pattern. The other group of Ss had four words that had no obvious common feature (nose, king, bell, yarn), and therefore they had to learn four associations.

Stage 2 was identical for the two groups. Four new words were presented, consisting of two rhyming pairs (boat and coat; cake and rake). It was predicted that an S who had the opportunity to use rhyme in stage 1 would learn to do so and would generalize the principle to stage 2, starting a criterion run of 10 perfect trials on trial 5. The other group, by comparison would be handicapped. The Ss were second- and fifth-grade children.

Condition	Grade 1		Grade 5	
	Stage 1	Stage 2	Stage 1	Stage 2
GrE (common feature)	20.0%	26.6%	53.0%	60.0%
GrC (no common feature)	0.0	13.0	6.6	53.0

The results are summarized in the accompanying tabulation. When a common feature was present, grade five Ss performed significantly better in both stages than did grade two Ss; but they did not perform better when there was no common feature (G_rC, stage 1). There was development with age of an ability to perceive and to use the economical principle, but there was no improvement in associative learning as such. What was the effect of training within the experiment? Did anyone *learn* to use the common feature in the course of stage 1 and then generalize the principle to stage 2? The answer is no. There was no significant change from stage 1 to stage 2 for either of the age groups having a common feature in stage 1; nor did those groups excel significantly compared to the other groups in stage 2. Put another way, the S either applied the rule at once in the training stage or he never did. In terms of development, the ability to do this increases; but apparently it does not increase by virtue of the kind of training given in this experiment. Massed practice with differential reinforcement, even in this simple task, did not help to disclose a principle.

It seems to me now that abstraction of spelling patterns with consequent transfer is the result of much exposure to them and takes place slowly over time. I think that this process is mainly one of perceptual abstraction which occurs with as little awareness on the learner's part as is the case with learning grammar and with as little dependence on external reinforcement. The Ss in the word-likeness experiments were seldom able to justify their choices in any intelligible way, even when the majority were correct. The successful Ss in the discrimination learning experiment, especially the fifth graders, did frequently remark on the common features of the word pairs. The question is, did the learning experiments just described test the same ability as did the tachistoscopic and word-likeness experiments? The Ss in the verbal discrimination learning task could have been given a follow-up test in which they would have been asked to judge word-likeness; the results of the two methods could then have been correlated. Unfortunately when the idea occurred to me, it was too late to retrieve the Ss.

I now see this work as needing to proceed in two directions: one, to continue to attempt to enhance experiences of observing spelling patterns, since I still think there must be ways of helping the abstraction to "roll out" of its diverse contexts; and two, to pin down more carefully the patterns and the rules that are actually effective in creating the "word-superiority" effect and its generalization in adult readers. Without the latter knowledge we cannot know exactly which features of orthographic structure we should attempt to enhance. It is also possible that there is some optimal developmental progression in internalizing the rule system that could be exploited in presenting reading matter so as to reveal higher-order structure.

Use of Interword Redundancy in a Verbal Task

Most of my students' and my own experiments on the economical use of structure in reading have been aimed at structure within the word, but I am keenly aware that a skilled reader makes use of syntactic and semantic relations between words. So does an unskilled reader; but I am not sure when he begins to use these relations to extract information, rather than merely to guess at what may follow. Must he perhaps learn to deal with words themselves as units first? It is possible, of course, that learning to use all types of structure goes on at the same time in reading. Adults and children by third grade or so appear to make use of phrase structure and other grammatical relations as tested by the eye-voice span (Levin & Kaplan, 1970). These *S*s were reading aloud, of course, and were producing all the words in a sequence; the interpretation of the results is not entirely clear, beyond the fact that the *S*s have a knowledge of grammar. I sought for a novel verbal task, therefore, that would reveal the extent to which children who presumably know something about word structure would be able to draw on interword relations to increase their economy of verbal problem solving. The task I chose was anagram solution, since a good deal is known about how adults solve anagrams.

If there is syntactic or semantic order in the array of information in an anagram task, will it be used economically by children in the third and fourth grade when they should be freed from letter-by-letter reading? Gibson, Tenney, and Sharabany (1971) performed experiments with children at this age level, investigating the effect of syntactic and semantic structure on anagram solution. In the first experiment the effect of syntactic structure and sentence meaning on the solution of a set of five anagrams was investigated. The anagrams, when solved, yielded a sentence such as "Sally helps Mom clean house." There were three groups of *S*s. The anagrams were presented to one group (SS, for sentence structure) one at a time in proper sentence order. There were six sets of this type, each set was arranged on a board so that one followed another. The letters, taken from a magnetized Scrabble set, could be moved around by the *S* during solution. One anagram was uncovered at a time and was left uncovered during solution. If an anagram had not been solved at the end of 90 seconds, the *E* arranged it in word order and *S* went on to the next anagram. The question was whether *S* would discover the sentence structure during the first few sets and look for structure in the remaining sets, thus facilitating solution.

A second group (NS, no structure) was given the same anagrams to solve, but they were not presented in sentence order. A third group (SS-NS) was presented with the first four sets in sentence order, but the last two sets were in scrambled order. If the sentence had been discovered during the first four sets, S might have been expected to continue to search for sentence structure that was no longer present. This group was given help in finding the sentence structure by being asked to read in order the words they had already solved before they uncovered each new anagram on a given board.

The mean summed times for solution of the first four sets varied for the three groups, being shortest for group SS-NS, next shortest for group SS, and longest for group NS. Only the difference between group SS-NS and the other two groups was significant, however. We were obliged to conclude that for these children the sentence structure was not detected and was not used without the hint given by reading the preceding words aloud. There was no interference for group SS-NS when compared to group NS on the last two scrambled sets, which were identical with those presented to group NS. However, 15 of the 16 Ss in group SS-NS took longer on board five than they had on board four, whereas the majority of the NS group improved their time, a difference which confirms the evidence that group SS-NS had previously been using the structure to facilitate solution. The fact that members of group SS almost uniformly failed to notice that the words made a sentence may be owing to the nature of the anagram task or to their immaturity. In a pilot experiment with adults in which more complex sentences were used, solution was facilitated when the anagrams were in sentence order. However, further confirmation of this result is needed.

In a second experiment the effect of semantic structure, specifically category membership, on anagram solution was investigated. That the solution of anagram problems by adults is facilitated by categorical relations has long been known (Rees & Israel, 1935). Since S must identify a solution as being a meaningful word, it stands to reason that knowing that the word will be an animal or a kind of fruit, etc., will assist solution. Six categories which were known to be familiar to third- and fourth-grade children were used. There were five anagrams for each category, and again five anagrams were presented on a board. There were two groups; in one the anagrams belonging to the same category were presented together on a board (group CS, category structure), whereas in the other the categories were scrambled so that none of the boards contained words of all one category (group NS, no structure).

Group CS had shorter mean times for all six boards, as Figure 2 shows. The curves suggest an increasing effect of category with practice, but the interaction was not significant; the facilitation was present and significant for group CS on the first board. The advantage appeared by the third anagram on a board and increased thereafter (a significant condition by trial interaction). Eleven of the 30 Ss in the CS group commented spontaneously on the presence of the category.

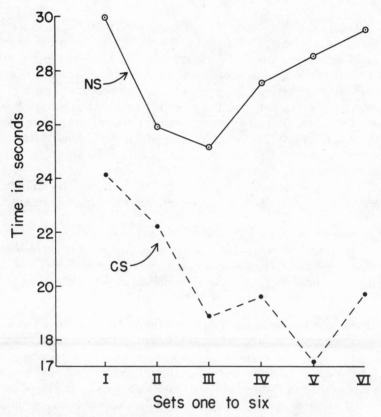

Figure 2.   Mean solution time per set as a function of order of presentation of the set.

The results make it plain that the semantic relationship of belonging to a common category can be used by fourth graders for economical solution of a novel verbal problem. But to speculate a bit, we have some reason to think that the children's solution strategies may have differed from the adults' strategies. I would like to indulge in this speculation because it brings me back to meaning and how it is processed—the problem with which I began.

Several strategies for solving anagrams are possible, the simplest being a purely trial-and-error approach of moving the letters about and waiting for a word to pop out by trying to pronounce an arrangement to see if it sounds like a word. The children on the whole appeared to be doing this (admittedly we lack hard evidence, as yet). When an acceptable pronunciation turned up that was not a word (e.g., KLIM when the word was MILK), they were likely to be stuck. How then did presence of a category help them? Safren (1962) suggested that when a set of anagrams is related by meaning, "associative strength activates existing response sets" to facilitate solution. It seemed that something like this did happen with the children; if a child perceived a relation between the first two anagrams, he went through a category list, trying the words in turn on the anagram to see if they would fit, as the following typical comments illustrate: "I'm trying to think of another silverware, but I can't." "It must be another color. I'm trying them." This method of solution, even if not cognitively very sophisticated, did often give results and the strategy would be reinforced.

Adults observed in our laboratory gave comments suggesting quite a different strategy. They deliberately put consonant clusters or consonants at possible places and vowels or vowel clusters in the center to achieve orthographic acceptability, and then they checked for semantic acceptability. Knowledge of a category would facilitate recognition of a word, since much of the processing of lexical features would be eliminated and there would also be no need of going through a whole category list. Word meaning for an adult, as I suggested earlier, may usefully be thought of as the pattern of abstract conceptual features that uniquely characterizes a word.

Whether meaning is more concrete for a child, I do not know; but I infer from the first experiment described in this paper that access to abstract meaning upon reading a word is not so direct for a child as it is for a mature reader, and that the child sounds the word, as he appeared to do with the anagrams, before getting to meaning.

In any case, the children did use category knowledge in a way that facilitated anagram solution. I believe we can conclude that a person will use the most economical cognitive strategy that is possible for his developmental level and that there is progress in developing more sophisticated and higher-order strategies.

Conclusion

This rather lengthy summary of a good deal of the research (my own and a number of my students') of the last ten years or so has forced me to take stock of my successes and my failures and to own up to a fair number of failures and gaps in the evidence. But it leaves me convinced that opportunistic research on unrelated problems is never as rewarding to either the researcher or to the consumer as is research set in a theoretical framework that provides a systematic program. I might have had a better program, but I find that I still see increasing specificity, optimization of attention, and economy of processing the information in stimulation as giving a useful direction to developmental research on problems of reading skill, namely, in determining both what it is and how it is attained.

REFERENCES

Baron, J., & Thurston, I. An analysis of the word-superiority effect. *Cognitive Psychology*, 1973, 4, 207-228.

Barron, R. W. Transfer of information processing strategies in a choice reaction time task. (Doctoral dissertation, Ohio State University.) Ann Arbor, Mich.: University Microfilms, 1971.

Cattell, J. M. Uber die Zeit der Erkennung und Bennenung von Schriftzeichen, Bildern und Farben. *Philosophische Studien*, 1885, 2, 635-650.

Chase, W. G., & Clark, H. H. Mental operations in the comparison of sentences and pictures. In L. W. Gregg (Ed.), *Cognition in learning and memory*. New York: Wiley, 1972. Pp. 205-232.

Clare, D. A. A study of principles of integration in the perception of written verbal items. Unpublished doctoral dissertation, Cornell University, 1969.

Clark, E. V. What's in a word? On the child's acquisition of semantics in his first language. In T. Moore (Ed.), *Cognitive development*. New York: Academic Press, 1973.

Erdmann, B., & Dodge, R. *Psychologische Untersuchungen über das Lesen, auf Experimenteller Grundlage*. Halle: M. Niemeyer, 1898.

Fries, C. C. *Linguistics and reading*. New York: Holt, 1963.

Garner, W. R. *Uncertainty and structure as psychological concepts*. New York: Wiley, 1962.

Gibson, E. J., Barron, R. W., & Garber, E. E. The developmental convergence of meaning for words and pictures. In appendix to final report, *The relationship between perceptual development and the acquisition of reading skill*. Project No. 90046, Grant No. OEG-2-9-420446-1071(010), Cornell University and United States Office of Education, 1972.

Gibson, E. J., Bishop, C. H., Schiff, W., & Smith, J. Comparison of meaningfulness and pronunciability as grouping principles in the perception and retention of verbal material. *Journal of Experimental Psychology*, 1964, 67, 173-182.

Gibson, E. J., Farber, J., & Shepela, S. Test of a learning set procedure for the abstraction of spelling patterns. In *The analysis of reading skill: A program of basic and applied research*. Final report, Project No. 5-1213, Contract No. OE 6-10-156, 1968.

Gibson, E. J., Gibson, J. J., Pick, A. D., & Osser, H. A developmental study of the discrimination of letter-like forms. *Journal of Comparative and Physiological Psychology*, 1962, 55, 897-906.

Gibson, E. J., & Guinet, L. Perception of inflections in brief visual presentations of words. *Journal of Verbal Learning and Verbal Behavior*, 1971, 10, 182-189.

Gibson, E. J., Osser, H., & Pick, A. D. A study in the development of grapheme-phoneme correspondences. *Journal of Verbal Learning and Verbal Behavior,* 1963, 2, 142-146.

Gibson, E. J., Osser, H., Schiff, W., & Smith, J. An analysis of critical features of letters, tested by a confusion matrix. In Final report on *A basic research program on reading.* Cooperative Research Project No. 639, Cornell University and United States Office of Education, 1963.

Gibson, E. J., Pick, A. D., Osser, H., & Hammond, M. The role of grapheme-phoneme correspondence in the perception of words. *American Journal of Psychology,* 1962, 75, 554-570.

Gibson, E. J., Poag, K., & Rader, N. The effect of redundant rhyme and spelling patterns on a verbal discrimination task. In appendix to final report on *The relationship between perceptual development and the acquisition of reading skill.* Project No. 90046, Grant No. OEG-2-9-420446-1071(010), Cornell University and United States Office of Education, 1972.

Gibson, E. J., Schapiro, F., & Yonas, A. Confusion matrices for graphic patterns obtained with a latency measure. In *The analysis of reading skill: A program of basic and applied research.* Final report, Project No. 5-1213, Cornell University and United States Office of Education, 1968. Pp. 76-96.

Gibson, E. J., Shurcliff, A., & Yonas, A. Utilization of spelling patterns by deaf and hearing subjects. In H. Levin & J. P. Williams (Eds.), *Basic studies on reading.* New York: Basic Books, 1970.

Gibson, E. J., Tenney, Y. J., Barron, R. W., & Zaslow, M. The effect of orthographic structure on letter search. *Perception and Psychophysics,* 1972, 11, 183-186.

Gibson, E. J., Tenney, Y. J., & Sharabany, R. Is discovery of structure reinforcing? The role of semantic and syntactic structure in anagram solution. In final report, *The relationship between perceptual development and the acquisition of reading skill.* Project No. 90046, Grant No. OEG-2-9-420446-1071(010), Cornell University and United States Office of Education, 1971. Pp. 48-64.

Gibson, E. J., Tenney, Y. J. & Zaslow, M. Is discovery of structure reinforcing? The effect of categorizable context on scanning for verbal targets. In final report, *The relationship between perceptual development and the acquisition of reading skill.* Project No. 90046, Grant No. OEG-2-9-420446-1071(010), Cornell University and the United States Office of Education, 1971.

Gibson, E. J., & Yonas, A. A developmental study of visual search behavior. *Perception and Psychophysics,* 1966, 1, 169-171. (a)

Gibson, E. J., & Yonas, A. A developmental study of the effects of visual and auditory interference on a visual scanning task. *Psychonomic Science,* 1966, 5, 163-164. (b)

Gibson, J. J., & Gibson, E. J. Perceptual learning: Differentiation or enrichment? *Psychological Review,* 1955, 62, 32-41.

Golinkoff, R. M. Children's use of redundant auditory information in the discrimination of nonsense words. Unpublished paper, Cornell University, December, 1972.

Golinkoff, R. M. Children's discrimination of English spelling patterns with redundant auditory information. Paper presented at the American Educational Research Association, 1974.

Hochberg, J. E., & Brooks, V. Pictorial recognition as an unlearned ability: A study of one child's performance. *American Journal of Psychology,* 1962, 75, 624-628.

Huey, E. B. *The psychology and pedagogy of reading.* New York: Macmillan, 1908. Republished by M.I.T. Press, 1968.

Kaplan, G., Yonas, A., & Shurcliff, A. Visual and acoustic confusability in a visual search task. *Perception and Psychophysics,* 1966, 1, 172-174.

Katz, J. J., & Fodor, J. A. The structure of a semantic theory. *Language,* 1963, 39, 170-210.

Levin, H., & Kaplan, E. L. Grammatical structure and reading. In H. Levin & J. P. Williams (Eds.), *Basic studies on reading.* New York: Basic Books, 1970. Pp. 119-133.

Lowenstein, A. A. Effects of instructions on the abstraction of spelling patterns. Unpublished master's thesis, Cornell University, 1969.

Luria, A. R. Speech development and the formation of mental processes. In M. Cole & I. Maltzman (Eds.), *A handbook of contemporary Soviet psychology.* New York: Basic Books, 1969. Pp. 121-162.

Moore, T. V. Image and meaning in memory and perception. *Psychological Monographs,* 1919, 27 (Whole No. 119).

Neisser, U. Decision time without reaction time: Experiments in visual scanning. *American Journal of Psychology,* 1963, 76, 376-385.

Neisser, U., & Beller, H. K. Searching through word lists. *British Journal of Psychology,* 1965, 56, 349-358.

Posner, M. I., & Mitchell, R. F. Chronometric analysis of classification. *Psychological Review,* 1967, 74, 392-409.

Rees, H. J., & Israel, H. E. An investigation of the establishment and operation of mental sets. In J. J. Gibson (Ed.), *Studies in psychology from Smith College. Psychological Monographs,* 1935, 46 (Whole No. 6). Pp. 1-26.

Reicher, G. M. Perceptual recognition as a function of meaningfulness of stimulus material. *Journal of Experimental Psychology,* 1969, 81, 275-280.

Rosinski, R. R., & Wheeler, K. E. Children's use of orthographic structure in word discrimination. *Psychonomic Science,* 1972, 26, 97-98.

Rothkopf, E. Z. Incidental memory for location of information in text. *Journal of Verbal Learning and Verbal Behavior,* 1971, 10, 608-613.

Rubenstein, H. *An overview of psycholinguistics.* Grant Report, Lehigh University, Bethlehem, Pa., 1971. To be published in *Current Trends in Linguistics,* Vol. 12. The Hague: Mouton.

Ryle, A. L. A study of the interpretation of pictorial styles by young children. Unpublished doctoral dissertation, Harvard School of Education, 1966.

Safren, M. A. Associations, sets, and the solution of word problems. *Journal of Experimental Psychology,* 1962, 64, 40-45.

Schapiro, F. Information extraction and filtering during perceptual learning in visual search. Unpublished doctoral dissertation, Cornell University, 1970.

Shepela, S. T. A developmental study of bimodal vigilance. Unpublished doctoral dissertation, Cornell University, 1971.

Tenney, Y. H. The child's conception of organization and recall: The development of cognitive strategies. Unpublished doctoral dissertation, Cornell University, 1973.

Vygotsky, L. S. *Thought and language.* Cambridge and New York: M.I.T. Press and Wiley, 1962. Edited and translated by Eugenia Hanfmann and Gertrude Vakar.

Wheeler, D. D. Processes in word recognition. *Cognitive Psychology,* 1970, 1, 59-85.

Yonas, A. The acquisition of information-processing strategies in a time-dependent task. Unpublished doctoral dissertation, Cornell University, 1969.

Zaslow, M. The effect of orthographic structure on letter search: A reexamination. Senior Honors Thesis, Cornell University, 1972.

Some Aspects of the First Stage of Reading[1]

JOHN J. GEYER
Rutgers University

PAUL A. KOLERS
Toronto University

Among its other features, reading involves a constellation of constructive processes in which meaning is attributed to written symbols. Such processing takes time. Various "systems" interact to transduce, store, and manipulate information. The skilled reader employs these operations flexibly to accomplish the task of the moment. Kolers (1970) concluded that at least three different competencies, types of performance in the skilled reader, can be differentiated. These are 1) visual operations resulting in the recognition of letters and individual words, 2) sensitivity to the grammatical relationships in connected text, and 3) the ready imposition and manipulation of "meanings." A skilled reader might operate at any of these levels for a particular task.

The visual operations resulting in the recognition of letters and words were studied in college students by Kolers and Katzman (1966), who presented letters rapidly to the same area of a viewing screen while varying the duration of presentation and the letters making up the sequences. When letter sequences were presented at fast rates, the students could often identify them as words better than as letters; in addition, the students sometimes reported all the letters correctly, but in the wrong order. At longer durations, errors of ordering never occurred, even when subjects failed to identify all letters correctly. Kolers and Katzman concluded that ordering letters and identifying them were separate processes and that the identification of words cannot depend wholly on identification of the individual letters. Word perception organizes a serial input.

From this and other evidence, Kolers (1970) suggested that a three-stage process is involved in the perception of serial letters. An initial

[1] This paper is based on a more extensive discussion by J. J. Geyer and P. A. Kolers, "Reading as information processing." In J. Voight (Ed.) *Advances in Librarianship,* Vol. 4, Academic Press, New York, 1974.

schematization provides a general framework of what the visual system will have to construct in order to represent what has been presented. A mechanism concerned with *ordering* the array works on the results of the schematization. Finally, the percept is constructed through an *impletion,* or filling-in, process.

This paper will review evidence indicating that these three components isolated by the procedures of Kolers and Katzman can be found when letters are presented as spatial arrays as well and that they are involved in normal reading. In the discussion which follows, the emphasis will be on visual and related organismic processes which underlie the specific linguistic content of reading. Our purpose is to present a schematic outline of an area of significant human performance while noting what we do *not* know about how we read.

Visual Operations: Schematization and Ordering

Reading differs from other language processes in that the visual system is the customary input modality. This section will discuss some hypothetical processes emerging from the recent experimental literature regarding these functions: the schematizing processes of *sharpening, orientation,* and *attentional focusing,* and the processes involved in the *ordering of input.*

Sharpening Processes

In the late 19th Century a popular analogy held that the eye was like a camera, and introductory textbooks until recent times contained illustrations showing the similarities. A basic contradiction recognized from the beginning was that while the eye is poorly designed as a camera, it is nevertheless a sensitive, flexible, and reliable light-processing device. For example, the opening and closing of the pupil of the eye in response to light intensity seems analogous to the f-setting of a camera. Many cameras are capable of a much wider range of adjustments than the 8 to 2 millimeters possible in the pupil. Yet the eye responds usefully to an enormous range of light intensity. The brightest light which does not cause pain is about a billion times brighter than the weakest light which can be seen. Changes in pupillary diameter can account for only a trivial portion of this range (Lindsay and Norman, 1972). Only recently have the neural mechanisms responsible for sensitivity control been identified in detail (Werblin, 1973).

Light entering the eye is bent first by the cornea and then focused to a variable degree by the lens, both of which have poor optical characteristics. In addition, the light must pass through two chambers filled with a jelly-like substance containing significant amounts of flotsam before reaching the retina. Most incredibly, the sensitive photochemical elements of the retina (the "film" of the camera analogy) face inward toward the brain so that the light must pass through several layers of neural tissue and blood vessels before effecting a neural response. By the time the light penetrates to the photochemicals, therefore, considerable blurring of the image occurs. Yet human visual acuity is so accurate that the separation between two stationary vertical lines can be detected when the visual angle subtended is about 10 seconds, a distance actually smaller than that between two elements of the receptor mosaic (Kolers, 1968).

The problem is not with the design of the eye but with the analogy. The eye is not a camera and a perfect retinal image is neither achieved nor necessary for good vision. Histologically the retina is an extension of the brain, performing essential processing at the periphery. Carrying out this processing, each eye in man contains approximately 130 million rods and 7 million cones, the receptor elements containing the photolabile pigments. (A commercial television picture, by way of comparison, is made up of about 250,000 elements). These receptors are organized into complex groups and considerable signal analysis is performed on the neural impulses in the retina. About one million fibers leave the retina, to carry these impulses to higher stations for further analysis. The several levels of the visual system do not act merely as relay stations but convert the impulses, selecting for such attributes as intensity, contrast, orientation, position, and movement. Clearly, the extensive processing within the visual system is such that the cortex does not receive a simple projection of the retinal image. Rather, the cortical representation and the perceptual experience associated with it are highly recoded abstractions.

Visual Attention

Perhaps the most important generalization stemming from the recent work in visual neurology is a new awareness of the *active* nature of the processes involved. By what processes and criteria do we choose from the multitude of stimuli impinging on us at all times those few to which we attend? How does the reader exclude distracting stimuli and how does he select and order those sequential portions of the visual field which constitute the appropriate input?

As yet there is little agreement as to specific systems responsible for selective attention in vision. All investigators would agree that major components are such gross peripheral functions as head and eye movements and the opening and closing of the lids, but this is a statement of little interest. Increasingly, interest is focusing on the phenomena which occur within the "stationary field"—that part of the world visible to a single glance or with the image stabilized on the retina.

One of the important issues on which investigators currently disagree concerns the degree to which voluntary processes determine which elements of the visual field are selected for further processing. Some investigators hold that attention is almost never voluntary; that it is determined almost wholly by the properties of the stimulus. This was the view underlying the work of the Gestalt psychologists who developed convincing examples of the principles governing stimulus organization. Such a view, however, must ignore increasing evidence that what the observer sees is governed to a large degree by what he expects to see and what he wishes to do. Many examples can be cited. Pictures, three-dimensional drawings, and optical illusions are seen quite differently by observers from different cultures (this interesting area is reviewed by Deregowski, 1972). If a two-way mirror is arranged so that an observer can see the scene ahead through the mirror as well as the scene reflected in the mirror from behind, he can voluntarily determine which image to attend to despite the fact that no change has occurred in the stimulus configuration or in such gross visual factors as accommodation, focus, or fixation.

Perhaps the best evidence for voluntary control of selective visual attention within the stationary field comes from experiments utilizing a stabilized retinal image. The eyes of an awake adult are normally in constant motion. In addition to pursuit and saccadic movements, the eyes maintain a constant low-amplitude, high-frequency motion called nystagmus, an entirely involuntary motion which disappears only in deep sleep. A fourth type of movement occurs when fixation is maintained. The eye actually drifts from the fixated point, snaps rapidly back, and drifts again. The pattern continues throughout the fixation without any awareness of it by the observer. The functional consequences of all four types of motion can be eliminated by the use of optical devices which produce a constant relationship between target and retina regardless of eye movements.

When a target is viewed under stabilized conditions it disappears. It does not simply fade away, however. Whole segments disappear together while what is left often preserves contours, and other structurally meaningful elements. Importantly, the observer can sometimes retard the fading of portions of the target by selectively attending to them. Thus, selective visual attention is an intentional process which is not wholly dependent upon eye movements nor wholly governed by the stimulus configuration. The observer can voluntarily preserve selected figural properties of the target and, in some cases, even implete parts of a disappearing figure. This latter process of impletion, or filling in, is demonstrated in ordinary vision by the impletion of the "blind spot," the region of the visual field corresponding to the area where the visual nerves pass through the retina.

Studies of vision under the conditions of stabilized viewing have important ramifications for an understanding of the reading processes and of visual perception in general. Although much remains to be understood, it is clear that vision is not the passive, receptive process envisioned by the camera analogy. Vision is an active, constructive, and intentional process *even within the stationary field*. Meaningfulness is projected forward and imposed on the visual scene.

In reading, the visual system is involved in the conversion of high density spatial arrays of symbols into interpretable relations, such as those characteristic of language. In sections below, it is suggested that two operations interact in the accomplishment of this task: an attentional focusing process which delimits the area of the stationary field attended to and an input ordering process operating in reading as a rapid attentional scan in the direction the language is written. These hypothetical operations by no means explain all the complexities of visual perception nor can their details be firmly documented. Further research, therefore, may well require modification of our ideas concerning the nature of these processes.

Attentional Focusing Processes

Kolers (1970) called attention to one of the earliest stages of visual recognition, in which a general framework, or schema, furnishes the information necessary for programing ordering and impletion. A visual attentional system which has recently experienced a resurgence of research interest may indicate some of the operations through which the schemata are formed. This system operates analogously to a variable-powered lens (Pribram, 1970). When the power setting is low, a large field of view is obtained but at a sacrifice of information concerning detail. As the focus is narrowed, more detail becomes available (Eriksen & Spencer, 1969). The phenomenon was known and studied by early psychologists as "attending broadly" and "attending narrowly" (discussed in Woodworth & Schlossberg, 1954). When urged to "attend broadly" to tachistoscopic presentations, subjects reported the beginning and ending letters of an array and a few letters from the center. More recently Mackworth (1965) showed that the visual system adjusts its "field size" to accommodate the amount of information in the field. When the load is excessive, the receptive field is narrowed to the more focally centered stimuli.

The attentional focusing process agrees with our conscious awareness of our visual experiences. The reader can see with a quick glance that the page overleaf is a page of print. In the context of the book he need only see its general form to know that it is not an illustration or a blank page. If the page were out of context, he might need to "look closer" to determine that it was actually print. He would have to "look very closely" to determine whether the period at the end of this sentence is perfectly round.

In an experiment which has become a modern classic, Sperling (1960) presented tachistoscopically from nine to twelve letters arranged in three rows. Exposure durations were too short for eye movements to take place. A high, medium, or low-pitched tone was sounded after the exposure to indicate which row subjects were to report. In the absence of a tone the subjects were able to report about five letters correctly, sampled from different parts of the visual field. These are the results that would be expected if subjects were employing a wide attentional focus. When a tone was sounded subjects responded by reporting the letters in the row indicated, demonstrating the attentional focusing phenomenon (Eriksen and Rohrbaugh, 1970). Under certain luminance conditions the effect could be obtained for several hundred milliseconds after the termination of the display, the ability to do so falling off with an increase in the delay of the tone.[2] Since the experimental technique rules out the possibility that effective eye movements could be involved, the experiment demonstrates several important considerations. The attentional focus effect in the experiment was task-related (that is, under the control of the subject) in both its temporal and spatial components. In addition, what has been called "input" in this paper was also temporally and spatially determined by the subject under unchanging visual conditions to meet changing task requirements. That is, "input" is not merely something that passively hap-

---

[2] Sperling's experiment was conducted to demonstrate a form of visual storage he has termed VIS or Visual Information Storage (Sperling, 1967). This store has the effect of lengthening the apparent duration of a tachistoscopic exposure for considerable periods beyond the termination of the light source. The effect is critically sensitive to the luminance conditions of the experiment and decreases as the conditions of normal reading are approached. It does not seem likely that it is involved in the normal reading processes nor would it seem to have any important function since time constraints are under the control of the reader.

pens; it is selected. From early visual levels, then, attentional processes involved in reading are active and intentional; they are not passive responses governed only by the visual scene.

In the tachistoscopic setting, a wide focus would be most effective where letter-order information is not important, where wide arrays are presented for durations too brief to allow the focusing and ordering processes to take place, and where the information requirements of the situation are very low. Since the subject initially focuses on a fixational target he would need to become familiar with the nature of the task before changing to a wide focal strategy.

These details are consistent with the experimental literature. At the briefest exposure durations from which letters can be recognized, order of report is random and accuracy of report favors the letters in the center, reflecting the sensitivity characteristics of the eye (Averbach & Sperling, 1968). Longer durations yield reports ordered from left to right (with readers of English) and report accuracy favors the items on the left. Using four-letter arrays (low information content) subjects changed from serial to parallel strategies (here equated with wide focus) as they gained experience with the task (Haber, 1969), and highly-practiced subjects were able to report two or three letters from the same 8 msec. exposures which were the necessary minimum for the report of a single letter (Kinsbourne & Warrington, 1962). Mewhort (1966) found that subjects tended to report the center letter best when the letters were widely spaced but the left letter best when letters were single-spaced. Letter spacing, which in reading determines word boundaries, may provide cues as to when order-preserving input strategies are important.

We can only speculate about the details of attentional focusing and its importance to the reading processes. With the focus at a wide setting, little information concerning detail is available and information about the order of elements within the stationary field is poorly preserved. Given the importance of letter order in printed language and the density of information on a printed page, it is unlikely that a wide field focus would be a useful strategy in most reading tasks but it could furnish the schemata necessary for appropriate ordering processes. Further research will be necessary before we can have much confidence in the role this attentional mechanism plays in normal reading and its contributions, if any, to reading disabilities.

Attentional Ordering Processes

While it is possible to design tachistoscopic experiments wherein subjects report horizontal arrays of letters randomly with fewer errors from the center of the array, these results are not obtained from unpracticed subjects given exposures of a tenth of a second or longer. Under these conditions, subjects typically report English from left to right with accuracy favoring the items first reported. This order-of-report effect was first reported by Glanville and Dallenbach (1929) who concluded that the responses were made from a "memory after-image"—a brief, fading store formed immediately after the perception of the letters. This store and its place in reading will be briefly discussed below as the Ready Store.

Interestingly, results opposite to those attributable to the order-of-report effect are obtained from experiments which tachistoscopically expose stimulus materials to the right or left of the point at which the subject is focusing, that is, to the right or left visual hemifield. Under these conditions, subjects report English words better from the right visual hemifield and Yiddish or Hebrew words (written from right to left) better from the left (Mishkin & Forgays, 1952; Orbach, 1953). That the effects are related to reading ability was shown by Forgays (1952) who found that the right field superiority for English increased as the school grade of the subjects increased and by Kimura (1959) who found a more pronounced right field superiority in college students than in poorly-educated army personnel of similar age.

The apparent contradictions in results obtained by presenting stimuli to the right and left visual hemifields and across the center of fixation have resulted in a very productive experimental effort.[3] The complexities of the results obtained are difficult to fit into any simple explanation although much has been learned which reinforces evidence from other sources indicating that the operation of the visual system is much more active and constructive than previously believed. Since the known optical properties and physiological sensitivities of the eye favor those items at the center of vision, the results must be due to processing factors, some of which are learned and sensitive to the directionality of language. Hershenson (1969) investigated this distinction and confirmed that even though letters near the fixation point were seen more clearly, identification was best for those letters on the left.

One explanation of the retinal hemifield results points to the importance of the beginning of a display. When letters are presented to the right

---

[3]This complex area of retinal hemifield effects on letter and word perception has been thoroughly reviewed by White (1969) up to that date. The functional interpretation presented in this section is necessarily oversimplified. Recent interpretations attempting to explain the effects at structural levels promise deeper understandings of the interactions of the cerebral hemispheres and, perhaps, some resolution of the debate concerning the causes of reading disabilities long associated clinically with handedness and "mixed lateral dominance."

visual field, the left-most letter is closer to the center of focus than it is when letters are presented to the left visual field. In the latter case, subjects must first attentionally scan to the left before they can begin processing in a left-to-right direction. Since the scan to the left-most element is in conflict with the direction of the report, perception in the left visual field suffers (White, 1969). This hypothesis, first suggested by Harcum and Finkel (1963), was tested by exposing English words and their mirror images to the left and right visual fields. The words were read best from the right field; the mirror images from the left, supporting the hypothesis.

There is good reason to believe, however, that the scanning process revealed in the presentations to the right and left hemifield occurs at a different level from the sequential processes which produce the order-of-report effect. This latter effect is produced when the stimulus consists of a number of elements requiring a number of responses. The effect is attributed to a limited storage time and to the possibility that reporting the first items may disrupt the storage of later items. No such response multiplicity is required to demonstrate response differences between the right and left visual hemifields. Such differences obtain for single English words and their mirror images, three-letter English words printed verti-cally (Goodglass & Barton, 1963), three-letter Yiddish words printed vertically (Barton, Goodglass, & Shai, 1965), Japanese words (Hirata & Osake, 1967), as well as for nonalphabetic visual forms requiring single responses (Egeth, 1971). In addition, order-of-report effects occur within the responses from both right and left hemifields (Heron, 1957).

Geyer (1966, 1970) suggested that two processes operating at differ-ent levels are involved. The first is a rapid attentional scan occurring concurrently with the exposure, and functioning in the selection and ordering of the elements of the visual field by converting spatial arrays into temporal sequences. Impletion processes operating on the ordered output of the attentional scan convert the stimuli to appropriate units which are then stored in the Ready Store. The order-of-report effects are produced by the limited time available for the organization of sequential responses. Working within a different experimental context, Mewhort (1967) advanced very similar ideas.

This interpretation finds support from a series of experiments inves-tigating the order-of-report effect in processing non-directional forms. Harcum, Hartman, and Smith (1963) presented to English-speaking sub-jects horizontal patterns of 10 circles, of which 5 had been filled-in. Subjects responded by filling in the appropriate circles on a response sheet. Without instructions, the subjects consistently marked their responses from left to right and produced the fewest errors on the left, the order-of-report effect. Instructions to mark responses from right to left produced differential accuracy favoring the right, but only if the instructions were given *prior* to the exposure. Instructions to respond from right to left given immediately *after* the exposure reduced the overall accuracy but retained the superior accuracy for items on the left. The experiment was repeated using Israeli subjects with the same results but in the reverse directions (Harcum & Friedman, 1963). Sperling (1960) reported the same pheonomenon in the vertical dimension.

Bryden (1960) also found that with non-directional material (geometric forms) lateral superiority was a function of order-of-report. With alphabetic material the effects of requiring a right-to-left report were to reduce the number of letters reported while preserving the left superiority. Bryden's subjects stated that in order to report the letters in a right-to-left direction, they first had to rehearse them silently in the normal order. These results strongly suggest that the direction of the initial scan can be programed to fit the requirements of the response task when the stimulus is not inherently ordered, but that the temporal order established by this early system can be altered by subsequent systems only with difficulty. The fact that many English letters carry more information in their right halves than their left (Kolers, 1969) may be related to the inherent directionality reported. The effect seems to be facilitative since Harcum (1964) found in presentations to the right and left hemifields that fewer errors were made on asymmetrical letters (B, G, K, etc.) than on symmetrical letters (H, Y, X, etc.)

As with the attentional focusing mechanism, further research will be required before the components underlying ordering in reading are fully understood. From the evidence, we can deduce tentatively that, in reading, the attentional scan involves a focus narrow enough to exclude the lines of print above and below and would input letters sequentially in the direction in which the language was written, thus preserving the order of the spatial array in its transduction to a temporal sequence. The operation of the system is extremely rapid. Estimates for similar processes are generally given as 10-15 msec. for each letter (Sperling, 1969). Geyer (1968) estimated the maximum rate as 8 msec. per letter space. (Letters are not recognized at these rates, of course, but are transferred to other systems where recognition processes occur at much slower rates.)

Direct tests of the early visual processes within contexts applicable to reading are difficult because effects are obscured in the report by processing at subsequent levels. One approach is to severely limit the amount of time available for such processes to take place. If the ordering of the input of a horizontal array of English letters is a left-to-right serial process, some minimal exposure duration should allow one letter to be reported and additional increments of time should result in reports of additional letters. These findings have been reported by several investigators (Averbach & Coriell, 1961; Sperling, 1963). Typically, subjects report an additional letter for each 10 to 15 msec. of added exposure duration until four or five letters are reported. Several hundred milliseconds of time are required for each additional letter beyond this maximum.

These results seem to agree with the idea of a rapid serial input followed by slower sequential responses to a fading trace store. Initially, longer exposure durations allow the input of additional elements which can be responded to before fading in the Ready Store. Once the storage-response rate interaction limit had been reached, additional exposure time would not be effective until it was adequate to allow the response to the first element to be made before the presentation terminated. From this point on, additional elements would be added to the report by increments of exposure duration equal to the response rate. That is, the critical factor would be the number of elements to which responses were made before the termination of the exposure, these being added to the relatively constant number available in the Ready Store. While retinal hemifield effects may seem far removed from the conditions of normal reading, the fact that they increase monotonically with elementary grade level and can differentiate between good and poor readers would make it seem likely that the processes involved are used in normal reading.

Orientation Processes

The flexibility of the human being as an information processor is such that compensations can be made for even gross violations of normal processing requirements. Text can be transformed, for example, in a number of ways (inversion, rotation, letter order, word order, etc.) without destroying its readability by skilled readers (Kolers, 1972a). Most readers would have little trouble in reading the following, for example:

slamina deggel-ruof era tar dna god ehT

The processes through which such transformations are read are important research questions in themselves; but, in addition, research concerning transformations can contribute to our understanding of normal reading. Processes which normally function in smooth and automatic congruence can be isolated by pitting them against one another. How do readers perceive language constancies despite differences in orientation and order of letters which radically change the image projected to the eye? Certainly cognitive functions such as judgment, estimation, and expectancy are involved. We cannot read transformed text unless we have the ability to read normal text and the powerful language systems would be fully used. Recent experimentation indicates that specifically visual functions may be involved as well. By recording the electrical activity of single cells in the visual system, scientists have isolated visual mechanisms which react selectively to objects of particular configurations and in particular orientations. Such mechanisms may play a part in compensating for such transforms as rotated or inverted letters, although there is as yet no evidence that they do. It is unlikely, however, that such mechanisms could function in compensating for other transforms such as reversed letter order and direction of reading. That transformations can be read at all, of course, rules out simplistic definitions of reading as learned responses to visual patterns, since it is unlikely that all geometrically transformed texts had ever been encountered previously.

Kolers and Perkins (1969a; 1969b) had subjects name letters transformed by inversion, rotation and mirror reflection and letters in normal orientation. The letters were named from left to right and in the reverse direction. Analysis of errors made showed that they clustered into subsets whose members were sensitive to visual confusion (such as p, q; b, d; h, y; t, f). The errors were clearly not due to confusion of their names but to confusions in visual processing. Speed of naming was affected primarily by an interaction between direction of reading and the direction in which the letters faced. That is, subjects could name letters faster when the characters were oriented in the direction in which the reading was performed, independently of whether the reading was leftward or rightward and of the vertical orientation of the letters. The evidence indicates that subjects developed an orientation set which was specific to the transformations rather than to the geometry of the letter forms. In naming the letters, subjects took into account information from the total context, including orientation sets and direction of reading. Smooth performance required a congruence between the components of the process.

Visual orientation sets also seem to be functioning in the recognition of transformed connected text. Kolers (1968b) compared native Hebrew speakers and native English speakers on their ability to read eight transformations of their languages. The order of difficulty of reading the various transformations was very similar for both groups, despite the fact that the texts differed in alphabet, language, and the direction in which the language is normally read. As with letters, it was the transformation imposed and not the specific geometry of the characters that determined the order of difficulty. The contribution of directional reading patterns is dramatically shown in the reading of transformations like the one reproduced above. This transformation may be read in a rightward direction as nonsense or in a leftward direction meaningfully. Despite the powerful effects of syntax and meaningfulness on reading, subjects read this transformation faster in a left-to-right direction (Kolers, 1972a).

Many mysteries remain in our understanding of how vision operates in the reading processes. The evidence of the recent past points strongly to the conclusion that visual processes are more active and intentional than was long believed and this has led to a renewed interest in how such processes develop. While the work in this area has contributed important insights concerning the task of learning to read and the etiology of specific reading disabilities, its full potential awaits a more precise understanding of the nature of vision. In addition, until we know more about vision, the cognitive processes for which vision is the mode of input will remain controversial.

Conversion-Impletion Processes

Following visual input, processing occurs which converts the visual information to a form compatible with ongoing cognitive systems. The processing at this level, then, is concerned with the recoding of input. Subsequent systems are responsible for response generation. The processing can be divided logically into two major stages: 1) a bounding or segmenting process which divides the incoming temporal order into suitable units, and 2) the conversion and impletion of the units into the form appropriate for the subsequent cognitive systems and for storage in the Ready Store. The detailed processes of word perception have been the subject of extensive experimentation and a substantial number of theoretical models has been advanced (compendia of recent models are contained in Kolers & Eden, 1968; Melton & Martin, 1972; Uhr, 1966; and Wathen-Dunn, 1967). All such models are considered tentative by their authors and few attempt to explain all aspects of the processes. How word recognition occurs at this level of processing is simply not known at present, although a significant body of evidence is rapidly accumulating.

Models explaining word perception processes fall into several categories. Some consider letter and word recognition as a special case of pattern recognition and are concerned typically with the geometry of the stimulus and with hypothetical smoothing processes which allow the recognition of objects in a variety of configurations and orientations. Early versions of this type of model often assumed that visual input is compared to a template stored in long term memory to effect recognition. The failure of template-matching models to reasonably account for even the simplest recognition processes (for example, the recognition of a single letter in a variety of type fonts and cursive scripts) has led to the abandonment of such simplified approaches to the complexities of human recognition processes (Neisser, 1967). More complex models have attempted to detail the distinctive features of the stimulus and how these features interact with feature analyzers within the organism. Gibson, Schapiro, and Yonas (1968), for example, have described a set of "distinctive features" for upper-case Roman letters such that each letter can be differentiated on the basis of the presence or absence of each feature. Unfortunately, however, distinctive feature models fall short of explaining the complexities of reading at this stage (Kolers, 1969); in fact, the very concept may be inappropriate for descriptions of visual objects (Kolers, 1972).

A rather different approach is taken by models of word recognition which seek to outline the nature of the coding involved in the conversion-impletion processes (e.g., Estes, 1972; Gardner, 1973; Morton, 1969; Newell, 1972; Rubenstein, Lewis & Rubenstein, 1971; Rumelhart & Siple, 1974; Spoehr & Smith, 1975; Wickens, 1972). Early models of this type tended to emphasize decoding processes which assumed that the major task of the reader (or listener) was to decode the visual or aural components in order to understand the meanings involved. Increasingly, however, these models are reflecting the fact that the perceiver must contribute his knowledge to the process; that the explicit message represents only cues to the underlying semantic structures (Freedle & Carroll, 1972). None of these models has achieved a consensus of expert opinion and their complexity precludes extensive discussion here. (The interested reader can find a review of this work in Smith & Spoehr, 1974). Much of the theoretical work in this area is limited in its applicability to normal reading by the common practice of presenting 3- and 4-letter series tachistoscopically under conditions which may encourage visual strategies not commonly employed in skilled normal reading. Nevertheless, the experimental work has contributed to an understanding of such questions of long-standing interest as the nature of the cues and units involved and the form of the converted information. This research will be briefly discussed.

Cues to Word Recognition and the Units Involved

In the late 19th Century one of America's first experimental psychologists, J. McK. Cattell, rejected the notion that we read words by putting together their letters and suggested that "general word shape" served as the cue for the recognition of a word. This argument, which served as one basis for the "Great Debate" over approaches to teaching reading (Chall, 1967), is still with us. The issues today are many-sided, but it is clear that there are many attributes which can serve as cues to word recognition. Much of the recent experimentation has replicated findings of the early psychologists, but under modern control conditions which contribute to confidence and have allowed an exploitation of the findings not possible to the original investigators.

Cattell's suggestion that "general word shape" formed the cue for word perception was based on his findings that the number of letters that can be reported from a brief tachistoscopic exposure is greater if the letters form a word than if they are random arrangements. The explanation assumed that two perceptual units, letters and words, were involved. Another classic experiment casts doubt on this dichotomy, however. Miller, Bruner, and Postman (1954) found a relatively constant increase in the number of letters reported from pseudowords as their letter order approximated more closely to that of English. Baddeley (1964) concluded that the effect was due to response and memorial processes, but recent studies have shown the effect to be perceptual as well (Hershenson, 1969; Reicher, 1969). Hershenson suggested that in addition to its effects on post-perceptual processes, letter-order redundancy may be involved in an internal attentional mechanism for organizing input.[4]

Gibson, Pick, Osser, and Hammond (1962) hypothesized that readers use their knowledge of letter order to group letters into an intermediate functional unit called the Spelling Pattern (SP). The SP is defined as a cluster of graphemes which has an invariant pronunciation according to the rules of English in a given linguistic environment (Gibson, 1965). A similar unit, but defined on its phonemic dimensions, has been proposed by Hansen and Rodgers (1965) and extended theoretically by Spoehr and Smith (1975). Gibson *et al.* (1962) showed that accuracy of report from tachistoscopic exposures was higher when six-letter arrays contained only SP's (e.g., GLURCK) than for letters randomly arrayed (e.g., CKURGL). Aderman and Smith (1971) confirmed this finding but found it to obtain only when the subjects expected SP's. This is evidence that the specific perceptual unit processed is determined by the expectancy of the subject, as suggested by Huey (1900) and Neisser (1967).

---

[4]Letter order redundancy refers to the fact that letters do not follow each other with equal probability in English. The probabilities associated with given letter combinations can be determined. Estimates of the average redundancy of letter order in English generally report a figure slightly over 50 percent (Garner, 1962; Hershenson, 1969).

Whatever the role of grapheme-phoneme relationships might be, several additional cues have been shown to be important to word recognition. The length of a word provides an important cue (Erdmann & Dodge, 1898; Hochberg, 1970; Wiegand, 1908). Kolers (1970) found that subjects reading transformed text tended to substitute words of the same length for those misread. Within the word, the initial letter furnishes a stronger cue than letters in subsequent positions (Goldscheider & Müller, 1893; Marchbanks & Levin, 1965; Zeitler, 1900).

In context with other words, the amount and nature of the context provide important cues to word recognition (Brown, 1970; Goodman, 1970). A number of studies have shown that tachistoscopic word recognition improves with the addition of sentence contexts presented prior to the exposure (Tulving & Gold, 1963; Tulving, Mandler, & Baumal, 1964; Morton, 1964a; Pollack, 1964). From studies of homographs presented with and without semantic and syntactic frames, Levin, Ford and Beckwith (1968; Ford & Levin, 1968) concluded that both semantic and syntactic information facilitated word perception.

It is probable that the various cues shown to influence word perception do not operate at the same level nor influence the process in the same way. Skilled readers perform in experiments in ways that demonstrate a rather precise knowledge of letter order probabilities. This knowledge, and the use of such additional cues as word boundaries and word length, are specific to the level concerned with the conversion and impletion processes. Syntactic and semantic context effects, on the other hand, operate directly in the verbal integration processes. Similar context effects, for example, have been shown for words presented aurally (Perfetti & Goodman, 1970; Stowe, Harris, & Hampton, 1963). It is probable that context, therefore, has its main effects through feedback processes which reduce alternatives and structure expectancies. This view is in agreement with recent interpretations of the literature suggesting that verbal labels do not directly facilitate visual processes but have their major effects at later memory stages. (Garner, 1972; Gibson, 1969).

The skilled reader in the ongoing reading task is processing information which combines redundancies in ways which allow the impletion of text from samples. That is, samples of the text are continuously processed for testing against what the reader expects (Giuliano, 1969). Syntactic and semantic constraints operate to reduce the number of possibilities to a minimum and letter order constraints combined with other cues allow the testing of possibilities from a minimal visual input. Thus, subjects often read words without noticing mispellings and other anomalies (Pillsbury,

1897), and good readers make errors which tend to preserve the syntactic and semantic aspects of the text.

The Form of the Converted Signal

A theoretical issue of considerable importance is the form of the signal at this stage of processing. Several investigators have examined this issue, but rarely can experimental results be ascribed to a particular system unconfounded by processes of subsequent systems. Geyer (1966) referred to the output of this stage as "an awareness of the stimulus," and Sperling (1969) used a computer analogy to describe the signal as consisting of "addresses of motor programs." Similarly vague descriptions are not unusual in the literature. The issue relates importantly to the question of whether reading is necessarily "decoding to speech" or whether it is possible to read "visually." While this question is far from settled, it now appears that the question itself may present a false dichotomy. Wickelgren (1969) concluded from a review of the literature that while the signal at this stage is no longer visual, it might be auditory, articulatory, or abstract in form.

The concern here is with that very narrow band of signals specific to language. To conclude that this signal is no longer visual does not imply that visual processes do not continue. There is, of course, a visual store operating in parallel which would maintain a copy of the visual aspects of the stimulus. We can remember visual scenes as visual scenes and can even call visual scenes from memory through visualization processes. These parallel processes will not be discussed here as their operations in the reading processes are little known, although undoubtedly important. For example, it has been shown that subjects maintain for lengthy periods detailed information about the pictorial aspects of sentences they have read and that such information plays a role in such "higher order" processes as memory for sentences (Kolers, 1974; Kolers & Ostry, 1974).

The decision as to whether the signal is articulatory, auditory, or abstract is more difficult and cannot be made finally at this time. Cohen and Granstrom (1968) rejected both visual and auditory codes as a base for a similar task. Hershenson (1969) found his results in agreement with several other investigators in the rejection of acoustic encoding, but he adds the suggestion that acoustic encoding may be involved when the percept is ambiguous or unknown. This implies that acoustic encoding is an added process used when demanded by the task.

There is a strong possibility that the impletion-conversion processes in the skilled reader can convert the signal to an abstract verbal form which is neither articulatory nor acoustic when this is appropriate to the task. Much of the evidence would be in agreement with this interpretation. In the present context that would mean essentially that skilled readers under appropriate circumstances can read "directly" to conceptualizations without any necessity to convert the text to a sound-based code. This view has been advanced by Brown (1970) and Kolers (1970) among others. Descriptions of the details of the process will have to await further work in both linguistics and psychology, however.

The Ready Store

The output of the impletion-conversion processes is the effective stimulus for subsequent response systems. This output has been organized into the response units which are expected to be appropriate to the task and converted into the compatible form. Verbal responses can be made directly to this signal. However, the high rate of operation of the input systems relative to the slower response systems makes direct response an untenable strategy except in the response time experiment requiring a single response and analogous natural events. Whenever multiple responses are required, and particularly in the continuous processing task of normal reading, a temporal buffer between input and output operations is required for smooth integration of the systems to occur (Geyer, 1968). Spatially separated stimulus components can be rapidly scanned for conversion to few and simplified percepts.

The role of the temporal buffer, here called the Ready Store (RS), is of fundamental importance in most reading tasks. In the tachistoscopic letter recognition task the rapid input systems can process several letters from a very brief exposure. These letters are stored in the RS and can be utilized for verbal responses until they fade. If the letters can be bounded into larger units by the impletion-conversion processes, the units are stored and processed from the RS. Storage is not limited to the products of single fixations, however. It is this capability of the RS to briefly hold the material from several fixations in coexistent storage which allows reading by phrases. As the bounding functions at earlier stages convert stimulus elements into larger units, the units stored in the RS are "chunked" on the basis of their syntactic and semantic properties into phrases. If the units have no such properties (e.g., random digits), chunking can be done on the basis of rhythm and stress.

In the continuous processing task of normal reading, the RS plays an additional important function. Ongoing reading is not a series of tachistoscopic exposures. We do not read in a simple S-R chain of look $\longrightarrow$ say $\longrightarrow$ move eyes $\longrightarrow$ look $\longrightarrow$ say . . . . Rather, the input and output systems operate with considerable independence, made possible by the buffering capacity of the RS. This independence of operation enables the input and output systems to function simultaneously, greatly enhancing the rate of reading. (This apparently simultaneous processing may involve rapid alternation of attention between the systems, but any such processes cannot be measured at present).

In typical oral reading, for example, the eyes make several fixations before the voice begins. Then both the eyes and the voice move forward through the text, the eyes remaining ahead of the voice. This phenomenon, known as the eye-voice span, has been long known and studied. The span is longer (measured in units of text) for good readers and for easier reading materials (Buswell, 1920; Fairbanks, 1937). Within limits, the eyes and voice operate independently. The voice may continue smoothly while the eyes "study" a difficult word. If the problem is resolved before the voice reaches the troublesome word, the eyes move ahead without any disturbance in the vocal output. At pauses for punctuation or breath, however, the eyes "mark time" to maintain the temporal relationship with the voice. During some punctuation pauses the eyes may refixate a point in the text where a previous error was made and return in time to begin reading again with no noticeable effect on the voice (Geyer, 1966). This remarkable independence of the visual system from those processes it subserves is possible through the temporal buffering action of the RS.

In the continuous reading act, speed of processing is determined by the slowest system, much as a convoy must pace itself to the slowest ship. When overt or covert speech is part of the process, these form the slowest system for many reading tasks. In this situation the task of the input systems is to keep a ready supply of effective stimuli available in the RS at all times. If the input systems move ahead too quickly, stimuli are lost before they can be responded to, necessitating regressive eye movements. Thus the optimal number of stimuli available in the RS at any moment is the number which can be responded to during a period of time equal to the maximum storage of a single item. This number will vary due to syntactic and semantic properties of the items, but if the processing proceeds smoothly the time between eyes and voice (the temporal eye-voice span) should remain relatively constant regardless of the number of textual units processed. Geyer (1968) confirmed that the average temporal eye-voice span for all subjects was very close to the predicted one second and that the relative constancy with which the temporal eye-voice span was maintained was highly related to eye movement patterns characteristic of good reading. Smooth continuous oral reading depends on the reader's ability to coordinate all systems in a temporal steady state centered on the buffering capabilities of the RS.

Summary

The research discussed above suggests that the processes of schematization, ordering, and impletion that Kolers (1970) postulated for the perception of serially presented letters operate as well in the perception of the horizontal arrays of letters encountered in normal reading. The gross levels at which these processes are accomplished and some of the operations involved are thought to be somewhat like the following:

An initial schema of the visual scene is formed which provides a general framework of the nature of the stimulus and allows the appropriate operations to be mobilized. Involved in this process is an attentional focusing mechanism which delimits the size of field. At the schematization stage the focus could be at a low-power setting, yielding a wide field with little detail. On the basis of this visual sample, the focus is narrowed to exclude extraneous portions of the field and to maximize detail. With focus narrowed, input by an extremely rapid attentional scan converts the spatial array to the ordered temporal sequence required for analysis by the next system. Signal sharpening and orientation processes operate at this level as well. All aspects of vision are current research fronts.

Visual information is converted to a phonemic form when that is necessary by processes which combine the ordered sequences with other information which allows percepts to be constructed. This conversion includes at least two processes: a) a bounding or segmenting process which groups stimulus elements (e.g., letters) into units (e.g., words) and b) converts the units to a phonemic form appropriate to the response. Thus an array of letters might be coded as separate phonemic elements or as a word, depending on the demands of the task. The processes involved are not passive decoding processes; they actively combine information from sources which allow garbled or missing visual information to be impleted. The nature of the processing, the units involved, and the form of the resulting percept are current research questions.

Percepts formed through the impletion processes are stored individually in the Ready Store. Each remains available to response systems for approximately one second before fading. In continuous processing the Ready Store acts as the major temporal buffer which allows the temporal integration of the rapid input systems with the slower operations of the response systems.

The act of reading serves purposes as varied as the ends language can be made to serve. Broadly considered, therefore, reading involves most of the major brain functions: sensation, attention, cognition, emotion, motor processes, etc. The systems suggesting in the sections above are concerned with only a narrow band of the total information flow in the reading act. These hypothetical processes need to be more firmly understood and related to other imporant components, before the reading processes can be structured in the formal and quantified models of complex behavior. Yet the general principles governing such models are apparent in the reading processes and are already useful in understanding these processes.

All of the processes suggested above (with the exception of the passive store) are active and task-related. Each requires information of three general types: a) stored information necessary to the specific process, b) feedback from subsequent or higher-order processes, and c) information from the environment. While it is convenient to group these processes into interactive levels or stages, these stages are not wholly one-directional but rather form recursive networks requiring reference to memory, to what has already been processed, to what is likely, and so on. Skilled reading is not a passive flow of information from visual input to verbal meaning. The introspectively conscious verbal flow is a by-product of constructive processes imposed by active systems moving foward through the text.

REFERENCES

Aderman, D., & Smith, E. E. Expectancy as a determinant of functional units in perceptual recognition. *Cognitive Psychology,* 1971, 2, 117-129.

Averbach, E., & Coriell, A. A. Short-term memory in vision. *Bell System Technical Journal,* 1961, 40, 309-328.

Averbach, E., & Sperling, G. Short-term storage of information in vision. In R. N. Haber (Ed.), *Contemporary theory and research in visual perception.* New York: Holt, 1968.

Baddeley, A. D. Immediate memory and the "perception" of letter sequences. *Quarterly Journal of Experimental Psychology,* 1964, 16, 364-367.

Barton, M. I., Goodglass, H., & Shai, A. Differential recognition of tachistoscopically presented English and Hebrew words in right and left visual fields. *Perceptual and Motor Skills,* 1965, 21, 431-437.

Brown, E. The bases of reading acquisition. *Reading Research Quarterly,* 1970, VI, 49-74.

Bryden, M. P. Tachistoscopic recognition of nonalphabetic material. *Canadian Journal of Psychology,* 1960, 14, 78-86.

Buswell, G. T. An experimental study of the eye-voice span in reading. *Supplemental Education Monographs,* 1920, 17, 1-104.

Chall, J. *Learning to read: The great debate.* New York: McGraw-Hill, 1967.

Cohen, R. L., & Granström, K. Interpolated task and mode of recall as variables in STM for visual figures. *Journal of Verbal Learning and Verbal Behavior*, 1968, 7, 653-658.

Deregowski, J. B. Pictorial perception and culture. *Scientific American*, 1972, 227, 82-88.

Egeth, H. Laterality effects in perceptual matching. *Perception and Psychophysics*, 1971, 9, 375-376.

Erdmann, B., & Dodge, R. *Psychologische Untersuchengun über das Lesen auf Experimenteller Grundlage*. Halle: Neimeyer, 1898.

Eriksen, C. W., & Rohrbaugh, J. W. Some factors determining efficiency of selective attention. *American Journal of Psychology*, 1970, 83, 330-342.

Eriksen, C. W., & Spencer, T. Rate of information processing in visual perception: Some results and methodological considerations. *Journal of Experimental Psychology Monographs*, 1969, 79, 1-16.

Estes, W. K. An associative basis for coding and organization in memory. In A. W. Melton & E. Martin (Eds.) *Coding processes in human memory*. New York: Witey, 1972.

Fairbanks, G. The relationship between eye movements and voice in oral reading of good and bad silent readers. *Psychological Monographs*, 1937, 48, 78-107.

Ford, B. L., & Levin, H. Homographs in a semantic context. In H. Levin, E. J. Gibson, & J. J. Gibson (Eds.), *The analysis of reading skill. A program of basic and applied research*. Ithaca, New York: Cornell University, 1968.

Forgays, D. G. The development of a differential word recognition. *Journal of Experimental Psychology*, 1952, 45, 165-168.

Freedle, R. O., & Carroll, J. B. Comprehension and acquisition: Reflections. In J. B. Carroll & R. O. Freedle (Eds.), *Language comprehension and the acquisition of knowledge*. New York: Wiley, 1972.

Gardner, G. T. Evidence for independent parallel channels in tachistoscopic perception. *Cognitive Psychology*, 1973, 4, 130-155.

Garner, W. R. *Uncertainty and structure as psychological concepts*. New York: Wiley, 1962.

Garner, W. R. Information integration and form of encoding. In A. W. Melton & E. Martin (Eds.), *Coding processes in human memory*. New York: Wiley, 1972.

Geyer, J. J. Perceptual systems in reading: A temporal eye-voice span constant. Unpublished doctoral dissertation. University of California, Berkeley, 1966.

Geyer, J. J. Perceptual systems in reading: The prediction of a temporal eye-voice span constant. In H. K. Smith (Ed.), *Perception and reading*. Newark, Delaware: International Reading Assn., 1968.

Geyer, J. J. Models of perceptual processsses in reading. In H. Singer & R. B. Ruddell (Eds.), *Theoretical models and processes of reading*. Newark, Delaware: International Reading Assn., 1970.

Geyer, J. J. Comprehensive and partial models related to the reading process. *Reading Research Quarterly*, 1972, 7, 541-587.

Gibson, E. J. Learning to read. *Science*, 1965, 148, 1066-1072.

Gibson, E. J. *Principles of perceptual learning and development*. New York: Appleton-Century-Crofts, 1969.

Gibson, E. J., Pick, A., Osser, H., & Hammond, M. The role of grapheme-phoneme correspondence in the perception of words. *American Journal of Psychology*, 1962, 75, 554-570.

Gibson, E. J., Schapiro, F., & Yonas, A. Confusion matrices for graphic patterns obtained with a latency measure. In H. Levin, E. J. Gibson & J. J. Gibson (Eds.) *The analysis of reading skill: a program of basic and applied research*. Ithaca, New York: Cornell University, 1968.

Giuliano, V. E. Analog networks for word association. In D. A. Norman (Ed.), *Memory and attention*. New York: Wiley, 1969.

Glanville, A. D., & Dallenbach, K. M. The range of attention. *American Journal of Psychology*, 1929, 41, 207-236.

Goldscheider, A., & Müller, R. F., Zur Physiologie und Pathologie des Lesens. *Zeitschrift für Klinische Medicin*, 1893, XXIII, 131-167.

Goodglass, H., & Barton, M. Handedness and differential perception of verbal stimuli in left and right visual fields. *Perceptual and Motor Skills*, 1963, 17, 851-854.

Goodman, K. S. Reading: A psycholinguistic guessing game. In H. Singer & R. B. Ruddell (Eds.), *Theoretical models and processes of reading*. Newark, Delaware: International Reading Assn., 1970.

Haber, R. N. Visual persistence and the processing of visual stimulation. Paper presented at a symposium on Visual Masking and Metacontrast during the International Congress of Psychology, London, 1969.

Hansen, D., & Rodgers, T. S. An exploration of psycholinguistic units in initial reading. *Technical Report No. 74*. Palo Alto, California: Stanford University Institute for Mathematic Studies in the Social Sciences, 1965.

Harcum, E. R. Effects of symmetry on the perception of tachistoscopic patterns. *American Journal of Psychology*, 1964, 77, 600-606.

Harcum, E. R., & Finkel, M. E. Explanation of Mishgin and Forgays' result as a directional-reading conflict. *Canadian Journal of Psychology*, 1963, 17, 224-234.

Harcum, E. R., & Friedman, S. M. Reversal reading by Israeli observers of visual patterns without intrinsic directionality. *Canadian Journal of Psychology*, 1963, 17, 264-273.

Harcum, E. R., Hartman, R., & Smith, H. F. Pre-versus post-knowledge of required reproduction sequence for tachistoscopic patterns. *Canadian Journal of Psychology*, 1963, 17, 264-273.

Heron, W. Perception as a function of retinal locus and attention. *American Journal of Psychology*, 1957, 70, 38-48.

Hershenson, M. Stimulus structure, cognitive structure, and the perception of letter arrays. *Journal of Experimental Psychology*, 1969, 79, 327-335.

Hirata, K. I., & Osaka, R. Tachistoscopic recognition of Japanese materials in left and right visual fields. *Psychologia*, 1967, 10, 7-18.

Hochberg, J. Components of literacy: Speculations and exploratory research. In H. Levin & J. P. Williams (Eds.), *Basic studies in reading*. New York: Basic Books, 1970.

Huey, E. B. *The psychology and pedogogy of reading*. Cambridge, Massachusetts: The M.I.T. Press, 1968.

Kimura, D. The effect of letter position on recognition. *Canadian Journal of Psychology*, 1959, 13, 1-10.

Kinsbourne, M. & Warrington, E. K. The effect of an aftercoming random pattern on the perception of brief visual stimuli. *Quarterly Journal of Experimental Psychology*, 1962, 14, 223-234.

Kolers, P. A. The recognition of geometrically transformed text. *Perception and Psychophysics*, 1968, 3, 57-64.

Kolers, P. A. Clues to a letter's recognition: Implications for the design of characters. *Journal of Typographic Research*, 1969, 3, 145-167.

Kolers, P. A. Three stages of reading. In H. Levin & J. P. Williams (Eds.) *Basic studies in reading*. New York: Basic Books, 1970.

Kolers, P. A. Experiments in reading. *Scientific American*, 1972, 227, 84-91.

Kolers, P. A. Two kinds of recognition. *Canadian Journal of Psychology*, 1974, 28, 51-61.

Kolers, P. A., & Eden, M., (Eds.). *Recognizing patterns: studies in living and automatic systems.* Cambridge, Massachusetts: The M.I.T. Press, 1968.

Kolers, P. A., & Katzman, M. T. Naming sequentially presented letters and words. *Language and Speech,* 1966, 9, 84-95.

Kolers, P. A., & Ostry, D. J. Time course of loss of information regarding pattern analyzing operations. *Journal of Verbal Learning and Verbal Behavior,* 1974, 13, 599-612.

Kolers, P. A., & Perkins, D. N. Orientation of letters and errors in their recognition. *Perception and Psychophysics,* 1969, 5, 265-269. (a).

Kolers, P. A., & Perkins, D. N. Orientation of letters and their speed of recognition. *Perception and Psychophysics,* 1969, 5, 275-280. (b).

Levin, H., Ford, B. L., & Beckwith, M. Homographs in grammatical frames. In H. Levin, E. J. Gibson & J. J. Gibson (Eds.), *The analysis of reading skill: A program of basic and applied research.* Ithaca, New York: Cornell, 1968.

Lindsay, P. H. & Norman, D. A. *Human information processing: An introduction to psychology.* New York: Academic Press, 1972.

Mackworth, N. H. Visual noise causes tunnel vision. *Psychonomic Science,* 1965, 3, 67-68.

Marchbanks, G., & Levin, H. Cues by which children recognize words. *Journal of Educational Psychology,* 1965, 56, 57-61.

Melton, A. W., & Martin, E., (Eds.). *Coding processes in human memory.* New York: Wiley, 1972.

Mewhort, D. J. K. Sequential redundancy and letter spacing as determinants of tachistoscopic recognition. *Canadian Journal of Psychology,* 1966, 20, 435-444.

Mewhort, D. J. K. Familiarity of letter sequences, response uncertainty, and the tachistoscopic recognition experiment. *Canadian Journal of Psychology,* 1967, 12, 309-321.

Miller, G. A., Bruner, J. S., & Postman, L. Familiarity of letter sequences and tachistoscopic identification. *Journal of General Psychology,* 1954, 50, 129-139.

Mishkin, M., & Forgays, D. G. Word recognition as a function of retinal locus. *Journal of Experimental Psychology,* 1952, 43, 43-48.

Morton, J. The effects of context on the visual duration threshold for words. *British Journal of Psychology,* 1964, 55, 165-180.

Morton, J. Interaction of information in word recognition. *Psychological Review,* 1969, 76, 165-178.

Neisser, U. *Cognitive psychology.* New York: Appleton-Century-Crofts, 1967.

Newell, A. A theoretical exploration of mechanisms for coding the stimulus. In A. W. Melton & E. Martin (Eds.), *Coding processes in human memory.* New York: Wiley, 1972.

Orbach, J. Retinal locus as a factor in recognition of visually perceived words. *American Journal of Psychology,* 1953, 65, 555-562.

Perfetti, C. A., & Goodman, D. Semantic constraints on the decoding of ambiguous words. *Journal of Experimental Psychology,* 1970, 86, 420-427.

Pillsbury, W. B. A study of apperception. *American Journal of Psychology,* 1897, 8, 315-393.

Pollack, I. Interaction of two sources of verbal context in word identification. *Language and Speech,* 1964, 7, 1-12.

Pribram, K. H. Perception and its disorders. *Research Publication ARNMD XLVIII,* 1970, 150-162.

Reicher, G. M. Perceptual recognition as a function of meaningfulness of stimulus material. *Journal of Experimental Psychology,* 1969, 81, 275-280.

Rubenstein, H., Lewis, S. S., & Rubenstein, M. A. Evidence for phonemic recoding in visual word recognition. *Journal of Verbal Learning and Verbal Behavior,* 1971, 10, 645-657.

Rumelhart, D. E., & Siple, P. The process of recognizing tachistoscopically presented words. *Psychological Review,* 1974, 81, 99-118.

Smith, E. E., & Spoehr, K. T. The perception of printed English: A theoretical perspective. In B. H. Kantowitz (Ed.), *Human information processing: Tutorials in performance and cognition,* New York: Wiley, 1974.

Sperling, G. The information available in brief visual presentations. *Psychological Monographs,* 1960, 74, No. 11.

Sperling, G. A model for visual memory tasks. *Human Factors,* 1963, 5, 19-31.

Sperling, G. Successive approximations to a model for short term memory. *Acta Psychologica,* 1967, 27, 285-292.

Sperling, G. Short-term memory, long-term memory, and scanning in the processing of visual information. In R. N. Haber (Ed.). *Information processing approaches to visual perception.* New York: Holt, 1969.

Spoehr, K. T., & Smith, E. E. The role of orthographic and phonotactic rules in perceiving letter patterns. *Journal of Experimental Psychology,* 1975, 104, 21-34.

Stowe, A. N., Harris, W. P., & Hampton, D. B. Signal and context components of word-recognition behavior. *Journal of the Acoustical Society of America,* 1963, 35, 639-644.

Tulving, E., and Gold, C. Stimulus information and contextual information as determinants of tachistoscopic recognition of words. *Journal of Experimental Psychology,* 1963, 66, 319-327.

Tulving, E., Mandler, G., & Baumal, R. Interaction of two sources of information in tachistoscopic word recognition. *Canadian Journal of Psychology,* 1964, 18, 62-71.

Uhr, L. (Ed.). *Pattern recognition.* New York: Wiley, 1966.

Wathen-Dunn, W. (Ed.). *Models for the perception of speech and visual form.* Cambridge, Massachusetts: M.I.T. Press, 1967.

Werblin, F. S. The control of sensitivity in the retina. *Scientific American,* 1973, 228, 70-79.

White, M. J. Laterality differences in perception: A review. *Psychological Bulletin,* 1969, 6, 387-405.

Wickelgren, W. A. Auditory or articulatory coding in verbal short-term memory. *Psychological Review,* 1969, 76, 232-235.

Wickens, D. D. Characteristics of word encoding. In A. W. Melton & E. Martin (Eds.), *Coding processes in human memory.* New York: Wiley, 1972.

Wiegand, C. F. Untersuchungen uber die Bedeutung der Gestalqualitat für die Erkennung von Wörten. *Zeitschrift für Psychologie,* 1908, XLVIII, 161-237.

Woodworth, R. S., & Schlosberg, H. *Experimental psychology.* New York: Holt, 1954.

Zeitler, J. Tachistoskopische Untersuchungen über das Lesen. *Philosophische Studien,* 1900, XVI, 380-463.

Reading as an Intentional Behavior[1]

JULIAN HOCHBERG
Columbia University

AND

VIRGINIA BROOKS
New York University

To the perception psychologist, reading is not an isolated behavior that can be understood adequately by itself. Depending as heavily as it does on the language skills and on directed visual search, reading text, as a perceptuomotor activity, has certain characteristics in common with listening to speech and with viewing scenes. The first characteristic shared by these three activities, which is more obvious in the case of reading than in the other two, is that these behaviors do not consist of automatic responses to the array or sequence of patterned stimulation that confronts the subject. The reader does not merely regard a block of text and immediately realize its message. He must *intend* to read the display, must "pay attention" to its meaning, if he is to be able to respond to its contents. What a phrase like "pay attention to" might mean in this context has not received much thought or experimental research, but it would seem to be of fundamental importance to any understanding of what the reading process is all about.

Let us consider briefly some of the more obvious ways in which intention affects reading: 1) As noted, if a person looks idly at a page of text, with no intention to read, he may recognize only those few words on which his gaze may rest. 2) An efficient reader may read text for meaning at up to 4,800 letters per minute, but at that rate he is very likely not to notice minor spelling errors or omissions; therefore, this figure certainly does not mean that each letter is actually looked at, even though comprehension scores may be very high. 3) In fact, if the task requires the reader to look at or near each letter—for example, if he is checking for misspellings or broken letters, as in proofreading—then his reading rate will slow down and his comprehension score will drop. Here, then, are two

[1] Supported by NICH and HD R01HD04213-01.

clearly separable reading tasks: one with intention to extract meaningful content from the printed page; the other with intention to pay attention to the letters and the spelling of the words that make up the printed page. These and other tasks, set either by the goals given the reader, or by the relative difficulty or unfamiliarity of the material, affect the reader's visual search patterns and performances (18, 2). Normally, of course, the subject is required neither to skim as lightly as possible nor to attend to each serif on each letter. Instead, his behavior is probably determined by the changing demands imposed by what he is reading—at one point, casting his eye far ahead; at another, looking at almost each individual letter. *Reading* is thus a very general term, covering a wide range of behaviors, involving diverse purposes and skills.

Skills in reading can be arranged in a logical hierarchy: the ability to discriminate letters and letter-groups, the ability to form grapheme-phoneme correspondences, and to spell out (1). In general, one might expect that these "lower" skills are to some degree necessary to the acquisition of higher ones—some minimum ability at letter-discrimination and at syllable- and word-recognition is needed in order for reading-for-meaning to proceed. Thus, it seems extremely likely that every practiced reader has had to acquire these "lower" skills at some stage in his career toward literacy, and that he can fall back upon them when the task requires it; for example, he can dissect some unfamiliar word or passage into its component letters, and then put it together again. But, these lower skills are probably used only occasionally. When the skilled reader reads normally, that is, when he uses his eyes to retrieve linguistic meaning from the printed page in as natural and content-oriented a way as he uses his ears to listen to speech, he probably looks at the text infrequently, compared to when he proofreads or compared to a less skilled reader. He "samples" the text in order to develop hypotheses about what the next string of symbols consists of, and to test those expectations at appropriate places further along in the text. This, of course, sounds more like what we think of as "skimming" than what we consider to be reading, but no hard distinction is really possible: "skimming" and "reading" represent points on a continuum of intention; they are not basically different activities. In fact, "skimming" is much closer to what the subject has learned to do when he is listening to speech or when he is looking at scenes, long before he comes to the special task of learning to read, that is, to the special task of using his eyes to "listen."

Before we consider how the various components of literacy might fit together in the intentional activity of normal reading, let us first examine in turn the prior behaviors of active listening and looking.

The first thing we should note about listening is that it, too, depends on the subject's attention. As a great deal of research has shown (7, 3, 21, 27), if a subject is asked to attend to one of two fairly rapid monologs that are being presented to him simultaneously, but in two different "channels" (e.g., one in a male voice and one in a female voice, or one in the right ear and one in the left ear), he *seems* to fail to "hear" the content of the unattended message; at least, he cannot recall it. Nor will the subject respond to some sets of words to which he has been instructed to respond, if they have been embedded in the unattended channel.

Such selective attention is often explained as being the result of a "filter" that passes the signals that are presented on the attended channel, but which attenuates or even blocks the other channel's signals. On closer examination, however, the filter analogy requires too many unlikely and complex properties to be very helpful. And in fact it is not true that we can say, *as a general statement,* that the content of the unattended message is unheard. For example, if both channels contain the same message, but the unattended one is delayed so that it lags behind the attended one, after a while most subjects realize that both messages are the same (27). As another example: if the subject's own name is presented in the unattended channel, he will tend to hear it even though it is not in the channel to which he has been instructed to attend. Now, while it is easy to see how one could "tune" a filter to select one frequency rather than another, or to select one ear rather than the other, it is hard to see how to construct a filter to work in terms of analyzed verbal meaning (9). For these and other reasons, Neisser (22) and Hochberg (14, 16) have argued that it is not necessary to invoke any filter at all in order to explain selective attention in listening; instead, we need to consider more closely what is really involved in attentive listening to speech.

The study of which sounds listeners confuse with each other, and which they can discriminate, lends some support to the proposition that we do not normally do much with the raw phonic elements of speech (20). We usually respond, instead, to larger packets of sounds, judging them to be one phoneme or another on the bases of certain distinctive features—distinctive features which tend to be those which distinguish the listener's own speech-producing actions, for example, tongue placement. The perception of word-sounds may be accomplished, therefore, by a process of "analysis of synthesis," that is, by matching certain features of the sensory input against corresponding features of one's plans to articulate speech.

Neisser (22) and Hochberg (16) propose that listening to speech follows the same outline as listening to word-sounds: In active listening, the subject has available to him in his own speech-generating repertory organized strings of language, that is, speech-generating plans which may be of the order of words, phrases, or even of sentences in length, depending on the cliché content of the language habitually used. The listener unfolds or reviews these units as he listens, checking the stimulus input relatively infrequently to confirm or revise his hypotheses. Speech sounds that were not anticipated in this fashion, nor encoded and stored as part of some such higher speech structure, present too much unorganized material to retain, exceed the memory-span for such unorganized and independent material, and cannot be recalled. This would explain what happens in the two-channel experiments, without recourse to any concept of a filter: the subject makes active anticipatory responses to the initial phonemes that he receives in the channel to which he is attending and stores the results of his testing of those expectations. Sounds that were uttered on the nonattended channel may be briefly stored as unrelated sounds, and will usually fade from memory while the subject reports the message received on the attended channel. As we should expect from our analysis of the situation, the experiment cannot be performed unless the verbal material presented is organized into redundant and predictable sequences (19). This argument is presented in more detail elsewhere (16). What is important to us here is that if listening to speech rests upon anticipating the results of having sampled redundant trains of sound, then something like this hypothesis-testing should also occur in reading, which is rooted in the listening and speaking processes.

Let us now turn to the skills that the subject must have acquired from his experiences in looking at scenes—skills which also antedate by many years his acquisition of reading abilities. Because our eyes register fine detail only within a very small region of the retina (the *fovea*), we must learn about the visual world by a succession of glances in different directions. Hence, like listening to speech, looking at scenes must occur by a temporal sequence of patterned stimulation. But whereas the listener only has the redundancy of ordered speech or music to guide his anticipations of what the next moment's stimulation will bring, the subject viewing a normal world has two sources of expectations: 1) Like the listener, he has learned something about the shapes to be expected in the world, and their regularities (14, 17); 2) The wide periphery of the retina, which is low in acuity and therefore in the detail that it can pick up, nevertheless provides an intimation of what will meet his glance when the observer moves his eyes to some region of the visual field. And because such changes in fixation point are executed by *saccadic movements*, whose endpoints are decided *before* the movement is initiated (i.e., saccades are *ballistic* movements), the contents of each glance is always, in a sense, an answer to a question about what will be seen if some specific part of the peripherally-viewed scene is brought to the fovea.

We do not know too much about the strategies and tactics of free eye-movement deployment in viewing scenes, but it seems safe to say that the major potentially informative parts of the scenes are scanned. This is followed by making whatever small excursions are necessary to fill in detail needed to decide what is being looked at. There is, in general, a relatively high number of large saccades, a great deal of recursion, and nothing at all that should make it easy for a subject to keep precise track of the temporal order in which any search of the visual field has been executed, that is, no mapping of spatial order into temporal sequence. But this is just the task that faces the child when he first learns to read: he has to put together letters into words by a sequence of small adjacent fixations. Surely this is an unaccustomed task for the visuomotor system.[2] It is one which needs whatever assistance can be provided and is one which the reader will try to escape as soon as he can (Hochberg, 1964).

The task of reading text, which requires the child to make many small, sequential, adjacent saccades, can be made easier in various ways. The strain can be reduced by using large type or by moving one's finger under the type, letter by letter; above all, and most useful to the attainment of literacy, by "guessing" at what some syllable, or some word, or even phrase would turn out to be. This last point is particularly important. Normal text is highly redundant in many ways, so that the subject does not have to *see* every part of a letter clearly, or every part of a word, in order to know what is being said. In short, the subject will—and *should*—tend to "guess" at what is vaguely seen in peripheral vision—and the more he knows about the redundancies of spelling, grammar, and idiom employed by the text, or *the more the text approaches the patterns of speech that he is normally prepared to generate,* the more he can correctly anticipate the message, the more likely that his guesses will be right, and the fewer the fixations that he actually needs to make. But the knowledge is essential: training for fewer fixations can be of little use if the anticipations are not correct to begin with, and if consequent reinforcement stemming from the correctness of the guess and from the relief of the onerous necessity for small saccades does not occur.

This reminds us of what is, of course, one of the primary characteristics of skill in reading: the fact that the practiced reader needs shorter and

---

[2] Adjustment to this task is not always satisfactorily achieved. Thus Taylor and Robinson (1963) found that inefficient early ocular motor activity may result in final motor habits which inhibit efficient reading after the original causes (difficulty with word identification and recognition) no longer exist.

fewer fixations in order to identify letters, to recognize words, to read text. How is this skill acquired, and on what psychological processes does it rest? Much of the research to this point has used the method of *tachisto-scopic presentation,* in which the subject is shown letters or other stimulus patterns at some short exposure. In some ways, though with many reservations (*15*), we may consider the tachistoscopic presentation as being analogous to a single fixation that is made in the course of the reading process. Many years ago, Cattell (*5, 6*) showed that the exposure required to identify each of a tachistoscopically-presented set of unrelated letters, increased as the number of letters increased. The exposure time required to recognize some familiar word or phrase is, however, no longer than that for a single letter. In other words, the skilled reader is "picking up" as a unit what the unskilled reader would have to identify by multiple fixations. Since then, it has been amply shown that subjects can recognize words and shapes with which they are familiar at shorter exposure times than are needed for material with which they are unfamiliar (*13, 25*). Here, then, is one obvious reason why the skilled reader can make fewer and shorter fixations in reading text. This does not mean, however, that he *sees* the letters any differently, that is, that his sensory processes have been affected. There are reasons to believe that these effects of familiarity occur because of the subject's *response bias:* he is more ready to respond with a given letter, word, or phrase even when only partial or no sensory basis for that response is actually present (*10*), and he can better *recall* familiar material. That is, as with speech sounds, we would expect that the arrangement of the letters of a completely unfamiliar word would soon be forgotten, whereas once the skilled reader has identified the stimulus as being a familiar word, he can generate all the individual letters in sequence whenever he is called upon to do so (assuming he can spell it), regardless of the number of letters involved. In support of this suggestion, we should note that it is possible to demonstrate effects of familiarity on tachistoscopic word-recognition under conditions in which those effects are almost certainly due to the differential availability of memory units by which the strings of letters may be encoded and subsequently regenerated, and not due to differential sensory processing (*12, 14*). And the demonstration by Graf and Torrey (*11*) that comprehension scores are higher for written material that is broken at major linguistic boundaries than are comprehension scores for material broken at minor boundaries might be interpreted as the effect of greater ease of storing the material in the former condition.

By responding to the few features seen in clear foveal vision with an entire word or phrase, the skilled reader, then, has largely relieved himself of the necessity of looking closely at the text. He therefore needs to fixate only those parts of the array, further along the page, that will enable him to make new guesses and to check his previous ones. The better the reader, the more widespread can be the fixations by which he samples the text—just so long as the text provides him with contextual redundancy and as long as his task permits him to attend to the meaning or content, rather than to spelling or to individual letters.

The question then becomes, what guides the skilled reader's fixations? How does he decide what the text in question is, without looking at each letter?

As in listening to speech, of course, the skilled reader's expectations of what he will find when he looks further along the page are based in part on the syntax, and on the meaning of what he has just read. In order for sampling to be possible, and for anything less than letter-by-letter reading to suffice, some redundancy, of course, is needed. With our present spelling and syntax, redundancy in the middle of long sentences is close to 100 percent. Like the listener, therefore, the reader can formulate and test speech fragments. He need not look at each letter because he can guess at the next n letters, and he knows enough about the constraints of language to make a profitable guess at how much further along he should look next in order to test these fragments and formulate new ones. Thus, it has been found that reading errors are influenced by associative factors and by language habits based on syntactic framework (8, 23, 24), which is what we would expect if readers' hypotheses are only intermittently tested. Call this determinant of fixation CSG for cognitive search guidance (15). Unlike the listener, however, the reader is not restricted to previous content as the source of his extrapolations because he can, in addition, use the information given in peripheral vision, as modified by his linguistic expectancies, to select the places at which he should seek successive stimulus input. Thus, at the very least, he should be able to anticipate, through the use of interword spaces that appear in the peripheral vision, where he must look in order to fixate the most informative portions of words (that is, their termini), and which words are likely to be short functors. Call such determinants of fixation PSG for peripheral search guidance. The practiced reader must move his eyes under the combined control of CSG and PSG.

The beginning reader, who really must look at most or all of the letters, probably makes little use of PSG. He is, therefore, less hampered than is the better reader when the information available in peripheral vision is interfered with, for example, by filling in the interword spaces so as to make the word boundaries indiscriminable when viewed peripherally (15). Readers with "tunnel vision," that is, lacking peripheral vision, have very low reading rates. But, the discovery of what actually guides a skilled reader's fixations and how these can be improved calls for more than a simple demonstration of the importance of peripheral vision. One possible avenue of research which we are currently exploring with Roger Nelson and Murray Glanzer, is to present the reader cinematically with a paragraph of text in which a simulated fixation point, that is, an area of clear vision containing four or five letters, appears successively at various places in the text. This procedure provides the reader with an incomplete sample of the page. The independent variables in this investigation are these: how the samples are taken; how the simulated fixation points are presented throughout the text; and the amount of information, if any, that is transmitted in the periphery of the field, that is, outside of the simulated fixation point. When the reader performs at or near his normal reading rate, we may assume that we have simulated his sampling procedure. In other words, we have given him the information he normally employs in terms of the units by which he normally reads.

This picture of skilled reading is one of successive extrapolations, not of information processing, letter by letter. If it is an accurate picture, it will explain why it appears as though really skilled readers are processing a tremendous amount of information per second; whereas, in fact, they are not—they merely know a great deal about the language and about writers. If we are to attempt to teach readers to make such extrapolations and to use them, we shall have to keep two things in mind: first, we must fit the text—which we are teaching them to anticipate—to the anticipations that their speech habits already provide; second, we cannot expect them to transfer such skilled reading habits to less idiosyncratic text until the appropriate habits of speech and knowledge have been built up.

But, are we talking about "skimming" or "reading?" In view of the fact that visual perception almost always entails a procedure of sampling from a display of stimulus information that is redundant for the perceptual task at hand—another way of saying this is that it is very hard to present the adult with a perceptual task to which none of his previous visual experience is relevant—it is hard to see how the distinction between skimming and reading can be maintained as an absolute one. That is, the distinction must be referred to the size of the units that the task requires the subject to process. For example, if the task is to detect burred or broken serifs in the text, each letter must be fixated more than once; anything less is skimming. But this is not how people normally read, whether for entertainment or for information. It is plausible that children should be encouraged to predict and anticipate what is coming next in reading. The exact methods for so encouraging them, however, should be the subject for empirical study and not for speculation. Empirical studies are also needed to determine what the goals and the appropriate units are for the different intentions that initiate and maintain reading behavior, if reading behavior—as opposed to symbol-recognition, orthography, or tachistoscopic-perception—is to be understood in a way that is theoretically satisfying or socially useful.

REFERENCES

1. Betts, E. A. "Reading: Perceptual Learning," *Education*. Indianapolis: Bobbs-Merrill, 1969.
2. Brandt, H. F. *The Psychology of Seeing*. New York: Philosophical Library, 1945.
3. Broadbent, D. E. *Perception and Communication*. London: Pergamon, 1958.
4. Buswell, G. T. *How People Look at Pictures*. Chicago: University of Chicago Press, 1935.
5. Cattell, J. McK. "The Time It Takes to See and Name Objects," *Mind*, 11 (1886), 63-65.
6. Cattell, J. McK. "The Inertia of the Eye and Brain," *Brain*, 7 (1886), 295-312.
7. Cherry, E. C. "Some Experiments on the Recognition of Speech, with One and Two Ears," *J. Acoust. Soc. Amer.*, 25 (1953), 975-979.
8. Clay, M. "A Syntactic Analysis of Reading Errors," *Journal of Verbal Learning and Verbal Behavior*, 7 (1968), 434-438.
9. Deutsch, J. A., and D. Deutsch. "Attention: Some Theoretical Considerations," *Psychological Review*, 70 (1963), 80-90.
10. Goldiamond, I. "Indicators of Perception: I. Subliminal Perception, Subception, Unconscious Perception: An Analysis in Terms of Psychophysical Indicator Methodology," *Psychological Bulletin*, 55 (1958), 373-411.
11. Graf, R., and J. W. Torrey. "Perception of Phrase Structure in Written Language," *Proceedings of the 74th Annual Convention of the American Psychological Association*, 1966, 83-84.
12. Hayes, W., J. Robinson, and L. Brown. "An Effect of Past Experience on Perception: An Artifact," *American Psychologist*, 16 (1961), 420 (Abstract).
13. Henle, M. "The Experimental Investigation of Past Experiences as a Determinant of Visual Form Perception," *Journal of Experimental Psychology*, 30 (1942), 1-22.
14. Hochberg, J. "In the Mind's Eye," in R. N. Haber (Ed.), *Contemporary Theory and Research in Visual Perception*. New York: Holt, Rinehart and Winston, 1968, 309-331.
15. Hochberg, J. "Components of Literacy: Speculations and Exploratory Research," in H. Levin and J. Williams (Eds.), *Basic Studies on Reading*, in press.
16. Hochberg, J. "Attention, Organization and Consciousness," in D. Mostofsky (Ed.), *Attention: Contemporary Theory and Analysis*. New York: Appleton-Century-Crofts, forthcoming.
17. Hochberg, J. "Units of Perceptual Analysis," in J. Mehler (Ed.), *Handbook of Cognitive Psychology*. Englewood Cliffs, N.J.: Prentice-Hall, forthcoming.
18. Judd, C. H., and G. T. Buswell. "Silent Reading: A Study of the Various Types," *Supplemental Educational Monographs*, 23 (1922).
19. Lawson, E. A. "Decisions Concerning the Rejected Channel," *Quarterly Journal of Experimental Psychology*, 18 (1966), 260-265.
20. Liberman, A. M. "Some Results of Research on Speech Perception," *J. Acoust. Soc. Amer.*, 29 (1957), 117-123.

21. Moray, N., and A. M. Taylor. "The Effect of Redundancy in Shadowing One of Two Messages," *Language and Speech,* 76 (1958), 376-385.

22. Neisser, U. *Cognitive Psychology.* New York: Appleton-Century-Crofts, 1967.

23. Rosenberg, S. "Associative Factors in the Recall of Connected Discourse," *Psychonomic Science,* 4 (1966), 53-54.

24. Samuels, S. J. "Effect of Word Associations on Reading Speed and Recall," *Proceedings of the 74th Annual Convention of the American Psychological Association,* 1966.

25. Solomon, R. L., and D. H. Howes. "Word Frequency, Personal Values, and Visual Duration Thresholds," *Psychological Review,* 58 (1951), 256-270.

26. Taylor, S. E., and H. A. Robinson. "The Relationship of the Ocular-Motor Efficiency of the Beginning Reader to His Success in Learning to Read," paper presented at the *American Educational Research Association Conference,* February 13-16, 1963.

27. Treisman, A. M. "Monitoring and Storage of Irrelevant Messages in Selective Attention," *Journal of Verbal Learning and Verbal Behavior,* 3 (1964), 449-459.

Word Recognition

Learning to Read[1]

ELEANOR J. GIBSON[2]
Cornell University

Educators and the public have exhibited a keen interest in the teaching of reading ever since free public education became a fact (*1*). Either because of or despite their interest, this most important subject has been remarkably susceptible to the influence of fads and fashions and curiously unaffected by disciplined experimental and theoretical psychology. The psychologists have traditionally pursued the study of verbal learning by means of experiments with nonsense syllables and the like—that is, materials carefully divested of useful information. And the educators, who found little in this work that seemed relevant to the classroom, have stayed with the classroom; when they performed experiments, the method was apt to be a gross comparison of classes privileged and unprivileged with respect to the latest fad. The result has been two cultures: the pure scientists in the laboratory, and the practical teachers ignorant of the progress that has been made in the theory of human learning and in methods of studying it.

That this split was unfortunate is clear enough. True, most children do learn to read. But some learn to read badly, so that school systems must provide remedial clinics; and a small proportion (but still a large number of future citizens) remain functional illiterates. The fashions which have led to classroom experiments, such as the "whole word" method, emphasis on context and pictures for "meaning," the "flash" method, "speed

[1] Reprinted from *Science,* 148 (1965) 1066-1072 with the permission of the author and the American Association for the Advancement of Science. The author is senior research associate in psychology at Cornell University. This article is adapted from a paper read at a conference on Perceptual and Linguistic Aspects of Reading, sponsored by the Committee on Learning and the Educational Process of the Social Science Research Council and held at the Center for Advanced Study in the Behavioral Sciences, Palo Alto, California, 31 October 1963.

[2] Now Susan Linn Sage Professor of Psychology, Cornell University.

reading," revised alphabets, the "return" to "phonics," and so on, have done little to change the situation.

Yet a systematic approach to the understanding of reading skill is possible. The psychologist has only to treat reading as a learning problem, to apply ingenuity in theory construction and experimental design to this fundamental activity on which the rest of man's education depends. A beginning has recently been made in this direction, and it can be expected that a number of theoretical and experimental studies of reading will be forthcoming (2).

Analysis of the Reading Process

A prerequisite to good research on reading is a psychological analysis of the reading process. What is it that a skilled reader has learned? Knowing this (or having a pretty good idea of it), one may consider how the skill is learned, and next how it could best be taught. Hypotheses designed to answer all three of these questions can then be tested by experiment.

There are several ways of characterizing the behavior we call reading. It is receiving communication; it is making discriminative responses to graphic symbols; it is decoding graphic symbols to speech; and it is getting meaning from the printed page. A child in the early stages of acquiring reading skill may not be doing all these things, however. Some aspects of reading must be mastered before others and have an essential function in a sequence of development of the final skill. The average child, when he begins learning to read, has already mastered to a marvelous extent the art of communication. He can speak and understand his own language in a fairly complex way, employing units of language organized in a hierarchy and with a grammatical structure. Since a writing system must correspond to the spoken one, and since speech is prior to writing, the frame work and unit structure of speech will determine more or less the structure of the writing system, though the rules of correspondence vary for different languages and writing systems. Some alphabetic writing systems have nearly perfect single-letter-to-sound correspondences, but some, like English, have far more complex correspondence between spelling patterns and speech patterns. Whatever the nature of the correspondences, it is vital to a proper analysis of the reading task that they be understood. And it is vital to remember, as well, that the first stage in the child's mastery of reading is learning to communicate by means of spoken language.

Once a child begins his progression from spoken language to written language, there are, I think, three phases of learning to be considered. They present three different kinds of learning tasks, and they are roughly sequential, though there must be considerable overlapping. These three phases are: learning to differentiate graphic symbols; learning to decode letters to sounds ("map" the letters into sounds); and using progressively high-order units of structure. I shall consider these three stages in order and in some detail and describe experiments exploring each stage.

Differentiation of Written Symbols

Making any discriminative response to printed characters is considered by some a kind of reading. A very young child, or even a monkey, can be taught to point to a patch of yellow color, rather than a patch of blue, when the printed characters YELLOW are presented. Various people, in recent popular publications, have seriously suggested teaching infants to respond discriminatively in this way to letter patterns, implying that this is teaching them to "read." Such responses are not reading, however; reading entails decoding to speech. Letters are, essentially, an instruction to produce a given speech sound.

Nevertheless, differentiation of written characters from one another is a logically preliminary stage to decoding them to speech. The learning problem is one of discriminating and recognizing a set of line figures, all very similar in a number of ways (for example, all are tracings on paper) and each differing from all the others in one or more features (as straight versus curved). The differentiating features must remain invariant under certain transformations (size, brightness, and perspective transformations and less easily described ones produced by different type faces and handwriting). They must therefore be relational, so that these transformations will not destroy them.

It might be questioned whether learning is necessary for these figures to be discriminated from one another. This question has been investigated by Gibson, Gibson, Pick, and Osser (3). In order to trace the development of letter differentiation as it is related to those features of letters which are critical for the task, we designed specified transformations for each of a group of standard, artificial letter-like forms comparable to printed Roman capitals. Variants were constructed from each standard figure to yield the following 12 transformations for each one: three degrees of transformation from line to curve; five transformations of rotation or reversal; two perspective transformations; and two topological transformations (see Fig. 1 for examples). All of these except the perspective transformations we considered critical for discriminating letters. For example, contrast V and U; C and U; O and C.

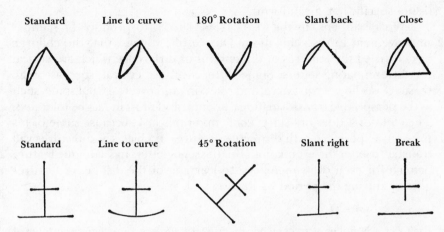

Figure 1.   Examples of letter-like figures illustrating different types of transformation.

The discrimination task required the subject to match a standard figure against all of its transformations and some copies of it and to select only identical copies. An error score (the number of times an item that was not an identical copy was selected) was obtained for each child, and the errors were classified according to the type of transformation. The subjects were children aged 4 through 8 years. As would be expected, the visual discrimination of these letter-like forms improved from age 4 to age 8, but the slopes of the error curves were different, depending on the transformation to be discriminated (Fig. 2). In other words, some transformations are harder to discriminate than others, and improvement occurs at different rates for different transformations. Even the youngest subjects made relatively few errors involving changes of break or close, and among the 8-year-olds these errors dropped to zero. Errors for perspective transformations were very numerous among 4-year-olds and still numerous among 8-year-olds. Errors for rotations and reversals started high but dropped to nearly zero by 8 years. Errors for changes from line to curve were relatively numerous (depending on the number of changes) among the youngest children and showed a rapid drop among the older—almost to zero for the 8-year-olds.

The experiment was replicated with the same transformations of real letters on the 5-year-old group. The correlation between confusions of the same transformations for real letters and for the letter-like forms was very high ($r = +.87$), so the effect of a given transformation has generality (is not specific to a given form).

What happens, in the years from 4 to 8, to produce or hamper improvement in discrimination? Our results suggest that the children have learned the features or dimensions of difference which are critical for differentiating letters. Some differences are critical, such as break versus close, line versus curve, and rotations and reversals; but some, such as the perspective transformations, are not, and must in fact be tolerated. The child of 4 does not start "cold" upon this task, because some of his previous experience with distinctive features of objects and pictures will transfer to letter differentiation. But the set of letters has a unique feature pattern for each of its members, so learning of the distinctive features goes on during the period we investigated.

Table 1.   Number of errors made in transfer stage by groups with three types of training.

Group	Type of training		Errors
	Standards	Transformations	
E1	Same	Different	69
E2	Different	Same	39
C	Different	Different	101

If this interpretation is correct, it would be useful to know just what the distinctive features of letters are. What dimensions of difference must a child learn to detect in order to perceive each letter as unique? Gibson, Osser, Schiff, and Smith (4) investigated this question. Our method was to draw up a chart of the features of a given set of letters (5), test to see which of these letters were most frequently confused by prereading children, and compare the errors in the resulting "confusion matrix" with those predicted by the feature chart.

A set of distinctive features for letters must be relational in the sense that each feature presents a contrast which is invariant under certain transformations, and it must yield a unique pattern for each letter. The set must also be reasonably economical. Two feature lists which satisfy these requirements for a specified type face were tried out against the results of

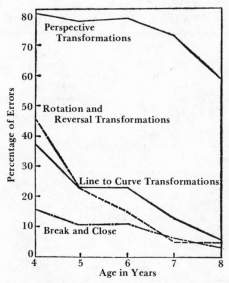

Figure 2.   Error curves showing rate of improvement in discriminating four types of transformation.

a confusion matrix obtained with the same type (simplified Roman capitals available on a sign-typewriter).

Each of the features in the list in Fig. 3 is or is not a characteristic of each of the 26 letters. Regarding each letter one asks, for example, "Is there a curved segment?" and gets a yes or no answer. A filled-in feature chart gives a unique pattern for each letter. However, the number of potential features for letter-shapes is very large, and would vary from one alphabet and type font to another. Whether or not we have the right set can be tested with a confusion matrix. Children should confuse with greatest frequency the letters having the smallest number of feature differences, if the features have been chosen correctly.

We obtained our confusion matrix from 4-year-old children, who made matching judgments of letters, programed so that every letter had an equal opportunity to be mistaken for any other, without bias from order effects. The "percent feature difference" for any two letters was determined by dividing the total number of features possessed by either letter, but not both, by the total number possessed by both, whether shared or not. Correlations were then calculated between percent feature difference and number of confusions, one for each letter. The feature list of Fig. 3 yielded 12 out of 26 positive significant correlations. Prediction from this feature list is fairly good, in view of the fact that features were

Features	A	B	C	E	K	L	N	U	X	Z
Straight segment										
Horizontal	+			+	+					+
Vertical		+		+	+	+	+			
Oblique /	+				+				+	+
Oblique \	+				+		+		+	
Curve										
Closed		+								
Open vertically								+		
Open horizontally			+							
Intersection	+	+			+	+			+	
Redundancy										
Cyclic change		+		+						
Symmetry	+	+	+	+	+			+	+	
Discontinuity										
Vertical	+				+				+	
Horizontal				+		+	+			+

Figure 3. Example of a "feature chart." Whether the features chosen are actually effective for discriminating letters must be determined by experiment.

not weighted. A multidimensional analysis of the matrix corroborated the choice of the curve-straight and obliqueness variables, suggesting that these features may have priority in the discrimination process and perhaps developmentally. Refinement of the feature list will take these facts into account, and other methods of validation will be tried.

Detecting Distinctive Features

If we are correct in thinking that the child comes to discriminate graphemes by detecting their distinctive features, what is the learning process like? That it is perceptual learning and need not be verbalized is probable (though teachers do often call attention to contrasts between letter shapes). An experiment by Anne D. Pick (6) was designed to compare two hypotheses about how this type of discrimination develops. One might be called a "schema" or "prototype" hypothesis, and is based on the supposition that the child builds up a kind of model or memory image of each letter by repeated experience of visual presentations of the letter; perceptual theories which propose that discrimination occurs by matching sensory experience to a previously stored concept or categorical model are of this kind. In the other hypothesis it is assumed that the child learns by discovering how the forms differ, and then easily transfers this knowledge to new letter-like figures.

Pick employed a transfer design in which subjects were presented in step 1 with initially confusable stimuli (letter-like forms) and trained to discriminate between them. For step 2 (the transfer stage) the subjects were divided into three groups. One experimental group was given sets of stimuli to discriminate which varied in new dimensions from the *same standards* discriminated in stage 1. A second experimental group was given sets of stimuli which deviated from *new standards*, but in the same dimensions of difference discriminated in stage 1. A control group was given both new standards and new dimensions of difference to discriminate in stage 2. Better performance by the first experimental group would suggest that discrimination learning proceeded by construction of a model or memory image of the standards against which the variants could be matched. Conversely, better performance by the second experimental group would suggest that dimensions of difference had been detected.

The subjects were kindergarten children. The stimuli were letter-like forms of the type described earlier. There were six standard forms and six transformations of each of them. The transformations consisted of two changes of line to curve, a right-left reversal, a 45-degree rotation, a perspective transformation, and a size transformation. Table 1 gives the errors of discrimination for all three groups in stage 2. Both experimental groups performed significantly better than the control group, but the group that had familiar transformations of new standards performed significantly better than the group given new transformations of old standards.

We infer from these results that, while children probably do learn prototypes of letter shapes, the prototypes themselves are not the original basis for differentiation. The most relevant kind of training for discrimination is practice which provides experience with the characteristic differences that distinguish the set of items. Features which are actually distinctive for letters could be emphasized by presenting letters in contrast pairs.

Decoding Letters to Sounds

When the graphemes are reasonably discriminable from one another, the decoding process becomes possible. This process, common sense and many psychologists would tell us, is simply a matter of associating a graphic stimulus with the appropriate spoken response—that is to say, it is the traditional stimulus-response paradigm, a kind of paired-associate learning.

Obvious as this description seems, problems arise when one takes a closer look. Here are just a few. The graphic code is related to the speech code by rules of correspondence. If these rules are known, decoding of new items is predictable. Do we want to build up, one by one, automatically cued responses, or do we want to teach with transfer in mind? If we want to teach for transfer, how do we do it? Should the child be aware that this is a code game with rules? Or will induction of the rules be automatic? What units of both codes should we start with? Should we start with single letters, in the hope that knowledge of single-letter-to-sound relationships will yield the most transfer? Or should we start with whole words, in the hope that component relationships will be induced?

Carol Bishop (7) investigated the question of the significance of knowledge of component letter-sound relationships in reading new words. In her experiment, the child's process of learning to read was simulated by teaching adult subjects to read some Arabic words. The purpose was to determine the transfer value of training with individual letters as opposed to whole words, and to investigate the role of component letter-sound associations in transfer to learning new words.

A three-stage transfer design was employed. The letters were 12 Arabic characters, each with a one-to-one letter-sound correspondence. There were eight consonants and four vowels, which were combined to form two sets of eight Arabic words. The 12 letters appeared at least once in both sets of words. A native speaker of the language recorded on tape the 12 letter-sounds and the two sets of words. The graphic form of each letter or word was printed on a card.

The subjects were divided into three groups—the letter training group (L), the whole-word training group (W), and a control group (C). Stage 1 of the experiment was identical for all groups. The subjects learned to pronounce the set of words (transfer set) which would appear in stage 3 by listening to the recording and repeating the words. Stage 2 varied. Group L listened to and repeated the 12 letter-sounds and then learned to associate the individual graphic shapes with their correct sounds. Group W followed the same procedure, except that eight words were given them to learn, rather than letters. Learning time was equal for the two groups. Group C spent the same time-interval on an unrelated task. Stage 3 was the same for the three groups. All subjects learned to read the set of words they had heard in stage 1, responding to the presentation of a word on a card by pronouncing it. This was the transfer stage on which the three groups were compared.

At the close of stage 3, all subjects were tested on their ability to give the correct letter-sound following the presentation of each printed letter. They were asked afterward to explain how they tried to learn the transfer words.

Figure 4 shows that learning took place in fewest trials for the letter group and next fewest for the word group. That is, letter training had more transfer value than word training, but word training did produce some transfer. The subjects of group L also knew, on the average, a greater number of component letter-sound correspondences, but some subjects in group W had learned all 12. Most of the subjects in group L reported that they had tried to learn by using knowledge of component correspondences. But so did 12 of the 20 subjects in group W, and the scores of these 12 subjects on the transfer task were similar to those of the letter-trained group. The subjects who had learned by whole words and had not used individual correspondences performed no better on the task than the control subjects.

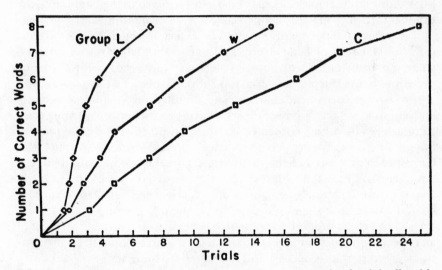

Figure 4.   Learning curves on transfer task for group trained originally with whole words (W), group trained with single letters (L), and control group (C).

It is possible, then, to learn to read words without learning the component letter-sound correspondences. But transfer to new words depends on use of them, whatever the method of original training. Word training was as good as letter training if the subject had analyzed for himself the component relationships.

Learning Variable and Constant Component Correspondences

In Bishop's experiment, the component letter-sound relationships were regular and consistent. It has often been pointed out, especially by advocates of spelling reform and revised alphabets (8), that in English this is not the case. Bloomfield (9) suggested that the beginning reader should, therefore, be presented with material carefully programed for teaching those orthographic-phonic regularities which exist in English, and should be introduced later and only gradually to the complexities of English spelling and to the fact that single-letter-to-sound relationships are often variable. But actually, there has been no hard evidence to suggest that transfer, later, to reading spelling-patterns with more variable component correspondence will be facilitated by beginning with only constant ones. Athough variable ones may be harder to learn in the beginning, the original difficulty may be compensated for by facilitating later learning.

A series of experiments directed by Harry Levin (10) dealt with the effect of learning variable as opposed to constant letter-sound relationships, on transfer to learning new letter-sound relationships. In one experiment, the learning material was short lists of paired-associates, with a word written in artificial characters as stimulus and a triphoneme familiar English word as response. Subjects (third-grade children) in one group were given a list which contained constant graph-to-sound relationships (one-to-one component correspondence) followed by a list in which this correspondence was variable with respect to the medial vowel sound. Another group started with a similarly constructed variable list and followed it with a second one. The group that learned lists with a variable component in both stages was superior to the other group in the second stage. The results suggest that initiating the task with a variable list created an expectation or learning set for variability of correspondence which was transferred to the second list and facilitated learning it.

In a second experiment, the constant or variable graph-sound relation occurred on the first letter. Again, the group with original variable training performed better on the second, variable list. In a third experiment adult native speakers of English and Spanish were compared. The artificial graphs were paired with nonsense words. Again there was more transfer from a variable first list to a variable second list than from a constant to a variable one. Variable lists were more difficult, on the whole, for the Spanish speakers, perhaps because their native language contains highly regular letter-sound relationships.

A "set for diversity" may, therefore, facilitate transfer to learning of new letter-sound correspondences which contain variable relationships. But many questions about how the code is learned remain to be solved, because the true units of the graphic code are not necessarily single letters. While single-letter-sound relations in English are indeed variable, at other levels of structure regularity may be discovered.

Lower- and Higher-Order Units

For many years, linguists have been concerned with the question of units in language. That language has a hierarchical structure, with units of different kinds and levels, is generally accepted, though the definition of the units is not easily reached. One criterion of a unit is recodability—consistent mapping or translation to another code. If such a criterion be granted, graphic units must parallel linguistic units. The units of the writing system should be defined, in other words, by mapping rules which link them to the speech code, at all levels of structure.

What then are the true graphic units? What levels of units are there? Exactly how are they mapped to linguistic units? In what "chunks" are they perceived? We must first try to answer these questions by a logical analysis of properties of the writing and speech systems and the correspondences between them. Then we can look at the behavior of skilled readers and see how units are processed during reading. If the logical analysis of the correspondence rules is correct, we should be able to predict what kinds of units are actually processed and to check our predictions experimentally.

Common sense suggests that the unit for reading is the single grapheme, and that the reader proceeds sequentially from left to right, letter by letter, across the page. But we can assert at once and unequivocally that this picture is false. For the English language, the single graphemes map consistently into speech only as morphemes—that is, the names of the letters of the alphabet. It is possible, of course, to name letters sequentially across a line of print ("spell out" a word), but that is not the goal of a skilled reader, nor is it what he does. Dodge (11) showed, nearly 60 years ago, that perception occurs in reading only during fixations, and not at all during the saccadic jumps from one fixation to the next. With a fast tachistoscopic exposure, a skilled reader can perceive four unconnected letters, a very long word, and four or more words if they form a sentence (12). Even first graders can read three-letter words exposed for only 40 milliseconds, too short a time for sequential eye movements to occur.

Broadbent (*13*) has pointed out that speech, although it consists of a temporal sequence of stimuli, is responded to at the end of a sequence. That is, it is normal for a whole sequence to be delivered before a response is made. For instance, the sentence "Would you give me your _____?" might end with any of a large number of words, such as "name" or "wallet" or "wife." The response depends on the total message. The fact that the component stimuli for speech and reading are spread over time does not mean that the phonemes or letters or words are processed one at a time, with each stimulus decoded to a separate response. The fact that O is pronounced differently in BOAT and BOMB is not a hideous peculiarity of English which must consequently be reformed. The O is read only in context and is never responded to in isolation. It is part of a sequence which contains constraints of two kinds, one morphological and the other the spelling patterns which are characteristic of English.

If any doubt remains as to the unlikelihood of sequential processing letter by letter, there is recent evidence of Newman (*14*) and of Kolers (*15*) on sequential exposure of letters. When letters forming a familiar word are exposed sequentially in the same place, it is almost impossible to read the word. With an exposure of 100 milliseconds per letter, words of six letters are read with only 20 percent probability of accuracy; and with an exposure of 375 milliseconds per letter, the probability is still well under 100 percent. But that is more than 2 seconds to perceive a short, well-known word! We can conclude that, however graphemes are processed perceptually in reading, it is not a letter-by-letter sequence of acts.

If the single grapheme does not map consistently to a phoneme, and furthermore, if perception normally takes in bigger "chunks" of graphic stimuli in a single fixation, what are the smallest graphic units consistently coded into phonemic patterns? Must they be whole words? Are there different levels of units? Are they achieved at different stages of development?

Spelling Patterns

It is my belief that the smallest component units in written English are spelling patterns (*16*). By a spelling pattern, I mean a cluster of graphemes in a given environment which has an invariant pronunciation according to the rules of English. These rules are the regularities which appear when, for instance, any vowel or consonant or cluster is shown to correspond with a given pronunciation in an initial, medial, or final position in the spelling of a word. This kind of regularity is not merely "frequency" (bigram frequency, trigram frequency, and so on), for it implies that frequency counts are relevant for establishing rules only if the right units and the right relationships are counted. The relevant graphic unit is a functional unit of one or more letters, in a given position within the word, which is in correspondence with a specified pronunciation (*17*).

If potential regularities exist within words—the spelling patterns that occur in regular correspondence with speech patterns—one may hypothesize that these correspondences have been assimilated by the skilled reader of English (whether or not he can verbalize the rules) and have the effect of organizing units for perception. It follows that strings of letters which are generated by the rules will be perceived more easily than ones which are not, even when they are unfamiliar words or not words at all.

Several experiments testing this prediction were performed by Gibson, Pick, Osser, and Hammond (*18*). The basic design was to compare the perceptibility (with a very short tachistoscopic exposure) of two sets of letter-strings, all nonsense or pseudo words, which differed in their spelling-to-sound correlation. One list, called the "pronounceable" list, contained words with a high spelling-to-sound correlation. Each of them had an initial consonant-spelling with a single, regular pronunciation; a final consonant-spelling having a single regular pronunciation; and a vowel-spelling, placed between them, having a single regular pronunciation when it follows and is followed by the given initial and final consonant spellings, respectively—for example, GL/UR/CK. The words in the second list, called the "unpronounceable" list, had a low spelling-to-sound correlation. They were constructed from the words in the first list by reversing the initial and final consonant spellings. The medial vowel spelling was not changed. For example, GLURCK became CKURGL. There were 25 such pseudo words in each list, varying in length from four to eight letters. The pronunciability of the resulting lists was validated in two ways, first by ratings, and second by obtaining the number of variations when the pseudo words were actually pronounced.

The words were projected on a screen in random order, in five successive presentations with an exposure time beginning at 50 milliseconds and progressing up to 250 milliseconds. The subjects (college students) were instructed to write each word as it was projected. The mean percentage of pronounceable words correctly perceived was consistently and significantly greater at all exposure times.

The experiment was later repeated with the same material but a different judgment. After the pseudo word was exposed, it was followed by a multiple-choice list of four items, one of the correct one and the other three the most common errors produced in the previous experiment. The subject chose the word he thought he had seen from the choice list and recorded a number (its order in the list). Again the mean of pronounce-able pseudo words correctly perceived significantly exceeded that of their unpronounceable counterparts. We conclude from these experiments that skilled readers more easily perceive as a unit pseudo words which follow the rules of English spelling-to-sound correspondence; that spelling patterns which have invariant relations to sound patterns function as a unit, thus facilitating the decoding process.

In another experiment, Gibson, Osser, and Pick (19) studied the development of perception of grapheme-phoneme correspondences. We wanted to know how early, in learning to read, children begin to respond to spelling-patterns as units. The experiment was designed to compare children at the end of the first grade and at the end of the third grade in ability to recognize familiar three-letter words, pronounceable trigrams, and unpronounceable trigrams. The three-letter words were taken from the first-grade reading list; each word chosen could be rearranged into a meaningless but pronounceable trigram and a meaningless and unpro-nounceable one (for example, RAN, NAR, RNA). Some longer pseudo words (four and five letters) taken from the previous experiments were included as well. The words and pseudo words were exposed tachistoscopically to individual children, who were required to spell them orally. The first-graders read (spelled out) most accurately the familiar three-letter words, but read the pronounceable trigrams significantly better than the unpro-nounceable ones. The longer pseudo words were seldom read accurately and were not differentiated by pronunciability. The third-grade girls read all three-letter combinations with high and about equal accuracy, but differentiated the longer pseudo words; that is, the pronounceable four- and five-letter pseudo words were more often perceived correctly than their unpronounceable counterparts.

These results suggest that a child in the first stages of reading skill typically reads in short units, but has already generalized certain regu-larities of spelling-to-sound correspondence, so that three-letter pseudo words which fit the rules are more easily read as units. As skill develops, span increases, and a similar difference can be observed for longer items. The longer items involve more complex conditional rules and longer clusters, so that the generalizations must increase in complexity. The fact that a child can begin very early to perceive regularities of correspon-dence between the printed and spoken patterns, and transfer them to the reading of unfamiliar items as units, suggests that the opportunities for discovering the correspondences between patterns might well be enhanced in programing reading materials.

I have referred several times to *levels* of units. The last experiment showed that the size and complexity of the spelling patterns which can be perceived as units increase with development of reading skill. The other levels of structure, both syntactic and semantic, contain units as large as and larger than the word, and that perception of skilled readers will be found, in suitable experiments, to be a function of these factors is almost axiomatic. As yet we have little direct evidence better than Cattell's original discovery (12) that when words are structured into a sentence, more letters can be accurately perceived "at a glance." Developmental studies of perceptual "chunking" in relation to structural complexity may be very instructive.

Where does meaning come in? Within the immediate span of visual perception, meaning is less effective in structuring written material than good spelling-to-sound corrrespondence, as Gibson, Bishop, Schiff, and Smith (20) have shown. Real words which are both meaningful and, as strings of letters, structured in accordance with English spelling patterns are more easily perceived than nonword pronounceable strings of letters; but the latter are more easily perceived than meaningful but unpronounceable letter-strings (for example, BIM is perceived accurately, with tachistoscopic exposure, faster than IBM). The role of meaning in the visual perception of words probably increases as longer strings of words (more than one) are dealt with. A sentence has two kinds of constraint, semantic and syntactic, which make it intelligible (easily heard) and memorable (21). It is important that the child develop reading habits which utilize all the types of constraint present in the stimulus, since they constitute structure and are, therefore, unit-formers. The skills which the child should acquire in reading are habits of utilizing the constraints in letter strings (the spelling and morphemic patterns) and in word strings (the syntactic and semantic patterns). We could go on to consider still superordinate ones, perhaps, but the problem of the unit, of levels of units, and mapping rules from writing to speech has just begun to be explored with experimental techniques. Further research on the definition and processing of units should lead to new insights about the nature of reading skill and its attainment.

Summary

Reading begins with the child's acquisition of spoken language. Later he learns to differentiate the graphic symbols from one another and to decode these to familiar speech sounds. As he learns to decode, he must progressively utilize the structural constraints which are built into it in order to attain the skilled performance which is characterized by processing of higher-order units—the spelling and morphological patterns of the language.

Because of my firm conviction that good pedagogy is based on a deep understanding of the discipline to be taught and the nature of the learning process involved, I have tried to show that the psychology of reading can benefit from a program of theoretical analysis and experiment. An analysis of the reading task—discriminatory and decoding aspects as well as the semantic and syntactical aspects—tells us *what* must be learned. An analysis of the learning process tells us *how*. The consideration of formal instruction comes only after these steps, and its precepts should follow from them.

REFERENCES

1. See C. C. Fries, *Linguistics and Reading* (Holt, Rinehart, and Winston, New York, 1963), for an excellent chapter on past practice and theory in the teaching of reading.

2. In 1959, Cornell University was awarded a grant for a Basic Research Project on Reading by the Cooperative Research Program of the Office of Education, U.S. Department of Health, Education, and Welfare. Most of the work reported in this article was supported by this grant. The Office of Education has recently organized "Project Literacy," which will promote research on reading in a number of laboratories, as well as encourage mutual understanding between experimentalists and teachers of reading.

3. E. J. Gibson, J. J. Gibson, A. D. Pick, H. Osser, *J. Comp. Physiol. Psychol.* **55**, 897 (1962).

4. E. J. Gibson, H. Osser, W. Schiff, J. Smith, in *A Basic Research Program on Reading*, Final Report on Cooperative Research Project No. 639 to the Office of Education, Department of Health, Education, and Welfare.

5. The method was greatly influenced by the analysis of distinctive features of phonemes by R. Jacobson and M. Halle, presented in *Fundamentals of Language* (Mouton, The Hague, 1956). A table of 12 features, each in binary opposition, yields a unique pattern for all phonemes, so that any one is distinguishable from any other by its pattern of attributes. A pair of phonemes may differ by any number of features, the minimal distinction being one feature opposition. The features must be invariant under certain transformations and essentially relational, so as to remain distinctive over a wide range of speakers, intonations, and so on.

6. A. D. Pick, *J. Exp. Psychol.*, in press.

7. C. H. Bishop, *J. Verbal Learning Verbal Behav.* **3**, 215 (1964).

8. Current advocates of a revised alphabet who emphasize the low letter-sound correspondence in English are Sir James Pitman and John A. Downing. Pitman's revised alphabet, called the Initial Teaching Alphabet, consists of 43 characters, some traditional and some new. It is designed for instruction of the beginning reader, who later transfers to traditional English spelling. See I. J. Pitman, *J. Roy. Soc. Arts* **109**, 149 (1961); J. A. Downing, *Brit. J. Educ. Psychol.* **32**, 166 (1962); _____, "Experiments with Pitman's initial teaching alphabet in British schools," paper presented at the Eighth Annual Conference of International Reading Association, Miami, Fla., May 1963.

9. L. Bloomfield, *Elem. Engl. Rev.* **19,** 125, 183 (1942).
10. See research reports of H. Levin and J. Watson, and H. Levin, E. Baum, and S. Bostwick, in *A Basic Research Program on Reading* (see *4*).
11. R. Dodge, *Psychol. Bull.* **2,** 193 (1905).
12. J. McK. Cattell, *Phil. Studies* **2,** 635 (1885).
13. D. E. Broadbent, *Perception and Communication* (Pergamon, New York, 1958).
14. E. Newman, *Am. J. Psychol.,* in press.
15. P. A. Kolers and M. T. Katzman, paper presented before the Psychonomic Society, Aug. 1963, Bryn Mawr, Pa.
16. Spelling patterns in English have been discussed by C. C. Fries in *Linguistics and Reading* (Holt, Rinehart, and Winston, New York, 1963), p. 169 ff. C. F. Hockett, in *A Basic Research Program on Reading* (see *4*), has made an analysis of English graphic monosyllables which presents regularities of spelling patterns in relation to pronunciation. This study was continued by R. Venezky (thesis, Cornell Univ., 1962), who wrote a computer program for obtaining the regularities of English spelling-to-sound correspondence. The data obtained by means of the computer permit one to look up any vowel or consonant cluster of up to five letters and find its pronunciation in initial, medial, and final positions in a word. Letter environments as well have now been included in the analysis. See also R. H. Weir, *Formulation of Grapheme-Phoneme Correspondence Rules to Aid in the Teaching of Reading,* Report on Cooperative Research Project No. 5-039 to the Office of Education, Department of Health, Education and Welfare.
17. For example, the cluster GH may lawfully be pronounced as an F at the end of a word, but never at the beginning. The vowel cluster EIGH, pronounced /A/ (/ej/), may occur in initial, medial, and final positions, and does so with nearly equal distribution. These cases account for all but two occurrences of the cluster in English orthography. A good example of regularity influenced by environment is [c] in a medial position before I plus a vowel. It is always pronounced /S/ (*social, ancient, judicious*).
18. E. J. Gibson, A. D. Pick, H. Osser, M. Hammond, *Am. J. Psychol.* **75,** 554 (1962).
19. E. J. Gibson, H. Osser, A. D. Pick, *J. Verbal Learning Verbal Behav.* **2,** 142 (1963).
20. E. J. Gibson, C. H. Bishop, W. Schiff, J. Smith, *J. Exp. Psychol.,* **67,** 173 (1964).
21. G. A. Miller and S. Isard, *J. Verbal Learning Verbal Behav.* **2,** 217 (1963); also L. E. Marks and G. A. Miller, *ibid.* **3,** 1 (1964).

Modes of Word Recognition[1]

S. JAY SAMUELS
University of Minnesota

THIS PAPER

1. Examines the strategies used by children in word recognition.
2. Reviews critically some of the classical research which has influenced current thinking about how words are recognized.
3. Presents a five stage model of how words are recognized by beginning readers.
4. Contrasts recent experimental findings of cues used in word recognition with some of the commonly held beliefs about cues used in word recognition.
5. Discusses some of the errors which can be found in classical studies on word recognition.
6. Reviews studies which find that letter-name knowledge has no effect on learning to read.
7. Presents data from experiments on the effect of phonic versus look-say methods of teaching reading along with findings regarding the perceptual unit of recognition.

When a word is presented visually and the experimental subject says the appropriate word, we say the word has been recognized. The purpose of this paper will be to examine the strategies used by children in learning to read words, to review critically some of the classical research which has influenced current thinking about how children recognize words, and to present some of the critical issues regarding word recognition.

---

[1] Preparation of this paper was supported in part by grants to the University of Minnesota, Center for Research in Human Learning, from the National Science Foundation (GS 1761), the National Institute of Child Health and Human Development (HD-01136), and the Graduate School of the University of Minnesota.

270

Strategies Used by Children in Learning to Read Words

Before the student has learned enough about reading to recognize words independently, the earliest stages of the learning to read process may be conceptualized within the framework of a five stage model.

1. *Stimulus presentation.* A stimulus complex is presented. This consists of the printed stimulus as it appears in a book or on a screen.

2. *Cue selection-discrimination learning.* Some aspect of the total stimulus complex is selected as the cue to which the response will be attached. In order to determine which aspect of the stimulus complex can be used to distinguish this word (or letter) from others, discrimination learning is involved. For example, the stimulus *h-i-p-p-o-p-o-t-a-m-u-s* may be presented and the student must learn to say the appropriate word. If this word is the longest among the list to be learned, then word length may be the cue. Reading is a complex act and numerous cues may be utilized (*23*). The cue upon which the learner focuses his attention may be a letter, letter group, word shape, in fact, any characteristic which helps to set this word apart from others.

3. *Visual recognition memory.* Having selected a cue, the learner must be able to recognize it again. Travers (*27*) has suggested that visual recognition memory of the cue is part of short term memory. Recent work on paired-associate learning has demonstrated the importance of visual recognition memory in associative learning (*1, 13*). An investigation of the relationship between visual recognition memory and reading achievement disclosed the two were significantly correlated (r = .35). To rule out the possibility that the correlation between visual recognition memory and reading simply reflected the well-known relationship between intelligence and reading achievement, the correlation between visual recognition memory and intelligence was computed. The correlation was found to be extremely small (*20*). Thus, visual recognition memory is related to reading achievement independent of intelligence. The correlation between visual recognition memory and paired-associate learning for the above students was r = .43.

4. *Response availability.* The appropriate response must be available for hookup with the cue if learning is to take place. By increasing response availability through the control of context and the associative connections between words, learning to read new words can be facilitated (*16, 22, 24*). For example, if the child can already read the word *green* and the new word to be learned is *grass*, response availability for the new word should be higher in the context *green grass* than if the word *grass* is presented by

itself. Reading speed and recall are also influenced by the associative connections between words (*17*). When third graders were given a high-association paragraph with sentences such as

> They were all happy to be together again. Outside the moon and stars shone brightly in the June sky, and the green grass sparkled in the night.

they read it significantly faster and with better recall than a group getting a low-association paragraph with sentences such as

> They were all relieved to be together again. Outside the moon and lake appeared clearly in the June evening and the green house sparkled in the valley.

Bormuth (*4*) and Ruddell (*15*) have found that linguistic variables can affect comprehension. It would be interesting to determine if some of the linguistic variables which affect comprehension also affect learning to read new words.

5. *Hookup or associative stage.* When the cue and the appropriate response are hooked up, we can say the learner is able to read or recognize the word, i.e., upon stimulus presentation he can say the correct word. According to Travers (*27*), the hooked up cue and response are part of long term memory.

The unskilled reader who is learning to recognize a word must select a cue, recall the cue, and have the appropriate response available for pairing with the cue. Various strategies have been described which beginning readers use to recognize a word. Some of these are listed below along with critical comments, many of which will be elaborated upon later in the paper.

1. *Recognition of words as sight words.* The words to be learned are presented to the student. His task is to learn to say the appropriate word which is associated with the visually presented stimulus. This procedure is often referred to as the look-say method and is frequently used in early reading training. What is of concern with the use of this method are the strategies used in learning and their subsequent effect on later learning. The words *boy* and *cat* may have been presented. Although the student learns to recognize the words, he may do so because he used letter *b* as the cue for *boy* and letter *c* as the cue for *cat*. Later when shown the words *ball* and *car* the student may call these words *boy* and *cat* because he relies on single letter cues *b* and *c* as cues for recognition.

2. *Unusual characteristics of words.* The learner may use as his cue for recognition some unusual or striking characteristic of the word. He may use word length as the cue to identify words in a list. For example, the learner may note that the short word is *cat* and the long word is *elephant*.

He may note the tail on the word *monkey*, or the spot of ink on a flash card. These may serve as cues to accurate recognition for a while. This strategy becomes ineffective when other long and short words are encountered.

3. *Word shape cues.* If lines are drawn about words printed in lower case, a characteristic outline or shape results. This outline can serve as a cue to recognition. If the same word were typed in upper-case, a less characteristic outline results and, consequently, is a less useful cue.

finger   finish   FINGER   FINISH

4. *Phonics.* Individual letters and letter clusters may be used as cues for sounds. These sounds may be combined sequentially to recognize the word. Critics of the phonic method of teaching word recognition claim that English is not a highly alphabetic language, that is, in English there is low correspondence between letters and sounds. This is true only at the level of individual letters. When individual letters as well as letter clusters and their positions in the word are taken into consideration, recent work in linguistics indicates that English has higher letter-sound correspondence than ever before realized.

5. *Context.* Word associations and information provided in the context of a sentence may provide the response necessary for recognizing the word. Red, white, and _____. Few English speaking people require the printed stimulus to recognize the missing word. While context provides an important cue for recognition and for learning to read a word, it is important to determine if the reader can recognize a word when it is presented in isolation. If the student does not visually attend to the stimulus when he says the word, he may not learn to read it.

When the beginning reader uses strategies such as recognizing words as sight words, using unusual characteristics of words and word shape as cues, he is learning strategies which not only are not useful for transfer but will have to be abandoned if he is to progress to the point where he can decode words on his own. Teachers who encourage their beginning students to use word shape and the whole word as cues have the mistaken belief that children ordinarily note a whole configuration. One reading textbook (26) states, "To start with a whole word is sound psychologically, for young children are not prone to be very analytical in their perceptions. Their natural tendency is to perceive total patterns."

If there is anything which discrimination studies indicate, it is that children select the easiest cue for recognition, and the easiest cue is frequently just a single letter of a word or some incidental detail. Children do not ordinarily attend to total patterns nor to all the letters in a word. It is only when single letter cues fail to distinguish one word from another that children attend to all the letters.

To determine which cues nonreaders and beginning readers use in word recognition, Marchbanks and Levin (12) had kindergarteners and first graders select the one word from a set of alternatives which was similar to a standard. The selection could be on the basis of word shape or letter cues. The results indicated that children preferred to use first letters, final letters, middle letters, and word shape (in that order of preference) as cues to word identification. This study is important because it demonstrates that the theories are untenable which propose that beginning readers recognize words as wholes primarily by shape. It also demonstrates the importance of letter cues in the word recognition of children.

Under which conditions will children use single letter cues or all the letters in the word as cues to recognition? To find the answer, Samuels and Jeffrey (21) gave kindergarteners a list of four words to learn to read. One group learned a list where the words were easy to visually discriminate from each other. This group was called the high discriminability group and their words were spelled DA, BE, MI, SO. Another group was called the low discriminability group and their words were difficult to visually discriminate from each other. The words were spelled SE, SA, ME, MA. A comparison between the two groups on speed of learning to read the words indicated that the group getting the list with highly discriminable words excelled. Then a test was given to determine the letters used as cues for recognition. The test revealed that the high discriminability group, which had learned more quickly, had used single letter cues as the basis for recognition. The low discriminability group, although learning less rapidly, had used both letters as the cue for recognition. When children in both groups were shown a word spelled MO, a word they had not seen before, those from the high discriminability group were apt to say the word was MI or SO depending on whether they used a first or last letter as a cue in recognition. Those in the low discriminability group tended to say the word was one they had not seen before. Thus, initial training on a list of words with low discriminability, which forced attention on all the letters, encouraged the child to adopt a strategy which provided a better basis for transfer to learning new words.

In teaching reading to beginning readers, a decision must be made between speed of initial learning and transfer. The decision to foster speed of initial learning at the expense of transfer may be a false economy. Initial speed of learning can be facilitated by using the look-say method with words which are highly discriminable from each other. For example, when given the sentence, "Yesterday our class went to a fire station," the beginning reader would probably learn to read the sentence using first or last letter cues. Although this strategy would lead to rapid learning, it also results in poor transfer to learning how to read new words. In learning to read, the principle of least effort operates. This means that the strategy is to select from the stimulus complex that cue which most easily elicits the correct response. Cues may be word length, shape, or single letters. These cues are irrelevant in that they provide no basis for learning new words and what is learned will before long inhibit future learning.

Teachers who begin the teaching of reading by having the learner recognize a basic group of words as sight words have noted that at first the learning is rapid, but soon the rate of learning new words slows down drastically. The initial rate of learning is rapid because numerous simple strategies provide cues for word recognition. Only so many words can be recognized by length, shape, and single letters before the strategies prove ineffective. When this occurs, the rate of learning new words decreases, and the learner remains on a learning plateau until he learns a rational system for decoding words from symbols to sounds.

One strategy for facilitating word recognition is to use color cues with each word as in the words-in-color system. With this system certain sounds are represented by particular colors. When a word is printed, it is spelled according to standard English orthography, but certain letters are in a particular color which represents the pronunciation. While this system may increase rate of initial learning, the critical question is one of transfer. If the learner focuses his attention on color and not letter shape, what happens when the color cues are removed? To answer this question, Samuels (19) had first graders and college students learn to read words printed in color or words printed in regular type. Samuels found that rate of learning the words in color was significantly faster than the words in regular type. But on the transfer tests—when the color cues were removed—the subjects had great difficulty in recognizing the words formerly in color. Thus, on the transfer tests the tables were turned. In comparing recognition between the words which were always in regular type to the words which had formerly been in color, recognition was superior for the words which had always been in regular type. What makes these results so surprising is that the college students knew the color cues were to be removed. Apparently, the color cue was so potent they were unable to focus attention on the relevant cue of letter shape. Again this study illustrates the principle of least effort in learning and the dangers of a false economy in which there is rapid learning at the expense of transfer.

Presently, many teachers are of the opinion that letter name knowledge facilitates learning to read. There is mounting evidence, however, that learning to decode words is not aided by letter name knowledge. The basis for the belief regarding the facilitating effect of letter name knowledge on reading may originate from the fact that causation is often mistakenly imputed to correlational findings. Bond and Dykstra (3) found in the first grade studies that reading achievement was highly correlated with letter name knowledge; in fact, it was the single best predictor of first grade reading success. Some ten years earlier, Nicholson (7) reported that the correlation between ability to identify lowercase letters upon entrance to first grade and the rate of learning to read words was r = .51, which was higher than the correlation between IQ (r = .36) and the rate of learning these words. In the same report (7), Linehan stated that letter name and letter sound training seemed to facilitate first grade reading achievement. Since the group which got letter name and sound training received auditory discrimination training as well, it is impossible to determine from this study if the facilitating effect was produced by the name, sound, or auditory discrimination training. Durrell (7) concluded, however, that reading difficulties could be prevented if, among other things, training in letter names and sounds was given.

Several critical questions must be answered regarding the finding that training in letter names and sounds facilitates learning to read words: 1) Is it letter names, letter sounds, or their combination which facilitates reading acquisition? 2) Can the correlational findings between letter names and sounds and reading be an artifact or product of some other factor? Ohnmacht (14) used a classroom setting to study the effect of letter name and sound training on reading. One group was given early training in letter names. A second group was given training in names and sounds, and a third group served as a control. She found that the group getting training on names and sounds was superior to the other groups in word knowledge and word discrimination. The group getting training in letter names was no better than the control on these reading measures. It appears, then, that letter name training in an experimental study does not facilitate reading acquisition.

Samuels was interested in the same question. He did a laboratory study (18) to determine what component of letter name knowledge, if any, facilitates reading acquisition. One of the explanations offered by educators as to why they believe letter name knowledge facilitates learning to read is that many letter names are similar to the letter sounds. It is possible, however, that reading acquisition may be influenced by the ability to visually discriminate one letter from another and not by knowledge of the letter names. To answer these questions, three groups of children midway through first grade were used. The visual discrimination group was given a paired-associate task in which the subjects had to visually discriminate four artificial letters from each other. The letter name group was given a paired-associate task with the same four letters but subjects had to learn letter names for each of the letters (S, M, E, A). The control group got an irrelevant paired-associate task. Then, the same transfer task was given to all the groups. This task consisted of learning to say the appropriate English word for words constructed out of the artificial letters (SE — SEE, SA — SAY, ME — ME, MA — MAY). Surprisingly, no significant differences were found among any of the groups. Since this finding ran counter to the correlational findings, the study was replicated twice, with different laboratory assistants and different first grade subjects, but always with the same results, i.e., no difference among the groups.

Results from Ohnmacht and Samuels studies suggest that letter name knowledge has no positive effect on reading acquisition and that the correlational findings between letter name knowledge and reading may be a product of some other factor. There is evidence (25) that paired-associate learning ability is significantly correlated with intelligence. Letter naming is a paired-associate task and may be taken as an index of intelligence. Since we already know that in the elementary school IQ is highly correlated with reading achievement, it is not surprising that letter name knowledge is also correlated with reading achievement. Another explanation is that the kind of home background which enables a child to enter first grade already knowing many of the letters of the alphabet would be the kind of home in which academic achievement would be emphasized. Again, it is well known that socioeconomic status and home environment are highly correlated with school achievement.

Although letter name knowledge does not seem to have any beneficial effect on reading, there is evidence that letter sound training does have a positive effect. The Linehan and Ohnmacht studies both suggested this, and a study by Jeffrey and Samuels (11), which will be discussed later, gives further evidence of this.

Classical Research Which Has Influenced Current Thinking

The research since the 1960's indicates that children tend to select a detail such as a letter as a cue for word recognition. This finding is at variance with the more commonly held belief that children use the whole word or word shape as the cue. How did this latter view originate?

Prior to 1900, Cattell, and Erdmann and Dodge published studies which led to the current belief that beginning readers use whole words and word shape as cues to word recognition. Over the years, partly to support the whole-word method of teaching reading, books on reading have continued to refer to these studies. Because of their importance, the errors which can be identified in these studies should be pointed out.

Erdmann and Dodge (8) were of the opinion that word length and shape were the primary cues used by skilled readers in word recognition. They came to this conclusion after finding that skilled readers could recognize words that were so far from the fixation point that individual letters could not be recognized, and words could be recognized even when letters were too small to be recognized individually.

It seems fallacious to assume that because skilled readers can recognize a word from its shape and length—under experimental conditions when other cues are missing—that shape and length are the primary cues adults rely on under normal conditions. Secondly, if Erdmann and Dodge are correct about adults using word shape and length as the primary cues, which is doubtful, it seems incorrect to assume, as many educators do, that these are the main cues children use in learning to read. Marchbanks and Levin (12) demonstrated that shape was the cue least used by children. Furthermore, it is apparent that a strategy of learning to read using word shape and length provides a poor basis for transfer to reading new words.

Cattell (6), in 1885, published a study which led to the present belief that beginning readers use the whole word in word recognition. The major finding in this study was that readers could recognize a short common word in slightly less time than it takes to recognize a single letter. There are several flaws in this study which should make the reader cautious about concluding that the results of this study apply to children learning how to read. In this study Cattell used a small number of highly educated adults. He had them read aloud as quickly as possible a passage from *Gulliver's Travels*, spell the letters contained in the words, and then read a passage consisting of 100 common nouns. The most serious error was that the time to pronounce the words is confused with the time it takes to recognize the words. Secondly, he used only skilled readers, and consequently, the findings are not valid for children.

In 1885, Cattell (5) also published a study in which he used a tachistoscope, thus eliminating the problem in the other study where the time to pronounce the word was confounded with the time to recognize the word. He found that in a fixed exposure time, two unconnected letters or two unconnected words could be recognized. Again he used adults, but he did mention one nine-year-old boy in the study who was described as being superior in reading ability to some of the adults.

The Cattell studies demonstrate that skilled readers do not engage in letter-by-letter processing. If they did, then the time for recognizing a word would be the sum of the time necessary for recognizing each of the letters. Many people have interpreted Cattell's results to mean that a skilled reader uses the entire word as the unit for recognition. This interpretation is not valid because Cattell's experiments were not designed to answer the question of what cues are actually used by skilled readers in word recognition. It is possible that Cattell's readers recognized just some of the letters in the word and were able to correctly identify the word from a partial percept. To infer from these studies that naive readers use the entire word as a cue in learning to read is an error, partly because naive readers were not used in these studies.

Second, it is now known that naive readers tend to select a detail rather than the entire word. Third, while it is known that the adult can perceive several letters together as a unit in word recognition, no one knows at the present time when beginning readers perceive these higher order units.

A higher order unit is a spelling pattern having invariant spelling-to-sound correspondence. For example, a higher order unit might be *gh* in words like *rough* or *tough*. Adults can recognize higher order units which conform to English spelling rules even when they are presented in nonsense words (*9*). The critical question is: How do beginning readers learn the higher order units?

In order to study how beginning readers learn higher order units, Gibson et al. (*10*) gave kindergarteners and first graders a task in which it was possible for them to learn patterns of spelling. The child was given a set of eight cards. Four of the cards had words with a higher order unit such as LACK, MUCK, DECK, and SOCK. The other four cards had words such as LAKE, MUCH, DEEK, and SOAK with no higher order unit. The cards were presented in pairs (e.g., LACK and LAKE), and the child simply had to point to one of the cards. If he pointed to the card with a higher order unit, that is, a word having CK, he was told that he was correct. In order to be able to consistently point to the correct card, the child had to learn a strategy for discriminating the higher order units. Although the task was difficult, Gibson found that for some of the children performance improved, indicating that they were learning how to discriminate and abstract the common spelling pattern.

The final topic which will be discussed relates to the findings of a laboratory study testing the effect of phonic versus look-say reading training on transfer to reading new words. In this study (11) kindergarten children were given phonic blend training and then were randomly assigned to a look-say, phonic, or control group. Look-say training consisted of learning to read a list of words. The letters of these words were used in new combinations to form the words used in the transfer list. Phonic training consisted of learning letter sounds. These letters were used in the transfer list of words. The control group got an irrelevant task to perform. Following training, all the subjects were given the same list of transfer words. First the subjects were shown the words and were asked to read them without any help. Then they were given instruction and the number of trials required for learning the entire list was computed. The results indicated that the phonic trained group was significantly better than the other two groups in number of words read without any help and speed of learning the entire list. There was no significant difference between the look-say and control groups on either of these measures, indicating that look-say training did not provide a basis for positive transfer to reading new words. A similar study (2) was done using college subjects. With one exception, the study using college subjects was identical to the one using kindergarten children. Some of the college subjects getting look-say training were able to read words on the transfer list on first presentation whereas virtually none of the look-say kindergarten subjects could do this. An analysis of how the college subjects did this revealed that those subjects who had used their knowledge of reading and who had learned letter sound correspondences on their own, were able to transfer this knowledge to reading the transfer list. Taken together, the two studies give strong support to the notion that knowledge of letter sound correspondence is an important basis for transfer to reading new words.

In the kindergarten study of the effect of phonic versus look-say training, a task analysis of the skills necessary for transfer to reading new words indicated that knowledge of letter-sounds as well as the ability to blend these sounds was required. As the data from the experiment revealed, the group getting both kinds of training was superior to the groups which did not get the necessary training. The implications of this experiment for the teaching of reading are that task analyses can be most helpful in planning instructional sequences. In doing task analyses, specific objectives are identified. Then, prerequisite skills necessary for the attainment of the objectives must also be identified. Carefully worked out and tested hierarchies of skills necessary for the attainment of the objectives for each stage in reading would be an important contribution to the field of reading instruction. The most simple task analyses suggest that for the objective of transfer to reading new words, knowledge of letter-sounds, ability to recognize higher-order units such as digraphs and blends and knowledge of their sounds, as well as the ability to blend these sounds into words are required.

REFERENCES

1. Bernbach, H. A. "Decision Process in Memory," *Psychological Review,* 74 (1967), 462-480.

2. Bishop, C. H. "Transfer Effects of Word and Letter Training in Reading," *Journal of Verbal Learning and Verbal Behavior,* 3 (1964), 215-221.

3. Bond, G. L., and R. Dykstra. *Coordinating Center for First Grade Reading Instruction Programs.* Final report, HEW Project No. X 001. Minneapolis: University of Minnesota, 1967.

4. Bormuth, J. R. "Readability: A New Approach," *Reading Research Quarterly,* 1 (Spring 1966), 79-132.

5. Cattell, J. "The Inertia of the Eye and Brain," *James McKeen Cattell–Man of Science,* Psychological Research, 1. Lancaster, Penna.: Science Press, 1947.

6. Cattell, J. "On the Time Required for Recognizing and Naming Letters and Words, Pictures, and Colors," *James McKeen Cattell–Man of Science,* Psychological Research, 1. Lancaster, Penna.: Science Press, 1947.

7. Durrell, D. D., et al. "Success in First Grade Reading, *Boston University Journal of Education,* 3 (1958), 2-47.

8. Erdmann, B., and R. Dodge. *Psychologische Untersuchungen über das Lesen auf Experimenteller Grundlage.* Halle: Neimeyer, 1968.

9. Gibson, E. J., et al. "The Role of Grapheme-Phoneme Correspondence in the Perception of Words," *American Journal of Psychology,* 75 (1962), 554-570.

10. Gibson, E., J. Farber, and S. Shepela. "Test of a Learning Set Procedure for the Abstraction of Spelling Patterns," *Project Literacy Reports #8.* Ithaca, N. Y.: Cornell University, 1967, 21-31.

11. Jeffrey, W. E., and S. J. Samuels. "The Effect of Method of Reading Training on Initial Reading and Transfer," *Journal of Verbal Learning and Verbal Behavior,* 6 (1967), 354-358.

12. Marchbanks, G., and H. Levin. "Cues By Which Children Recognize Words," *Journal of Educational Psychology,* 56 (1965), 57-61.

13. Martin, E. "Relation Between Stimulus Recognition and Paired-Associate Learning," *Journal of Experimental Psychology,* 74 (1967), 500-505.

14. Ohnmacht, D. C. "The Effects of Letter Knowledge on Achievement in Reading in the First Grade," paper presented at American Educational Research Association in Los Angeles, February 7, 1969.

15. Ruddell, R. B. "An Investigation of the Effects of the Similarity of Oral and Written Patterns of Language Structure on Reading Comprehension," doctoral dissertation, Indiana University, 1963.

16. Samuels, S. J. "The Effect of Experimentally Learned Word Associations on the Acquisition of Reading Responses," *Journal of Educational Psychology,* 57 (1966), 159-163.

17. Samuels, S. J. "Effect of Word Associations on Reading Speed, Recall, and Guessing Behavior on Tests," *Journal of Educational Psychology,* 59 (1968), 12-15.

18. Samuels, S. J. "Letter-Name Knowledge vs. Letter-Sound Knowledge as Factors in Reading Acquisition," *Reading Teacher,* 24 (1971), 604-608.

19. Samuels, S. J. "Relationship Between Formal Intralist Similarity and the von Restorff Effect," *Journal of Educational Psychology,* 59 (1968), 432-437.

20. Samuels, S. J., and R. Anderson. "Visual Recognition Memory, Paired Associate Learning, and Reading Achievement," *Journal of Educational Psychology.* 65 (1973), 160-168.

21. Samuels, S. J., and W. D. Jeffrey. "Discriminability of Words and Letter Cues Used in Learning to Read," *Journal of Educational Psychology,* 57 (1966), 337-340.

22. Samuels, S. J., and M. C. Wittrock. "Word Association Strength and Reading Acquisition," *Journal of Educational Psychology,* 60 (1969), 248-252.

23. Singer, H. "Conceptualization in Learning to Read," *New Frontiers in College-Adult Reading,* The 15th Yearbook, National Reading Conference. Milwaukee: National Reading Conference, 1966, 116-132.

24. Staats, A. W. *Learning, Language, and Cognition.* New York: Holt, Rinehart and Winston, 1968.

25. Stevenson, H. W., et al. "Intercorrelations and Correlates in Children's Learning and Problem Solving," *Monographs of the Society for Research in Child Development,* 33 (1968), 1-68.

26. Tinker, M., and C. McCullough. *Teaching Elementary Reading.* New York: Appleton-Century-Crofts, 1962.

27. Travers, R. M. C. "Perceptual Learning," *Review of Educational Research,* 37, 599-617. Washington, D. C.: American Educational Research, 1967.

Reactions to Modes of Word Recognition

JOANNA P. WILLIAMS*
University of Pennsylvania

Professor Samuels has reported on a topic that is of fundamental importance. Whatever one's ultimate definition or criterion of "reading" may be, word recognition must clearly be included as one of the primary and major component skills. The strategies that a reader actually utilizes in word recognition are far from explicitly delineated at the moment. Since the question is central to any genuine understanding of reading, however, our current hypotheses and rather tentatively held conclusions ought to be given further serious examination.

Samuels has provided us with an extensive list of the various cues and strategies that may be used in word recognition—word length, initial letter, overall shape, context—and he has done an admirable job of explaining how each one of these might be employed as the effective cue by a beginning reader. His warning that "children select the easiest cue for recognition" and that the easiest cue is sometimes an "incidental detail" is very well taken. Moreover, one should not expect that other, more relevant cues will also be picked up by the child. One of Samuels' own experiments illustrates this point. Subjects learned to read words printed in color more easily than words printed in regular type; however, when color cues were removed, they could not recognize the words that had previously appeared in color. In this case, the color cue was so salient that it overrode the relevant cue. Taber and Glaser (9) did a similar study in a programed instruction context, in which children learned a paired-associates list of printed color names. The actual color was the supporting cue and was faded out gradually over the series of learning trials. Again, in this experiment, there was little evidence that the children had in fact responded during training on the basis of anything besides the color cue.

One of Samuels' major points was that in developing training strategies, one must often choose between a criterion of speed of initial learning and a criterion in terms of the ability to transfer to new, un-

---

* Now at Teachers College, Columbia University.

trained material. Surely we would not be satisfied if our instructional gains were focused solely on the materials actually encountered in training. Samuels' data, indicating that initial training on a word list of low discriminability leads to the development of a better transfer strategy, are most convincing. It appears to me that the development of an effective teaching strategy must be one that is based on good answers to two questions: 1) what cues must the child attend to, in order to solve the criterion task—which we assume will be a transfer task; and 2) how can we ensure that he will attend to those cues?

I also appreciate having Samuels' description and evaluation of the early work done by Cattell and by Erdmann and Dodge. It is well to be reminded what these old data, from which so many conclusions and implications have been drawn, actually consist of. It is important to note, as Samuels points out, that a demonstration of what a skilled reader does is not necessarily what a beginner will do. But an even more important point, I believe, is that what a subject—naive or sophisticated about reading—*can* do, under certain specified, artificial, arbitrary laboratory conditions, is not at all the same as what that subject *does* do in an ordinary reading situation. To confound these two questions is very misleading, and it is sad to see how often there has been this confusion. Not that this confounding is limited to research in reading, of course: the literature in child development is full of similar instances in which estimates of normative or average performance are confused with data on maximal performance.

I should like to turn now to a discussion of additional data that are relevant to our discussion of word recognition. Before a child can recognize a word, he must have learned to some degree how to differentiate the written symbols, or graphemes, that he finds on the printed page. Gibson (5) has suggested that improvement of visual discrimination depends on learning the distinctive features of the forms to be discriminated, i.e., those dimensions of difference that distinguish the stimuli. Precise specification of the critical features of letters of the alphabet, of course, will be a difficult task.

It is obvious in any case that the graphemic characteristics of the word provide an important category of cues in word recognition (12). One of my students, Margaret Ackerman, and I (1) did an experiment concerned not with the nature of the critical features themselves, but rather with the effectiveness of different training methods in ensuring that attention is focused on the features, whatever they may be.

In this experiment we compared simultaneous and successive discrimination tasks involving highly similar letters (*b* and *d*) and dissimilar letters (*s* and *b*). First grade urban children were used as subjects. In simultaneous training, the two letters were presented at the same time, and on every trial, the subject was reinforced for responding to the same one of these stimuli, regardless of its spatial position. In the successive discrimination problem, on the other hand, only one letter was presented on each trial. The subject learned to press the left of two response buttons when *b* was presented, and the right button when *s* was presented. The response measure was the number of trials required to reach a criterion of nine consecutive correct responses. We found that with highly similar stimuli (*b* and *d*), the successive problem was *less* difficult than the simultaneous problem; while with dissimilar stimuli (*s* and *b*) the successive problem was *more* difficult. Because these findings were unexpected, we replicated the study—and got the same results. Our notion is that for the *s-b* comparison, distinctive cues are easily identified (such as size), and so, in simultaneous training, the subject has from the start some basis for comparison and differentiation. However, *b* and *d* are notoriously confusing to a first grader, and the cues that are to be used in the solution of this discrimination problem must be developed during the training. It is possible that simultaneous training in this case presents the subject with so much information at one time that the identification of some critical feature which can be used in comparison will be hindered.

In a follow-up study, we found that the same results held on a paired-associates task in which trigrams were paired with color names. This task, we felt, simulated the decoding part of the reading task, in which the child must learn to associate phonemes with their graphic representations. An approximation of the simultaneous discrimination problem was attained by the use of the trigrams *bad* and *dab,* which would be paired, for example, with *red* and *blue*. In the successive training condition, *bab* and *dad* were the critical trigrams. Again, successive training proved superior. We are speculating on the implications that might be drawn for the development of workbooks and other practice materials.

Now let us turn from comparisons of training methods to more descriptive data. Samuels mentioned a study of Marchbanks and Levin (8) which assessed the relative importance of several graphemic cues in children's matching responses. These investigators asked middle-class children in kindergarten and first grade to select, from a group of three letter and five letter "pseudowords," the one similar to that which had just been exposed to them and withdrawn from sight. They found that the specific letters are much more important in determining recognition than is the overall shape of the word. The beginning letter was the most salient cue, followed by the final letter.

Ellen Blumberg, David Williams, and I (3) did the same type of study with disadvantaged urban children to see what true nonreaders would do. Our kindergarten sample had had no formal reading training and had little or no knowledge of the alphabet. We found that these children showed *no* preference for any of the cues; they matched on a random basis. Our first grade sample, which had had some reading training, behaved exactly as did Marchbanks and Levin's middle-class children. That is, individual letters, especially the initial letter, provided the important cues.

What implications are there here for instruction? In view of these and other findings, there really seems to be no justification for developing instructional methods or primer materials based on the use of overall shape as the primary cue. Shape seems a poor choice after reading training is begun, for when children know the alphabet, individual letters become quite salient. Moreover, if one's instructional strategy were to attempt to capitalize on tendencies seen before any instruction is given, shape would be a poor choice, for there was no tendency at all on the part of our nonreaders to utilize this cue.

We also tested some adults on this task. The data were quite different from those of the children; the adults' choices were much more complex. Surprisingly, although the task as presented seemed wholly visual, half of the subjects reported some use of an "aural" strategy—rhyme, for the most part. The other half reported that they used a purely visual strategy, and again surprisingly, half of these described their strategy as one in which they tried to match on the basis of overall shape. This had been the *least* salient cue for the children.

These results remind us once more that it should not be assumed that adults and children behave in the same manner on this type of visual matching task. Indeed, it is most interesting to note the fact that the most widely used reading method over the past thirty years (the look-say or whole word) has stressed identification of words on the basis of overall shape and configuration. But it is adults and not children who sometimes show this strategy in word recognition.

The second general basis for word recognition lies in the relationship between the graphic characteristics and the nature of the spoken language. Early work focused on the correspondences between individual letters and the sounds they represented. However, English spelling is quite irregular when individual letters and sounds are considered. This fact suggested that thinking of correspondences in terms of single letters was not useful, which led in turn to a search for a more appropriate unit. It appears that clusters of letters do have more stable relationships with sound patterns, and it has been suggested that these "spelling patterns" are critical units for perception (5). That is, while the letter *c* alone is not sufficient to signal a consistent pronunciation, initial *ca* or *ce* does correlate well with specific phonemic patterns.

Eleanor Gibson's hypothesis (5) that spelling-to-sound invariance accounts for the fact that "pronounceable" pseudowords such as *glurck* are more easily recognized in a tachistoscopic exposure than are unpronounceable pseudowords such as *crurgl* has not held up, largely on the basis of her own research showing that deaf children behave in the same way as normals (6). This leaves us with the question of what it actually is that makes certain "spelling patterns" or letter clusters more easily recognized than others. Perhaps it will turn out after all not to depend heavily on the spoken language.

Here may be an appropriate point to bring up another experiment that dealt with methods of training. Sometimes assumptions have been made and accepted wholeheartedly with little or no objective data to support them. Such is the character of the recommendation, made by Bloomfield (2) and echoed by almost all other proponents of linguistics reading methods, that only simple, single grapheme-phoneme correspondences be presented to the beginning reader. Evidently this untested assumption seemed commonsensical enough to go unquestioned until Levin and Watson (7) proposed an equally commonsensical point of view. They argued that a child must learn that there are variations in correspondences in English, and that if he is presented with multiple correspondences early in instruction, he will be more likely to develop a useful problem-solving approach to the reading task (that is, a "set for diversity").

These contradictory points of view were tested in an experiment in which fifth and sixth graders learned multiple correspondences in a modified paired-associates paradigm (*10*). The two methods used were: *successive,* where only one of two phonemes which mapped to a particular grapheme was presented for the first half of the training trials, and the other phoneme for the last half of training, and *concurrent,* where both phonemes associated with each grapheme were presented on each of the six trials. When they were asked how many sounds went with each form, subjects were much more accurate at identifying as multiple correspondences the ones that had been trained concurrently. Presumably, then, in attempting to read new words, children would more readily identify such graphemes as multiple and so try out more than one phoneme for them, thereby making it more likely that they would succeed in reading the word.

Additional support of the "set for diversity" hypothesis came from analysis of the errors on another test, in which the subject was to identify all the phonemes that were associated with each grapheme. Here, there were fewer omissions on concurrent items than on consecutive ones. These effects were large, and they remained over two variations in the procedure (which equated first the number of presentations of each type of correspondence and secondly the strength at the end of training of the two successive correspondences).

A second important question, of course, is how much of the material presented in training was actually learned. In terms of this simple performance criterion, there were again differences in favor of concurrent training, but here the effect was small and unstable. Further work indicated that first-graders, tested early in their first semester of reading instruction on a similar task (in which the stimuli were homographs), showed a similar pattern.

Admittedly, much more research is needed in order to apply such findings as these to actual instruction. For one thing, few programs teach letter-sound correspondences in isolation. Further work is in progress, focusing on spelling patterns presented in the context of words. At present, however, in the absence of sufficient data on which to base a final decision, it would seem reasonable to provide at least some variation—some kind of concurrent training—when presenting multiple grapheme-phoneme correspondences. Certainly the data indicate that critical questioning of some of the time-honored assumptions and recommendations is desirable.

There is a third general category of cues that is used in word recognition: the context in which the word appears. That is, a reader makes use of the information contained in the rest of the sentence in his efforts to recognize the word. For example, in the sentence "He walked toward the . . . ," there are certain limitations, of both a grammatical and a semantic nature, on the words that can complete the sentence in an acceptable fashion. Investigators have found that it is indeed easier to recognize a word when it is presented in context than when it is presented alone. For example, Samuels has demonstrated that recognition speed for the response item in a word pair can be facilitated or interfered with by an appropriate selection of stimulus items.

More emphasis is being placed on context, or, to state it another way, the search for cues when units larger than a single word are considered. Only a few years ago, psychologists were comfortable with a very simple and narrow definition of reading, one that concentrated on what was *distinctive* about reading. Such definitions put major emphasis on the decoding process, of course.

Today the focus has shifted. Decoding is necessary but not sufficient, and other aspects of "reading"—notably, of course, comprehension—have been attracting attention (*11*). The emergence of such interest undoubtedly reflects the very strong influence of cognitive psychology. Reading now tends to be tied to information-processing and other related concepts. Definitions also seem to be growing more general and less focused on what is unique to reading. One can reasonably describe skilled reading, I believe, as a process in which the reader samples the cues on the printed page. Using these partial cues together with previous knowledge both about printed pages and about the world, the reader forms hypotheses (or expectations), which are confirmed or disconfirmed by subsequent samplings.

It is clear that whatever the definition of reading, the processes involved for the proficient reader and for the beginner do not completely overlap. Language has a hierarchical structure, and whether we are considering the processing of speech or of text, the identification of the "processing units" is of prime concern. It seems obvious that there are different types of units and different levels of units which depend in part on the characteristics of the reader—his proficiency, his purpose, and so forth. (They also depend on the nature of the material to be processed.) The specification of these units, intraword and beyond, how they are structured and how they are identified and recognized, will continue to be a central focus of the research in this area.

As would be expected, research interest has been shifting to the adult, skilled reader. Certainly, many of the issues arising from cognitive theory are more pertinent to the reader who has some proficiency, that is, an individual who is past the point at which decoding skills have become fully established and automatized. Moreover, a good bit of work on the visual recognition processes has already been accomplished, and it is to be expected that there would be a major push to do the same kind of initial "mapping out" with respect to the other aspects of reading.

I am concerned about this shift in interest, in that findings may not relate very closely to the behavior of the beginning reader, let alone to any ultimate concern with instruction in beginning reading. Other recent interests in the psychology of reading also seem to be leading away from questions of literacy training. The notion, for example, that speaking and writing are both derived directly from underlying linguistic structures, as opposed to the more common view that speech is primary and that writing

is simply (or complicatedly) a representation of speech, is most provocative (4). Such questions are tremendously fascinating and obviously deserve study. But, again, what about the five year old? How will he gain
from this kind of research?

We cannot afford to lose interest in fundamental investigations of the
behavior of the beginning reader, investigations that focus on the basic
processes of word recognition that are clearly so crucial to the five year
old. More work of the type that is so well represented by Samuels' experiments is sorely needed.

REFERENCES

1. Ackerman, M. D., and J. P. Williams. "Simultaneous vs. Successive Discrimination
   Training as a Function of Stimulus Similarity," paper presented at meetings of the
   American Educational Research Association, February 1969.
2. Bloomfield, L., and Clarence L. Barnhart. *Let's Read: A Linguistic Approach*. Detroit:
   Wayne State University Press, 1961.
3. Blumberg, E. L., D. V. Williams, and J. P. Williams. "What Cues Are Used in Visual
   Word Recognition?" paper presented at meetings of the Eastern Psychological Associa-
   tion, April 1969.
4. Francis, N. "Commentary on Chapters One Through Three," in H. Levin and J. P.
   Williams (Eds.), *Basic Studies on Reading*. Harper and Row, 1970.
5. Gibson, E. J., et al. "A Developmental Study of the Discrimination of Letter-Like
   Forms," *Journal of Comparative and Physiological Psychology*, 55 (1962), 897-906.
6. Gibson, E. J., A. Shurcliff, and A. Yonas. "Utilization of Spelling Patterns by Deaf and
   Hearing Subjects," in H. Levin and J. P. Williams (Eds.), *Basic Studies on Reading*.
   Harper and Row, 1970.
7. Levin, H., and J. Watson. "The Learning of Variable Grapheme-to-Phoneme Corre-
   spondences: Variations in the Initial Consonant Position," *A Basic Research Program on
   Reading*, U. S. Office of Education Cooperative Research Project No. 639. Ithaca, New
   York: Cornell University, 1963.
8. Marchbanks, G., and H. Levin. "Cues by which Children Recognize Words," *Journal of
   Educational Psychology*, 56 (1965), 57-61.
9. Taber, J. I., and R. Glaser. "An Exploratory Evaluation of a Discriminative Transfer
   Learning Program Using Literal Prompts," *Journal of Educational Research*, 55 (1962),
   508-512.
10. Williams, J. P. "Successive vs. Concurrent Presentation of Multiple Grapheme-
    Phoneme Correspondences," *Journal of Educational Psychology*, 59 (1968), 309-314.
11. Williams, J. P. "From Basic Research on Reading to Educational Practice," in H. Levin
    and J. P. Williams (Eds.), *Basic Studies on Reading*. New York: Harper and Row, 1970.
12. Williams, J. P., and H. Levin. "Word Perception: Psychological Bases," *Education*, 87
    (1967), 515-518.

The Effect of Pictures and Contextual Conditions on Learning Responses to Printed Words*

HARRY SINGER
University of California, Riverside

S. JAY SAMUELS and JEAN SPIROFF
University of Minnesota

Introduction

In teaching children to recognize new words, teachers may either present a word alone, in association with a picture, embedded in a sentence, or in a combination of sentence context plus a picture. Evidence has been presented regarding the efficacy of each of these conditions on the acquisition of reading responses. But, the evidence is contradictory; consequently, some explanations and prescriptions for teaching children to recognize printed words are in direct conflict.

On one side of the controversy, Samuels (1967) found that in comparison with words alone, presenting pictures in association with words apparently interfered with acquisition of reading responses. His explanation was that pictures distracted children from focusing attention on the printed words and that to be able to focus is critical if an individual is to acquire correct responses to printed words. However, Hartley (1970) concluded from her experimental instruction of beginning first graders that she could not generalize about the relative effectiveness of printed words presented alone, with a picture, or with oral context on the identification of those words.

*Reprinted from *Reading Research Quarterly*, 9, 4, 1973-1974, 555-567. This research was supported by grants from the Research Committee of the Academic Senate, University of California, Riverside and from the National Institutes of Child Health and Human Development to the Minnesota Reading Research Project. The Center for Research in Human Learning, at the University of Minnesota, has also supported this research.

In contrast to Samuels' focal attention hypothesis, Goodman (1965) formulated a linguistic or contextual hypothesis based on his demonstration that contextual constraints facilitated identification of words children could not recognize when the words were presented in isolation. He explained that performance on the novel words improved because the syntactic and semantic constraints of the sentences provided cues for anticipating the unknown words. Consequently only a confirming response from perceiving all or part of the word was necessary for the reader to progress. Or, if negative feedback was obtained when the response selected for the perceived word was tested for consistency of meaning with the direction of thought, then spontaneous correction of the erroneous response would occur. Weber (1970) observed that in reading connected discourse, errors made by first graders during oral reading were often predictable from syntactic or semantic constraints in the words preceding the error.

In an observational study of reading development, Biemiller (1970) concluded that during grades 1 and 2, children progressed through 3 stages in learning to recognize printed words. In the first stage, children used contextual constraints for anticipating or guessing unknown words. In the second stage, children either used analytical techniques such as structural analysis or phonics to recognize unknown words or they gave no response. The third stage represented an integration of the first 2 stages and resulted in a superior performance in word recognition. Barr (1972) related the development of these stages to a concomitant shift in instruction from emphasis on context for recognizing the whole word to stress upon a more analytical response, such as use of grapheme-phoneme correspondence rules.

The focal attention hypothesis acknowledges that pictures or context can cue or prompt a correct response to printed words; but, if the reader depends upon these cues to anticipate the unknown words, he may not acquire appropriate responses to the graphic features of the word itself. Consequently, in connected discourse, he may seem to know the word because he correctly anticipates it; but when tested on the word in isolation, his inability to identify the word will reveal that he did not acquire an accurate response to the word itself. In contrast, Goodman's contextual hypothesis states that children do not need to have the word presented in isolation—that presenting new words in context is all that is needed for children to acquire correct oral responses to them.

This study was an attempt to resolve the focal attention versus context controversy. Pedagogically, the controversy can be reduced to the question of what instructional conditions will best help a child learn to recognize a new word. For example, in learning to recognize new words, wha effect do pictures have? Similarly, in learning to recognize new words, what effect does context have? Furthermore, does a combination of pictures and context enhance the recognition of new words?

Designwise, this is a 2-factor study with grade level and the experimental treatments the factors. Grades 1 and 2 were used in order to determine whether developmental changes occur in the use of cues for identifying words.

Method and Procedures

Subjects. 80 grade 1 and 84 grade 2 children from a metropolitan school system were used during the seventh month of the school year.

Design. A 2 (grades 1 and 2) x 4 (treatments) factorial design was used. Subjects in each grade were randomly assigned to each of the 4 experimental conditions. The 4 conditions were *word-picture, word-no picture, sentence-picture,* and *sentence-no picture.*

Materials. The warm-up materials consisted of two 5x8 index cards, each with a picture of a girl and her name printed below in an artificial alphabet.

Training stimuli for the *word-picture* treatment consisted of four 5x8 cards. Each card had either a picture of a cup, cat, bat, or bed on it and the corresponding word beneath the picture in an artificial alphabet. Training stimuli for the *word-no picture* treatment had 4 cards with the same words, but no picture. Training stimuli for the *sentence-picture* condition had 4 cards with a picture of either a cup, cat, bat, or bed, and a sentence using the word. All words were printed in the standard English alphabet, except for the words for cup, cat, bat, and bed. The sentences were "Fill the cup," "The cat sleeps," "The bat flies," and "The bed is pretty." Training stimuli for the *sentence-no picture* condition consisted of 4 cards with the same sentences, but without pictures.

Test stimuli for all 4 conditions were identical. There were four 5x8 index cards, each containing a single word, either *cup, cat, bat,* or *bed* printed in the artificial alphabet. The cards were bound on a ring. Each set of 4 training cards was followed by a set of 4 test cards. Training and test cards were arranged in 3 random orders on the ring. Each of the treatments was on a separate ring.

Procedure. The entire procedure—warm-up, training, and testing— was completed by the examiner at one sitting, working individually with

experiment proper, a study-test procedure was used.
rials, the subject was asked to look at the word, to put his
e word, and to tell the examiner what the word was. If no
forthcoming within 7 seconds, the subject was told the word
niner. If the response was incorrect, the correct response was

uring the test trials, only the 4 target words were shown in the
icial alphabet; no cues accompanied the words. All 4 treatment
oups received the same conditions on the test trials. The subject was told
to look at the word, to put his finger under it, and to state what the word
was. No feedback of any kind was given on the test trials. Study and test
trials were alternated for a maximum of 12 trials. However, if the child got
all 4 correct on 2 successive trials, the procedure was stopped.

Results

Two separate analyses were computed: one for the trials to criterion
and the other for number of correct responses in the test trials.

An analysis of variance, Tables 1a and 1b, shows that for both trials to
criterion and for number of correct responses, grade level and treatments
were significant. However, the grade level by treatment interactions were
not significant for either trials to criterion or for number correct in the test
trials. In other words, the pattern of responses for children in both grade
levels was the same. Because there was no interaction effect, the results for
grades 1 and 2 were combined in order to compare the differences among
the treatments.

Table 1a. Analysis of variance for effect of 4 treatments at 2 grade levels on trials
to criterion.

Source of Variance	Degrees of Freedom	Sum of Squares	F-Ratio	P-value
Grade	1	57.90	6.14	<.01
Treatment	3	253.24	8.95	<.001
Grade x Treatment	3	28.14	.99	<.39
Error	156	1471.92		

Table 1b. Analysis of variance for effect of 4 treatments at 2 grade levels on number of correct responses on test trials.

Source of Variance	Degrees of Freedom	Sum of Squares	F-ratio	P-value
Grade	1	1020.59	7.23	<.007
Treatment	3	3375.86	7.97	<.001
Grade x Treatment	3	104.18	.25	<.86
Error	156	22021.03		

The means and standard deviations for trials to criterion and number of correct responses for each of the 4 treatments are shown in Table 2.

Table 2. Means and standard deviations for total sample on trials to criterion and number of correct responses for 4 treatments.

| | Treatments | | | |
	Word – No Picture	Word – Picture	Sentence – No Picture	Sentence – Picture
Trials to Criterion				
Mean	8.0	9.69	10.32	11.45
SD	3.78	3.55	3.08	1.41
Number Correct				
Mean	34.98	28.43	26.23	23.29
SD	11.43	12.52	13.61	10.78

Table 2 reveals that the *word-no picture* condition had the fewest trials to criterion, 8.02. The means then rise for *word-picture,* 9.69; *sentence-no picture,* 10.32; and *sentence-picture,* 11.45. As shown in Table 3, a Neuman-Keuls test on trials to criterion indicated that the *word-no picture* treatment required significantly fewer trials to criterion compared with each of the other treatments. The *word-picture* required significantly fewer trials in comparison with *sentence-picture.* There was no significant difference between *word-picture* and *sentence-no picture.* But, neither was there any difference between the *sentence-no picture* and the *sentence-picture* treatment.

Table 3.   Neuman-Keuls comparisons of treatments.

| | | Number of Correct Responses | | |
	Sentence – Picture	Sentence – No Picture	Word – Picture	Word – No Picture
Sentence – Picture		NS	NS	p<.01
Sentence – No Picture			NS	p<.01
Word – Picture				p<.05

| | | Trials to Criterion | | |
	Word – No Picture	Word – Plus Picture	Sentence – No Picture	Sentence – Plus Picture
Word – No Picture		p<.05	p<.01	p<.01
Word – Picture			NS	p<.05
Sentence – No Picture				NS

On number of correct responses, the *word-no picture* condition had an average of 34.98 correct responses, while the other treatments had 28.43 for *word-picture*, 26.23 for *sentence-no picture*, and 23.29 for *sentence-picture*. As indicated in Table 3, the Neuman-Keuls test showed that the *word-no picture* condition had significantly more correct responses than any other conditions. None of the other conditions were significantly different from each other.

Discussion

The results disclosed that the *word-no picture* treatment required significantly fewer trials to criterion. Furthermore, more correct responses were given with this treatment when compared with all the other conditions. Moreover, as the number of cues which were associated with the target word changed from pictures to sentence and increased from sentence to sentence plus pictures, the number of trials required to reach criterion consistently increased and the number of correct responses in the test trials consistently decreased. (See Figures 1a and 1b.) Thus, the results of the present study support Samuels' focal attention hypothesis that to facilitate the acquisition of word recognition responses, visual attention must be focused on the printed word.

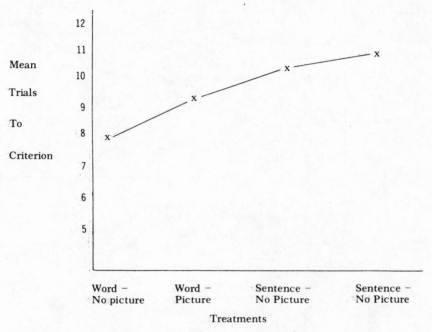

Figure 1a.   Mean trials to criterion for 4 treatments.

However, in a previous study, Samuels (1967) found that *word-picture* was superior in the study trials, but not in the test trials. That is, in the *word-picture* condition, children tended to use the picture to correctly anticipate the target words. Hence, they were learning to use pictures as a type of context cue to identify the target words, which is analogous to using sentence cues to anticipate words as fluent readers usually do in the *process of reading*. But, in the word condition, children had only the target word to attend to and hence *learned* to identify the target word better. In short, the *word-picture* group was learning to use the picture as a cue to identify the target word, while the *word-no picture* group had to learn to respond only to the graphic stimuli of the target word.

In the present study, the context condition consisted of a printed sentence. In 3 of the 4 sentences, definite syntactic and semantic constraints were available for predicting the target words. If contextual

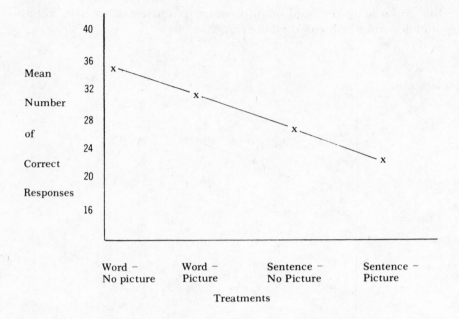

Figure 1b.   Mean number of correct responses for 4 treatments.

constraints are sufficiently predictive, a child may be able to give the correct response to the target words without having to perceive the words themselves. A question arises whether by providing the context orally, the teacher can facilitate a correct response without distracting the child's attention from the printed word. However, Hartley (1970) tested the effect of oral context on word recognition and found that oral context was not superior to word alone or word plus picture in either the study trials or the test trials.

In general, the evidence does not support Goodman's (1965) contention that sentence context facilitates acquisition of correct responses as compared with recognition of the unknown word in isolation. Even though he did demonstrate that adding sentence context to unknown words enables individuals to identify words they could not recognize when the same words were presented in isolation, he did not provide any evidence that through the use of context, readers had, in fact, *learned* to recognize the unknown word.[1] Nevertheless, the evidence in the present experiment clearly shows that many individuals eventually reached criterion and exhibited correct responses under *each treatment,* but the addition of pictures, context, or pictures plus context makes the learner *less* efficient in acquiring reading responses.

A question which we may wish to consider is why do the picture and context conditions make the learner less efficient? The answer seems to lie in the fact that on the study trials, pictures as well as context enabled the student to give the correct response without having to visually attend to the graphemes. On the test trials, when the pictures and the verbal context were no longer present, the learner was unable to identify the words because the eliciting cues had been removed. Apparently, then, the pictures and verbal context provided sufficient cues for the student to give the correct oral response. On the other hand, the superiority of the *word-no picture* condition is explained by the fact that the only cues that the child could attend to were the graphic stimuli of the words themselves, and visual attention is an essential condition needed for learning to identify the words.

The paired-associates laboratory paradigm used in this study is analogous to some of the instructional processes used in the classroom to teach children to recognize words. In a test of the focal attention hypothesis for reading acquisition in a classroom situation, Samuels (1967) found that learning to recognize words was superior when no picture was present. Furthermore, he found that poor readers were significantly more distracted by pictures than were good readers. The good readers had apparently learned that pictures were an irrelevant cue and that, in order to recognize a word, attention had to be focused on the target word itself. That is, the individual has to perceive and learn to give correct responses to graphemes.

According to Zeaman and House (1967), one of the major constructs which can be used to explain differences in acquisition rate is that of focal attention strategies. In fact, Estes (1970) states that the construct of focal attention is more useful than the construct of individual differences in intelligence to explain variation in rate of acquisition. If we apply the focal

---

[1] Goodman's results can be attributed to the *process of reading,* in which semantic and syntactic constraints can be used for predicting unknown words. With a minimum of sampling of the unknown words, a high percent of accuracy in identifying them can be attained. The present study emphasizes the *processes of learning* in which focal attention on the unknown words is a prerequisite to such subsequent processes as discrimination, hooking-up responses to graphemes, and reinforcement of correct responses. Thus, the Goodman-Samuels controversy can be at least partially resolved by realizing that they are referring to 2 different, but interrelated, processes: the reading process and the learning process.

attention construct to reading, high IQ children, who also tend to be the better readers, seem to learn at a faster rate because they focus their attention on the relevant attributes of the stimulus sooner than low IQ children. Use of contrastive spelling patterns may also serve to focus attention on relevant attributes of graphic stimuli (Fries, 1962). Indeed, use of such distinctive features was successful in laboratory instruction for learning and transfer of grapheme-phoneme correspondences (Gibson, 1965). Also, Skailand (1970) found that low socioeconomic kindergarten pupils taught to respond to stimuli which were arranged in contrastive spelling patterns recalled about twice as many syllables and words as those children who were taught by the whole-word method or by single grapheme-phoneme combination.

Thus, the evidence consistently supports Samuels' focal attention hypothesis. When confronted by a novel word, the poor reader who has pictures or context available but who does not know which are the relevant stimuli nor how to respond to them tends to search for or rely upon pictures or contextual cues for eliciting a correct oral response for the unknown word. If the word can be correctly identified from these cues alone, the reader no longer has a need to attend to the word itself. Under these conditions, he is less likely to acquire and associate responses to the graphic stimuli.

While this study has demonstrated that for the purpose of teaching children to identify a word it is best to present that word in isolation, it is not to be implied that this is the only method which should be used in teaching children to read. The child needs to get ample practice reading meaningful and interesting material in context so that he will develop strategies for using semantic and syntactic constraints in passages as aids in word identification. Indeed, to become a fluent reader, an individual must be able to mobilize semantic and syntactic constraints for antici-pating words. He must also learn how to test his predictions by using the graphemic cues present in the text. There is evidence that these strategies which facilitate the word identification process can be trained (Samuels, Dahl, and Archwamety, 1974).

Summary and Conclusions

The purpose of the present investigation was to test Samuels' focal attention hypothesis for learning to recognize printed words. A 4-treatment (*word-no picture, word-picture, sentence-no picture,* and *sentence-picture*) by 2-level (grades 1 and 2) factorial design was used to test the effects of the treatments on learning to recognize words printed in an artificial alphabet. A whole-word method, employing a paired-associate anticipation procedure, was the technique used for teaching 80 first and 84 second graders who were randomly assigned to the 4 treatments.

The analysis of variance indicated that grade level and treatment effects were significant for trials to criterion and for correct responses on the test. The results were interpreted as supporting Samuels' focal attention hypothesis for acquiring reading responses for novel words. In general, efficiency in learning to associate responses to graphic stimuli is significantly greater when the word is presented in isolation than when presented in sentence context or in association with a picture, or both.

REFERENCES

Barr, Rebecca C. The influence of instructional conditions on word recognition errors. *Reading Research Quarterly,* Spring, 1972, 7, 509-529.

Biemiller, Andrew. The development of the use of graphic and contextual information as children learn to read. *Reading Research Quarterly,* Fall 1970, 6, 75-96.

Estes, William K. *Learning theory and mental development.* New York: Academic Press, 1970.

Fries, Charles C. *Linguistics and reading.* New York: Holt, Rinehart, and Winston, 1962.

Gibson, Eleanor. Learning to read. *Science,* May 1965, 148, 1066-1072.

Goodman, Kenneth S. A linguistic study of cues and miscues in reading. *Elementary English,* October 1965, 42, 639-643.

Hartley, Ruth N. Effects of list types and cues on the learning of word lists. *Reading Research Quarterly,* Fall 1970, 6, 97-121.

Samuels, S. Jay. Attentional processes in reading: the effect of pictures in the acquisition of reading responses. *Journal of Educational Psychology,* December 1967, 58, 337-342.

Samuels, S. J.; Dahl, P.; & Archwamety, T. Effect of hypothesis/test training on reading skill. *Journal of Educational Psychology,* 1974, 66, 835-844.

Skailand, Dawn B. A comparison of four language units in teaching beginning reading. Unpublished doctoral dissertation, University of California, Berkeley, 1970.

Weber, Rose-Marie. First graders' use of grammatical context in reading. In Harry Levin and Joanna Williams (Eds.) *Basic Studies on Reading.* New York: Basic Books, 1970. Pp. 147-163.

Zeaman, D., & House, B. J. The relation of IQ and learning. In R. M. Gagne (Ed.) *Learning and Individual Differences.* Columbus, Ohio: Charles E. Merrill, 1967. Pp. 192-212.

Cognition

Conceptualization in Learning to Read[*]

HARRY SINGER
University of California at Riverside

Children have learned to read by means of a wide variety of methods and materials. During the history of American reading instruction (Smith, 71), the unit of initial instructional emphasis has varied by increasing in a surprisingly systematic way from the letter (alphabet method) to word parts (phonic method) to the whole word (word method) and finally to the sentence and paragraph (language arts method).[1] But, there is still only a paucity of knowledge about how children actually do learn to read (Mac-Kinnon, 52).

However, it is known that regardless of any of the strategies that have been employed for teaching reading, the average pupil in progressing through the grades does cumulatively learn to recognize words that have not been specifically taught. That is, the pupil develops general word recognition ability, the ability to transform printed stimuli into mental processes so that meaning can be associated with these stimuli. For example, even though the basal reader method emphasizes the development of a sight word vocabulary, pupils recognize at successively higher grade levels an increasingly greater percentage of words than those to which they have been systematically exposed (Gates, 23). Apparently, experience in supplemental reading and the developmental word recognition lessons of the basal reader have been successful in teaching pupils more than just the correspondence among the seen, heard, and spoken words when they are learning to read orally by means of the controlled basal reader vocabulary. In fact, scrutiny of the lesson plans in the teacher's

---

[*]Reprinted from George B. Schick and Merrill M. May (Eds.), *New Frontiers in College-Adult Reading*, Fifteenth Yearbook of the National Reading Conference, 1966, 116-132. Reprinted with permission.

[1]Such a wide range of approaches to teaching reading in the first grade now exists that 27 somewhat different studies at this grade level were supported by the U.S. Office of Education at a total cost of approximately $600,000 (Durrell, 16).

manual which accompanies the basal reader reveals that pupils are explicitly taught to abstract and generalize recurring word parts, such as initial consonants, blends, phonograms, syllables, and affixes. Consequently, either by instructional design or by utilizing their own learning "strategies" (Bruner et al., 8), pupils could thus acquire a mediational response system for selecting, perceiving, and processing printed verbal stimuli. The symbolic responses or concepts in this mediational response system can then be mobilized in varying combinations for recognizing many more printed words than those employed in the original formation of the mediational response system. Since the pupil would not need to develop a separate mediational response for each printed word that he can recognize, the possibility of "cognitive strain" would be reduced (Bruner, et al., 8). Of course, if the formation of a conceptualized mediational response system is not attained, then the pupil's rate of learning to recognize words would be relatively slow because he would be limited to recognition of just those words for which he had developed specific responses.

Whether reading is taught through a basal reader method or through some other method, a complex conceptual system and mental organization would have to be postulated to explain how individuals do learn to read. Because there are many factors which enter into the development of general reading ability (Holmes, 30, 32, 35; Holmes and Singer, 36, 37, 38; Singer, 66), each method of teaching reading can be relatively successful because it stresses one or another of the many variables that are related to attainment of speed and power of reading (Holmes, 32). However, all the necessary elements for reading are present in the materials employed by each method so that pupils in learning to read through any of these methods could have used their capabilities for selecting their own unit of perception, their own conceptualized mediational response systems, and developed their own mental organization for attaining speed and power of reading (Holmes and Singer, 36; Singer, 63, 66). Probably the acquisition of such response systems could be facilitated by an instructional strategy which capitalizes upon the cognitive capabilities of the learner (Singer, 67).

Some Related Research

Although many factors have to be postulated in order to account adequately for the attainment of reading behavior, the formation and use of concepts are, in fact, related to a significant portion of the variance in each subsystem of reading (Singer, 63, 64). From the many studies on conceptualization and the relationship between conceptualization and reading ability, which have been reviewed elsewhere (Singer, 63), only one investigation that is quite germane to a theoretical formulation of the role of conceptualization in learning to read will be reviewed again in this paper. Also, two more recent reports on the relationship between conceptual ability and reading achievement will be summarized.

Capacity for conceptualization was specifically related to reading achievement by Kress (43). After matching 25 pairs of children who were between the ages of 8 and 11, above average in intelligence and comparable on all subscales except the Similarities subscale of the Wechsler-Bellevue Intelligence Test, but who were significantly different on a word recognition test and the Stanford Achievement Test (Paragraph Meaning), Kress administered to each subject a battery of clinical tests of concept formation, which included the Goldstein-Scheerer, the Hanfmann-Kasanin, and the Wisconsin Card Sorting Tests. Responses to the WISC Similarities test were scored for concrete, functional, and abstract levels. Kress summarized the results of these concept formation tasks by stating that in contrast to the "achieving readers," the "non-readers" tend to lack a) versatility and flexibility, b) originality in establishing suitable hypotheses for testing, c) initiative for exhausting all solutions, d) persistence in problem solving under changing conditions, e) ability to draw inferences from relevant clues, f) ability to shift set when new standards are introduced, g) ability to analyze the factors present, h) adequate labels for common concepts, and i) adequate concepts for dealing with language. On the other hand, the non-readers tend to exhibit a) a tendency to cling to previous acceptable solutions, b) an abnormal need for success and avoidance of failure, c) a dependence on the physical characteristics of the objects, and d) a tendency to be more concrete and less abstract in conceptual functioning.

Jan-Tausch (41) also concluded that "retarded readers are retarded because of limitations to concrete thinking," but he conceded that other causes of reading retardation, such as poor vision, hearing, ego development, and instruction could be inferred from his data.

Recently, Robinson (60) hypothesized that rigidity in perception and conceptualization might be an important factor in reading retardation. She suggested that while most individuals are flexible in perceptual and conceptual modes, some pupils might rely mainly upon a single perceptual and conceptual style which, if non-modifiable, would require adaptation of instructional methods in order for these pupils to be successful in learning to read.

The evidence clearly indicates that there is a relation between conceptualization and learning to read, which is usually not a function of the method of teaching reading. Therefore, any theory which purports to explain how individuals learn to read would need to state explicitly the way in which the formation and use of concepts might enter into the development and dynamics of general reading ability. The following is an attempt at such a theoretical formulation. Also, an attempt will be made to integrate this theoretical formulation with the substrata-factor theory of reading.

Conceptual Ability in the Substrata-Factor Theory of Reading

In the process of learning to read, an individual develops and utilizes his ability to select and organize symbolic stimuli into perceptual units. Through conceptualization, the process of discriminating, abstracting, generalizing and organizing common elements (Hull, 39), relationships (Smoke, 72), or crucial aspects of a complex figure (Osgood, 56), an individual reduces a variety of stimuli into fewer categories, which simplify and facilitate his learning task by easing the "cognitive strain" (Bruner et al., 8). Gradually he thereby builds up a conceptual-readiness (Leeper, 48; Russell, 61; Vinacke, 75) to respond to stimuli with a symbolic mode of reaction (Heidbreder, 29) or mediated response (Osgood, 56; Morris, 53). The concept that is formed could vary in span (Zaslow, 78), consistency (Reed, 58), or level of generality (Hanfmann and Kasanin, 26; Goldstein et al., 25; Reichard, et al., 59; Zaslow, 78). These categories are internally linked together into a hierarchical system (Long and Welch, 49, 50) which enables an individual to organize broader units of response on a higher-order conceptual level and through such a superordination process to synthesize disparate elements (Bruner and Oliver, 10). An individual can then utilize this hierarchical system to select and respond to a perceptual unit. Through this circularity of perceptual processes and conceptualization, reinforced by successful practice, a coherent and flexible system develops, in which all the parts—when the individual attains maturity—psychosynchromesh as the individual compounds and recompounds them into working systems. These working systems are momentary organizations to meet the demands of the task-stimuli of the reading material and the reader's purpose (Holmes, 31). Thus, an individual acquires the ability to transform printed symbols into a complex of mental processes, known as his *word-recognition-substrata,* to which meaning can be associated.

If an individual lacks the capacity to conceptualize because of brain damage (Goldstein, et al., 25; Nielsen, 55; Werner and Garrison, 76), personality disorganization (Cameron, 12), or if his level of conceptual capability is inadequate at the time of instruction (Barnard, 3; Kress, 43; Piaget, 57; and Zaslow, 78), then the stimuli of the printed page during the process of learning to read may not be merged into concepts but remain a "succession of object like beads on a string" (Russell and Groff, 62). Furthermore, if a teacher believes that early reading experiences consist of acquiring "mechanics" of reading, then the teacher may aim to develop this ability by calling upon memorization, rather than higher thought processes (Gans, 19), but if a teacher does stress conceptualization by grouping stimuli into common elements, pupils will tend to attain greater transfer (Gates, 20); or, despite the organization of instruction, pupils who have the capability may still achieve the necessary generalizations (Carroll, 13, 14).

Concomitantly with the development of a word-recognition-substrata, an individual learns to associate meanings, the residuals of his experiences with the referents of the symbolic stimuli, to the transformation of the printed symbols. These associations are fused or arranged into thought sequences and integrated into a broader working system of symbolic reasoning. If a communications network is developmentally established and integrated, then there can be cumulative transfer of meaning from the kinesthetic to the auditory and the visual modalities (Holmes, 33). Consequently, a conceptual system could be formed by selecting and interrelating meanings across these modalities. Then, this conceptual system could be mobilized for responding to stimulus input through the kinesthetic, auditory, or visual modalities (Singer, 63; Singer and Balow, 70).[2]

Defined from the above theoretical analysis, reading is a processing skill that consists of a) transformation of printed stimuli into a word-recognition-substrata, b) association of meaning to the transformed stimuli, c) synchromeshing of a) and b) into a harmonious working system. This working system is a momentary organization of substrata processes that is controlled by the demands of the task-stimuli, the individual's level of maturity in reading, his purposes, his values (Holmes, 34; Athey, 2), and his biological support system (Davis, 15). Thus, through a succession of working systems, the individual is able to attain speed, comprehension, and power in reading. Interference, faulty functioning, or failure in any of the above subsystems, a), b), or c), serves to reduce achievement in speed and/or power of reading.

The remainder of this paper will be divided into three sections to explain in greater detail how conceptualization may operate in the inter-

---

[2] Bruner's (9) identification of enactive, iconic, and symbolic modes of representation is similar to the above formulation of kinesthetic, auditory, and conceptual modalities.

related subsystems of 1) word recognition, 2) word meaning, and 3) reasoning-in-context. In each of these broadly defined subsystems of general reading ability, flexibility in conceptualization will also be explicated.

Word Recognition

In the early stages of learning, the individual is confronted with a wealth of unfamiliar details which require fine discriminations for consequent perceptual accuracy and conceptual adequacy. Errors in responses to words at this primary level of development can often be attributed to perceptual immaturity, inadequate functioning of perceptual processes, incompletely developed word recognition concepts, or some combination of these factors. For example, a child may not be able to discriminate the fine differences between *e* and *o*, especially when these letters occur in the middle of a word and have to be discriminated from the other letters, as well as from each other, as in the words *net* and *not*. Or he may not have a correct kinesthetic or orientational concept of the so-called reversal letters of *b, d, p, q, u,* and *n.* Further errors may result from inadequate auditory discrimination of vowels, as in *pan* and *pin,* in which the slight change in pitch may not reach the level of awareness for some children.

The kinds of errors and their frequencies might not only arise from determinants within the individual, but also from interaction between these determinants and the method of instruction (Bond, 5; Fendrick, 18). If an individual with a sensory deficiency is exposed to a method of instruction which requires proficiency in that same sensory mode but is not able to compensate through a self-acquired method nor has had instruction adapted to his major mode of learning, he is likely to accumulate a disability in reading, in addition to a *negative* learning set in this area.

In diagnosing word recognition errors, care must be taken not to confuse various levels within a particular mode. For example, an individual may have good auditory acuity, that is, a peripheral auditory system in good functioning order, but his auditory conceptual system may not be operating adequately or at a sufficiently mature level to enable an individual to learn to respond well through that mode. In other words, an individual may have satisfactory acuity, but lack of ability to organize the auditory stimuli, as Kyme (44) has demonstrated. Although Kyme's study was in the area of musicality or aesthetic judgment, there is some evidence that there may be analogous levels of functioning for language in the auditory modality (Singer, 63). The discrepancy between peripheral and central functioning or integration in the auditory mode may also be true in the kinesthetic and visual modes.

Characteristics of Task-Stimuli and Modes of Conceptualization

Because of the nature of printed stimuli of language and his capabilities, the individual can learn to conceptualize such verbal stimuli through emphasis upon different modes, such as auditory, visual, kinesthetic, or a combination. That is, some aspects of printed language can be sounded out and auditorily grouped, such as *see, tea,* tidy; other parts of words may have identical letter configurations, such as l*ight,* s*ight,* r*ight,* and can be organized into visual concepts; and all printed stimuli have characteristic lines or curves which the eye can follow and integrate into a general response because of kinesthetic features (Hebb, 28), such as the up-and-down-and-across characteristics in *t*ree, a*t*e, boa*t*. [3]

However, any one word does not necessarily fit into a particular conceptual category, nor do two individuals necessarily develop the same conceptual responses or organization of responses. When a word does fall into multi-categories, an individual may form and draw upon several concepts and coordinate them into a working system to solve the word recognition task. For example, the word "right" may have an auditory unit or phonogram, "ri;" a visiogram, "gh" (silent); and a phonogram, "t," for one person, but another individual may have developed a larger gestalt, "r" and "ight." Still another person may perceive this word by its entire configuration and respond to it by means of a "whole word" process. Whatever concepts are formed, an individual will have to organize them into a working system to meet the demands of the task-stimuli.

Flexibility in word recognition. Conceptualizations in different modes enable a reader to recognize words in a variety of ways. Multimodal conceptualization of responses to words is necessary since words and parts of words do not fit into any one mode. Thus, if an individual starts to sound out a word, he may find that he has to stop at *a particular* boundary-point within the word because the next part could not be integrated as an auditory component; then, if he has the necessary visual or kinesthetic concept, he can utilize it. Finally he has to blend or synthesize all his responses together to form the whole word. In some instances a reader may fill in a missing word by calling upon his word sense. The conditions necessary for flexibility are a) a variety of processes that can be

---

[3] An appropriate name for kinesthetically formed images of printed stimuli, the writer suggests, is "kinesthetograms."

organized into a working system appropriate to the task-stimuli, b) a mental process which enables an individual to sense the necessity for shifting from one process to another, or to resolve discrepancies that may arise from a narrow response unit by calling upon a broader conceptual response, c) a fairly evenly developed cross-section of abilities, and d) a growing feeling of confidence in and mastery over the processes involved in learning to read.

Obviously, if an individual has only one approach, he can not shift to another. If he encounters a barrier to his one technique, he must stop because he has no other approach to circumvent the barrier or to make it permeable. For example, an individual may have a phonetic approach which works very well with c-a-t and such words, if properly applied, but which will not function with r-i-g-h-t. Or an individual may be able to sound out "ri," but reaches a barrier for "gh" if he systematically tries to sound out each letter. However, he may be able to circumvent this barrier if he knows "ight" as a phonovisiogram or he may be able to break the barrier if he knows the visiogram "gh" (silent) and passes on to the last letter of the word.

Even if an individual does have a broad word-recognition-substrata of phonics, syllabification, affixes, blending, and rhyming processes, he must also have some mechanism which institutes a reorganization of his word-recognition-substrata. If he does not reorganize, then he might persistently bump against the barrier. Sometimes in oral reading a child may be observed as he reaches such a barrier; instead of shifting to another approach, he backs up to the beginning of the sentence, as though he were going to get a running start of context clues to overcome the barrier by sheer ideational force.

The mechanism or process which institutes the switching or reorganization process might be termed "flexibility-in-manipulating-verbal-symbols." A necessary component of this process is the ability to generalize or conceptualize within limits appropriate to the task-stimuli of each mode. At the extremes of this conceptual span are the over-generalizer and the undergeneralizer (Zaslow, 78).

The overgeneralizer, the person whose generalization within a particular mode is very broad, will tend to be frustrated in certain situations. For example, he may recognize correctly m*eat* and s*eal*, but not br*ead*, if his generalization includes *all* vowel combinations of "ea," instead of only those which do not follow "r." Bright children may be in this classification early in learning (Carroll, 13, 14).

The undergeneralizer, the person whose concept in a particular mode is narrow, will tend to have difficulty in recognizing words, even though they are in his hearing or meaning vocabulary, which he might have recognized if his concept were broader. For example, the under-generalizer might recognize *seat,* but not be able to recognize b*eat,* even though he is able to substitute consonants, that is, he may not have developed a category for "*eat.*" He might consequently think that the word recognition processes for each word are unique. This approach is probably characteristic of certain brain-damaged individuals who lack capacity for conceptualization.

The flexible generalizer, the person whose concept is inclusive but within appropriate boundaries, will tend to apply his concept when appropriate but shift to another readily when the first does not apply. For example, he may have acquired the concept that when two vowels are together, as in b*oat,* the first vowel says its name and the second is silent, but he knows there are exceptions, such as "pneumatic" or "oil."

Differences in mode of conceptualization. Differences exist not only *between* individuals in each mode, but also within the *same* individual. Kling (42), for example, computed a correlation for college students of .03 between auditory and visual discriminations for nonverbal stimuli.

Comparison of individuals on any one aspect of word recognition results in a distribution whose shape reflects the general level of maturity for that process. At the fourth grade, for instance, knowledge of letter sounds is negatively skewed (Gates, 22) because this ability has already reached maturity in most of the subjects. But syllabification, a process still being developed at the fourth grade, yields a normal curve of distribution.

Measurements made repeatedly on the same individual in all three modes would probably reveal intraindividual differences in learning mode; over a period of time, these measurements would theoretically reveal a gradient-shift from kinesthetic-to-auditory-to-visual dominance in mode of learning ability (Holmes, 31). However, individuals, in general, do not necessarily need to develop to perfection in any one word recognition process. Instead, by means of a combination of fairly well developed skills in the various processes or modes, they can achieve sufficient accuracy in word recognition so that they are not handicapped at all *in transforming any word into mental processes for the purpose of arousing and associating meaning.*[4]

Emotional and personality factors. The degree of stress which an individual feels he is under while reading will tend to influence the breadth of

---

[4] This hypothesis may explain Triggs's (74) otherwise puzzling results. Triggs reported that mean scores from a cross-sectional investigation on syllabication and rhyming, subtests of the Diagnostic Reading Test, rose steadily through the twelfth grade. Performance on these variables dropped slightly from grade 12 to college, however, while comprehension still continued to improve.

his "cognitive map" (Tolman, 73). For example, in reading orally he might feel unduly self-conscious and consequently be very sensitive to his errors. These feelings, in turn, could feed back into and constrict his mental processes. This constriction would then operate against fluency in reorganization or selection of alternate routes required by the characteristics of the task-stimuli. But, under less emotion-provoking conditions, such as in silent reading, when he found himself blocked in one approach, he is more likely, if he has the necessary abilities, to fluently reorganize his word-recognition-substrata and mobilize a working system that is more appropriate for solving the particular word recognition task. Of course, a basic assumption for this flexibility is that the individual had been taught or had learned multiple routes to the goal of success in word recognition.

However, sometimes experiences in emotion-provoking situations may perseverate or be aroused in silent reading situations. For example, a child might have learned from a perfectionist, a teacher or parent or both, and as a consequence might feel that he is unable to read whenever he could not transform all the stimuli into corresponding oral responses that perfectly match the characteristics of the stimuli. Then, in reading silently, even at the 95 percent level of word recognition accuracy or at a level at which he could accurately attain ideas from the material, he would still not read with a feeling of enjoyment or satisfaction, for he would tend to recall the voice-of-conscience whenever he stumbled or slurred over a word.

At the other extreme, a permissive or laissez-faire atmosphere, could also result in inaccurate responses to printed words. In this environment an individual might not acquire the necessary motivation to make fine discriminations between and within words. Furthermore, the individual in this learning atmosphere might not receive sufficient correction for his errors. Because of this lack of motivation and feedback, the individual might be hindered from developing a learning set (Harlow, 27) for improving his word recognition abilities.

Fixation in development of word recognition. If an individual's ability in one area is disproportionately better developed than his abilities in other word recognition processes, he is likely to use his most developed ability, whether or not it is appropriate to the task-stimuli; that is, he might leap-before-looking, so to speak. Consequently, such an individual would continually experience frustration, until his other word recognition abilities had developed to the point where they could be mobilized into a working system for attaining word recognition.

However, some individuals might become fixated at a particular level of development in word recognition. For example, such an individual might use a combination of context, whole word recognition, or spelling, if the first two did not work. Because this combination could work for many words, he might not feel the necessity for expanding his repertoire of word recognition abilities.

Although a "gradient-shift" (Holmes, 31) might be a general characteristic of development towards maturity in which an individual reorganizes his word recognition processes and shifts from an inefficient to a more efficient and effective method of processing stimuli (Gates, 21; Singer, 66), a fixated individual would not fit into this developmental process. The manifestation would show up mostly in speed of reading. However, there could also be an interference in comprehension or in continuity of thought because an excessive concentration of energy had been utilized in overcoming word-barriers and because a maximum span of attention had been surpassed.

Summary on word recognition. Normal development of a word recognition subsystem is dependent upon adequately functioning kinesthetic, auditory, and visual perception and conceptual processes, plus an integrated and flexibly operating intercommunications network among these processes (Holmes, 33; Singer, 63). Facilitation of this development results not only from conceptualization of responses to printed stimuli, but also from considerable practice and experience in a moderately motivating and emotionally satisfying atmosphere for learning to read. Under these organismic and environmental conditions, an individual could form highly organized and flexible word-recognition-substrata which function so harmoniously and rapidly that the processes mobilized for this subsystem not only psychosynchromesh but also require a minimum of mental energy. Therefore, a maximum of mental energy could be devoted to the reasoning-in-context aspects of reading.

However, when a strange or unfamiliar word does appear, an individual has to mark time in his mental processing of the content and switch most of his mental energy to the operation of his word-recognition-substrata. This reduces his speed of reading and may interfere in his comprehension to the extent that he will have to re-read (Bayle, 4). When he has built a bridge over this gap in the continuity of his word-recognition-processing, the reader can then switch most of his mental energy back to his reasoning-in-context substrata or processes that are mobilized for attaining the central thought, integrating dispersed ideas, inferring from explicit or implicit premises in a passage, and such processes that go beyond word recognition and association of meaning to the recognized words.

Word Meaning

If an individual can recognize words, but not have any meaning to associate with these words, the result is known as "word calling." That is, an individual could learn to recognize a word as a whole word, or grasp the word from context, or utilize some combination of word-recognition-processes to transform it, but be unable to associate meaning to it, not because of some lack of association process (Holmes, 33) but because he simply has not had experience, direct or vicarious with the referent or referents of the word. Consequently, meanings for words should be developed concomitantly or even ahead of their appearance in reading material so that the word-recognition-substrata and the meaning-substrata can be integrated. However, in general, at about age 11, development of word recognition surpasses the development of meaning (Gates *et al.*, 24).

Some linguistic elements, such as affixes and roots, have generalized meaning, which can be utilized not only for unlocking the meaning of a word by analyzing it into its constituent elements and then synthesizing these elements (Hunt, 40) but also can be integrated into the word-recognition-substrata. Consequently these linguistic elements have a dual function.

In the early stages of learning to read, pictures may also enter into the two subsystems of word recognition and word meaning. They may serve as clues for word recognition and enable an individual to recall and associate a word with its object-referent. But, the picture is only a cue to some intermediate verbal transformation. That is, the individual must learn to make a verbal response to the picture and this verbal response then mobilizes the necessary word recognition or word meaning reaction.

Prior to the sixth grade, auditory cues for responses to pictures, as measured by a "reading capacity" test (Durrell and Sullivan, 17; Alden, 1), lead the individual to mobilize a quantitatively if not qualitatively different mental organization from that which is mobilized for response to a visual verbal type of reading test, such as the Gates Reading Survey (Singer, 63, 69). After the fifth grade, the two subsystems of listening comprehension and reading achievement, as assessed by the above types of tests, tend to merge. A possible hypothesis for this merger consists of two components: normally during the early stages of learning to read, the individual a) gradually develops his word-recognition-substrata and b) slowly acquires a greater degree of intercortical facilitation and communication between his auditory and visual modalities. When the developmental gradients of these two processes merge at the sixth grade level, the individual can not only transform printed stimuli into ideas at any level, concrete, functional, or verbal-conceptual, in accordance with the context and his level of intelligence, but he can also receive increased stimulation from his auditory modality. Therefore, he can better associate his listening vocabulary with his word recognition processes and his reading vocabulary.

Reasoning-In-Context

As an individual develops word-recognition-substrata to overcome the barrier presented by words in the form of printed symbols, he becomes increasingly able to use reading as a means of acquiring facts, forming concepts, and relating them as generalizations (Brownell and Hendrickson, 7). That is, he uses his reasoning-in-context substrata, an organized working system of mental abilities and processes, to learn from the printed page.

In a modern instructional program, word-recognition-substrata, word-meaning-substrata, and reasoning-in-context substrata are developed simultaneously. But, as a result of mental capability, training, and practice, the time and mental energy required for word-recognition-substrata in the process of reading gradually decrease while the time and energy employed for word-meaning-substrata and reasoning-in-context substrata gradually increase. This development eventually reaches a point where the mature and competent reader is relatively unconscious of the organization and dynamics of his word-recognition-substrata as he reads. He is almost unaware of the processes because his word recognition subsystems are effectively mobilized, efficiently synchromeshed, and, when necessary, flexibly and readily reorganized in response to the stimuli of the printed page and his motivation in reading. Consequently he can then focus his mental energy upon comprehending the ideas conveyed by the words. Thus, he can read rapidly and fluently, unhindered by barriers to word recognition, and only limited by his word-meaning-substrata and his ability to reason-in-context.

Conceptual ability enters not only into the formation of word-recognition-substrata but also operates in word-meaning-substrata and in reasoning-in-context-substrata. For, as he reads, an individual can inductively form concepts (Werner and Kaplan, 77), hierarchically integrate previously formed concepts (Long and Welch, 49), deductively "verify and strengthen the structure of a concept" (Russell, 61:162), reorganize a concept (Brownell, 6) or create concepts (Leeper, 48). An individual can thus use reading as one means of developing his concepts from "simple to complex, concrete to abstract, undifferentiated to differentiated, discrete to organized, and from ego-centric to more social" (Russell, 61:249).

Speed and/or power of reading require not only fluency in word recognition but also flexibility in conceptual organization (Murphy, 54), in addition to other types of flexibility (Laycock, 45, 46, 47). That is, to comprehend some passages an individual not only has to conceptualize, but he also has to change, modify or reorganize a previously formed concept. For example, a young child could have learned through his experience that home is a place where parental conflict exists. When he reads a story about parental relationships, he might find that the ideas in this story do not coincide with his concept of home. If he persists with this experientially-determined generalization, he might not "get it," re-read the passage to clarify the meaning (Bayle, 4), or even continue to read with the conflict unresolved. Consequently, lack of conceptual flexibility could adversely affect his speed and/or power of reading. For either reading component, the effect may be exhibited more at the judgmental or evaluative than at the factual level (McKillop, 51).

Another element of flexibility is the ability to shift from one concept to another in the process of reading. That is, a competent reader selects the relevant words and organizes them into concepts; he also uses previously formed concepts in responding to the material. The flexible reader modifies his conceptual span and appropriately shifts from one idea to another. If he has an overly broad span, he will probably attempt to include too much of the material into his concept and encounter confusion; if he has a narrow span, he will tend to exclude material and perhaps not arrive at a concept but only a sequence of events. In either extreme, the reader will not form the intended idea. In general, the ability to form an optimum span and adequate conceptual level is a function of mental age and normal developmental processes (Zaslow, 78).

Thus, in learning to read, an individual with the necessary capacities can develop a conceptualized mediational response system. Then, in accordance with his purposes and the demands of the task-stimuli, he can mobilize this system together with other subsystems into a mental organization for attaining speed and power of reading. Although each individual forms a working system that is composed of his unique strengths and weaknesses, he must mobilize at least minimum amounts of certain common subsystems, if he is to read at all (Holmes and Singer, 36, 38). Consequently, each individual's working system varies around a basic, developmental working system that is the common route to maturity in speed and power of reading (Buswell, 11; Holmes, 30; Singer, 63, 66; Holmes and Singer, 36, 38).

Summary and Implications

A theoretical formulation of the role of conceptualization in the acquisition of reading behavior was presented and an attempt was made to integrate this theoretical formulation with the substrata-factor theory of reading.

Theory is designed not only for explanation, but also for prediction (Singer, 68). Already plans have been made to test at the kindergarten level the predictive validity of an instructional strategy based upon the above theoretical formulation (Singer and Balow, 70). Eventually, a longitudinal investigation should be undertaken to test the developmental implications of this theory of conceptualization in learning to read. In the meantime, the theory can be used as a cognitive guide for teaching reading (Singer, 64, 65, 66, 67).

REFERENCES

1. Alden, Clara L., Helen B. Sullivan, and D. D. Durrell, "The Frequency of Special Reading Disabilities," *Education*, 62:32-39, September, 1941.

2. Athey, Irene, *Reading Personality Patterns at the Junior High School.* Unpublished doctoral dissertation, University of California, Berkeley, 1965.

3. Barnard, Maryline, *Reading Disability and Levels of Perceptual Efficiency: An Experimental Study.* Unpublished doctoral dissertation, University of Southern California, 1958.

4. Bayle, Evalyn L., "Nature and Causes of Regressive Eye Movements in Reading," *Journal of Educational Psychology*, 11:16-35, September, 1942.

5. Bond, Guy L., *The Auditory and Speech Characteristics of Poor Readers,* Teachers College Contributions to Education, No. 657, 1935.

6. Brownell, W. A., "Learning as Reorganization: An Experimental Study in Third Grade Arithmetic," *Duke University Research Studies in Education*, No. 3, 1939.

7. Brownell, W. A., and G. Hendrickson, "How Children Learn Information, Concepts, and Generalizations," *Yearbook of the National Society for the Study of Education*, 49: Part 1, 1950.

8. Bruner, J., *A Study of Thinking*, New York: Wiley, 1956.

9. Bruner, J., "The Course of Cognitive Growth," *American Psychologist*, 19:1-15, January, 1964.

10. Bruner, J. and Oliver, Rose., "Development of Equivalence Transformations in Children," *Monographs of the Society for Research in Child Development*, 28:125-143, 1963.

11. Buswell, Guy T., *Fundamental Reading Habits: A Study of Their Development,* Supplemental Educational Monographs, No. 21, 1922.

12. Cameron, N., "Reasoning, Regression, and Communication in Schizophrenics," *Psychological Monographs*, 50: No. 1, 1938.

13. Carroll, Herbert A., "Generalization of Bright and Dull Children: A Comparative Study with Special Reference to Spelling," *Journal of Educational Psychology*, 21:489-499, October, 1930.

14. Carroll, Herbert A., *Generalization of Bright and Dull Children*, New York: Teachers College Contributions to Education, Columbia University, Bureau of Publications, No. 439, 1930.

15. Davis, Frank R., "The Substrata-Factor Theory of Reading: Human Physiology as a Factor in Reading." In J. A. Figurel (Editor), *Proceedings of the Ninth Annual Conference of the International Reading Association*, 1964, 292-296.

16. Durrell, D. D., "The First Grade Cooperative Studies: History." In J. A. Figurel, *Reading and Inquiry. Proceedings of the Tenth Annual Convention of the International Reading Association*, Newark, Delaware, 1965.

17. Durrell, D. D., and Helen B. Sullivan, *Manual for Durrell-Sullivan Reading Capacity Test*, New York: World Book, 1937.

18. Fendrick, P., *Visual Characteristics of Poor Readers*. Teachers College Contributions to Education, No. 656, 1935.

19. Gans, Roma, *A Study of Critical Reading Comprehension in the Intermediate Grades*, Teachers College Contributions to Education, No. 811, 1940.

20. Gates, Arthur I., *Generalization and Transfer in Spelling*. New York: Teachers College, Columbia University, Bureau of Publications, 1935.

21. Gates, Arthur I., *The Improvement of Reading*, New York: MacMillan, 1947.

22. Gates, Arthur I., *The Manual of Directions for Gates Reading Diagnostic Test*. New York: Teachers College, Columbia University, Bureau of Publications, 1953.

23. Gates, Arthur I., "The Word Recognition Ability and the Reading Vocabulary of Second and Third Grade Children," *Reading Teacher*, 15:443-448, May, 1962.

24. Gates, Arthur I., G. L. Bond, and D. H. Russell, "Relative Meaning and Pronunciation Difficulties of the Thorndike 20,000 Words," *Journal of Educational Research*, 32:161-167, November, 1938.

25. Goldstein, K., and M. Scheerer, "Abstract and Concrete Behavior: An Experimental Study with Special Tests," *Psychological Monographs*, 53: No. 2, 1941.

26. Hanfmann, Eugenia, and J. A. Kasanin, "Conceptual Thinking in Schizophrenics," *Nervous Mental Disorders Monographs*, No. 67, 1942.

27. Harlow, Harry, "The Formation of Learning Sets," *Psychological Review*, 56:51-65, 1949.

28. Hebb, D. O., *Organization of Behavior*, New York: John Wiley, 1949.

29. Heidbreder, Edna, "Toward a Dynamic Psychology of Cognition," *Psychological Review*, 52:1-22, January, 1945.

30. Holmes, Jack A., *Factors Underlying Major Reading Disabilities at the College Level*, Unpublished doctoral dissertation, University of California, Berkeley, 1948.

31. Holmes, Jack A., *The Substrata-Factor Theory of Reading*, Berkeley, California Book, 1953. (Out of Print)

32. Holmes, Jack A., "Factors Underlying Major Reading Disabilities at the College Level," *Genetic Psychology Monographs*, 49:3-95, February, 1954.

33. Holmes, Jack A., "The Brain and the Reading Process." In Claremont College, *Reading is Creative Living, Twenty-Second Yearbook of the Claremont Reading Conference*. Claremont, California: Curriculum Laboratory, 1957, 49-67.

34. Holmes, Jack A., "Personality and Spelling Ability," *University of California Publications in Education*, 12:213-292, 1959.

35. Holmes, Jack A., "The Substrata-Factory Theory of Reading: Some Experimental Evidence." New Frontiers in Reading, *Proceedings of the Fifth Annual Conference of the International Reading Association*. New York: Scholastic Magazines, 1960, 115-121.

36. Holmes, Jack A., and Harry Singer, *The Substrata-Factor Theory: The Substrata Factor Differences Underlying Reading Ability in Known Groups*. Final report covering contracts 538 and 538A, Office of Education, U.S. Department of Health, Education, and Welfare, 1961.

37. Holmes, Jack A., and Harry Singer, "Theoretical Models and Trends Toward More Basic Research in Reading," *Review of Educational Research*, 34:127-155, April, 1964.

38. Holmes, Jack A. and Singer, Harry, *Speed and Power of Reading in High School*. U.S. Department of Health, Education, and Welfare: Office of Education. A publication of the Bureau of Educational Research and Development. Superintendent of Documents, Catalog No. FS 5.230:30016. U.S. Government Printing Office, Washington, D.C. 20402, 1966.

39. Hull, Clark L., "Quantitative Aspects of the Evolution of Concepts," *Psychological Monographs*, No. 123, 1920.

40. Hunt, Jacob T., "The Relation Among Vocabulary, Structural Analysis, and Reading," *Journal of Educational Psychology*, 44:193-202, April, 1953.

41. Jan-Tausch, James, "Concrete Thinking as a Factor in Reading Comprehension." In J. A. Figurel (Editor), *Challenge and Experiment in Education*, Proceedings of the Seventh Annual Conference of the International Reading Association, 1962, 161-164.

42. Kling, Martin, *Auditory and Visual Discriminations*, Unpublished Master's thesis, University of California, Berkeley, 1956.

43. Kress, R. A., *An Investigation of the Relationship Between Concept Formation and Achievement in Reading*, Unpublished doctoral dissertation, Temple University, 1955. *Dissertation Abstracts*, 16:573-574, 1956.

44. Kyme, George H., *The Value of Aesthetic Judgments in the Assessment of Musical Capacity*, Unpublished doctoral dissertation, University of California, Berkeley, 1954.

45. Laycock, Frank, *An Experimental Study of Flexibility in Reading Rate Among Candidates for College Matriculation*. Unpublished doctoral dissertation, University of California, Berkeley, 1947.

46. Laycock, Frank, "Flexibility in Reading Rate and Einstellung," *Perceptual and Motor Skills*, 8:123-129, June, 1958.

47. Laycock, Frank, "The Flexibility Hypothesis in Reading and the Work of Piaget." In J. A. Figurel (Ed.), *Challenge and Experiment in Education*, Proceedings of the Seventh Annual Conference of the International Reading Association, New York: Scholastic Magazines, 1962, 241-243.

48. Leeper, R. W., "Cognitive Processes," In S. S. Stevens (Ed.), *Handbook of Experimental Psychology*. New York: Wiley, 1958, 730-757.

49. Long, L., and L. Welch, "The Higher Structural Phases of Concept Formation in Children," *Journal of Psychology*, 9:59-95, January, 1940.

50. Long, L., and L. Welch, "Influences of Levels of Abstractness on Reasoning Ability," *Journal of Psychology*, 13:41-59, January, 1942.

51. McKillop, Anne S., *The Relationship Between the Reader's Attitude and Certain Types of Reading Responses*. New York: Teachers College, Columbia University, Bureau of Publications, 1952.

52. MacKinnon, Archie R., *How Do Children Learn to Read?* Toronto: Copp, Clark, and Company, 1959.

53. Morris, C. W., *Signs, Language and Behavior*, New York: Prentice-Hall, 1946.

54. Murphy, P. G., "The Role of the Concept in Reading Ability," *Psychological Monographs*, 44:21-73, 1933, No. 3.

55. Nielsen, J. M., *A Textbook of Clinical Neurology*, New York: Paul B. Hoeber, 1951.

56. Osgood, Charles, *Method and Theory in Experimental Psychology*, New York: Oxford University, 1956.

57. Piaget, J., "Principal Factors Determining Intellectual Evolution from Childhood to Adult Life." In *Factors Determining Human Behavior, Harvard Tercentenary Conference of Arts and Sciences*, Cambridge: Harvard University, 1937, 32-48.

58. Reed, H. B., "Factors Influencing the Learning and Retention of Concepts—I. The Influence of Set." *Journal of Experimental Psychology*, 36-71-87, 1946.

59. Reichard, Suzanne, M. Schneider and D. Rapaport, "The Development of Concept Formation in Children," *American Journal of Orthopsychiatry*, 14:156-162, January, 1944.

60. Robinson, Helen M., "Perceptual and Conceptual Style Related to Reading," In J. A. Figurel (Ed.), *Improvement of Reading Through Classroom Instruction*, Proceedings of the Ninth Annual Conference of the International Reading Association, 1964, 26-28.

61. Russell, David H., *Children's Thinking*, New York: Ginn, 1956.

62. Russell, David H., and Patrick J. Groff, "Personal Factors Influencing Perception in Reading," *Education*, 75:600-603, May, 1955.

63. Singer, Harry, *Conceptual Ability in the Substrata-Factor Theory of Reading*, Unpublished doctoral dissertation, University of California, 1960.

64. Singer, Harry, "Substrata-Factor Theory of Reading: Theoretical Design for Teaching Reading," In J. A. Figurel (Ed.), *Challenge and Experiment in Reading*, Proceedings of the Seventh Annual Conference of the International Reading Association, New York: Scholastic Magazines, 1962, 226-232.

65. Singer, Harry, "Substrata-Factor Evaluation of a Precocious Reader," *Reading Teacher*, 18:288-296, January, 1965.

66. Singer, Harry, *Substrata-Factor Reorganization Accompanying Development in Speed and Power of Reading*. Final report on Project No. 2011, U.S. Office of Education, 1965.

67. Singer, Harry, "A Theory of Human Learning for Teaching Reading: A Discussion of Professor Arthur Staats's 'Integrated Functional Learning Theory for Reading,' " in Albert J. Kingston (Ed.), *Use of Theoretical Models in Research*, Newark, Delaware: International Reading Association, 1966.

68. Singer, Harry, "Symposium on the Substrata-Factor Theory of Reading: Research and Evaluation of Critiques," In J. A. Figurel (Ed.), *Reading and Inquiry*, Tenth Annual Convention of the International Reading Association, Newark, Delaware: International Reading Association, 1965.

69. Singer, Harry, "Validity of the Durrell-Sullivan Reading Capacity Test," *Educational and Psychological Measurement*, 125:479-491, Summer, 1965.

70. Singer, Harry, and Irving H. Balow, *Evaluation of a Horizontal vs. Vertical Reading Readiness Program*, Research Proposal for Extramural Funds, University of California, Riverside, 1965. (Multilith)

71. Smith, Nila B., *American Reading Instruction*, Newark, Delaware: International Reading Association, 1965.

72. Smoke, Kenneth, "An Objective Study of Concept Formation," *Psychological Monographs*, 42, No. 4 (Whole No. 191), 1932.

73. Tolman, Edward, "Cognitive Maps in Rats and Men," *Psychological Review*, 55:189-208, 1948.

74. Triggs, Frances O., "The Development of Measured Word Recognition Skills, Grade Four Through the College Freshman Year," *Educational and Psychological Measurement*, 12:345, 349, Autumn, 1952.

75. Vinacke, W. E., "The Investigation of Concept Formation," *Psychological Bulletin*, 48:1-31, 1951.

76. Werner, H., and Doris Garrison, "Perceptual Behavior of Brain-Injured and Mentally Defective Children: An Experimental Study by Means of the Rohrschach Technique," *Genetic Psychology Monographs*, 31:51-110, 1945, No. 2.

77. Werner, H., and Edith Kaplan, "The Acquisition of Word Meaning: A Developmental Study," *Monographs of the Society for Research in Child Development*, 15, No. 1 (Whole No. 51), 1950.

78. Zaslow, Robert W., *A Study of Concept Formation in Brain Damaged Adults, Mental Defectives and Normals of Different Age Levels*, Unpublished doctoral dissertation, University of California, Berkeley, 1957.

Comprehending What We Read:
An Outsider Looks In[*]

JOEL R. LEVIN
University of Wisconsin

I do not profess to be an expert in reading. This statement applies not only to my personal reading speed and comprehension, but also to my familiarity with the reading and perception literature in the respective fields of education and psychology. What I would like to do, as an outsider looking in, is to share with you some potential educational applications that grew out of a symposium entitled "Issues in Imagery and Learning" held at the 1971 Western Psychological Association meeting in San Francisco. The focus of the symposium was on visual imagery in children and its reported positive relationship with learning and memory.

The bulk of the experimentation in which imagery processes have been engaged and inferred (through the use of pictorial and image-evoking materials) has incorporated associative learning tasks in laboratory settings. In a few experiments, comprehension of sentences and sentence-embedded materials has been investigated. A recurring result is that materials which are concrete, imageable and dynamic are easier to remember than those which are not (e.g., Paivio, 1969; Rohwer, 1967).

A sentence is assumed to make its constituents more memorable by virtue of the organization it bestows on them. It has been hypothesized that the success of the organization depends upon the extent to which increased contextual meaning and imagery is produced (Levin, 1972). A collection of sentences should impose an organization on its constituents

*Reprinted from *Journal of Reading Behavior*, 4, Fall 1971-1972, 18-27. Reprinted with permission of the author and the National Reading Conference, Inc. Supported in part as a Research and Development Center by funds from the United States Office of Education, Department of Health, Education, and Welfare. Center No. C-03/Contract OE 5-10-154. This paper was adapted from a symposium presentation, "Issues in Imagery and Learning: Verbal and Visual Variables," at the annual meeting of the Western Psychological Association in San Francisco, April 1971. The author is grateful to Mrs. Arlene Knudsen for typing the final draft of the paper, as well as to the referees for improving the paper's clarity.

in analogous fashion. In this paper, I will restrict my attention to reasonably concrete materials. That is, sentences like "Continuous fraud negates implied sincerity" are probably less concrete and imageable than sentences like "Giddy spinsters terrify squealing infants" (Davidson, 1966). Paivio (1970) has presented data which support this notion by showing that the former type of sentence is accompanied by longer imagery latencies (i.e., a greater amount of time is required to form a mental image of the sentence's contents) as well as by inferior recall of the general meaning of the sentence (though not necessarily the individual words).

Consider the school-age child who cannot comprehend—and consequently will not remember—the content of what he reads. I am not referring to the child who cannot identify (decode) the words, although the ensuing discussion may in fact be relevant when considering this type of reading disability as well. Neither am I referring to the child who can identify the words correctly, but cannot derive meaning from them because they are foreign to his experiential vocabulary (see Wiener & Cromer, 1967). For now, I will focus my attention on the child who can identify the words, knows the meaning of individual words, but has difficulty in integrating the separate meanings into an organized whole. The child to whom I am referring possesses average or above average decoding and vocabulary skills, but performs poorly on tasks which involve reading comprehension.

Wiener and Cromer (1967) have considered this type of reading disability in what they have called a "difference" model. Unlike the traditional view that all reading problems result from either disorders (generally organic) or deficits (lack of prerequisite identification and/or vocabulary skills), these authors have argued that at least two other models of reading difficulty need to be considered: the "disruption" model, where emotional and psychological barriers which are interfering with the reading process must be removed; and the "difference" model.

The "difference" model asserts that:

> . . . reading difficulty is attributable to *differences* or mismatches between the typical mode of responding and that which is more appropriate, and thus has the best payoff in a particular situation. This model assumes that the individual would read adequately if the material were consistent with his behavior patterns; thus, a *change* in either the material or in his patterns of verbalization is a prerequisite for better reading (Wiener & Cromer, 1967).

Take another look at the last sentence. It says that a "difference" between good and poor readers is attributable to the way in which they respectively input what they read. Good readers typically comprehend; poor readers do not. In order for poor readers to perform more like good readers, one of two events must occur: a) the reading materials must be changed in some way (e.g., their content, their structure, their representational mode, and the like); or b) poor readers must learn (be taught) to employ some of the "habits" of good readers. [The same two recommendations have been made elsewhere with regard to making the performance of children who are poor *learners* more like that of children who are good *learners* (e.g., Levin, Rohwer and Cleary, 1971; Rohwer, 1970).]

At the imagery and learning symposium, I recommended that a distinction be made between two different approaches to the study of facilitative variables in children's learning (Levin, 1972). In one line of research, learning materials are manipulated or organized pre-experimentally to render them more or less memorable. Specifically, verbal and imaginal representations which have been imposed on the to-be-learned materials are known to affect performance on learning tasks. Rohwer's (1967) extensive investigation of semantic and syntactic aspects of verbal "elaboration," and Paivio's (1969) manipulation of the concreteness-image evocativeness of learning materials exemplify this kind of paradigm. Frase's efforts to vary properties of prose materials (e.g., Frase, 1969; Frase and Washington, 1970; Maroon, Washington, and Frase, 1971) are of particular relevance here.

A second class of experiments has examined the effect of prelearning instructions, usually in the form of a strategy or mnemonic, which induce changes in the character of the learner's behavior. A technique is introduced by the experimenter which, if adopted by the subject, will likely facilitate the ensuing task. The comparative effectiveness of various strategies (notably those requiring subject-generated verbalizations and imagery) has been studied, summaries of which may be found in the reports of Bower (1972) and Levin (1972).

In the remainder of this paper, I will distinguish between the two approaches as they relate to reading comprehension, which, in fact, I have already done vis-à-vis the Wiener and Cromer (1967) quote referred to earlier. The reader will be helped in making this distinction through the use of appropriate section headings, examples, and explicit references.

Changing the Reading Materials

Cromer (1970) wanted to see if changing the structure (i.e., organization) of reading materials would benefit subjects who had the necessary vocabulary skills, but who exhibited poor comprehension. As a partial validation of the reading difficulty models mentioned previously, Cromer selected samples of poor-reading junior college students with either "deficit" or "difference" problems. The two groups of poor readers were relatively closer in mean IQ (Deficit: 110.4; Difference: 111.3) than in mean vocabulary, where the Deficit group's average score (154.4) was lower then that of the Difference group (158.9). The mean vocabulary score of the Difference group corresponded to the median score for college freshmen.

Subjects read stories in which the sentences were "organized" in various ways. In two of the conditions, the sentences appeared either in regular form, e.g.,

"The cow jumped over the moon"

or in predetermined phrase groups, e.g.,

"The cow jumped   over the moon"

The latter groupings were based on agreed-upon phrase boundaries as prescribed by Lefevre (1964).

The basic finding of the Cromer (1970) study was that when the story was presented in regular sentence form, there were large differences in comprehension between the poor-reading groups and matched (in IQ) groups of good readers. However, when the phrase groupings were employed, the performance of the Difference poor readers was as high as that of the good readers. The Deficit group's performance remained low, in accordance with the reading difficulty models. That is, the different organization of the materials helped only those subjects who read poorly for reasons other than vocabulary deficits. Thus, changing the organization of printed materials facilitated the performance of poor readers (Cromer, 1970).

Another question which may be asked is whether poor readers comprehend story passages better when they are presented in alternative modes (e.g., in auditory or pictorial, as opposed to printed form). In a study by Oakan, Wiener and Cromer (1971), for example, it was found that poor readers comprehended slightly more when they *listened* to stories than when they *read* them themselves, while for good readers, the reverse was true. Sticht's work (e.g., Sticht, 1971) dealing with poor readers' preference for, and performance on, listening materials lends support to these findings.

Rohwer and Matz (1975) used two groups of subjects, one from a white middle-class population and the other from a black lower-class population. The two groups differed substantially in IQ and (presumably) in reading achievement. Story passages were read to subjects in the company of either regular printed sentences or line drawings which appeared in sequence as each sentence of the story was read. For the better readers (middle-class whites), it made little difference whether print or pictures accompanied the story. Performance was good under both conditions. For the poorer readers (lower-class blacks), when the story was accompanied by printed sentences, performance was very poor; when pictorial representations were used, performance was as good as that of the better readers. Saying that these children cannot comprehend *written* stories is quite different from saying that they cannot comprehend stories.

The same type of argument is used by Jensen (1969) in discussing the differing correlation between Level I and Level II abilities in middle- and lower-class populations. The correlation between IQ (a Level II measure) and learning ability (a Level I measure) is hypothesized to be quite strong for middle-class children and quite weak for lower-class children. An implication of this is that middle-class children with low IQs probably are slow learners as well; the same statement cannot be made with confidence for lower-class children with low IQs, however.

The results of both the Cromer (1970) and the Rohwer and Matz (1975) studies may be represented by the all-purpose model in Figure 1. When learning or comprehension is assessed by a single method, only the subjects from Population I will demonstrate mastery. When a different method is employed, the difference between the two populations may diminish.

This, of course, gets at the heart of the aptitude-treatment interaction (ATI) debates, the one difference here being that Method B is better than Method A for *both* populations, but comparatively less so for subjects in Population I. Till now, the ATIers have been mainly concerned with the detection of disordinal (cross-over) interactions, such that Method A works best for Population I and Method B works best for Population II. This type of ATI has not been easy to demonstrate, however (Bracht, 1970; Cronbach and Snow, 1969).

An ATI stance is certainly applicable to the ordinal interaction model portrayed in Figure 1. It simply says that variations in the nature of instructional materials are not as crucial for "good" students as they are for "poor" students. This should not imply that variations in the quality of the organization or mode of the materials will have *no* effect on the performance of good students (see, for example, Maroon et al., 1971). In the Oakan et al. (1971) experiment already cited, good readers comprehended substantially less when they read stories which were transcriptions of poor readers' efforts to read the normal passage. These transcribed stories included ". . . all of the poor reader's pauses, false starts, errors, mispronunciations, omissions, etc." Furthermore, as noted earlier, when the good readers were tested for comprehension after *listening* to stories read to them. their performance was worse than when they read the stories themselves.

An explanation provided by the authors is that in reading the passages themselves, good readers are able to go back and re-read any misunderstood parts of the sentence which, of course, is not possible when listening to a single spoken version of the same story. It is also probable that when good readers read, they are employing well-developed organizational strategies which are conducive to comprehension, and as the authors suggest:

> . . . if poor readers typically do not organize their input into certain efficacious patterns, they may have considerable difficulty understanding what they read . . . (Oakan et al., 1971).

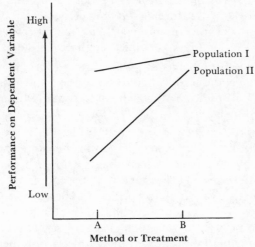

Figure 1.   Hypothesized Ordinal Interaction between Aptitude (Population) and Treatment (Imposed Independent Variable) to Account for Some Recent Findings.

There are two major recommendations which follow from the ordinal ATI model in Figure 1. The first is that it is incumbent upon us to find the optimal presentations of learning materials for children who appear to be slow learners. Given a sufficient variety of presentations, many children tabbed as "nonlearners" will emerge as "learners." At the same time, others will not. It is only this latter group whom we may legitimately regard as "nonlearners" and who will require greater remediation than merely changes in materials.

The Rohwer and Matz (1975) study cited earlier demonstrated that children from middle and lower social class groups differ only slightly in comprehension when pictures accompany an auditory version of a story. If both good and poor readers can comprehend stories based on pictorial representations, then it is reasonable to ask whether good readers are doing something pictorial-like when they are reading regular printed materials, while poor readers are not. This brings us to the second (and potentially more important) recommendation indicated by the model in Figure 1.

Changing the Reader's Behavior

Until now we have been discussing changes in learning materials which improve the performance of poor readers. Attention will now be directed toward presumed differences in the behavior of good and poor readers. If differences can be identified, then it might prove fruitful to instruct or induce poor readers to employ the habits of good readers.

What are some of the habits of good readers? That visual imagery constitutes a likely candidate has been first mildly, and then strongly, suggested in a pair of studies by Richard Anderson and his associates at the University of Illinois.

The first experiment (Anderson and Hidde, 1971) extends some recent findings dealing with sentence comprehension. Bobrow and Bower (1969), for example, found that subjects who were asked either to "disambiguate" (determine the contextual meaning of a multiple-meaning word) or to "continue" (construct a logical consequence of a provided sentence) a list of sentences, exhibited recall superior to subjects who were asked to peruse the same sentences for spelling errors. Similarly, Begg and Paivio (1969) reported that subjects were better able to detect semantic changes—as opposed to lexical changes which had little effect on meaning—in a repeated list of sentences, especially when the materials were relatively concrete. The importance of "meaning" in comprehension has been demonstrated in these and similar experiments (e.g., Bobrow, 1970; Levin and Horvitz, 1971). By the same token, the role of "imagery" cannot be discounted.

In the Anderson and Hidde (1971) study, college students were asked to rate either the pronunciability or imagery vividness of thirty sentences. On a surprise test for recall of as many sentences as the subject could remember, it was found that the imagery-rating group recalled far more sentences and sentence parts (e.g., verbs and objects) than did the pronunciability-rating group.

This is interesting in light of the fact that subjects in the latter group actually read each sentence aloud (three times) in rating its pronunciability while those in the former group did not. [At the same time, the possibility that repeating the sentence over and over was interfering (rather than imagery facilitative)—as has been shown to be the case in intentional learning paradigms with older subjects (e.g., Rohwer and Bean, 1973; Bobrow and Bower, 1969)—should be considered.] Within the imagery-rating group, a moderate relationship was found between subjects' reported vividness of a sentence's imagery and its probability of being recalled.

Anderson's second study provides more direct evidence that visual imagery improves reading comprehension. In that experiment (Anderson and Kulhavy, 1972), high school seniors were given a written passage to read either with or without instructions to visualize what they were reading. Although the experimental manipulation (i.e., instructions to use imagery) was not effective as a "main effect," a pronounced relationship between subjects' reported frequency of imagery throughout the passage and amount of information recalled about it (independently of their instructional conditions) was found. Thus, those subjects who reported having used imagery extensively recalled more of what they read than those who reported having used little or no imagery.

In a recently completed study with fourth graders (Levin, 1973), by inducing imagery in one group and not in another, we manipulated the degree to which presumably non-imagery producers (poor readers) generated visual images while reading. As predicted, the imagery strategy improved comprehension, and in accordance with the Wiener and Cromer (1967) model, "difference" poor readers (those with adequate vocabulary skills) benefitted more than "deficit" poor readers (those lacking prerequisite vocabulary skills). The interpretation of such results is similar to Cromer's (1970) and, of course, has important implications with regard to the teaching of reading to children with a diversity of poor-reading causes. The training of imagery production in children in need of an organizational framework looms as a reasonable strategy.

Much of what I have been saying has been suggested or implied by others before (e.g., Bugelski, 1969; Hafner, 1960; Huey, 1908). Nonetheless, the possibility of employing visual imagery as an aid to comprehension has not received widespread publicity. In one of the standard reading tests, among the authors' suggestions for improving the reading of low achievers may be found:

> Word recognition practice, phrase practice and expression practice should require response to meaning and imagery. Reading is getting ideas from the printed word; all aspects of reading instruction should focus upon meanings and reactions to meanings (Durrell and Hayes, 1969; Durrell and Brassard, 1969).

These comments appear on the primary (Grades 1-3.5) and intermediate (Grades 3.5-6) versions of the Durrell Test, and are apparently intended for "deficit" poor readers. However, a generalization of the imagery idea from comprehension of words to comprehension of sentences and paragraphs is not included in Durrell's (1969) suggestions on the advanced (Grades 7-9) version of his test. This is regrettable since a greater proportion of poor readers are probably of the "difference" variety at this age.

As educators, we should continually be seeking ways to improve the learning process and make it more enjoyable. Changing the characteristics of reading materials or changing the reader's characteristic behaviors seem to be two reasonable (and not necessarily mutually exclusive) possibilities. While the former approach caters to individual differences through the presentation of differentially effective organizations, the latter approach promises the greater educational payoff beyond the confines of the well-organized textbook, the optimally sequenced teaching machine, and the multi-talented teacher. Equipped with efficient organizational strategies, the child will be less dependent on the quality of stimuli in his environment, for he will be capable of reorganizing, elaborating and concretizing relatively disorganized, unelaborated and abstract materials.

REFERENCES

Anderson, R. C. and Hidde, J. L. Imagery and sentence learning. *Journal of Educational Psychology*, 1971, *62*, 526-530.

Anderson, R. C. and Kulhavy, R. W. Imagery and prose learning. *Journal of Educational Psychology*, 1972, *63*, 242-243.

Begg, I. and Paivio, A. Concreteness and imagery in sentence meaning. *Journal of Verbal Learning and Verbal Behavior*, 1969, *8*, 821-827.

Bobrow, S. A. Memory for words in sentences. *Journal of Verbal Learning and Verbal Behavior*, 1970, *9*, 363-372.

Bobrow, S. A. and Bower, G. H. Comprehension and recall of sentences. *Journal of Experimental Psychology*, 1969, *80*, 455-461.

Bower, G. H. Mental imagery and associative learning. In L. Gregg (ed.), *Cognition in Learning and Memory*, 1972. New York: John Wiley and Sons.

Bracht, G. H. Experimental factors related to aptitude-treatment interactions. *Review of Educational Research*, 1970, *40*, 627-645.

Bugelski, B. R. Learning theory and the reading process. In *The 23rd Annual Reading Conference*, 1969, University of Pittsburgh Press, Pittsburgh.

Cromer, W. The difference model: A new explanation for some reading difficulties. *Journal of Educational Psychology*, 1970, *61*, 471-483.

Cronbach, L. J. and Snow, R. E. *Individual differences in learning ability as a function of instructional variables*. Final report, USOE, Contract No. OEC-4-6-061269-1217, March 1969.

Davidson, R. E. Semi-grammaticalness in the free learning of sentences. Unpublished doctoral dissertation, University of California, Berkeley, 1966.

Durrell, D. D. *Durrell listening-reading series, advanced lavel*. New York: Harcourt, Brace and World, 1969.

Durrell, D. D. and Brassard, M. B. *Durrell listening-reading series, intermediate level*. New York: Harcourt, Brace and World, 1969.

Durrell, D. D. and Hayes, M. T. *Durrell listening-reading series, primary level*. New York: Harcourt, Brace and World, 1969.

Frase, L. T. Paragraph organization of written materials: The influence of conceptual clustering upon the level and organizational of recall. *Journal of Educational Psychology*, 1969, *60*, 394-401.

Frase, L. T. and Washington, E. D. Children's ability to comprehend text. Paper presented at the annual meeting of the American Psychological Association, Miami, September 1970.

Hafner, L. E. An experimental study of the effect on various reading achievement scores of teaching selected context aids to a group of fifth grade pupils. Unpublished doctoral dissertation, University of Missouri at Columbia, 1960.

Huey, E. B. *The psychology and pedagogy of reading*. New York: Macmillan, 1908.

Jensen, A. R. How much can we boost IQ and scholastic achievement? *Harvard Educational Review*, 1969, *39*, 1-123.

Lefevre, C. A. *Linguistics and the teaching of reading*. New York: McGraw-Hill, 1964.

Levin, J. R. When is a picture worth a thousand words? In *Issues in Imagery and Learning: Four Papers*. Madison: Wisconsin Research and Development Center for Cognitive Learning, 1972.

Levin, J. R. Inducing comprehension in poor readers: A test of a recent model. *Journal of Educational Psychology*, 1973, *65*, 19-24.

Levin, J. R. and Horvitz, J. M. The meaning of paired associates. *Journal of Educational Psychology*, 1971, *62*, 209-214.

Levin, J. R., Rohwer, W. D., Jr., and Cleary, T. A. Individual differences in the learning of verbally and pictorially presented paired associates. *American Educational Research Journal*, 1971, *8*, 11-26.

Maroon, S., Washington, E. D., and Frase, L. T. Text organization and its relationship to children's comprehension. Paper presented at the annual meeting of the American Educational Research Association, New York, March 1971.

Matz, R. and Rohwer, W. D., Jr. Visual elaboration of text. Paper presented at the annual meeting of the American Educational Research Association, New York, March 1971.

Oakan, R., Wiener, M. and Cromer, W. Identification, organization, and reading comprehension for good and poor readers. *Journal of Educational Psychology*, 1971, *62*, 71-78.

Paivio, A. Mental imagery in associative learning and memory. *Psychological Review*, 1969, *76*, 241-263.

Paivio, A. *Imagery and language.* Research Bulletin No. 167, University of Western Ontario, London, 1970.

Rowher, W. D., Jr. *Social class differences in the role of linguistic structures in paired-associate learning: Elaboration and learning proficiency.* Final report, USOE, Contract No. OE 6-10-273, November 1967.

Rowher, W. D., Jr. Images and pictures in children's learning: Research results and educational implications. *Psychological Bulletin,* 1970, *73,* 393-403.

Rohwer, W. D., Jr., and Bean, J. P. Sentence effects and noun-pair learning: A developmental interaction during adolescence. *Journal of Experimental Child Psychology,* 1973, *15,* 521-523.

Rowher, W. D., Jr., and Matz, R. Improving oral comprehension in white and in black children: Pictures versus print. *Journal of Experimental Child Psychology,* 1975, *19,* 23-36.

Sticht, T. G. *Learning by listening in relation to aptitude, reading, and rate-controlled speech: Additional studies.* HumRRO Technical Report 71-5, April 1971.

Cognitive Development and Reading[*]

DAVID ELKIND
University of Rochester

Cognitive development and reading achievement is a very large topic and one that can hardly be covered, at least with any completeness, in a brief paper such as this one. Instead, what I would like to do is to examine two more circumscribed issues beneath the more general rubric of the title. One of these issues has to do with beginning reading and the child's conception of the letter, while the second has to do with advanced reading and the child's construction of meaning. Hopefully, the discussion of these two issues will provide some concrete examples of how knowledge about cognitive development can contribute to our understanding of reading achievement.

The Child's Concept of a Letter and Beginning Reading

One of Piaget's most important contributions to education was his demonstration of the difference between the way in which children and adults see the world. The well known "conservation" experiments are a case in point. Most adults are amazed to discover that young children believe that changing the shape of a piece of clay will change the *amount* of the clay. Adult amazement at the child's lack of conservation suggests that most adults believe that children see the world in much the same way that they do, and that any differences are at best a matter of experience and familiarity.

Where does this assumption, that children see the world as we do, come from? In many ways, it is an adult form of egocentrism, a failure to take the child's point of view. While the child's egocentrism derives from an inability to reconstruct the point of view of another person, adult egocentrism results from inability to recall or reconstruct the course of

*Reprinted from Malcolm Douglass (Ed.), *Claremont Reading Conference Thirty-Eighth Yearbook*, 1974, 10-20. With permission of the author and the Claremont Reading Conference, Inc., Claremont Graduate School, Claremont, California.

one's own cognitive growth. Once we attain *conservation,* for example, we are no longer aware of the fact that it was even a problem or that we ever doubted the constancy of a quantity across a change in its appearance.

This phenomenon, the loss of awareness of our own part in the construction of reality, is what Piaget means by *externalization.* To illustrate this phenomenon, consider the test for the conservation of liquid quantity. The apparatus consists of two wide low beakers and a tall narrow one. The two low beakers are filled equally high with colored liquid and the child being examined is asked to state whether the amounts in the two beakers are the same. After the child agrees that this is the case, the examiner pours the liquid from one glass into the tall beaker and asks the child if the amount in the tall beaker is the same, more or less, than that in the low container.

Reactions to this demonstration follow a predictable course. Young children (usually 4-5) say that the amount in the tall glass is more, while somewhat older children (usually 6-7) say that the amount in the low container is the same as the amount in the tall container despite the unequal levels. The child arrives at this conclusion with the aid of reason because there is no way, by merely looking at the two containers, that he could be sure that they contained equal amounts. The child arrived at the equality by reasoning from the fact that the quantities were the same before, nothing was added or removed, so they are the same now.

What is significant about this developmental progression, from the present point of view, is that once the child attains conservation he is no longer aware of his own part in the process. Although conservation is a deduction, a conclusion from reasoning, the child takes it to be a perceptual given, a piece of reality that has nothing at all to do with him. He *externalizes* the results of his own mental activities and assumes that what he has constructed exists outside of and independently of himself.

In general this process of externalization serves a useful adaptive purpose and allows the individual to operate more effectively in the environment. Externalization only becomes a problem when we try to teach the young, that is, when we try to short circuit the natural educational process. In that case we as adults, who have conceptualized and externalized many facets of the world, find it difficult to appreciate the difficulties children encounter in their attempts at making sense out of their world. Piaget's works on number, space, time and so on, have demonstrated the problems children encounter in mastering concepts which, to adults, appear self evident.

This long preamble was necessary to demonstrate what seems to me to be a basic error in much beginning reading instruction. The error centers about the concept of the letter which is, in many ways, the basic "unit" of reading. To the adult the letter appears as a discrete object which is an arbitrary representation of one or more sounds. But the "letter," as the adult knows it, is an externalized conception and it is no more "out there" than is the equality between liquids in tall and narrow containers. The letter we know and see as adults is not the letter known to the beginning reader.

From the child's point of view, the concept of the letter poses many of the same cognitive problems as attaining concepts of number, space and time. Before the age of six or seven, most children lack a true unit or number concept because they cannot coordinate two dimensions or relationships simultaneously. Such coordinations are basic to the construction of a unit concept because a unit is by definition, both like every other unit and different from it in its order of enumeration. It is generally not until about the age of six or seven, when children attain what Piaget calls concrete operations, that most children grasp that one and the same numeral has ordinal and cardinal properties. That is to say, only after the child attains concrete operations does the child grasp that any given numeral (say 6) represents both a *position* in a series *and* a class property (sixness which is shared by all groupings of six things).

In many ways the child's difficulties in grasping the concept of a letter are even more difficult than the hardships he encounters in constructing the concept of a number. Like numbers, letters have an ordinal property which is their position in the alphabet. And letters also have a cardinal property which is their name (A, B, C, etc.) and which each letter shares with all other letters of the same name (all B's are B and so on). Letters are even more complicated than numbers because, in addition to their ordinal and cardinal properties, they also have phonic contextual properties. This is true in the number system as well as to the extent that the position of a number will determine whether or not it is sounded. It is probably fair to say, nonetheless, that the positional rules regarding letters and sounds are probably more complex than the positional rules in arithmetic. No one doubts that the positional rules of arithmetic involve reason and logic and I am simply arguing that the same holds true for the child's construction of phonic context rules.

Many different kinds of evidence support this logical analysis of the difficulties in early reading. Phonetic languages, such as Japanese, Hebrew, Serbo-Croatian, etc., are apparently much easier to learn to read than is English. Clearly this is not a matter of discrimination and association because in Japanese there are some 5000 characters and some fifty ideographs. Hebrew, in addition to its alphabet, also has a whole set of independent phonetic symbols. In a phonetic alphabet, the logical difficulties are removed because one and the same element always has one and the same sound regardless of its position or phonetic context. The letter in a phonetic alphabet is still a complex concept but a less complicated one than the concept of the letter in English.

In addition to this cultural evidence, we have published a body of research which also points to the logical difficulties inherent in beginning reading. We have shown that reading achievement and logical ability load on the same factor (Elkind, Horn and Schneider, 1965); that average readers are superior to slow readers, of comparable overall intelligence, in logical ability (Elkind, Larson & Van Doorninck, 1965) and that training children in logical skills has a significant positive effect upon some aspects of reading achievement (Elkind & Deblinger, 1969). All of these findings are consistent with the view that the letter is a complex logical construction that requires concrete operations for its full elaboration.

To test this hypothesis in still another way, we have begun, in the last few years, to look at the cognitive competencies of children who read early, that is, children who read before they enter kindergarten. One of our hypotheses was that if reading involves concrete operations, which are usually attained at age 6-7, then early readers should show these abilities at an early age. In addition to assessing children's cognitive abilities we were also interested in the personal social characteristics of these children and in the educational-emotional climate that prevails in their homes.

We have now completed two studies of early readers, one with 16 (Briggs & Elkind, 1973) early readers and in another with 38 (Briggs & Elkind, 1974). In both studies the early readers were matched with non-early reading control children on such things as age, sex, IQ and socioeconomic status. All the children were given a large battery of achievement and intelligence tests as well as personality and creativity tests. In addition, their parents were interviewed. In both studies we found that early reading children were superior to nonearly reading children on Piagetian measures of conservation. They were also better on certain ITPA scales such as sound blending.

It is important to emphasize, however, that cognitive construction of a letter is only one of the requirements for successful early reading. Our parent interview data suggest that a rich background of early experience with spoken and written language provided by homes where books and magazines are plentiful, where parents read and read to the children, is also important for successful reading. In addition the data on early readers also suggest that emotional attachment to an adult who is a model of reading behavior and who rewards the child's reading activities is of considerable importance in early reading. Learning to read is a dull and unrewarding task, and social motivation to please significant adults appears to be a necessary, if not a sufficient, factor in learning to read.

In talking about cognitive development and early reading, it is therefore, important to avoid the two extremes that are sometimes advocated when cognitive "readiness" is discussed. One extreme is "early intervention" in the effort to train children of preschool age in cognitive abilities they have not yet attained. I have seen no evidence that such early intervention has any lasting effectiveness. But the alternative extreme, allowing children to learn in their own time and in their own way, is also unwarranted. Children need instruction in learning to read, but only after they have demonstrated the requisite cognitive abilities.

In summary, there appears to me to be at least four requirements for successful beginning reading: a) a language rich environment; b) attachment to adults who model and reward reading behavior; c) the attainment of concrete operations; and d) an instructional program. All other things being equal, namely, that the children in question are of at least average intellectual ability and are free of serious emotional or physical handicaps, the presence of these four characteristics should ensure that most children will learn to read with reasonable ease and eventual enjoyment.

Advanced Reading and the Construction of Meaning

It has already been suggested that the intellectual processes involved in beginning reading are analogous to those involved in concept formation. A child who is learning to read has to coordinate similarities and differences and construct concepts of letters which are both like every other letter in that they represent sounds but different in the particular sounds they stand for. Concept formation also involves inferential processes and these can be observed in beginning reading as well. Many errors in beginning reading such as reading "where" for "when" are not discrimination errors, but rather inferential errors. The child is inferring the whole from observing the part (the wh.-). Such inferential errors are high level cognitive errors inasmuch as the child is doing what more advanced and accomplished readers do. These processes should be encouraged by temporarily sacrificing accuracy for fluency. After a child is a fluent reader he can always correct for accuracy, but the reverse is less likely to be the case.

Once the concept formation and inferential aspects of reading have become automatized, and children can recognize printed words with ease and rapidity, they enter the phase of rapid silent reading. In silent reading the major cognitive task is no longer concept formation and inference but rather, interpretation, the construction of meaning. In constructing meanings, the child has to relate representations, in this case printed words, with his own concepts and ideas. Success in interpretation, or comprehension, will depend upon a different set of characteristics than learning to read and these will be described below.

Visual independence. Rapid silent reading and comprehension requires, at the very outset, that the visual verbal system become independent of the sensory motor system. Rapid reading involves fewer motor fixations and wider visual segments of scanning and this in turn means less motor involvement and more conceptual inferential activity. In effect, in rapid silent reading the brain does more work and the eyes do less. We have some recent evidence that supports the importance of visual independence in advanced reading.

In one study (Elkind, Horn & Schneider, 1965), we found that while tactile discrimination of sandpaper letters was positively related to reading achievement among beginning readers, it was negatively correlated with reading achievement among advanced readers. Apparently, motoric identification and discrimination of letters, as advocated by Fernald (1921) and Montessori (1964) is beneficial in the beginning phases of learning to read but the coordination of visual and motor processes has to be given up if more rapid reading is to develop. Put more concretely, it is helpful for a beginning reader to use his finger as a marker to direct attention and exploration of printed matter. But once he becomes an advanced reader, using a finger as a marker would impede his reading. Rapid reading requires a certain independence from the tactile motor system.

Some recent data (Elkind & Meyer, 1974) on perceptual exploration and memory demonstrate this growth of visual independence in another way. Children at different age levels (from age 4 through age 8) were shown large cards upon which were pasted 16 pictures of familiar objects. On one card the pictures were pasted in an upright position whereas on another the same pictures were pasted at 180° from their normal position. At each age level half of the children were shown the card with the picture upright while the other half were shown the card with the pictures 180° to the upright. Each child had two tasks: to name each of the figures on the card and then, to recall as many of the figures as he could once the card was turned over.

Results showed that among young children (age 4-5) there was a significant difference in recall scores in favor of the figures rotated 180°. This difference, however, diminishes as children grow older and disappears at about the age of 8 or 9. A similar pattern appears to hold true for limited hearing children who use finger spelling and vocalization in communication (Elkind & LaFrance, 1974). What these data suggest is that in young children the motoric system is still tied to the visual system. In identifying the 180° figures, these children may implicitly try to "right" the figures which produces increased motoric involvement. Our hypothesis is that the increased motoric involvement and attendant heightened attention account for the superior memory for upside down figures in young children. Among older children, in whom identification can occur without implicit motoric "righting" this attentional advantage for upside down figures is no longer present.

There is thus some direct as well as indirect evidence that rapid, silent reading involves the attainment of considerable visual independence from the tactile motor system. Apparently this occurs even among limited hearing children who use finger spelling as well as vocalization to communicate. Although many limited hearing children seldom go beyond the fourth or fifth grade reading level, this is probably more a conceptual matter than one of visual-motor dependence. Indeed, among older deaf children, the rapidity with which they finger spell and read finger spelling is very much like rapid reading. Visual independence amounts to a kind of automatization of the visual aspects of reading in which the visual scanning process is relatively independent of tactile motor input.

Meaning construction. A second prerequisite to advanced silent reading is facility in meaning construction. From a cognitive development point of view, reading comprehension is not a passive process of decoding written symbols. On the contrary, it must be regarded as a constructive activity analogous to creative writing. Elsewhere (Elkind, Hetzel & Coe, 1974) we have described three types of learning which are: a) the construction of concepts (knowledge), b) the construction of representations (including language), and c) the construction of meanings (the coordination of knowledge and representations). The point is that meaning is not given or inherent in written or spoken words but rather has to be given meaning by the reader or listener who interprets them within his own storehouse of knowledge. The silent reader gives meaning to the words he reads by relating these to the conceptual system he has constructed in the course of his development. The richness of meaning that he derives from his reading will depend both upon the quality of the material he is reading and upon the breadth and depth of his conceptual understanding. Satisfaction in reading often derives, in part at least, from the degree of fit between the material being read and the conceptual level of the subject who is reading it.

A recent doctoral dissertation (Schlager, 1974) supports this position. In her dissertation Dr. Schlager chose 33 books that had won Newbery awards for excellence. She then went to a number of libraries and determined how frequently each of the books had been checked out over the preceding three year period. On the basis of these data she was able to select the five most frequently chosen books and the five least frequently chosen books from her original list. Dr. Schlager then analyzed the books from the standpoint of their congruence with the conceptual systems of the age group for which they were written. She found that the five most frequently chosen books were congruent with the cognitive level of the children for whom they were written while this was not true for the five least chosen books. Apparently, other things being equal, children prefer stories which can be given meaning within their own cognitive organization at the time.

It should be said, too, that comprehension, or the construction of meanings, is also helped by the child's own efforts at giving meaning to (i.e. representing) his own experiences. The more opportunity children have to experience the effort and satisfaction of representing their own thoughts verbally and otherwise, the better prepared they will be for interpreting the representations of others. In contemporary education, teachers often seem reluctant to have children write creatively or otherwise. But I am very much of the opinion that the more children write, the more they will get from their reading. At all levels of reading proficiency, writing and reading are reciprocal processes of meaning construction which mutually reinforce and benefit one another.

Receptive discipline. A third prerequisite to effective silent reading seems, at first statement, to be a contradiction to what has just been said about the reader being an active participant in the process. Effective reading comprehension would seem also to require a receptive attitude, a willingness to respond to the representations of others. Good readers, like good listeners, have to be simultaneously passive (being receptive to the representations of others) and active (interpreting those representations within their own conceptual framework).

Many young people are poor readers for the same reason that they are poor listeners, they are more interested in representing their own thoughts and ideas than they are in interpreting the thoughts and ideas of others. They lack what might be called *receptive discipline.* A young person demonstrates receptive discipline when he attends fully to the representations of others and resists following his own free associations and tangents. Many so called "slow readers" have problems with receptive discipline and not with rapid reading.

Receptive discipline is not innate and can be facilitated and taught. Text material that is of interest to the reader and at his level of competence facilitates a receptive attitude. Another way to encourage receptive discipline is to have goals for non-recreational reading. When a young person, or an adult for that matter, knows that he will have to re-present what he has read to a group, he is likely to be more attentive than if this were not a requirement. These are but a few examples of techniques that might be employed to encourage receptive discipline. Whatever techniques are used to instill it, the attainment of receptive discipline would seem to be an important ingredient for successful reading comprehension.

Summary

In this paper I have tried to outline what cognitive developmental theory and research would seem to suggest as some of the prerequisites for beginning and rapid reading. As far as beginning reading is concerned, there is evidence to believe that concrete operations, a language rich environment, attachment to adults who model and reward reading behavior, and appropriate instruction are all involved in successful beginning reading. With respect to advanced reading, there is evidence to suggest that visual independence, meaning construction and receptive discipline are all involved in rapid silent reading and successful comprehension. While we are still far from having a complete understanding of beginning or advanced reading, analysis of the cognitive aspects of this process promises to add significantly to our understanding of reading achievement.

REFERENCES

Briggs, C., & Elkind, D. Cognitive Development in Early Readers. *Developmental Psychology,* 1973, *9,* 2, pp. 279-280.

Briggs, C., & Elkind, D. Characteristics of Early Readers, 1974 (in preparation).

Elkind, D., & Deblinger, J. Perceptual training and reading achievement in disadvantaged children. *Child Development,* 1969, *40,* pp. 11-19.

Elkind, D., Hetzel, D., & Coe, J. Piaget and British Primary Education, 1974 Educational Psychologist, 1974, *11,* 1-10.

Elkind, D., Horn, J., & Schneider, G. Modified word recognition, reading achievement and perceptual decentration. *Journal of Genetic Psychology,* 1965, *107,* 235-251.

Elkind, D., & LaFrance, P. Figural orientation and memory in limited hearing children, 1974 (in preparation).

Elkind, D., Larson, M. E., & Van Doorninck, W. Perceptual learning and performance in slow and average readers. *Journal of Educational Psychology,* 1965, *56,* pp. 50-56.

Elkind, D., & Meyer, J. Figural orientation and memory in children, 1974 (in preparation).

Fernald, G. The effect of kinesthetic factors in the development of word recognition in the case of non readers. *Journal of Educational Research*, 1921, *IV*, pp. 355-77.

Montessori, M. *The Montessori Method.* New York: Schocken, 1964.

Schlager, N. *Developmental Factors Influencing Children's Responses to Literature.* Unpublished doctoral thesis. Claremont Graduate School, Claremont, California, 1974.

Perceptual Decentration Learning and Performance in Slow and Average Readers[*]

DAVID ELKIND, MARGARET LARSON, AND WILLIAM VAN DOORNINCK[**]
Child Study Center, University of Denver

The present study is the second in a series aimed at applying Piaget and Morf's (1958) logical model of perceptual development to the problem of reading. In order to make such an application plausible and to fit the present study within the context of the previous investigation, the major propositions of Piaget's theory will be reviewed, and the results of the previous investigation will be briefly summarized.

Without going into great detail, Piaget holds that the perception of the young child is *centered* in the sense that it is caught and held by the dominant aspects of the visual field. In each case, the dominant aspects of the field are determined by Gestalt-like principles such as those of "good form," "continuity," "closure," etc., which Piaget calls *field effects*. With increasing age, however, the child' perception becomes progressively *decentered* in the sense that it is gradually freed from its earlier domination by field effects. Perceptual decentration is brought about by the development of a higher order perceptual organization, whose structural fundament is a system of internalized perceptual actions that Piaget speaks of as *perceptual regulations*. Perceptual regulations enable the child to act on the perceptual configuration without manipulating it in actuality. The ability, for example, to mentally unscramble the letters ulbe (blue) could be an operational criterion for the presence of perceptual regulations.

According to Piaget, the system of perceptual regulations is in many ways analogous, though not identical with, the system of mental operations which mediates concept formation.[1] Both perceptual regulations and mental operations enable the child to combine elements and relations

---

[*]Reprinted from *Journal of Educational Psychology, 56,* 1, 1965, 50-56. Copyright 1965 by the American Psychological Association. Reprinted with permission.

[**]David Elkind is now at the University of Rochester.

[1]The lack of perfect "fit" between perception and logic is the reason that Piaget and Morf (1958) call the activities of perception only *partially isomorphic* with those of conception.

in ways that would be impossible on the plane of sensori-motor action. Given a row of buildings of different heights, a child having attained the level of perceptual regulations can mentally order them as to size, although this would be manifestly impossible for the child to accomplish in reality. Such a feat is analogous, on the conceptual plane, to that of the child, who, having attained the level of mental operations, can put himself mentally in the place of another person and take that person's point of view. In addition to enabling the child to mentally manipulate his world, perceptual regulations and mental operations are also alike in that their manner of activity lends itself to description by symbolic logic. Although the fit in the case of perceptual activity is less perfect than in the case of conceptual activity, logic still provides a useful way of describing the perceptual functioning of older children and adults.

In order to make the process of perceptual decentration concrete, and to show how it can be described in logical terms, the problem of figure-ground reversal will be analyzed from this point of view. From the standpoint of logic, figure-ground reversal would seem to require an operation called *logical multiplication*. This is the operation utilized whenever a new class is to be formed of those individuals who are simultaneously members of two separate classes. For example, logical multiplication of the class of Protestants (P) and the class of Americans (A) gives the following: $A \times P = AP, A\bar{P}, \bar{A}P, \bar{A}\bar{P}$, or, in words, the class of American Protestants, the class of persons who are American and not Protestant, the class of persons who are Protestant and not American, and the class of persons who are neither Protestant nor American.

To illustrate the way in which logical multiplication can account for figure-ground reversal, recall for a moment the classic Rubin vase-profiles drawing and let C = the contour lines, V = the vase area, and P = the profile areas. Logical multiplication of the contours and areas gives the following: $C \times V \times P = CVP; CV\bar{P}; C\bar{V}P; \bar{C}VP; C\bar{V}\bar{P}; \bar{C}\bar{V}P; \bar{C}\bar{V}\bar{P}$. Not all of these logical possibilities are, however, perceptual possibilities. A contour line, for example, can be "thought of" in isolation, but cannot be "perceived" without at the same time giving form to a figure. This is the sense in which logic is a less perfect fit for perceptual activity than it is for conceptual operations. On the other hand, logical multiplication does provide the possibilities for seeing either vase or profiles as figure. The combination $CV\bar{P}$, the combination of the contour and the vase area without the profile areas, gives rise to the perception of the vase. Contrariwise, the combination of $C\bar{V}P$, the combination of the contour and profile areas without the vase area, gives rise to the perception of the profiles. Logical multiplication of contours and areas could thus provide the combinations necessary to experience figure-ground reversal.[2]

With respect to reading, perceptual decentration in the form of logical multiplication would seem to be required to overcome perhaps the most difficult problem in learning English phonics. The problem is that in English, one and the same letter can stand for more than one sound while the same sound can be represented by more than one letter. To grasp this fact, it would seem necessary, from the standpoint of the perceptual decentration theory, for the child to logically multiply all sound and letter combinations and from the resulting combinations choose those that are operative in English. To illustrate, let l = any single letter or letter combination and let s = any single sound or sound combination. Logical multiplication of the two would result in the following classes: s x l = sl, s$\bar{\text{l}}$, $\bar{\text{s}}$l, $\bar{\text{s}}\bar{\text{l}}$, or in words, the combination of the sound and the letter, the combination of the sound without the letter, the combination of the letter without the sound, and the combination of neither sound nor letter, i.e., the null class. Repetition of this process over all letters and sounds would provide the child with all the possible combinations that occur in English phonics and thus yield the necessary elements for a mastery of reading.[3]

If this interpretation of the way in which children learn to master phonics seems overly intellectual, it might be well to recall some of the evidence from current psycholinguistic research. By the age of 4 (Berko, 1958) children have already abstracted many grammatical rules and usages such as those for pluralization and possession. That young people have actually formed rules is shown by the phenomena of *regularization* whereby youngsters transform an irregular ending into a common one, such as "feets" for "feet." If children at the age of 4 are abstracting complex rules of grammatical inflection and word combination, it does not seem farfetched that at the ages of 6 and 7 they would be able to form various combinations of letters and sound via logical multiplication. In addition, this logical interpretation of reading could explain the success of the Pitman (1961) 44-letter International Teaching Alphabet (ITA) with beginning and retarded readers. In effect, the Pitman alphabet eliminates the need for logical multiplication by having a single letter for every sound

---

[2] Obviously, figure-ground reversal can be, and has been, interpreted from the physiological point of view. In a test between the developmental predictions of a physiological "satiation" theory (Kohler & Wallach, 1944) and the Piaget decentration theory, however, the predictions of the Piaget theory were upheld by data which at the same time contradicted the expectations based on the satiation position (Elkind & Scott, 1962).

[3] This analysis of reading in terms of Piaget's theory is our responsibility and any ambiguities or errors in it should not be attributed to Piaget, who, insofar as we know, has not addressed his theory to this particular problem.

and vice versa. The success of this alphabet with beginning and retarded readers certainly suggests that the child's difficulty in learning to read is not one of perceptual discrimination. This follows because the addition of 18 additional discriminations eases rather than complicates the learning process.

On the basis of the earlier theoretical analysis of reading and the above mentioned indirect evidence for the role of perceptual activity in reading, an investigation (Elkind, Horn, & Schneider, 1965) was undertaken to test in a more direct fashion the notion that learning to read involves a kind of logical activity. One hundred and eighty elementary school children were given a battery of tests including: a) a number of figural perception tasks which in previous studies (Elkind, Koegler, & Go, 1962; Elkind & Scott, 1962) provided construct validity for the notion of perceptual decentration, b) a number of verbal perceptual tasks (scrambled words, run-on sentences, and reading words upside down) which in theory required perceptual decentration, and c) a set of standard reading achievement measures. Factor analysis of the results showed a common factor present among all the measures employed in the study. This finding was consistent with the hypothesis that a common factor, namely decentration, underlay success on ambiguous figural and verbal tests as well as on measures of reading achievement.

It might be argued, however, that the common factor revealed by the factor analysis was nothing other than general intelligence and that the postulation of a general decentration factor was entirely superfluous. Since no controls for intelligence were incorporated in the factor analysis, such an objection is perfectly warranted. Indeed, it was to answer this objection that the present study was undertaken. In the present investigation we attempted to control for the intelligence factor by using matched groups of slow and average readers. Specifically, our hypothesis was that slow readers would perform at a lower level and show less learning ability on a measure of figural decentration than would average readers of comparable intelligence.

Method

Subjects

The subjects were 60 children from an elementary school in suburban Denver. Thirty of the subjects were at grade level or better in reading achievement while the other 30 subjects were either 1 or 2 years retarded in their reading and were receiving remedial reading instruction. The children were chosen from the entire school population and were closely matched as to age, sex, and a nonverbal measure of IQ (the Otis, 1952, Alpha). Four grade levels were represented in the sample and the mean ages and IQs, together with the corresponding standard deviations for each grade level, are presented in Table 1. As can be seen from Table 1, the groups were almost identical with respect to the matching variables.

Table 1. Means and standard deviations for age and IQ for slow and average readers and for four grade levels

Grade level	N	Mean age[a]	SD[a]	Mean IQ[a]	SD[a]
3					
Average	8	106.6	3.35	110.8	8.47
Slow	8	107.0	4.44	110.8	7.95
4					
Average	7	119.6	2.67	106.4	4.44
Slow	7	119.7	4.40	105.9	3.40
5					
Average	9	131.3	2.87	105.9	5.20
Slow	9	131.4	2.83	104.7	3.83
6					
Average	6	142.2	2.34	112.5	6.10
Slow	6	142.3	3.04	111.8	5.93

[a]In months.

Tests and Procedures

The tests and procedures were the same as those employed in previous studies of perceptual decentration (Elkind et al., 1962; Elkind, Koegler, Go, & Van Doorninck, 1965). Two sets of 8 x 10 inch cards containing ambiguous figures in black and white and a set of cardboard shields—cut so that when they were placed over the drawings of Set B the hidden (reversed) figures were immediately apparent—were the test materials. The average correlation between the two sets of figures, based on a separate study (Elkind, 1964) of 171 children aged 6-12 was .50 ($p <$ .05).

Each child was pretested on one set of cards (Form A) immediately prior to training. The testing consisted of showing the child the cards one at a time and asking him, "What do you see? What does it look like?" The child's *pretraining* score was the number of figures, of the 21 possible, that he perceived on the first, pretraining presentation of Set A. Immediately after being presented with Set A, the child was trained on the second set of cards (Set B). Training involved providing the child with successively more direct and revealing clues to the perception of figures not spontaneously detected. The first clue, given after the child's spontaneous response, was the statement,

Some children see more than one thing.
Do you see anything else besides a _____
[whatever the child had seen]?

If this clue did not prompt a reversal of figure and ground, a second clue was given,

Sometimes children see a _____ [whatever figure he had not detected] in the picture. Do you see a _____?

If the child replied that he did see the figure, he was asked to point out the parts to insure that he was not responding to suggestion. Those children who still did not see the "hidden" figure were then given a third clue. This time the cardboard shield was superimposed on the drawing and the previous question was repeated. The youngster was again asked to point out the parts to insure that he actually saw the reversed figure. Each child was trained to the criterion of being able to point out all the figures in Set B. The child's *learning* score was the number of clues he required to reach this criterion. Immediately after training the child was again tested on Set A. The number of figures detected in Set A after training was the child's *posttraining* score.

Statistical Analysis

Two separate analyses of variance were computed. The first analysis was of the pre- and posttraining scores on Set A. For these scores it was possible to analyze the main effects of Age, of Reading Group (slow and average), and Time of Testing (i.e., pre- or posttraining) and the interaction effects by means of a Lindquist (1953) Type III design.

The second analysis was of the learning scores and involved determining the effects of Age and Reading Group on the number of clues required to see all the figures in Set B.

In order to have equal numbers of subjects in each cell and to increase the N within it, the third and fourth grade subjects were combined into a younger age group, while the fifth and sixth grade subjects were combined into an older age group for both slow and average readers.

Results

Analysis of Pre- and Posttraining Score Variance (See Table 2)

Effect of age. As shown in Table 2, the *F* for age was nonsignificant. This was an unexpected finding since previous work with the ambiguous figures always showed a regular increase with age in the ability to perceive the hidden figures. Possible explanations for this finding will be presented in the discussion section.

Table 2. Analysis of variance of pre- and posttraining scores for age (A), reading group (R), and time of testing (T)

Source	df	SS	MS	F
Between subjects	59	667.47		
A	1	10.77	10.77	2.26
R	1	388.80	388.80	81.51*
A X R	1	.57	.57	.12
Error B	56	267.33	4.77	
Within subjects	60	1,444.0		
T	1	1,190.70	1,190.70	249.62*
AT	1	10.87	10.87	2.28
RT	1	4.04	4.04	.85
ART	1	12.65	12.65	2.65
Error W	56	225.74	4.77	
Total	119	2,111.47		

*$p < .01$.

Table 3. Pre- and posttraining mean scores and differences for two reading groups and two age levels

Reading group	N	Age level	Pre-training	Post-training	d[a]
Slow	15	Younger	8.67	15.30	6.46*
	15	Older	9.67	15.07	5.40*
Average	15	Younger	11.47	19.27	7.80*
	15	Older	13.33	18.87	5.47*

[a]The significance of these differences was tested by means of a Scheffé test described by Winer (1962).
*$p < .01$.

Effect of reading group. The *F* for the reading group factor was 81.51 and was significant beyond the .01 level. Examination of the means for the slow and the average readers revealed that the average readers had higher mean scores than the slow readers at both age levels. Table 3 presents these data.

Effect of time of testing. For Time of Testing, the *F* was 249.62 and was significant well beyond the .01 level. For both the average and slow reading groups the training produced a significant improvement in performance between the first and the second administration of Set A (cf. Table 3).

Interactions. None of the interactions was significant.

Analysis of Learning Scores (See Table 4)

Effect of age. The *F* for Age was 5.96 and was significant at the .01 level. Inspection of Table 5 indicates that this *F* resulted from the fact that the older children in both the slow and the average reading groups took fewer trials to reach criterion than did the younger groups.

Effect of reading group. The *F* for Reading Group was 55.49 and was significant at the .01 level. The mean number of training trials required by the slow group was significantly greater than the number required by the average group at both of the age levels employed in the study. Table 5 presents this information.

Interaction of Age and Reading Group. The *F* for this interaction was .64 and was not significant.

Table 4.   Analysis of variance of learning scores for age (A) and reading group (R)

Source	df	SS	MS	F
A	1	39.78	39.78	5.96*
R	1	370.01	370.01	55.49**
(Cells)	(3)	(414.06)		
A X R	1	4.27	4.27	.64
Error W	53	353.59	6.67	
Total	59	767.65		

*p < .05.
**p < .01.

Discussion

The results of the present study have shown that with respect to figural decentration, slow readers were significantly less adept than average readers of comparable age, intelligence, and sex. Slow readers had lower pretraining scores, required more and more direct clues to reach the learning criterion during training, and transferred the effects of training to a significantly lesser extent than did the average readers. These findings are thus in general agreement with the hypothesis that reading involves the ability to decenter perception and that the more decentered a child's perception the better his reading ability. Moreover, the fact that the slow and average groups were equated for IQ suggests that the ability to decenter perception is not the same as general intelligence as measured by a nonverbal test. While these results do not *prove* the role of perceptual decentration in reading, nor the validity of the logical analysis of this process, they do provide further evidence for the construct validity of the notion of decentration and for the fruitfulness of the logical model of perception for generating testable hypotheses. Before describing some of the implications of these results, several of the incidental findings need to be interpreted.

Table 5. Learning score means and differences for two age levels and two reading groups

Age group	Reading group		d^a
	Slow	Average	
Younger	17.13	11.80	5.33*
Older	15.13	10.53	4.60*
Total	16.13	11.16	4.97*

[a]The significance of these differences was tested by means of a Scheffé test described by Winer (1962).

* $p < .01$.

In one respect the results of the present study do not support work previously done with the two sets of ambiguous pictures. In all the previous investigations (Elkind, 1964; Elkind et al., 1962; Elkind et al., 1965; Elkind & Scott, 1962) there was a regular increase with age in the untutored ability to reverse figure and ground and to perceive the hidden figures. In the present study, however, no significant age differences in performance scores were found even though two age levels were represented in the investigation. This finding can be explained by reference to

Table 3 which shows that there was an increase with age in the pretraining performance of the average but not in the pretraining performance of the slow readers. This suggests that one reason for the nonsignificant F for age was the inclusion of slow reading children whose ability to reverse figure and ground does not, apparently, spontaneously increase with age.

Turning to the posttraining performance scores, Table 3 shows that neither the average nor the slow reading groups made much improvement with age. For the average group this fact can be explained on the basis of the ambiguous picture test itself. As shown in a previous study (Elkind et al., 1962), training brings most average reading children close to the maximum ambiguous picture test score by the third grade. For the average readers, then, the lack of improvement with age in posttraining scores was probably more a function of the low ceiling of the test than of the lack of change in the children under investigation. For the slow readers, however, this explanation does not hold since their posttraining scores did not approach the maximum attainable score at any age level. Such a finding adds support to the previous conclusion that slow readers have a special disability with respect to perceptual decentration.

This last remark returns us to the general implications of the present investigation. From the practical point of view, the findings suggest that even in kindergarten, children might profit from instruction and practice in perceptual decentration activities such as recognizing pictures of things upside down and finding hidden figures of the Gottshaldt variety. This hypothesis should, of course, be tested. From the theoretical point of view, the findings suggest that a simple discrimination theory of perception is inadequate to deal with the problem of learning the symbols of English phonics and that the role of *perceptual activity*—mental manipulation of perceptual givens—will have to be taken into account to fully describe the role of perception in reading.

REFERENCES

Berko, Jean. The child's learning of English morphology. *Word,* 1958, *14,* 150-177.
Elkind, D. Ambiguous pictures for the study of perceptual development and learning. *Child Development,* 1964, *35,* 1391-1396.
Elkind, D., Horn, J., & Schneider, Gerrie. Modified word recognition, reading achievement and perceptual de-centration. *Journal of Genetic Psychology,* 1965, *70,* 235-251.
Elkind, D., Koegler, R. R., & Go, Elsie. Effects of perceptual training at three age levels. *Science,* 1962, *137,* 7.
Elkind, D., Koegler, R. R., Go, Elsie, & Van Doorninck, W. Effects of perceptual training on unmatched samples of brain injured and familial retarded children. *Journal of Abnormal Psychology,* 1965, *70,* 107-110.

Elkind, D., & Scott, L. Studies in perceptual development: I. The de-centering of perception. *Child Development,* 1962, *33,* 619-630.

Kohler, W., & Wallach, H. Figural after-effects, *Proceedings of the American Philosophical Society,* 1944, *88,* 269-357.

Lindquist, E. F. *Design and analysis of experiments in psychology and education.* Boston: Riverside Press, 1953.

Otis, A. S. *Self administering test of mental ability: Alpha, short form.* Yonkers-on-Hudson: World Book, 1952.

Piaget, J., & Morf, A. Les isomorphismes partiels entre les structures logiques et les structures perceptives. In J. Piaget (Ed.), *Etudes d'épistémologie génétique.* Vol. 6. Paris: Presses Universitaries de France, 1958, Pp. 51-116.

Pitman, I. J. Learning to read. *Journal of the Royal Society of Arts,* 1961, *109,* 149-180.

Winer, B. *Statistical principles in experimental design.* New York: McGraw Hill, 1962.

Affect

Reading Research in the Affective Domain

IRENE ATHEY

University of Rochester

In the past decade, America has invested a large proportion of its educational resources in searching for new solutions to the problem of reading failure. The magnitude of the problem and the importance of the outcome for our national life would certainly seem to warrant such outlays. Further, the extent and complexity of the problem demand that these resources be deployed in the conduct of research and training programs which have been shown to maximize both short- and long-term payoff. Under these circumstances, research and training programs which focus on the perceptual, cognitive, and linguistic variables of reading would seem to have clear priority. Not only is their relevance to reading readily apparent, but it is also relatively easy to devise ways to improve the level of achievement on these variables.

Judged against these criteria, research programs dealing with the relation of personality variables to reading does not seem to carry the same urgency. Some reading experts are skeptical that such relationships exist, for the research in this area has, indeed, proved inconclusive, often contradictory. Even when relationships are clearly demonstrated, they are not immediately translatable into a course of action which is likely to be perceived as desirable and feasible by educators and parents.

For some psychologists, however, the subject may have its own intrinsic interest and appeal, regardless of its immediate utilitarian value. But a stronger case can be made if we consider that, by increasing our knowledge of the affective life of the child, we broaden our understanding of his total functioning in the academic situation. In other words, the intellectual variables involved in reading do not operate in isolation but are modified by the individual's attitudinal and personality characteristics.

Nor is it true that personality variables are unresponsive to training, and therefore beyond the purview of the teacher. Although there has been a tendency, following psychoanalytic thinking, to accept the assumption that the basic parameters of the personality are laid down before the child comes to school and are, in any case, the responsibility of the parents rather than the teacher, still it remains a fact that teachers, whether they realize it or not, can have a tremendous influence on those aspects of the affective domain which have to do with learning. We have no statistics, for example, on how many children who have the requisite cognitive skills for reading are still unable to read, or how many children who are perfectly capable of reading do not choose to read outside school, either for information or pleasure. Such information would bring the importance of the affective domain into much sharper focus.

Briefly then, if a defense of this particular area of research were needed, it would include the following arguments: 1) Affective, attitudinal, and personality factors may have both a direct and an indirect influence on the cognitive variables involved in reading. 2) Affective, attitudinal, and personality factors shown to be related to reading are susceptible to intervention treatment by researchers, and especially by teachers whose associations with the young reader are both intensive and continuous. 3) The problems of reading are so complex and so urgent that we cannot afford to neglect any promising line of research which may lead ultimately to improved reading performance.

Fortunately, a persistent minority among reading researchers has continued to pursue the questions of reading and personality. In fact, the volume of research on this topic has increased steadily since the 1920s. Much of the literature has come from the clinic, where the interaction and compounding of emotional and learning problems have been the object of intensive study. During the past thirty years, however, clinical studies have tended to be outweighed by a steadily increasing number of research investigations, using subjects at all levels of reading proficiency and a variety of experimental measures.

This chapter presents a brief exposition of several personality theories and a review of certain studies which may suggest certain lines of research that could be pursued with advantage in order to clarify the role of affective factors in reading.

Affective Variables and Models of Reading

Theories and models of reading are usually concerned primarily, if not exclusively, with the perceptual and linguistic aspects of reading. In these theories and models, reading is considered as a form of information processing. However, information processing theories rarely take account of affective variables, although most theorists assume them to be operating at the same time as the information is being processed. Two

exceptions to this general statement are the substrata-factor theory of
Holmes (1954, 1960, 1961) and Singer (1965) and Ruddell's psycholinguistic model (1970, 1976) described elsewhere in this volume. But
these models merely acknowledge the existence of affective factors during the act of reading. They do not explain how such factors operate to
change what is seen and what is understood (i.e., how the information is
interpreted by the reader).

Moreover, it is difficult to see how affective variables could be integrated into an information-processing model without the benefit of knowing how these variables operate within the context of the personality
theory from which they are derived. It is not enough to show that good
readers differ from poor readers on some personality dimension, such as
self concept. The more difficult (but more important) step is to show the
implications of this difference (as suggested by the motivational or personality theory) for the cognitive functioning of good and poor readers.
This is difficult for a number of reasons. For one thing, personality
theories often tend to be of the armchair variety. They employ a network
of concepts which may have utility for the clinician in terms of developing
new insights into clients' problems, but do not lend themselves readily to
experimental testing. Moreover, these concepts can be translated into
measuring instruments only with great difficulty, if at all. For example,
the concept of "superego" may be very useful for theoretical and practical
purposes, but no satisfactory measure of the superego has, as yet, been
devised. Sometimes the instrument may be satisfactory in terms of its
technical requirements (reliability, validity, etc.), but its relationship to the
theory is tenuous. For example, a test designed to measure "anxiety" may
be a valid and useful instrument in and of itself, but whether it is a valid
measure of "drive" as postulated in Hull's motivational theory is more
doubtful. [In fact, Eysenck (1955, 1957) has demonstrated that the Manifest Anxiety Scale, which purports to be such a measure of "drive," seems
to be measuring a trait he calls "neuroticism," and possibly other related
dimensions such as introversion-extraversion.]

Another difficulty arises from the fact that personality theories, when
they do concern themselves with the intellectual life of the individual,
tend to deal with it in a global fashion and seldom address themselves to
such relatively limited aspects of cognitive functioning as reading. It is not
surprising, therefore, that we have no measures readily available for use
in personality-based reading research.

Given this situation, two possible courses of action seem to present
themselves for the researcher interested in this area. Since theories and
models of reading are not very helpful, a more promising line of attack

would seem to be through personality theory. Obviously, some personality theories are more suitable than others for this purpose. The first task, therefore, is to select a theory which holds some promise of potential application to reading; next, to deduce one or more hypotheses about reading behavior which are hypotheses clearly derivable from the theory; and finally, to select or construct valid measures of the concepts contained in the hypothesis.

A second course of action might be to take some of the personality variables whose relationship with reading seems to have been demonstrated more consistently in the research literature (e.g., self-concept), and to attempt a theoretical integration of these isolated variables into reading theories or models, showing at what points in the reading process and in what ways these variables are operating. In this alternative strategy, the researcher is developing his or her own theory of the role of personality variables in reading.[1] One suspects that a possible outcome of this exercise may be the formulation of several different models for different groups of readers. Entwisle (1971) has pointed out that a model of any aspect of human functioning is the ultimate abstraction, since it assumes that the processes in question operate in the same way for everyone. The truth probably lies toward the opposite extreme; that is to say, it is more likely that we need a different model for every reader, since every reader must function in a somewhat different way from every other in assimilating the information presented in print. Indeed, this was an underlying assumption of Holmes' substrata-factor theory. He considered his research on known groups to be a step in the direction of understanding *individual* differences among readers.

Neither of these strategies is easy, and neither gives promise of immediate or great payoff. Neither enjoys the same prestige as research in the cognitive and linguistic variables related to reading. But they deal with questions which must be answered before we can fully understand what is happening during reading. Moreover, they are questions which hold their own intrinsic interest for many psychologists who do not discount or underrate the role of intellectual factors.

The Search for a Personality Theory

Pursuing the first of the strageties mentioned above requires the identification of a personality theory which has the potential for generating hypotheses applicable to reading and also includes well-defined,

---

[1] "Reading" is here taken to include the comprehension as well as the decoding aspects.

measurable concepts. Each of the sections below presents a brief exposition of a theory which appears to meet these specifications and a review of some studies designed to test hypotheses derived from the theory.

Self Concept Theory

The notion of the self concept appears to have its roots in several personality theories, especially those which adopt an organismic or phenomenalistic approach. It has been defined as a set of "self percepts which have acquired meaning and which have been related to other self percepts . . . the individual's picture of himself, the perceived self with accrued meanings" (Super et al., 1963:18). Since the person cannot ascribe meanings to himself in a vacuum, the self concept usually consists of the picture of the self in some situation, role, or web of relationships.

> The *self concept system* is made up of the various self concepts, the pictures which the individual has of himself in different roles and in different types of situations. Thus it should be noted that it is incorrect to write of the self concept as though each person had just one; each person has a number of self concepts, but one self concept system at any point in time. This system may be well or poorly organized. It is therefore proper to refer to the self concept system, or to the concept of self as fireman, wage-earner, father, or citizen: the self concept system is general and inclusive, the self concept more specific and limited (Super et al., 1963:19).

Although this is a useful distinction, in the literature the term *self concept* is often used in a global way to include such aspects as body image, level of aspiration, social influence, and personal values. In conducting research studies, the measure employed to assess self concept is usually a self report instrument consisting of items covering a wide range of behaviors, or a subscale of a standardized personality inventory. However, it has become increasingly apparent that, while the total self concept may be positive or negative, the correlations among some aspects of the self concept may be quite low (Akeret, 1965). During the past decade, therefore, several attempts have been made to develop measures which differentiate the dimensions of the self concept.

Self concept has been found to be consistently related to reading achievement, in spite of the variety of measures used to assess both factors. Reviews of the research on this relationship and/or discussion of its educational implications may be found in Abrams (1969), Athey and Holmes (1969), Berretta (1970), Cohn and Kornelly (1970), Griffiths (1970-71), Jackson (1972), Maxwell (1971), Miller and Windhauser

(1971), Palardy (1969), Purkey (1970), Sebeson (1970), and Toews (1972).

In general, the research literature suggests that good readers tend to have more positive self concepts than poor readers (Athey & Holmes, 1969; Hallock, 1958; Lockhart, 1965; Lumpkin, 1959; Malmquist, 1958; Padelford, 1969; Seay, 1960; Stevens, 1971; Zimmerman & Allebrand, 1965). More specifically, feelings of adequacy and personal worth, self-confidence and self-reliance seem to emerge as important factors in the relationship with reading achievement. Conversely, underachieving readers tend to be characterized by immaturity, impulsivity, and negative feelings concerning themselves and their world (Blackham, 1955; Bodwin, 1957; Schwyhart, 1967; Toller, 1967). The work of Bricklin (1963) and Sopis (1965) suggests that the relationship may be defined in terms of particular reading difficulties and the self image *as a reader*. Wattenberg and Clifford (1964) suggest that indices of the sense of personal worth and competence, if used in kindergarten, would add significantly to reading prediction.

The Tennessee Self-Concept Scale (Fitts, 1965) includes components measuring Family Self, Social Self, Physical Self, Personal Self, and Moral-Ethical Self, as well as the Total Self Concept score. This scale was used by Hebert (1968) with 50 ninth-graders. However, the only significant correlation with reading comprehension appearing in this report is for Total Self-Concept.

Cummings (1970) found a significant relationship between scores on the Thomas Self-Concept Values Test and the California Reading Test for 48 third grade children. The pattern of self-concept value factors was different, however, for groups of readers scoring highest and lowest in their classrooms and farthest above or below the level anticipated for them.

Dennerll (1971) found reading achievement to be significantly related to the self concept of ability and of reading, but not to global self concept, suggesting that differentiation of the self concept may be well established by the fifth grade. Although the girls in this study were higher achievers than the boys, and the high SES students were higher achievers than the low SES students, sex and socioeconomic status were not significantly related to self concept. Possibly, some other variable, such as aspiration level, locus of control, or value system may be operating to obscure the relationship. Although, in general, poor achievers have lower aspiration levels than high achievers, sometimes their aspiration levels may be unrealistically high. For example, Ruhly (1970) performed a series of covariance analyses on a large number of variables presumably related to reading for 128 white boys in the second grade. Of the three variables relating to self concept (self adequacy, role expectations, and total self concept), only role expectations proved significant, and that in a reverse direction; low readers reported greater role expectations than did high readers, reflecting what would appear to be an unrealistic level of aspiration among the former.

Since the relationship between reading and self concept appears to be well documented, a number of investigators have attempted to improve the self concept of poor readers either prior to, or concurrently with, remedial instruction in reading (Hedges, 1971; Krim, 1968; P. W. Smith, 1969). The interaction of reading, self concept, and race or nationality has also been studied (Bell et al., 1972; Frerichs, 1971; Padelford, 1969; Phillips, 1972; Pratz, 1969; Reynolds, 1970; Schoeller & Pearson, 1970; M. E. Smith, 1970; Wiggins, 1971).

Self-Consistency Theory

Lecky (1951) is one of the few personality theorists who have touched on reading directly in the exposition of their theories. Lecky's theory views "all psychological phenomena as illustrations of the single principle of unity" (p. 152), namely, the need to maintain self-consistency among the perceptions, beliefs, and actions of the individual. Faced with conflicting data, the organism will 1) reject the conflicting information outright, 2) modify it to fit the prevailing belief structure, or 3) change the prevailing belief structure to accommodate the conflicting information. Which of these alternatives ensues is dependent on the strength of the prevailing belief structure and the degree to which it is cherished by its owner. Hence some beliefs are extremely resistant to change, even when confronted with powerful contradictory evidence, because they are crucial to the person's belief system and therefore necessary to the maintenance of his self-consistency.

> Resistance is the opposite of assimilation and learning, and represents the refusal to reorganize the values, especially the ego values . . . . To the educator, it appears as an obstacle to learning. But if we would really understand these resistances, we must see them not as neurotic or abnormal manifestations, but as wholly natural devices for avoiding reorganization (p. 162).

The implications of self-consistency theory for reading may be seen in the following example:

> For years the deficiency of boys in reading, as compared with girls who receive the same instruction, has been widely recognized, particularly in elementary courses. We have discovered that this difference is due not to

a lack of ability on the part of the boys, but to a lack of reading material which is suitable for boys. The boy from six to eight years old, just beginning to learn to read, is mainly concerned with maintaining the conception of himself as manly. He likes to play cowboy, G-man and Indian. He tries not to cry when he gets a bump. Yet this boy, when the reading lesson begins, must stand up before his companions and read that "the little red hen says 'Cluck! Cluck!' "—or something equally inconsistent with his standards of how he should behave. To be obliged to read such material aloud, especially in the presence of others, is not consistent with his view of masculine values. If a boy is trying to maintain a standard of manliness on the playground, he does not abandon that standard merely because he walks from the playground into the classroom. When books on railroads and airplanes are provided, they serve to support these values and are assimilated eagerly. The point is, of course, that the assumed defect in reading never was a defect except from the standpoint of an unenlightened school system, but on the contrary was a manifestation of a wholesome, normal, and desirable resistance (pp. 162-163).

Lecky would not maintain, of course, that this affront to masculinity is the sole, or even the major, cause of reading disability among boys. The extent to which it is a primary cause, or one of a syndrome of causal factors, remains a matter of speculation, and an open question for research.

Any test of Lecky's theory requires the construction of a valid measure of self-consistency. Lecky developed a personality inventory, which he called the *Individuality Record,* designed to demonstrate the existence of a self-consistent attitudinal posture toward various aspects of the environment, which would be especially evident within the limits of prescribed belief systems. A modified version of this inventory might be used to test Lecky's hypothesis about reading failure among both adults and children.

If Lecky's hypothesis is correct with respect to young boys who are learning to read, then there should be a correlation between the severity of the reading problem and the degree and kind of "masculine" behavior exhibited (e.g., in play). If such a correlation were established, it would also be incumbent on the researcher to show that such behavior was less prevalent among boys who did not have a reading problem or to suggest possible differences to account for the presence and absence of reading failure in the two groups of "masculine" boys.

Lecky's theory should have wider implications than this, however. Reading may be conceived of more broadly as an intellectual, or academic, activity, rather than as a "feminine" activity. Conceived this way, it may conflict with the value systems of girls, as well as boys. Research might be designed to show that a belief system which emphasized the inherent value and pleasure of reading would differentiate good and poor readers, regardless of intelligence or sex.

Lecky does not address the problem of how the "ideal" self, as opposed to the self concept, is related to self-consistency, especially when a discrepancy exists between them. (Such a discrepancy is often viewed as a symptom of maladjustment among personality theorists.) It would seem that data on the "ideal" self would provide important clues to the dynamics of the individual's belief system, whether an ideal-self discrepancy existed or not. Reduction of the discrepancy may be brought about in either or both of two ways: the "ideal" is lowered so that it is more attainable (the individual becomes more accepting of his limitations) or the "self" is raised to that it conforms more nearly to the ideal (Fennimore, 1968). Such changes can give us much information about the individual's changing belief-system over time. Where an ideal-self discrepancy persists, this may mean that the individual would like to emulate his ideal, other things being equal, but that other values have greater priority. He would like, for instance, to be cooperative, but this conflicts with some other value such as "getting ahead." In this case, we have some information about the position of this particular value in the total value-system, i.e., whether it is central or peripheral, and thus, how resistant it may be to change. This would be an important consideration, if the beliefs about the self and the ideal self were shown to be related to reading.

Working within the framework of Lecky's theory, Fillmer et al. (1971-72) related the various subscales of the Tennessee Self-Concept Scale to reading scores on the Stanford Achievement Test and to measures of two- and three-dimensional perception. Significant relationships were found between reading and two of the self-concept measures, moral-ethical self and self-criticism. Several of the self-concept measures were highly related to visual perception. The authors suggest several hypotheses, all consonant with Lecky's theory, to account for this phenomenon.

Another study which seems to have some bearing on the theory is that of Bakan (1971) who hypothesized that, when a student values academic achievement, his self-esteem is affected by the consistency with which he achieves. From a total of 639 junior high school students she selected 112 with average GPAs and rank-ordered them in terms of the consistency of grades gained over a four-year period. Both the achievement level and the self-concept-of-ability scores (Brookover scale) of the highly inconsistent group showed a greater decrement over time than the highly consistent group. This result is interesting because it suggests that all-round average achievement has a greater positive effect on both self concept and subsequent achievement than superior achievement in some areas compensated by inferior achievement in others. Apparently, junior high school students have not yet come to appreciate William James' aphorism that the sense of self-worth must reside in one or two chosen areas in which a person performs well.

Khan (1969, 1970) and Khan and Roberts (1971), in a longitudinal study exploring affective correlates of academic achievement, found certain affective characteristics to have high factorial stability over time, and to predict achievement scores better than grades. The highest predictor for both sexes was a factor labeled Achievement Anxiety which appeared to reflect a low value for competition and striving for advancement.

As Lecky pointed out, self consistency refers to the relative tenacity of values, beliefs, and attitudes. An important consideration, therefore, is the position of the individual's belief about his academic ability in his hierarchy of values and beliefs, since the core beliefs would be most resistant to change. If this determination were made prior to a treatment program designed to change beliefs about reading, presumably those cases in which reading was a peripheral value would be most subject to change.

Competence Theory

In a classic paper entitled "Motivation reconsidered: The concept of competence," published in 1959, Robert White postulated a basic, lifelong drive in all animals, including man, for ordering and mastering the environment. Ordering the environment reduces the uncertainty about what can be expected to happen, and hence gives the individual better powers of prediction and control. Mastering the environment satisfies a basic need to perceive oneself as having an effect on what happens to him, and therefore capable of reducing the uncertainty still further. Other writers (e.g., Erikson, 1950; Jahoda, 1958) have come to view the feeling of ability to master the environment (at least to some degree) as essential to mental health.

The feeling of competence, according to White, is a source of satisfaction which is independent of extrinsic rewards, punishments, or social expectancies. The need to organize and manipulate the environment is innate; but the ways in which it finds expression are determined by the child's experiences, especially his experiences with significant others. Erikson has proposed a stage theory showing the basic requisites and interactions which produce a developing sense of mastery in relation to the environment. Since learning to read is an activity participated in by every "normal" member of our culture, Erikson's theory is particularly appropriate because it concentrates upon the development and functioning of the normal or healthy personality, rather than upon behavioral aberrations.

Erikson conceives of the whole psychological span of human life as a series of eight periods or stages, the first four of which are pertinent to the present discussion. Each stage is characterized by its own peculiar developmental task, which is imposed partly by the individual's own maturation and partly by the expectations of the society in response to that maturation. The developmental task—or crisis, as Erikson calls it—has both a positive and a negative dimension, and the successful accomplishment of a particular stage depends upon achieving a workable balance between the two. For example, the first developmental task, which will lay the foundation for the emerging personality, is "the firm establishment of enduring patterns for the balance of basic trust over basic mistrust" (1959, p. 63). The healthy personality contains both elements, but trust predominates for the most part over mistrust. The outcome of each stage for a given individual depends upon the nature of his experiences during that stage. Thus, whether the child develops basic trust depends upon the quality of the maternal relationship and upon the parents' conveying to the child "an almost somatic conviction that there is a meaning to what they are doing" (1950, p. 222). A drastic loss of mother love at the time when basic trust is being established may lead to acute infantile depression or to a mild depressive coloring of the personality for the whole remainder of life.

The second psychosocial task, which occurs in the second or third year of life, is the establishment of autonomy versus shame and doubt. The sense of autonomy is built on the child's new-found mastery over his physical environment through the use of movement and over his social environment through the use of language. However, these new abilities need room to grow and operate. Impatient or belittling adults can stunt the growth of autonomy and tip the balance in the direction of a lasting sense of shame or self-doubt. As in the case of basic trust, too much autonomy can be detrimental, since it will assuredly bring the individual into conflict with society. Whatever the resolution of the crisis, this stage is critical to the formation of the child's self concept.

At the age of four or five, the child must use his newly-gained autonomy to initiate his own activities and social interactions. He must be allowed to do this without continually being made to feel guilty about the actions he performs in reality or in fantasy. Again, the way this crisis is resolved will affect the child's later career as a "self-starter."

The fourth stage is probably the most interesting for teachers because it coincides with the elementary school period. This is the stage of "industry versus inferiority," in which the mastery of the skills deemed important by the society, and the establishment of a good relationship with those who teach these skills, are the central tasks and crucial to the child's sense of identity. The enjoyment of work and a sense of pride in one's own creations are the principal items of learning during this period.

Erikson elaborates on several other important features of the stages. First, it should be noted that no crisis is resolved once and for all but is a continuing theme throughout life. At any given age the particular conflict designated is the dominant issue for that stage. Second, the stages occur in a fixed sequence, and the emergence of each new level of social interaction is dependent on the degree to which the preceding stages have been successfully negotiated. This means that some children who have reached the age of school entrance may be struggling with residual conflicts from earlier periods and are thus ill-equipped to start establishing the work patterns typical of the "industry versus inferiority" period.

Erikson does not refer specifically to reading as one of the skills to be mastered, though it would seem to follow from his general description of this period. The school's priorities today are such that learning to read could be considered as the *major* developmental task of the early elementary school years. As Margaret Mead (1958) has pointed out, "At whatever point the society decides to stress a particular adjustment, it will be at this point that adjustment becomes acute to the individual" (p. 347). There can be no doubt that in American culture learning to read is a major adjustment which the child must make to retain his own and others' respect. It is a part of the process of "growing up," a *sine qua non* of maturity, and a product of socialization processes almost as important as learning to walk and talk.

If this interpretation of Erikson's theory is correct, it gives rise to a number of hypotheses with respect to the relationship of reading to certain aspects of psychosocial development. Specifically, the following hypotheses, if confirmed at the elementary school level, would support the validity of the interpretation:

1. Good readers may be expected to exhibit strong feelings of self-esteem, a firm conviction of their own worth, while poor readers will display feelings of inferiority and inadequacy, especially in the school (reading) situation.
2. Good readers will obtain higher scores on measures of basic trust, autonomy, and initiative, or a composite of all three, than poor readers.

3. Good readers will value and enjoy school work, whereas poor
    readers will tend to dislike school-related activities.
4. Good readers will identify (but not *over*-identify—see Erikson, p.
    88) with their teachers, while poor readers will reject teachers as
    identification models.
5. Good readers will be relatively free from anxiety and neurotic
    manifestations, while poor readers will have a higher anxiety level
    and exhibit more symptoms of maladjustment.

These are a few of the hypotheses that might be generated from
Erikson's theory, and no doubt the reader will think of others. A research
study designed to test these hypotheses would call for the construction of
valid measures of Erikson's psychological constructs—basic trust, autonomy, etc.—since no suitable measures currently exist. Behavior rating
scales might be the most appropriate method of measuring these particular constructs in children.

We find that much of the research in this area does indeed support
the above hypotheses. For convenience, the studies have been summarized under the following headings: Autonomy, Environmental mastery, Accurate perception of reality, Attitudes toward learning, and
Anxiety.

Autonomy

Shatter (1956) found that fourth grade boys who were retarded
readers made significant gains in reading and in maturity, independence,
and self-reliance as a result of a group therapy program. McGinnis (1965)
found that parents of good readers manifested attitudes favoring growth
of independence and exposed their children to democratic practices and
environmental activities which would encourage such growth. Conversely, Carrillo (1957) found poor readers to show lack of independence,
avoidance of leadership opportunities, and a poor attitude to responsibility. On a nonverbal task requiring the subject to place himself in relation
to a triangle with points labeled *parents, teacher,* and *other children,* poor
readers placed themselves within the triangle significantly more frequently (Henderson, Long, and Ziller, 1965).

Anderson (1972) hypothesized that Self-Directed Activity (SDA) as
observed in 14 fourth-grade "natural classroom environments" would
lead to superior quality of response on the Directed-Reading-Thinking
Activity devised by Stauffer. In addition to this finding, some interaction
effects among sex, race, and teacher estimates of SDA were observed,

suggesting that high SDA in girls is acceptable to the teacher, but in boys may be perceived as a threat to authority. The author concluded that approaches to reading which provide maximum opportunity for SDA are generally superior to those that do not.

Henderson and Long (1971) obtained scores on the Children's Self-Social Constructs Test and behavior ratings by teachers for 95 black children at school entrance. At the end of first grade significant differences were found on these measures among three groups differing in academic achievement: repeaters, promoted nonreaders, and readers. The readers displayed a pattern of mature, realistic independence. Berger (1968) has also remarked on the importance of promoting a positive identity and sense of independence among college students with reading problems.

Environmental Mastery

Blackham (1955) found ninth grade overachievers in reading to have a greater amount of intellectual energy at their disposal, to be more spontaneous and creative, and to be able to make finer intellectual discriminations. Tabarlet (1958) found fifth grade children, two or more years retarded in reading, to be inferior to normal readers in interpersonal skills, social participation, satisfactory work and recreation, and adequate outlook and goals. Carter (1964) reviewed the later careers of retarded readers of normal intelligence, and found that their vocational mobility and aspirations tended to remain horizontally oriented. Norman and Daley (1959) found clusters of items suggesting feelings of "environmental deprivation" and maltreatment to differentiate poor male readers in the sixth grade, while Spache concluded from two studies (1954, 1957) that the typical retarded reader in the primary grades had less insight into the human dynamics of a situation and manifested less solution-seeking behavior. Abrams (1964), likewise, concluded that nonreaders were more impulsive and less able to respond appropriately to environmental stimuli than good readers.

Accurate Perception of Reality

Environmental mastery would seem to be dependent to some extent on the degree to which the individual perceives his environment accurately and realistically. There is some suggestion in the literature that poor readers may be less aware of (Margulies, 1942) and more prone to entertain erroneous conceptions of their environment (Jackson, 1944), specifically of their teachers and peers (Holzinger, 1967). They have been found deficient in ego strength, defined as "the ability to gauge reality and synthesize behavior in appropriate goal-directed activity" (Barber, 1952). Ramsey (1962) and Lasswell (1967) have remarked that poor readers are less realistic in their estimates of themselves as readers, while Bouise (1955) and Van Zandt (1963) have demonstrated a similar lack of realism with respect to educational and vocational aspirations. In a series of carefully documented case studies, Shrodes (1949) has described changes in student self-awareness and growth of insight into the motivations governing behavior as the result of a course of bibliotherapy.

Holzinger (1967) found that poor readers in the first grade scored significantly lower on peer and teacher perception, while those in the fourth grade, in addition to the above measures, were also significantly lower on self perception. There is some suggestion that poor readers may be more interested in the world of fantasy than in the realities of the school situation. Gates (1936), for example, observed 26 cases of recessive behavior, including chronic mind-wandering and daydreaming, among 100 poor readers.

Attitudes Toward Learning

Since reading is the basis of learning most other school subjects, it seems logical to suppose that when the child finds reading a pleasurable experience, his positive attitudes toward reading will rapidly become generalized to most other subjects. Conversely, his expanding interests should lead to a deeper love of reading as a primary source of information and enjoyment. Such burgeoning curiosity may find many other avenues of expression besides reading, of course, but in this society reading still remains one of the major vehicles for satisfying a desire for knowledge.

The available evidence tends to support the view that good readers are likely to be more intellectually oriented (Gates, 1936; Granzow, 1954; Witty, 1950), exhibit higher aspirations (Lasswell, 1967) and drive for achievement (Bauer, 1956), and to show more curiosity (Maw & Maw, 1962) and more positive attitudes toward school in general (Carter, 1964; Granzow, 1954) and reading in particular (Groff, 1962; Healy, 1965; Ketcham, 1966). Johnson (1959) found that by categorizing first grade children as "eager" or "reluctant" readers, he could predict reading success in the second grade, even though the two groups made comparable scores in initial reading readiness tests. Attitudinal factors have similar implications for remedial reading (Peter, 1963).

Biel (1945) and others have hypothesized that the known sex difference in the number of reading disability cases may be attributable in part to the difficulty boys experience in identifying with women teachers in the primary grades (cf. Lecky's theory of self-consistency). Gowan (1955) and Fliegler (1957), after reviewing the literature on gifted underachievers, point out that the underachiever is usually characterized by an inability to identify with authority figures, or to create warm relationships with either teachers or peers. Dorney (1963) found that delinquent adolescent boys improved significantly in their attitude toward authority figures after a course of reading instruction.

As part of a longitudinal study of the relationship of preschool social-emotional functioning to later intellectual achievement, Kohn and Rosman (1972) examined two dimensions of their Social Competence Scale—Interest-Participation versus Apathy-Withdrawal and Cooperation-Compliance versus Anger-Defiance. An earlier study by Silverman (1968) confirmed the hypothesis that 103 nursery school children who scored high on Apathy-Withdrawal were having later learning difficulties as measured by a group achievement test administered in second grade. (The Anger-Defiance dimension was not predictive). In the Kohn and Rosman study, nearly 300 children were followed for one year in day care centers and for two years in the first and second grades of New York City schools. The earlier finding was confirmed: Children high in Apathy-Withdrawal were low achievers compared to children high in Interest-Participation. By the end of second grade, girls (but not boys) high on Anger-Defiance were also exhibiting low achievement patterns. The importance of interest and participation in school-related activities demonstrated in this study is consonant with the earlier findings of Kagan and his colleagues (Kagan et al., 1958; Sontag et al., 1958).

Anxiety

Smith and Carrigan (1959) have suggested that anxiety is an important dimension in reading disability, its role being to excite some functions such as fluency, and to depress others such as word recognition and day-to-day memory. A number of investigators have found a significant negative relationship between reading comprehension and anxiety (Cowen, et al., 1965; Frost, 1965; Neville, Pfost, and Dobbs, 1967; Pacheco, 1964; Phelps, 1967) or neuroticism (Savage, 1966). Other authors have suggested that the influence of anxiety may lie in its interaction with other variables such as perceptual rigidity (Simula, 1964), introversion (Vehar, 1968), intelligence (Scarborough, Hindsman, & Hanna,

1961), socioeconomic status (Dukes, 1964), and disparity of reading and arithmetic performance (Lynn, 1957).

Cotler (1969) evaluated the effects of positive and negative reinforcement and test anxiety on the reading performance of 189 boys in the fourth, fifth, and sixth grades. He concluded that "test anxiety or its equivalent can no longer be ignored as a relevant variable" in reading performance, whereas reinforcement (in this case money) was not a significant variable. In two further experiments, Cotler and Palmer (1970, 1971) found that anxiety and academic achievement were related in middle-class boys, but not girls or lower-class boys. Using the galvanic skin response (GSR) as an index of anxiety, Rugel (1971) found that the level of arousal in second and third graders increased as the reading task increased in difficulty from independent to instructional to frustration levels. At the college level, Maxwell (1971) has remarked on a syndrome among underachieving students whose most salient features are self-deprecation, lack of a clear system of goals and values, vulnerability to disparagement by others, immature relations with parents, lack of insight into personal problems, and a pervasive anxiety or depression—in brief, all the dimensions hypothesized from Erikson's theory.

On the other hand, it should be noted that some researchers (e.g., Anderson, 1964; Shapiro, 1968) have failed to find any relationship between reading ability and anxiety, so the role of anxiety in reading success or failure remains in some doubt.

Social Learning Theory

Rotter's theory (1966) is based on his observations that certain accepted principles of reinforcement theory do not adequately reflect human behavior unless a concept of *expectancy* is added. Rewarding a behavior does not strengthen the behavior directly but the expectancy that the behavior will produce future rewards. In animals and very young children, the expectation of reward is strongly linked to frequency of reward. In human beings, at least those who have begun to form concepts and have some awareness of complex causes, many factors can influence the expectation of reward—past experience, current information, one's estimate of the probabilities of the situation, etc.

Rotter suggests that one of the most important factors contributing to this expectancy is the individual's belief in the extent to which he can affect the outcome. Clearly, his belief will vary from situation to situation, or so one might assume. But Rotter finds that some people have a general disposition to believe in their own efficacy to control events, while others seem to be perpetually at the mercy of forces beyond their control.

Since Rotter first drew attention to the phenomenon about fifteen years ago, a body of literature on "locus of control" has accumulated. (For the interested reader, there are two reviews by Joe, 1971, and Throop & Macdonald, 1971.) Coleman (1966) used a measure of internal-external control in the report on the *Equality of Educational Opportunity* and found that, among disadvantaged children, students with high achievement scores were higher on the internal attitudes than the poor achievers. In general, "internals" seem to spend more time in academic activities and have higher educational aspirations than "externals," but the research has not been extended to the subject of reading. Entwisle (1971) has suggested that "control beliefs" may be especially important for reading, since middle-class parents teach their children from the beginning to expect order and meaning in their daily lives and to develop alternative strategies for dealing with problems which appear to violate this order, whereas poor children's early education may be deficient in these respects. The expectancy that reading will not only be a system with its own internal meaning and consistency, but also a tool to help solve other problems, must have important consequences for the excitement and desire to learn which children bring to reading. On the other hand, when reading is not seen as having these characteristics, it becomes "one more thing" imposed on unwilling victims by powerful authority figures.

Attitudes like these are probably first learned in the home. It would be unrealistic to expect that parents whose lives are wrapped in hopelessness will imbue their children with feelings of self-determination and conquest. If such attitudes are as important to reading as Entwisle and others suggest, it becomes a matter of urgency that the school develop strategies for changing the feelings of apathy and helplessness which impede learning.

Several studies (e.g., Milner, 1963; Bee et al., 1969; Feshbach, 1975) have shown how the hidden curriculum of the middle-class home inculcates a general expectancy for success in solving problems and for achieving in school. Other studies have shown that internals (those who see themselves as able to exert control on their lives) spend more time in academic activities (Chance, 1965; Crandall, Katkovsky, & Crandall, 1965), consistently attain higher course grades and achievement scores (McGhee & Crandall, 1968), and have higher academic confidence and educational aspirations (Gurin et al., 1969; Lao, 1970).

However, in spite of the above studies, the relationship of locus of control to reading remains relatively unexplored. One might expect that internals would be superior on reading comprehension tasks which involved some risk-taking or hypothesis-testing. The interaction of locus of control and sex (Joe, 1971) and socioeconomic level (Entwisle, 1971) should also be considered.

Expectancy Theory

This theory differs from the previous one in that the expectancies here are those of other people *for* the individual, not the individual's expectations *about* other people. Rosenthal has taken the ancient adage that we all try to live up (or down) to other people's opinions of us, and has attempted to give it the status of a scientific principle which can be demonstrated in a variety of situations. The first such demonstration was recorded in *Pygmalion in the Classroom* (1968) in which children identified as "late-bloomers" were later found to grow intellectually, the inference being that such growth was a direct result of teachers' expectations that it would occur.[2] The phenomenon has been observed elsewhere (Brookover et al., 1967). Rubovitz and Maehr (1973) observed the behavior of student teachers who had been led to believe that certain children were "gifted" or "non-gifted." They found that teacher behavior toward students did change as a function of expectations, but it was also affected by other variables such as the student's race. The major difference was in the quality rather than the amount of attention given. A significant interaction was also found with teacher personality. The more dogmatic the teacher, the greater the tendency to react positively to "gifted" white students and negatively to "gifted" black students.

It appears that teachers' expectations do affect their behavior toward students and hence, we may infer, students' perceptions of those expectations. Palardy (1969) and Purkey (1970) discuss a number of research studies showing that students' self perceptions are positively correlated with their perceptions of the teacher's feelings toward them. Moreover, the more positive the children's perceptions of their teacher's feelings, the better their academic achievement and the more desirable their classroom behavior tends to be. Mantaro (1971), for example, found that the learner's perception of certain dimensions of the interpersonal relations

---

[2] Students who plan to conduct research in this area should be aware of the methodological problems. See Claiborn (1969), Elashoff and Snow (1970), and Thorndike (1968) for critiques.

between himself and his teacher (regard, empathy, and congruence) were positively related to both self concept and reading performance.

Such studies are usually conceived within the framework of some other theory than expectancy theory. This fact emphasizes the relationships among the various theories and the interaction of the variables involved. The researcher may start his inquiry from the vantage point of any one of the above theories, but sooner or later he must take cognizance of the effects of other variables which have a prominent position in some other theory. If this leads to a study of the interaction of various factors, it must also lead to some integration of the theories, and so to an increased understanding of the total dynamics of the behavior studied.

Cognitive Style Theory

The notion that people may differ in their style of conceptualization was introduced in a 1963 monograph by Kagan and his colleagues. The Conceptual Style Test (CST) was devised to separate those possessing the "analytic attitude" from those whose perceptual organization is of a more global nature. It requires the child to respond to a series of three-picture items by grouping the objects depicted in one of two possible ways.

The analytic-global distinction is further related to a number of personality dimensions, among which the reflectivity-impulsivity distinction seems particularly relevant to reading; for Kagan suggested that the discrimination of stimuli called for in the reading task would favor analytic children over those who are "restless and impulsive, unable to accept the sedentary and reflective requirements of the reading situation." The suggestion was timely, in that innercity children who most frequently manifested severe reading disabilities were often found to be hyperactive and impulsive. Subsequent research has attempted to verify this hypothesis and to assess the efficacy of programs designed to train children in the analytic attitude.

Reflective children do seem to adopt more efficient strategies, such as focusing on the stimulus attributes of a perceptual task, generating plausible hypotheses, and asking questions designed to extract more relevant information, than do impulsive children (McKinney, 1973). Other writers agree that impulsive children "do not scan the field for distinctive features as systematically as do reflectives" (Ault, Crawford, & Jeffrey, 1972). Supporting evidence comes from Nuessle's finding (1972) of a relationship between developmental differences in focusing and developmental differences in reflectivity-impulsivity, and Kagan's study (1965) showing that reflective children learned letters and words more easily than impulsive children. Kagan further noted that children with reading disabilities were more likely to be impulsive than reflective (Kagan, 1966).

As might be expected, conceptual style has been found to correlate with response time. Kagan et al. (1964) have found stable individual differences in response time in about two thirds of the samples tested, and there has been some speculation as to the reinforcement history of children manifesting these conceptual styles. Weiner and Adams (1974), for example, have suggested that reflective children are likely to have experienced failure, whereas frustration is the more probable antecedent of impulsive behavior. Accordingly, a number of programs have been developed to help children increase their response time and adopt a more reflective approach to cognitive tasks, with some measure of success (Briggs & Weinberg, 1973; Egeland, 1974; Kagan, Pearson, & Welch, 1966; Robertson & Keeley, 1974; Zelniker, Cochavi, & Yered, 1974).

As previously indicated, there has been some suggestion that conceptual style may be related to class or ethnic background. Wagner and Wilde (1973) found four intercorrelated dimensions of cognitive style to differentiate middle-class from lower-class children. Ethnic background and sex, on the other hand, did not seem to be significant variables. Nor, in general, does conceptual tempo appear to be related to intelligence (Messer, 1974), although this may not be true for specific populations.

Much research has been generated since the concept of cognitive style was first introduced into the literature, and new questions are constantly being posed about its relationship to other variables. To the extent that reading involves discrimination tasks and hypothesis-generating behavior, the research on cognitive style would seem to have direct implications for the reading field. There is a need to establish which components of reading are most susceptible to the influence of cognitive style, especially where styles may be modified by training. Moreover, it should be borne in mind that the hypothesized relationships between reflectivity-impulsivity and accuracy of response did not hold for one third of the children studied who fell into the category of fast-accurate or slow-inaccurate. Not only should these children be studied further, but the advantage of being fast-accurate or even fast-inaccurate (as opposed to slow-accurate) in relation to different kinds of tasks warrants consideration. The student who is interested in this topic will find a sizable literature, but there are several reviews (Kagan & Kogan, 1970; Messer, 1974; Rosenfield, 1975) which may be consulted with advantage. In brief, this appears to be one of the more fruitful areas for future research on reading and the affective domain.

Conclusion

This chapter has presented a brief exposition of some of the personality theories which have given rise to hypotheses related to achievement in general and/or reading in particular and of some of the research studies conducted within the framework of those theories. It does not claim to be exhaustive in either respect. On the one hand, probably any theory of personality could be used as a starting point for the derivation of testable hypotheses about some aspect of reading. On the other hand, the achievement-related research which could appropriately have been included in any one of these sections was quite voluminous. The reader should, therefore, regard this chapter as a preliminary foray into some of the more promising lines of investigation from which to proceed in the exploration of more fruitful theory and new directions for research.

REFERENCES

Abrams, J. C. A study of certain personality characteristics of nonreaders and achievers. Unpublished doctoral dissertation, Temple University, 1955.

Abrams, J. C. Further considerations on the ego functioning of the dyslexic child—a psychiatric viewpoint. In Spache, G. D. (Ed.), *Reading Disability and Perception*. Proceedings of the 13th Annual Convention of the International Reading Association. Newark, Del.: International Reading Association, 1969, 13 (3), 16-21.

Akeret, R. U. Interrelationships among various dimensions of the self concept. In Lindzey, G., and Hall, C. S. (Eds.), *Theories of Personality: Primary Sources and Research*. New York: Wiley, 1965, 491-493.

Anderson, D. J. Manifest anxiety level and reading achievement: A study of the relationships between the manifest anxiety level and the reading achievement of fifth and sixth grade boys. Unpublished doctoral dissertation. New York University, 1964.

Anderson, W. W. Self-directed activity as a variable in reading instruction. *Reading World*, 1972, 12(1), 3-14.

Athey, I. J., and Holmes, J. A. *Reading Success and a Personality Value-Systems Syndrome: A Thirty-Year Then and Now Study at the Junior High School Level*. U. S. Office of Education, Contract No. S-248, Bureau of Research, No. 5-8027-2-12-1, 1967. (Published by University of California Press, 1969.)

Ault, R., Crawford, D., and Jeffrey, W. E. Visual scanning strategies of reflective, impulsive, fast-accurate, and slow-inaccurate children on the Matching Familiar Figures Test. *Child Development*, 1972, 43, 1412-1417.

Bakan, R. Academic performance and self concept as a function of achievement variability. *Journal of Educational Measurement*, 1971, 8(4), 317-319.

Barber, L. K. Immature ego development as a factor in retarded ability to read. Unpublished doctoral dissertation, University of Michigan, 1952.

Bauer, E. B. The interrelatedness of personality and achievement in reading. Unpublished doctoral dissertation, University of California at Berkeley, 1956.

Bee, H. L., Van Egeren, L., Streisguth, A. P., Nyman, B. A., and Leckie, M. S. Class difference in maternal teaching strateties and speech patterns. *Developmental Psychology*, 1969, 1, 726-734.

Bell, D. B., Lewis, F. D., and Anderson, R. F. Some personality and motivational factors in reading retardation. *Journal of Educational Research,* 1972, 65(5), 229-233.

Berger, A. Identity, confusion, and reading instruction. *Journal of the Reading Specialist,* 1968, 7(4), 170-174.

Berretta, S. Self-concept development in the reading program. *Reading Teacher,* 1970, 24(3), 232-238.

Biel, J. E. Emotional factors in the treatment of reading difficulties. *Journal of Consulting Psychology,* 1945, 9, 125-131.

Blackham, G. J. A clinical study of the personality structures and adjustments of pupils underachieving and overachieving in reading. Unpublished doctoral dissertation, Cornell University, 1955.

Bodwin, R. F. The relationship between immature self-concept and certain educational disabilities. Unpublished doctoral dissertation, Michigan State University, 1957.

Bouise, L. M. Emotional and personality problems of a group of retarded readers. *Elementary English,* 32 (1955), 544-548.

Bricklin, P. M. Self-related concepts and aspiration behavior of achieving readers and two types of nonachieving readers. Unpublished doctoral dissertation, Temple University, 1963.

Briggs, C. H., and Weinberg, R. Effects of reinforcement in training children's conceptual tempos. *Journal of Educational Psychology,* 1973, 65, 383-394.

Brookover, W. B., Erickson, E. L., and Joiner, L. M. Self concept of ability and school achievement: III. Relationship of self concept to achievement in high school. U. S. Office of Education, Cooperative Research Project. Final Report, Contract No. 2831, 1967.

Carrillo, L. W. The relation of certain environmental and developmental factors to reading ability. Unpublished doctoral dissertation, Syracuse University, 1957.

Carter, P., Jr. A descriptive analysis of the adult adjustment of persons once identified as disabled readers. Unpublished doctoral dissertation, Indiana University, 1964.

Chance, J. E. Internal control of reinforcement and the school learning process. Paper read at the annual meeting of the Society for Research in Child Development, Minneapolis, 1965.

Claiborn, W. L. Expectancy effects in the classroom: a failure to replicate. *Journal of Educational Psychology,* 1969, 60 (5, Part 1), 377-383.

Cohn, M., and Kornelly, D. For better reading—a more positive self-image. *Elementary School Journal,* 1970, 70(4), 199-201.

Coleman, J. S., et al. *Equality of Educational Opportunity.* National Center for Educational Statistics, Department of Health, Education, and Welfare. OE-38001, 1966. (ED 012 275).

Cotler, S. The effects of positive and negative reinforcement on the reading performance of male elementary school children. *Genetic Psychology Monographs,* 1969, 80, 29-50.

Cotler, S., and Palmer, R. J. The relationships among sex, sociometric, self, and test anxiety factors and the academic achievement of elementary school children. *Psychology in the Schools,* 1970, 7(3), 211-216.

Cotler, S., and Palmer, R. J. Social reinforcement, individual difference factors, and the reading performance of elementary school children. *Journal of Personality and Social Psychology,* 1971, 18(1), 97-104.

Cowen, E. L., Zax, M., Klein, R., Izzo, L. D., and Trost, M. A. The relationship of anxiety in school children to school record, achievement, and behavioral measures. *Child Development,* 1965, 36, 685-695.

Crandall, V. C., Katkovsky, W., and Crandall, V. J. Children's belief in their control of reinforcement in intellectual-academic achievement situations. *Child Development,* 1965, 36, 91-109.

Cummings, R. N. A study of the relationship between self concepts and reading achievement at third-grade level. Unpublished doctoral dissertation, University of Alabama, 1970.

Dennerll, D. E. Dimensions of self concept of later elementary children in relationship to reading performance, sex role, and socioeconomic status. Unpublished doctoral dissertation, University of Michigan, 1971.

Dorney, W. P. The effectiveness of reading instruction on the modification of certain attitudes toward authority figures of adolescent delinquent boys. Unpublished doctoral dissertation, New York University, 1963.

Dukes, B. M. Anxiety, self-concept, reading achievement, and creative thinking in four socioeconomic status levels. Unpublished doctoral dissertation, University of Alabama, 1964.

Egeland, B. Training impulsive children in the use of more efficient scanning techniques. *Child Development,* 1974, 45, 165-171.

Elashoff, J. D., and Snow, R. E. A case study in statistical inference: Reconsideration of the Rosenthal-Jacobson data on teacher expectancy. Department of Health, Education, and Welfare, Report No. Tr-15, Bureau No. BR-5-0252, December 1970. (ED 046 892)

Entwisle, D. R. Implications of language socialization for reading models and for learning to read. *Reading Research Quarterly,* 1971 (Fall), 7(1), 111-167.

Erikson, E. H. *Childhood and Society.* New York: Norton, 1950.

Erikson, E. H. Identity and the life cycle. In Klein, G. S. (Ed.), *Psychological Issues,* New York: Basic Books, 1959, 18-171.

Eysenck, H. J. A dynamic theory of anxiety and hysteria. *Journal of Mental Science,* 1955, 101, 28-51.

Eysenck, H. J. *Dynamics of Anxiety and Hysteria.* London: Routledge and Kegan Paul, 1957.

Fennimore, F. Reading and the self concept. *Journal of Reading,* 1968, 11 (6), 447-451, 481.

Feshbach, N. D. Some interpersonal factors associated with successful and problem readers. Paper presented at the annual meeting of the Society for Research in Child Development, Denver, Colorado, 1975.

Fillmer, H. T., Busby, W. A., and Smittle, P. Visual perception and self-concept: new directions in reading. *Journal of Reading Behavior,* 1971-72, 4(3), 17-20.

Fitts, W. H. *Manual: Tennessee Self-Concept Scale.* Nashville, Tenn.: Counselor Recordings and Tests, 1965.

Fliegler, L. A. Understanding the underachieving gifted child. *Psychological Reports,* 1957, 3, 533-536.

Frerichs, A. H. Relationship of self-esteem of the disadvantaged to school success. *Journal of Negro Education,* 1971, 40(2), 117-120.

Frost, B. P. Intelligence, manifest anxiety, and scholastic achievement. *Alberta Journal of Educational Research,* 1965, 11, 167-175.

Gates, A. I. The role of personality maladjustment in reading disability. *Journal of Genetic Psychology,* 1941, 59, 77-83.

Gowan, J. C. The underachieving gifted child—a problem for everyone. *Exceptional Children,* 1955, 21, 247-249.

Granzow, K. R. A comparative study of underachievers, normal achievers, and over-achievers in reading. Unpublished doctoral dissertation, Iowa State University, 1954.

Griffiths, A. N. Self-concept in remedial work with dyslexic children. *Academic Therapy,* 1971, 6(2), 125-133.

Groff, P. J. Children's attitudes toward reading and their critical reading abilities in four content type materials. *Journal of Educational Research,* 1962, 55, 313-317.

Gurin, P., Gurin, G., Lao, R. C., and Beattie, M. Internal-external control in the motivational dynamics of Negro youth. *Journal of Social Issues,* 1969, 25, 29-53.

Hallock, G. A. Attitudinal factors affecting achievement in reading. Unpublished doctoral dissertation, Wayne State University, 1958.

Healy, A. K. Effects of changing children's attitudes toward reading. *Elementary English,* 1965, 42, 269-272.

Hebert, D. J. Reading comprehension as a function of self-concept. *Perceptual and Motor Skills,* 1968, 27, 78.

Hedges, R. E. An investigation into the effects of self-directed photography experiences upon self concept and reading readiness achievement of kindergarten children. Unpublished doctoral dissertation, Syracuse University, 1971.

Henderson, E. H., and Long, B. H. Personal-social correlates of academic success among disadvantaged school beginners. *Journal of School Psychology,* 1971, 9(2), 101-113.

Henderson, E. H., Long, B. H., and Ziller, R. C. Self-social constructs of achieving and nonachieving readers. *Reading Teacher,* 1965, 19, 114-118.

Holmes, J. A. Factors underlying major reading disabilities at the college level. *Genetic Psychology Monographs,* 1954, 49, 3-95.

Holmes, J. A. The substrata-factor theory of reading: some experimental evidence. In Figurel, J. A. (Ed.). *New Frontiers in Reading.* Proceedings of the Fifth Annual Conference of the International Reading Association. New York: Scholastic Magazines, 1960, 115-121.

Holmes, J. A. Personality characteristics of the disabled reader. *Journal of Developmental Reading,* 1961, 4, 111-122.

Holmes, J. A., and Singer, H. *Substrata-Factor Differences Underlying Reading Ability in Known Groups.* Report of a Cooperative Research Project to U. S. Office of Education, Contract Nos. 538, SAE-8176 and 538, SAE-8660, 1961.

Holzinger, M. Personality and behavioral characteristics of able and less able readers of elementary school age. Unpublished doctoral dissertation, University of Minnesota, 1967.

Jackson, J. A survey of psychological, social, and environmental differences between advanced and retarded readers. *Journal of Genetic Psychology,* 1944, 65, 113-131.

Jackson, R. Building reading skills and self concepts. *Reading Teacher,* 1972, 25(8), 755-758.

Jahoda, M. *Current Concepts of Positive Mental Health.* New York: Basic Books, 1958.

Joe, V. C. Review of the internal-external control construct as a personality variable. *Psychological Reports,* 1971, 28, 619-640.

Johnson, D. E. Reading behavior, achievements, and attitudes of first grade boys. Unpublished doctoral dissertation, Stanford University, 1959.

Kagan, J. Reflection-impulsivity and reading ability. *Child Development,* 1965, 36, 609-628.

Kagan, J. Reflection-impulsivity: The generality and dynamics of conceptual tempo. *Journal of Abnormal Psychology,* 1966, 71, 17-24.

Kagan, J., and Kogan, N. Individual variation in cognitive processes. In P. H. Mussen (Ed.), *Carmichael's Manual of Child Psychology* (3rd. ed.), 1970, Vol. 1, 1273-1365.

Kagan, J., Moss, H. A., and Sigel, I. E. Psychological significance of styles of conceptualization. In Wright, J. C., and Kagan, J., (Eds.), *Basic Cognitive Processes in Children.* Monograph of the Society for Research in Child Development, 1963. (Reprinted in *Cognitive Development in Children: Five Monographs of the Society for Research in Child Development,* 1970).

Kagan, J., Pearson, L., and Welch, L. Modifiability of an impulsive tempo. *Journal of Educational Psychology,* 1966, 57, 359-365.

Kagan, J., Rosman, B., Day, D., Albert, J., and Phillips, W. Information-processing in the child: Significance of analytic and reflective attitudes. *Psychological Monographs,* 1964, 78, No. 1.

Kagan, J., Sontag, L. W., Baker, C. T., and Nelson, V. L. Personality and IQ change. *Journal of Abnormal and Social Psychology,* 1958, 56, 261-266.

Ketcham, C. A. Factors in the home background and reader self-concept which relate to reading achievement. Unpublished doctoral dissertation, Lehigh University, 1966.

Khan, S. B. Affective correlates of academic achievement. *Journal of Educational Psychology,* 1969, 60(3), 216-221.

Khan, S. B. Affective correlates of academic achievement—a longitudinal study. *Measurement and Evaluation in Guidance,* 1970, 3(2), 76-80.

Khan, S. B., and Roberts, D. M. Factorial stability of academically relevant affective characteristics. *Measurement and Evaluation in Guidance,* 1971, 3(4), 209-212.

Kohn, M., and Rosman, B. L. Relationship of preschool social-emotional functioning to later intellectual achievement. *Developmental Psychology,* 1972, 6(3), 445-452.

Krim, L. F. Underachieving readers in an elementary school summer reading improvement program: a semantic differential measure of their change in attitude toward school, self, and aspiration. Unpublished doctoral dissertation, University of Denver, 1968.

Lao, R. C. Internal-external control and competent and innovative behavior among Negro college students. *Journal of Personality and Social Psychology,* 1970, 14, 263-270.

Lasswell, A. Reading group placement: its influence on enjoyment of reading and perception of self as a reader. Paper presented at annual conference of American Educational Research Association, New York, 1967.

Lecky, P. *Self-Consistency: A Theory of Personality.* New York: Island Press, 1951.

Lockhart, H. M. Personality and reading readiness. *Illinois School Research,* 1965, 2, 9-11.

Lumpkin, D. D. The relationship of self-concept to achievement in reading. Unpublished doctoral dissertation, University of Southern California, 1959.

Lynn, R. Temperamental characteristics related to disparity of attainment in reading and arithmetic. *British Journal of Educational Psychology,* 1957, 27, 62-67.

Malmquist, E. Factors related to reading disabilities in the first grade of the elementary school. *Acta Universitatis Stockholmiensis,* Stockholm Studies in Educational Psychology, No. 2, Stockholm: Almquist and Wiksell, 1958.

Mantaro, C. A. An investigation of the relationship between interpersonal relationships perceived by a pupil to exist between himself and (1) his reading achievement, (2) his self concept. Unpublished doctoral dissertation, Syracuse University, 1971.

Margulies, H. "Rorscharch responses of successful and unsuccessful students." *Archives of Psychology,* No. 271, 1942.

Maw, W. H., and Maw, E. W. Children's curiosity as an aspect of reading comprehension. *Reading Teacher,* 1962, 15, 236-240.

Maxwell, M. The role of attitudes and emotions in changing reading and study skills behavior of college students. *Journal of Reading,* 1971, 14(6), 359-364, 420-422.

McGhee, P. E., and Crandall, V. C. Beliefs in internal-external control of reinforcement and academic performance. *Child Development,* 1968, 39, 91-102.

McGinnis, D. J. A comparative study of the attitudes of parents of superior and inferior readers toward certain child-rearing practices. *National Reading Conference Yearbook,* 1965, 14, 99-105.

McKinney, J. Problem-solving strategies in impulsive and reflective second-graders. *Developmental Psychology,* 1973, 8, 145.

Mead, M. Adolescence in primitive and modern society. In Maccoby, E. E., Newcomb, T. M., and Hartley, E. D. (Eds.), *Readings in Social Psychology* (3rd ed.). New York: Holt, 1958, 341-350.

Messer, S. Reflectivity-impulsivity: a review. Unpublished paper, 1974.

Miller, C. D. An exploratory investigation of self concepts of high-achieving, average achieving, and low-achieving groups of junior high pupils as perceived by the pupils and their teachers. Unpublished doctoral dissertation, University of Colorado, 1963.

Miller, W. H., and Windhauser, E. Reading disability: tendency toward delinquency. *The Clearing House,* 1971, 46(3), 183-187.

Milner, E. A study of the relationship between reading readiness in grade one school children and patterns of parent-child interaction. *62nd Yearbook of the National Society for the Study of Education,* Chicago: University of Chicago Press, 1963, 108-143.

Neville, D., Pfost, P., and Dobbs, V. The relationship between test anxiety and silent reading gain. *American Educational Research Journal,* 1967, 4, 45-50.

Norman, R. D., and Daley, M. F. The comparative personality adjustments of superior and inferior readers. *Journal of Educational Psychology,* 1959, 50, 31-36.

Nuessle, W. Reflectivity as an influence on focusing behavior of children. *Journal of Experimental Child Psychology,* 1972, 14, 265-276.

Pacheco, A. D. Anxiety and reading achievement in sixth grade children. Unpublished doctoral dissertation, Colorado State University, 1964.

Padelford, W. B. The influence of socioeconomic level, sex, and ethnic background upon the relationship between reading achievement and self concept. Unpublished doctoral dissertation, University of California at Los Angeles, 1969.

Palardy, J. M. For Johnny's reading sake. *Reading Teacher,* 1969, 22(8), 720-724.

Peter, Sister M. The role of intelligence, personality, and selected psychological factors in remedial reading progress. Unpublished doctoral dissertation, University of Rochester, 1963.

Phelps, R. E. The measurement of manifest anxiety in young children and its relationship to later reading achievement. Unpublished doctoral dissertation, University of Connecticut, 1967.

Phillips, S. O. The relative effectiveness of three instructional approaches upon the reading habits and attitudes and academic performance of disadvantaged black college freshmen. *Reading World,* 1972, 12(1), 25-40.

Pratz, O. R. A study of the affective correlates of academic achievement in school children of different countries. Unpublished doctoral dissertation, University of Texas at Austin, 1969.

Purkey, W. W. *Self Concept and School Achievement.* Englewood Cliffs, N.J.: Prentice-Hall, 1970.

Ramsey, W. A study of salient characteristics of pupils of high and low reading ability. *Journal of Developmental Reading,* 1962, 5, 87-94.

Reynolds, S. C. The relationship between ability to read and the meaning and expression of emotion: a study of lower-class, institutionalized boys with antisocial behavior problems. Unpublished doctoral dissertation, Columbia University, 1970.

Robertson, D., and Keeley, S. Evaluation of a mediational training program for impulsive children by a multiple case study design. Paper presented at the American Psychological Association Conference. New Orleans, August, 1974.

Rosenfield, S. Cognitive style and the reading process. Paper presented at the International Reading Association conference, New York City, 1975.

Rosenthal, R., and Jacobson, L. *Pygmalion in the Classroom: Teacher Expectation and Pupils' Intellectual Development.* New York: Holt, Rinehart, and Winston, 1968.

Rotter, J. G. Generalized expectancies for internal versus external control of reinforcement. *Psychological Monographs,* 1966, 80, No. 1 (Whole No. 609).

Rubovits, P. C., and Maehr, M. L. Pygmalion black and white. *Journal of Personality and Social Psychology,* 1973, 25(2), 210-218.

Ruddell, R. B. Psycholinguistic implications for a systems of communication model. In Singer, H., and Ruddell, R. B. (Eds.). *Theoretical Models and Processes of Reading.* Newark, Del.: International Reading Association, 1970, 239-258.

Ruddell, R. B. Language Acquisition and the Reading Process. In Singer, H., and Ruddell, R. B., (Eds.). *Theoretical Models and Processes of Reading* (2nd ed.). Newark, Del.: International Reading Association, 1976.

Rugel, R. P. Arousal and levels of reading difficulty. *Reading Teacher,* 1971, 24(5), 458-460.

Ruhly, V. M. A study of the relationship of self concept, socioeconomic background and psycholinguistic abilities to reading achievement of second grade males residing in a suburban area. Unpublished doctoral dissertation, Wayne State University, 1970.

Savage, R. D. Personality factors and academic attainment in junior school children. *British Journal of Educational Psychology,* 1966, 36, 91-92.

Scarborough, O. R., Hindsman, E., and Hanna, G. Anxiety level and performance in school subjects. *Psychological Reports,* 1961, 9, 425-430.

Schoeller, A. W., and Pearson, D. A. Better reading through volunteer reading tutors. *Reading Teacher,* 1970, 23(7), 625-630, 636.

Schwyhart, F. K. Exploration of the self-concept of retarded readers in relation to reading achievement. Unpublished doctoral dissertation, University of Arizona, 1967.

Seay, L. C. A study to determine some relations between changes in reading skills and self-concepts accompanying a remedial program for boys with low reading ability and reasonably normal intelligence. Unpublished doctoral dissertation, Texas State College, 1960.

Sebeson, L. Self concept and reading disabilities. *Reading Teacher,* 1970, 23(5), 460-464.

Shapiro, M. A. Relationships among extraversion, neuroticism, academic reading achievement, and verbal learning. Unpublished doctoral dissertation. Rutgers—The State University, 1968.

Shatter, F. An investigation of the effectiveness of a group therapy program, including the child and his mother, for the remediation of reading disability. Unpublished doctoral dissertation, New York University, 1956.

Shrodes, C. Bibliotherapy: a theoretical and clinical experimental study. Unpublished doctoral dissertation, University of California at Berkeley, 1949.

Silverman, H. The prediction of learning difficulties and personality trends in preschool children. Unpublished doctoral dissertation, Columbia University, 1968.

Simula, V. L. An investigation of the effects of test anxiety and perceptual rigidity upon word recognition skill of second grade children. Unpublished doctoral dissertation, Indiana University, 1964.

Singer, H. Substrata-factor reorganization accompanying development of general reading ability at the elementary-school level. U. S. Office of Education, Cooperative Research Project, Final Report, Contract No. 2011, 1965.

Smith, M. E. The effects of an experimental program to improve self concept, attitudes toward school, and achievement of Negro fourth, fifth, and sixth grade students. Unpublished doctoral dissertation, University of Michigan, 1970.

Smith, P. W. Self concept gain scores, and reading efficiency terminal ratios as a function of specialized reading instruction or personal interaction. In Figurel, J. A. (Ed.), *Reading and Realism.* Proceedings of the 13th Annual Convention of the International Reading Association. Newark, Del.: International Reading Association, 1969, 13(1), 671-674.

Smith, D. E. P., and Carrigan, P. M. *The Nature of Reading Disability.* New York: Harcourt, Brace, 1959.

Sontag, L. W., Baker, C. T., and Nelson, V. L. Mental growth and personality development: a longitudinal study. *Monographs for Research in Child Development,* 1958, 23 (2, Serial No. 67).

Sopis, J. F. The relationship of self-image of a reader to reading achievement. Unpublished doctoral dissertation, New York University, 1965.

Spache, G. D. Personality characteristics of retarded readers as measured by the Picture-Frustration Study, *Educational and Psychological Measurement,* 1954, 14, 186-192.

Spache, G. D. Personality patterns of retarded readers, *Journal of Educational Research,* 1957, 50, 461-469.

Stevens, D. O. Reading difficulty and classroom acceptance. *Reading Teacher,* 1971, 25(1), 52-55.

Super, D. O., Starishevsky, R., Matlin, N., and Jordaan, J. P. *Career Development: Self Concept Theory.* New York: College Entrance Examination Board, 1963.

Tabarlet, B. E. A study of mental health status of retarded readers. Unpublished doctoral dissertation, Louisiana State University, 1958.

Thorndike, R. L. Review of *Pygmalion in the Classroom. American Educational Research Journal,* 1968, 5, 708-711.

Throop, W. F., and Macdonald, A. P. Internal-external locus of control: a bibliography. *Psychological Reports,* 1971, 28, 175-190.

Toews, A. Emotions and reading difficulties. *School and Community,* 1972, 58(8), 35.

Toller, G. S. Certain aspects of the self-evaluations made by achieving and retarded readers of average and above average intelligence. Unpublished doctoral dissertation, Temple University, 1967.

VanZandt, W. A study of some home-family-community factors related to children's achievement in reading in an elementary school. Unpublished doctoral dissertation, Wayne State University, 1963.

Vehar, M. A. Extraversion, introversion, and reading ability. *Reading Teacher,* 1968, 21, 357-360.

Wagner, S., and Wilde, J. E. Learning styles: can we grease the cogs in cognition? *Claremont Reading Conference,* 1973, 37, 135-142.

Wattenberg, W. W., and Clifford, C. Relation of self-concepts to beginning achievement in reading. *Child Development,* 1964, 35, 461-467.

Weiner, A. S., and Adams, W. V. The effect of failure and frustration on reflective and impulsive children. *Journal of Experimental Child Psychology,* 1974, 17, 353-359.

White, R. W. Motivation reconsidered; the concept of competence, *Psychological Review,* 1959, 66, 297-333.

Wiggins, R. V. A comparison of children's interest in and attitude towards reading material written in Standard and Black English forms. Unpublished doctoral dissertation, Ohio State University, 1971.

Witty, P. A. Reading success and emotional adjustment, *Elementary English Review,* 1950, 27, 296.

Zelniker, T., Cochavi, D., and Yered, J. The relationship between speed of performance and conceptual style: The effect of imposed modification of response latency. *Child Development,* 1974, 45(3), 779-784.

Zimmerman, L., and Allebrand, C. N. Personality characteristics and attitudes toward achievement of good and poor readers, *Journal of Educational Research,* 1965, 59, 28-30.

Reading Success and Personality Characteristics in Junior High School Students*

IRENE ATHEY
University of Rochester

JACK A. HOLMES
University of California at Berkeley

Theoretical Background

Although a continuous flow of articles attests to the increasing interest in the relationship of reading and personality factors, few researchers in this area derive their hypotheses directly from a comprehensive personality theory. The probable reason is that most personality theorists do not address themselves directly to problems of school learning, and certainly not to specific subject areas such as reading. Similarly, theories and models of reading are equally unpromising as sources of personality-related hypotheses, since their primary concern is with cognitive and linguistic factors.

Erikson's psychosocial theory (1959) would appear to be one of the more fruitful theories in this regard because it specifies the personality dimensions which are successively established from birth and especially during the crucial period when learning to read is considered a "developmental task" by the society. In brief, all those components of "the healthy personality" which precede or are concurrent with learning to read should, on this theory, be positively related to reading. Consequently, it was anticipated that the factors derived in this study would resemble those components.

Holmes' substrata-factor theory (1960) presents a model intended to portray the organization of the human mind engaged in the process of

*This research was supported by a grant from the U.S. Office of Education, Contract No. S-248, Bureau of Research, No. 5-9027-2-12-1. For the complete report see Athey and Holmes (1969).

reading. Incoming information is processed and stored in "substrata factors" which, neurologically speaking, may resemble subsystems of brain cell-assemblies (Hebb, 1949). These subsystems become interfacilitated by firing in phase. In this way, diverse appropriate subsets of information learned under different circumstances at different times, and hence stored in different parts of the brain, may be brought simultaneously into awareness when triggered by appropriate stimuli. A knowledge of the affective aspects of the incoming information is part of the substrata factor, and may be at the conscious or unconscious level. As a matter of fact, the affective (attitudinal, emotional, etc.) reactions to specific subsets of information are often deep-seated and inaccessible to consciousness, especially when the information is related to a person's views of himself and the nature of the physical and social world. Holmes calls these primitive belief systems "the deep-seated value systems, the fundamental ideas that the individual holds of himself, and his developing relationship to his environment . . . mobilizers [since they] function to select from one's repertoire of subabilities those which will maximize one's chances of solving a specific problem in particular, and forwarding the realization of self-fulfillment in general" (1960, p. 116). From Holmes' theory, it was therefore hypothesized that, if specific personality constellations related to reading could be isolated, they would be concerned with the individual's sense of self-worth and his attitudes toward other aspects of his home and school environment.

Finally, it was anticipated that the identified factors would contribute to the prediction of the criterion variable, reading achievement.

Purpose of the Study

The major purposes of the study were: 1) To integrate Erikson's theory on the development of a healthy personality with Holmes' theory of reading, and to derive from the integrated theory testable hypotheses regarding the contribution of specified personality characteristics to reading success. 2) To validate the findings, first by a double cross-validation; second, by a longitudinal study on the same sample; and third, by a longitudinal replication using cross-sectional samples 30 years later.

Hypotheses

The hypotheses derived from the integrated Erikson-Holmes theory stated: 1) That successful readers would exhibit those qualities which characterize the "healthy personality" (viz., positive self-concept, autonomy, basic trust, mastery of the environment, and freedom from neurotic anxiety), and 2) that each of these qualities would, as "mobilizers," make a significant contribution to reading success.

Tests

The Stanford Achievement Test, Paragraph Meaning, Form V (1932) was used as the reading criterion.

A double cross-validation following two-way item analysis of the University of California Inventory selected those items which exhibited discriminating power with respect to reading. A third and consolidating item analysis determined the content of the new inventory.

Samples and Procedures

In all, five samples were used in the study. Two samples were drawn from the longitudinal study (1933-1935) at the Institute of Human Development, University of California, Berkeley, and one of these (N = 160) was studied longitudinally in Grades 7, 8, and 9 (1933-1935); the other sample (N = 130) was used for cross-validation purposes. In addition, three comparable samples were selected from Grades 7, 8, and 9 in 1966 (N's = 143, 158, 112).

The study comprised three major phases: Construction of reading personality scales; Longitudinal validation; and Cross-sectional replication after 30 years.

First phase: Construction of reading-personality scales (the THEN phase)

1. *Item analysis.* The upper and lower 27 percent of Grade 9 (1935) students on the reading distribution were used to make an item analysis of the initial 328 items on the personality protocols of the *University of California Inventory.*
2. *Initial cross-validation.* The significant items were cross-validated on a totally new Grade 9 (1935) sample.
3. *Reciprocal cross-validation.* Procedures 1 and 2 were repeated, using the upper and lower 27 percent of the second sample for the item analysis; and the original sample was now used for the second cross-validation.

4. *Item analysis of pooled samples.* A third consolidating item analysis was performed on the 27 percent of the best and worst readers in the pooled Grade 9 samples (N = 290). An item was retained if it was a) significant at the 5 percent level and b) discriminated in the same direction in this *and* the two former analyses. Of the original 328 items, 70 survived the triple analyses.

5. *Pearson correlation.* All subjects in the two samples were rescored on the 70 discriminating items, and the resulting scores were correlated with reading. These correlations were all significant and also stable for the cross-validating samples. Table 1 demonstrates the improvement in correlation, and hence in predictive validity, obtained by selecting from the total inventory those items which discriminated between good and poor readers.

6. *Factor analysis.* The items were intercorrelated and submitted to a principal components factor analysis to determine whether they would cluster into scales descriptive of the personality characteristics hypothesized from theory. Seven factors were isolated and subsequently purified to form four scales which were interpreted as: I. *Social Independence,* II. *Self-Concept,* III. *School Dislikes,* and IV. *Self-Decision.*

Table 1.   Correlations between reading and the original and new scales of the U.C. inventory (1933 Samples)

Original scales (328 items)	Boys (N=78)	Girls (N=69)	Total (N=147)
Social maladjustment	.196	−.053	.072
Personal inferiority	−.019	−.308	−.157
Overstatement	−.185	−.267	−.220
Family maladjustment	.042	.029	.039
Physical symptoms	−.086	−.102	−.092
Fears	.087	.056	.047
Generalized tensions	−.182	.183	−.019
School maladjustment	−.001	−.133	−.047
New scale (70 items)	Boys (N=81)	Girls (N=79)	Total (N=160)
Same sample	.548	.455	.497
	(N=65)	(N=65)	(N=130)
Cross-validating sample	.455	.663	.563

Second phase: Longitudinal validation (the THEN phase)

7. *Correlation.* The personality protocols at the Grade 7 and 8 levels for the original Grade 9 sample were rescored for the purified scales. Correlations with reading were computed and compared for the three years (see Table 2).

Table 2. Comparison of correlations for personal-values inventory scales and reading for 7th, 8th, and 9th grades

		Grades	
Reading and	7th r_{cx}	8th r_{cx}	9th r_{cx}
I. Social Independence			
1933, '34, '35[a]	.219*	.211*	.219*
1966[b]	.062	.024	.238*
II. Self-Concept			
1933, '34, '35	.256*	.086	.388*
1966	.169*	.161*	.188*
III. School Dislikes			
1933, '34, '35	.136	.077	.077
1966	.095	.003	.059
IV. Self-Decision			
1933, '34, '35	.209*	.257*	.345*
1966	.308*	.427*	.221*
Total "Pure" Factors (I-IV)			
1933, '34, '35	.322*	.288*	.465*
1966	.245*	.317*	.318*

*Significantly different from zero ($a = .05$).

[a] 1933, 1934, 1935: N = 120.

[b] 1966: $N_7 = 143$, $N_8 = 158$, $N_9 = 112$.

Third phase: Cross-sectional Replication (the NOW phase)

8. *Correlation.* The same personality scales and the same reading criterion test used in the *then* phase were administered to new samples in Grades 7, 8, and 9 in 1966. The 30 (3 grades x 4 scales + 3 totals for the *then* and *now* samples) means and correlations were

examined within and between the longitudinal and the cross-sectional samples for the two groups.

9. *Multiple correlation.* For each of the six years (Grades 7, 8, and 9 in 1933-1935 and in 1966), the best predictor scales were included in multiple correlations using reading as the criterion variable.

10. *Socioeconomic status.* Finally, a comparison of the correlations of S.E.S. versus the new personality scale with reading was made.

Results and Conclusions

1. An integrated personality and reading theory can provide a strong theoretical framework within which research in this area may be pursued in meaningful directions.

2. Specific personality characteristics, hypothesized from an integrated Erikson-Holmes theory, have been shown to be consistently related to reading in the 7th, 8th, and 9th Grades and for two similar age groups separated by some 30 years.

3. Social independence, a positive self-concept, and the desire and ability to make one's own decisions (with freedom from anxiety for making those decisions) constitute a syndrome that is clearly related to reading at the junior high school level.

4. The new personality inventory correlated more highly with reading achievement than did the socioeconomic status of the subjects (see Table 3).

5. *On the average, the best estimate is that these value-saturated personality scales account for 13 percent of the variance of reading success at the junior high school level* (see Table 4).

6. The combined techniques of item analysis, two-way cross-validation, and factor analysis provide an effective method for constructing new value-saturated personality scales that can be shown to have a specific and demonstrated relationship to reading achievement.

7. The newly constructed scales should be extended in line with the theoretical aspects hypothesized from personality theory. Since Erikson's

theory has provided valuable insights into the possible mutual development in the *individual* of reading and certain aspects of personality in accordance with the mobilizer hypothesis of Holmes, further research should examine other promising concepts such as basic trust and initiative. The present findings suggest the need for constructing valid and reliable scales to measure these concepts in order to extend the application of the integrated theory, especially to minority groups and earlier age levels.

8. Research in the area of personality as it relates to reading is difficult and arduous but, if pursued relentlessly, it can produce reliable and valid results of psychological and educational significance.

Table 3.   Comparative correlations between reading and (a) total (I-IV) inventory and (b) socioeconomic status

Variables	THEN Sample	r_{cx}
	7th *(1933)*	
Total (I-IV) Inventory		.322
Socioeconomic Status		-.170*
	8th *(1934)*	
Total (I-IV) Inventory		.288
Socioeconomic Status		-.277*
	9th *(1935)*	
Total (I-IV) Inventory		.465
Socioeconomic Status		-.240*

*The correlation is negative simply because the socioeconomic scale weights the occupations in an inverse order:

    I & II.   Professionals, proprietors, managers with some college education.

       III.   Small shopkeepers, clerks, salespersons, skilled workers of high educational status.

       IV.   Skilled manual workers.

       V.   Unskilled workers with minimal education.

Table 4.　　Comparison of multiple R's, derived from a best weighting of the subscales of the inventory for predicting reading achievement, with zero-order r's derived by summing raw scores of subscales of the inventory and correlating the total with reading achievement

Sample	$\beta{\cdot}r$	$\beta{\cdot}r$	$\beta{\cdot}r$	Comparable correlations	
				Unadjusted	Adjusted
7th Grade					
1933 $\overline{R}_{C{\cdot}II,\ I,\ IV}$ = (.21) (.26) + (.16) (.22) + (.12) (.21)				= .337[a]	302
1933 $r_{C{\cdot}(I\text{-}IV)}$ ·				.322	322
1966 $\overline{R}_{C{\cdot}IV,\ II,\ I}$ = (.31) (.31) + (.17) (.17) + (−.02) (.06)				= .350	322
1966 $r_{C{\cdot}(I\text{-}IV)}$ ·				.245	245
8th Grade					
1934 $\overline{R}_{C{\cdot}IV,\ I,\ II}$ = (.23) (.26) + (.19) (.21) + (.04) (.09)				= .324	286
1934 $r_{C{\cdot}(I\text{-}IV)}$ ·				.288	288
1966 $\overline{R}_{C{\cdot}IV,\ II,\ I}$ = (.44) (.43) + (.19) (.16) + (−.05) (.02)				= .464	447
1966 $r_{C{\cdot}(I\text{-}IV)}$ ·				.317	317
9th Grade					
1935 $\overline{R}_{C{\cdot}II,\ IV,\ I}$ = (.36) (.39) + (.33) (.35) + (.04) (.22)				= .512	493
1935 $r_{C{\cdot}(I\text{-}IV)}$ ·				.465	465
1966 $\overline{R}_{C{\cdot}I,\ IV,\ II}$ = (.17) (.24) + (.20) (.22) + (.18) (.19)				= .343	305
1966 $r_{C{\cdot}(I\text{-}IV)}$ ·				.318	318

[a]I. Social Independence, II. Self-Concept, IV. Self-Decision, (I-IV). Total of "Pure" Factors (including III. School Dislikes).

REFERENCES

Athey, I., and Holmes, J. A. *Reading Success and Personality Characteristics in Junior High School Students.* Berkeley: University of California Press, 1969.

Erikson, E. H. Identity and the life-cycle. In Klein, G. S. (Ed.), *Psychological Issues,* New York: Basic Books, 1959, 18-171.

Hebb, D. O. *The Organization of Behavior.* New York: Wiley, 1949.

Holmes, J. A. The substrata-factor theory of reading: Some experimental evidence. In Figurel, J. A. (Ed.). *New Frontiers in Reading.* Proceedings of the Fifth Annual Conference of the International Reading Association. New York: Scholastic Magazines, 1960, 115-121.

Cultural Interaction

Achieving School Failure: An Anthropological Approach to Illiteracy and Social Stratification[*]

R. P. MCDERMOTT[**]

Stanford University

Introduction

This chapter is divided into four sections. The first defines a problem and asks a question. The problem is that children from minority communities appear to regenerate their parents' pariah status by learning how to act in ways condemned by the larger host community. The question asks where this learning comes from and whether or not it represents a rational adaptation to socialization attempts by host schools.

The second section examines the production of pariah-host social organizations in terms of what both pariah and host members must know about the daily business of treating each other as pariahs and hosts. Early experiences in the politics of everyday life determine the categories children develop for use in deciding how to act in similar situations at future times. In other words, the politics of everyday life socialize the identities, statuses and abilities of children and, as such, are the source of the persistence of social organizations, including pariah groups, across generations.

*Reprinted from George Spindler (Ed.), *Education and Cultural Process: Toward an Anthropology of Education*. New York: Holt, Rinehart, and Winston, 1974, 82-118. With permission of author and Holt, Rinehart, and Winston, Publisher. Comments on an earlier draft of this chapter were generously offered by Eric Arrow, Jacob Bilmes, Nancie Gonzalez, Robert McDermott, Harry Singer, and Stanley Wanat. I am most heavily indebted to Henry Beck, Harumi Befu, Charles Frake, Karl Pribram, and George Spindler for constant stimulation, encouragement and constructive criticism during the past two years. Even with their excellent counsel, however, the paper may harbor errors for which I am alone responsible.

**Now at Rockefeller University.

The third section discusses an example. Specifically, the social organization of learning to read in a host teacher and pariah student classroom is examined in terms of the politics of everyday life. For black American children in white-administered schools, it is argued that competence in reading and competence in classroom politics are inversely proportional. Inability to read is positively condemned by the host population and assures oppression and the assignment of pariah status by the host community. Nevertheless, not learning to read is accompanied by all the social skills essential to a peer-defined political success within the classroom. In peer group terms, it represents more of an achievement than a disability. Accordingly, the hypothesis examined is that a significant number of what are usually described as reading disabilities represent situationally induced inattention patterns which make sense in terms of the politics of the interethnic classroom. Pariah children learn not to read as one way of acquiring high status and strong identity in a host classroom.

The fourth section describes a starting point for culturally induced learning disabilities in terms of cultural or communicative code differences and conflicts. Specifically, it is hypothesized that minor differences in communicative codes can lead to disasters in everyday life. On the basis of communicative code conflicts, teachers classify their students into ability groups. Although in no way related in the first grade to potential reading or social leadership skills, the teacher's classificatory schema has great influence as a self-fulfilling prophecy. Many pariah children adapt to the senseless and degrading relational messages given them by unknowing teachers with different communicative codes by shutting down their attention skills in response to teacher tasks such as reading. Communicative code conflicts between black children and white teachers are discussed in detail, and the high rate of black school failure is tentatively explained.

The Ontogeny of Pariah Minorities

Most modern nations harbor one or more *pariah groups* "actively rejected by the host population because of behavior or characteristics positively condemned" by host group standards (Barth 1969:31). Host standards can be violated by an absurd collection of traits ranging from skin color and occupational specialties to culinary and sexual preferences. What is interesting is the persistence of both host group standards and pariah groups across generations. Even in the face of efforts by modern states to subdue the arbitrary and oppressive standards of host groups and to accommodate minority behavior patterns by programs of rationalization and equalization, pariah groups endure. For example, America has blacks, Native Americans, and Hispanic people; Japan has the Koreans (Mitchell 1967) and the racially indistinct Burakamin (DeVos and Wagatsuma 1966); Norway, the Lapps (Eidheim 1969); Northern Ireland, the Catholics; India, the outcasts; and Israel, the Oriental Jews. In all these groups, each generation of children will renew their parents' life styles, apparently oblivious to the condemnation and oppression that pariah status vis-à-vis the host group will bring down upon their heads.

How does this happen? How is pariah status acquired by each new generation? Despite years of special education, minority American children continue to speak low esteem dialects, fail in school, and attain occupational specialties which run afoul of public morality and legality. Apparently, the acquisition of pariah behavior patterns is a very complex process rooted in everyday life and is not going to be altered by formal training in a classroom for a few hours a week. Indeed, most pariah behavior patterns need not be altered. Black language, for example, bears a pariah label, but it is a perfectly efficient mode of communication with special social functions within the black community (Labov 1969). To treat it as an inferior or deprived language is wrong. To meddle with its use by way of a language arts program in order to homogenize it with the host language is not only wrong, but also naive. It indicates that we understand very little about how people acquire models of and guides to behavior in their own society and how these models are used to generate social structures complete with stratification. This chapter will attempt a better understanding of the acquisition of social structure (Cicourel 1970a)—how children acquire what has to be known in order to act in a culturally or subculturally appropriate way in specific social situations (Frake 1962, 1973).

Two positions are usually taken on the acquisition of pariah social status. To the distant observer and the pariah group member, it seems an obvious case of host populations working to defeat the efforts of each and every pariah child to break the degradation that bonds him without reason from his first day out of the womb. The child is simply tagged as he enters the world in such a way that the tag is available for all to see. Negative differential behavior is then applied to all the tagged regardless of acquired skills. Racial markers can, of course, do this job most efficiently: witness black America. Similar systems have been attempted without racial markers. Tattooing is one possibility. The Japanese of the Tokugawa era attempted another by having all members of the pariah Burakumin wear leather squares on the outside of all their garments

(Cornell 1970). The point is that pariah children are made visible to all, defined as deviant because of their visibility, and treated badly as a result.

There is a good reason for viewing the ascriptive system just described as too simple a representation of the acquisition of a particular status in a social structure. First, such clear-cut boundaries between host and pariah groups are seldom defined. Racial boundaries are not available in most societies in which there are pariah group problems. In fact, most observers must live in an area for a long time before they can start distinguishing between groups. The codes are subtle. Religion, language, dress and the minutiae of nonverbal communication very often function as markers for ascription. Even where biological boundaries can be drawn, as may be the case for outcastes in India, it takes either a native's eye or an anthropometrist's calipers to do the job (Beteille 1972). In such cases, identification involves much social work on the part of the interactants. The host population must be keyed to spotting certain cues, and the pariah population must in some way send off the cues which will allow them to be identified and abused.

A second problem with viewing status ascription as a simple tagging process is that in most contemporary societies such overt ascription is frowned upon by both legal constitutions and popular ideologies. Formal organizations which operate according to ascriptive criteria are officially prohibited. Japan and America stand out as two countries which have done a great deal to minimize overt ascription with universal schooling and uniform testing procedures for the placement of personnel in both the public and private sectors of their economies (Azumi 1969; Parsons 1959). Yet pariah boundaries remain firm, even within the school systems themselves (Shimahara 1971; Cicourel and Kitsuse 1963). Again it appears that something more than ascription is going on. How else could it be that, even after the demise of formal institutional powers to identify and operate against pariah people, pariah groups survive? The host population does not simply slot a child on the basis of its parentage and then keep a careful eye out for the child so that he never advances a slot. Rather, it seems as if the child must learn how to do it himself; he must learn a way of acting normally which the host population will be able to condemn according to the criteria the hosts have learned for evaluating, albeit arbitrarily, their own normal behavior. Pariah status appears almost as achieved as ascribed.

An alternative to the distant observer's view of the acquisition of pariah social status is the view of a host population native who usually sees in pariahs an obvious case of inferior persons begetting inferior persons. The argument is that pariah children acquire their low status because they are inferior. Unfortunately, each new pariah generation often reaffirms the soundness of the host's classificatory schema by apparently learning the codes of behavior essential to the schema's maintenance. Although there is no evidence that host classifications are accurate assessments of the natural order of people and their abilities, the host perception of pariah group behavior may not always be totally blinded by prejudice. Hosts may merely see what is there for them to see given the standards of evaluation that they use uniformly on all people regardless of race or ethnic identity. The question is, how is it that what is there for them to see is in fact there?

Consider an extreme example. The Burakumin minority in Japan has suffered a long history of political suppression due to its participation in condemned occupational specialties (Ninomiya 1933). Since the formal breakdown of the caste system during the Mejii Restoration a century ago, many Burakumin have attempted unsuccessfully to pass into the mainstream of Japanese life. At present, they are physically, linguistically, religiously, and, for the most part, occupationally indistinct from other Japanese. They can be discovered only on the basis of either their present or past residence in known Burakumin ghettos. Accordingly, most Japanese teachers are unaware of a child's Burakumin status in the early grades (Shimahara 1971). Yet, by puberty, a Burakumin identity will be visible and of increasing importance, as there is an increasing differential in the performances of Burakumin as opposed to non-Burakumin pupils. They lag behind on I.Q. and achievement tests and daily attendance, and they are the first to engage in delinquent activities (DeVos and Wagatsuma 1966; Brameld 1968). How does host group prejudice work against an invisible group? Obviously, it does not. It may be that unconscious host group standards work against Burakumin children in some subtle ways, however, for the children are eventually made visible, sorted out and condemned. But this is not obvious to a liberal and enlightened Japanese teacher, who, through no apparent fault of his own, winds up doing exactly the same job that a prejudiced teacher might do: he winds up failing many more Burakumin than non-Burakumin. The host-group stand appears strong. The teacher has only reacted to what was available for him to see, namely, obviously inferior performances by many Burakumin children. Again, pariah status seems almost as achieved as ascribed.

This Burakumin example sheds great light on this ascription versus inherent acquisition issue. The Burakumin child experiences teachers as prejudiced beings who inflict failing biographies on Burakumin children. The children are perhaps correct given the subtleties of interclass or interethnic communication. They are incorrect in viewing their school records as products of a blind ascription, for their invisibility protects them from such a fate. Host teachers have equally confusing experiences with school failure. They are correct in not assuming complete blame for the high rate of Burakumin school failure. Nevertheless, they are incorrect in viewing school failure as the result of an inherent acquisition, the unfolding of an inferior genetic stock or, at best, the unfolding of an inferior socialization process that leaves the child deprived. First, the Burakumin do not represent a gene pool (Taira 1971). Second, the social disadvantage perspective is almost as simplistic as the ascription stand, for it has never been able to account for how children with failing school records do so well in complex settings outside of school. Learning to talk and learning to behave sensibly in everyday life are far more complex than the tasks learned in school, and most so-called disadvantaged children excel at both, at least to the extent that such children have been carefully studied. Disadvantage is indeed a too simple, and often biased, account of minority school failure. Burakumin children do not come to school disadvantaged; they leave school disadvantaged. The question is, without some ascriptive mechanism working against them, how does this school failure and consequent disadvantage come about? In other words, if neither ascription nor inherent acquisition can completely account for pariah school failure, then how can the acquisition of pariah status be conceived?

A third position is possible. From their respective vantage points, both the pariah and the host groups are correct. To the pariah group, host behavior is indeed oppressive. To the host group, pariah behavior is indeed inadequate. If we understand how the two groups find this out about each other, we will have located the central problem. What is it that pariah people do that has host people react in oppressive ways, even if they do not want to be oppressive? And what is it that host people do that has pariah people react in antithesis to host expectations, even as they struggle to behave adequately according to host standards? If such misunderstandings take place very often in the early grades, the results can be disastrous. Once a host teacher treats a child as inadequate, the child will find the teacher oppressive. Often, once a child finds a teacher oppressive, the child will start behaving inadequately. After such a point, relations between the child and the teacher regress—the objectionable behavior of each will feed back negatively into the objectionable behavior of the other.

It is in this context that a third position makes sense: a child must achieve his pariah status. It is neither ascribed to the child nor naturally acquired by him in the sense that puberty is acquired. First, some form of miscommunication between a child and his teacher must take place. If this is not repaired quickly, a mutually destructive or regressive one-to-one relationship (Scheflen 1960) will be established between the teacher and the child. When teacher-student communication is complicated by interethnic code differences, regressive relations occur with enough frequency to result in the children forming alternatives to the teacher's organization of the classroom. Within the confines of these new social organizations, the children work at becoming visible. As a result, they leave themselves open to even further condemnation. The teacher's role as the administrator in charge of failure becomes dominant. And the children's revolt grows. School work gets caught in this battle, and a high rate of school failure results. A great deal of social work must be performed by both teachers and students in order for so many failures to occur. Whether the records list all passing or all failing grades, student records represent achievements in the sense that many difficult battles in the politics of everyday life had to be fought in their making. Teachers do not simply ascribe minority children to failure. Nor do minority children simply drag failure along, either genetically or socially, from the previous generation. Rather, it must be worked out in every classroom, every day, by every teacher and every child in their own peculiar ways.

Viewing school failure as an achievement implies that school failure can be understood as a rational adaptation by children to human relations in host schools. The rest of this chapter will be aimed at showing just that. The next section will consider, theoretically, how human relations are worked out face-to-face in the classroom. These relations have fantastic implications for the social organization of the classroom—who gets to interact with whom, when, and about what and who gets to learn from whom, when, and about what. In short, face-to-face relations help to organize status and abilities in the classroom. In the last two sections, the interference of interethnic human relations on learning to read is examined for black Americans.

The Social Organization of Status and the Politics of Everyday Life

It is considered a social fact (although actually it is either a native or a professional sociological model, but it is always treated as a fact) that there are different groups in the social organizations of modern states, and some of these are defined as pariah groups. It is this social fact that most social scientists want to explain. Beneath this fact, however, there are many other facts made of the little stuff of everyday life that helps produce larger social facts or patterns available for observation. A social organization is not a thing in itself as Durkheim would have us believe. Rather, it is an accomplishment, the product of great work in the everyday life of innumerable social actors. The term "social organization" is a shorthand term for the organization of social actions performed by social actors (Garfinkel 1956:181; cf. also, Miller, Galanter, and Pribram, 1960:98). The term social organization glosses all the hard work of social actors attempting to deal with each other. It hides all the achievements of everyday life. Social organizations are daily accomplishments, daily products of actors working out rational ways of dealing with each other.

If a social organization shows a division into pariah and host groups, then this is a division produced in everyday life; in their daily dealings, pariah and host people must classify each other into different groups and then treat each other in accordance with the dictates of their classification. Such a division cannot be taken by itself as a topic of our inquiry, for it is a mere gloss of the social acts that make it look like a fact. We must go deeper and ask how this fact is available for seeing and naming by either host or pariah members or the ethnographer. Let us examine, then, not that fact of such pariah-host relationships, the resource, but the fact of the fact, the topic; let us ask how it is that the persons involved in such relationships manage to organize and produce such relationships and to take them as the substance of everyday life (Beck 1972); let us "examine not the factual properties of status hierarchies, but the *fact* of the factual properties of status hierarchies" (Zimmerman and Pollner 1970:83). How is it then that host and pariah people, and the sociologists who study them, come to see their existence as related groups as facts?

The question we started with was how do the children of each generation acquire pariah status. This question has shifted somewhat in our discussion, and we must now ask how children learn to uniformly produce pariah-host statuses in their interactions with each other and their teachers. The designated statuses are not simple, cut and dried slots into which members of different groups are easily placed. *Statuses* do not specify everything that occurs in an interaction; rather they are the labels "used by the observer and actor as practical language games for simplifying the task of summarizing a visual field and complex stimuli that are difficult to describe in some precise, detailed way" (Cicourel 1970b:21). Status labels never reduce the complex stimulus fields so much that social life becomes easy. There is always interaction work to be done; social life is always in process.

One's place in a society is not easily acquired. Even if it is the lowest place on the stratification ladder, it is not simply worn as a piece of clothing. A selective way of seeing oneself in the position and of seeing others in relation to oneself must be developed. As Becker has written, an actor acquires a "symbolic mansion" established and maintained in interaction with other human beings; the symbols develop early in ontogeny and prescribe for the actor what situations he should attend, "what he should do in a particular social situation, and how he should feel about himself as he does it" (Becker 1962:84). Statuses, therefore, must be learned. Depending on how they are learned, a child develops specific identities and abilities for use in specific situations. First they are learned in the home in everyday interaction with family members. Many of these first statuses, identities, and abilities undergo considerable alterations in school on the basis of everyday interaction with class members and especially the teacher. School-specific social and intellectual skills must therefore be understood in terms of the politics of everyday life in the classroom. If the skills developed at home are relevant to what happens in the classroom, or if new skills must be developed, they will be visible, and they will make sense in terms of the politics of the classroom.

The *politics of everyday life* are built on messages of relationship passed between two or more social actors. According to Bateson's classic distinction, communication involves not only the transfer of information, but also the imposition of a relationship (Bateson 1972). A communicative act not only has a content which it reports, it also has command aspects which stipulate the relationship between the communicants. An army sergeant sends out messages of relationship with his uniform and an annoyed wife with her hands on her hips. These relational messages form the context for the transfer of information by classifying its intent (Watzlawick, Beaven, and Jackson 1967:54). Such a context is read by the interpreter of a communicative act before the content of a message is attended. Thus, with open arms one sets a context which can be interpreted as specifying a love relationship, and everything said after that point will be measured for its value in this context; open arms with a gun in each hand asserts a different context and the information transferred, assuming one does not flee in fear of being shot, is understood differently. In both contexts the host may inform his guest that he has been anxiously awaiting his arrival, but the information transferred would be quite different depending upon the message of relationship sent off before any words were spoken.

Children are extremely well equipped by school age for entrance into the politics of everyday life. Messages of relationship are handled competently by neonates (Caudill and Weinstein 1969) and constitute the only form of communication allowed the child in its early years (Blurton-Jones 1972). Love, hate, support, antagonism, trust and deference are some of the relational messages transferred in daily life. Indeed, apparently few concerted practical activities are possible without the communication of such messages; even a slight eruption in their flow can cause a social breakdown (Garfinkel 1963). Children are especially expert in handling these messages as they have not yet developed competence in the verbal arts of saying what is not meant and interpreting what is not intended. Relational messages are more rooted in nonverbal channels which allow for more leakage and clues to deception than verbal channels (Ekman and Friesan 1969), and children decipher these without hindrance from message content.

At school age, the point at which children start acquiring their institutional biographies, relational messages continue in their dominance over information transfer. This is a decisive and delicate time in a child's life. School success, an essential ingredient in any child's avoidance of pariah status, is dependent upon high levels of information transfer. In these early stages of school, depending upon how the politics of everyday life are handled, the child defines his relations with his classmates and his teachers. These relations, remember, define the context of whatever information is to be transferred by a communicant. If the wrong messages of relationship are communicated, reading, writing, and arithmetic may take on very different meanings than they do for the child who is more successful in getting good feelings from the politics of the classroom. The wrong messages of relationship can result in learning disabilities. More will be said on this issue later. At present it is only essential to realize that children deal seriously in relationships, are profoundly affected by their abilities to do relational work, and acquire a social status and attendant skills on the basis of their successes and failures.

Let us try to describe the setting in which relational work is performed. Its general properties are really well known. Goffman (1963) has described the "primal sociological event" as one in which a person with an obvious stigma, no nose, for example, encounters a person without a stigma; in such a case, a tremendous amount of work must go into unspoken arrangements about how the two are to look at each other, at the nose, around the nose, or at the ground. Looking in this situation carries powerful relational messages. One has the power to induce confusion, embarrassment, anger, fright, trust, or love. The eyes will tell the stigmatized whether he has met a person with a similar stigma, with an acquaintance and understanding of the stigma, or with a fear or hate of the stigma. Goffman's point is that we all suffer from stigma of sorts. Every interaction is marked by some hiding and some probing. How much must be hidden, how much probing can go on, or indeed, whether hiding and probing are necessary at all, is dependent upon the messages of relationship exchanged. A policeman's uniform usually invokes hiding on ego's part and allows for probing on the policeman's part. Sexually suggestive clothing does the opposite. In the first case, ego shuts down, and in the second, an opening up is usually called forth. Situations in which these same cues invoke the opposite reactions can be imagined. The effort is to make as much sense as possible of the person's actions, to infer his intentions, and to then react sensibly given the intentions of both interactants (Schutz 1953).

The cues available in any situation are endless. People can send messages with their ecological setting, e.g., whether they are in a bar or a church (Barker 1968; J. McDermott 1969; Sommer 1969); with their posture (Scheflen 1964); with their spacing vis-à-vis their interpreter (Hall 1966); with their odor (Largey and Watson 1972); with their gaze (Kendon 1967); with their tone of voice (Crystal 1972; Laver 1968); with their sequencing of body and voice rhythms (Condon and Ogston 1966, 1971; Byers 1971; Kendon 1970, 1973); and so on. Everything available to the senses of the actors constitutes a possible contribution to the sense and rationality of an interaction.

More than the success of the interaction rides on how sensibly it can be made. Something important happens to the way in which the stigmatized person is going to interpret his next interaction; if one is treated to understanding and sympathy on one occasion, the next occasion will be attended and scanned for messages in a very different way than if the original interaction resulted in a fight. The selective perception skills that are carried from one situation to another of similar type, following Cicourel (1970b), are called status. In addition to his status, the stigmatized individual's feelings can undergo alteration. In talking about formative experiences during puberty, Erikson has noted that "it is of great relevance to the young individual's identity formation that he be responded to and be given function and status as a person whose gradual transformation makes sense to those who begin to make sense to him" (1968:156). Both status and identity are developed in daily interactions. A great deal is at stake in each and every one of them, for status and identity breakdowns are also developed in daily interactions.

An example of the social organization of status and identity in a classroom may be helpful here. Teachers often break their classes into ability groups in order to simplify their administration of the classroom. Not only the level of work engaged in, but also the people interacted with and the kind of feedback received from the teachers all depend upon the group to which the child is assigned. In this way, the teacher organizes the statuses and identities of the children in the class. What is most interesting is that the children seldom reject their assignment—even if they are assigned the lowest status in the classroom achievement hierarchy, they most often accept it as if it makes sense. If the child does not like his assignment, he may buckle down and work harder to catch the rest of the class. But revolt is seldom attempted. The reason is that the teacher generally assigns children to groups according to the same criteria that the children themselves use in their dealings with each other, and the same criteria that the children's parents and the rest of their community use in their dealings with the children. In short, the teacher handles the children in a way the children are used to being handled. Politically, the teacher, the children and the child's community are in harmony. Even if being placed in a low ability group is not good for the child's ego, the results of grouping, if it makes sense, will not be disastrous. The politics of everyday life in the classroom will be identical to the politics of everyday life outside the classroom, and the children's world will be in order.

The social organization of status and identity sometimes does not go so smoothly. Consider the case of an intense, bright child who arrives in school unable to keep up in reading because of some developmental lag specific to processing printed information. When this child is assigned to the lowest ability group, it makes no sense to him. He is treated as a gifted learner and a sociometric star outside the classroom; anything less than equivalent treatment in the classroom will be inadequate to the child's way of evaluating his place in the world. Of course, he revolts and "a negative motivational cycle" begins to take shape (Singer and Beardsley 1970). Later, the possibilities of a host group teacher successfully grouping minority children into the same ability groups that the minority community might inself perceive will be considered. From the high rate of revolt and "negative motivational cycles" in minority classrooms, the possibilities seem slim. The point here is that the politics of everyday life socially organize a classroom. Ability groupings help a teacher to isolate into accessible units children who are to receive fairly similar messages of relationship from the teacher. If the wrong children are assigned to the low ability groups, they will reject the messages of relationship forwarded from the teacher. They will demand a political reorganization of the classroom, one that is more commensurate with their statuses and identities outside the classroom. In the early weeks of a school year, the politics of the classroom feed the teacher's perception, and the classroom is organized accordingly. Then the children reorganize the class according to their own perceptions. If the teacher is insensitive to their demands, the remainder of the year can be occupied in small battles over each child's status and identity within the classroom. Whether or not anything is ever accomplished in the classroom depends upon how quickly these battles can be resolved. Thus, the development of abilities and disabilities also depends upon the politics of daily classroom life.

The specific division of abilities and disabilities among any pariah and host groups should be understood in terms of the politics of everyday life. It is in the very small political arenas constituted by dyads and only slightly larger groups that social organizations are produced. If we want to understand a large scale organizational division within a social organization, we must start asking how this division is produced. Pariah and host group members acquire different skills and produce the different behavior that makes for the organizational division between pariah and host groups. The division looks so real that we professional social scientists study it, and lay social scientists, or natives, perceive and use it as a model for their dealings with each other. In fact, the division is dependent for its existence on the daily differential use of abilities and disabilities by host and pariah group members. The employment of these abilities and disabilities depends upon man's delightful capacity to attend to, think about, and manipulate only certain selected aspects of his environment. Just what parts of an environment are attended and mastered depends upon the social meaning of the environment as recorded in the experiences of the developing child. For example, reading materials can or cannot be attended depending upon whether looking in a book is an acceptable activity in a particular social milieu and whether books contain information helpful to operating in a particular social environment. The social organization of reading materials will now be considered in more detail.

A Biobehavioral Ethnography of Reading Disabilities

Black children in America have a high rate of learning disabilities. Rates of functional black illiteracy are estimated around 50 percent (Thompson 1966) as compared to 10 percent for white Americans and only 1 percent for Japan (Makita 1968). The high rates of these disabilities do not point to a high rate of genetic inferiority, neurological damage, language deprivation, or any of the other intrapsychic causes suggested in social and behavioral science literature. Rather, the high rates of learning disorders point to learned patterns of selective inattention developed in the politics of everyday life in the classroom. Status and identity work is a dismal failure in early elementary school for many black children with white teachers and, as a result, they turn off, in the sense that they physiologically shut down. As a yoga or Zen master (Kasamatsu and Hirai

1966) may do for an entire environment, black children disattend reading materials and join their peers in the student subculture within the class. Reading disabilities and school failure result.

School failure is an important place to start an inquiry into the acquisition of pariah status, and social science literature on pariah group persistence across generations has often centered on school failure and its causes. Most of the work has centered on the children, independent of the schools they attend, as if there was something naturally wrong with their brains. To paraphrase crudely, the cause of pariah groups is that pariah children do not seem to think too well. This deprivation theme should be fairly offensive to social science; after all, has not a century of anthropology shown that to understand people is to discern difference and not deprivation? Yet the anthropological argument is difficult. Pariah children fail, and fail miserably. How can we claim that they are neither damaged nor deprived? One answer is that we have been measuring achievements with a biased set of standards. Achievements are realized only in particular situations. Rather than attempting to measure the development of absolute capacities that a child uses for all situations through time, perhaps we should center on the situations in which and for which particular skills are acquired. In other words, if we examine the classroom as a set of situations or an "occasion corpus" (Zimmerman and Pollner 1970), a child's failing performance on classroom tests might appear to be something of a situational achievement. Deprivation hypotheses are considerably weakened, if, instead of just looking at the skills stored in children's bodies, we look also at the social contexts in which the skills are turned into achievements.

Medicine, education, and psychology have all produced deprivation hypotheses for social scientists to adopt. Of late, pariah children have been described as genetically inferior (Jensen 1969). Another claim has it that an unspecified number suffer brain damage due to the poverty and ignorance that burdened their mothers in pregnancy and birth (Birch and Gussow 1970). Social science itself has had a hand in claiming that pariah children suffer perceptual handicaps (C. Deutsch 1968; Jensen 1966) and conceptual and linguistic handicaps (M. Deutsch 1963; Bernstein 1964; Entwisle 1971) due to low social class and its associated life-style. All these disciplines assume to discover facts out of context, raw facts about the world and the behavior of its inhabitants. Of course there are no such things. All behavior is context-bound. More important, all behavior is indexical or dependent upon our interpretation of the context in which the behavior is situated (Bar-Hillel 1954; Beck 1972; Cicourel, in press). Yet all assume that facts are available for all to see, and that these facts are invariable. In the case of learning disabilities, each discipline has assumed that whatever is located in the heads of the children studied is invariable. Whether a discipline uses a perceptual, cognitive, or language test, a projective technique or a sociometric status score, each has assumed that it describes the skills the individual has acquired for all occasions and tasks. That is, of course, incorrect. Each of these disciplines assumes too much.

My proposal is that each of these disciplines is describing the same social processes and merely indexing them differently. Scores on perceptual, intelligence, attitude, language competence, and even neurological tests are all remnants of the normal and practical work of persons in a particular situation. Ways of perceiving, thinking, feeling, talking, and the activities of the neural wetware processing our perceiving, thinking, feeling, and talking are all dependent upon the situations in which the person is placed. Testing offers a particular situation which may record little more than the way the subject defines the testing situation in response to the way in which the subject understands the tester's definition of the situation. In short, test scores always have discernible roots in the social world in which they take place (Cicourel, in press). We cannot expect tests to necessarily reveal very much about intrapsychic events and the capabilities of any subject. But tests can, if they are properly read, tell a great deal about interpsychic, social procedures in which a subject is engaged. For example, Cazden (1970) has described black children who do badly on language complexity tests in formal situations, and very well in informal situations; the opposite holds true for white children. What we can learn from such tests has nothing to do with a child's capacity to talk; but there is a great deal of information about social organization stored in this little test. Social organizations are made by people knowing approximately what to do in particular situations; a social organization is a cognitive phenomenon. When we look to tests for information about social organization, about the thinking underlying the social acts to be performed during the test, then they are very revealing.

Reading tests can significantly reveal the dynamics of social organization. Pariah children do very badly at them, almost certainly for social reasons. Reading is an act which apparently aligns the black child with the "wrong" forces in the social universe. In the classroom social organization produced by the politics of everyday life, reading takes its place as part of the teacher's "ecology of games" (Long 1958). To read is to accept these games and all the statuses and identities that accompany them. Not to read is to accept peer group games and their accompanying statuses and identities. In other words, given a particular social organization, reading failure is a social achievement. Conventional testing procedures could never reveal this trend. The battle grounds on which it is determined whether a child learns to read or not are drawn by the statuses and identities made available by the teacher and the peer group, in short, by social relations. If the teacher and the children can play the same games, then reading and all other school materials will be easily absorbed.

The success of educational settings directed by ethnic (Alitto 1969; Hostetler and Huntington 1971) and dialect (Fishman and Leuders-Salmon 1972) minorities for themselves illustrates this point nicely. If the children and the teacher generate their behavior from a shared set of interpretive procedures, efficient classroom learning can almost be assumed. This record contrasts, however, with educational settings designed and administered by outsiders to a community. Such settings often result in school failure. Centuries of failure in the white education of American Indians and blacks and Japanese failures in the education of Korean and Truk natives (Fisher 1961) illustrate this contrasting situation. If the classroom is divided into two separate worlds with teachers and students occupying different ecologies of games, school failure appears to be inevitable. The identities and statuses offered by a school system without roots in the community are apparently not worth seeking or are worth avoiding. For many children in such a situation, a social reorganization of the classroom becomes the main alternative to following the teacher's dictates.

An essential question at this point is how the politics of everyday life get inside a child's body and dictate what shall be perceived. This question can now easily be handled by recent advances in neuropsychology. Not all biology is reductionist, and there is good reason to attempt a view of social life by an examination of the biological foundations of behavior. Geertz alerted us to this possibility in his account of the dynamic, feedback relationship between biology and culture.

> As our central nervous system—and most particularly its crowning curse and glory, the neocortex—grew up in great part in interaction with culture, it is incapable of directing our behavior or organizing our experience without the guidance provided by systems of significant symbols . . . Such symbols are thus not mere expressions, instrumentalities, or correlates of our biological, psychological, and social existence; they are prerequisites of it. Without men, no culture, certainly; but equally, and more significantly, without culture, no men (1965:61).

Attention is the mechanism by which our bodies help us divide the world into significant and insignificant. As Wallace has suggested, man has created a rich and elaborate world for himself "by a process of selective attention to his total environment" (1965:277). Apparently, man suffers tremendous limitations in his ability to process all the information available to him at any one instant. Selection is a ubiquitous and unending process throughout our central nervous systems. Significance is stored not only in the social world, in the symbols out there, but in our equipment for decoding and interpreting the world. As Pribram has indicated, "societies are made up of persons whose brains shape the interactive matrix" (1969:37). What is organized in social organizations are individuals inter-preting the world, human brains attending to some aspects of the social world and not to others.

A brief account of the psychophysiological concept of attention will hopefully suggest the importance of attention patterns for social scientists and detail for us how patterns of inattention can result in reading dis-abilities. The central nervous system has been increasingly conceived as a set of models depicting the world outside the body, in terms of which an organism attends, perceives, thinks, and acts (Sokolov 1969; Pribram 1971; MacKay 1972). Stimuli enter the body and if they are uninformative no attention will be paid to them. If the match is improper, the central nervous system will orient in search of new information which will either restore or redefine the model. In such a case, the organism is said to be "looking to see," and different parts of the brain will be activated in processing the new stimuli until harmony is again established (Pribram 1970). First a decision is made to look for a stimulus and only then is a second decision made as to whether or not the proper stimuli occur (Dewey 1896; N. Mackworth and Bagshaw 1970).

The human system is best discussed in terms of the feedback relations between pertinence, attention, and memory storage. Physiologists are not easily given to talking about pertinence centers in the brain, but they do talk about the efferent control of afferent stimuli on the basis of what central mechanisms deem to be the most pertinent information at any particular time. Central control of the models is called up from memory with plans. Furthermore, there is central control right down at the recep-tor sites as to what sort of information makes it to the brain for considera-tion and possible action (Pribram 1970, 1971; Rothblatt and Pribram 1972). The central nervous system is thus intimately involved in the organizational work that goes into the construction of significance in the world. The same symbols that are processed by our bodies are those processed in our social systems. Our bodies are the nodes in the com-municative network that is society, and the work of these various nodes produces what has come to be seen as social organization. Statements of

this proposition are unfortunately rare, but the trend is apparently changing (Bateson 1972; Beck 1971a,b). Nevertheless, we still have only a few
anecdotes interrelating the organization of social events and the organization of neurological events. Pribram has given one delightful example:

> For many years there was an elevated railway line (the "el") on Third
> Avenue in New York that made a fearful racket: when it was torn down,
> people who had been living in apartments along the line awakened
> periodically out of a sound sleep to call the police about some strange
> occurrence they could not properly define. The calls were made at the
> times the trains had formerly rumbled past. The strange occurrences
> were, of course, the deafening silence that had replaced the expected
> noise (1971:50).

A model of the world for a particular time and place existed in the central
nervous systems of many people up and down the Third Avenue El.
When the environment did not supply the essential information, the
people began orienting and paying attention. In this case, our ecology
worked its way into our bodies and told us when to listen, namely at the
time when the El had previously roared by; our social system then worked
its way into our bodies and told us what to hear when we listened, perhaps
a thief or another strange occurrence requiring police assistance. Society
and ecology are merely two aspects of the environment with which we
communicate. They send us messages about the adequacy of the internalized models of the time and space criteria in terms of which we
perceive, think and act. We all live in a world of information which we
decode according to the dictates of context. Much of this context is
encoded in our memory and evidenced in our attention patterns.

There are many Third Avenue El trains in our lives. In every classroom in America, there is an organization of ecological and social happen-
ings mediated by various neurologies with memory and attention biases
wired into the wetware. To study one is to study the other, to study the
brain is to study social organization, and vice versa. In this biobehavioral
inquiry into reading disabilities, however, both systems are obviously
involved. The epidemiological contours of reading disabilities run along
ethnic and cultural lines and suggest that they are indeed socially organized. Yet unlike most behavior that we see as socially organized,
reading skills or their diminution due to brain insult or socially induced
inattention, obviously, rather than implicitly, involve neurological organization. Indeed, the picture we are developing of reading as a "psycholinguistic guessing game" (Goodman 1970; Wanat 1971) fits exactly the
picture we have of the structure of the brain's activity in all behavior. In an

excellent paper, J. Mackworth has laid the two side by side: reading involves

> a selective process that involves partial use of available language cues
> selected from the perceptual input on the basis of the reader's expecta-
> tion, an interaction between thoughts and language . . . ; the neuronal
> model anticipates the future probability and meaning of the next
> stimulus. A neuronal mechanism checks the meaning and nature of an
> incoming stimulus against the predictions of the neural model. Thus
> construction of a neural model is an active process, involving a two-way
> exchange of messages from environment and brain (1972:704, 708).

Both the environment and the brain are socially constructed. When a child is unable to read, part of the environment is not being processed by the brain. Because the epidemiology of reading disabilities follows a social organization, it is possible to claim that the organization of the proper neurological models for reading also follows a social organization. A brief look at the social organization of classrooms for black children in America will indicate how their brains appear disabled for reading. *In the politics of everyday life, black children in America learn how not to read; they learn how not to attend to printed information and as a result show high rates of reading disabilities.* The implications of this high rate of illiteracy for the acquisition of pariah status is obvious.

Almost a half a century ago, attention was a major focus of classroom research. Primarily this old research attempted to document whether or not children were paying attention to their teachers by noting their gaze direction during lessons. This is not a very efficient method of studying attention, for receptor orientation gives little information about just what a child is attending to during a boring lecture. The literature is significant, however, in documenting contrasting receptor attention patterns be-tween middle American host schools then and minority classrooms now. In their check of gaze direction, it was shown that more than 90 percent of the host children had their eyes fixed on their teachers or their work at any given time (Jackson 1968). This contrasts considerably with estimates obtained from the contemporary classrooms that share in the early cen-tury pedagogical style of the teacher directing all attention in the class-room. M. Deutsch (1963) has found that teachers in Harlem elementary schools spent more than half their day calling children to attention. Attention patterns indeed appear to define the "scene of the battle" in pariah group education (Roberts 1970). School does not seem to work for many teachers and pariah children, and formal roles and statuses are not identically defined by teachers and students. The call for attention appears far more often and seems to have far less effect than it did in the twenties when these earlier studies were carried out.

There is much social organization in these attention and inattention patterns. In primate studies, attention patterns have recently been used to delineate the social organization of dominance hierarchies (Chance 1967). The more one baboon visually attends to another baboon, the more responsible it is to the leader's every movement. Similarly, in the classroom where teachers and students produce leadership patterns for each other, attention is an issue. To attend to a teacher is to give the teacher a leadership role in the classroom: to attend to the peer group is to subvert the teacher's role. In the older studies, the primary fact is that all the children paid homage to the teacher's leadership role by attending, physically at least, to the teacher's activities. In schools populated by pariah children, this leadership role is much more subject to negotiation: some teachers can pull it off and some cannot; some children give their attention and others do not. It is in the context of this battle for attention that we must consider the nature of pariah reading disabilities. In many pariah classrooms, the politics of everyday life has been escalated into war games; there are teacher games and peer group games, and every student must make his choice. One takes sides by attending or not attending. Those who attend learn to read; those who do not attend do not learn how to read.

Attention patterns increasingly shift from teacher games to peer group games as a pariah child moves through elementary school. In addition to the often reported facts that pariah children learn less and misbehave more often as they get older, data on shifts in the perceptual, language structure and function, and attitude patterns of children in school are now available. The next few years promise to bring us far more information, not only on American blacks, the focus of all the work to be briefly discussed here, but on other pariah groups as well.

Perception

Much of the transmission of social know-how that occurs in the early years of school amounts to perceptual learning. Apparently different cultures learn how to perceive differently. This is especially the case for materials represented in two dimensions which apparently allow for more variability than the three-dimensional world of movement and action (Segall, Campbell, and Herskovits 1966; Forge 1970). Learning how to read involves a great deal of perceptual learning. Many children reverse their letters when first learning how to write, for there really is not much difference between p, d, g and b; o and e; u, n, m, v and w. Normals master these subtle differences, and disabled children continue to have difficulty distinguishing these forms after the first grade. Careful attention must be paid to differences in rotation, line-to-line curve, dimension and line-breaking transformations in order to make the proper distinctions between the letters which signal differences in word form and meaning. We develop these skills and store them deep in our nervous system. The more we read, the less work it takes to distinguish the different forms. The eye apparently learns just what to look for and orients only when a drastically misshapen form appears; the difficulties of proofreading illustrate just how well a good reader is programmed to read for meaning and to notice typographic irregularities only when they are given special attention.

Some black children do not permanently develop the essential skills for letter differentiation. In a test designed to analyze a child's competence at handling the perceptual transformations essential to letter discrimination, Gibson (1965) has shown that most children have trouble with rotation and line-to-curve transformations at age five. By age seven most children have mastered these transformations. This is the case for both black and white children. However, black children I tested at twelve years of age showed a mixed range in these skills; those who could read performed well, and those who could not read performed very poorly, scoring below younger black children on the same test. These children had apparently learned how not to see, or, more specifically, learned how not to look in order that they might not see. Reading apparently became a call for inattention, and they submerged the skills essential for a successful attending to reading materials.

Language Structure and Function

This shift in the perceptual properties of many black children is accompanied by subtle but highly significant changes in language structure and function. The brilliant work of Labov and his associates in Harlem has revealed that our language is indeed socially organized. The way in which our vocal chords allow for a passage of air to reverberate into the ears of other social actors depends greatly on just who the interactants are and how they are related. Depending upon who is doing the talking and who is doing the listening, not only will different points of information be passed, but the way of saying it may be remarkably different. Pariah children often learn to use one speech code or register for dealings with pariah people and another for host people; the differences in the code may be subtle lexemic markers as in Japan (Donoghue 1971), subtle phonemic shifts as between social classes and ethnic groups in New York City's Lower East Side (Labov 1964a), gross dialect shifts as between whites and blacks in America, or major language shifts as between French and English speakers in Canada or the Lapps and Norwegians in Norway (Eidheim 1969).

American blacks acquire a nonstandard or dialect English which is more often mutually intelligible with white English. When there is an intelligibility breakdown, the result can be disastrous. Gumperz gives the following example from a postbellum southern teacher's diary:

> I asked a group of boys one day the color of the sky. Nobody could tell me. Presently the father of one of them came by, and I told him of their ignorance, repeating my question with the same result as before. He grinned: "Tom, how sky stan'?" "Blue," promptly shouted Tom (1970:4).

This gross level of language interference was, of course, attributed by the teacher to the child's stupidity, and the teacher probably unconsciously related to the child the subordinate status that accompanies being "stupid" in a classroom.

For the most part, however, black and white verbal codes are mutually intelligible in content. Switching does not cause a problem at the structural level; rather the codes function to differentiate the games being played and the meaning attached to the behavior of various other actors in the game. Messages of relationship are differently stored in the codes. Indeed, using one and not the other is itself a powerful relational message. Switching codes causes a problem, then, for an actor's definition of situation. If an actor defines himself in terms of the ecology of games played by the peer group, then taking on the code which demands participation in the ecology of teacher and book games demands an existential leap and is neither easily nor healthily performed.

The differentiation of codes according to grammar alone deals only with what is systematically possible. Learning should not be blocked. Children merely learn new codes. The differentiation of codes on the basis of appropriateness is apparently a much more difficult chasm to bridge. When the social organization of communicative behavior is divided by two definitions of what is culturally appropriate, the one definition belonging to the teacher and the other to the pupils, communication across codes is much more limited than if codes are merely structurally at odds. It is not difficult to learn that "What color is the sky?" and "How sky stan'?" are equivalent, but, when your teacher deems you ignorant for using the one and your peer group shuns you for using the other, then the job of switching codes is difficult indeed.

The ecology of peer group games is well defined by the growth of a highly elaborate linguistic code restricted to peer group members. Labov has performed a masterful task in isolating these games in his delineation of the stages of acquisition of nonstandard English:

1. Up to age 5: basic grammatical rules and lexicon are taken from parents.
2. Age 5 to 12 the reading years: peer group vernacular is established.
3. Adolescence: "The social significance of the dialect characteristics of his friends become gradually apparent."
4. High school age: "The child begins to learn how to modify his speech in the direction of the prestige standard in formal situations or even to some extent in casual speech" (Labov 1964b:91).

The second and third stages are, of course, most important for a consideration of the implications of the school and the peer group registers for learning. The implications are not so obvious; what difference does it make if children use one register for interacting with teachers and reading materials and another for interacting with each other? The importance of these two registers lies in the fact that during the school years the two become mutually exclusive. As children participate more in their peer groups, the less importance is attached to school games. The more children participate in the ecology of games defined by their peers, the more deviant their linguistic registers; it is these linguistic features which help to mark off the peer group from the ecology of the schools.

Labov has documented these trends beautifully. Participation in peer groups, especially those with formal organizations such as street gangs, are accompanied by major phonological and grammatical shifts. One of the many charts presented in his Harlem study is reproduced here (Labov et al. 1968:182):

Percent of Standard Verb Agreement for Club Members, Lames and Whites

Present Tense Forms of Verb	Club Members	Lames	Whites
has (3rd sg.)	19	60	100
doesn't (3rd sg.)	03	36	32
were (2nd sg. + pl.)	14	83	100
does (3rd sg.)	00	13	100
says (3rd sg.)	04	00	100
(No. of subjects	31	10	8)

This illustrates the implications that peer group status has for the speech register employed by black adolescents. Lames do not participate in formally organized peer groups although they are in contact with the gangs and are part of the black speech community. In school, Lames are still open to interpreting favorably some cues from the teacher's ecology. The Inwood whites are of a low social class, but they do not show the extreme alienation patterns which characterize black children in school. Club members show the most extreme deviance from the standard English linguistic code, Inwood whites the least, and Lames fall in between. The same rank ordering can be made for the three groups' participation in school. This is not to say that linguistic difference causes alienation from school; rather it is a standard for nonacceptance of the ecology of games played in white schools. The rise in status of a black child in his peer group, the adoption of the peer group's linguistic register, and alienation from school all develop together.

In terms of this inquiry into reading disabilities, participation in peer group formal organizations and the employment of their linguistic registers are of great importance, for they correlate very well with reading scores. Labov and Robins (1969:57, 167) have shown perfectly the relation between the acquisition of reading skills and the participation in the peer group ecology of games. Not one out of 43 gang members was able to achieve a reading score on grade level and most are more than two years behind the national average. Participation in the peer group ecology of games appears indeed to be exclusive of a participation in the school ecology of games of which reading is a part. Printed materials appear to send few meaningful cues to those interested in improving their status among their peers.

Attitudes

Labov's findings are not limited to classrooms which harbor members of formally organized gangs in Harlem. In two classrooms in suburban New York City, the exact same trends were found. The children were not unaware of the trends, and their significance was readily apparent in the children's attitudes towards each other. This should not surprise us at all. In my high school, I remember that most of us could define others and make very accurate estimates of their grade point averages on the basis of clothes worn, speech patterns, and some postural cues. Our expertise was perhaps not as loaded as that of black children, for their expertise not only defines others but also determines who is to be popular or not. A series of sociometric tests administered in an all black, bottom track, sixth grade were consistent in placing nonreaders at the center of all peer group activities. Similar tests in an all black, nontracked, fifth grade also showed nonreaders at the center of most activities. Reading skills do not recommend an actor for leadership. Indeed, the acquisition of such skills can exclude an actor from the peer group ecology of games.

Ethnographic Summary

Many topics have been briefly touched in this short description of the black classroom, but its thrust can be summarized. Learning disabilities occur at very high rates in the American black population. The distribution of these disabilities overlaps with the distribution of social behavior that leads to the acquisition of nonmarketable and pariah biographies, behavior such as participation in street gangs and classroom subcultures specializing in disruption and failure. This nascent pariah population shows subtle shifts in its perceptual, linguistic, and attitude patterns. What the children are doing is learning to behave in new, culturally appropriate ways in educational settings, new ways which will determine their acquisition of pariah status vis-a-vis the host population. These new ways of behaving involve the development of new cues to be sent out in interaction with other humans, such as new phonemes and morphemes, and the development of new perceptual and evaluative skills, such as the abilities to hear new phonemes and perceive group leaders without confusion. What is being learned are new attention patterns, new ways of seeing, hearing, and construing the meaning of particular items of behavior shared with others in the subculture. When some items are attended, others are disattended, some of them actively so. Learning to behave in a culturally appropriate way in black classrooms in white school systems apparently involves learning to attend to cues produced in the peer group and learning to disattend teacher and school produced cues, such as shouts for attention or the introduction of tasks such as reading. These attention patterns are deeply programmed in the central nervous system. When the child attempts to attend to cues outside his learned competence, he fails. In this way, many black children fail in reading, and they appear neurologically impaired. Obviously, they are usually not impaired at all; they have merely learned to attend to different stimuli in a school situation. Ironically and tragically, for their successful and rational adaptation to the school situation, they are categorized as impaired and treated as inferiors. Thus they acquire pariah status.

Biculturation and the Acquisition of Pariah Status

Now that we have some notion of how a black classroom is organized
in American schools and what black children must know in order to act in
a subculturally appropriate way in the classroom, we must ask how this
know-how is produced. Why is it that the social world of many black
children is organized without a place for printed materials? Some observers might point to genes or to various kinds of deprivation leading to
cognitive or motivational breakdowns. Others, especially radical
educators (Holt 1969; Kohl 1967), black leaders, and P.T.A. groups, point
to "underachieving schools" and the failure of teachers to do the job.
Implicit in much of this rhetoric is the claim that racism is the primary
factor in the failure of whites to educate black children; white teachers
expect black children to fail and subtly induce their expectations into the
children who indeed do fail.

These are the two alternatives offered by the literature: the children
fail because there is something wrong with their heads; or the children fail
because the schools are disasters and the teachers are racists. The first
argument is far too simple. Gene pools (Montagu 1964) and cognitive and
motivational systems are not easily located, and no one has shown why any
of these systems fail in school and not in other settings in the social world.
The second literature is a little more difficult to dismiss. Obviously, it is not
only the schools that fail, for they serve different groups the same product
with differential success. When racism is appended to the charge of school
underachievement, the argument is intuitively more forceful. However,
we have little idea just what racism means of late or, more importantly,
how it works especially for the mostly well-meaning, hard-working, and
ideologically nonracist teachers that staff our urban schools.

The proposal of this chapter is that reading disabilities are products
of the way in which the people in the classroom use their categories for
interaction to produce statuses and identities, or ways of attending
stimuli, in the classroom setting. Although racist categories work their way
into the production of the social organization of black-white relations, a
teacher does not have to be a racist for the politics of everyday life to
produce a classroom rigidly divided between teacher and peer group
games. Any formal differences in the communicative styles of the teacher
and the children can introduce havoc to their relations and the messages
of relationship they consequently send to each other.

Consider the following important example. Two black Americans
attending a Chicago college were introduced to each other. A film, shot at
the rate of 24 frames per second, was made of their shaking hands. There

was a definite rhythm to their handshake; for three frames their hands went up and for three frames down, and so on. Two Polish Americans at the same college produced a different but also fairly rhythmic interaction. One Pole and one black from each dyad produced a disastrous interaction (Leonard 1972): five up, one down, one up, two down, etc. There was no rhythm to their interaction. There they were, joined together at the hands, but with apparently little idea about what to do with each other. An analysis of the conversational false starts indicates that they also had little idea of what to say to each other. Rational and stigma-free interactions are difficult to make out of such material. Apparently, our communicative codes go into our bodies and establish rhythms and expectations about the rhythms of others. Interacting with a person with a slightly different code or rhythm can be a fatiguing and upsetting experience. On a one-to-one basis, these difficulties can be worked out or negotiated until the two interactants have managed consistent or rational ways of dealing with each other. In a classroom in which a teacher often stands one-to-thirty against a code of difference, negotiations are often not possible and at best limited (Byers, personal communications).

Communicative code differences in a classroom setting can have tremendous effects. A teacher out of phase with his students will undoubtedly fail in the politics of everyday life. Rational interaction with the group will hardly be possible. As a result, the teacher will fall back on his formal authority as a teacher, his so-called "role" to instruct the children in their classroom behavior. The children often reject this authority role and develop an idiosyncratic code. such as the nonstandard peer group code Labov has described. The children's actions make much sense. When rational interaction with a teacher is not possible, that is, when his position of authority makes no sense in terms of his relations with the children, they produce an alternative system and disown the teacher's authority. Reading skills get caught in this battle over which cues are to be attended—peer group cues or teacher cues.

This paper has suggested how a child learns to produce a pariah status in his work in everyday life. It has offered an example of this work in detailing how a large number of black children acquire statuses, identities, and behavioral patterns which produce a pariah biography. The statuses, identities, and behavioral patterns developed by black children in white school systems produce learning disabilities and enable the host population to exclude the black child from participation in the more lucrative institutions of American society. How are these statuses, identities and behavioral patterns produced? Three tasks remain if this question is to be answered.

Communicative Code Differences and the Inhibition of School Learning

First, examples of how minor differences in communicative codes can induce a selective inattention to school material must be given. One of the first reports of such interference was offered by Spindler (1959) in his work on the self-fulfilling prophecies of teachers unconsciously dominating classroom social organization. He showed how middle-class teachers attended to middle-class children and labeled them as the most talented and ambitious of the children in their classes. School success followed along identical lines, but more subtle evaluations of talent divided the populations along different lines. In this case, lower class children gave up trying and acquired failing "institutional biographies" (Goffman, 1963) because of an inability to give evidence of their intelligence in terms of the limited code that the teachers used to evaluate children.

A more specific example has been recently offered for a St. Louis elementary school with black teachers and black children. The effects of little things were in no way little in this school. Rist offers the following account of the classroom after it had been divided into three "ability groups," the fast, slow and nonlearners at Tables 1, 2, and 3, respectively:

> The organization of the kindergarten classroom according to the expectation of success or failure after the eighth day of school became the basis for the differential treatment of the children for the remainder of the school year. From the day that the class was assigned permanent seats, the activities in the classroom were perceivably different from previously. The fundamental division of the class into those expected to learn and those expected not to permeated the teacher's orientation of the class (1970: 423).

Assignment to each of the tables was based on the teacher's subjective evaluations which, after dissection by Rist, were shown to be rooted in the teacher's evaluation of the children's physical appearance and interactional and verbal behavior. At Table 1 are centered children with newer and cleaner clothes and more of them on cold days, slightly lighter skin, and processed hair. Children with reciprocal traits were positioned at lower tables. Class leaders or direction givers also clustered at Table 1. The children at the low tables spoke less in class, in heavy dialect when they did, and almost never to the teacher. What is most unfortunate is that by the third grade the children at the lower tables were still at the lower tables. Once the child is tracked, it is almost impossible for him to break loose. The lower his table, the less he gets in instructional time. In addition, teacher expectations follow him from year to year. Apparently, the acquisition of a school biography is completed within the first week of school, and all on the basis of a teacher's ethnocentric evaluation of a child's mannerisms.

A similar analysis can probably be carried out for every year of schooling that a child undergoes. Each year, more are sorted out until the "select few" reach college. The word "select" should not be taken in its elitist sense. By the time they enter college, some people may be more select because their enculturation to school equips them to do college work. We should not make the mistake, however, of thinking that the select few were selected for any reason other than that they were most like their teachers. Given Labov's speech data, we can see that the children at Table 3 are not the interactional and verbal dullards that the teacher supposed them to be. By the sixth grade, assuming Labov's data are predictive, the children at Table 3 will talk the most and be the best dressers and the most popular individuals in every class. Their native equipment for leading and learning is in perfect shape, although by the sixth grade it is understandably directed away from school. Why these children are not selected in their early years by teachers has to do with how well prepared both they and their teachers are for working out the conflicting points in their communicative code. The children are often more adaptable than their teachers. They are able and willing to develop new codes; indeed, they do so every day in the playgrounds. However, if the new code is used to degrade the children, as is the case for the children in "lower" ability groups, they will take flight and cut themselves off from whatever rewards the new code has to offer them. If a modus vivendi is not reached in the early grades, the children at the lower tables will create their own subculture defined partly in opposition to the classroom culture attempted by the teacher.

Pariah children invariably share some minor traits which help them to identify each other and to distinguish themselves from the host population. A particular phoneme, lexeme, or body movement can do the job. Invariably, these traits are at most minuscule factors in cognitive development. Even a dialect barrier great enough to produce mutual unintelligibility is not enough to stop German children from speaking and reading High German (Fishman and Leuders-Salmon 1972). Dialect differences between black children and white school officials and books, often claimed as a source of reading failure (Baratz and Shuy 1969), apparently present little formal interference to the reading process (Melmud 1971). It depends on what is done with the differences. In host-pariah teacher-student relations, the differences are used to do a great deal, and are allowed to intervene in interactions to the extent that they cut off the possibility of sense being made between the pair. The child gets stuck in a low ability group for reasons he cannot understand and the teacher finds the child's behavior equally incomprehensible. In such a case the teacher grasps onto a formal definition of the teacher's role in order to make sense of the situation: the teacher develops status or interaction skills in accordance with the definition of the teacher as a person to be listened to and learned from under any circumstances. Faced with this senseless rigidity of the teacher's role, the child develops his status and identity in the alternative source offered by his peer group. Recall the disabled child assigned low status in the classroom despite a high degree of acceptance outside the classroom. The child shut down his learning skills and turned to abnormal behavior (Singer and Beardsley 1970). The same senseless assignment to ability groups is often made in the inter-ethnic classroom. The host teacher has different standards of evaluation than the minority child. Accordingly, the wrong children are often as-signed to the low ability groups. Their assignment does not make sense to them, and they understandably shut down their learning skills and revolt. The difference between what happens to the disabled child who perceives a senseless status assignment and a minority child in an identical situation is that the minority child is never alone. The teacher invariably makes mistakes on a number of the children, and the ensuing revolt can develop earlier and more powerfully when a large number of chilren is involved.

The children in an interethnic classroom have three choices. They can take school as a source of identity; thus, the children at Table 1. They can take the peer group as a source of identity and fight the system; thus, the children at Tables 2 and 3 transformed by late elementary school into the gangs Labov has described. The third and perhaps the worst choice is represented by the children at the lower tables who accept the teacher's definitions and passively fail through school into pariah status. They also fail in their identity work. For the children to dispute the messages of relationship offered by a teacher to the lower ability groups causes havoc in the classroom but solid ego development in the children's own commu-nity. For the children to passively accept subordinate status creates class-room calm, but a weak ego. Either way, learning is blocked; in the first case by active selective inattention and misbehavior, in the second case with motivational lag and selective inattention. Neither group learns to read.

Black-White Communicative Code Differences

A second task is to describe possible points of conflict in black and white communicative skills and the difficulties of biculturation or the

acquisition of competence in both codes. Work on this topic is just beginning, but already there are indications that the use of time and space in
black culture is distinct from the use of time and space in white culture.
Regardless of what these codes are an adaptation to, the point is that
blacks and whites slice up the world in slightly different ways. When the
black child enters a host school, he is asked to alter his codes drastically for
spacing his body vis-a-vis (Aiello and Jones 1971; Hall 1971; Scheflen
1971; Johnson 1971) and his timing in conversation (Lewis, 1970; Gumperz and Herasimchuk, 1972; Leonard, 1972). This is very important, for
it is in terms of these time and space coordinates that people send each
other messages of relationship. If these code differences are not worked
out, the teacher and students will tie into or punctuate (Bateson 1972;
Watzlawick et al. 1967) each other in all the wrong ways.

Punctuation breakdowns are the stuff of the self-fulfilling prophecies
described above. The child moves or speaks in the wrong way at the wrong
time according to the teacher's code, and he will be branded hyperactive,
out of control, or stupid. The teacher will appear equally disoriented
according to the child's code and may well be branded cold and unfair.
Slight differences in time and space use do not have to result in such a
disaster, but they often do.

In an exciting article, Byers and Byers (1972) have described how
black-white code differences can lead to pupil-teacher breakdown. The
teacher in question is considered unbiased and talented. Byers and Byers
filmed her interaction with four four-year-old girls, two black and two
white. In the sequence analyzed, she looks at the black and white children
almost an identical number of times. However, the black children look at
the teacher more than three times as often as the white children. One
might postulate that the children are anxious about their performance, or
perhaps they are hyperactive, etc. Byers and Byers have a much more
interesting conclusion to offer, after they add the most important information that the white children established eye contact with the teacher
almost twice as often as the black children who are straining three times as
hard to catch the teacher's eyes. This is very crucial, for it is during eye
contact that the teacher can send the children messages of reassurance
and affection, messages such as, "I love you," "You are doing well," "How
smart!", or at least, "You are making sense to me." Why do these black and
white eyes punctuate each other in all the wrong ways?

Consider what social work is performed by a glance of the eyes. The
eyes are engaged in gathering information about the content and report
of any interaction that a body is engaged in. Constant surveillance makes
people uncomfortable, perhaps because it is a statement of distrust, a sign

of one's unwillingness to suspend belief that nothing threatening is about to occur. So the eyes are used in brief spurts only, in passing glances. What is more interesting is that these glances are very well timed to occur at moments of maximum information transfer. Eye glances are paced by conversational rhythms, intonation patterns, and body movements and are sequenced rather neatly to other rhythms between two people. The white girls in the interaction that Byers and Byers have described appear to know just when to look at the white teacher in order to gain access to her eyes and whatever relational messages she is to dispense. The black girls do not appear to have the same information. They appear to be working off a slightly different interaction rhythm. Of course, this is just as Leonard's (1972) analysis of the black-white handshake and Gumperz's and Herasimchuk's (1972) analysis of black-white intonation rhythms predicted. Interaction is indeed an action between people, and if not perfectly timed the interaction will fail. In the case of this teacher and these children, the white-white interaction is successful, and the white-black interaction fails. For all their interactional work, the two black girls receive little relational support, and it is not difficult to predict that they will someday direct their interactional work towards each other. In time, achievement will be located in the peer group, and not in the teacher.

More blatant examples of teacher-student battles over time and space use exist in every American classroom in which teachers generally monopolize 85 percent of class space and 100 percent of class time (Sommer 1969). From the first to the last grade, the teacher attempts to dictate when and where a child should speak or move. In ghetto schools, this often leads to constant and open welfare. Teachers spend an inordinate amount of a child's six years in elementary school fighting with the class about just who is going to say and do what at a particular moment; manuals guiding a new teacher in instructional methods in such a school detail at length exactly how a teacher must rigidly structure time and space (Trubowitz 1968; Board of Education 1966). The children fight this particular structure to the extent that it stifles them; if their function and status in the structure do not make sense to them, that is, if the politics of classroom life do not make sense, they reject the structure and all that comes with it, including literacy.

A large percentage of American blacks are especially adept at making the code shifts essential to smooth interactions with whites. This is no easy task, for enculturation into two cultures, or biculturation (Valentine 1971), can have its drawbacks for ego development. The bicultural child must acquire two sometimes mutually exclusive ways of knowing how to act appropriately, one way for when whites are present and another for when the interaction matrix is all black. Where code shifting is most difficult is apparently in the bureaucratic setting in which the white code, in addition to being the only acceptable medium of information exchange, is also the medium for the expression of host group power and host group access to the essential and even luxurious utilities of the ecosystem that is contemporary America. The police station, the welfare office, the job interview and the classroom are all situations which demand complete subservience to host group codes. In each of these situations, people are being processed rather than negotiated with in an attempt to establish rationality. The rationale is already set. The bureaucrat has it down and the pariah does not. The bureaucrat already has the role defined, and the pariah must fit in if he is to be processed successfully. Even when the bureaucrat attempts to negotiate a rational interaction—to approach his public as he would normal people in everyday life, he is unable to do so because of the sheer numbers of people that must be processed. The teacher, for example, must deal with 30 children at a time, and the give and take that characterizes everyday life become impossible. Consequently, the teacher's code becomes the classroom code, and children are evaluated in its terms.

In the classroom, the teacher has the power; the teacher has the tools to supply the institutional biography that the child needs to escape his pariah origins. Teachers are quick to point this out to children and daily tell them that there is no success without school. If the child attempts biculturation, he adapts to the teacher's code, accepts the teacher's messages of power and dominance, and works hard at school. Many black children do not go this route. They reject the teacher's code and transform their minor differences in time and space use into large differences defining the classroom as the scene of the battle between the races. Code differences do not have to develop in this fashion, but they most often do. It is a measure of the teacher's adaptability in the early grades. The more sensible student-teacher relations can be made in the early grades, the less difference code differences will make. If the teacher fights the children with his formal authority from the early grades on, the children will equate the teacher's code with senseless suppression; it will become a difference that makes a difference. The children will reject the new code and seek the more rewarding alternatives offered by the peer group.

Host group teachers do not produce code differences. Both the teacher and his students partake in long ethnic traditions in their first years of life, and they then bring these traditions to school. The question is, how are ethnic differences made to make a difference? In the earlier grades, teachers make the difference as they are apparently not as adaptable as their students. In later years, as peer group lines solidify and code differences become the focus of most classroom social and political work, the children enforce the distinction between the teacher's code and their own code. In making their code make a difference, they are learning how to produce pariah status vis-à-vis the host group; they are learning to appear like "one-of-those"; they are producing a pariah biography which will haunt them until the next generation again plays the politics of everyday life in the classroom.

Identity and Mobility

The third task cannot be properly dealt with until we have detailed accounts of the politics of everyday life for many pariah groups both here in America and in other cultures. The third task is to explain why blacks do not fare as well as other minorities in classroom politics. All ethnic groups, Jews, Japanese, or Italians, for instance, bring some differences to the classroom. Shouldn't they all lead to communicative breakdowns, degrading relational messages between students and teachers, and, finally, learning disabilities? Yes, and indeed they do. Some groups have worked out ingenious strategies for by-passing host group discriminatory powers. American Catholics, for example, appear to have always understood the complexities of moving through host schools. Accordingly, they have always maintained their own school systems which have functioned not only as socializing agents, but also as protection against the sorting efforts of host group members. Whether or not their diplomas were equivalent in quality to host diplomas, Irish, Italian, and other Catholic Americans have always equipped their children with the institutional biographies required for at least minimally upward mobility.

The strategies of each group for identity work in the face of unacceptable messages of relationship in the classroom are probably deeply rooted in its history. The reasons for its having to develop such strategies exist in the politics of the classroom. If group identity work is necessitated by a breakdown in teacher-student relations, strategies as to what will be attended to and what will be acted upon will be worked out among the students. Learning abilities and disabilities are developed in such a context. School learning is almost always set back; the question is whether the group opts for learning how not to learn, the case described in this paper, whether the group merely opts to learn only about its own materials, as is the case for Hasidic Jews and the Pennsylvania Dutch, or whether the group overcomes the degrading messages and does scholastically better than host children even according to host group standards. The last case is most intriguing because of the records achieved by American Jews and American Japanese. Both groups have soared over mobility barriers and appear to have well escaped pariah status because of their mastery of the American school system. Of course, both groups reached the American shores with tremendous entrepreneurial skills and established traditions of literacy. Nevertheless, the essential question remains unanswered; namely, what did the Jews and the Japanese know that other pariah groups did not know? Alternatively, it can be asked what the host group knew about Jews and Japanese that it apparently does not know about other minorities (Spindler, personal communication). The point is that ethnic identity work defines what is to be learned and how it is to be learned, what is to be read and the strategies used for the reading act. What is different about the ethnic identity work of one group rather than another? Such a question will keep the next generation of scholars busy. If we achieve an answer, we will know a great deal.

Summary

Pariah groups are continually regenerated by host and pariah children learning how to assign *meanings* to particular social acts and how to *act appropriately* on the basis of the meanings assigned. These meanings are programmed into the *central nervous system* as patterns of *selective attention* to the stimuli particular to some acts and not to others. Patterns of selective attention, glossed in everyday language as *abilities, statuses* and *identities,* shape a child's *institutional biography* and define whether the child, his abilities, statuses and identities, are to be assigned to a pariah or a host group in any situation.

The conclusion of this chapter is that the patterns of selective attention and inattention demonstrated by pariah children in school represent rational adaptations to the politics of everyday life in the classrooms. School failure and delinquency often represent highly motivated and intelligent attempts to develop the abilities, statuses, and identities that will best equip the child to maximize his utilities in the politics of everyday life. If the teacher is going to send degrading messages of relationship regardless of how the game is played, the child's best strategy is to stop playing the game.

The ability to read is taken up in some detail since it is one program which defines the boundary between pariah and host groups. Specifically, it is suggested that the politics of everyday life induce patterns of inattention for the reading task in particular groups. Host teachers and pariah children find each other occasionally unintelligible because of vocal and body language code differences and stereotypes. These differences are escalated into cues for intergroup conflict when degrading messages of relationship are appended by the teacher to the child's use of his own code for interpreting and generating behavior. The child is engaged in identity and status work and often rejects these messages as meaningless. The child then develops patterns of inattention to the teacher, the teacher's tasks such ae behaving "properly" and reading, and, eventually, most stimuli generated by the host group. The high rate of black American illiteracy and pariah group membership is explained in this way.

REFERENCES

Aiello, J., and S. Jones, 1971, "Field Study of the Proxemic Behavior of Young Children in Three Subcultural Groups," *Journal of Personality and Social Psychology* 19(7):351-356.

Allitto, S., 1969, "The Language Issue in Communist Chinese Education." In C. Hu, ed., *Aspects of Chinese Education.* New York: Teachers College Press.

Azumi, K., 1969, *Higher Education and Business Recruitment in Japan.* New York: Teachers College Press.

Baratz, J., and Shuy, R., eds., 1969, *Teaching Black Children To Read.* Washington, D.C. Center for Applied Linguistics.

Bar-Hillel, Y., 1954, "Indexical Expressions," *Mind* (n.s.) 63:359-379.

Barker, R., 1968, *Ecological Psychology.* Stanford, Calif.: Stanford University Press.

Barth, F., 1969, "Introduction." In F. Barth, ed., *Ethnic Groups and Boundaries.* Boston: Little, Brown and Company.

Bateson, G., 1972, *Steps to an Ecology of Mind.* New York: Ballantine Books.

Beck, H., 1971a, "The Rationality of Redundancy," *Comparative Political Studies* 3(4):469-478.

Beck, H., 1971b, "Minimal Requirements for a Biobehavioral Paradigm," *Behavioral Science* 16:442-456.

Beck, H., 1972, "Everyman Meets the Epistemologist." Paper presented at the 1972 Annual Meeting of the American Political Science Association.

Becker, E., 1962, *The Birth and Death of Meaning.* New York: The Free Press.

Bernstein, B., 1964, "Elaborated and Restricted Codes," *American Anthropologist* 66(6, part 2):55-69.

Beteille, A., 1972, "Race, Class and Ethnic Identity," *International Social Science Journal* 23(4):519-539.

Birch, H., and J. Gussow, 1970, *Disadvantaged Children: Health, Nutrition and School Failure.* New York: Harcourt Brace Jovanovich.

Blurton-Jones, N., 1972, "Nonverbal Communication in Children." In R. Hinde, ed., *Nonverbal Communication.* London: Cambridge University Press.

Board of Education, New York City, 1966, *Getting Started in the Elementary School.*

Brameld, T., 1968, *Japan: Culture, Education and Change in Two Communities.* New York: Holt, Rinehart and Winston, Inc.

Byers, P. 1971, "Sentics, Rhythms, and a New View of Man." Paper presented to the 138th Annual Meeting of the American Association for the Advancement of Science, Philadelphia, December 30, 1971.

Byers, P., and H. Byers, 1972, "Nonverbal Communication and the Education of Children." In C. Cazden, et al., eds., *Functions of Language in the Classroom,* New York: Teachers College Press.

Caudill, W., and H. Weinstein, 1969, "Maternal Care and Infant Behavior in Japan and America," *Psychiatry* 32:12-43.

Cazden, C., 1970, "The Situation: A Neglected Source of Social Class Differences in Language Use," *Journal of Social Issues* 26(2):35-60.

Chance, M., 1967, "Attention Structure as the Basis of Primate Rank Orders," *Man* (n.s.) 2(4):503-518.

Cicourel, A., 1970a, "The Acquisition of Social Structure." In J. Douglas, ed., *Understanding Everyday Life.* Chicago: Aldine.

Cicourel, A., 1970b, "Basic and Normative Rules in the Negotiation of Status and Role, *Recent Sociology* 2:4-45.

Cicourel, A., 1974, "Ethnomethodology." In T. Sebeok, ed., *Current Trends in Linguistics,* vol. 12. The Hague: Mouton.

Cicourel, A., and J. Kitsuse, 1963, *Educational Decision Makers.* New York: Bobbs-Merrill.

Condon, W., and W. Ogston, 1966, "Sound Film Analysis of Normal and Pathological Behavior Patterns," *Journal of Nervous and Mental Disease* 163(4):338-347.

Condon, W., 1971, "Speech and Body Motion Synchrony of the Speaker-Hearer." In D. Horton and J. Jenkins, eds., *The Perception of Language.* Chicago: Charles Merrill.

Cornell, J., 1970, " 'Caste' in Japanese Social Structure," *Monumenta Nipponica* 15(1-2):107-135.

Crystal, D., 1972, "Prosodic and Paralinguistic Correlates of Social Categories." In E. Ardener, ed., *Social Anthropology and Language.* London: Tavistock.

Deutsch, C., 1968, "Environment and Perception." In M. Deutsch, et al., eds., *Social Class, Race and Psychological Development.* New York: Holt, Rinehart and Winston, Inc.

Deutsch, M., 1963, "The Disadvantaged Child and the Learning Process." In A. Passow, ed., *Education in Depressed Areas.* New York: Teachers College Press.

DeVos, G., and H. Wagatsuma, eds., 1966, *Japan's Invisible Race.* Berkeley: University of California Press.

Dewey, J., 1896, "The Reflex Arc in Psychology," *Psychological Review* 3(4):357-370.

Donoghue, J., 1971, "An Eta Community in Japan: The Social Persistence of an Outcaste Group." In G. Yamamato and T. Ishida, eds., *Modern Japanese Society.* Berkeley: McCuthchan.

Eidheim, H., 1969, "When Ethnic Identity Is a Social Stigma." In F. Barth, ed., *Ethnic Groups and Boundaries.* Boston: Little, Brown and Company.

Ekman, P., and W. Friesen, 1969, "Nonverbal Leakage and Clues to Deception," *Psychiatry* 32(1):88-106.

Entwistle, D., 1971, "Implications of Language Socialization for Reading Models and for Learning to Read," *Reading Research Quarterly* 7(1):111-167.

Erikson, E., 1968, *Identity: Youth and Crisis.* New York: Norton.

Fisher, J., 1961, "The Japanese Schools for the Natives of Truk." In G. Spindler, ed., *Education and Culture.* 1963, New York: Holt, Rinehart and Winston, Inc.

Fishman, J., and E. Leuders-Salmon, 1972, "What Has Sociology To Say to the Teacher." In C. Cazden, et al., eds., *Functions of Speech in the Classroom.* New York: Teachers College Press.

Forge, A., 1970, "Learning to See in New Guinea." In P. Mayer, ed., *Socialization.* London: Tavistock.

Frake, C. O., 1962, "The Ethnographic Study of Cognitive Systems." In S. Tylor, ed., *Cognitive Anthropology.* New York: Holt, Rinehart and Winston, Inc., 1969.

Frake, C. O., 1975, "How to Enter a Yakan House." In M. Sanches and B. Blount, eds., *Sociocultural Dimensions of Language Use.* New York: Academic Press.

Garfinkel, H., 1956, "Some Sociological Concepts and Methods for Psychiatrists,"*Psychiatric Research Reports* 6:181-196.

Garfinkel, H., 1963, "A Conception of, and Experiments with, 'Trust' as a Condition of Stable Concerted Actions." In O. Harvey, ed., *Motivation and Social Interaction.* New York: Roland Press.

Geertz, C., 1965. "The Impact of the Concept of Culture on the Concept of Man." In E. Hammel and W. Simmons, eds.,*Man Makes Sense.* Boston: Little, Brown and Company.

Gibson, E., 1965, "Learning To Read," *Science* 148:1066-1072.

Goffman, E., 1963, *Stigma.* Englewood Cliffs, N.J.: Prentice-Hall, Inc.

Goodman, K., 1967, "Reading: A Psycholinguistic Guessing Game." In H. Singer and R. Ruddell, eds., *Theoretical Models and Processes of Reading.* Newark, N.J.: International Reading Association.

Gumperz, J., 1970, "Sociolinguistics and Communication in Small Groups," *Language-Behavior Research Laboratory Working Paper no. 38.* Berkeley, Calif.

Gumperz, J., and E. Herasimchuk, 1973, "The Conversational Analysis of Social Meaning." In R. Shuy, ed., *Sociolinguistics: Current Trends and Prospects.* Washington, D.C.: Georgetown University Press.

Hall, E., 1966, *The Hidden Dimension.* New York: Anchor Books.

Hall, E., 1971, "Environmental Communication." In H. Essor, ed.,*Behavior and Environment.* New York: Plenum Press.

Holt, J., 1969, *The Underachieving School.* New York: Pitman.

Hostetler, J., and G. Huntington, 1971. *Children in Amish Society: Socialization and Community Education.* CSEC. New York: Holt, Rinehart and Winston, Inc.

Jackson, P., 1968, *Life in the Classroom.* New York: Holt, Rinehart and Winston, Inc.

Jensen, A., 1966, "Social Class and Perceptual Learning," *Mental Hygiene* 50:226-239.

Jensen, A., 1969, "How Much Can We Boost I.Q. and Scholastic Achievement?" *Harvard Educational Review* 39:1-123.

Johnson, K., 1971, "Black Kinesics," *Florida FL Reporter* 9(1,2):17-20, 57.

Kasamatsu, A., and T. Hirai, 1966, "An Electroencephalographic Study on the Zen Meditation," *Folia Psychiat, Neurolog, Japonica* 20:315-336.

Kendon, A., 1967, "Some Functions of Gaze-Direction in Social Interaction," *Acta Psychologica* 26:22-63.

Kendon, A., 1970, "Movement Coordination in Social Interaction," *Acta Psychologica* 32:100-125.

Kendon, A., 1973, "The Role of Visible Behavior in the Organization of Social Interaction." In M. von Cranach and I. Vine, eds., *Social Communication and Movement.* London: Academic Press.

Kohl, H., 1967, *36 Children.* New York: New American Library.

Labov, W., 1964a, "Phonological Correlates of Social Stratification," *American Anthropolgist* 66(4, part 2):164-176.

Labov, W., 1964b, "Stages in the Acquisition of Standard English." In R. Shuy, ed., *Social Dialects and Language Learning.* Champaign, Ill.: National Council of Teachers of English.

Labov, W., 1969, "The Logic of Nonstandard English,"*Florida FL Reporter* 7(1):60-75, 169.

Labov, W., P. Cohen, C. Robins, and J. Lewis, 1968,*A Study of the Nonstandard English of Negro and Puerto Rican Speakers in New York City,* Cooperative Research Project No. 3288.

Labov, W., and C. Robins, 1969, "A Note on the Relation of Reading Failure to Peer-group Status in Urban Ghettos," *Florida FL Reporter* 7(1):54-57, 167.

Largey, G., and D. Watson, 1972, "The Sociology of Odors," *American Journal of Sociology* 77(6):1021-1034.

Laver, J., 1968, "Voice Quality and Indexical Information," *British Journal of Disorders of Communication* 3:43-54.

Leonard, C., 1972, "A Method of Film Analysis of Ethnic Communication Style." Paper presented to the American Ethnological Society Meetings, Montreal, April 6.

Lewis, L., 1970, "Culture and Social Interaction in the Classroom," Language-Behavior Research Laboratory Working Paper no. 38. Berkeley, Calif.

Long, N., 1958, "The Local Community as an Ecology of Games." In N. Polsby, et al., eds., *Politics of Social Life,* 1963. Boston: Houghton Mifflin Company.

MacKay, D., 1972, "Formal Analysis of Communicative Processes." In R. Hinde, ed., *Nonverbal Communication.* London: Cambridge University Press.

Mackworth, J., 1972, "Some Models of Reading Process: Learners and Skilled Readers," *Reading Research Quarterly* 7:701-733.

Mackworth, N., and M. Bagshaw., 1970, "Eye Catching in Adults, Children and Monkeys." *Perception and Its Disorders, ARNMD,* 48:201-203.

Makita, K., 1968, "The Rarity of Reading Disability in Japanese Children," *American Journal of Orthopsychiatry* 38:599-614.

McDermott, J., 1969, "Deprivation and Celebration: Suggestions for an Aesthetic Ecology." In J. Edie, ed., *New Essays in Phenomenology.* New York: Ballantine.

Melmud, R., 1971, "Black English Phonology: The Question of Reading Interference," Monographs of the Language-Behavior Research Laboratory. Berkeley: University of California.

Miller, G., E. Galanter, and K. Pribram, 1960, *Plans and the Structure of Behavior* New York: Holt, Rinehart and Winston, Inc.

Mitchell, R., 1967, *The Korean Minority in Japan.* Berkeley: University of California Press.

Montagu, A., ed., 1964, *The Concept of Race.* New York: Crowell-Collier and Macmillan.

Ninomiya, S., 1933, "An Inquiry Concerning the Origin, Development, and Present Situation of the *Eta* in Relation to the History of Social Classes in Japan," *Transactions of the Asiatic Society of Japna* (second series) 10:47-145.

Parsons, T., 1959, "The School Class as a Social System," *Harvard Educational Review* 29(4):69-90.

Pribram, K., 1969, "Neural Servosystem and the Structure of Personality," *Journal of Nervous and Mental Disease* 149(1):30-39.

Pribram, K., 1970, "Looking to See." *Perception and Disorders, ARNMD* 48:150-162.

Pribram, K., 1971, *Languages of the Brain.* Englewood Cliffs, N.J.: Prentice-Hall, Inc.

Rist, R., 1970, "Student Social Class and Teacher Expectations," *Harvard Educational Review* 40:411-451.

Roberts, J., 1970, *Scene of the Battle: Group Behavior in Urban Classrooms.* New York: Doubleday Company.

Rothblat, L., and K. Pribram, 1972, "Selective Attention: Input Filter or Response Selection," *Brain Research* 39:427-436.

Scheflen, A., 1960, "Regressive One-to-one Relationships," *Psychiatric Quarterly* 23:692-709.

Scheflen, A., 1964, "The Significance of Posture in Communication Systems," *Psychiatry* 27:316-331.

Scheflen, A., 1971, "Living Space in an Urban Ghetto," *Family Process* 10(4):429-450.

Schutz, A., 1953, "Common .Sense and Scientific Interpretation of Human Action." In M. Natanson, ed., *The Philosophy of the Social Sciences,* 1963. New York: Random House.

Segall, M., D. Campbell, and M. Herskovits, 1966, *The Influence of Culture on Visual Perception.* Indianapolis: Bobbs-Merrill.

Shimahara, N., 1971, *Burakumin: A Japanese Minority and Education.* The Hague: Martinus Nijhoff.

Singer, H., and B. Beardsley, 1970, "Motivating a Disabled Reader," Thirty-seventh yearbook of the Claremont College Reading Conference.

Sokolov, E., 1969, "Modeling Properties of the Nervous System." In M. Cole and I. Maltzman, eds., *Handbook of Contemporary Soviet Psychology.* New York: Basic Books.

Sommer, R., 1969, *Personal Space,* Englewood Cliffs, N.J.: Prentice-Hall, Inc.

Spindler, G., 1959, "The Transmission of American Culture." In G. Spindler, ed., *Education and Culture,* 1963. New York: Holt, Rinehart and Winston, Inc.

Taira, K., 1971, "Japan's Invisible Race Made Visible," *Economic Development and Cultural Change* 19(4):663-668.

Thompson, L., 1966, *Reading Disability.* Springfield, Ill.: Charles C. Thomas.

Trubowitz, S., 1968, *A Handbook for Teaching in the Ghetto School.* New York: Quadrangle.

Valentine, C., 1971, "Deficit, Difference and Bicultural Models of Afro-American Behavior," *Harvard Educational Review* 41(2):137-158.

Wallace, A., 1965, "Driving to Work." In M. Spiro, ed., *Context and Meaning in Cultural Anthropology.* New York: The Free Press.

Wanat, S., 1971, *Linguistic Structure and Visual Attention in Reading,* Research Reports. Newark, Delaware: International Reading Association.

Watzlawick, P., J. Beaven, and D. Jackson, 1967, *Pragmatics of Human Communication.* New York: Norton.

Zimmerman, D., and M. Pollner, 1970, The Everyday World as a Phenomenon. In J. Douglas, ed., *Understanding Everyday Life.* Chicago: Aldine.

Dialect in Relation to Oral Reading Achievement: Recoding, Encoding, or Merely a Code?[1]

MARILYN S. LUCAS AND HARRY SINGER
University of California at Riverside

Dialect has been a prominent suspect for the past ten years as a causal factor in the disparity between achievement of the majority group (Anglo) and certain minority groups such as blacks and Mexican-Americans (Goodman, 1965; Baratz & Shuy, 1969; Brown, 1970; Wolfram, 1970; Baratz, 1971). These minority groups on the average achieve at a lower level than their Anglo peers, and the gap tends to increase with continued school experience (Tireman, 1948; Coleman, 1966; Singer, 1970; Carter, 1970).

Controversy on Dialect Interference in Reading

The views on the issue of dialect interference with reading achievement can be organized into three categories:

1. A general hypothesis that dialect interferes with learning to read has been stated by Goodman (1968), Bailey (1966) and Labov (1969).[2]

2. Differentiating the interference hypothesis, Chomsky (1970, p. 14), has argued on theoretical grounds that dialect differences in syntax and lexical items, but not in phonology, are likely to interfere in reading comprehension.

3. The contrasting hypothesis is that dialect per se is not a major cause of reading problems for children speaking non-standard dialects (Venezky, 1970; Gumperz, 1970).

---

[1] Reprinted from *Journal of Reading Behavior*, 7, No. 2, Summer 1975, 137-148. With permission of authors and the National Reading Conference. This study was supported by University of California Intramural Research Grant No. 1018.

[2] Goodman recently concluded this hypothesis was false (Goodman & Buck, 1973).

Review of Research

Empirical studies for resolving the controversy on the relationship between dialect and reading achievement are scanty for black children and even scantier for Mexican-American children (Tireman, 1948; Rosen & Ortego, 1969a). There is nevertheless a climate of opinion that Mexican-American dialect does interfere with reading achievement (Carter, 1970; Rosen, 1970).

A critical shortcoming of most reports on Mexican-American children is their tendency to equate the concepts of bilingualism and dialect (Tireman, 1948; Ramirez, 1970; Entwisle, 1971; Rosen & Ortego, 1969b). Dialect essentially refers to variations of speech in a given language community, while bilingualism indicates a person who speaks two languages. Actually, there is a "monoglot-bilingual-equilingual" continuum whose extremes are defined by those speakers who are monoglot in a given language, such as Spanish, and those who have attained the "standard" dialect in the majority *and* minority language, such as English and Spanish (Singer, 1956). Differentiating these concepts should clarify interpretation of results. Also, more evidence, based upon more carefully defined samples, may help resolve the controversy on the influence of dialect in reading achievement.

To satisfy the definition requirements of a dialect (Gaeng, 1971), we chose our sample according to the following criteria: children born in the United States who speak predominantly English, and whose speech varies from the larger community but results in no communication interferences for the average English-speaking listener as assessed by a linguist.

Sample: The sample was randomly chosen from children of Spanish surname attending two public schools in Riverside, California. The children resided in the community in which these schools are located. One of the communities consists of Mexican-American families who had moved out of the *barrio,* which is located in another part of Riverside. The other community consists of acculturated Mexican-Americans who had lived in the community for two or three generations or longer. All but three of the children in the sample were born in the Riverside area; the remaining three were born in the Southwestern United States.

Ten children from grades 1-3, selected from each school, made up a total sample of 60 children. Although 13 percent of the original group of parents did not give permission for their children to participate in the study, whatever sampling bias resulted from the necessity of securing parental consent was distributed across the three grades and the two schools.

Design and Procedures[3]

The purpose of the study was to test the null hypothesis that in Mexican-American children dialect is not significantly related to oral reading ability. For this purpose, a correlation design was employed.

Instruments:

1. *Oral reading* was assessed by taping performance on the Gates-McKillop Reading Diagnostic Test (Gates & McKillop, 1962).

2. *Language background:* a bilingual speaker interviewed parents and scored a Language Background Scale devised for this study. The interviewer rated each parent, the child, and any other adults with whom the parents or children frequently interacted (i.e., grand-parents or other relatives living in the home) according to the language most often used: Spanish only, English only, or a combination of the two. From these data, a scale was constructed with an arbitrary weight assigned to each language combination on the scale (Spanish only - 4, Spanish with some English - 3, English with some Spanish - 2, English only - 1). Weighted scores were then separated according to the child's *listening environment* (speech of parents to each other, to the child, and to significant others) and *speaking environment* (speech of the child to parents, other children, and significant others in the home).

3. *Spontaneous language responses* of the child were assessed by taping the subject's responses to selected pictures from the Children's Apperception Test (Bellak & Bellak, 1949).

4. *Language processing abilities in English* were measured by seven selected subtests of the Illinois Test of Psycholinguistic Abilities (ITPA), Revised Edition.

Analysis of Results

Mean scores and standard deviations in oral reading, presented in Table 1, are consistent with previously reported trends in reading achievement for Mexican-Americans (Tireman, 1948; Singer, 1970).

---

[3] Appreciation is expressed to Sandra Prasad, Grace Ritchie, Bette Flushman, Donna Shannon, and Sharon King for their assistance in conducting the parent interviews and testing the children, and to Kathy Williams and Shelley Cauffiel for their assistance in data analysis. Thanks is also expressed to Tom Armbruster, graduate student in Education and Linguistics, for his linguistic analysis of the taped oral reading and spontaneous speech of the children. The cooperation of Dr. Allan Metcalf, Chairman of the Linguistics Committee, University of California, Riverside Unified School District, and of the children, parents, and staffs of the schools involved, is gratefully acknowledged.

Table 1.   Oral reading scores by grade and school

	School A		School B		Schools A & B	
Grade	1.9	3.9	1.9	3.9	1.9	3.9
Mean	1.77	3.41	1.98	3.49	1.88	3.45
SD	.22	.80	.95	1.08	.68	.93

Since Tables 1 and 2 showed no consistent statistically significant differences between schools in results on oral reading, language background scale and ITPA subtests, the samples from the two schools were combined. These language scale results also indicated that our sample had satisfied the selection criterion.

The mean ITPA scores are consistent with expectations based upon previous studies of Mexican-American children (Jorstad, 1971; Kirk, 1971; Killian, 1971).

Table 3 indicates:

1. Ability to infer pictured relationships and understand spoken English vocabulary is significantly related to oral reading in grade 1;

2. Ability to process English syntactical structures and memory for auditory sequences is significantly related to oral reading at grade 3;

3. Degree of dialect in the home, as measured by the language background scale, is not significantly related either to oral reading performance or to performance on the ITPA in the first grade;

4. In third grade, there is a significant negative relationship between the amount of Spanish heard in the home and syntactic ability, and a significant positive relationship between syntactic ability and oral reading ability.

Table 4 lists only those correlations which are germane to the relationship between dialect and oral reading. The only significant correlations are at the third grade level: language background is negatively related to syntax, and syntax, in turn, is positively related to oral reading. In other words, those children who experienced more Spanish in the home tended to be lower in syntactic ability. Therefore, we infer that language background working through syntax affects oral reading performance. More specifically, we hypothesize that the intermixture of Spanish and English syntax heard in the home tends to reduce the Mexican-American child's ability to perform in English syntax, and this relative inability interferes with the processing of language involved in oral reading.

Table 2. Language background and ITPA Scores by Grade and School (Grades 1 and 3)

Grade	School A		School B		Schools A & B	
	1	3	1	3	1	3
Language Scale:						
Listening						
Mean	2.14	2.20	2.69	2.56	2.43	2.40
SD	.87	.92	.54	.48	.75	.44
Speaking						
Mean	1.33	1.32	1.67	1.26	1.51	1.29
SD	.77	.28	.72	.39	.74	.34
ITPA Subtests:						
Visual Reception						
Mean	33.0	32.4	33.2	36.0	33.1	34.2
SD	8.79	8.83	5.22	2.54	7.04	6.59
Auditory Reception						
Mean	30.6	32.6	33.3	31.6	31.95	32.1
SD	5.62	6.31	7.09	8.28	6.38	7.18
Visual Association						
Mean	37.8	31.3	38.8	33.4	38.3	32.4
SD	3.97	6.62	6.01	6.22	4.99	6.34
Auditory Association						
Mean	31.0	36.4	29.3	39.8	30.2	33.1
SD	4.5	5.32	8.68	11.93	6.78	9.61
Auditory Sequential Memory						
Mean	35.6	37.9	36.8	38.2	36.2	38.1
SD	4.9	4.79	6.97	5.92	5.90	5.25
Visual Closure						
Mean	30.9	31.3	32.7	37.8	31.8	34.55
SD	5.51	6.43	6.18	6.63	5.78	7.18
Grammatic Closure						
Mean	31.5	29.4	30.2	24.8	30.9	27.1
SD	6.00	7.90	7.57	9.14	6.68	8.64

Table 3.   Correlations of reading, language background and ITPA subtests (combined schools)

	Grade 1			Grade 3		
		Language Background			Language Background	
	Oral Reading (N = 20)	Listening (N = 17)	Speaking (N = 17)	Oral Reading (N = 20)	Listening (N = 18)	Speaking (N = 18)
ITPA Subtests						
Visual Reception (essential visual relationships)	−.320	.069	.062	−.191	−.075	−.144
Auditory Reception (vocabulary)	.497*	−.375	.032	.334	−.206	−.072
Visual Association (picture relationships)	.446*	−.177	.063	.243	.042	.048
Auditory Association (verbal analogies)	.428	−.227	−.226	.257	−.631**	−.217
Auditory Sequential Memory (memory for digits)	.124	−.250	−.137	.481*	−.002	−.154
Visual Closure (hidden partial figures)	.079	−.069	−.267	.182	−.047	−.495*
Grammatic Closure (completion of oral sentences)	.412	−.023	.198	.539*	−.526*	−.143
Oral Reading	−−−−	−.157	−.096	−−−−	−.165	−.151

*correlations significant at the .05 level
**correlations significant at the .01 level

Table 4.   Correlations of language background, syntax and reading

	Grade 1	Grade 3
Language Background (Listening) x ITPA Grammatic Closure (Syntax)	−.023	−.526*
ITPA Grammatic Closure (Syntax) x Oral Reading	.412	.539*
Language Background (Listening) x Oral Reading	−.157	−.165

*correlations significant at the .05 level

Discussion

General intelligence may be related both to performance on some ITPA subtests and to oral reading skill. Moreover, poorer performance in syntactic ability associated with a higher degree of Spanish heard in the home can be attributed to intragroup variations in cognitive capability or to dialect interference, or to some interaction of these determinants. Since syntax is theoretically a function of a basic cognitive capability (Slobin, 1966), there appears to be no way to independently assess syntax and cognitive capability.

Our results cannot be attributable to dialect differences in phonology. Dialect differences in phonology do interfere with recognition of words presented in isolation but not in context (Melmed, 1971); in our study, the oral reading test presented words in context and consequently minimized the probability of phonological interference. Moreover, if such differences were significant in oral reading achievement, we would expect them to be of greater import in lower than in higher grades because of the greater emphasis on sound-symbol correspondence in the lower grades. However, our data indicate no significant relationship between degree of Spanish language background and oral reading achievement of first graders.

The only significant relationship between bilingual background and oral reading was an indirect one, found at grade three: syntactic ability was negatively related to Spanish language experience and positively related to oral reading achievement. This finding and other changes in correlations between grades one to three in our study are consistent with systematic changes at successive elementary grade levels that have been found elsewhere to occur in abilities predictive of reading achievement in normative groups (Singer, 1965). Consequently, we can hypothesize that in grades 1-3 the changes in the relationship between language processing ability and reading are a function not of phonological, but of syntactical abilities, which become significantly related to oral reading achievement as the child progresses in school and encounters linguistically more complex reading tasks.

However, syntactic errors made by children in our study appeared to be similar to those made by less linguistically mature children (for example "theirselves" for "themselves," "mouses" for "mice")[4,5] Since differences between Mexican-Americans and Anglos in syntactical ability tend to be overcome by adulthood (Holland, 1960; Metcalf, 1972), the syntactical differences found in our study may be dialect interferences in oral reading achievement that occur in elementary grades, but are less likely to be operative in subsequent years.

Other factors, such as environmental and emotional problems connected with belonging to a nondominant cultural group, may also interfere with and further reduce the reading performance of Mexican-American children (Guerra, 1965; Ramirez, 1969, 1970; Schwartz, 1969; Henderson & Merritt, 1969) particularly if teachers respond negatively to language and reading responses of Mexican-American children. There is evidence that oral reading responses of dialectally different children are likely to be misinterpreted as errors by some teachers (Hughes, 1967; Labov, 1969; Shuy, 1969; Stewart, 1969). For other teachers, dialect differences may have been overemphasized as a causal factor for "inadequate responses" (Crowl & MacGinitie, 1970) or "bothersome" language behavior (Hughes, 1967). Goodman (1970) has suggested that teachers may misjudge the linguistic proficiency of speakers of "low-status" dialects because of their expectation models. For all of these teachers, dialect may have simply become a *code word* that implied low achievement and led to a self-fulfilling prophecy. For example, instructional decisions may have resulted in such reactions as downward adaptation of the curriculum and consequently reduced achievement in reading as it does in arithmetic (Balow, 1964), or initiation of procedures to

---

[4] For a comprehensive listing of Spanish-English errors, see Lado (1964) and Stockwell et al. (1965a, b).

[5] "Error" is defined here as an incorrect response on the Illinois Test of Psycholinguistic Abilities closure subtest.

modify a child's pronunciation may have exacerbated rather than ameliorated the effect of dialect on reading achievement. Therefore, a testable hypothesis is that teacher attitude, behavior, and evaluation of dialectally different children's oral language and reading responses mediate the degree of the relationship between their dialect and oral reading achievement.

Summary and Conclusion

Throughout the past decade, dialect has been emphasized as a causal factor of reading deficiencies in such minority groups as blacks and Mexican-Americans. But a search of the literature has not revealed any hard evidence to support this contention. On the contrary, our evidence indicates that dialect differences in their phonological aspect are not significantly related to oral reading achievement. What we did find is that degree of Spanish heard at home was negatively related to syntactical ability, which in turn was positively related to oral reading achievement. Consequently, dialect is at least indirectly associated with, if not a causal factor in, interference with oral reading performance. Therefore, a differentiated concept of the relationship between dialect, language development, and oral reading achievement is necessary. In general, we would agree with the hypothesis that dialect variation is of importance to oral reading to the extent that dialects differ on the syntactic level, but that dialect differences in phonological rules are irrelevant (Chomsky, 1970; Stewart, 1969). However, this hypothesis has to be qualified further: whether syntactical or lexical differences in dialect affect oral reading performance is also a function of the child's linguistic development and the nature of the reading task. As the dialectally different child progresses on the linguistic continuum in his second language, he will, of course, tend to have less difficulty performing in that language. Furthermore, the less the reading task involves words in isolation, lexical unfamiliarity, or syntactical complexity, the less will be the impact of dialect on oral reading achievement.

REFERENCES

Bailey, Beryl. In Bereiter, C. and S. Engelmann. *Teaching disadvantaged children in the preschool.* Englewood Cliffs, N.J.: Prentice-Hall, 1966.

Balow, Irving. The effects of homogeneous grouping in seventh grade arithmetic. *The Arithmetic Teacher,* March, 1964, 2, 186-191.

Baratz, Joan. A review of research on the relationship of black English to reading. Paper presented at International Reading Association meeting, Atlantic City, 1971.

Baratz, Joan and Shuy, R. W., eds. *Teaching black children to read.* Washington, D.C., Center for Applied Linguistics, 1969.

Bellak, L. and Bellak, S. S. *Manual of instructions for the Children's Apperception Test.* New York: C.P.S. Co., 1949.

Brown, Eric. The bases of reading acquisition. *Reading Research Quarterly,* Fall, 1970, 6(1), 49-74.

Carter, T. P. *Mexican-Americans in school: a history of educational neglect.* Princeton: College Entrance Examination Board, 1970.

Chomsky, N. Phonology and reading. In H. Levin and Joanna P. Williams, eds. *Basic Studies in Reading.* New York: Basic Books, 1970.

Coleman, James. *Equality of educational opportunity.* Superintendent of Documents. Catalog No. FS 5.238:38000. Washington, D.C.: U.S. Government Printing Office. 1966.

Crowl, T. K. and MacGinitie, W. H. White teachers' evaluations of oral responses given by white and Negro ninth-grade males. *Proceedings of the 75th Annual Convention,* American Psychological Association, 1970.

Entwisle, Doris R. Implications of language socialization for reading models and for learning to read. *Reading Research Quarterly,* Fall, 1971, 7(1), 111-167.

Gaeng, P. *Introduction to the principles of language.* New York: Harper and Row, 1971.

Gates, A. I. and McKillop, Anne S. *Gates-McKillop Reading Diagnostic Tests.* New York: Columbia University, Teachers College Press, 1962.

Goodman, K. S. Dialect barriers to reading comprehension. *Elementary English,* December, 1965, 42(8), 853-860.

Goodman, K. S. Study of children's behavior while reading orally. Final Report, Project S425, Contract OE-6-10-136, 1968.

Goodman, K. S. Comprehension-centered reading. *Claremont Reading Conference, 34th Yearbook,* 1970, 125-134.

Goodman, K. S. and Catherine Buck. Dialect barriers to reading comprehension revisited. *The Reading Teacher* 1973, 27, 6-12.

Guerra, Manuel H. Why Juanito doesn't read. *California Teachers' Association Journal,* October, 1965, 17-19.

Gumperz, J. J. Verbal strategies in multilingual communication. In J. E. Alatis, ed. *21st Annual Round Table, Bilingualism and Language Contract: Anthropological, Linguistic, Psychological and Sociological Aspects.* School of Languages and Linguistics Monograph Series on Languages and Linguistics, No. 23, 128-148. Washington, D.C.: Georgetown University Press, 1970.

Henderson, R. W. and Merritt, C. C. Environmental backgrounds of Mexican-American children with different potentials for school success. *Journal of Social Psychology,* 1969, 74, 101-106.

Holland, W. R. Language barrier as an educational problem of Spanish speaking children. *Exceptional Children,* September, 1960, 27, 42-49.

Hughes, Anne. An investigation of certain socio-linguistic phenomena in the vocabulary, pronunciation and grammar of disadvantaged preschool children, their parents and their teachers in the Detroit public schools. Unpublished doctoral dissertation, Michigan State University, 1967.

Jorstad, Dorothy. Psycholinguistic learning disabilities in 20 Mexican-American students. *Journal of Learning Disabilities,* March, 1971, 4(3), 143-149.

Killian, L. R. WISC, Illinois Test of Psycholinguistic Abilities and Bender Visual-Motor Gestalt Test performance of Spanish-American kindergarten and first grade school children. *Journal of Consulting and Clinical Psychology,* 1971, 37(1), 38-43.

Kirk, S. A. and Kirk, Winifred. *Psycholinguistic learning disabilities: diagnosis and remediation.* Urbana: University of Illinois Press, 1971.

Labov, W. Some sources of reading problems for Negro speakers of non-standard English. In Joan Baratz and R. W. Shuy, eds. *Teaching black children to read*. Washington, D.C.: Center for Applied Linguistics, 1969, 117-137.

Lado, R. *Language testing: the construction and use of foreign language tests.* New York: McGraw-Hill, 1964.

Melmed, P. J. Black English phonology: the question of reading interference. Berkeley: University of California. *Monographs of the Language-Behavior Research Laboratory,* No. 1, February, 1971.

Metcalf, A. Mexican-American English in Southern California. *Western Review,* 1972, *9,* 13-21.

Ramirez, M. Identification with Mexican-American values and psychological adjustment in Mexican-American adolescents. *International Journal of Social Psychiatry,* 1969, *15*(2), 151-156.

Ramirez, M. The bilingual program bandwagon and the psychodynamics of the Chicano child. *Claremont Reading Conference, 34th Yearbook,* 1970, 68-72.

Rosen, C. L. Assessment and relative effects of reading programs for Mexican-Americans. Unpublished manuscript, University of Georgia, 1970 (estimated date).

Rosen, C. L. and Ortego, P. D. Issues in language and reading instruction of Spanish-speaking children. Newark, Delaware: International Reading Association, 1969(a).

Rosen, C. L. and Ortego, P. D. Language and reading problems of Spanish-speaking children in the Southwest. *Journal of Reading Behavior,* Winter 1969, *1*(1), 51-70 (b).

Schwartz, A. J. Comparative values and achievement of Mexican-American and Anglo pupils. Center for the Study of Evaluation, University of California at Los Angeles, Graduate School of Education, Report No. 37, February, 1969.

Shuy, R. W. A linguistic background for developing beginning reading materials for black children. In Joan Baratz and R. W. Shuy, eds. *Teaching black children to read*. Washington, D.C.: Center for Applied Linguistics, 1969, 117-137.

Singer, H. Bilingualism and elementary education. *Modern Language Journal,* December, 1956, *40*(8), 444-458.

Singer, H. Substrata factor reorganization accompanying development of general reading ability at the elementary school level. Final Report, Contract No. 2011, U. S. Office of Education, 1965.

Singer, H. Effect of integration on achievement of Anglos, Negroes, and Mexican-Americans, Paper presented at the Annual Convention of the American Educational Research Association, Minneapolis, Minnesota, March 3-6, 1970.

Slobin, D. Comments on "Developmental psycholinguistics," In F. Smith and G. A. Miller, eds. *Genesis of language: a psycholinguistic approach.* Cambridge, Massachusetts: MIT Press, 1966.

Stewart, W. A. On the use of Negro dialect in the teaching of reading. In Joan C. Baratz and R. W. Shuy, eds. *Teaching black children to read*. Washington, D.C.: Center for Applied Linguistics, 1969.

Stockwell, R. P., J. D. Bowen and J. W. Martin. *The Grammatical Structures of English and Spanish.* Chicago: University of Chicago Press, 1965. (a)

Stockwell, R. P. and J. D. Bowen. *The Sounds of English and Spanish.* Chicago: University of Chicago Press, 1965. (b)

Tireman, L. S. Teaching Spanish-speaking children. Albuquerque: University of New Mexico Press, 1948.

Venezky, R. Non-standard language and reading. Madison, Wisconsin: University of Wisconsin, Research and Development Center for Cognitive Learning, Working Paper No. 43, 1970.

Wolfram, W. Sociolinguistic alternatives in teaching reading to non-standard speakers. *Reading Research Quarterly,* Fall, 1970, *6*(1), 9-33.

The Influence of Students' Speech Characteristics on Teachers' Evaluations of Oral Answers*

THOMAS K. CROWL
Richmond College
City University of New York

WALTER H. MACGINITIE
Teachers College
Columbia University

The importance of vocal cues as a basis for forming attitudinal judgments about a speaker has been dramatically demonstrated in a series of studies in which listeners who heard tape recordings of bilingual or bidialectal speakers formed significantly different attitudes toward the *same* speaker, depending on what language or dialect the speaker was speaking (Anisfeld, Bogo, & Lambert, 1962; Anisfeld & Lambert, 1964; Lambert, Anisfeld, & Yeni-Komshian, 1965; Lambert, Frankel, & Tucker, 1966; Lambert, Hodgson, Gardner, & Fillenbaum, 1960).

In studies involving listeners' judgments about speakers, it has frequently been found that listeners tend to agree with one another with respect to the judgments they make, not only in cases where these judgments are accurate but also in cases where these judgments are inaccurate. (See Kramer, 1963; Sanford, 1942, for comprehensive reviews.) Agreement among listeners with respect to the errors they make in judging a speaker's characteristics is probably the most forceful evidence of vocal stereotyping.

Williams, Whitehead, and Miller (1972) recently investigated the concept of vocal stereotyping within an educational context by examining relationships between teachers' expectations of student academic performance and teachers' attitudes toward students' speech. Using students from three ethnic groups, the study found that students whose speech was

---

*Reprinted from *Journal of Educational Psychology,* 1974, *66,* 3, 304-308. With permission of the authors and the American Psychological Association.

judged to be more nonstandard were also expected to perform worse academically than students whose speech was judged to be more standard.

It is important to note that the study referred to above focused on expectations of student performance. The present investigation was designed to find out if students' actual (not expected) academic performance is judged differently by teachers as a function of students' speech characteristics. An attempt was made to examine some important practical ramifications of the phenomenon of vocal stereotyping. This was done by changing the level of conceptual focus from the listeners' attitudinal judgments and expectations about a speaker to the level of overt behavior actually exhibited by listeners toward a speaker as a function of the speaker's vocal characteristics. The present study was directed at two general questions: Do differences in students' speech characteristics lead to differential judgments by teachers about students' academic performance? If so, is it possible to identify specific characteristics of teachers who are most susceptible to vocal stereotyping?

Method

Selection of Speech Sample

Speech samples of two groups of ninth-grade boys were used in the study, one group consisting of six white students of an upper-middle socioeconomic background and the other group consisting of six black students of a lower socioeconomic background. It was felt that only after evidence had been gathered which demonstrated differential judgments on the basis of rather gross speech differences would it be feasible to try to isolate specific speech characteristics associated with differential teacher judgments.

In order to control the content of students' answers while varying the speech characteristics of the students, 12 predetermined answers were used for each of two questions:

Why do we celebrate Thanksgiving?
What is the difference between a discovery and an invention?

The predetermined answers were based on answers actually given by another group of white ninth graders of upper-middle socioeconomic level. The answers were worded in standard English, with the mean number of words being 18.3. Tape recordings were made of all students in the study speaking all answers.

To insure that each student's ethnic group could be accurately identified from his speech, 12 judges drawn from the same population of teachers who participated in the study listened to the tapes and were asked to identify each student's ethnic group. The overall accuracy of individual judges' identifications was high, ranging from 75% to 100%, with a mean of 88.4%.

Students were provided with a typed set of the predetermined answers and were given an unlimited amount of time to rehearse the answers and to ask the experimenter about the meaning or pronunciation of words or about the general procedures for taping. Answers were taped as often as necessary until both the experimenter and the student agreed that each written answer had been spoken verbatim and in a natural-sounding manner.

Preparation of Tapes

By splicing together segments from the original recordings, two tapes were compiled in such a way that on each tape (*a*) each of the 24 answers occurred once, (*b*) half of the answers to each question were given by black students and half by white students, (*c*) each student gave one answer to each question, and (*d*) for any given answer, the ethnic group of the respondent on one tape was reversed on the other tape. Answers to the Thanksgiving question preceded answers to the "discovery" question on Tape A; on Tape B, this order was reversed. The beginning of each tape contained a set of instructions and four answers spoken by the experimenter to one practice question.

Subjects

The subjects consisted of 62 white teachers who had one or more years' teaching experience and who volunteered to participate. Overall, there were more female than male subjects ($n = 35$ and 27, respectively); the modal age was 25-34 years ($n = 31$); the modal number of years teaching experience was 1-5 years ($n = 27$); the most frequent grade level taught was either elementary ($n = 30$) or senior high school ($n = 25$); the highest academic degree held was either a bachelor's degree ($n = 25$) or a master's degree ($n = 36$); and classes most frequently taught by the subjects were comprised of 75%-100% white students ($n = 45$).

Experimental Procedure

The study was presented in the guise of a project for gathering data concerning grading practices of experienced teachers in order to establish norms for grading oral answers. Teachers were instructed to grade each answer in terms of "how well it really answers the question," using a scale where 10 = excellent and 1 = completely wrong. Recordings were presented to subjects either individually or in small groups, with half of the subjects randomly assigned to listen to Tape A and half to Tape B. After grading the answers, each subject filled out an anonymous biographical data sheet. In terms of sex, age, total years teaching experience, most frequent grade level taught, highest academic degree held, and ethnic group of students most frequently taught, the subjects in both groups were remarkably similar.

Results

By summing the ratings given by the subjects across both tapes, it was possible to compare the mean rating for answers when spoken by black students with the mean rating for the same answers when spoken by white students. An analysis of variance with repeated measures was initially carried out using the ratings of answers to each question separately. Since the results of the separate analyses were virtually identical, the data were combined and reanalyzed. In all analyses, the pooled interaction of individual subjects and individual students was used as the error term. The difference between subjects' ratings of the same answers spoken by black students ($M = 5.48$, $SD = 2.60$) and by white students ($M = 5.82$, $SD = 2.59$) was significant ($F = 13.22$, $df = 1/600$, $p < .001$). Thus, it was concluded that white teachers were influenced in their evaluations of students' oral answers by the speech characteristics of students whose ethnic group could be identified from their speech.

The finding of a significant difference between the ratings assigned by the two groups of subjects ($F = 21.74$, $df = 1/600$, $p < .001$) was unanticipated in view of the marked similarity of the two teacher groups in terms of biographical data and was particularly surprising in view of the comparability of the two groups' ratings of the practice answers. Also unanticipated was the significant interaction between the ethnic group of student and of teacher group ($F = 14.19$, $df = 1/600$, $p < .001$), indicating that subjects' ratings of answers with respect to the students' ethnic group differed, depending on which tape had been listened to by the subject. Although the same students and the same answers appeared on both tapes, answers assigned to black students on Tape A were assigned to white students on Tape B, and vice versa. It had been assumed that some of the predetermined answers were inherently better answers than others, but it had also been assumed that random assignment would result in the answers on each tape being similar in quality for the two ethnic groups. In light of the above findings, the assumption of similar distribution of answer quality was tested.

In order to examine the effect of answer quality without the effect of students' voices, written versions of the answers used in the study were presented to 42 student teachers. An analysis of the mean ratings of the answers in written form indicated that the answers assigned to white students on Tape A ($M = 6.10$, $SD = 2.80$) received significantly higher ratings ($t = 4.42$, $p < .001$) than did answers assigned to black students on Tape A ($M = 5.62$, $SD = 2.81$). Since the ethnic group of the student giving a particular answer was reversed on the two tapes, the above finding also indicated that the answers assigned to black students on Tape B received significantly higher ratings in their written form than did answers assigned to white students on the same tape.

If the inherent quality of the answer was the only factor affecting subjects' ratings of oral answers, one would expect white students' answers to receive higher ratings on Tape A and black students' answers to receive higher ratings on Tape B. In fact, white students' answers did receive higher ratings on Tape A (White, $M = 6.22$, $SD = 2.72$; Black, $M = 5.52$, $SD = 2.66$). But black students' answers did *not* receive higher ratings on Tape B (Black, $M = 5.44$, $SD = 2.54$; White, $M = 5.42$, $SD = 2.40$). In view of the evidence cited above, it appears that inherently superior answers spoken by black students were not perceived as any better than inherently inferior answers spoken by white students; or conversely, inherently inferior answers spoken by white students were perceived as being as good as inherently superior answers spoken by black students.

Since differences in students' speech characteristics led to significantly different judgments of the quality of students' academic performance, an attempt was made to identify specific characteristics of those teacher subjects who were most susceptible to vocal stereotyping. No significant differences were found, however, between ratings assigned to answers spoken by students of different ethnic groups by male or female subjects, by subjects younger than or older than 35 years of age, by subjects with less than or more than five years teaching experience, by subjects who were elementary school teachers or nonelementary school teachers, or by subjects having taught classes comprised of less than or more than 25% black students.

Discussion

In most previous studies of vocal stereotyping, subjects have been explicitly instructed to judge a speaker's characteristics on the basis of vocal cues, and it has usually been tacitly assumed that the other kinds of behavior of a listener toward a speaker would vary as a function of the way in which the listener perceived the speaker. The current study did not make the task of judging the speaker's characteristics explicit. On the contrary, subjects were specifically instructed to evaluate the content of the speech and implicitly asked to ignore the characteristics of the speaker. A different kind of behavior—namely, evaluating answers—was measured directly, and it was inferred that differences between evaluations of answers containing the same words were a function of the listener's perception of the speaker. The overall findings of the study supported the notion that the content of the same oral answer is evaluated differently when spoken by different persons whose difference in ethnic group is identifiable from their speech.

The results of the current study are consistent with many previous findings regarding vocal stereotyping. In this study, listeners judged the content of answers spoken by black students as inferior to the content of answers spoken by white students. Such a judgment is, by definition, erroneous since the verbal content of black students' and white students' answers was the same. The results also support the findings from studies of bilingual and bidialectal speakers (Lambert et al., 1960, 1965, 1966), inasmuch as listeners of a majority ethnic group reacted unfavorably toward members of a minority ethnic group. Although no measures of subjects' attitudes toward blacks in general were obtained, it is unlikely that negative attitudes would have been expressed. The subjects participating in the study, who were experienced teachers attending graduate courses during the summer, probably comprised a group with rather liberal views. It should also be noted that subjects participating in the study came from a total of 22 different states, with only one subject from a southern state.

Some differences in vocal cues between the two sets of answers may have been directly associated not with the different ethnic and socioeconomic backgrounds of students used in the study but rather with the experimental procedure itself. For example, the fact that students rehearsed their answers might have added an automatic quality to the recordings, although anecdotal evidence from subjects indicated that teachers were not aware that the answers were not spoken spontaneously. Also, while the wording of answers in standard English was useful in eliminating rating biases associated with nonstandard grammar, it is possible that the recorded answers given by students who may characteristically speak nonstandard English may have sounded incongruent. Again, however, anecdotal evidence suggested that this possibility was somewhat remote since most teachers indicated that during the experiment they were not even aware that the students came from different ethnic and socioeconomic backgrounds.

Within an educational context, the findings of the study are consistent both with the recent finding that students with more nonstandard speech are expected to perform worse academically than students whose speech is judged as more standard (Williams et al., 1972) as well as with the much earlier finding of Michael and Crawford (1927) that ratings of students' speech are positively correlated with students' academic performance.

While the findings of the study have implications concerning the nature of teacher-student interaction in the classroom and should alert teachers to a possible source of bias that might go undetected, it must be remembered that the experimental conditions of the study differed in a number of obvious and important ways from a typical classroom situation. In evaluating oral answers in a classroom, teachers have visual as well as vocal cues on which to base their judgments, students' responses are spoken spontaneously rather than after practice in saying them naturally, and the teacher often is already well acquainted with the student who is giving an answer. Also, controlling the content of answers may have diminished differences that might actually be found among students such as those used in the study, because vocabulary and grammatical differences were purposely eliminated. It is difficult to know how the combination of cues transmitted from the student to the teacher might detract from an unbiased appraisal of a student's academic performance.

An important way in which the experimental conditions probably did correspond to a classroom situation is the fact that the teachers' attention was not drawn specifically to the speech characteristics of students. Despite the fact that students' speech differences were not highlighted, vocal stereotyping occurred. An immediate practical concern emanating from the finding of vocal stereotyping are the grades actually assigned to students and the impact these grades may have on the student's perception of himself and his subsequent attitudes toward school and academic performance. Although statistically significant, the magnitude of the difference between ratings assigned to speakers of different ethnic groups was only .34 on a 10-point scale. Nevertheless, if teachers engage in vocal stereotyping without being aware that they are stereotyping, the potential cumulative influence of a student's speech on the teacher's judgment of the student could be considerable, particularly when one considers the frequency of student-teacher verbal interaction in the classroom. Even though teachers may not be recording marks in a grade book every time a student speaks, it may be that the teacher makes some kind of judgment about what kind of person the student is, and these subtle judgments may ultimately affect the teacher's behavior toward a student.

It should be noted that it was not possible to identify specific characteristics of teachers who were most susceptible to vocal stereotyping, but all of the teachers in the study were white and very few of them had had much experience teaching black students. It should also be noted that the lower scores assigned to black students' answers may reflect, at least in part, differences in the perceptual ability of white teachers to apprehend black students' speech. The result of not being able to apprehend as easily what a student is saying might lead to the assignment of a lower score. Certainly, it would seem fruitful to carry out similar kinds of investigations with different populations, such as black teachers or teachers from various geographic regions or dialect areas.

REFERENCES

Anisfeld, E., & Lambert, W. E. Evaluational reactions of bilingual and monolingual children to spoken languages. *Journal of Abnormal and Social Psychology,* 1964, **69**, 89-97.

Anisfeld, M., Bogo, N., & Lambert, W. E. Evaluational reactions to accented English speech. *Journal of Abnormal and Social Psychology,* 1962, **65**, 223-231.

Kramer, E. Judgment of personal characteristics and emotions from nonverbal properties of speech. *Psychological Bulletin,* 1963, **60**, 408-420.

Lambert, W. E., Anisfeld, M., & Yeni-Komshian, G. Evaluational reactions of Jewish and Arab adolescents to dialect and language variations. *Journal of Personality and Social Psychology,* 1965, **2**, 84-90.

Lambert, W. E., Frankel, H., & Tucker, G. R. Judging personality through speech: A French-Canadian example. *Journal of Communication,* 1966, **16**, 305-321.

Lambert, W. E., Hodgson, R. C., Gardner, R. C., & Fillenbaum, S. Evaluational reactions to spoken languages. *Journal of Abnormal and Social Psychology,* 1960, **60**, 44-51.

Michael, W., & Crawford, C. C. An experiment in judging intelligence by voice. *Journal of Educational Psychology,* 1927, **18**, 107-114.

Sanford, F. H. Speech and personality. *Psychological Bulletin,* 1942, **39**, 811-845.

Williams, F., Whitehead, J. L., & Miller, L. M. Relations between language attitudes and teacher expectancy. *American Educational Research Journal,* 1972, **9**, 263-277.

Section Three

MODELS

Introduction to Models

Four types of models (psycholinguistic, information processing, developmental, and affective) have been selected for this section. In an accompanying article, Holmes explicates basic assumptions underlying construction of the substrata-factor model. The same questions can be asked about the other models. What are the assumptions upon which they are constructed? How do differences in their basic assumptions affect their construction and explanation of reading?

Models should first be understood in relation to their purpose, what they are trying to explain, and judged on how adequately they accomplish this purpose. Then they should be evaluated in a broader context. In the following papagraphs of this introductory section are some questions, procedures, and criteria to use in conducting this broader evaluation.

Although all of the models depict variables and their interrelationships for responding to and processing of print, they differ in structure. What are the structural differences among the models and how do these differences affect their explanations for processing responses and deriving meaning from printed words?

Models also differ in modes of processing stimuli. For example, mature readers do not just respond passively to print but appear to actively select and even sample print, not only when scanning or skimming but also when engaged in systematic, sequential reading. Do the models account for this two-way processing of print? Another example is that some aspects of reading involve linear processing while other phases of reading entail simultaneous processing of responses to print. Are these variations in processing modes taken into consideration in the construction of the models?

Additional criteria can be employed for assessing the validity of models. Are they heuristically useful and susceptible to self-correction? For example, what research and instructional hypotheses have been or can be derived from the model? What is the explanatory power of a model? Using logical analysis to test explanatory power and comprehensiveness of a model, ask how each model explains the following reading phenomena:

1. Developmental differences in acquisition of identification and processing of a word, a sentence or a paragraph.
2. Decoding, recoding, associating and testing meaning, storage and retrieval, and encoding of responses to print.
3. The role of reasoning processes, such as concept formation, problem-solving, critical and creative thinking in comprehending and evaluating printed communications.

4. The way in which cognitive and affective processes interact in response to the reader's purpose and the demands of the task.
5. Developmental changes in perception, language, cognition, culture, and values.
6. What occurs when a word can or cannot be recognized from contextual constraints and minimal cues? Or when a change occurs from one purpose to another, for example, from reading relatively easy material rapidly and superficially to reading difficult material slowly and more analytically? Or when a reader is or is not deriving meaning from print?

Models can provide pedagogical insights. What implications for diagnosis and improvement of reading can be drawn from each model? What guidance do models provide for instruction in word identification, sentence meaning, or paragraph comprehension?

Only a representative group of models could be included in this section. Below is an annotated list of references to other models.

REFERENCES TO OTHER MODELS

Davis, Fred (Editor). *Literature of Research in Reading with Emphasis on Models*. Targeted Research and Development Program in Reading, Report No. 2. U. S. Department of Health, Education, and Welfare, Washington, D. C.: Contract No. OEC-0-70-4790 (508), Project No. 0-9030, 1971.

    The result of a year-long review of the literature, this volume contains papers on language development, learning to read, and models related to the reading process.

Kavanagh, James, and Ignatius Mattingly (Editors). *Language by Ear and by Eye*. Cambridge, Massachusetts: M.I.T. Press, 1973.

    Chapters in this book, the Proceedings of an Invitational Conference called by the National Institute of Child Health and Human Development, are on linguistic theory, writing systems, speech perception, auditory processing of speech, component processes in reading, and an information processing model (Philip Gough's model reprinted in this section).

Levin, Harry, and Eleanor Gibson. *The Psychology of Reading*. Cambridge, Massachusetts: M.I.T. Press, 1975.

    Levin and Gibson review research and critically analyze several information processing models. They challenge the theoretical position that the fluent reader predicts and confirms prediction by sampling print, asking such critical questions as, what specifically does the reader predict? How does the reader know what to sample and where to search for information to confirm or disconfirm predictions?

    Rejecting attempts to construct *the* model of *the* reading process, Levin and Gibson prefer to stress these principles of reading: reading involves selection of word features, active strategies, and economy in processing by reducing alternatives.[1]

    The Levin-Gibson concept of "reduction of alternatives" raises these questions: What are the alternatives? How does the reader decide on what alternatives to act upon? What test is used by the reader to determine whether the alternative selected is appropriate?

Singer, Harry. Theoretical Models of Reading: Implications for Teaching and Research. In H. Singer and R. B. Ruddell (Editors), *Theoretical Models and Processes of Reading* (First Edition). Newark, Delaware: International Reading Association, 1970.

    Singer briefly reviews models organized under the categories of a) teaching, b) processing, and c) skills types of models. He finds that some models deal with only part of the reading process (perceptual, cognitive, neurological) while others are intended to be comprehensive. After discussing implications of models for research and teaching, he suggests variables, processes, and cultural contexts that need to be included in a comprehensive model of reading.

---

[1] Stanley Wanat. Conceptual Frameworks for Analyzing Reading. Unpublished paper, State University of New York at Stony Brook, 1975.

Psycholinguistic Models

Psycholinguistic Implications for a Systems of Communication Model[*]

ROBERT B. RUDDELL
University of California at Berkeley

The role of psycholinguistics in studying language skills learning is undoubtedly more powerful than either that of linguistics or psychology considered separately. Although the linguist has offered a description of language competency through possible systems for describing and generating sentences and the psychologist has pursued learning theory from various viewpoints, the psycholinguist is interested in exploring the psychological reality of linguistic descriptions. In brief, the viewpoint of the psycholinguist as described by Miller is that of accepting "a more realistic conception of what language is" (3). A major goal of the psycholinguist which may be realized in the distant future is the development of a theory or theories of language performance.

The relationship between psycholinguistics and reading instruction is apparent if one views the former discipline as developing an understanding and explanation of language processing and the latter as having its central focus on the enhancement of the ability to decode and comprehend language. This relationship is even more obvious as one considers the definition of reading as a complex psycholinguistic behavior which consists of decoding written language units, processing the resulting language counterparts through structural and semantic dimensions, and interpreting the deep structure data relative to an individual's established objectives.

A central problem, however, in attempting to relate the findings of linguistics and psycholinguistics to the language skill of reading is ironi-

---

*Reprinted from *Psycholinguistics and the Teaching of Reading*, Kenneth S. Goodman and James T. Fleming, editors. Newark, Delaware: International Reading Association, 1969, 61-78.

452

cally that of communication. The many dimensions of these two disciplines have caused the reading specialist and reading researcher to ask how the multitude of individual components are related to one another and in turn to language skills development. The purpose of this discussion is to provide an overview of selected linguistic and psycholinguistic variables related to decoding and comprehending language, to briefly examine their psychological reality, and in summation to incorporate these variables into a systems of communication model.

Transformational and semantic theories have proposed that language may be viewed on several levels. The first level is considered to be the surface structure and encompasses morphemic and syntactic structures which are realized in the form of the graphemic, morphographemic, phonemic, and morphophonemic systems. It is at this level that reading instruction considers the decoding process. The second level consists of structural and semantic readings which make provision for processing language for interpretation. The various transformational and rewrite rules and the structural reading, as well as an individual's mental dictionary of semantic readings, are considered to be incorporated into this level.

The third and least-understood level consists of the deep structure of language where it is hypothesized that the syntactic and semantic components of the language are integrated for language interpretation and stored in memory. This article will initially examine the decoding process, representing one dimension of the surface structure level. Next, the comprehension process encompassing the syntactic dimension of surface structure, the structural and semantic readings, and the deep structure will be considered. A minor emphasis will be given to the role of affective mobilizers and cognitive strategies in language processing. And finally, a systems of communication model will be presented to summarize the discussion relative to reading and language skills processing.

The Decoding Process

One of the central tasks of early reading instruction is that of discovering the nature of the correlation between printed units and their oral counterparts. Instructional approaches have placed varying degrees of emphasis on a variety of decoding units. These include careful control of "regularities" and "irregularities" in grapheme-phoneme correspondences, notably vowels; spelling sound units which are related to an intermediate level unit known as the morphophoneme; and a phonologically based unit known as the vocalic-center group which closely approximates the syllable and in certain instances the smallest significant meaningful language unit or morpheme.

Most reading programs place some degree of emphasis on these various units at some point in the program although the exact structure and sequencing of these units may not always be obvious. Nevertheless, decoding skills have been taught successfully by placing special emphasis on one or a combination of these units. Perhaps a more scientific statement would be that children have learned to decode while being instructed through these various approaches. The latter statement leaves open the possibility that in some manner children are independently able to arrive at an optimal decoding unit depending upon their own cognitive strategy and the particular decoding approach used. But the key question at this point asks what research evidence is available to support a particular perceptual unit or units leading to decoding skill development in reading instruction. Parallel questions not considered in this discussion ask if a variety of units should be considered in the instructional program, at what point in a developmental sequence should they be introduced for maximum utilization, and is there any relationship between specific linguistic units and learner characteristics.

Grapheme-phoneme correspondences. The recommendation that initial words be introduced on the basis of grouped grapheme-phoneme consistencies has been proposed by Soffietti (47), Fries (12), Smith (49), Hall (20), and Bloomfield (4). These individuals have expressed the opinion that the inconsistencies of the English orthography place a limitation on the acquisition of sound-symbol correspondences as presently developed in widely used reading textbooks. Although the results have been inconsistent in investigations varying the degree of emphasis on sound-symbol correspondences and related generalizations, some early studies have revealed superior results for phonic emphasis at early grade levels, particularly in word recognition (3, 26, 48). More recently the work of Hayes (22), Ruddell (40), Hahn (19), Tanyzer and Alpert (51), Mazurkiewicz (29), and Downing (9) have lent support to the value of greater consistency in the introduction of sound-letter correspondences. Additionally, the consistent replication of research findings discussed by Chall (6) also supports the logical expectation that an approach to decoding which helps the child grasp the nature of the English writing code would be of value.

From the standpoint of information transfer the research by Samuels and Jeffrey (43) emphasizes the value of sound-letter correspondence units. In their research pseudo letters were designed to represent English phonemes and kindergarten subjects were taught to decode on the basis of sound-letter correspondences and on the basis of "whole words." The findings indicated that subjects taught by the first method were more effective in transferring their skills to "new words" than were those subjects taught by the second method. The emphasis on individual correspondences appears to provide a lower error rate and more effective decoding skill than does attention to word identification based on single features.

In a later study the same researchers (23) replicated aspects of the above study with similar findings. However, they attributed their results in part to one aspect of the experimental treatment which taught the subjects to blend phonemes represented by the pseudo letters into words. These findings are similar to those of Silberman (44) in that subjects were unable to transfer correspondence information to new words unless they had received phonic-blend instruction. The findings may be interpreted to suggest that sound blending places the phonemes in a natural sound-unit context constituting a more elaborated decoding unit which is of value in transferring sound-letter correspondence informaton to new letter patterns and words.

Morphographemic-morphophonemic correspondences. If a decoding program is to account for the nature of the English writing system, it is necessary to consider spelling units or letter patterns which provide for prediction of sound correspondences beyond the grapheme-phoneme correspondence level. Venezky (52), Wardhaugh (53), and Reed (38) have discussed this concern with reference to the morphophoneme. This unit represents an intermediate unit between the phoneme and morpheme and may be thought of as a sound-spelling pattern unit or morpho-phonemic-morphographemic system. For example, in considering the words "extreme" and "extremity," one might point to the second *e* grapheme and note that there is little regularity in its representation of a given sound. However, when one considers these two words on the morphophonemic level, a very regular pattern is immediately obvious. In the alternations extreme-extremity, obscene-obscenity, supreme-supremity, one observes a consistent shift in the sound value (/iy/ to /i/) with the addition of the suffix *-ity*. Although some reading programs have developed a few alternations—such as that found in the final *e* marker (sit /i/, site /ay/)—very little consideration has been given to detailed study and research in this area.

Venezky has emphasized that a distinction needs to be made between spelling-sound patterns based on the spelling system and those based on phonological habits. In the first case children probably need to be taught the generalization that the letter c represents /s/ when followed by $e, i,$ or y (e.g., city/sitiy/) and represents /k/ otherwise (e.g., cat/kæt/). However, the generalization that final consonant s is pronounced as /z/ following voiced sounds (e.g., dog$s$ /z/), as / əz/ after /s, z, š, ž, č, ǰ/ (e.g., buzze$s$ / əz/), and as /s/ in all other contexts (e.g., hop$s$ /s/) is phonological in nature. For this reason the native speaker will automatically produce this change and there would seem to be little need to teach it.

An intensive research effort is needed to examine the contribution of the value of morphophonemic generalizations for reading instruction. One basic question might explore the possible advantage of near simultaneous introduction of contrasting letter patterns representing different but consistent vowel values (e.g., bat, bate), in contrast to sequencing grapheme-phoneme correspondences on the basis of "consistent" vowel correspondences (e.g., bat, mat), as is the case in many recently published reading programs. The research by Levin and Watson (28), although limited in scope, has demonstrated possible value in establishing a "set for diversity" in decoding and may be interpreted to lend some support to the former consideration.

Vocalic-center group, morpheme. Hansen and Rodgers (21) have posited that a linguistic unit identified as the vocalic-center group provides for high transfer value in decoding. This unit defined as "a vowel nucleus with 0-3 preceding and 0-4 following consonants" (39) is phonologically rather than semantically based. In most cases, however, this unit would parallel that of the syllable as defined by the lexicographer. The rationale for considering such a unit is that phonological segmentation is of greater significance than morphological segmentation for the early reader. Rodgers has reported one experiment in which children were asked to repeat disyllabic words (e.g., toas-ter) and bimorphemic words (e.g., toast-er) after the investigator. Their errors were found to favor redivision along the syllabic or phonological rather than along morphological breaks. It should be pointed out, however, that many words classified along phonological boundaries (e.g., quick-ly) will also be classified in an identical fashion along morphological boundaries (e.g., quick-ly).

Other research, notably that of Gibson and her colleagues (14), has explored the presence of a higher order unit formed by grapheme-phoneme correspondences. This research has demonstrated that children in the early stages of reading have developed higher-order generalizations which provide for decoding pseudolinguistic letter patterns following English spelling expectancies. The children appeared to perceive regularities in sound-letter correspondences and transfer these to decoding unfamiliar trigrams even though taught by what the researchers refer to as the "whole word" approach.

Additional work by Gibson, et al. (*13*), has demonstrated that adult subjects perceive pseudolinguistic trigrams more easily when they follow English spelling generalizations or pronounceable units (e.g., *BIF*) than when they are less pronounceable (e.g., *IBF*) or more meaningful (e.g., *FBI*). Because the task of the reader is that of decoding written letter patterns and transferring them into oral counterparts, pronounceable letter combinations would seem to be of significant value. On the other hand, meaningful trigrams, such as *FBI*, require the reader to work with three units rather than one. It was noted that the latter type of trigram was more easily recalled than the pronounceable unit. The ease in recall of the meaningful unit was attributed to known and exhaustible storage categories while the pronounceable trigram syllables would call for an extremely large number of categories and be more difficult to retrieve. The researchers concluded that pronounceability was the better grouping principle for reading. This conclusion lends support to the validity of the previously discussed vocalic-center group and in certain instances the corresponding morpheme.

At this point the discussion has considered several decoding units and their psychological real value for developing decoding skills. It would appear that the following units are psychologically real decoding units as used by early readers: grapheme-phoneme correspondences; morpho-graphemic-morphophonemic patterns; and vocalic-center groups and in some cases corresponding morphemes. Upon initial examination the above units appear to be mutually exclusive. This condition may not be obvious, however, when operationalized in the instructional program. The great majority of linguistically influenced programs which attempt to control for sound-letter correspondences do not teach correspondences in isolation. For the most part, this learning is accomplished through initial consonant substitution, final consonant substitution, and vowel substitution contrasts. For example, the matrix in Figure 1 accounts for emphasis on initial consonants b/b/ and m/m/ in context; medial vowels a /æ/ and i/i/ in context; morphophonemic pattern contrast with a vowel shift from /æ/ to /ey/; and utilizes the vocalic-center groups and corresponding morphemes.

	-at	*-ate*	*-it*
b-	b*a*t	b*a*t*e*	b*i*t
m-	*m*at	mate	*m*it

Figure 1.   Commonalities in decoding units

This example greatly oversimplifies the discussion but serves to illustrate the operational economy which is possible in teaching various decoding generalizations. Most programs, however, attempt to place specific emphasis on a particular unit of analysis by controlling letter-sound relationships with substitutions of correspondences in initial, medial, and final positions.

It is thus possible to view the decoding process as establishing an understanding of the relationship between grapheme-phoneme correspondences, which form the larger morphographeme and morphophoneme units which, in operational form, can in turn formulate the pronunciation of the vocalic-center group and, in some instances, the corresponding morpheme.

The Comprehension Process

In examining the process of comprehension, the two general areas of relational meaning and lexical meaning are of primary concern. With the former, one is concerned with the importance of structural relationships in sentences and, with the latter, the importance of semantic considerations realized through denotative and connotative meanings and non-linguistic signs.

Research related to the comprehension process has been prompted by the extensive sentence knowledge which the English speaker possesses. For example, he can recognize grammatical from nongrammatical sentences, *The car struck the tree* versus *The struck tree the car;* comprehend different sentences having the same constituent structures, *John is eager to please* versus *John is easy to please;* identify ambiguous sentences with identical surface structure, *They are frying chickens* versus *They are frying chickens;* and understand sentences with similar meaning but possessing different surface structures, *The girl struck the robber* versus *The robber was struck by the girl.* Additionally, the English speaker can comprehend as well as generate a phenomenally large number of novel sentences. These facts alone suggest that language production and comprehension must be characterized by a rule governing nature. But what evidence is present which will provide for the validation of language generalizations proposed by language scholars?

Relational meaning—surface structure. Recent psycholinguistic research has sought to explore the psychological reality of surface structure constituents or the way in which language patterns tend to "chunk" into syntactic categories. Glanzer (*16*) has shown that pseudosyllable-word-pseudosyllable patterns are more easily learned when the connnecting word is a function word (e.g., *of, and*) than when it is a content word (e.g., *food*). This finding supports the view that the resulting constituent group is a more natural word group and thus more easily processed.

The work of Johnson (*24*) dealing with a paired associate learning task has shown that adult subjects make a larger number of recall errors between phrases (e.g., *The valiant canary . . . ate the mangy cat.*) than within phrases (e.g., *The . . . valiant . . . canary,* etc.). This finding suggests that phrases may operate as psychologically real units. The experiment of Fodor and Bever (*11*) also supports this contention. In their investigation, a clicking noise of brief duration was made as a sentence was read. Regardless of the placement of the click (e.g., during a word occurring immediately before or after a phrase boundary), the subjects indicated that the click occurred at the phrase boundary. Thus their conclusion supports the viewpoint that perceptual units correspond to sentence constituents as designated by the linguist.

The recent work of Ammon (*1*) has revealed that third grade and adult subjects require more time to process and respond to phrases. Suci et al (*50*) reported similar findings, thus providing additional support for sentence constituents as meaningful processing units.

Relational meaning—deep structure. The transformational theory has proposed that sentences are processed from the surface structure level to an underlying or deep structure for comprehension purposes. This deep structure is realized through transformational and rewrite rules and is then integrated with the semantic component to convey meaning.

The work of Miller (*32*) has demonstrated that when subjects are asked to transform sentences from one form into another (e.g., active affirmative to passive or active affirmative to passive negative), a positive relationship is present between transformation time and the complexity of the transformation. This finding supports the contention that transformations possess psychological reality in that the greater the number of transformations the greater is the distance between the surface and deep structure of a sentence.

Mehler (*30*) has shown that after subjects have been asked to memorize a series of complex sentences varying in grammatical type, they tend to recall the sentence but in a simpler grammatical form. For example, a sentence in the passive may be recalled in its active form. These findings suggest that a recoding of the sentence has occurred and that the semantic form is maintained but the deep syntactic marker indicating the passive form has been forgotten.

The role of transformations in sentence comprehension has also been demonstrated in the research of Gough (*18*) and Slobin (*46*). These researchers have shown that sentence comprehension varies in increasing difficulty (speed in determining truth value of sentence) in the following order—active affirmative, passive, negative, and passive negative. Thus, the available evidence does give support to the reality of deep sentence stucture. Additional support will be derived from the discussion of short- and long-term memory presented later in this paper.

Lexical meaning. It should be obvious at this point that this discussion of surface and deep structure has placed little emphasis on the role of lexical meaning. Some evidence is present in the previously discussed work of Gough (*18*) and Slobin (*46*) to suggest the importance of this language component. It is of interest to note, for example, that passive sentences were comprehended with greater ease than negative sentences even though the former are thought to be syntactically more complex. This unexpected finding may be attributed in part to the semantic difference between the passive and the negative and to the semantic similarity between the passive and the active. In instances requiring a true or false determination, negative sentences seem to be difficult to comprehend. Slobin has emphasized that not only is syntax important in comprehending sentences but semantic considerations must also be accounted for. His research has shown that the differentiation in difficulty between active and passive can largely be eliminated by clarifying the role of nouns in the subject and object positions. This clarification can be accomplished by reducing the possibility of semantic reversibility (e.g., Reversible: The *girl* struck the *boy*. The *boy* was struck by the *girl*. Nonreversible: The *boy* picked the apple. The *apple* was picked by the *boy*.) Such findings suggest that much more is involved in sentence understanding than relational meaning.

One would expect structure words to play an important role in narrowing possible semantic alternatives in the sequence of a sentence context. For example, the word *the* not only cues a noun which follows but may also clarify or emphasize the semantic nature of the noun (e.g., *The* dog was in our yard versus *Some* dog was in our yard). Miller (*32*) and Miller et al (*34*), demonstrated that words in context following a similar grammatical pattern are perceived more accurately than when in isolation. These findings suggest that the contextual constraint serves to narrow the possible range of appropriate words. Additional support for the importance of context in narrowing semantic possibilities is found in the research of Goodman (*17*). He has shown that although children may be unable to decode words in isolation, they deal successfully with the same words in a running context. Research by Ruddell (*41*) has shown that reading comprehension of fourth grade children is significantly higher on passages utilizing basic high-frequency patterns of their oral language structure in contrast to passages using low-frequency and more-elaborated construction. These findings may be interpreted to support the importance of contextual associations which provide sufficient delimiting information to enable a child to determine the semantic role of a word and further to recognize and comprehend it in the sentence.

The importance of the connotative dimension of word meaning obtains support from the research by Samuels (*42*). Fifth and sixth grade subjects were found to perform significantly higher in comprehending a reading passage containing words of high association value than a control group reading a passage containing low association value words.

Although effort is being made in developing a semantic theory which parallels the previously discussed deep structure, progress has been understandably slow because of the extremely complex nature of relating the semantic and structural components. Katz and Fodor (*25*) have characterized the form of a semantic theory as linguistic description minus grammar. They have postulated that a semantic component in language serves to assign meaning to each sentence through semantic markers. For example, semanticists have constructed semantic categories such as object—nonobject, animate—inanimate, human—nonhuman, and male—female. A semantic marker (*37*) such as *male* represents the content of words like *man, boy,* or *father* in contrast to words like *car, truth,* and *girl.* In some respects this approach resembles the game of 20 questions which provides for narrowing the definition of the meaning under consideration. A sequence of such semantic markers constituting the dictionary would thus provide a semantic reading and define the conceptual content of words. By then utilizing a set of projection rules, the readings of lexical items would be integrated with the grammatical relationships as indicated by the deep structure to derive the semantic characterizations of sentence constituents. Postal (*37*) expresses the view that such characterizations will explain semantic properties such as ambiguity (e.g., I observed the ball.), paraphrase (e.g., John is a farmer. *John* is someone who farms.), synonymy (e.g., not living; dead), or anomaly (e.g., John married a potato pancake.).

A difficulty which is apparent in the Katz and Fodor discussion of sentence meaning is the ambiguity resulting from the limited sentence context. To use an example from Katz and Fodor, the sentence "The bill is large," can mean a sizeable debt or the unusual size of a bird's beak. To know that the sentence is ambiguous is only a first step toward the understanding of its meaning. The meaning difficulty is resolved in a larger verbal context such as "Oh, I see you bought a new dress," or "My, what an unusual bird." The ambiguity may also be accounted for in a nonlinguistic fashion if one is purchasing clothing at a store or visiting a zoo. To describe rules, however, which will define the larger verbal context and nonlinguistic meaning represents an enormous task for the psycholinguistic researcher.

Short- and long-term memory. The importance of memory in language processing is also of significant concern as one considers surface and deep structure. Miller and Chomsky (35) have proposed that a short- and long-term memory are operative in language processing. It is further proposed that the limited short-term memory deals with the less complex surface structure of sentences while the long-term memory handles the more involved, deep structure of sentences.

Miller (32) has demonstrated that subjects have great difficulty in processing sentences containing self-embedded structures (e.g., The rat that the cat that the dog worried killed ate the malt, etc.) in contrast to right-recursive sentences (e.g., This is the dog that worried the cat that killed the rat that ate the malt, etc.). Because the deep structure of these sentences is identical, Miller attributes this variation in difficulty to the heavy demand placed on the short-term memory by the surface structure of the self-embedded sentence.

It would thus seem logical that because of the limited short-term memory (33), a deep language structure and a long-term memory component are essential for information processing over running discourse. The previously cited work of Mehler may be interpreted to support this viewpoint in that complex sentences presented to subjects were recalled in a simpler form. It would thus seem that after a sentence is processed in the deep structure, the underlying meaning is retained with little regard for the structure. It would also appear that the deep underlying structure is basic to comprehending sentences.

Affective and Cognitive Dimensions

Affective mobilizers. A system of communication must in some manner account for an individual's interests, attitudes, and values which become operationalized as his objectives and goals. As an individual confronts a verbal task, his motivation reflected in his persistence and drive is extremely important. This viewpoint is supported by Durkin's research (8) which has identified the preschool reader as an individual who is serious and persistent, possesses the ability to concentrate, and is of a curious nature. In a study of achieving and nonachieving elementary school readers, Kress (27) has reported that the former group demonstrated more initiative in exhausting solutions and was found to persist in problem solving under changing conditions. The research of Piekarz (36) has indicated that the high-level reader, in contrast to the inferior reader, provides significantly more responses in interpreting a reading passage, a trait thus indicating greater involvement and participation. The high-level reader is also more objective and impersonal in synthesizing information sought. The research of Athey (2) has demonstrated the importance of value systems as mobilizers for reading at the junior high school level.

One would also expect life objectives to influence an individual's store of concepts and in turn his semantic dimension of language processing. The reality of this view is reflected in functional varieties of language. The lexicon of the organic chemist varies markedly from that of the newscaster, and both in turn differ from that of the farm laborer.

The affective mobilizers operationalized as the objectives and goals of the individual would thus be expected to influence language processing at the surface-structure level, through the structural and semantic readings, and at the deep-structure level.

Cognitive strategies. As an individual participates in the communication act, he is constantly required to perceive and organize experiences. He must develop a symbol-processing system which will provide for conceptualization of experience. Bruner et al. (5) have shown that a cognitive strategy is of basic importance to the conceptualization process. Kress (27) concluded from a concept formation study of elementary school children that achieving readers were superior to nonachievers in versatility and flexibility, ability to draw inferences from relevant clues, and ability to shift set when new standards were introduced. From an extensive review of research on conceptualization, Singer (45) concluded that an important dimension in comprehending language consists of changing, modifying, and reorganizing a previously formed concept.

Thus the cognitive strategy of an individual is considered to be operationalized as a process of evaluating the adequacy of information, data gathering, hypothesis building, organizing and synthesizing data, and hypothesis testing. Additionally, the utilization of these factors must be guided by a constant awareness of the need to shift one's strategy to account for other approaches to problem solutions.

A Systems of Communication Model

Although care must be exercised in attributing psychological reality to a competence model or linguistic description, the research presented in this discussion lends some degree of support to the reality of surface structure, language processing through structural and semantic readings, deep structure, short- and long-term memory, and the importance of affective mobilizers and cognitive strategies. Thus, in a limited degree, evidence is present to suggest the general nature of a model of performance.

The language model in Figure 2 has been formulated in order to integrate the previous discussion and express relationships between the various psycholinguistic factors involved in the communication process. On the extreme left of the model the basic communication skills are identified. The rectangular line encloses a hypothetical representation of the systems involved in encoding and production processes of speech or writing and the decoding and comprehension processes of listening or reading.

Near the bottom of the rectangle, the affective mobilizers and the cognitive strategies are noted. The mobilizers represent individual interests, attitudes, and values and become operationalized as goals and objectives in the communication setting. The strategies represent an individual's approach to the language-processing task as determined in part by his objectives. The vertical arrows are entered at key parts of the model from the affective and cognitive dimensions and indicate that during language processing the reader is constantly interacting with each phase of the communication model. These aspects of the model would enable the individual to shift his attention, for example, to the structural aspects of a sentence in order to obtain added relational data to determine the specific semantic dimension of a given word.

The model becomes more meaningful as the act of reading is traced through the various dimensions. In the early stages of reading, the child encounters the English writing system. The objective of the instructional program is to help him understand the nature of the code. This objective

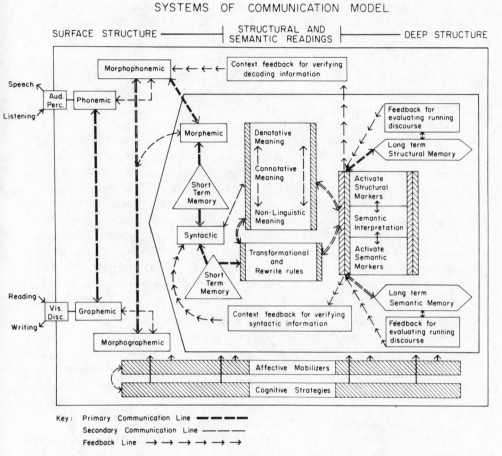

SYSTEMS OF COMMUNICATION MODEL

SURFACE STRUCTURE ——————| STRUCTURAL AND | —————— DEEP STRUCTURE
                          | SEMANTIC READINGS |

Figure 2.   Systems of Communication Model

may be accomplished by establishing the relationship between the graphemic and morphographemic systems and the phonemic and morphophonemic systems, respectively. The development of cognitive strategies should lead the child to examine alternatives to decoding words. For example, after an unsuccessful attempt to utilize the grapheme-phoneme relationships in decoding, it may be necessary to examine clues at the morphographemic-morphophonemic level or to utilize the context feed-back from the interpretation derived from the deep structure of the sentence. The more advanced reader may move directly from the morphographemic level through the morphophonemic system to the morphemic level or directly from the morphographemic level to the morpheme with a minimal use of the morphophonemic system (*10*).

The organized sound patterns directly involve the morphemic system. At this point the short-term memory is effected, and the syntactic system begins to "chunk" the language units through the constituent structures for transformational and rewriting purposes. Following the transformation and rewriting of the sentence in its most basic form, the semantic aspect of the model is encountered, and the meaning of the various morphemes are considered through a semantic reading utilizing the denotative, connotative, and nonlinguistic dictionary components. The semantic and structural meanings are then meshed through the semantic interpretation or projection rules, and the meaning is established. Simultaneously, the appropriate semantic markers and structural markers are attached, and the semantic and structural contexts are placed in long-term memory. If at the point of semantic projection some difficulty is encountered and the sentence appears to be ambiguous, the reader may return to the morphophonemic level or the syntactic level to verify the surface structure realization for a specific morpheme or constituent structure, respectively.

As a new sentence appears in the running context, the communication is processed in the same fashion. Previous information, which has been stored in the long-term semantic and structural memories, is available for mobilization to the semantic-interpretation level to aid in evaluating the running discourse relative to the objectives established by the reader.

Just as one has examined the act of reading which involves the factors inside the rectangular line, one could proceed through the model in a similar fashion for the decoding and comprehension processes of listening. The encoding and productive processes of writing and speech can be examined by starting with the long-term semantic and structural memories, progressing to the semantic interpretation or projection, and moving from right to left through the model.

In conclusion, the field of psycholinguistics holds significant promise in developing an understanding of language processing which in turn should generate valuable knowledge about the reading process and other communication skills. This result is suggested in the overview of research presented in this discussion providing support for the psychological reality of selected linguistic units. Formulations such as those realized in the systems of communication model should enable reading researchers and specialists to work more profitably toward a theory of reading.

REFERENCES

1. Ammon, P. R. "The Perception of Grammatical Relations in Sentences: A Methodological Exploration," *Journal of Verbal Learning and Verbal Behavior,* 7 (1968), 869-875.

2. Athey, Irene J. "Reading-Personality Patterns at the Junior High School Level," unpublished doctoral dissertation, University of California at Berkeley, 1965.

3. Bear, D. E. "Phonics for First Grade: A Comparison of Two Methods," *Elementary School Journal,* 59 (1958), 394-402.

4. Bloomfield, L. *Language.* New York: Holt, Rinehart and Winston, 1933.

5. Bruner, J., J. Goodnow, and G. Austin. *A Study of Thinking.* New York: Wiley Press, 1956.

6. Chall, Jeanne S. *Learning to Read: The Great Debate.* New York: McGraw-Hill, 1967.

7. Clifton, C., I. Kurca, and J. J. Jenkins. "Grammatical Relations as Determinants of Sentence Similarity," *Journal of Verbal Learning and Verbal Behavior,* 4 (1965), 112-117.

8. Durkin, Dolores. "Children Who Learn to Read Before One," *Reading Teacher,* 14 (1961), 163-166.

9. Downing, J. A. "The I.T.A. (Initial Teaching Alphabet) Reading Experiment," *Reading Teacher,* 18 (November 1965), 105-110.

10. Edfeldt, A. W. *Silent Speech and Silent Reading.* Stockholm: Almgrist and Wiksell, 1959.

11. Fodor, J. A., and T. G. Bever. "The Psychological Reality of Linguistic Segments," *Journal of Verbal Learning and Verbal Behavior,* 4 (1965), 414-420.

12. Fries, C. C. *Linguistics and Reading.* New York: Holt, Rinehart and Winston, 1963.

13. Gibson, Eleanor J., et al. "A Comparison of Meaningfulness and Pronounceability as Grouping Principles in the Perception and Retention of Verbal Material," *A Basic Research Program on Reading.* Ithaca, New York: Cornell University, Cooperative Research Project No. 639, 1963.

14. Gibson, Eleanor J., H. Osser, and Anne D. Pick. "A Study of the Development Grapheme-Phoneme Correspondences," *A Basic Research Program on Reading.* Ithaca, New York: Cornell University, Cooperative Research Project No. 639.

15. Gibson, Eleanor J., et al. "The Role of Grapheme-Phoneme Correspondences in the Perception of Words," *American Journal of Psychology,* 75 (1962), 554-570.

16. Glanzer, M. "Grammatical Category: A Rote Learning and Word Association Analysis," *Journal of Verbal Learning and Verbal Behavior,* 1 (1962), 31-41.

17. Goodman, K. S. "A Linguistic Study of Cues and Miscues in Reading," *Elementary English,* 42 (1965), 639-643.

18. Gough, P. G. "Grammatical Transformations and Speed of Understanding," *Journal of Verbal Learning and Verbal Behavior,* 4 (1965), 107-111.

19. Hahn, H. T. "Three Approaches to Beginning Reading Instruction," *Reading Teacher,* 19 (May 1966), 590-594.

20. Hall, R. A., Jr. *Sound and Spelling in English.* Chilton Books, 1961.

21. Hansen, D. N., and T. S. Rodgers. "Exploration of Psycholinguistic Units in Initial Reading," in Goodman (Ed.), *The Psycholinguistic Nature of the Reading Process.* Detroit: Wayne State University Press, 1968, 59-102.

22. Hayes, R. B. "ITA and Three Other Approaches to Reading in First Grade," *Reading Teacher,* 19 (May 1966), 627-630.

23. Jeffrey, W. E., and S. J. Samuels. "Effect of Method of Reading Training on Initial Learning and Transfer," *Journal of Verbal Learning and Verbal Behavior,* No. 3, 7 (1967), 354-358.

24. Johnson, N. F. "The Psychological Reality of Phrase-Structure Rules," *Journal of Verbal Learning and Verbal Behavior,* 4 (1965), 414-420.

25. Katz, J. J., and J. A. Fodor. "The Structure of a Semantic Theory," *Language*, 39, No. 2 (1963), 170-210.

26. Kelly, Barbara Cline. "The Economy Method Versus the Scott, Foresman Method in Teaching Second Grade Reading in the Murphysboro Public Schools," *Journal of Educational Research*, 51 (1958), 465-469.

27. Kress, R. A. "An Investigation of the Relationship Between Concept Formation and Achievement in Reading," unpublished doctoral dissertation, Temple University, 1955.

28. Levin, H., and J. Watson. "The Learning Variable Grapheme-to-Phoneme Correspondences," *A Basic Research Program on Reading*. Ithaca, New York: Cornell University, Cooperative Research Project No. 639, 1963.

29. Mazurkiewicz, A. J. "ITA and TO Reading Achievement When Methodology Is Controlled," *Reading Teacher*, 19 (May 1966), 606-610.

30. Mehler, J. "Some Effects of Grammatical Transformation on the Recall of English Sentences," *Journal of Verbal Learning and Verbal Behavior*, 2 (1963), 346-351.

31. Miller, G. A. "Some Preliminaries to Psycholinguistics," *American Psychologist*, 20 (1965), 15-20.

32. Miller, G. A. "Some Psychological Studies of Grammar," *American Psychologist*, 17 (1962), 748-762.

33. Miller, G. A. "The Magical Number Seven, Plus or Minus Two," *Psychological Review*, 63 (1956), 81-97.

34. Miller, G. A., G. A. Heise, and W. Lichten. "The Intelligibility of Speech as a Function of the Context of the Test Material," *Journal of Experimental Psychology*, 41 (1951), 329-335.

35. Miller, G. A., and N. Chomsky. "Finitary Models of Language Users," in R. D. Luce, R. Bush and E. Galanter (Eds.), *Handbook of Mathematical Psychology*, 11. New York: Wiley Press, 1963.

36. Piekarz, Josephine A. "Getting Meaning From Reading," *Elementary School Journal*, 56 (1956), 303-309.

37. Postal, P. M. "Underlying and Superficial Linguistic Structure," *Harvard Educational Review*, 34 (1964), 246-266.

38. Reed, D. W. "A Theory of Language, Speech, and Writing," *Linguistics and Reading*, Highlights of the Pre-convention Institutes. Newark, Delaware: International Reading Association, 1966, 4-25.

39. Rodgers, T. S. "Linguistic Considerations in the Design of the Stanford Computer Based Curriculum in Initial Reading." Institute for Mathematical Studies in the Social Sciences, Technical Report No. 111, USOE Grant Number OE5-10-050, 1967.

40. Ruddell, R. B. "A Longitudinal Study of Four Programs of Reading Instruction Varying in Emphasis on Regularity of Grapheme-Phoneme Correspondences and Language Structure on Reading Achievement in Grades Two and Three." University of California, Berkeley, 1968. Supported by the USOE, Projects 3099 and 78085.

41. Ruddell, R. B. "The Effect of the Similarity of Oral and Written Patterns of Language Structure on Reading Comprehension," *Elementary English*, 42 (1965), 403-410.

42. Samuels, D. J. "Effect of Word Associations on Reading Speed, Recall, and Guessing Behavior on Tests," *Journal of Educational Psychology* (in press).

43. Samuels, S. J., and W. E. Jeffrey. "Discriminability of Words and Letter Cues Used in Learning to Read," *Journal of Educational Psychology*, 57, No. 6 (1966), 337-340.

44. Silberman, H. F. *Exploratory Research on a Beginning Reading Program*, Technical Memorandum, No. TM-895/100/00. Santa Monica: System Development Corporation, 1964.

45. Singer, H. "Conceptualization in Learning to Read: New Frontiers in College-Adult Reading," in G. B. Schick and M. M. May (Eds.), *Fifteenth Yearbook of the National Reading Conference.* National Reading Conference, Milwaukee, 1966, 116-132.

46. Slobin, D. I. "Grammatical Transformations and Sentence Comprehension in Childhood and Adulthood," *Journal of Verbal Learning and Verbal Behavior,* 5 (1966), 219-227.

47. Soffietti, J. P. "Why Children Fail to Read: A Linguistic Analysis," *Harvard Educational Review,* 25 (Spring 1955), 63-84.

48. Sparks, Paul E., and L. C. Fay. "An Evaluation of Two Methods of Teaching Reading," *Elementary School Journal,* 57 (April 1957), 386-390.

49. Smith, H. L., Jr. *Linguistic Science and the Teaching of English.* Cambridge: Harvard University Press, 1959.

50. Suci, G. J., P. R. Ammon, and P. Gamlin. "The Validity of the Probe-Latency Technique for Assessing Structure in Language," *Language and Speech,* 10 (1967), 69-80.

51. Tanyzer, H. J., and H. Alpert. "Three Different Basal Reading Systems and First Grade Reading Achievement," *Reading Teacher,* 19 (May 1966), 636-642.

52. Venezky, R. F. "English Orthography: Its Graphical Structure and Its Relation to Sound," *Reading Research Quarterly,* 2 (Spring 1967), 75-106.

53. Wardaugh, R. "Linguistics—Reading Dialogue," *Reading Teacher,* 21 (February 1968), 432-441.

Behind the Eye:
What Happens in Reading*

KENNETH S. GOODMAN
University of Arizona

A child, eyebrows knit, haltingly speaks as he stares intently at the small book he is holding, "See Tom. See Tom . . ." He stops, apparently unable to continue. "We haven't had that next word yet," he states in a troubled voice to his teacher.

"Mary is only seven, but she can read anything," says the doting mother to her friend. "Read us that article from the *Times*," she says to the little girl. The child reads an article on national politics, with great speed and animation, while the friend listens appreciatively. She stumbles occasionally, as the going gets rough now and then, but is apparently untroubled by the task. "Did you understand all that dear?" her awed listener asks. "She has a little difficulty putting it into words, but I'm sure she understands," interposes the mother.

"I give up," the weary graduate student mutters to himself as he sits at the small table in the library stacks. He's just finished his third reading of the article his professor has assigned. He forces himself to formulate, out of the conceptual jumble he finds himself lost in, a few questions to raise in class. "Maybe the class is too advanced for me," he wonders. "Why don't these guys write so people can understand?"

"I can't make head or tail out of this damn thing." A best-selling writer is speaking long-distance to his attorney. "It's some kind of release I'm supposed to sign giving this producer the film rights to my latest book. But it's full of all kinds of parties of the first part and whereas's."

"Read it to me," says the lawyer. The author begins. "The undersigned, who shall be known as . . ." The attorney listens, interrupts a few

---

*Reprinted from Kenneth S. Goodman and Olive S. Niles (Eds.), *Reading Process and Program*. Commission on the English Curriculum, Urbana, Illinois: National Council of Teachers of English, 1970, 3-38. Copyright 1970 by the National Council of Teachers of English. Reprinted with permission.

470

times to ask for repetition, and is ready by the time his caller has finished to offer his legal advice. He clarifies the meaning of the document to the author, restates the legal terminology in phrases his client finds meaningful, dictates a clause to be added to protect the author's rights.

Reading is obviously involved in each of these episodes. But, at what point does it become reading and at what point does it cease to be reading and become something else, thinking perhaps, or concept formation, or the acquisition of knowledge?

Is the child who is limited to calling the names of word shapes he has been taught in any sense a reader? If he is not, at what point does he become one? Is it when he has a larger sight-word repertoire? How large? Is it when he has learned how to "attack" new words? If, like the hypothetical Mary above, he can "read" things he can't understand, is he reading?

To what extent must a reader arrive at the meaning the writer intended? If he must fully *comprehend,* then our graduate student is a non-reader. Even if a moderate level of comprehension is required he has fallen short of the mark. Are all readers then only semiliterate?

Who has read the legal document? The lawyer who is hundreds of miles away from it and who cannot even see it, or his client who holds it in his hand? Or did reading require both of their contributions? Shall we call what the author did reading, and his attorney's contribution interpretation? Or shall we say that the author was word-calling and the lawyer comprehending?

The issues which are raised in these episodes are neither simple nor easily answered. To a certain extent, of course, we can be arbitrary. We can define reading to be anything we choose. But if our definition is to be useful, it must be one we can use consistently; it must be inclusive of that which is relevant and exclusive of that which is not. It must also be productive. Definitions which are too narrow or too broad or too vague or too specific tend to cut off or dissipate inquiry rather than promote it. Further, a definition must be consistent with reality.

To move us toward a definition of reading, it may help to list certain evident aspects of the process:

- Reading begins with graphic language in some form: print, script, etc.
- The purpose of reading is the reconstruction of meaning. Meaning is not in print, but it is meaning that the author begins with when he writes. Somehow the reader strives to *reconstruct* this meaning as he reads.

- In alphabetic writing systems there is a direct relationship between oral language and written language.
- Visual perception must be involved in reading.
- Nothing intrinsic in the writing system or its symbols has meaning. There is nothing in the shape or sequence of any letters or grouping of letters which in itself is meaning.
- Meaning is in the mind of the writer and the mind of the reader.
- Yet readers are capable through reading of reconstructing a message which agrees with the writer's intended message.

A Definition of Reading

At this point, we're ready to state a definition of reading: *Reading is a complex process by which a reader reconstructs, to some degree, a message encoded by a writer in graphic language.*

In this definition it is no more significant that the reader starts with graphic input[1] than that he ends with meaning. To understand this process, we must understand the nature of the graphic input. We must understand how language works and how language is used by the reader. We must understand how much meaning depends on the reader's prior learning and experience in the reconstruction of meaning. We must understand the perceptual system involved in reading. As we come to see the reader as a user of language, we will understand that reading is a psycholinguistic process, an interaction between thought and language.

Written Language: The Nature of the Graphic Input

Written English is, of course, an alphabetic system. It uses a set of letters almost directly adapted from the Latin. The Latin alphabet in turn was derived from the Greek. Most modern languages are written with alphabets derived from the same group of ancient, related alphabets. Alphabetic writing differs from other systems in that the system is a representation not of meaning directly, but of oral language. In original intent, the units of written language (letters) represented the sound units of speech rather than meanings as in pictographic and other systems.

Oral language is produced in a time sequence, but written language must be arranged spatially. Though various arrangements are possible, and used in other systems, in English print is arranged from left to right

---

[1] As we think of reading as an information seeking process, it will help to think of the graphic material as input and meaning as output. Oral reading produces speech as a second output.

and top to bottom in successive lines. White space separates patterns of letters just as oral patterns are marked by intonation contours, pauses, pitch sequences, and relative stressing. Larger patterns require markings, punctuation, to set them off from other patterns. Again, intonational features are replaced to some degree in print by periods, commas, and other graphic signals. In this feature, as in a number of others, there is no one-to-one correspondence between oral and written language. The intonation pattern of a question like "Do you understand?" is distributed over the whole oral sentence, while graphically it is represented only by a capital letter at the beginning and a question mark at the end. It is marked as different from the statement form only at the end. (Contrast Spanish which puts a question mark at both ends.)

Relationships between Oral and Written English

While written language is a secondary form, both historically and in the personal history of any individual, it must be seen as a different but parallel form to oral language, since both for the literate user are fully capable of meeting the complex needs of communication. Written language has the advantage, only recently made possible for oral language, of being perfectable and preservable. Oral language on the other hand is more easily and more rapidly produced in a wider range of circumstances.

Having said that English uses an alphabetic writing system, we must now caution that the set of relationships between oral and written English is not a simple small set of letter-to-sound correspondences (or phoneme-to-grapheme ones, to use linguistic terms). For several reasons, to be accurate, we must say that the relationships are between patterns of sounds and patterns of letters. The most significant of these reasons is that spelling patterns are basically standard and stable while oral language changes over time and space.

Spellings are standard. Standard spellings were developed by printers in the early years of the development of printing and the spread of literacy. Though Americans may differ from the British in the spellings of a very few words like "labor" (labour), there is great agreement on word spellings among speakers of all English dialects. *Pumpkin* is the spelling whether one says *punkin, ponkin, pumpkin* or whatever. This is, of course, a considerable advantage, since written communication between speakers of diverse English dialects is made more effective. Any other arrangement would require establishment of a standard dialect upon which to base spelling. Subsequently either the dialect would need to be protected from change or periodical updating of the spelling system to catch up with the changes would be required. If this could be accomplished, the spelling system would be highly suited for the one dialect's speakers, but increasingly dysfunctional for all others. Change is always going on in language. It cannot in any case be closed off. No lesser man than Napoleon tried and failed to keep language from changing.

Oral language sequences. Another factor in making the relationships between oral and written English complex has to do with the nature of oral language sound sequences. For example, note these related words: *site, situate,* and *situation.* In *site,* we have a well known pattern with a vowel-consonant-e. (V-C-e) The *e* serves as a pattern marker. Notice that the relationship of the prior vowel to a sound is not clear without the rest of the spelling pattern. But when, through affixes, the word *situate* is formed, a sound sequence occurs after the /t/ which requires a shift in the oral form to a *ch* sound /č/. The same shift occurs in the word sequence *don't you.* We must either change the spelling to *ch* or retain the *t* and lose the close letter-sound correspondence. Similar shifting is required in moving to *situation* where the sound becomes *sh* /š/. The spelling system has alternatives. It may retain the close correspondence of sounds and letters and thus change spellings as the sounds shift. Or it may retain the letters even when the sound shifts and thus preserve the derivational character of the word relationships. The system tends to do the latter perhaps because speakers of the language seem to shift as required so automatically that they are not bothered by the spelling discrepancy. It simply sounds too strange to his ears for a speaker of English to say *situation* differently. This may be illustrated with this nonsense word offered in three alternate spellings: *boft, boffed, bofd.* The final consonant cluster is pronounced the same by native speakers of English. Because /f/ precedes the final consonant, the latter is produced as /t/; spelling cannot induce a speaker to abandon that pronunciation.

Much has been written about regular and irregular relationships between oral and written English. The distinction loses its meaning if we understand that the patterns of correspondence are complex, but systematic. Some examples above have already illustrated this complex-regularity. Here is another: *s* may not frequently represent the sound *sh* /š/, but when it does, as in *sure* and *sugar,* the circumstances are consistent ones and it is thus every bit as regular in its representation as it is in *sister. Hymn, damn, bomb, sign,* appear irregularly spelled, but they are not so if we consider the "silent letters" relate to derived forms such as *hymnal, damnation, bombard, signal.*

A number of early applications to reading materials which stressed linguistics tended to apply a rather narrow view of regular letter-sound correspondence. The Bloomfield-Barnhart materials, the SRA Linguistic Readers, and the Harper-Row Linguistic Science Readers are examples. The Merrill Linguistic Readers, based on the work of C. C. Fries, had a somewhat broader view of regularity as represented in spelling patterns.

The Nature of Language

If we are to define and understand reading, we must understand the nature of language itself. Paradoxically, language is learned so early and so well that we tend to take its functioning for granted.

How Language Works

Language is always a means and only rarely an end in itself. We are so distracted, as we use it, by meaning (the end for which language is the means) that we are quite unaware of how language works to convey meaning. Consider, for example, a simple statement: *John hit Bill.* In either oral or written form, it is not the symbols, phonemes, or letters but the systematic structuring of these symbols that makes comprehension of meaning possible.

The listener or reader must recognize the patterns *John, hit,* and *Bill* and he must also recognize the pattern of patterns which makes a statement of relationships possible. The difference between *John hit Bill* and *Bill hit John* is in the sentence patterns or syntax. Nothing else tells the listener or reader whether Bill or John hit John or Bill. Grammar, the system of language, makes it possible for language to convey the most complex relationships humans conceive.

All language is patterned: the patterns are the sequences in which the elements may occur. In *John hit Bill,* it is pattern alone which tells the listener who was hitting and who was being hit.

In English, pattern is itself the single most important aspect of grammar. Other languages make more use of word changes (inflections) such as affixes to carry extensive portions of the grammatical system. In such languages the nominative and accusative endings might have differentiated the aggressor from the victim in the example above. English preserves such a system in its pronouns. *I hit him* and *He hit me* use different forms in grammatical cases. But notice that we still would not say *Him hit I.* Pattern is still preserved.

Certain English words and word parts serve as pattern markers. In a statement like *A man was feeding his dogs,* we have a pattern: A _____ was _____ing his _____s. The pattern markers, function words like *A, his,* and *was,* and inflectional endings like *ing,* and *s* set the pattern up. In themselves none of these elements carry meaning. But without the grammatical pattern they create, we cannot express even the simplest relationship between the words that do carry meaning.

How Language Is Used

When a child undertakes to learn to read at the age of five or six, he is already a skilled user of language. He has somehow learned to generate language to communicate his thoughts, emotions, and needs to his family and peers. Further, he is able to comprehend what other people say to him. To state that he has learned by imitation does not accurately represent the case. He has, in fact, devised language for himself which moves toward the norms of adult language because the more it does, the more effective he is in communication.

Moreover, he has not simply acquired a collection of words or sentences to use when the occasion is appropriate. He has learned the rules by which language is produced. Language is rule-governed. As long as a child can only produce language he has already heard, his language capability is severely limited. Infinite numbers of sentences are possible in a language. If a child had to hear them and learn them before he could use them, language learning would be a much slower process than it is. But a small number of rules govern language production. These are the rules that tell the child which noun to put before and which after a transitive verb when he runs up to a teacher on the playground and says, "John hit Bill." They are the rules that make it possible for him to say, "When I hit him, he hits me back," getting *hit* and *hits* in the right position and making one clause subordinate to another. They are the rules that make it possible for him to say things he has never heard anyone say before and be sure that other speakers of the language will understand.

Generating language. In speaking or in writing, meaning in the mind of the originator creates a deep language structure (a set of base forms) and activates a set of rules which transform that structure and generate a signal, either graphic or oral. This process must be a complete one. The signal must have a surface structure which is complete. All essential elements must be present, and extraneous ones must not be. We might describe this whole process as *encoding.* A structured code signal has been produced. The user of a language has so well learned this encoding procedure that it is virtually automatic. Meaning, as a language user formulates it, literally creates an automatic chain of events which results in language code. A model of speech, quite simplified, is reprinted in Figure 1.

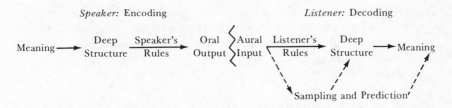

Figure 1. Spoken Language.

Note in this model that the speaker's output is not the same as the listener's input. What is said is not precisely what is heard, just as in reading what is written is not precisely what is read. This relationship might be compared to the relationship of fetus and mother. Her bloodstream nourishes the uterine wall from which the fetus draws its nourishment, through its own bloodstream. But, the two bloodstreams are not connected.

Note also that meaning is not in the oral output or the aural input. Meaning is only in the minds of the speaker and the listener. The listener (like the reader) must recreate meaning for himself from the input he has obtained.

Language has been learned by the listener in the context of experience as it was used in those situations by people around him. His ability to recreate meaning depends on his ability to associate those experiences and the concepts he has formed through them with the language.

The speaker in generating language must produce a sound sequence which is decodable by the listener. In this oral language signal, the sounds must be sufficiently well articulated and the structure sufficiently complete that the listener has all the information he needs.

At first appearances, it would seem that listening would be a kind of mirror image of speech with the process simply reversed to get from surface structure of aural language to meaning.

In fact, however, the listener may, through a process that combines sampling and prediction, leap to the deep structure and meaning without using all the information available to him. He acquires strategies as a language user that enable him to select only the most productive cues. His user's knowledge of language structure and the redundancy[2] of that structure make it possible for him to predict and anticipate the

---

[2] Redundancy means, here, that each bit of information may be conveyed by several cues in the language. For example, notice in this sentence how many cues indicate the plural nature of the subject: *Two boys are eating their sandwiches.*

grammatical pattern on the basis of identifying a few elements in it. The context in which the language occurs, created by the previous meanings he has gathered, allows him to predict the meaning of what will follow. All these combine to make listening related to but a very different process from speaking.

Perception in Listening and Reading

Before we compare listening and reading, let's explore how perception operates in listening. Every language uses a small number of sound units, which some linguists label phonemes. These are in reality bundles of sounds which are treated by listeners as the same. Just as we call many different colors and shades of colors red, we hear many different sounds as /t/. Two colors could be quite similar, but one would be called red and the other orange, while two other more dissimilar colors might be both called red. In the same way the *phoneme* is a perceptual category. As a language is learned these categories become functional. The child learns to treat certain differences as significant and others as insignificant. *In short, he not only learns what to pay attention to, but, equally important, what not to pay attention to.* So the native speaker of Japanese learning English does not distinguish *late* from *rate* because he has learned to ignore a difference which isn't significant in Japanese. Similarly, a speaker of English has difficulty differentiating the Spanish *pero* (but) from *perro* (dog).[3]

Perception in language is and must be both selective and anticipatory. To be aware of what is significant in language one must ignore what is not. Perception, to be functional in listening, must be augmented by anticipation. The sounds are so fleeting and follow each other so rapidly that time does not allow for each to be fully perceived and identified. Mastery of the phonological system, however, and of the grammatical system as well, enables the listener to use partial perceptions and sample the input. Under some circumstances, of course, the partial perceptions may be too fragmentary or distorted and the listener may have to ask for repetition. But, to be quite blunt, what we think we hear is as much what we expect to hear as it is what we do hear.

Contrast the task of repeating even a short sequence in a foreign language with a comparable or longer one in a known language. The foreign language simply doesn't correspond to available perceptual categories, nor can we fit what we do catch into any system that would aid prediction.

---

[3] If you don't hear the difference, then you don't know Spanish phonemes, which is the point here.

Perception in language use cannot be viewed then as a simple series of sound perceptions or word perceptions. It must be understood in relation to the grammatical structure of the language, and to the structure of the meaning which is being communicated.

All that has been said in comparing speaking and listening basically applies to the parallel language processes, writing and reading.

The writer generates his signal in exactly the same way that the speaker does. In the last stage, these generative processes differ. In speech, a series of phonological rules determines the exact sound sequences which will be uttered. In writing, instead of phonological rules a set of graphotactic rules (spelling if you prefer) produces the exact grapheme sequences.

As we have indicated earlier, though both speaking and writing must produce complete signals, writing is usually polished and perfected to a greater degree than speech through editing by the author. Furthermore, the reader works from a more or less permanent graphic input while the listener must contend with input that in most cases perishes as it is produced. Rereading is possible. Relistening requires that the speaker cooperate in repeating what he has said.

But reading, like listening, is a sampling, predicting, guessing process. Proficient readers, in fact, learn to use the reading process much more rapidly than they normally use the listening process. Listening is held pretty much to the rate at which speech is produced. That, of course, is much slower than the processing of average proficient readers.

In the guessing game which is reading, three types of information are used. Each has several subtypes. They are used in reading simultaneously and not sequentially.

Information Used during the Reading Process

I. Grapho-phonic Information
    A. Graphic Information: The letters, spelling patterns and patterns of patterns created through white space and punctuation. A word or suffix represents a graphic pattern; a phrase or sentence is a pattern of patterns.
    B. Phonological Information: The sounds, sound patterns and patterns of patterns created through intonation (pitch, stress, pause). Read any line on this page and note how these work.
    C. Phonic Information: The complex set of relationships between the graphic and phonological representations of the language. Notice here we are speaking of the relationships and not an instructional program for teaching them.

II. Syntactic Information
   A. Sentence Patterns: The grammatical sequences and interrela-
       tionships of language. The ____s ____ed the ____s, is an example
       of a sentence pattern common in English.
   B. Pattern Markers: The markers which outline the patterns.
       1. Function Words: Those very frequent words which, though
           themselves relatively without definable meaning, signal the
           grammatical function of the other elements. Examples: *the,
           was, not, do, in, very, why, but.*
       2. Inflections: Those bound morphemes (affixes) which con-
           vey basically grammatical information. Examples: *ing, ed, s.*
       3. Punctuation—Intonation: The system of markings and
           space distribution and the related intonation patterns. Pitch
           and stress variations and variable pauses in speech are rep-
           resented to some extent by punctuation in writing.
   C. Transformational Rules: These are not characteristic of the
       graphic input itself, but are supplied by the reader in response
       to what he perceives as its surface structure. They carry him to
       the deep structure and meaning. If he is to recognize and derive
       meaning from a graphic pattern, he must bring these gram-
       matical rules into the process.

III. Semantic Information
   A. Experience: The reader brings *his* prior experiences into play in
       response to the graphic input.
   B. Concepts: The reader organizes the meaning he is reconstruct-
       ing according to his existing concepts and reorganizes experi-
       ence into concepts as he reads.
   C. Vocabulary is largely a term for the ability of the child to sort out
       his experiences and concepts in relation to words and phrases in
       the context of what he is reading.

All of these kinds of information are available to the reader at the
same time in graphic language. In the sampling process, they support
each other much as they do in listening. Particular cues take on strategic
importance in relation to the full array of information in the input which
they could not have in isolation. In a list a word like *the,* for example, is a
word with little or no referential meaning. It summons forth, from the
reader's stockpile of information, no experiences or concepts. But put *the*
into a sentence and it becomes a grammatical cue of some importance. In
these sequences: *He hurried to farm* (his land) and *he hurried to the farm, farm*

is marked as a noun in the second sequence by *the,* whereas in the first, *farm* is a verb and the reader will expect an object to follow.

The relationship between oral and written language is of more significance in reading than in listening. Particularly in learning to read the language he speaks, a child may draw on his oral language competence as he develops control over written language. The alphabetic character of the writing system makes it possible to match sound sequences already known with less familiar graphic sequences.

A possible simplified model for reading in early stages might look like this:

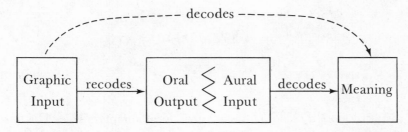

Figure 2. Early reading[4]

The child here recodes graphic input as speech (either outloud or internally) and then, utilizing his own speech as aural input, decodes as he does in listening. Notice the model assumes some direct decoding from print to meaning, even at early stages.

Some writers on the topic of reading have assumed that for instructional purposes these two aspects, recoding and decoding, are separable. And indeed, materials and methods have been built on that assumption. As a prereading program, instruction is provided to the child in matching letters and sounds (i.e., synthetic phonics, Sullivan's programed reading) or in matching spelling patterns and sound patterns (e.g., Fries Linguistic Readers) or in matching oral names with graphic shapes (sight vocabulary). But in all of these types of recoding instruction, the reader is

---

[4] In this diagram, *recode* is used to mean going from code to code (aural to graphic); *decode* is reserved for processes that go from code (in either form) to meaning. In this sense, comprehension and *decoding* are virtual synonyms while word-calling and sounding-out are *recoding* processes. A third term, *encode,* is used to mean going from meaning to code (again either written or oral). In our early example of the writer and his attorney, the writer could only *recode* printed language as oral language. But the lawyer could *decode* from language to meaning. Then he could *encode* meaning in an oral language form his client could *decode* (comprehend).

confined to words or word parts and may not sample the syntactic or semantic information that would be available in full language. What's more, the process is one in which meaning cannot result. Thus by our tentative definition given earlier, recoding in itself is not reading.

In any case, a second instructional phase would be needed to help the learner adapt his recoding strategies and techniques to the full language situation in which all information is available and decoding may result.

Reading does eventually become a parallel process to listening which then would have this appearance:

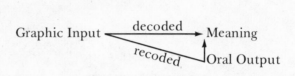

Figure 3.   Proficient reading

In this model, recoding has at best a supplementary role. The basic decoding is directly from print to meaning, though there is some echo of speech involved as the reader proceeds even in silent reading. At times, the reader may find it helpful to recode print as speech and then decode. (The reverse may also be true for literate speakers. They may occasionally "write it down," recoding speech as graphic input and then decoding.)

When silent reading becomes proficient, it becomes a very different process from oral reading. It is much more rapid and not tied to encoding what is being read as speech. In silent reading, the reader sweeps ahead, sampling from the graphic input, predicting structures, leaping to quick conclusions about the meaning and only slowing down or regressing when subsequent sampling fails to confirm what he expects to find.

Oral reading which is fluent and accurate may involve simultaneous recoding and decoding. But for most proficient silent readers, who don't have much occasion for oral reading, oral reading apparently follows this model:

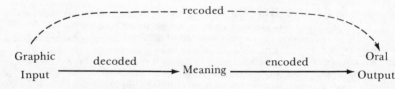

Figure 4.   Oral reading

Primarily oral output is produced *after* meaning has been decoded and hence, though comprehension may be high, the oral output is often a poor match for the graphic input. The reader sounds clumsy and makes numerous errors.

The diagram on page 491 illustrates in some detail the psycholinguistic process which is silent reading. This model represents the *proficient* reader, but it also represents the competence which is the goal of reading instruction.

Reading is an active process in which the reader selects the fewest cues possible from those available to him and makes the best choices possible. If he is highly proficient, he will have good speed and high comprehension; reading will be a smooth process. If he is less proficient or if he is encountering unusually difficult material (as in the case of the graduate student in our early examples), reading will be less smooth and will involve considerable cycling back to gather more cues and make better choices.

Meaning is the constant goal of the proficient reader and he continually tests his choices against the developing meaning by asking himself if what he is reading makes sense. The process does not require that he perceive and identify every cue. In fact that would be both unnecessary and inefficient. But it does require that the reader monitor his choices so he can recognize his errors and gather more cues when needed.

Such traditional terms as *word recognition, sounding out,* and *word attack* stem from a view of reading as a succession of accurate perceptions or word identifications. Such a view is not consistent with the actual performance of proficient readers.

The Application of Reading

Reading, if it is successful, is, as we have shown, not a passive process. The reader is a language user who interacts with the graphic input. Successful reading yields meaning which becomes the means to further ends. The reader may follow directions, respond to questions, read further. The extent and direction of application depend on the nature and purpose of what is read. Literary materials, because of their aesthetic, stylistic qualities, yield a kind of pleasure and satisfaction which creates further appetite for literature. Plot and story line in literature propel the reader forward. "I just couldn't put it down," he may say.

Informational materials may have a similar effect; new knowledge leads to a desire for more knowledge. Or such material may meet a small but immediate need, as for example when the reader needs to clarify a particular fact in the encyclopedia.

Language and thought are interactive in reading, but at some point thought processes leap out and away from the message of the writer.

In this interaction a reader may be involved in cycles of reading, reflective thinking, flights of fancy and then more reading. In certain kinds of materials, recipes for example, the reader may follow a *read* and *do* cycle. He reads and then gathers his ingredients; then he reads again and performs step one and so forth.

Though reading and the application of the fruits of reading are separable, it must always be remembered that reading is never pursued for its own sake, even in literature. If the reader finds no "payoff," he will not continue to read. This is as true in the stages in which reading is being acquired as it is in the stages of proficient reading.

Materials used in the teaching of reading at all stages must necessarily be meaningful. Children with different purposes and interests will need a variety of materials to keep them reading. Ironically, development of reading competence is best achieved when the learner's focus is on the content of materials and not on reading itself. Social studies, science, mathematics, literature and other materials contribute well to the child's reading development while serving other curricular ends, if their conceptual load is not too heavy.

Adaptation in Reading

By the time he undertakes to become literate in his native language every child has acquired considerable competence[5] in its basic communicative use. The basic form of his language, that used in common discourse and conversation, is his means of communication, expression, thinking, and learning. It makes sense to start with this common discursive language in reading. Experience stories, directions, labels, signs are examples of early reading materials that use common language.

Children have not necessarily acquired the same kind of competence in dealing with other specialized forms of language. Literature utilizes one such special form. The language of literature has its own special set of rules and contingencies. Poetic license makes it possible for the poet to reverse some key language priorities for the sake of meter, rhyme, or

---

[5] We use *competence* here, as some linguists do, to represent the basic, developed capacity for using language. *Performance* is a behavioral indicator of that *competence* but behavior should not be confused with the abilities that make performance possible.

mood. Similarly, literary prose employs structures and language devices differently from common language.

The strategies which the child has learned in listening transfer well to reading common language. To deal with literary language he will need to modify his strategies and perhaps acquire some new ones.

A good deal of prereading experience with literature will help the child build a strong base for reading literature for himself. Some children grow up in a world of literature: they are surrounded by books; their parents read to them; they acquire favorites which they soon know by heart. By the time such children come to school, they have a feel for the peculiarities of literary language and a sense of what to expect from it. They can predict in literary language as they can in more common language. For the large number of children who lack such background, teachers can begin to build it through oral reading to the children and other devices while the more basic literacy ability is being built.

Subsequently, children can begin to read literary language. As they do so, they will necessarily modify the techniques and strategies they use in reading to accommodate the structure of literary language. Even then, it will probably make the most sense to start with literary forms and themes which are most like common language and move to literary forms which deviate more. Folk and fairy tales may be pleasurable to the child because of their familiarity. But the archaic language, the unusual structure, and the allegorical nature of their plots may combine to make them unsuitable for early literature reading. One possibility, of course, is to rewrite them for young children in order to eliminate these problems. A criticism of that approach is that in the process their qualities as literature may be lost and they may become dull and lacking in color and characterization. In a similar sense, adaptations of great works of literature for children too young to handle the original may make them more readable but destroy their essential merits. In both cases, such critics conclude it might be better to postpone reading such materials until the child's reading competence has reached a point where he is ready to learn to cope with the special demands they make on him.

Research into literary style is beginning to suggest that writers employ less common language structures frequently to achieve a sense of individuality and distinction. If this is true, then some specific assistance to children in recognizing and predicting these structures may greatly enhance their ability to read particular authors.

In the past several decades, a large and varied literature especially written for children of various ages has been produced. Such literature makes it possible to guide youngsters through material which they can

select to suit their own interests and levels of ability. In the process, they
will build their ability to deal with more sophisticated literature. A number
of publishers have organized better selections in kits with multiple copies
of each title and teacher guide material.

Schools present the learners with the need for dealing with a number
of other special forms of language. Textbooks, in general, use language in
special ways which vary from common language use. They tend, particularly in elementary and secondary schools, to present a very large number
of topics, facts, and concepts rapidly and superficially. Reading to learn
may well stimulate learning to read, but only if the concept load (roughly
the number of new ideas presented) is not so heavy as to cause the reader
to lose any sense of meaning. *Textbook reading, through the elementary years at*
least, probably requires considerable introductory, preparatory work on the part of
the teacher. Concepts and ideas can be introduced through demonstration,
experimentation, concrete illustration. Vocabulary can be developed orally in relationship to these experiences. Then, and only then, is the child
ready for the task of reading about the same concepts in the text. He reads
them not so much to gain new concepts as to reinforce them. In the
process, he learns to handle the unusual language uses of textbooks. If
textbooks are well written and handled well in elementary schools, he
may, by the time he is in high school, be able to initiate study at times
through a textbook with the teacher following up and reteaching the
concepts he meets in the books.

Another alternative is to change our thinking about how textbooks
are used in elementary and junior high schools. Part of the problem with
textbooks is that they move rapidly from topic to topic, a fact inherent in
the nature of the task they undertake. Consequently, they present a large
vocabulary of terms not well developed in context. Perhaps multimedia
approaches would help; kits and coordinated packages containing film
loops, audio and video tapes, transparencies, and other materials as well
as reading materials could replace the single text. The texts could become
elements in resource kits to provide more specific focus on single concepts
or depth treatment of groups of related concepts.

Children will encounter problems in learning to deal with other kinds
of reference books too. The need for reference skills, use of index,
contents and glossary is obvious. Less obvious problems involve strategies
for dealing with specialized vocabulary and language structures. Ency-
clopedias, for example, employ distinctive writing styles. There are also
key problems for the reader in learning to modify his whole reading style
to reference reading. Even graduate students do not always have effective
techniques for selecting and reading from reference works only those

portions germane to their needs. Skimming is one of several gross sampling strategies needed for specific use in some kinds of reference work.

Science, mathematics, social studies, music, art, industrial arts, home economics, in fact all school subjects, require learners to handle special kinds of language. It cannot be assumed that general reading competence leads automatically to these special abilities. Using a recipe, following a set of plans, interpreting a contour map, following a laboratory procedure—all present special reading problems. The abilities required must, of course, be developed in the context of the tasks. To pick an example, a reader can't learn how to read a recipe unless he is really making something. And the best test of the effectiveness of the reading will be the way the final product tastes. The implication is apparent. *Every teacher of whatever subject and level must be prepared to help children to meet new demands on their reading competence and to develop the special strategies which these demands require.* [6]

A special word needs to be said about vocabulary. Every time a learner pushes into a new field or into a new subject area within an old one, he encounters new vocabulary or new uses for old terms. That problem is a by-product of his quest for knowledge. The vocabulary is unfamiliar because the ideas and concepts it expresses are unfamiliar. Like new concepts, new vocabulary learned in relationship to the new knowledge must be built on the base of pre-existing vocabulary. If the new vocabulary is more effective in manipulating the new ideas it will be absorbed, and old language may be modified or set aside. *Vocabulary development outside of the context of new ideas and pre-existing language is not possible.*

What we commonly call a vocabulary problem is never simply a matter of putting a verbal label on an object. In reality, it may represent a variety of different problems.

1.   The reader encounters a printed form he does not recognize for a word in his oral vocabulary. This is the simplest vocabulary problem since he has experiences and concepts to relate to his oral vocabulary.

2.   The reader encounters a printed form which is not familiar and not in his oral vocabulary. But the concept is a known one. He has other language forms to express it. In this case the problem is to associate new language with old.

---

[6] Of course it will also help to assure that materials children are asked to read are written well. Poor writing is not likely to be easily read.

3. The reader encounters a printed form which is unfamiliar, has no oral counterpart for him, and represents a concept which is new to him. He may in fact lack relevant experience on which to base such a concept. This is the case in which vocabulary must follow conceptual development. Otherwise, we have a fourth possibility.

4. A written form is familiar and may even have an oral equivalent, but the reader has no meaning for it. Within narrow limits he may even use it to answer test questions correctly without understanding what he is reading.

5. The final possibility exists as readers become proficient. They may encounter printed forms and come to attach concepts to them without ever encountering them in oral speech. One does not have to be able to pronounce a word to understand it.

Objectives of the Reading Curriculum

Once we have defined reading and discussed it as a process, a next step in considering reading curricula is to restate this process as a series of objectives. First, however, an important distinction must be made. That is the distinction between language competence and language performance.

Competence and Performance

Much has been said in curricular literature about behavioral objectives. In this view, the ultimate objective of instruction is always to change behavior (which we treat as a synonym for performance). But this view fails to take into account the concept that there is underlying all performance a basic competence. It is this underlying competence, and not the behavior itself, which we seek to build through education.

Above we delineated some variations involved in vocabulary. To use this as an example, in expanding vocabulary we must not mistake performance, the uttering of words, for competence, the understanding which must underlie the effective use of words. Too often school lessons change performance (behavior) but only superficially get at competence, and thus a change is a temporary or meaningless one.

While we must seek evidence in performance of the competence which learners have achieved, we must be very cautious of either equating performance and competence or of interpreting performance too directly and simplistically.

In language and reading this distinction is particularly important. Vocabulary, to continue the example, is going to develop in direct ratio to the experience and interest that a learner has. *Low vocabulary yield in the performance of children in certain task situations cannot be directly interpreted to mean that the child has a small vocabulary.* It may mean only that the topic or topics were not ones which interested him; it might also mean that for various reasons such as fear, unfamiliarity of the situation or the interviewers, or disdain for the task or teacher, the child simply did not perform in any way representative of his competence.

Here is another example: There are periods in the development of reading competence when oral reading becomes very awkward.[7] Readers who have recently become rapid, relatively effective, silent readers seem to be distracted and disrupted by the necessity of encoding oral output while they are decoding meaning. Ironically, then "poor" oral reading performance *may* reflect a high degree of reading competence rather than a lack of such competence.

Relevance

The language user, though he may be a beginner as far as literacy is concerned, brings to the task of learning to read the sum total of his life's experiences and the language competence he has already acquired. He has learned language well no matter what rung on the socioeconomic ladder his dialect occupies. To make it possible for each learner to fully capitalize on these resources the reading curriculum must be relevant to him. It must make it possible for him to build on his strengths, not put him at a disadvantage by focusing on his weaknesses.

All learners have had experiences. A learner is only disadvantaged if the school rejects his experiences as unsuitable to build learnings on while accepting those of other children. Similarly language difference is not a disadvantage unless the school rejects certain dialects and insists that a child must speak and read in a dialect in which he is not competent.

Remedial reading classes and clinics invariably have more boys than girls, more blacks than whites, more minority group youngsters than is proportional in the population these programs serve. This is not so much an indication of real weakness in these groups as it is of the failure of school reading programs to adequately reach them.

---

[7] Kenneth S. Goodman and Carolyn L. Burke, *Study of Children's Behavior While Reading Orally,* Final Report, Project S 425, USOE, March 1968.

Too much time has been spent trying to find weaknesses and deficiencies in children which might explain their lack of success in learning to read. A flexible, relevant reading curriculum would capitalize on the strengths of children of both sexes and of all shapes, sizes, colors, ethnic and cultural backgrounds, dispositions, energy levels, and physical attributes. Every objective in reading must be relevant to the pupils we are teaching.

Comprehension: The Prime Objective in Reading

Essentially, the only objective in reading is comprehension. All else is either a skill to be used in achieving comprehension (for example, selecting key graphic cues), a subcategory of comprehension (for example, critical reading) or a use to be made of comprehension (e.g., appreciation of literature).

Comprehension depends on the successful processing of three kinds of information: grapho-phonic, syntactic, and semantic. A series of abilities is necessary to make this process successful. How these abilities operate within this process is illustrated in the tentative Model of Reading (Figure 5).[8]

Reading instruction has as its subsidiary objectives development of these skills and strategies:

Scanning: The ability to move from left to right and down a page, line by line.

Fixing: The ability to focus the eye on the line of print.

Selecting: The ability to select from graphic input those key cues which will be most productive in the information processing. For example, initial consonants are the most useful letters in words.

Predicting: The ability to predict input on the basis of grammar and the growing sense of meaning from prior decoding. (Prediction and selection operate together since each is dependent on the other.)

Forming: The ability to form perceptual images on the basis of selection and prediction. The reader must combine what he sees with what he expects to see to form a perceptual image.

Searching: The ability to search memory for phonological cues and related syntactic and semantic information associated with perceptual images. The reader brings to bear his language knowledge and his experiential and conceptual background as he reads.

Tentative choosing: The ability to make tentative choices (guesses) on the basis of minimal cues and related syntactic and semantic input. It is

---

[8] The author is indebted to William Gephart for the original flow chart for this model and to William Page for the current version.

crucial that the reader use the least amount of information possible to make the best guess possible. To do so, he will need well developed strategies that become almost automatic.

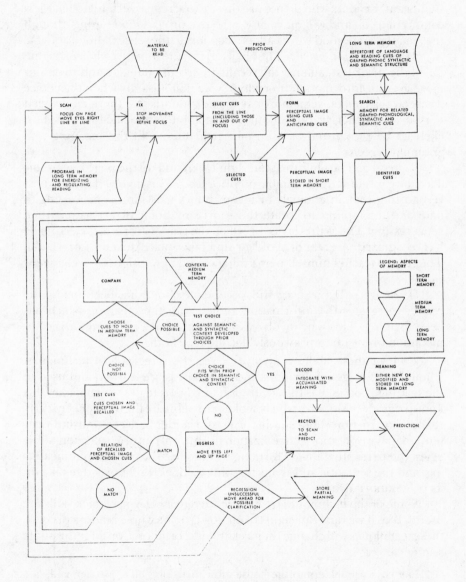

Figure 5.   The Goodman Model of Reading

Testing—semantic and syntactic: The ability to test choices against the screens of meaning and grammar. Literally the reader says to himself: "Does that make sense?" "Does that sound like language to me?" This involves the crucial ability to recognize his own errors when they are significant. Readers who do not use these two screens will tend to have low comprehension and will make little effective progress in reading, though they may become good word callers (recoders in the sense defined above).

Testing—grapho-phonic: The ability to test the tentative choice, if it has failed the prior test, against the recalled perceptual image and to gather more graphic information if needed. Note that it is only when the choice has been rejected on semantic or syntactic grounds that there is any need to resort to further grapho-phonic information. A miscalled word is most likely to be recognized as a mistake if it doesn't fit the meaning and grammar screens.

Regressing: The ability to scan right to left and up the page line by line if a choice is found unacceptable on prior tests. This involved the reader's recognizing that an anomaly or inconsistency exists in his processing to date and attempting to locate the source or point of error and then reprocessing. This is the device by which the reader corrects the errors he has recognized. A great deal of learning takes place through correction. The reader teaches himself new strategies and new insights as well as new words.

Decoding: When a successful, acceptable choice has been made, the reader integrates the information gained with the meaning which has been forming. This may involve assimilation of new meaning or accommodation of meaning previously decoded, or both.

Each of these abilities involves a set of strategies and techniques. Though phonic generalizations and sight words are learned and used in the reading process, it is the acquisition of key strategies which makes this knowledge develop and which makes it useful to the reader. In early reading instruction children will form associations between oral and written language (phonics generalizations). But only in the selection strategies, the perceptual image forming techniques, the grapho-phonic testing, and the semantic and syntactic contexts does this knowledge take on its true importance.

Some of the techniques we have tended to label word attack skills are useful. But, if we raise our sights from words to the whole reading process, these techniques will change their relative importance. Consider this short sequence:

> The boys stumbled into the house after their long hike. Mother said, "You must really be *fatigued*. Sit here and rest while I get lunch ready."

When she returned with the food, Mother discovered they were so fatigued that they had fallen asleep.

Now, if we assume that *fatigued* is an unknown word to be "attacked," we will tend to employ phonics, structural analysis and other techniques that can work within the context of the word to achieve its recognition. This will be a problem, if, as is likely, the reader has not heard the word and therefore cannot match it with an equivalent.

If on the other hand, we are concerned about the same problem as it actually is encountered in the reading process, we will see that the meaning of the passage can come through rather clearly without the identification of this word. In fact, it is quite likely that in this short sequence the reader had become aware that the word must mean something like "tired." Should he assume another definition, *hungry* for example, subsequent reading might cause a correction. All of the syntactic and semantic information which the reader has going for him makes him relatively independent of the grapho-phonic information.

Developing Sophistication in Reading

Adequate functioning of the reading process depends on development in a number of areas, both mechanical and intellectual. A deficiency in any one of these can affect the quality of the child's reading and lessen its meaning for him.

Techniques and Strategies

If a reader does not develop independence in the use of the strategies and techniques required for adequate functioning of the reading process then special attention may be required. Cycles of skill instruction could be planned which would move the learner from language to a focus on the technique or knowledge which he needs and then back to language so that he can test the technique as he attempts to read.

To pick a simple example, suppose that a child is not aware that initial consonants are the most useful graphic cues. Instruction might help him by selecting from reading material words which start in various ways. Then the reader would return to the reading material to utilize the technique of selecting initial consonant cues.

If on the other hand children become overdependent on specific techniques, then again they can be guided within the full scope of reading materials to put the techniques in proper perspective in relationship to other techniques and available information. Suppose a child had become too reliant on initial consonants and was using neither meaning and syntax nor other graphic cues well. He could be helped to move away from his overdependence while the weak strategies were being developed at the same time.

Sequencing of skill instruction in reading has often been strongly advocated by publishers and curriculum workers. But the reading process requires that a multitude of skills be used simultaneously. As we have indicated, many of these skills are already employed by the learner in listening. *Any sequence will necessarily be arbitrary.*

Flexibility

In discussing adaptation, we indicated the need for developing general reading strategies and special reading strategies for literature, science, social studies and other language uses. The key to this development is experience of the learner with a wide variety of materials, and guidance from the teacher as it is needed to help develop specific strategies to handle the requirements of these special reading materials. This is only one kind of flexibility needed. A second kind of flexibility has to do with reading purpose. The reader needs to gain flexibility in the way his reading process functions in relation to the outcome he desires.

If he desires a high degree of comprehension with great detail then he will be more demanding of himself and more painstaking. If at the opposite extreme he is only concerned with getting a quick notion of the general drift of what he is reading, he will use test processes more freely, sample more widely, and not bother to worry about errors as he reads. If speed reading courses have any validity it must be in their ability to get readers to break out of a single inflexible reading style and into a more variable one.

A Sense of the Significance of Reading

A child who was a beginning reader was once asked why she thought it was important to know how to read. "You might park some place," she said, "and there might be a No Parking sign there. And a man might come out and say, 'Can't you read?' "

The story illustrates a small child's view of the great importance of being able to read in a literate society. An individual in a literate society has many, many encounters every day that require the comprehension of written language. Success with adult illiterates in building literacy has been achieved by building the instructional program around their most pressing needs: signs, applications, labels, directions, and other mundane things which readers take for granted.

A lesser, but still important motivation for the acquisition of reading comes from the pleasure and satisfaction it provides. This is not to say that simply by telling children how much fun reading is they can be motivated to learn. Rather, they can be led to discover this for themselves. The enjoyment of a good story will whet the appetite for more. The satisfaction of getting the information needed from a reference work will stimulate the reader to make greater use of reading as a source of information.

In aiding children to see the significance of reading, we should avoid the temptation of preselecting all the material for them. Children, like adults, have varied tastes and interests. What most children like or profit from may be totally uninteresting to one child. If a child is to find himself in reading, a wide range of topics, formats, and even quality must be represented in the material available to him.

In the multimedia world in which today's children become literate, reading need not be isolated from or exalted above other media. Television, movies, radio can and do actually stimulate reading. Today's readers have seen and heard events that their parents and grandparents encountered only through their newspapers. They bring a much broader background and range of interests to reading than any earlier generations. Above all, motivation for reading requires that schools make themselves relevant to today's children.

Critical Sense

To read critically is to read skeptically. The reader asks himself not only, "Do I understand what this means?" but "Do I buy it?" Implicit in critical reading is a set of values and criteria which is constantly brought into play throughout the process.

Three things are requisite to developing critical reading competence. First, the reader must develop a set of appropriate criteria to judge what he is reading, or at least he must have general criteria which will help him deal with matters such as plausibility, credibility, ulterior motives of the writer or publisher, and so forth. Second, he must see critical reading as necessary and possible for himself. Third, he must be aware of the devices which writers use to appeal emotionally and subtly to him as a means of influencing him.

Much of the reading required of children in school deters rather than promotes critical reading. If there is always one right answer to a question, if the teacher settles an argument by pointing out that the book has given the information on page 38 (implying that books are never wrong), if children are led to believe that they are not competent to judge the merits of their social studies or science books, then the teacher cannot turn around and ask children to read an essay in their reading text critically. One either reads critically or one does not. *The strategies required to read critically must be developed for all reading tasks and not just for special ones designed for instruction.*

Some of the most effective users of language in our country are paid high salaries by Madison Avenue agencies to convince the public that they cannot possibly exist without their clients' products. The same *tactics* have been used with remarkable success to sell political candidates. Only a truly critical reader or listener can hope to ferret out fact from propaganda.

Conclusion

Everyone agrees that reading is a critical area in education. Everyone agrees that methods must be found and curricula developed to teach all children to read effectively. Energy and money are expended for materials, clinics, special teachers by school systems and by parents. That private clinics flourish and that schools are increasing their efforts are mute evidence that the problems of reading instruction have not been solved.

The state of reading instruction today is that of an art. Skilled teachers and specialists have the know-how to help *most,* but not all, of their pupils.

There is no simple breakthrough in reading just around the corner which will change instruction to a foolproof science. As more is understood about reading and learning to read, it becomes ever clearer how complex these processes are. No simple antitoxin can be injected into nonreaders to make them readers. But progress will come as misconceptions disappear in favor of sound understanding. Materials and curricula based on scientific insights will replace those built on tradition, trial-and-error and expediency. And a reading curriculum will evolve tied to an effective theory of reading instruction.

The basis for such progress now exists. If parents, teachers, and administrators can resist simplistic panaceas and keep up sustained efforts to achieve more effective reading instruction, then the next decade can be the one in which the major problems are solved.

Reading: A Psycholinguistic Guessing Game[*]

KENNETH S. GOODMAN[**]
Wayne State University

As scientific understanding develops in any field of study, preexisting, naive, common sense notions must give way. Such outmoded beliefs clutter the literature dealing with the process of reading. They interfere with the application of modern scientific concepts of language and thought to research in reading. They confuse the attempts at application of such concepts to solution of problems involved in the teaching and learning of reading. The very fact that such naive beliefs are based on common sense explains their persistent and recurrent nature. To the casual and unsophisticated observer they appear to explain, even predict, a set of phenomena in reading. This paper will deal with one such key misconception and offer a more viable scientific alternative.

Simply stated, the common sense notion I seek here to refute is this: "Reading is a precise process. It involves exact, detailed, sequential perception and identification of letters, words, spelling patterns and large language units."

In phonic centered approaches to reading, the preoccupation is with precise letter identification. In word centered approaches, the focus is on word identifications. Known words are sight words, precisely named in any setting.

This is not to say that those who have worked diligently in the field of reading are not aware that reading is more than precise, sequential identification. But, the common sense notion, though not adequate, continues to permeate thinking about reading.

Spache (8) presents a word version of this common sense view: "Thus, in its simplest form, reading may be considered a series of word perceptions."

[*]Paper read at the American Educational Research Association, New York, February 1967, and published in the *Journal of the Reading Specialist*, May 1967. Reprinted with permission of the author and publisher.

[**]Now at the University of Arizona at Tucson.

The teacher's manual of the Lippincott *Basic Reading* (6) incorporates a letter by letter variant in the justification of its reading approach: "In short, following this program the child learns from the beginning to see words exactly as the most skillful readers see them . . . as whole images of complete words with all their letters."

In place of this misconception, I offer this: Reading is a selective process. It involves partial use of available minimal language cues selected from perceptual input on the basis of the reader's expectation. As this partial information is processed, tentative decisions are made to be confirmed, rejected, or refined as reading progresses.

More simply stated, reading is a psycholinguistic guessing game. It involves an interaction between thought and language. Efficient reading does not result from precise perception and identification of all elements, but from skill in selecting the fewest, most productive cues necessary to produce guesses which are right the first time. The ability to anticipate that which has not been seen, of course, is vital in reading, just as the ability to anticipate what has not yet been heard is vital in listening.

Consider this actual sample of a relatively proficient child reading orally. The reader is a fourth grade child reading the opening paragraphs of a story from a sixth grade basal reader (5):

"If it bothers you to think of it as baby sitting," my father said, "then don't think of it as baby sitting. Think of it as homework. Part of your education. You just happen to do your studying in the room where the baby brother is sleeping, that's all." He helped my mother with her coat, and then they were gone.

So education it was! I ~~opened~~ ^{hoped©} a _{the} dictionary and picked out a

word that sound~~ed~~ ^s good. "<u>Phil/oso/phi/cal</u>" ^{PH————— He} ~~I~~ yelled. Might

as well study ~~word meanings first~~. "~~Philosophical~~ ^{what it means 1. Phizo 2. Phiso/soophical} : showing calmness

and courage in ~~the~~ face of ill fortune." ^{his 1. fort 2. future 3. futshion} I mean I really yelled it. I guess a fellow has to work off steam once in a while.

He has not seen the story before. It is, by intention, slightly difficult for him. The insights into his reading process come primarily from his errors, which I choose to call miscues in order to avoid value implications. His expected responses mask the process of their attainment, but his unexpected responses have been achieved through the same process, albeit less successfully applied. The ways that they deviate from the expected reveal this process.

In the common sense view that I am rejecting, all deviations must be treated as errors. Furthermore, it must be assumed in this view that an error either indicates that the reader does not know something or that he has been "careless" in the application of his knowledge.

For example, his substitution of *the* for *your* in the first paragraph of the sample must mean that he was careless, since he has already read *your* and *the* correctly in the very same sentence. The implication is that we must teach him to be more careful, that is, to be more precise in identifying each word or letter.

But now let's take the view that I have suggested. What sort of information could have led to tentatively deciding on *the* in this situation and not rejecting or refining this decision? There obviously is no graphic relationship between *your* and *the*. It may be, of course, that he picked up *the* in the periphery of his visual field. But, there is an important non-graphic relationship between *the* and *your*. They both have the same grammatical function: they are, in my terminology, noun markers. Either the reader anticipated a noun marker and supplied one paying no atten-tion to graphic information or he used *your* as a grammatical signal ignoring its graphic shape. Since the tentative choice *the* disturbs neither the meaning nor the grammar of the passage, there is no reason to reject and correct it. This explanation appears to be confirmed by two similar miscues in the next paragraph. *A* and *his* are both substituted for *the*. Neither are corrected. Though the substitution of *his* changes the mean-ing, the peculiar idiom used in this dictionary definition, "in the face of ill fortune," apparently has little meaning to this reader anyway.

The conclusion this time is that he is using noun markers for grammatical, as well as graphic, information in reaching his tentative conclusions. Altogether in reading this ten page story, he made twenty noun marker substitutions, six omissions and two insertions. He corrected four of his substitutions and one omission. Similar miscues involved other function words (auxiliary verbs and prepositions, for example). These miscues appear to have little effect on the meaning of what he is reading.

In spite of their frequency, their elimination would not substantially improve the child's reading. Insistence on more precise identification of each word might cause this reader to stop seeking grammatical information and use only graphic information.

The substitution of *hoped* for *open* could again be regarded as careless or imprecise identification of letters. But, if we dig beyond this common sense explanation, we find 1) both are verbs and 2) the words have *key* graphic similarities. Further, there may be evidence of the reader's bilingual French-Canadian background here, as there is in subsequent miscues (*harms* for *arms, shuckled* for *chuckled, shoose* for *choose, shair* for *chair*). The correction of this miscue may involve an immediate rejection of the tentative choice made on the basis of a review of the graphic stimulus, or it may result from recognizing that it cannot lead to the rest of the sentence, "I hoped a dictionary . . ." does not make sense. (It isn't decodable). In any case, the reader has demonstrated the process by which he constantly tests his guesses, or tentative choices, if you prefer.

Sounds is substituted for sound*ed*, but the two differ in ending only. Common sense might lead to the conclusion that the child does not pay attention to word endings, slurs the ends or is otherwise careless. But, there is no consistent similar occurrence in other word endings. Actually, the child has substituted one inflectional ending for another. In doing so he has revealed 1) his ability to separate base and inflectional suffix, and 2) his use of inflectional endings as grammatical signals or markers. Again, he has not corrected a miscue that is both grammatically and semantically acceptable.

He for *I* is a pronoun for pronoun substitution that results in a meaning change, though the antecedent is a bit vague, and the inconsistency of meaning is not easily apparent.

When we examine what the reader did with the sentence *"Might as well study word meanings first,"* we see how poorly the model of precise sequential identification fits the reading process. Essentially this reader has decoded graphic input for meaning and then encoded meaning in oral output with transformed grammar and changed vocabulary, but with the basic meaning retained. Perhaps as he encoded his output, he was already working at the list word which followed, but the tentative choice was good enough and was not corrected.

There are two examples, in this sample, of the reader working at unknown words. He reveals a fair picture of his strategies and abilities in these miscues, though in neither is he successful. In his several attempts at *philosphical,* his first attempt comes closest. Incidentally, he reveals here that he can use a phonic letter-sound strategy when he wants to. In subsequent attempts he moves away from this sounding out, trying other possibilities, as if trying to find something which at least will sound familiar. Interestingly, here he has a definition of sorts, but no context to work with. *Philosophical* occurs as a list word a number of times in the story. In subsequent attempts, the child tried *physica, physicacol, physical, philosovigul, phizzlesovigul, phizzo sorigul, philazophgul.* He appears to move in concentric circles around the phonic information he has, trying deviations and variations. His three unsuccessful attempts at *fortune* illustrate this same process. Both words are apparently unknown to the reader. He can never really identify a word he has not heard. In such cases, unless the context or contexts sufficiently delimit the word's meaning, the reader is not able to get meaning from the words. In some instances, of course, the reader may form a fairly accurate definition of the word, even if he never recognizes it (that is matches it with a known oral equivalent) or pronounces it correctly. This reader achieved that with the word *typical* which occurred many times in the story. Throughout his reading he said *topical.* When he finished reading, a check of his comprehension indicated that he knew quite well the meaning of the word. This phenomenon is familiar to any adult reader. Each of us has many well-defined words in our reading vocabulary which we either mispronounce or do not use orally.

I've used the example of this youngster's oral reading not because what he's done is typical of all readers or even of readers his age, but because his miscues suggest how he carries out the psycholinguistic guessing game in reading. The miscues of other readers show similarities and differences, but all point to a selective, tentative, anticipatory process quite unlike the process of precise, sequential identification commonly assumed.

Let's take a closer look now at the components the reader manipulates in this psycholinguistic guessing game.

At any point in time, of course, the reader has available to him and brings to his reading the sum total of his experience and his language and thought development. This self-evident fact needs to be stated because what appears to be intuitive in any guessing is actually the result of knowledge so well learned that the process of its application requires little conscious effort. Most language use has reached this automatic, intuitive level. Most of us are quite unable to describe the use we make of grammar in encoding and decoding speech, yet all language users demonstrate a high degree of skill and mastery over the syntax of language even in our humblest and most informal uses of speech.

Chomsky (3) has suggested this model of sentence production by speakers of the language:

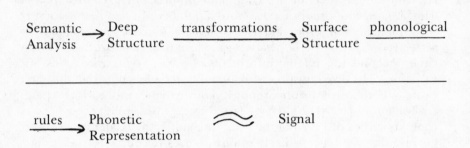

A model structure of the listener's sentence interpretation, according to Chomsky, is:

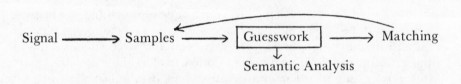

Thus, in Chomsky's view encoding of speech reaches a more or less precise level and the signal which results is fully formed. But in decoding, a sampling process aims at approximating the message and any matching or coded signal which results is a kind of by-product.

In oral reading, the reader must perform two tasks at the same time. He must produce an oral language equivalent of the graphic input which is the *signal* in reading, and he must also reconstruct the meaning of what he is reading. The matching in Chomsky's interpretation model is largely what I prefer to call a recoding operation. The reader recodes the coded graphic input as phonological or oral output. Meaning is not normally involved to any extent. This recoding can even be learned by someone who doesn't speak the language at all, for example, the bar-mitzvah boy may learn to recode Hebrew script as chanted oral Hebrew with no ability to understand what he is chanting; but when the reader engages in semantic analysis to reconstruct the meaning of the writer, only then is he decoding.

In oral reading there are three logical possible arrangements of these two operations. The reader may recode graphic input as oral language and then decode it. He may recode and decode simultaneously. Or, he may decode first and then encode the meaning as oral output.

On the basis of my research to date, it appears that readers who have achieved some degree of proficiency decode directly from the graphic stimulus in a process similar to Chomsky's sampling model and then encode from the deep structure, as illustrated in Chomsky's model of sentence production. Their oral output is not directly related to the graphic stimulus and may involve transformation in vocabulary and syntax, even if meaning is retained. If their comprehension is inaccurate, they will encode this changed or incomplete meaning as oral output.

The common misconception is that graphic input is precisely and sequentially recoded as phonological input and then decoded bit by bit. Meaning is cumulative, built up a piece at a time in this view. This view appears to be supported by studies of visual perception which indicate that only a very narrow span of print on either side of the point of fixation is in sharp focus at any time. We might dub this the "end of the nose" view, since it assumes that input in reading is that which lies in sharp focus in a straight line from the end of the nose. Speed and efficiency are assumed to come from widening the span taken in on either side of the nose, moving the nose more rapidly or avoiding backward movements of the eyes and nose, which, of course, must cut down on efficiency.

This view cannot possibly explain the speed with which the average adult reads, or a myriad of other constantly occurring phenomena in reading. How can it explain, for example, a highly proficient adult reader reading and rereading a paper he's written and always missing the same misprints. Or how can it explain our fourth grader seeing, "Study word meanings first," and saying, "Study what it means"?

No, the "end of the nose" view of reading will not work. The reader is not confined to information he receives from a half inch of print in clear focus. Studies, in fact, indicate that children with severe visual handicaps are able to learn to read as well as normal children. Readers utilize not one, but three kinds of information simultaneously. Certainly without graphic input there would be no reading. But, the reader uses syntactic and semantic information as well. He predicts and anticipates on the basis of this information, sampling from the print just enough to confirm his guess of what's coming, to cue more semantic and syntactic information. Redundancy and sequential constraints in language, which the reader reacts to, make this prediction possible. Even the blurred and shadowy images he picks up in the peripheral area of his visual field may help to trigger or confirm guesses.

Skill in reading involves not greater precision, but more accurate first guesses based on better sampling techniques, greater control over language structure, broadened experiences and increased conceptual development. As the child develops reading skill and speed, he uses increasingly fewer graphic cues. Silent reading can then become a more rapid and efficient process then oral reading, for two reasons: 1) the reader's attention is not divided between decoding and recoding or encoding as oral output, and 2) his speed is not restricted to the speed of speech production. Reading becomes a more efficient and rapid process than listening, in fact, since listening is normally limited to the speed of the speaker.

Recent studies with speeded up electronic recordings where distortion of pitch is avoided have demonstrated that listening can be made more rapid without impairing comprehension too.

Though the beginning reader obviously needs more graphic information in decoding and, therefore, needs to be more precise than skilled readers, evidence from a study of first graders by Goodman (4) indicates that they begin to sample and draw on syntactic and semantic information almost from the beginning, if they are reading material which is fully formed language.

Here are excerpts from two primer stories (1, 2) as they were read by a first grade child at the same session. Ostensibly (and by the intent of the authors) the first, from a second preprimer, should be much easier than the second, from a third preprimer. Yet she encountered problems to the point of total confusion with the first and was able to handle exactly the same elements in the second.

Note, for example, the confusion of *come* and *here* in "Ride In." This represents a habitual association in evidence in early reading of this child. Both *come* and *here* as graphic shapes are likely to be identified as *come* or *here*. In "Stop and Go," the difficulty does not occur when the words are sequential. She also substitutes *can* for *and* in the first story, but encounters no problem with either later. *Stop* stops her completely in "Ride In," a difficulty that she doesn't seem to know she has when she reads "Stop and Go" a few minutes later. Similarly, she calls (ride) *run* in the first story, but gets it right in the latter one.

RIDE IN

Run
~~Ride~~ in, Süe.
Run
~~Ride~~ in here.
Come   here
~~Here~~ I ~~come~~, Jimmy.
Can Come
~~And~~ ~~here~~ I (stop.)

STOP AND GO

Jimmy said, "Come here, Sue,
too
Look at my ~~toy~~ (train.)

See it go.
toy
Look at my lit/tle ~~train~~ go."
toy
Sue said, "Stop the ~~train~~.
Come
Stop it ~~here~~, Jimmy."
toy
Jimmy said, "I can stop the ~~train~~.
toy
See the ~~train~~ stop."
too.
Sue said, "Look at my ~~toy~~.
toy.
It is in the ~~train~~.
too
See my little red ~~toy~~. Jimmy.
toy
It can ride in the ~~train~~."
toy
Jimmy said, "See the ~~train~~ go.
Look at it go."
Suzie   too
~~Sue~~ said, "Look at my little red ~~toy~~.
toy
See it go for a ~~train~~ ride."
Suzie   too
~~Sue~~ said, "My little red ~~toy~~!
said   too
© Jimmy, my ~~toy~~ is not here.
toy
It is not in the ~~train~~.
toy
Stop the ~~train~~, Jimmy.
too
Stop it and look for my ~~toy~~."

Though there are miscues in the second story, there is a very important difference. In the first story she seems to be playing a game of name the word. She is recoding graphic shapes as phonological ones. Each word is apparently a separate problem. But in "Stop and Go" what she says, including her miscues, in almost all instances makes sense and is grammatically acceptable. Notice that as *Sue* becomes better known she becomes *Suzie* to our now confident reader.

A semantic association exists between *train* and *toy*. Though the child makes the same substitution many times, nothing causes her to reject her guess. It works well each time. Having called (train) *toy*, she calls (toy) *too* (actually it's an airplane in the pictures), not once, but consistently throughout the story. That doesn't seem to make sense. That's what the researcher thought too, until the child spoke of a "little red *too*" later in retelling the story. "What's a 'little red too,'" asked the researcher. "An airplane," she replied calmly. So a train is *toy* and a plane is a *too*. Why not? But, notice that when *toy* occurred preceding *train*, she could attempt nothing for *train*. There appears to be a problem for many first graders when nouns are used as adjectives.

Common sense says go back and drill her on *come, here, can, stop, ride, and;* don't let her go to the next book which she is obviously not ready to read.

But the more advanced story, with its stronger syntax, more fully formed language and increased load of meaning makes it possible for the child to use her graphic cues more effectively and supplement them with semantic and syntactic information. Teaching for more precise perception with lists and phonics charts may actually impede this child's reading development. Please notice, before we leave the passage, the effect of immediate experience on anticipation. Every one of the paragraphs in the sample starts with "Jimmy said" or "Sue said." When the reader comes to a line starting *Jimmy,* she assumes that it will be followed by *said* and it is not until her expectation is contradicted by subsequent input that she regresses and corrects her miscue.

Since they must learn to play the psycholinguistic guessing game as they develop reading ability, effective methods and materials used by teachers who understand the rules of the game, must help them to select the most productive cues, to use their knowledge of language structure, to draw on their experiences and concepts. They must be helped to discriminate between more and less useful available information. Fortunately, this parallels the processes they have used in developing the ability to comprehend spoken language. George Miller (7) has suggested

". . . psycholinguists should try to formulate performance models that will incorporate . . . hypothetical information storage and information processing components that can simulate the actual behavior of language users."

I'd like to present now my model of this psycholinguistic guessing game we call reading English. Please understand that the steps do not necessarily take place in the sequential or stretched-out form they are shown here.

1. The reader scans along a line of print from left to right and down the page, line by line.
2. He fixes at a point to permit eye focus. Some print will be central and in focus, some will be peripheral; perhaps his perceptual field is a flattened circle.
3. Now begins the selection process. He picks up graphic cues, guided by constraints set up through prior choices, his language knowledge, his cognitive styles, and strategies he has learned.
4. He forms a perceptual image using these cues and his anticipated cues. This image then is partly what he sees and partly what he expected to see.
5. Now he searches his memory for related syntactic, semantic, and phonological cues. This may lead to selection of more graphic cues and to reforming the perceptual image.
6. At this point, he makes a guess or tentative choice consistent with graphic cues. Semantic analysis leads to partial decoding as far as possible. This meaning is stored in short-term memory as he proceeds.
7. If no guess is possible, he checks the recalled perceptual input and tries again. If a guess is still not possible, he takes another look at the text to gather more graphic cues.
8. If he can make a decodable choice, he tests it for semantic and grammatical acceptability in the context developed by prior choices and decoding.
9. If the tentative choice is not acceptable semantically or syntactically, then he regresses, scanning from right to left along the line and up the page to locate a point of semantic or syntactic inconsistency. When such a point is found, he starts over at that point. If no inconsistency can be identified, he reads on seeking some cue which will make it possible to reconcile the anomalous situation.
10. If the choice is acceptable, decoding is extended, meaning is assimilated with prior meaning, and prior meaning is accommodated, if

necessary. Expectations are formed about input and meaning that lie ahead.

11. Then the cycle continues.

Throughout the process there is constant use of long- and short-term memory.

I offer no apologies for the complexity of this model. Its faults lie, not in its complexity, but in the fact that it is not yet complex enough to fully account for the complex phenomena in the actual behavior of readers. But such is man's destiny in his quest for knowledge. Simplistic folklore must give way to complexity as we come to know.

REFERENCES

1. Betts, Emmett A. "Ride In," *Time to Play,* Second Preprimer, Betts Basic Readers (3rd ed.), Language Arts Series. New York: American Book, 1963.

2. Betts, Emmett A., and Carolyn M. Welch. "Stop and Go," *All In A Day,* Third Preprimer, Betts Basic Readers. New York: American Book, 1963.

3. Chomsky, Noam. Lecture at Project Literacy, Cornell University, June 18, 1965.

4. Goodman, Yetta M. College of Education, Wayne State University, doctoral study of development of reading in first grade children.

5. Hayes, William D. "My Brother is a Genius," *Adventures Now and Then,* Book 6, Betts Basic Readers (3rd ed.), Emmett A. Betts and Carolyn M. Welch. New York: American Book, 1963, 246.

6. McCracken, Glenn, and Charles C. Walcutt. *Basic Reading,* teacher's edition for the preprimer and primer. Philadelphia: B. Lippincott, 1963, vii.

7. Miller, George A. "Some Preliminaries to Psycholinguistics," *American Psychologist,* Vol. 20, No. 18, 1965.

8. Spache, George. *Reading In The Elementary School.* Boston: Allyn and Bacon, 1964, 12.

One Second of Reading*

PHILIP B. GOUGH
University of Texas

Suppose the eye of a moderately skilled adult reader (henceforth, the Reader) were to fall on this sentence, and that he were to read it aloud. One second after his initial fixation, only the first word will have been uttered.[1] But during that second, a number of events will have transpired in the mind of the Reader, each the evident result of processes of amazing complexity. If we knew the train of events, we would know what the processes must accomplish and thus something of their nature. If we knew this, we would know what the child must learn to become a Reader.

Accordingly, this paper is concerned with two topics. First, it tries to describe the sequence of events that transpire in one second of reading, in order to suggest the nature of the processes that link them. Second, it attempts to relate this description to some facts about the acquisition of reading. The description of the chain of events is intended to be exhaustive in the conviction that the complexity of the reading process cannot otherwise be fully appreciated. Thus it is detailed by choice, speculative by necessity, and almost certainly flawed. I hope these are virtues, for much of what is written about reading is either too vague to be tested or too banal to bother, and an analysis that can be attacked in detail can yield detailed knowledge. The consideration of research on reading in children, on the other hand, is anything but complete. Quite apart from the familiar methodological shortcomings which abound in this research, most of it is aimed at a level of description too gross to be of any use here.

---

*Reprinted from J. F. Kavanagh and I. G. Mattingly (Eds.) *Language by Ear and by Eye.* Cambridge, Mass.: MIT Press, 1972, 331-358. With permission of author and MIT Press.

[1] This estimate is based on my reading, as naturally as possible, 50 sentences drawn from the *Daily Texan* and presented tachistoscopically. The median interval between stimulus and response onset was just over 700 msec, and the average initial word required roughly 300 msec to produce.

So rather than presenting an unavoidably dreary review of the literature, I have attempted to interpret the acquisition of reading in terms of the present model, and to fit selected experimental results into the resulting framework.

The Reading Process

Reading begins with an eye fixation. The Reader's eyes focus on a point slightly indented from the beginning of the line, and they remain in that fixation for some 250 msec (Tinker 1958). Then they will sweep 1-4 degrees of visual angle (say 10-12 letter spaces) to the right, in a saccadic movement consuming 10-23 msec, and a new fixation will begin. Barring regressions, and ignoring return sweeps (which take 40-54 msec), this sequence will be repeated as long as reading continues [up to at least six hours according to Carmichael and Dearborn (1947)]. When the initial fixation is achieved, a visual pattern is reflected onto the retina. This sets in motion an intricate sequence of activity in the visual system, culminating in the formation of an icon.

Iconic Representation

The existence of the icon, a relatively direct representation of a visual stimulus that persists for a brief period after the stimulus vanishes, has been amply demonstrated (Sperling 1960, 1963). I take the icon to be a central event, presumably corresponding to neural activity in the striate cortex (cf. Haber & Standing 1969). I further assume that the icon is an "unidentified" or "precategorical" visual image, a set of bars, slits, edges, curves, angles, and breaks, perhaps corresponding to the output of simple cells like those identified by Hubel and Wiesel (1962).

Whatever the form of its contents, the iconic buffer has a substantial capacity. Sperling (1963) has shown that it can hold at least 17 of 18 letters presented in three rows of six. In the case of ordinary reading matter, it can be estimated that the useful content of the icon will include everything in an oval roughly two inches wide and an inch high, or about 20 letter-spaces of the line under fixation.[2]

The decay of the icon has been intensively studied (cf. Haber 1968, 1969). It is known to persist for several seconds if the stimulus is followed

---

[2] I am indebted to Kent Gummerman for this estimate. It is based on "a) acuity data for viewing in the horizontal meridian (Feinberg 1949), b) Wertheim's (1894, p. 185) 'iso-acuity' ellipses that show areas of equal acuity in all directions, and c) the conservative assumption that a letter can be resolved if the thickness of its component lines can be resolved by the eye" (Gummerman, personal communication).

by darkness, but for less than half a second if in light (Sperling 1963). It can be erased or masked by a following patterned stimulus (Liss 1968; Spencer 1969).

The *formation* of the icon, on the other hand, has scarcely been studied at all. One reason is that it is excruciatingly difficult to investigate; the question of how long it takes to form an icon is no less than the question of how long it takes us to sense something. Simple threshold data are uninformative, for they only indicate how much (i.e., what duration of) visual energy is necessary to initiate the train of events which results in the icon. Masked threshold data tell no more, for they are naturally interpreted as indicating how long one icon exists before it is replaced by another. As far as I can see, the only relevant published data are to be found in studies of visually evoked potentials (e.g., Dustman and Beck 1965). If a flash of light is presented to the eye, it is reflected in detectable changes in electrical potential at the occipital cortex no less than 50 msec later;[3] Dustman and Beck (1965) have suggested that wave components with mean latencies of 57 and 75 msec are related to awareness of the light. Assuming that patterned visual information is processed no faster than a flash of light, we might infer (acknowledging the length of the leap) that the icon could not be formed in less than 50 msec, and that its full development may require closer to 100 msec.[4]

Given these assumptions, we are led to suppose that the Reader's initial fixation yields an icon containing materials corresponding to the first 15 to 20 letters and spaces of the sentence (e.g., "Suppose the eye of a"). This icon will become fully "legible" in something like 100 msec. It will last until it is replaced by the icon arising from the Reader's second fixation, some 250 msec later.

In the meantime, the lines, curves, and angles of the first icon will be recognized as familiar patterns. I assume they are identified as letters.

Letter Identification

Letter recognition is very rapid. There is striking evidence that even unrelated letters can be recovered from the icon at rates of 10-20 msec per letter.

One such datum was provided by Sperling (1963), who found that if a random matrix of letters was followed immediately by a patterned mask,

---

[3] There is an early component of the wave at approximately 43 msec, but Dustman and Beck feel that it is not correlated with stimulus awareness.

[4] Presumably the latency of the icon will vary with the intensity of the stimulus (and perhaps with its complexity).

the number of letters reported increased linearly with the duration of the matrix, one letter every 10 msec, up to a limit imposed by memory. Since premask stimulus duration is directly related to icon duration, this result presumably reflects the rate of readout of letters from the icon into a more durable register.

Given that simple recognition thresholds have been shown to be lower for words [and even pronounceable nonsense syllables (Gibson, Osser et al. 1963)] than for random strings like Sperling's, it would be interesting to see if their letters can be read out even more rapidly. To my knowledge, the relevant experiment has not yet been conducted.[5] But there are data that suggest a comparable rate of letter identification with meaningful materials.

First, Scharf, Zamansky et al. (1966) found the masked recognition threshold (using Sperling's own mask) for familiar five-letter words to be roughly 90 msec (under high luminance). This fact provides little comfort for any assumption that read-out of letters from the icon is more efficient for meaningful or pronounceable materials than for random strings of letters; Sperling's results show that under the same circumstances, four or five unrelated letters can easily be registered.

Second, Michael Stewart, Carlton James, and I (Stewart, James et al. 1969) found that visual recognition latency—the time between presentation of a word and the beginning of its pronunciation—increases steadily with word length in letters, from 615 msec for three-letter words to 693 msec for ten-letter words. The function is negatively accelerated; the increase in latency with length is greater with short words than long. But the data are compatible with the assumption that letters of words are read out of the icon at a rate of 10-20 msec per letter.

Third, W. C. Stewart and I (Gough and Stewart 1970) have measured how long it takes readers to decide that a given string of letters is a word or not. One of the variables we manipulated was word length. We found that four-letter words are acknowledged some 35 msec faster than six-letter words, again consistent with the assumption that each additional letter requires an additional 10-20 msec for readout from the icon.

These data, among others, suggest that letters are recovered from the icon *as* letters, that the evident effects of higher levels of organization (like spelling patterns, pronounceability, and meaningfulness) on word recognition and speed of reading should be assigned to higher, and later, levels

---

[5] Gilbert (1959) came close when he presented linguistic segments (words and phrases) of various lengths for various durations, and examined the amount recovered as a function of length of material and exposure duration. But his materials were presented by film, so that control over stimulus quality and duration was crude, and he presents only a rough general description of his materials.

of processing. It is worth noting that if this analysis is correct, then it can be, at best, a half-truth to say that we do not read letter by letter.

Suppose that letters are identified and read out of the icon at a rate of 10 to 20 msec per letter, starting the moment the icon is formed. Since the icon should endure for some 250 msec, between one and two dozen letters could be identified from it even if readout were strictly serial. With a conservative estimate of three fixations per second, and assuming the average word to contain seven letters, even the lower value of letter transfer (i.e., 12 per fixation) would yield a reading speed in excess of 300 words per minute.

I see no reason, then, to reject the assumption that we do read letter by letter.[6] In fact, the weight of the evidence persuades me that we do so serially, from left to right (cf. White 1969). Thus I will assume that the letters in the icon emerge serially, one every 10 or 20 msec into some form of character register.

How the letters get here and what form they take once they have arrived are intriguing questions. But more important is what is done with them. Clearly, letters are not the stuff of which sentences are made. They must be associated with meanings; they must be mapped onto entries in the mental lexicon. The specification of the mechanism by which this is accomplished is, as I see it, the fundamental problem of reading.

The Mapping Problem

There are two superficially appealing possibilities. First, one might assume that the lexicon is directly accessible from the character register, that the Reader goes "directly" from print to meaning. This possibility is appealing to some theorists (cf. Kolers 1970) at least in part because of the nonalphabetic (i.e., neither phonemic nor syllabic) character of many orthographies. Since readers of such orthographies have to learn thousands of arbitrary associations between printed and spoken words, they could as easily learn direct associations between the orthographic words and their meanings and circumvent the spoken word altogether. And if they can do it, so can we.

We can, indeed, but only at great (and quite unnecessary) expense. Every potential Reader has a lexicon that is accessible through phonological information; he can understand the spoken word. Presumably, then, each of his lexical entries contains a phonological representation, and he has a retrieval mechanism that can address the entry through that representation. If he learns to assign such a representation to the printed word,

---

[6] Elsewhere (Gough 1968) I have tried to argue that the traditional arguments against this notion are without foundation.

the mapping problem is solved, and he quickly becomes a Reader. If he does not, he must add an orthographic representation to each of the tens of thousands of lexical entries (to say nothing of constructing a completely new retrieval mechanism to make use of them). The Reader of a nonalphabetic orthography might do this, for his is Hobson's choice. But we have a significant alternative, for while the orthography of English is complex and its rules are numerous, no one has seriously proposed that the number of these rules approaches within a factor of 100 the size of our lexicons. If there is any principle of cognitive economy, it surely must demand that we do not acquire tens of thousands of supererogatory associations, and we must not go straight from print to meaning.

The second possibility is, in this respect, appropriate: it is that we go from print to meaning by way of speech. On this view, the Reader applies orthographic rules to the contents of the character register, converting them to speech, and then listens to himself. All the Reader must add to his cognitive equipment are the orthographic rules. Nothing needs to be added to the lexicon; no new retrieval system needs to be constructed.

The advantages of this hypothesis are obvious. It is a venerable one, and it has prompted any number of studies of subvocal activity during reading (Conrad 1972). But I find it untenable, for I do not believe that the device it proposes can work fast enough. Recall that M. Stewart, C. T. James, and I (1969) found that production latency for a three-letter word is in excess of 600 msec. A highly motivated and practiced subject can push this down to 500 msec. Subtracting the 32 msec our voice key consumes, the 10 msec or so it requires for a nervous impulse to travel from the midbrain to the larynx (Ohala 1970), and another 5 or 10 for it to get to the midbrain from the motor cortex, one is still left with well over 400 msec for an instruction to speak to be assembled. Even ignoring the additional time required for a circuit through some version (however abstract) of an auditory loop, a Reader would not understand a printed word for better than 400 msec after his eye fell on it.

Clearly, we do not know just how long it takes to understand a word. But what may be relevant evidence was obtained several years ago in a study by Rohrman and myself (Rohrman and Gough 1967). We asked subjects to decide if pairs of words were synonymous or not, and measured the latencies of their decisions. On some trials, we announced that a pair would be presented in two seconds by saying "set"; on others, the warning signal was one member of the pair to be judged. We found that giving the subject one member in advance reduced his decision latency by roughly 160 msec. If it is assumed that simultaneous presentation of the pair requires a serial search for the two meanings, and that giving one word in advance eliminates only the retrieval of its meaning from the total decision process, then this result indicates that the meaning of a printed word is located in something on the order of 160 msec. (This result is, in light of the present model, fascinating: if the icon of the word was formed in 100 msec, then it suggests that the meaning of a word is located as fast as its letters can be read out of the icon.) This interpretation is clearly open to question, but if the estimate is anywhere near the true value, then the Reader understands a word well before he can begin to utter it, and the speech-loop hypothesis cannot possibly hold.

In light of these considerations, I am led to a third hypothesis, one that claims the advantages of both (and the disadvantages of neither) at the small price of a charge of abstraction. Suppose it is assumed that the Reader maps characters, not onto speech, but rather onto a string of systematic phonemes, in the sense of Chomsky and Halle (1968). Systematic phonemes are abstract entities that are related to the sounds of the language—the phonetic segments—only by means of a complex system of phonological rules. Thus it is easy to imagine that formation of a string of systematic phonemes would necessarily take place at some temporal distance from (i.e., some time before) the posting of motor commands, and the prohibitive cost of passage through the speech loop would be eliminated. Moreover, since lexical entries must contain, in addition to their semantic and syntactic features, a lexical representation in systematic phonemes, it seems reasonable to assume that the speaker of a language employs, in the comprehension of speech, retrieval mechanisms that access the lexical entries through these lexical representations. If characters are converted into comparable representations, then available retrieval mechanisms could be engaged, and the search for meaning in reading would require no costly new apparatus.

Obviously, this hypothesis is highly speculative, and I can offer no experimental evidence in support of it.[7] But Halle (1969) and N. Chomsky (1970) argue persuasively for a similar view, and I know of nothing to preclude it. More important, it provides the basis for a coherent account of a central problem in the acquisition of reading, as I will attempt to show later.

Thus, I will assume that the contents of the character register are somehow transposed into abstract phonemic representations. If, as

---

[7] Since this paper was delivered, Herbert Rubenstein has reported that subjects take longer to decide that a nonsense word which is homophonic with some English word is *not* a word than to make the same decision about nonsense items which are not homophonic with any English lexical item. This result is, in my view, persuasive evidence for the hypothesis that the printed word is mapped onto a phonemic representation by the Reader.

Chomsky and Halle argue, the orthography of English directly reflects this level of representation, little processing will be required; otherwise, more complex transformations [e.g., the grapheme-phoneme correspondence rules of Venezky (1970)] will yield a string of systematic phonemes that can be used to search the mental lexicon.

Lexical Search

Whether the preceding hypothesis is correct remains to be seen. But whether by this mechanism or by some other, lexical entries are ultimately reached; the Reader understands the words of the sentence. Too little is known about word comprehension to suggest how it is accomplished or even to constrain speculation in any serious way. So I will adopt what I take to be the simplest assumption: that the words of the sentence are understood serially, from left to right.

Apparent objections to this hypothesis lie in the prevalence of lexical ambiguity. First, if words are understood one at a time, then it seems likely that they will frequently be misunderstood, at least until context demands and receives assignment of a new reading. Second, it would seem that prior context would determine the course of lexical search, a procedure not incorporated in the present model.

The first is no real objection, for words often are misunderstood momentarily, and the presence of lexical ambiguity in a sentence demonstrably increases the difficulty of processing the sentence. For example, Foss (1970) has found that if subjects are asked to monitor a sentence for the presence of a given phoneme, their reaction time to the target is increased if it follows an ambiguous item. As to the second point, several experiments in our laboratories have failed to find evidence that the disruptive effect of ambiguity can be eliminated by prior context. Foss has found the same increase in phoneme monitor latency after an ambiguous word even when that word is preceded by a context that completely disambiguates it. In pilot studies, several of my students have found that it takes longer to decide if a pair of words are related when one is ambiguous than if it is not, even when the unambiguous word is presented first (e.g., *prison-cell* takes longer than *prison-jail*). Thus we have (as yet) found no evidence that disambiguation takes place until *after* lexical search.

Such evidence suggests that the abstract phonemic representation is assigned the first lexical entry that can be found. This is consistent with the results of Rubenstein, Garfield, and Millikan (1970) and Gough and Stewart (1970) which show that words are acknowledged to be words more rapidly if they are ambiguous than if they are not (with form and frequency equated). This result suggests that the various readings of a polysemous word are stored separately in the mental dictionary, rather than under a single heading (as they are in Webster's). Interestingly, Rubenstein, Lewis, and Rubenstein (1971) have found that this result does not hold for systematically ambiguous items (i.e., items like *plow*, in which the ambiguity lies only in grammatical category); consistency demands the assumption that these constitute single entries with alternative syntactic features specified.

Thus, lexical search would appear to be a parallel process, with the race going to the swift. When the first entry is located, its contents are accepted as the reading of the word until it proves incompatible with subsequent data; in the case of a systematically ambiguous word, its grammatical category can remain unspecified until further information is provided. In either event, the contents of the lexical entry yielded by each successive word must be deposited somewhere to be organized into a sentence. Primary memory is a likely spot.

Primary Memory

A small-capacity buffer storage system where 4 to 5 verbal items are maintained for a matter of seconds is postulated in many current models of memory (cf. Norman 1970). An item entering this primary memory [PM] (Waugh and Norman 1965) is generally thought to be subject to any of four fates. If it is ignored, it will simply (and rapidly) decay; on the other hand, it can be renewed through rehearsal. When the PM is full, an item in residence must be displaced if a new item is to enter. Finally, it may be transferred or copied into a more permanent store, the secondary memory.

There is one impediment to the assumption that the PM is the temporary repository for the content of a lexical entry. It is widely assumed that the contents of the PM are primarily acoustic or articulatory or phonemic (e.g., Baddeley 1966; Conrad 1964), largely because it is readily shown that verbal items are easily confused on this basis in short-term memory. I find this argument shaky.

First, confusion based on supraphonological properties of items in short-term memory can be demonstrated quite easily. Cornbleth, Powitzky, and I have found that lists of six nouns are more easily remembered if all are singular or plural than if singulars and plurals are mixed in a list; a variety of controls show that the effect cannot be attributed to confusion at the phonological level. The same appears to be true of verbs and tense, *mutatis mutandis*. If confusion data suggest that phonological information is in the PM, then reasoning from appropriate data leads to the same conclusion regarding syntactic or semantic properties. Second, Craik (1968) has shown that the immediate memory span is virtually identical for words of one to four syllables. This clearly suggests that the capacity of the PM is not defined by acoustic, articulatory, or even phonemic parameters, for all of these surely must vary from one-syllable to four-syllable words.

These data, I think, justify the assumption that the contents of lexical entries, including phonological, syntactic, and semantic information, are deposited in the PM, presumably one entry to a cell. The PM thus would become the working memory for the mechanisms of sentence comprehension.

There are many observations consistent with the assumption that the PM and the comprehension device interact in some such fashion. Three might be noted. First, it is obvious that far more words may be retained in sentences than out of them; sentences are remembered better than lists. In the present model this would be explained by assuming that when words are processed into sentences, the resulting structure is allocated to a further storage system with a much greater capacity. I am inclined to identify it with the secondary memory of the memory theorists, and to propose that items pass into secondary memory only when they are related to one another, or integrated in some fashion akin to comprehension. But that is another matter. For the present purpose, it suffices to assume that when a sentence is understood, it is deposited in the Place Where Sentences Go When They Are Understood (PWSGWTAU).

Second, when the contents of the PM are integrated, the PM can be cleared and new items entered. Support for this notion comes from a series of recent experiments by John Mastenbrook and myself, in which we have found that if a subject is asked to recall a five-word sentence together with five unrelated words, his recall is significantly greater if the sentence is presented before the list than vice versa, independent of recall order. This is easily explained in the present model: if the list is registered first, PM is full when the sentence arrives, and it can be processed only at the cost of some items from the list, whereas if the sentence arrives first, it is quickly understood and the PM is cleared when the list arrives.

Third, the model predicts that any sentence whose initial words exceed the capacity of PM before they can be understood (i.e., before their grammatical relations can be discovered) will prove incomprehensible. This is just the case with sentences self-embedded to a degree of 2 or more.

The evidence, then, supports the assumption that the PM provides a buffer memory for the comprehension device. In my opinion, we have no good idea how that device works; the question is being studied and debated intensively (cf. Gough 1971). For the present purpose, it suffices to assume that some wondrous mechanism (which we might dub *Merlin*) operating on the information in the PM, tries to discover the deep structure of the fragment, the grammatical relations among its parts. If Merlin succeeds, a semantic interpretation of the fragment is achieved and placed in the ultimate register, the PWSGWTAU. If Merlin fails, we would assume that the fixation will be maintained to provide further processing time, or that a regressive eye movement would be called for. This is obviously consistent with the well-known facts about eye movements and difficulty of material (cf. Tinker 1958).

Assuming success, the obtained deep structure provides the basis for the formation of a superficial structure containing the formatives from PM; application of phonological rules to this structure will yield instructions for the pronunciation of the fragment, and the Reader will begin to speak.

At this moment, some 700 msec have passed since the Reader's eye fell on the sentence. By this time, he is probably into his third fixation, perhaps 30 spaces into the sentence. The material from the first fixation is in the ultimate register (the PWSGWTAU); that from the second fixation is crowding into the PM.

I have tried to summarize the history of the 700 msec in Table 1, where the contents of each of the proposed stages of processing are specified at 100-msec intervals. Obviously, most of the entries are little more than plausible guesses. But the table suggests just how much must have happened. Some 20 to 25 letters have been internalized as characters, and converted into abstract phonemes. Perhaps a half dozen lexical entries have been located, and their contents copied into PM. The grammatical relations between some portion of these have been discovered, and the construction of a deep structure has begun. The semantically interpreted items have been inserted into a surface phrase-marker, and that, in turn, has been translated into motor commands.

On the outside, the Reader has rotated his eyes a few millimeters and he has begun to move his mouth. But on the inside, there has been a rapid succession of intricate events. Clearly, this succession could only be the product of a complex information processing system. That which has been proposed herein is outlined in Figure 1. It contains components that are asked to perform amazing feats with amazing rapidity, and precisely in concert. It remains to be seen whether this model bears any resemblance to reality. But it does suggest the complexity of the system that must be assembled in the mind of the child who learns to read.

Table 1. Level of representation as a function of time

Msec	Material under Fixation	Level of Processing: Lines, Curves, Angles	Level of Processing: Letters	Level of Processing: Systematic Phonemes
000	Suppose the eye	Suppose the eye	s	
100	" " "	"		
200	" " "	"	. . pose th . . .	sŭb = p
300	ose the eye of a mod	ose the eye of a mod	. . . e the e . . .	. . . = pōz#ð . . .
400	" " "	"	. . . e eye o . . .	. . . z#ðē#i . . .
500	of a moderately skil	of a moderately skil	. . . ye of a . . .	. . . i#tv#æ . . .
600	" " "	of a moderately skil	. . . e of a . . .	. . v#æ#m . . .
700	" " "	"	. . . oderate . . .	. . #modě . . .
800	tely skilled adult r	tely skilled adult re	. . . erately . . .	. . . ěræt# . . .
900	" " "	"	. . . led adu . . .	. . . #ly#s . . .
1000	adult reader (hencef	"	. . . d adult . . .	. . . skɨld . . .

Table 1. (Continued)

Msec	Level of Processing: Lexical Entries	Level of Processing: Semantic Representation	Level of Processing: Phonetic Representation	Vocalization
000				
100				
200				
300	$\begin{bmatrix} +V_t \\ +ment \\ \cdot \\ \cdot \end{bmatrix}$			
400	$\begin{bmatrix} +V_t \\ +ment \\ \cdot \\ \cdot \end{bmatrix} \begin{bmatrix} +Art \\ +Def \\ \cdot \\ \cdot \end{bmatrix}$			
500	$\begin{bmatrix} +V_t \\ +ment \\ \cdot \\ \cdot \end{bmatrix} \begin{bmatrix} +Art \\ +Def \\ \cdot \\ \cdot \end{bmatrix} \begin{bmatrix} +N_c \\ +Conc \\ \cdot \\ \cdot \end{bmatrix}$	$\text{IMP}(_s \text{ you will suppose } [_s$		
600	$\begin{bmatrix} +Art \\ +Def \\ \cdot \\ \cdot \end{bmatrix} \begin{bmatrix} +N_c \\ +Conc \\ \cdot \\ \cdot \end{bmatrix} \begin{bmatrix} +Prep \\ +Poss \\ \cdot \\ \cdot \end{bmatrix}$	$\ldots \text{ suppose } [_s \text{ the eye } (_s$	səpʰōwz	

Table 1 (Continued)

Msec	Level of Processing: Lexical Entries	Level of Processing: Semantic Representation	Level of Processing: Phonetic Representation	Vocalization
700	[+Prep +Poss · · ·] [+Art −Def · · ·]	. . . the eye (s X [s	ōwzðiyáy	"Su . . ."
800	[+Prep +Poss · · ·] [+Art −Def · · ·] [+Adj +Deg · · ·]	. . . eye (sX [s] has eye	zðiyáyəv	". . . ppo . . ."
900	[+Prep +Poss · · ·] [+Art −Def · · ·] [+Adv +Deg · · ·]	. . . X [s X be Y (Y mod)	ðiyáyəv	". . . se . . ."
1000	[+Art −Def · · ·] [+Adv +Deg · · ·] [+Adj +Anim · · ·]	. . . X be skilled (sskil . . .	áyəvə	". . . se . . ."

SUPPOSE THE EYE...   "SUPPOSE..."

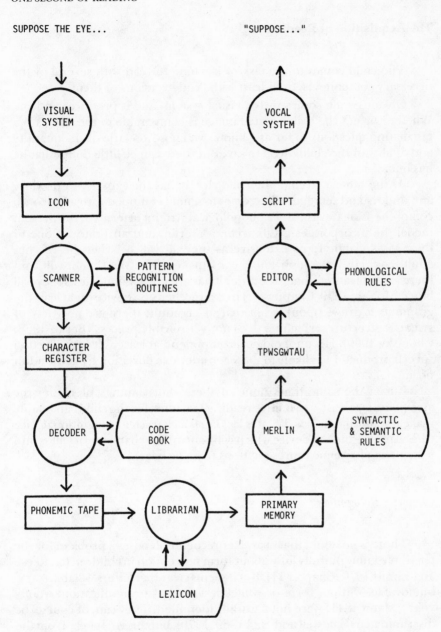

Figure 1.   A model of reading

The Acquisition of Reading

The child comes to the task of learning to read with several of the necessary components, or at least with crude versions of them.

Obviously, he comes with a visual system, and it produces an icon. Whether or not the child's visual image is comparable to the adult's is a fascinating question; so far as I know, we know too little of the quantity and quality of the child's icon to say. But there can be little doubt that he has one.

At the other extreme, the child clearly has the capacity to produce and understand sentences. He comes to school equipped with a lexicon, a comprehension device, and a phonological system; in terms of the present model, he incorporates a Librarian, a Merlin, and an Editor. None of these is as elaborate or extensive as they all will be when he reaches adulthood. His lexicon obviously contains fewer entries than it will, and there are indications that the entries it has are not as complete as they will be (cf. McNeill 1970, Chapter 8). His comprehension device (or at least the grammar it draws upon) is not that of an adult; there are a variety of syntactic structures which he does not yet reliably process (Berko 1958; Chomsky 1969). His phonological component, at least as it is engaged in speech production, is likely to show considerable deviation from the adult norm.

But at the same time, none of these shortcomings precludes the assembly of (at least) a primitive reading machine, for the child can readily make use of what he has. What is lacking is a character recognition device (the Scanner) and the device which will convert the characters it yields into systematic phonemic representations (the Decoder).

Character Recognition

There is no doubt that character recognition poses a problem for the child. We know pitifully little about form perception in children (cf. Reese and Lipsitt 1970, Chapter 11). But it seems clear that letters—"lank, stark, immovable, without form or comeliness, and as to signification, wholly void" (Mann 1841)—are not naturally identified. They can, of course, be discriminated (Caldwell and Hall 1969, 1970), but this is a far cry from the absolute identification demanded by the reading process. For example, while children will make relatively few mistakes in copying a pattern like a letter (Asso and Wyke 1971), indicating that they are quite capable of simultaneous discrimination, they find the same distinction inordinately difficult in a successive discrimination task (Rudel and Teuber 1963).

The difficulties posed for the child by letters that are mirror images of one another (e.g., "b-d, p-q") and, to a lesser extent, by those that are inversions (e.g., "b-p") have long been noted (cf. Monroe 1932). There have been a number of studies assessing methods of teaching children these distinctions (e.g., Hendrickson and Muehl 1962). And almost as often, this problem has been taken as a symptom of reading disability (cf. Orton 1937).

In one sense, it must be such a symptom. An inability to reliably identify "b" cannot fail to be a handicap in reading. But as E. Gibson has pointed out, the discrimination our orthography demands of the child runs directly counter to virtually all of his perceptual experience, in which objects differing only in orientation are equivalent. Moreover, Corballis and Beale (1971) have argued persuasively that such equivalence is deeply rooted in the bilateral symmetry of our anatomy. Thus these distinctions must pose a problem for every child, and there is every indication that this is the case.

Aside from orientation, the features that distinguish (or fail to distinguish) one letter from another in the child's icon are little understood. Gibson's studies of letter confusions in early readers and adults (Gibson, Schapiro et al. 1968) have suggested a set of features that may well be those used by the character recognition device. What remains to be disclosed, however, are the features by which the prereader will distinguish the same patterns. This knowledge would indicate which subcomponents of the character recognition device are available in the prereader, and which are not, and we might get some idea of what it takes to assemble the complete device.

It would be comforting to think that character recognition (or better, the lack of it) was the chief impediment to learning to read, for it can be taught (at least with patience). The unwary might be tempted to find support for this in the infamous fact that knowledge of the alphabet is the single best predictor of reading achievement (Bond and Dykstra 1967). But Samuels (1971) has reported the results of several studies that found no evidence that teaching the alphabet facilitates learning to read.

It remains to be seen, however, if the correlation is entirely spurious. Teaching of the alphabet, the ABC's, dates at least to the time of Socrates (Mathews 1966), and I find it difficult to believe that a tradition that appears to serve no other purpose would survive if it did not serve this one. Whether by means of alphabet books, blocks, or soup, character recognition must be mastered. It is obviously a necessary component of reading; equally obvious, it is not a sufficient one. Given character recognition, the fundamental problem arises, that which is commonly referred to as *decoding*.

Decoding

The Reader converts characters into systematic phonemes; the child must learn to do so. The Reader knows the rules that relate one set of abstract entities to another; the child does not. The Reader is a decoder; the child must become one. The decoding metaphor is familiar, and it would be difficult to argue that it is unappropriate. But if we take seriously the notion that characters are decoded to systematic phonemes, there is an interesting consequence. We can no longer think of the child as a clerk to whom we hand the code, for there is no direct way to display the rules constituting it. We cannot show him that this character goes with that systematic phoneme, for there is no way to isolate a systematic phoneme. We cannot tell him, "This goes with That," for we have no way of representing That.

In short, we cannot teach him the code. This is not to say that he cannot acquire it; every Reader before him has done so. But the child must master the code through a sort of cryptanalysis rather than through memorization. Viewed in this light, what is necessary for the child to learn to read is that he be provided with a set of pairs of messages known to be equivalent, one in ciphertext (writing) and one in plaintext (speech). They must be provided in sufficient quantity to enable him to arrive at a unique solution, and that is all.

A full solution of the code (i.e., one equivalent to that we ascribe to the Reader) can be achieved only if the child correctly identifies the alphabets of the plaintext and of the ciphertext. If we assume that the child has lexical representations in the form of systematic phonemes, the former should pose no special problem. (There is, however, some evidence to suggest that this may be a facile assumption (Savin 1972). It remains to be seen whether evidence of this sort is indicative of a different sort of phonological organization in the child, or the result of something much more superficial.)

If the child has mastered the character recognition problem as discussed above, then he has isolated the alphabet of the ciphertext, and his problem is reduced to a tractable one: that of searching for correspondences between the message pairs. But if, for some reason, he has not realized the unity of the letters, then he is faced with a cryptanalytic task of demonstrably greater difficulty, that of working out the cipher alphabet and the code simultaneously. In this connection, the Look-and-Say method obviously comes to mind. In light of the present analysis this method is not totally unreasonable. It provides the essential ingredients for the child's cryptanalysis (i.e., pairs of spoken and written messages). The trouble with it is that it does not appropriately define the problem for the child-cryptanalyst.

The Look-and-Say method confronts the child with a problem of paired-associate (PA) learning. We know that subjects confronted with the PA task will "solve" it as efficiently as they can; they will select some cue, some feature of each stimulus, and associate the defined response with that cue. That cue can be any feature or property of the stimulus item that distinguishes it from the others; in the case of visual material, it might be length, or area, or the presence of a curved line. I know of no reason to suppose that the child is different from the sophomore subject in this respect. Confronted with a word (the Look) to which he must associate a response (the Say), he should be likely to seize upon any feature of the word that differentiates it from the others he must master.

An egregious example of this can be found in a study reported by Coleman (1970) as part of his effort to collect a data base for a technology of reading. One of Coleman's concerns was to rank words that might be used in basic reading programs in order of the ease with which the child could learn to read them. So several hundred words were taught to different children by the look-say method, and the number of errors to criterion was taken as the basic datum. The words *kitten* and *no* were found to be the easiest of all. When it is noted that the words were presented in short lists, and that *kitten* is the only word as long as six letters, it is easy to see why these words were easy (and it is not that they are intrinsically so).

Given the manner in which lists are learned, it seems clear that the Look-and-Say method would not force the child to map characters onto phonemes until simpler strategies will no longer work, and that will not happen until the list reaches a substantial length. At this point, we would expect that some children will tackle the cryptanalysis and learn to read, but we should not be surprised to see others resign in frustration. And that, of course, is what is known to happen with the Look-and-Say method.

It is clearly preferable to confront the child with the mapping problem from the start, and to suggest to him that it is solvable. One way is through phonics. In this method (or better, class of methods), the child is explicitly directed to the ciphertext alphabet, and conceivably to the plaintext as well. The method requires that he pair letters (and clusters of letters) with spoken syllables; to the extent that he segments those syllables, such learning might provide material for the necessary cryptanalysis.

It is important to realize, though, that phonics does not teach the mapping required to become a Reader. What the Reader knows is the mapping between characters and systematic phonemes; what the child is taught in phonics is to name a letter (or letter pair) with a syllable that contains the appropriate systematic phoneme. When a child "sounds out" a new word, it is apparent to any auditor that the child is not converting letters into underlying phonemic representations. Rather he is searching for something that he can hear as a word.

In the present analysis, phonics is not a method of teaching the child grapheme-phoneme correspondence rules. The rules he learns are not the rules he must master, but rather heuristics for locating words through the auditory modality. The lexical representations of those words then provide data for the induction of the real character-phoneme rules. Skill in phonics gives the child a means of naming a word *in loco parentis;* it provides him with a valuable means of data collection.

The crucial variable in the cryptanalytic problem is the character of the data: the nature and number of message pairs. Other things equal, the shorter the messages, the fewer the potential solutions; so cryptanalysis is facilitated if the shortest possible messages are provided first. Virtually every method takes advantage of this fact by beginning reading instruction with short words. [It is interesting to note that Jacotot, one of the intellectual ancestors of Gestalt psychology, advocated beginning with a book and gradually working back to the letter, whatever that means (Mathews 1966).] Cryptanalysis is also facilitated if the messages are arranged such that covariation is apparent; if a change in a ciphertext is also accompanied by a change in the corresponding plaintext, the solution is obvious.

From this perspective, the various so-called Linguistic Methods [like those advocated by Bloomfield (1942) and Fries (1963)] appear to be optimal, for they offer the child a sequence of message pairs in which only one element is varied at a time. What is surprising, at least on first inspection, is that this method has not been shown to be superior. Indeed, there is no compelling evidence that any reasonable method of reading instruction yields results different from the others. This is encouraging, in one sense, for it means that children can manage to learn to read under any method, so long as they are provided the appropriate data, and the present hypothesis predicts just that. But it is also frustrating, for differential predictions are the stuff of which theories are made.

The trouble is, of course, that Methods are not methods. That is, a Method describes little more than an orientation on the part of a teacher, and perhaps the use of a particular basal reading series (Chall 1967). What are desperately needed are experimental studies of reading acquisition in detail, where we know what was presented to the child, when, in what manner, and how often.

There have been very few, and they are not very revealing. The first (that I know of) was conducted by Bishop (1964), using adult subjects. It was intended to compare the transfer effects of word and letter training. One group of subjects was taught to an eight-item paired-associate list, where each stimulus consisted of four Arabic characters (e.g., ف | و ﺏ) drawn from a set of twelve, and each response was a disyllabic Arabic word (e.g., /faru/). A second group was taught to name each of the twelve characters with its appropriate phoneme (i.e., they were given instruction in Arabic phonics). A third learned an irrelevant task. When all groups were then asked to learn a new eight-item PA list (in which the characters were recombined to form novel words), the phonics group learned it most rapidly. This is scarcely surprising (though it may have been when the study was conducted), for it seems clear that the whole-word group had little reason to detect correspondences, since other strategies requiring no intellectual effort would suffice perfectly well. (In fact, we might have expected to see negative transfer in this group, save for the fact that training and transfer stimuli had no initial characters in common.) What is more interesting is that the word group performed better than the control; some subjects evidently took on the cryptanalysis even though it was not necessary. But these subjects were college students, and it is not obvious that children would go to the same trouble.

A more promising study was conducted with kindergarteners by Jeffrey and Samuels (1967). They employed an artificial alphabet of six nonsense figures. Three (call them A, B, C), were identified with the consonants /m, s, b/, three (X, Y, Z) with the vowels /e, i, o/. One group of subjects, the Word Group, was taught a four-item PA list: AX-/mo/, BX-/so/, CY-/be/, CZ-/bi/. A Letter Group was taught four isolated correspondences: A-/m/, B-/s/, Y-/e/, and Z-/i/. A control group was taught an unrelated task.

Prior to training, all groups were familiarized with the alphabet, and given practice on "blending" the sounds to be used in the ultimate transfer list, AZ, BZ, BY, and AY. Then each group was given its training. On the transfer list, the phonics group performed significantly better than the others, which did not differ. In this study, the Letter Group was given what amounts to phonics instruction, and the Word Group might be thought of as representing a linguistic method. If this were so, the phonics instruction would seem to be the superior method of (at least) initial instruction. But there is a serious flaw in this analogy, for the Word Group was mistreated.

The Letter Group was exposed to just those four elements that would be involved in the transfer; the Word Group, on the other hand, confronted items composed of six. But more important, the organization of those elements fell short of that which could be expected to yield successful cryptanalysis.

The message pairs which the Word Group was allowed to use may be arranged in a matrix, arrayed by initial and final ciphertext element:

	X	Y	Z
A	/mo/	—	—
B	/so/	—	—
C	—	/be/	/bi/

This display makes clear the structure of the correspondence rules, and it is conceivable that they might be induced by someone who knew that CY can be decomposed to C and Y, and that /be/ consists of /b/ plus /e/. (In fact, the Word Group produced something like eight correct responses—of a possible 80—on the initial transfer trial, so more than one of the 20 must have induced something.) But there is nothing to demand it, for memorizing only four item-item correspondences will solve the problem. In fact, to achieve the solution of the code implicit in this matrix would require the identification of *six* rules. It is surely reasonable for the learner to prefer rote memory in this instance.

Such considerations lead to the hypothesis that the child would most readily learn the true system of correspondences when it provides the simplest solution to the cryptanalytic problem. For example, if, in a design like that of Jeffrey and Samuels, the child had been forced to learn not just four items, but all six lying outside a diagonal of this matrix, then the principled solution would be as simple as the associative one, and we would expect significantly greater transfer to novel items (i.e., the diagonal items).

This analysis suggests that the child's task bears a striking resemblance to those studied in adults under the rubric of miniature linguistic systems. Since the seminal experiments of Esper (1925, 1933), this literature has grown too large to review here (see Smith and Braine, 1972). But it provides abundant evidence for the principle proposed here: The greater the advantage afforded by induction of structure (over rote memory), the more frequent the induction. In the present case, we should expect to see that if Jeffrey and Samuels had not only more completely filled the matrix but enlarged it (in either dimension), the Word Method would have yielded dramatically better results (cf. Foss 1968; Palermo and Parrish 1971). And when one considers that the real task confronting the child involves a matrix in multiple dimensions, the consequences are even more apparent. There have been other studies of teaching methods (e.g., Hartley 1970)—in this experimental sense—but they add little to this picture.

How the child solves the decoding problem is a mystery, but many do. If one does, he should be able to understand and produce any word that conforms to the rules he has mastered. Yet it has long been observed that there are children who can read and pronounce words, children who can decode, but yet do not seem to *read* connected discourse. They "bark at print"; they are "word-callers" or "parrot-readers." Evidently, solving the decoding problem does not automatically make the child a Reader.

The Speed Problem

There is a natural interpretation of this problem within the present model. To understand a sentence, it does not suffice to obtain lexical entries, place them in the PM, and pronounce them. If the words of a sentence are to be integrated into a semantic reading, they must be deployed in the PM together.

To be sure, we adults can tolerate substantial delays between words without apparent disruption of comprehension; if the delays are brief enough, as in hesitation pauses, we may not even be aware of them. This is to be expected if the PM is indeed the repository for material waiting to be understood, for it will hold that material for a short while. But Martin (1968) has shown that pauses of as little as two seconds interfere with our ability to perceive sentences in noise, and we have found some evidence in pilot studies that repetition of words within sentences reduces our capacity to remember them.

It seems reasonable to suppose that the child's ability to comprehend sentences is affected in the same way. Furthermore, if—as some evidence suggests (Haith, Morrison, et al. 1970)—the child's PM is much smaller than our own, then pauses between words will prove even more disruptive for the child's comprehension. There is an obvious source of pauses in reading sentences: if words are identified slowly, then pauses are inevitable. There is abundant evidence that children do not identify words as rapidly as adults, and that the poor reader does not identify words as rapidly as the good one.

The hypothesis that temporal word spacing will significantly diminish sentence comprehension in the child would be easy to test. But I think that naturalistic observation of children reading aloud suggests that temporal spacing is a ubiquitous problem in early reading. If it takes too long to read a given word, the content of the immediately preceding words will have been lost from the PM, and comprehension will be prevented. If the word in question is read aloud, it will necessarily be read as a citation form, and the child's oral reading will sound like a list just because he is, in fact, reading a list.

To prevent this, the child who would understand must try to read rapidly, and if he cannot quickly identify a word, he must guess. The result will frequently be an oral reading error. These errors have been the subject of considerable study (Weber 1968), and seemingly contradictory conclusions have been drawn from them. On the one hand, it has been argued [e.g., by Goodman (1970) and elsewhere] that reading is normally a kind of guessing game, in which the reader uses the printed word for little more than hints as to whether he is thinking the right thoughts or not. In this view, oral reading errors are nothing but a manifestation of normal function, not a symptom of malfunction, and thus they should not be squelched. On the other hand, it has been argued (Biemiller, 1970), that at least in the early stages of reading, oral reading errors are an indication that the child is avoiding the decoding problem, and thus a sign that he is unable to identify what lies before him.

From the present point of view, Biemiller is closer to the truth. A guess may be a good thing, for it may preserve the integrity of sentence comprehension. But rather than being a sign of normal reading, it indicates that the child did not decode the word in question rapidly enough to read normally. The good reader need not guess; the bad should not.

In the model I have outlined, the Reader is not a guesser. From the outside, he appears to go from print to meaning as if by magic. But I have contended that this is an illusion, that he really plods through the sentence, letter by letter, word by word. He may not do so; but to show that he does not, his trick will have to be exposed.

REFERENCES

Asso, D., and M. Wyke, 1971. Discrimination of spatially confusable letters by young children. *J. Exp. Child Psych.* 11:11-20.

Baddeley, A. D., 1966. Short-term memory for word sequences as a function of acoustic, semantic, and formal similarity. *Quart. J. Exp. Psychol.* 18:362-365.

Berko, J., 1958. The child's learning of English morphology. *Word,* 14:150-177.

Biemiller, A., 1970. The development of the use of graphic and contextual information. *Reading Res. Quart.* 6:75-96.

Bishop, C. H., 1964. Transfer effects of word and letter training in reading. *J. Verbal Learning and Verbal Behavior* 3:215-221.

Bloomfield, L., 1942. Linguistics and reading. *Elementary English,* 18:125-130; 183-186.

Bond, G. L., and R. Dykstra, 1967. The cooperative research program in first-grade reading instruction. *Reading Res. Quart.* 2:4, 5-126.

Caldwell, E. D., and V. C. Hall, 1969. The influence of concept training on letter discrimination. *Child Development* 40:63-71.

Caldwell, E. D., and V. C. Hall, 1970. Concept learning in discrimination tasks. *Develop. Psych.* 2:41-48.

Carmichael, L., and W. F. Dearborn, 1947. *Reading and Visual Fatigue.* Boston: Houghton Mifflin.

Chall, J., 1967. *Learning To Read: The Great Debate.* New York: McGraw-Hill.

Chomsky, C., 1969. *The Acquisition of Syntax in Children from 5 to 10.* Cambridge, Mass.: M.I.T. Press.

Chomsky, N., 1970. Phonology and reading. In H. Levin and J. P. Williams (eds.), *Basic Studies on Reading.* New York: Basic Books, pp. 3-18.

Chomsky, N., and M. Halle, 1968. *The Sound pattern of English.* New York: Harper and Row.

Coleman, E. B., 1970. Collecting a data base for a reading technology. *J. Ed. Psych. Monographs* 61:4, Part 2, pp. 1-3.

Conrad, R., 1964. Acoustic confusions in immediate memory. *Brit. J. Psych.* 55:75-84.

Conrad, R., 1972. Speech and reading. In James F. Kavanagh and Ignatius Mattingly (Eds.), *Language by Ear and by Eye.* Cambridge: M.I.T. Press.

Corballis, M. C., and I. L. Beale, 1971. On telling left from right. *Sci. Amer.* 224:96-104.

Craik, F. I. M., 1968. Two components in free recall. *J. Verbal Learning and Verbal Behavior* 7:996-1004.

Dustman, R. E., and E. C. Beck, 1965. Phase of alpha brain waves, reaction time and visually evoked potentials. *Electroenceph. Clin. Neurophysiol.* 18:433-440.

Esper, E. A., 1925. A technique for the experimental investigation of associative interference in artificial linguistic material. *Language Monogr.,* vol. 1.

Esper, E. A., 1933. Studies in linguistic behavior organization: I. Characteristics of unstable verbal reactions. *J. Gen. Psych.* 8:346-379.

Feinberg, R., 1949. A study of some aspects of peripheral visual acuity. *Amer J. Optometry and Arch. of Amer. Acad. Optometry* 26:49-56, 105-119.

Foss, D. J., 1968. Learning and discovery in the acquisition of structured material. *J. Exp. Psych.* 77:341-344.

Foss, D. J., 1970. Some effects of ambiguity upon sentence comprehension. *J. Verbal Learning and Verbal Behavior* 9:699-706.

Fries, C. C., 1963. *Linguistics and Reading.* New York: Holt, Rinehart, and Winston.

Gibson, E. J., 1965. Learning to read. *Science,* 148:1066-1072.

Gibson, E. J., F. Schapiro, and A. Yonas, 1968. Confusion matrices for graphic patterns obtained with a latency measure. In *The Analysis of Reading Skill: A Program of Basic and Applied Research.* Final report, Project No. 5-1213, Cornell University and U.S.O.E., pp. 76-96.

Gibson, E. J., H. Osser, and A. Pick, 1963. A study in the development of grapheme-phoneme correspondences. *J. Verbal Learning and Verbal Behavior* 2:142-146.

Gilbert, L. C., 1959. Speed of processing visual stimuli and its relation to reading. *J. Ed. Psych.* 55:8-14.

Goodman, K. S., 1970. Reading: A psycholinguistic guessing game. In *Theoretical Models and Processes of Reading*, H. Singer and R. R. Ruddell (eds.), Newark, Del.: International Reading Association, pp. 259-272.

Gough, P. B., 1968. We don't read letter-by-letter? Paper presented at a Consortium on Psycholinguistics and Reading, Convention of the International Reading Association, Boston.

Gough, P. B., 1971. (Almost a decade of) experimental psycholinguistics. In *A Survey of Linguistic Science*, W. O. Dingwall (ed.), College Park: Linguistics Program, Univ. of Maryland.

Gough, P. B., and W. C. Stewart, 1970. Word vs. non-word discrimination latency. Paper presented at Midwestern Psychological Association.

Haber, R. N. (ed.), 1968. *Contemporary Theory and Research in Visual Perception*. New York: Holt, Rinehart and Winston.

Haber, R. N. (ed.), 1969. *Information-Processing Approaches to Visual Perception*. New York: Holt, Rinehart and Winston.

Haber, R. N., and L. B. Standing, 1969. Direct measures of short-term visual storage. *Quart. J. Exp. Psych.* 21:43-54.

Haith, M. M., F. J. Morrison, K. Sheingold, and P. Mindes, 1970. Short-term memory for visual information in children and adults. *J. Exp. Child Psych.* 9:454-469.

Halle, M., 1969. Some thought on spelling. In *Psycholinguistics and the Teaching of Reading*. K. S. Goodman and J. T. Fleming (eds.), Newark, Del.: International Reading Association.

Hartley, R. N., 1970. Effects of list types and cues on the learning of word lists. *Reading Res. Quart.* 6:97-121.

Hendrickson, L. N., and S. Muehl, 1962. The effect of attention and motor response pretraining on learning to discriminate b and d in kindergarten children. *J. Ed. Psych.* 53:236-241.

Hubel, D. H., and T. N. Wiesel, 1962. Receptive fields, binocular interaction and functional architecture in the cat's visual cortex. *J. Physiol.* 160:106-154.

Jeffrey, W. E., and S. J. Samuels, 1967. Effect of method of reading training on initial learning and transfer. *J. Verb. Learning and Verbal Behavior* 6:354-358.

Kolers, P. A., 1970. Three stages of reading. In *Basic Studies on Reading*, H. Levin and J. P. Williams (eds.), New York: Basic Books, pp. 90-118.

Liss, P., 1968. Does backward masking by visual noise stop stimulus processing? *Perception and Psychophysics* 4:328, 330.

McNeill, D., 1970. *The Acquisition of Language*. New York: Harper and Row.

Mann, 1841; cited by Mathews (1966), p. 77.

Martin, J. G., 1968. Temporal word spacing and the perception of ordinary, anomalous, and scrambled strings. *J. Verbal Learning and Verbal Behavior* 7:1954-157.

Mathews, M. M., 1966. *Teaching to Read: Historically Considered*. Chicago: University of Chicago Press.

Monroe, M., 1932. *Children Who Cannot Read*. Chicago: University of Chicago Press.

Norman, D. A. (ed.), 1970. *Models of Memory*. New York: Academic Press.

Ohala, J., 1970. Aspects of the control and production of speech. UCLA: Working Papers in Phonetics, vol. 15.

Orton, S. T., 1937. *Reading, Writing, and Speech Problems in Children*. New York: W. W. Norton.

Palermo, D. S., and M. Parrish, 1971. Rule acquisition as a function of number and frequency of exemplar presentation. *J. Verbal Learning and Verbal Behavior* 10:44-51.

Reese, H. W., and L. P. Lipsitt, 1970. *Experimental Child Psychology.* New York: Academic Press.

Rohrman, N. L., and P. B. Gough, 1967. Forewarning, meaning, and semantic decision latency. *Psychonomic Sci.* 9:217-218.

Rubenstein, H., L. Garfield, and J. A. Millikan, 1970. Homographic entries in the internal lexicon. *J. Verb. Learning and Verbal Behavior* 5:487-492.

Rubenstein, H., S. S. Lewis, and M. A. Rubenstein, 1971. Homographic entries in the internal lexicon: Effects of systematicity and relative frequency of meanings. *J. Verbal Learning and Verbal Behavior* 10:57-62.

Rudel, R. G., and H.-L. Teuber, 1963. Discrimination of direction of line in children. *J. Comp. Physiol. Psychol.* 56:892-898.

Samuels, S. J., 1971. Letter-name versus letter-sound knowledge in learning to read. *The Reading Teacher,* 24:604-608.

Savin, Harris B., 1972. What the child knows about speech when he starts to learn to read. In James F. Kavanagh and Ignatius Mattingly (Eds.), *Language by Ear and by Eye.* Cambridge: M.I.T. Press.

Scharf, B., H. S. Zamansky, and R. F. Brightbill, 1966. Word recognition with masking. *Perception and Psychophysics,* 1:110-112.

Smith, K. H., and M. D. S. Braine, 1972. Miniature languages and the problem of language acquisition. In *The Structure and Psychology of Language,* T. G. Bever and W. Weksel (eds.), New York: Holt, Rinehart and Winston.

Spencer, T. J., 1969. Some effects of different masking stimuli in iconic storage. *J. Exp. Psych.* 81:132-140.

Sperling, G., 1960. The information available in brief visual presentations. *Pschol. Monogr.,* 74: No. 11 (whole No. 498).

Sperling, G., 1963. A model for visual memory tasks. *Human Factors,* 5:19-31.

Stewart, M. L., C. T. James, and P. B. Gough, 1969. Word recognition latency as a function of word length. Paper presented at Midwestern Psychological Association.

Tinker, M. A., 1958. Recent studies of eye movements in reading. *Psych. Bull.* 55:215-231.

Venezky, R. L., 1970. *The Structure of English Orthography.* The Hague: Mouton.

Waugh, N. C., and D. A. Norman, 1965. Primary memory. *Psych. Rev.,* 72:89-104.

Weber, R., 1968. The study of oral reading errors: A survey of the literature. *Reading Res. Quart.* 4:96-119.

Wertheim, T., 1894. Ueber die indirekte Sehschärfe. *Z. Psychologie u. Physiologie der Sinnesorgane* 7:172-187.

White, M. J., 1969. Laterality differences in perception: A review. *Psych. Bull.* 72:387-405.

Is Reading a Letter-by-Letter Process?
A Discussion of Gough's Paper*

WILLIAM F. BREWER
University of Illinois

Gough has given us a most provocative paper. He has attempted to build an explicit model of the reading process and provide a millisecond by millisecond account of what is going on in the mind of the reader. Given our current level of knowledge in this area, this is clearly a courageous thing to do. By proposing an explicit theory of the reading process and taking a firm stand on the fundamental issues in reading research, Gough has performed an extremely valuable service. He states that his model is intended to be an exhaustive description of the reading process, and I intend to take him at his word. In order to explore his model I would like to go through it stage by stage and see how well it accounts for those things we do know about the reading process.

A quick look at the history of theories in this area reveals the ingenious nature of Gough's overall strategy. In the late 1800s it appears that reading was thought to be a serial processing of the letters making up words and then a serial combination of these words into sentences. However, this position was overthrown by a series of studies coming out of Wundt's laboratory soon after the founding of experimental psychology. Perhaps the most influential work opposed to the letter-by-letter theory was a series of studies carried out by James McK. Cattell (1885a, 1885b, 1886a, 1886b). Cattell rejected the letter-by-letter (serial) theory of word perception in favor of the whole-word (parallel) approach on the basis of the following kinds of evidence: a) Words in prose passages can be read almost as fast as lists of letters. b) The immediate visual apprehension span for letters in prose is much greater than for random letters. c) Latencies to initiate pronunciation of words are shorter than those for letters. d) Visual recognition thresholds for words are lower than the thresholds for letters.

---

*Reprinted by permission from J. F. Kavanagh and I. G. Mattingly (Eds.) *Language by Ear and by Eye*. Cambridge, Massachusetts: MIT Press, 1972, 359-365.

For the most part, serious research on the reading process stopped with the rise of behaviorism; however, among those few who continued to work in the area, Cattell's arguments were considered to have shown that word perception is parallel, not serial (Woodworth 1938). In light of this brief history of models of reading Gough's general strategy becomes clear. He has chosen to use the recent work in psycholinguistics and visual information processing to develop a new sophisticated letter-by-letter model of reading. Gough did not take the time to criticize Cattell's position, but I would expect him to make the following types of arguments: a) The fact that words in prose passages can be read almost as fast as lists of letters does not indicate equal perceptual processing time; higher-order linguistic variables make the response output times of words faster than those of letters. b) The fact that the immediate visual apprehension span for letters in prose is much greater than that for random letters does not reflect the speed of perceptual processing but simply the fact that the letters processed from a random string are not formed into higher-order units and therefore many are lost in recall. c) The slower initiation of pronunciation of letters than of words is not due to slower perceptual processing but to a slower response system for letter naming. d) I am not sure how Gough would handle the effects of linguistic structure on visual recognition thresholds, but probably he would develop some form of response bias explanation. Overall it looks as if Cattell's parallel processing model was resting on a rather weak foundation.

In his new serial processing theory Gough has developed an inflow model with letter-by-letter processing at the lower levels and has rigorously separated this stage from the higher-order linguistic processing. Gough eloquently expressed the motivation behind his approach when he stated that he didn't "see how the syntax can go out and mess around with the print." It is hard not to be in sympathy with this comment, but I have chosen instead to live with the paradox of having higher-order linguistic processes find their way downstream where they should not be. Thus, for the rest of this paper I would like to update Cattell's arguments and help him put down this rejuvenated letter-by-letter model.

Gough's model begins by assuming a regular mechanical left-to-right progression of eye fixations. While we still do not have detailed knowledge about the location of fixations in reading, it seems clear that there are systematic differences in the rate and duration of fixations due to the linguistic characteristics of the material being read (Huey 1908; Hochberg 1970; Mehler, Bever et al. 1967; Woodworth 1938). Thus, an adequate model of reading will have to include some mechanism to allow an interaction between the higher linguistic processing and the control of eye fixations. It is not clear how Gough's linear inflow model can handle this problem.

The next stage of information processing in the model is the development of an icon in 100 msec that lasts for 250 msec and can hold roughly 20 letter-spaces of material. While none of these time parameters is too well established currently, these estimates are certainly fairly typical of those in the literature.

The next stage is crucial in the development of an updated serial model of the reading process. In order to make a letter-by-letter model function in real time, the rates of letter processing have to be extremely rapid. Gough uses the evidence from Sperling (1963) that icon readout takes place at a constant rate of one letter every 10 msec. There are a large number of problems with this very fast icon readout time. In order to obtain this estimate of readout time, Sperling (1963) assumed that a visual noise field stops the ongoing perceptual processing. It is not at all certain that a visual noise mask does operate this way (Haber 1970b; Kahneman 1968). If one accepts the use of a visual noise mask, then there is some evidence to support the 10-msec icon readout (Sperling 1963; Scharf, Zamansky et al. 1966).

However, there is also a variety of evidence to suggest that icon readout may not be serial. Sperling (1967) has reported evidence that he interprets as opposing his earlier hypothesis of strict serial readout. Haber (1970a) has obtained evidence for serial processing in word perception with naive subjects, but not with practiced subjects, who show parallel processing in the same task. Eriksen and Spencer (1969) have used sequential presentation of letters at varying rates to test the serial readout hypothesis and have found evidence in favor of parallel processing. Gough reports a study done in his laboratory that shows that the latency to initiate pronunciation of visually presented words is longer for long words than short words. This replicates the results of Cattell (1886b) and Eriksen, Pollack et al. (1970). Gough uses the evidence from his study to support a serial 10-msec icon readout. However, the experiment by Eriksen et al. included a control condition using stimuli of similar visual complexity which differed in length of verbal response to show that most of the longer latencies must be due to increased time of motor programming, rather than to increased time of visual processing. Overall it appears that the evidence for the crucial 10-msec letter readout component of the model is not very strong.

Because Gough's model does not allow any higher-order processing components to interact with the letter readout level, there should be no difference between words and nonwords in rate of visual processing. However, there are now a large number of studies which show that forced-choice letter recognition is better and letter search times are faster for words than for nonwords. (Aderman and Smith 1971; Krueger 1970a,b; Reicher 1969; Smith 1969; Wheeler 1970). Some of these studies [e.g. Wheeler (1970)] have gone to enormous lengths to show that the effect is due to the word-nonword difference, and not to response bias from some higher level of organization.

There are several additional types of information that I find hard to reconcile with the model. In reading for meaning, typographical errors are frequently not noticed. An early study by Pillsbury (1897) explored the phenomenon in some detail and showed that subjects frequently give a phenomenological report of having seen a word that has not appeared. It is hard to see how Gough's model can deal with this interaction of higher-order levels with the perceptual processing of letters. A similar problem for the model is the subjects' phenomenological report that they can see much more at a given exposure duration if the material is in higher-order units such as words or sentences (Huey 1908; Neisser 1967).

After the letters have been processed they are mapped onto systematic phonemes. As one of several types of processing this may be a reasonable hypothesis. However, Gough's model makes this the exclusive path from the letters to meaning. Thus *any* evidence showing direct processing of words without a phonological transformation is incompatible with the model. Therefore the fact that we can read with understanding homophones such as "chute" and "shoot" cannot be dealt with, since visual information must have been used to retrieve the appropriate meaning. The studies on reading with deaf subjects reported by Gibson, Shurcliff et al. (1970) and by Conrad (1972) also show that reading can take place without a stage of phonological transformation. However, it seems clear that any successful model also needs a system that allows direct translation from the orthography to a phonological level, since adult readers can pronounce words they have never seen before. The arguments that Gough makes in favor of mapping onto the level of systematic phonemes have some merit, but some of the simplicity is lost in those cases where the orthography does not reflect the level of systematic phonemes, since the model will require additional apparatus to handle these instances. Gough's arguments against a mapping from the orthography to speech are not very convincing. If he is willing to use a system as abstract as the level of systematic phonemes in his model, then it seems only fair to allow other theorists a level of speech that is abstract enough to avoid the time parameter difficulties he outlines. In fact Sperling (1967) has proposed a model that maps onto speech, containing a buffer of motor-instruction programs which deal with these time difficulties. In general it looks as if there is enough evidence to reject models that postulate only a letter-to-sound mapping or only a letter-to-meaning mapping, but beyond that there is little constraint about how the systems might function.

After information has reached the level of systematic phonemes, the meanings of individual words are retrieved word by word, from left to right. The assumption is made that the order of lexical search is not affected by previously processed information. This is a most intriguing assumption. At the level of awareness it is certainly the case that the particular reading given to a word is determined by previous information. For example, take the word *light* in the following two sentences: a) *The painter said the new paint was lighter, but his assistant still had trouble picking it up.* b) *The weight lifter said the dumbell was light, but when we came closer we could see that it was actually painted a dark blue.* In the first sentence the first five words give "*lighter*" the reading "pale" and the remainder of the sentence shifts the reading to "not heavy." In the second sentence the initial reading is "not heavy" and the final reading shifts to "pale." Thus, it is clear that at the level of awareness both preceding and following information contribute to the reading given a particular lexical item.

However, the fact that the conscious reading is determined by preceding information does not eliminate the possibility that there is an unconscious lexical search that operates without regard to previous context and then sends one appropriate reading up to the level of awareness. In fact Foss's (1970) finding that response to a probe is slow for a word following an ambiguous word, regardless of the presence or absence of disambiguating context, is consistent with Gough's model. But in general not enough is known about the order of lexical search to constrain model building at this level.

After lexical lookup the information is taken to a buffer that can handle both syntactic and semantic information. It is clear that there has to be a place where the syntactic and semantic relations of the reading matter are worked out, and Gough chooses to identify this with the primary memory box that is part of most current models of memory. One possible problem for the model is the fact that the contents of primary memory are typically available to conscious observation, whereas the intricate syntactic and semantic processing that must go on in sentence understanding appear to be unavailable to conscious observation. But this is another area where there simply is not enough knowledge to put much constraint on alternative models.

The final stage in the model is TPWSGWTAU. This is the place where all sentences go if they have led a good life; if they have not been good they are consigned to a regressive eye-movement.

In summary I think Gough has made a gallant attempt to provide an explicit model of the reading process. However, it is obvious that we have consistently locked horns over the possibility of higher-order processes interacting with lower-order processes. Gough has given new life to the letter-by-letter approach to reading and I have tried to do the same for Cattell's criticisms of such a model. Whatever the merits of Gough's particular model, I think the attempt has been most productive in bringing to the surface some of the fundamental issues in building a psychological model of the reading process.

REFERENCES

Aderman, D., and E. E. Smith, 1971. Expectancy as a determinant of functional units in perceptual recognition. *Cog. Psych.* 2:117-129.

Cattell, J. McK., 1885a. The inertia of the eye and brain. *Brain,* 8:295-312.

Cattell, J. McK., 1885b. Ueber die Zeit der Erkennung und Benennung von Schriftzeichen, Bildern und Farben. *Philosophische Studien,* 2:635-650. (Translated as: On the time required for recognizing and naming letters and words, pictures and colors. In A. T. Poffenberger (ed.), *James McKeen Cattell: Man of Science. Vol. 1. Psychological Research.* Lancaster, Penn.: Science Press, 1947, pp. 13-23.)

Cattell, J. McK., 1886a. The time taken up by cerebral operations. III. The perception-time. *Mind,* 11:377-392.

Cattell, J. McK., 1886b. The time taken up by cerebral operations. IV. The will-time. *Mind,* 11:524-534.

Conrad, R., 1972. Speech and reading. In James F. Kavanagh and Ignatius Mattingly (Eds.), *Language by Ear and by Eye.* Cambridge: MIT Press.

Eriksen, C. W., M. D. Pollack, and W. E. Montague, 1970. Implicit speech: Mechanism in perceptual encoding? *J. Exp. Psych.* 84:502-507.

Eriksen, C. W., and T. Spencer, 1969. Rate of information processing in visual perception: Some results and methodological considerations. *J. Exp. Psych. Monograph,* 79, No. 2, Part 2.

Foss, D. J., 1970. Understanding comprehending. Paper presented at the meetings of the Midwestern Psychological Association, Cincinnati, Ohio, April 30.

Gibson, E., A. Shurcliff, and A. Yonas, 1970. Utilization of spelling patterns by deaf and hearing subjects. In H. Levin and J. P. Williams (eds.), *Basic Studies on Reading.* New York: Basic Books, pp. 57-73.

Haber, R. N., 1970a. How we remember what we see. *Sci. Amer.* 222:5, 104-112.

Haber, R. N., 1970b. Note on how to choose a visual noise mask. *Psych. Bull.* 74:373-376.

Hochberg, J., 1970. Components of literacy: Speculations and exploratory research. In H. Levin and J. P. Williams (eds.), *Basic Studies on Reading.* New York: Basic Books, pp. 74-89.

Huey, E. B., 1908. *The Psychology and Pedagogy of Reading.* New York: Macmillan. Reprinted: Cambridge, Mass.: MIT Press, 1968.

Kahneman, D., 1968. Method, findings, and theory in studies of visual masking. *Psych. Bull.* 70:404-425.

Krueger, L. E., 1970a. Search time in a redundant visual display. *J. Exp. Psych.* 83:391-399.

Krueger, L. E., 1970b. Visual comparison in a redundant display. *Cog. Psych.* 1:341-357.

Mehler, J., T. G. Bever, and P. Carey, 1967. What we look at when we read. *Perception and Psychophysics,* 2:213-218.

Neisser, U., 1967. *Cognitive Psychology.* New York: Appleton-Century-Crofts.

Pillsbury, W. B., 1897. A study in apperception. *Amer. J. Psych.* 8:315-393.

Reicher, G. M., 1969. Perceptual recognition as a function of meaningfulness of stimulus material. *J. Exp. Psych.* 81:275-280.

Scharf, B., H. S. Zamansky, and R. F. Brightbill, 1966. Word recognition with masking. *Perception and Psychophysics,* 1:110-112.

Smith, F., 1969. The use of featural dependencies across letters in the visual identification of words. *J. Verbal Learning and Verbal Behavior,* 8:215-218.

Sperling, G., 1963. A model for visual memory tasks. *Human Factors,* 5:19-31.

Sperling, G., 1967. Successive approximations to a model for short term memory. *Acta Psych.* 27:285-292.

Wheeler, D. D., 1970. Processes in word recognition. *Cog. Psych.* 1:59-85.

Woodworth, R. S., 1938. *Experimental Psychology.* New York: Holt.

General Discussion of Papers by Gough and Brewer[*]

Gough made a number of points in response to Brewer's discussion. 1) He conceded that he had neglected to put in his model an arrangment for advance control of eye movement according to the difficulty of the material being read, but pointed out that his model does provide for regression after failure in grammatical processing. 2) By "icon" he did *not* mean a "little picture in the eye" but a little picture in the head, as yet unanalyzed. 3) As for Brewer's objection to left-to-right processing, he did not see that the reader's ability to deal with misspelled words, or words with missing letters, is a real difficulty for his model; such words merely mean that provision for "further inferential processing" is required. In support of the left-to-right model, he referred to one of his own studies, in which reaction time increased the further to the right in the test word a substitution of an asterisk for a letter was made. The special case where the word was intact had the shortest reaction time. Again, when the task was to find a target letter, reaction time increased as the target was shifted from left to right. (This finding contradicts the early studies referred to by Norman, in which no difference was noted between words or fragments of words.) 4) The replication of Sperling's (1960) experiment by Scharf, Zamansky et al. (1966), using Sperling's masks, revealed no difference between the processing of words and individual letters. 5) He did not see any conflict between his position and the conclusion of Eriksen and Spencer (1969) that it is longer before one can begin report of a short word than of a long word. 6) Cattell's (1886) finding that words take less time to process than single letters is not really relevant, but his other finding, that six-letter words take longer to recognize than four-letter words, *is* relevant. There is, in fact, an extensive literature on the processing of visual displays, summed up in White's (1969) review. 7) He conceded that the existence of homophones might require some change in his model. 8) The reading of deaf is not necessarily like the reading of normal persons, and his model

*Reprinted by permission from J. F. Kavanagh and I. G. Mattingly (Eds.) *Language by Ear and by Eye*. Cambridge, Massachusetts: MIT Press, 1972, 367-371.

does not pretend to explain it. 9) He considered irrelevant Norman's argument that one can go directly from objects to their own representation, and that therefore the same might be true for words. 10) As for the findings of Miller and Isard (1963), he acknowledged that grammatical constraints do operate during reading; the question was at what level. He did not think that they operate in reading very far "downstream." 11) Context does not appear to operate in advance of the linguistic processing of a sentence, as Foss and one of his (Gough's) students have shown. 12) Gough could not imagine a comprehension device without a buffer (Miller suggested that the buffer be called "context").

Posner referred to an experiment by Eriksen, Pollack et al. (1970) using sequences of numerals as stimuli. Reaction time seemed to be related to the number of syllables in the names of the numerals. Gough said he had experimented with various syllable lengths, both separately and as part of another experiment, and had not discovered any such effects. He had also done experiments with digraphs representing single sounds, like *th*. Here, too, no evidence of effect on reaction time had been noted. Only the number of letters per word affected reaction time. Syllables and digraphs must apparently be dealt with further "upstream."

Lotz noted that competent readers paraphrase when they read aloud. He suggested that this could mean processing by the phonological component, the semantic component, and then the phonological component again. Gough said that the meaning of a sentence was recovered "upstream" from its actual utterance. Lotz also added that the process of writing was closely connected to linguistic processing. Experiments with the subvocal behavior of a subject who is writing would be of great interest.

In response to a question by LaBerge, Gough said that his displays always use lower-case letters. LaBerge pointed out that to use upper-case would force the subject to ignore what he knew about patterns of lower-case letters. Jenkins and Kolers referred to an experiment by Tinker (1963), later replicated by Kolers, in which no change was observed in the rate of reading aloud of texts in which the proportion of uppercase to lower-case letters varied from 0 to 100 percent. But this, Kolers said, does not mean that there was no change in the difficulty of the task, since the subjects may have done more internal processing if this were required to maintain their customary reading rate.

Liberman reminded the group of the linguistic distinction between the phonological level and the phonetic level. The phonetic level describes the behavior of the articulators, but it must also be represented in the central nervous system. Activity at the phonetic level does not necessarily result in any actual or implicit articulation. The fact that one takes pleasure in the phonetic patterns of verse, and that we notice phonetic features of the text, e.g., "the rain in Spain" sentence, suggests as Mattingly pointed out in his paper that the phonetic level, as just defined, is engaged during reading, and that Gough could incorporate this in his model without a major revision. Gough was not convinced, and Miller remarked that one does not read verse at 400 words per minute.

Conrad questioned Gough's suggestion that reading by the congenitally deaf may be a different process from ordinary reading. Gough said that his model is an attempt to describe the normal, 400-word-per-minute reader. Lloyd said that by this definition the reading of the deaf is slower and qualitatively poorer than that of normal readers. Liberman said that the difference is more than just a question of speed. The linguistic competence that deaf people acquire by reading is quite different from the linguistic competence of normal persons. Moreover, their writing is generally poor.

Kolers questioned the serial character of Gough's model. Different readers, reading the same text, have different and quite complex eye-movement patterns. There must be some way in which this incoherent input is sorted out. Gough stuck by his model and referred to evidence that readout of connected text under appropriate conditions—threshold with masking—is no better than readout of unrelated letters. There was no influence from the syntactic level.

Brewer said that Pillsbury's (1897) experiment, in which subjects saw words that were not there, was evidence of higher-level processing. Gough thought that Pillsbury's subjects were simply doing something different from ordinary reading. He did not deny that a speaker would reconstruct text if he had to.

Mattingly said that he found the developmental section of Gough's paper, which had not so far been discussed, extremely interesting, and that the notion of the beginning reader as a cryptanalyst is a useful insight in considering what the pupil can do and what the teacher can help him do. Jenkins agreed, remarking that one thing which helps the cryptanalyst is volume: "It may be it is necessary to get, in some sense, the cognitive load up high enough and the volume of input and possibly matches up high enough to give the kid a corpus that is big enough to work on and enough motivation to solve that problem."

Savin questioned the value of the block diagram models with buffers that investigators of information processing produce. What is really important to know is the *form* of the information in the buffer: was it circles and lines, or letters? Information processing experiments are not helpful here.

Jenkins suggested that a reaction time experiment using verbal suffixes of differing length, like *ed* and *ing,* would help to indicate the extent to which processing in reading is serial.

Posner questioned whether reaction time methods are the most appropriate for studying the internal stages of reading. It is not necessarily obvious, as the case of the Eriksen result suggests, what units are being processed. He mentioned the Reicher (1969) and Wheeler (1970) studies in which identification of letters was shown to be 10 percent more accurate in verbal context than in isolation as an example of an alternative approach. This experiment, Gough admitted, would create great difficulties for his serial model, but it had not been replicated. But Gibson called attention to a similar experiment by Smith (1969).

Gough said that his model implied that the time for lexical lookup would be highly dependent on word length, but this did not seem to be the case. He referred to an experiment that he and Rohrman had done, which showed that the time required to decide whether two words were synonyms when presented simultaneously differed by 160 msec from the time required when one of the words was presented in advance. This means that the subject is "getting to meaning" as fast as possible, if it is assumed that the icon requires some time to set up and that readout is letter by letter.

Liberman said that he was puzzled by the question of whether syntactic and semantic constraints affect the reading process. They are certainly very important in speech perception. Once the reader has access to the phonology, what happens from then on is the same as what happens with a listener.

REFERENCES

Cattell, J. McK., 1886. The time taken up by cerebral operations. III. The perception time. *Mind*, 11:377-392.

Eriksen, C. W., M. Pollack, and W. Montague, 1970. Implicit speech: Mechanism in perceptual encoding? *J. Exp. Psych.* 84:503-507.

Eriksen, C. W., and T. Spencer, 1969. Rate of information processing in visual perception: Some results and methodological considerations. *J. Exp. Psych. Monograph*, 79, No. 2, Part 2.

Miller, G., and S. Isard, 1963. Some perceptual consequences of linguistic rules. *J. Verbal Learning and Verbal Behavior* 2:217-228.

Pillsbury, W. B., 1897. A study in apperception. *Amer. J. Psych.* 8:315-393.

Reicher, G., 1969. Perceptual recognition as a function of meaningfulness of stimulus material. *J. Exp. Psych.* 81:276-280.

Rohrman, N. L., and P. B. Gough, 1967. Forewarning, meaning, and semantic decision latency. *Psychonomic Sci.*, 9:217-218.

Scharf, B., H. S. Zamansky, and R. F. Brightbill, 1966. Word recognition with masking. *Perception and Psychophysics*, 1:110-112.

Smith, I., 1969. The use of featural dependencies across letters in the visual identification of words. *J. Verbal Learning and Verbal Behavior*, 8:215-218.

Sperling, G., 1960. The information available in brief visual presentations. *Psych. Monog.*, 74, No. 11 (Whole No. 498).

Tinker, M. A., 1963. *Legibility of Print*. Ames: Iowa State University Press.

Wheeler, D. D., 1970. Processes in word recognition. *Cog. Psych.* 1:59-85.

White, M. J., 1969. Laterality differences in perception: A review. *Psych. Bull.* 72:387-405.

Toward a Theory of Automatic
Information Processing in Reading[*]

DAVID LABERGE AND S. JAY SAMUELS
University of Minnesota

Among the many skills in the repertoire of the average adult, reading is probably one of the most complex. The journey taken by words from their written form on the page to the eventual activation of their meaning involves several stages of information processing. For the fluent reader, this processing takes a very short time, only a fraction of a second. The acquisition of the reading skill takes years, and there are many who do not succeed in becoming fluent readers, even though they may have quickly and easily mastered the skill of understanding speech.

During the execution of a complex skill, it is necessary to coordinate many component processes within a very short period of time. If each component process requires attention, performance of the complex skill will be impossible, because the capacity of attention will be exceeded. But if enough of the components and their coordinations can be processed automatically, then the load on attention will be within tolerable limits and the skill can be successfully performed. Therefore, one of the prime issues in the study of a complex skill such as reading is to determine how the processing of component subskills becomes automatic.

Our purpose in this paper is to present a model of the reading process which describes the main stages involved in transforming written patterns into meanings and relates the attention mechanism to processing at each of these stages. In addition, we will test the model against some experimental findings which indicate that the role of attention changes during advanced states of perceptual and associative learning.

*Reprinted by permission from *Cognitive Psychology*, 6, 1974, 293-323. Copyright 1974 by Academic Press, Inc. This research was supported by a grant (HD-06730-01) to the authors from the National Institutes of Child Health and Human Development, and in part by the Center for Research in Human Learning through National Science Foundation Grant GB-17590.

This paper is divided into four sections in which we 1) briefly summarize the current views of the attention mechanism in information processing, 2) set forth a theory of automaticity in reading and evaluate it against some data, 3) discuss factors which may influence the development of automaticity, and 4) discuss some implications of the model for research in reading instruction.

Attention Mechanisms in Information Processing

In view of the fact that the present model places heavy emphasis on the role of attention in the component processes of reading, it may be well to review briefly the way the concept has been used by researchers in the recent past.

The properties of attention most frequently treated by investigators are selectivity and capacity limitation. Posner and Boies (1971) list alertness as a third component of attention, but this property has been investigated mostly in vigilance tasks and less often in the sorts of information processing tasks related closely to reading. The property of attention which has generated the most theoretical controversy is its limited capacity. When early dichotic listening experiments indicated that subjects select one ear at a time for processing messages, Broadbent (1958) proposed a theory which assumed that a filter is located close to the sensory surface. This filter allows messages from only one ear at a time to get through. However, later experiments indicated that well-learned significant signals such as one's own name (Moray, 1959) managed to get processed by the unattended ear. This led Treisman (1964) to modify the Broadbent theory and allow the filter to attenuate the signal instead of blocking it completely. In this way, significant, well-learned items could be processed by the unattended ear. Deutsch and Deutsch (1963), on the other hand, described a theory which rejected the placement of a selective filter prior to the analysis or decoding of stimuli and instead placed the selection mechanism at a point much later in the system, after the "importance" or "pertinence" (Norman, 1968) of the stimulus has been determined.

In the present model, it is assumed that all well-learned stimuli are processed upon presentation into an internal representation, or code, regardless of where attention is directed at the time. In this regard, the model is similar to the models of Deutsch and Deutsch and of Norman. However, the present theory proposes in addition that attention can selectively activate codes at any level of the system, not only at the deeper levels of meaning, but also at visual and auditory levels nearer the sensory surfaces. The number of existing codes of any kind that can be activated by attention at a given moment is sharply limited, probably to one. But the number of codes which can be simultaneously activated by outside stimuli independent of attention is assumed to be large, perhaps unlimited. In short, it is assumed that we can only attend to one thing at a time, but we may be able to process many things at a time so long as no more than one requires attention.

It is this capability of automatic processing which we consider critical for the successful operation of multicomponent, complex skills such as reading. As visual words are processed through many stages en route to meaningfulness, each stage is processed automatically. In addition, the transitions from stage to stage must be automatic as well. Sometimes a stage may begin processing before an earlier one finishes its processing. Examples of these interrelations between stages of processing are treated in the research of Sternberg (1969) and Clark and Chase (1972). In the skill of basketball, ball-handling by the experienced player is regarded as automatic. But ball-handling consists of subskills such as dribbling, passing, and catching, so each of these must be automatic and the transitions between them must be automatic as well. Therefore, when one describes a skill at the macrolevel as being automatic, it follows that the subskills at the microlevel and their interrelations must also be automatic.

Our criterion for deciding when a skill or subskill is automatic is that it can complete its processing while attention is directed elsewhere. It is especially important in such tests that one take careful account of all attention shifts. On many occasions, people appear to be giving attention to two or more things at the same time, when, in fact, they are shifting attention rapidly between the tasks. An example is the cocktail party phenomenon in which a person may appear to be following two conversations at the same time, but in reality he is alternating his attention.

The way we attempt to manage this problem in the laboratory is to test automaticity with procedures that control the momentary attention state of the subject (LaBerge, Van Gelder, & Yellott, 1970). Typically, we present a cue just prior to the stimulus the subject is to identify, and this induces a state of preparation for that particular stimulus. Most of the time he receives the expected stimulus, but occasionally he receives instead a test stimulus unrelated to the cue. The response to the unexpected test stimulus requires that the subject switch his attention as well as process the test stimulus. If the processing of the test stimulus requires attention, then the response latency will include both time for stimulus processing and time for attention switching. If, however, the stimulus processing does not require attention (i.e., it is automatic), then the response latency will not include stimulus processing time, assuming that the stimulus processing is completed by the time attention is switched.

Model of Automaticity in Reading

With these considerations of attention in mind, we turn to a description of a model of automatic processing in reading. This model is based on the assumption that the transformation of written stimuli into meanings involves a sequence of stages of information processing (Posner *et al.*, 1972). Although the overall model has many stages and alternative routes of information processing, we hope that the way it is put together will permit us to isolate small portions of the model at a time for experimental tests without doing violence to the model regarded as a whole. Our strategy here is to capture the basic principles of automaticity in perceptual and associative processing with simple examples drawn from initial processing stages of reading and then indicate how these examples generalize to more complex stages of reading.

We shall consider first the learning, or construction, of visual codes in reading, which includes the perception of letters, spelling patterns, words, and word groups. After presenting some relevant data, we will attempt to detail the rest of the model, showing how the visual stage fits into the larger picture. Then we will describe an experiment which attempts to demonstrate the acquisition of automaticity in the kind of associative learning utilized in the decoding and simple comprehension of words.

Model of Grapheme Learning

Now let us consider in some detail the learning of a perceptual code. It is assumed that incoming information from the page is first analyzed by detectors which are specialized in processing features such as lines, angles, intersections, curvature, openness, etc., as well as relational features such as left, right, up, down, etc. (Rumelhart, 1970). For present purposes, it is not necessary that we stipulate the exact mapping of these features onto properties of physical stimuli. In fact, to do so would emphasize a punctate view of the feature detectors, whereas we wish to provide for the possibliity, following Gibson (1969), that relational aspects may be important in this kind of learning. However, it should be pointed out that it is sometimes difficult to define relational properties in a clear way.

VISUAL MEMORY

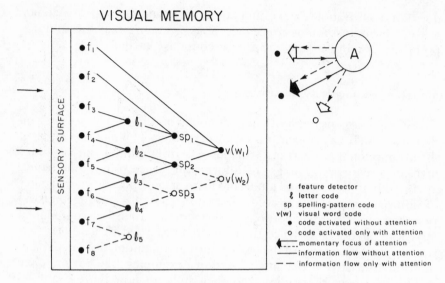

Figure 1.   Model of visual memory showing two states of perceptual coding of visual patterns. Arrows from the attention center (A) to solid-dot codes denote a two-way flow of excitation: attention can activate these codes and be activated (attracted) by them. Attention can activate open-dot codes but cannot be activated (attracted) by them.

In Figure 1 we present an abbreviated sketch of the role of visual perception in the reading model. In this schematic drawing, graphemic information enters from the left and is analyzed by feature detectors, which in turn feed into letter codes. These codes activate spelling-pattern codes, which then feed into word codes, and word codes may sometimes give rise to word-group codes. Some features activate spelling patterns and words directly (e.g., f_1 and f_2). These features detect characteristics such as word shape and spelling-pattern shape. This hierarchical coding scheme draws heavily on the notions of Gibson (1971), Bower (1972), Johnson (1972), and others, but particularly on the model described by Estes (1972).

The role of the attention center of Figure 1 is assumed to be critical early in the learning of a graphemic code, but expendable in later states of learning. Arrows from the attention center indicate a two-way flow of information between the center and each visual code in long-term memory. Every visual code in long-term memory is represented by the symbol O or ●. The open circle indicates codes that are activated only with the assistance of attention. The filled circles indicate codes which may be activated without attention. The lines leading from the visual codes to attention represent the flow of information that occurs when a code has been activated or "triggered" by stimuli. The lines leading from the attention center to visual codes represent the activation of these units by attention. When a stimulus occurs and activates a code, a signal is sent to the attention center, which can "attract" attention to that code unit in the form of additional activation. Only the well-learned, filled-circle codes can attract attention. If attention is directed elsewhere at the time a visual code is activated by external stimulation, attention will not shift its activation to that visual code, unless the stimulus is intense or unless the code automatically activates autonomic responses or other systems which mediate the "importance" (Deutsch & Deutsch, 1963) or "pertinence" (Norman, 1968) of that code to the attention center.

The many double arrows emanating from the attention center, therefore, indicate potential lines of information flow to every well-learned code in visual long-term memory. At any given moment, however, the attention center activates only one code. This characteristic of the model represents the limited-capacity property of attention.

As conceptualized here, attentional activation may have three different effects on information processing. First of all, it can assist in the construction of a new code by activating subordinate input codes. For example, in Figure 1, successive activation of features f_7 and f_8 is necessary to synthesize letter code l_5. Secondly, activation of a code prior to the presentaton of its corresponding stimulus is assumed to increase the rate of processing when that stimulus is presented (LaBerge *et al.*, 1970). Finally, activation of a code can arouse other codes to which it has been associated, as will be described later in connection with Figure 3.

Some of the most common patterns we learn to recognize are letters, which are represented in Figure 1 as l_1, l_2, etc. We assume that the first stage of this learning requires the selection of the subset of appropriate features from the larger set of features which are activated by incoming physical stimuli. For example, assume that a child is learning to discriminate the letters t and h. The length of the vertical line is not relevant to the discrimination of these two letters. Instead he must note the short horizontal cross of the t and the concave loop in the h. These are the distinctive features of these letters when considered against each other. In the model, we represent the selection of features of a given letter by the lines leading from particular features to a particular letter. In this example, the length of the vertical line is an irrelevant feature, but when these two letters are compared with other letters, for example the letter n, the length of the vertical line becomes a relevant feature. We assume that this kind of adjustment in feature selection continues as the rest of the alphabet is presented to the child. One feature that seems to be irrelevant for all letters is thickness of line. It would appear, then, that many features are selected for a given letter, and in many cases letters share features in common. Therefore, the relationship between the feature and letter code levels shown in Figure 1 is somewhat simplified for economy of illustration. Figure 1 shows only two lines leading from features into a given letter; typically a letter is coded from more than two feature detectors, and a given feature may feed into more than two letters.

As a first stage of perceptual learning, selection of relevant features is similar to the initial stages of concept learning tasks (e.g., Trabasso & Bower, 1968) in which the subject searches for the relevant dimension before he selects a response. The rate of learning to select the appropriate features of a pattern may be quite slow the first time a child is given letters to discriminate. However, after a child has experienced several discrimination tasks, he may develop strategies of visual search which permit him to move through this first stage of perceptual learning at an increasingly rapid rate.

In the second stage of perceptual learning, as conceived here, the subject must construct a letter code from the relevant features, a process which requires attention. By rapid scanning of the individual feature detectors, perhaps along with some application of Gestalt principles of organization (e.g., proximity and similarity), a higher-order unit is formed. If the pattern has too many features, organization into a unit code might not be manageable. This would mean that when the letter is itself organized into a superordinate code, it would consist of several components, instead of one unit. However, when the features do permit organization into a unitary code, this code is of a short-term nature at first and is quickly lost when the eye shifts to other patterns, or when attention activates another visual code. But every time the subject organizes the features into that particular letter code, some trace of this organization between features and letter code is laid down. The dashed lines in Figure 1 between features and a letter represent the early state of establishment of these traces, and the solid lines represent later states of trace consolidation.

In the early trials of learning we assume that attention activation must be added to external stimulation of feature detectors to produce organization of the letters into a unit. In the later trials, we assume that features can feed into letter codes without attentional activation, in other words, that the stimulus can be processed into a letter code automatically.

For example, contrast the perception of the familiar letter a with the unfamiliar Greek letter γ. Let us assume that the visual stimulus, a, first activates the feature detectors f_3 and f_4. These features automatically activate the letter code l_1, which corresponds to the letter a. When the Greek letter, γ, is presented, assume that features f_7 and f_8 are activated. However, these features do not excite the letter code l_5 by themselves. Nevertheless, when this unfamiliar letter is presented, the feature detectors f_7 and f_8 induce the attention center to switch attention activation to themselves, because they are already linked to the attention center (by learning or heredity). The resultant scanning or successive activation of these features by attention produces sufficient additional activation to organize and arouse the letter code l_5. Were the subject to activate and not organize the features, then the Greek letter would not be perceived as a unit but merely as a set of features, f_7 and f_8.

If the subject is induced to organize the separate features into a unit when it is presented to him, the lines linking features f_7 and f_8 will presumably become strengthened, until after many such experiences they eventually become as strong as those lines linking features f_3 and f_4 with letter code l_1, which represents a highly familiar pattern such as the letter a. When this is accomplished, the Greek letter, γ, can be perceived as a unit without requiring attention to the scanning of its component features.

When this unitization becomes automatic, there is nothing to prevent the subject from exercising the option of attending to the features of the Greek letter, much as he can choose to pay attention to the curved lines in the familiar letter a if he chooses. This optional attentional activation at either the feature level or the letter level is implied in the model by the placement of dots at both feature detectors and letter codes.

At this point it would appear appropriate to mention that there may exist another stage of learning located between feature selection and the unitizing stages of perceptual learning. Quite possibly the subject may learn to scan features more rapidly with practice, and eventually the scanning itself may become automatic. Experiments which measure the learning of patterns by shortened reaction time in matching tasks or by increased accuracy in tachistoscopic exposures would then be revealing the learning of a scanning path for features and not necessarily the gradual formation of a unit. One way to test for feature scanning as opposed to unit formation might be to estimate how much short-term memory capacity is taken up when a letter is presented. For example, to identify each letter by a series of feature tests may require about four or five binary decisions (Smith, 1971), implying that each letter is represented by as many components. Even if a subject stores only three or four letters visually in short-term memory, this means he would have to be storing 12-20 feature chunks, which seems unlikely given the limits set by Miller (1956) at seven plus or minus two.

One might be tempted to move the argument up one level in the visual hierarchy and maintain that letters are the visual units normally coded in reading. This would leave the formation of higher-order units to other systems such as the phonological system. This position is close to the one taken by Gough (1972), who makes a strong attempt to reconcile letter-by-letter visual scanning with the apparently high rates of word processing by fluent readers.

One could even move the argument up another level to consider spelling patterns as the typical units of visual perception in reading, a position preferred by Gibson (1971), although she maintains that these units must eventually be reorganized into still higher-order units.

The critical point being made here is that automaticity in processing graphemic material may not necessarily mean that unitizing has taken place. Scanning pathways may have been learned to the degree that they can be run off automatically and rapidly, whatever the size of the visual code unit involved. The present model as depicted in Figure 1 adapts itself to the view that a letter may be a cluster of discrete features which are scanned automatically. One simply equates the symbol l_1 with the term (f_3, f_4), to indicate that the code at the letter level is a cluster of feature units. The interpretation of automaticity is the same. For the dashed lines linking features with letters, the features cannot be adequately scanned without the services of attention; for the solid lines, the features are scanned automatically. For present purposes of exposition, however, we find it more convenient to refer to letters, spelling patterns, and words as unit codes, but we hope that the reader will keep in mind that there is an alternative view of what it is that is being automatized in perceptual learning of this kind.

Before extending the model to other stages of processing, such as sounding letters, spelling patterns, and words or comprehension of words, we will describe briefly an experiment which attempted to measure automaticity of perception and use it as an indicator of amount of perceptual learning of a graphemic pattern.

Indicators of automatic perceptual processing. One way to test recognition of a letter is to present two letters simultaneously and ask the subject to indicate if they match or not (Posner & Mitchell, 1967). In order to determine whether a person can automatically recognize a letter pattern, we must present a pair of patterns at a moment when he is not expecting them. The way this was done in a recent study (LaBerge, 1973b) was to induce the subject to expect a letter, e.g., the letter *a*, by presenting it first as a cue in a successive matching task. If the letter which followed the cue was also an *a*, he was to press a button, otherwise not. Occasionally, following the single letter cue *a*, the subject was given a pair of letters other than the letter expected, e.g., the stimulus (b b). If these letters matched, he was to press the button, otherwise not, regardless of what the cue was on that trial. In terms of Figure 1, the state of the subject at the moment he expects the letter *a* may be represented by the attention arrow activating l_1, which we shall assume corresponds to the letter code *a*. The perceptual analyzers are primed to process the stimulus *a* and when it occurs, the speed of recognition should be increased. However, when a pair of different letters, (b b), is presented, corresponding to l_4, for example, the attention arrow leading to l_4 now becomes activated and the arrow to l_1 deactivated. The time required for this change is often referred to as switching time and may be as large as 80 msec in some cases (LaBerge, 1973a). The important prediction by the model is that familiar letters corresponding to l_4 will have already processed features f_6 and f_7 into the letter code l_4 by the time attention is switched from l_1 to l_4, whereas unfamiliar letters such as l_5 will not have achieved this capability of processing features f_7 and f_8 into l_5 before attention is switched to l_5.

Therefore our indicator of automaticity in the perception of letter pattern is the extra time it takes to perceptually process a letter once attention has been shifted to that letter. If this time is negligible, then we conclude that the letter code is activated automatically from external stimulation of its features before attention was switched to it. If this time is substantial, then we conclude that attention was needed to synthesize the features into the letter code. Of course we do not have direct means of assessing the amount of attention time involved in perceptual coding. However, we do have good estimates of the total time it takes to code and match highly familiar letters in these tasks, which for adults we assume must be quite automatic by now. Using familiar letters as controls, we can measure the differences between match latencies for unfamiliar and familiar letters and use this as an estimate of the extra attention time required to process unfamiliar letters. Then, as further training is given, we may note the convergence of the latencies of the unfamiliar to the familiar letters and use this as an indicator of perceptual learning.

In the experiment by LaBerge (1973b), the unfamiliar letters were [↳ ↲ ↱ ↰] and the familiar letters used as controls were [b d p q]. Other groups of letter patterns, e.g., [a g n s], were used as cues to focus the subject's attention at the moment a pair of test letters was given according to the procedure just described. Referring to Figure 1, a letter from the familiar test group could be represented by a letter code such as l_4, and a letter from the unfamiliar test group by l_5. A letter from the group [a g n s] could be represented by l_1, which represents the momentary focus of attention. We expected that latencies of unfamiliar test letter matches would be longer than the familiar letter matches at first, but we expected that the amount of the difference would decrease with practice if perceptual learning were taking place.

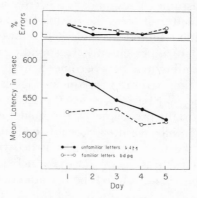

Figure 2.   Mean latency and percent errors of matching responses to unfamiliar and familiar letter patterns.

The results from the 16 college-age subjects are shown in Figure 2. The initial difference in latency between unfamiliar and familiar letters was 48 msec and the difference clearly decreased over the next four days. In terms of the model in Figure 1, we would say that the dashed lines between features f_7 and f_8 and l_5 were strengthened over days and approached the automatic level of learning of the lines connecting f_6 and f_7 with l_4.

The finding that unfamiliar letters improved with practice more than did familiar letters offers support for the hypothesis that something is being learned about the unfamiliar letters over the days of training. Evidence that subjects are learning automatic processing of the unfamiliar letters is supported by a special testing condition presented to another group of 16 subjects. In this condition, the familiar and unfamiliar patterns were presented both as cues and target stimuli so that we could assess the time taken to detect the letter when the subject expected that letter. In terms of the model in Figure 1, we assume for the unfamiliar letter that the attention arrow to l_5 is activated at the time the letter is presented. Similarly, when a familiar letter, l_4, is cued, the attention arrow is focused on l_4 in preparation for that letter to be presented.

A comparison of latencies of these successive matches showed that the time to make an unfamiliar match equals the time to make a familiar match. This means that under conditions when the subject is attending to these letters, differences between perceptual learning of letters are not revealed. Only under conditions when the subject is attending elsewhere at the moment when the test letter is presented do these differences emerge.

Taken together, the data from these two conditions strongly suggest that what is being learned over days is a perceptual process that operates without attention, namely an automatic perceptual process. Whether the process be a unitizing one or a quick scanning of features, or perhaps something else, is not decided by these data. The main conclusion is that what is being improved with practice is automaticity.

Apparently, acquiring automaticity is a slow process in contrast to the relatively quick rate of acquiring accuracy in paired associate learning (Estes, 1970). For a five-year old, one suspects that achievement of automatic recognition of the 26 letters of the alphabet may indeed be a slow learning process, assuming that the child is no better than the college adult at this task. It may be that the child can learn to distinguish letters with accuracy with relatively few exposures, but it is costing him a considerable amount of attention to do it. Apparently, considerably greater amounts of exposure to the graphemes are necessary before the child can carry out letter recognition automatically, a feat he must learn to do if he is to acquire new skills involving combinations of these letters.

For other studies which support the hypothesis that visual processing may occur without attention, the reader is referred to Eriksen and Spencer (1969), Posner and Boies (1971), Egeth, Jonides, and Wall (1972), and Shiffrin and Gardner (1972). An experiment by LaBerge, Samuels, and Petersen (1973) treats perceptual learning of unfamiliar letter-like patterns which are more complex than the ones described here with similar results.

Theoretical Relationships between Visual and Phonological Systems

We turn now to a consideration of other processing systems which presumably operate on the inputs from visual codes. Of course the model we are describing step-by-step is not considered to be complete at this time. Rather we expect that it will have to be modified a good deal as the appropriate experimental tests are made. However, we hope that the present model will help clarify some of the locations of our ignorance and point the way to the kinds of experimental and theoretical operations most likely to remove that ignorance.

In Figure 3 we describe the structure of the phonological memory system and the more important lines of associative activation, both direct and indirect, leading from the visual codes. Evidence that recognition of visually presented words typically involves phonological recoding is given by Rubenstein *et al.* (1971) and Wicklund and Katz (1970). A model of the articulatory response system is also briefly sketched to represent direct links between phonological memory and the overt articulation of words. The structures in the visual memory system are abbreviated in Figure 3 for economy of exposition.

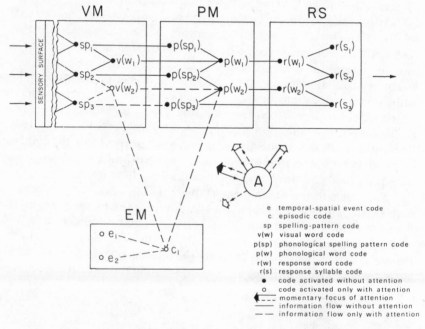

Figure 3.   Representation of associative links between codes in visual memory (VM), phonological memory (PM), episodic memory (EM), and the response system (RS). Attention is momentarily focused on a code in visual memory.

The phonological memory system is assumed to contain units closely related to acoustic and articulatory inputs. If we were to represent these systems separately, we would be strongly tempted to construct the acoustic system in a fashion similar to the visual system, with features, phonemes, syllables, and words structured in a hierarchy. The structure of the articulatory system is roughly suggested within the response system of Figure 3, in the form of a hierarchy of response output nodes arranged in a mirror image of the hierarchies for the sensory systems. For example, to respond with a word, one gives attention to $r(w_1)$ which then automatically feeds into the syllabic units $r(s_1)$ and $r(s_2)$, and perhaps from these into phonemes. For present purposes, we feel that we can trace the flow of information from the visual system to the phonological system without making specific assumptions about the precise relationships between the acoustic and articulatory systems. Following Gibson (1971), therefore, we lump these under the general heading of the phonological system.

The input to the phonological memory system is assumed to come from at least six sources: units in visual memory, response memory, semantic memory, and episodic memory, as well as from auditory stimulation and articulatory response feedback. Of course, additional activation can be provided from the attention center to any well-learned unit in phonological memory as is the case for units in visual memory. The sources of input of main interest here are the codes of the visual system. Associations between visual codes and their phonological counterparts are indicated by the lines drawn between the visual and phonological systems. Solid lines denote automatic associations; dashed lines denote associations that require additional activation by attention to generate an association. For example, a visually coded word $v(w_1)$, e.g., "basket," automatically activates its phonological associate, $p(w_1)$, e.g., /basket/, while another visual word code $v(w_2)$, e.g., "capstan," requires additional activation by attention before it can activate its phonological associate $p(w_2)$, e.g., /capstan/. Another way that the phonological code $p(w_1)$ can be activated by the visual system is by way of the component spelling patterns sp_1 ("bas") and sp_2 ("ket"), which may be associated with the phonological units $p(sp_1)$, (/bas/), and $p(sp_2)$, (/ket/). Once $p(sp_1)$ and $p(sp_2)$ are activated, they in turn activate and organize a blend into the phonological word unit, $p(w_1)$, (/basket/). This blend is accomplished by the two connecting lines presumably learned to automaticity by a great deal of practice in hearing and speaking these two syllabic components in the context of the word unit.

Thus we have specified two different locations in which the unitizing of a word might take place, one in the visual system and the other in the phonological system. For the experienced reader, the particular location used is optional. If he is reading easy material at a fast pace, he may select as visual units words or even word groups; if he is reading difficult material at a slow pace, he may select spelling patterns and unitize these into word units at the phonological level.

Exactly how these options are executed is a matter for speculation at present. Our best estimate of the role of the attention activator during fast reading is one in which no attention is given to the visual system, and the highest visual unit available is the one that automatically activates its corresponding phonological code. For slow reading, we suspect that the attention arrow is directed to the visual system where smaller units are given added activation, resulting in the activation of smaller phonological units. These phonological units then are blended automatically into larger phonological units.

The dashed lines in Figure 3 leading to the episodic memory system represent an indirect way that a visual code may activate a phonological code. This memory system, labeled "episodic" by Tulving (1972), is closely related to the temporal-contextual-information store of Shiffrin and Geisler (1973). It contains codes of temporal and physical events which can be organized with visual and phonological codes into a superordinate code, indicated here by c_1. These codes represent associations that are in the very earliest stages of learning. The dashed lines connected with the episodic code represent the fact that attention is required to activate the code. With further practice, direct lines may be formed between visual and phonological codes, for example the line joining $v(w_2)$ with $p(w_2)$. This link is represented by a dashed line to indicate that additional activation by attention still is necessary for the association to take place. The solid lines joining visual and phonological codes, of course, represent well-learned associations that occur without attentional activation. Of course, all three types of associations, episodic, nonautomatic direct, and automatic direct, are assumed to be at the accuracy level.

The initial association between a new visual pattern and its phonological response is considered to be a fast learning process (Estes, 1970). It may not occur on the first trial, but when it does occur, it appears to happen in an all-or-none manner. For this state of learning, progress is indicated customarily by percent correct or percent errors. When the subject has achieved a criterion of accurate performance, the visual code still requires attention whenever retrieval occurs through the episodic memory code or through a direct dashed-line connection, even if the perceptual coding of the visual stimulus itself is automatic. Further training beyond the accuracy criterion must be provided if the association is to occur without attention, represented by the solid lines. The letter-naming experiment soon to be described will serve as an illustrative example of the associative learning this model is intended to represent.

Theoretical Relationships between Visual, Phonological, and Semantic Systems

Once a visual word code makes contact with the phonological word code in reading, we assume that the meaning of the word can be elicited by means of a direct associative connection between the phonological unit, $p(w_1)$, and the semantic meaning unit, $m(w_1)$, as shown in Figure 4. Most of the connections between phonological word codes and semantic meaning codes have already been learned to automaticity through extensive experience with spoken communications. In fact, authors of children's books purposely select vocabularies in which words meet this condition. This takes the attention off the processing of meaning and frees it for decoding. However, for a child in the process of learning meanings of words, we assume that the linkage between a heard word and its meaning may be coded first in episodic memory. This is represented in Figure 4 by the organization of $p(w_3)$ and $m(w_3)$ and event e_1 and e_2 into the episodic code c_2. Additional exposures to a word along with activations of its meaning would begin to form a direct link between the phonological unit and its meaning, represented by the dashed line between $p(w_2)$ and $m(w_2)$.

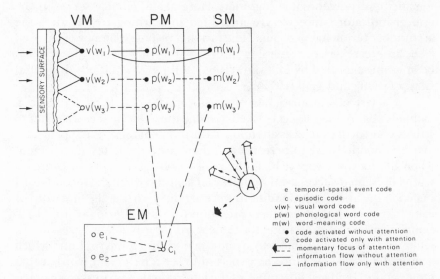

Figure 4.   Representation of three states of associative learning involving codes in visual memory (VM), phonological memory (PM), semantic memory (SM), and episodic memory (EM). Attention is momentarily focused on a code in episodic memory.

At these two states of learning, attention is needed to activate the association of a heard word into its meaning, but with enough practice, a word should elicit its meaning automatically, as illustrated by the solid line joining $p(w_1)$ with $m(w_1)$.

At this point we may mention that the association between the phonological form of a word and its meaning may go in the other direction, so that activation of a meaning unit could automatically excite a phonological unit. However, we are not prepared to specify in any detail how this is done. We simply wish to indicate that generating speech by activation of semantic structures also appears to be automatic, at least in the general sense in which we are using the term here.

We should note the possibility in the model that a visual word code may be associated directly with a semantic meaning code (Bower, 1970; Kolers, 1970). That is, a unit, $v(w_1)$, may activate its meaning, $m(w_1)$, without mediation through the phonological system. The fact that we can quickly recognize the difference in the meaning of such homonyms as "two" versus "too" seems to illustrate this assumption.

Indicators of automatic associative processing. The way we are currently measuring the role of attention in associative processing is similar in principle to the method already described in this paper for testing automaticity of perceptual recognition. Here again, latency serves as the critical indicator, since we are interested in learning trends after the accuracy criterion has been met. The fact that response latency of a paired associate decreases considerably after accuracy has been achieved has been well-established by Millward (1964), Suppes *et al.* (1966), Judd and Glaser (1969), and Hall (1972).

In a test of automatic associative processing used by LaBerge & Samuels (1973), the subject is asked to name the letter he sees. In order to strictly control the subject's attention at the moment the letter appears, we give him another task to perform and then insert the letter at a moment when he does not expect it. Eight subjects observed pairs of common words presented successively and pressed a button when the second word matched the first word. Conditions were arranged so that the first word of each pair prepared the subject's attention for the following word. Occasionally, instead of presenting the same word for a match, we presented a letter and asked the subject to name it aloud into a microphone which activated a voice key. Since he expected to see a particular word at that moment, we could test how much of the letter-naming process was carried out before attention was shifted to the letter. Of course, this test of automaticity required a control condition with letters whose names were already at the automatic level of associative learning.

The two sets of letters were the same as the ones used in the perceptual learning study. The familiar set was [b d p q] and the unfamiliar set was [⌊ ⌌⊦⌐]. The names for the familiar set were bee, dee, pea, and cue, and the names for the unfamiliar set were one, two, four, and five. The overall latency of naming a letter pattern presumably includes perceptual coding time, association time, and residual response time. However, we were interested in differences only in association time. After determining that the residual-response component was equal for the familiar and unfamiliar letters, we had only to equate the familiar and unfamiliar letters with respect to perceptual coding time. To do this we gave the subjects preliminary training on perceptual matching of the unfamiliar patterns until they were recognized as fast as familiar patterns. These matching tests were given under automatic test conditions already described. When the criterion had been met on matching tests, the subjects were given a card for about two minutes on which were drawn the new patterns along with their corresponding names. They then began a series of daily tests of naming these new letters along with tests in which familiar letters were named. After each day's test block, intensive training blocks were given in which a trial consisted of a small circle as a cue followed by one of the eight letters which the subject named. Figure 5 shows the results of this experiment over 20 days of testing and training.

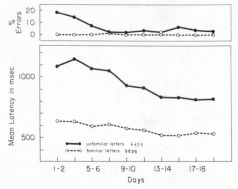

Figure 5.   Mean latency and percent errors of naming responses to unfamiliar and familiar letter patterns.

It is evident that the latency difference of a naming response to the new and old letters is quite large at first and converges over days of training. All eight subjects showed convergence. This convergence continues when accuracy appears to be stationary. Additional tests conducted

under conditions in which the subject was attending to the naming operation prior to the stimulus onset showed no difference in latencies of
familiar and unfamiliar letters. In view of these findings, we believe that
Figure 5 provides an indication of the gradual learning of automatic
naming associations.

In Figure 6 is shown a model of three levels of associative learning for
this experiment. Any one of the familiar letters may be designated as l_4
and its name by $n(l_4)$; any of the unfamiliar letters may be designated by l_6
and its name by $n(l_6)$. At first the subject may associate the unfamiliar
letters with their names by some mnemonic strategy, rule, or image. This
state of learning is represented by the lines which connect with the
episodic code c_1. Later, as learning progresses, a direct link may be
formed. This is indicated by the type of line joining l_5 with $n(l_5)$. Dashed
lines, of course, indicate that attention must be focused on the letter to
provide the additional activation needed to complete the association and
excite the phonological name unit. The solid line joining the familiar

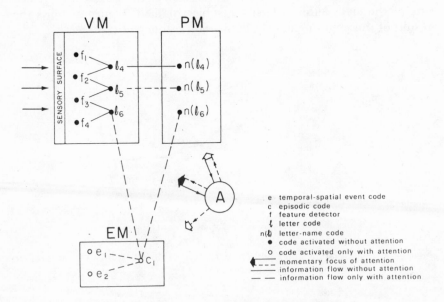

Figure 6.   Representation of three states of associative learning between codes in
               visual memory (VM), phonological memory (PM), and episodic mem-
               ory (EM). Attention is momentarily focused on a code in visual mem-
               ory.

letter l_4 with its name $n(l_4)$ represents an automatic association, which allows the stimulus activation of l_4 to then excite $n(l_4)$ while attention is directed elsewhere.

The results shown in Figure 5 are consistent with this model of automatic association. However, at the end of 20 days of practice, the college subjects did not name unfamiliar letters as fast as they named the familiar letters, a finding which leads us to conclude that the subjects were still using some degree of attention to make the association. Apparently, it would take a great many more days to bring letter naming of these rather simple letters to the level of automaticity already achieved by the familiar letters. We are tempted to generalize to classroom routines in elementary schools in which letter naming is directly taught and tested only up to the accuracy level. A child may be quite accurate in naming or sounding the letters of the alphabet, but we may not know how much attention it costs him to do it. This kind of information could be helpful in predicting how easily he can manage new learning skills which build on associations he has already learned.

We agree that higher-order reading skills are based more on sounding letters than naming them. Had we instructed the subjects to sound the letters instead of name them, we would regard the expected convergence of latency of the unfamiliar sounds to the latency of the familiar sounds as indicating the gradual development of automaticity in sounding letters. In this case, we would designate the sound of a visual letter code l_5 in Figure 6 as $p(l_5)$ instead of $n(l_5)$, etc. We assume that the three states of learning to associate a name with a letter would generalize to the case of learning to sound that letter and to sounding spelling patterns and words as well.

Turning to the association of word sounds with word meanings illustrated in Figure 4, it is possible to perform learning experiments using indicators of automaticity of associating meanings in much the same way as we did for associating names. The only major difference in procedure is that instead of asking the subjects to name a letter, we ask him to press a button if the word is a member of a particular category of meaning (Meyer, 1970).

General model of automaticity in reading. In Figure 7 all the memory systems relevant to this theory of reading are shown together. We may use this sketch to trace some of the many alternative routes that a visually presented word could take as it proceeds toward its goal of activating meaning codes. A given route is defined here not only in terms of the particular systemic code encountered along the way, but also in terms of whether or not attention adds its activation to any of these codes. A few of the possible optional processing routes may be described as follows:

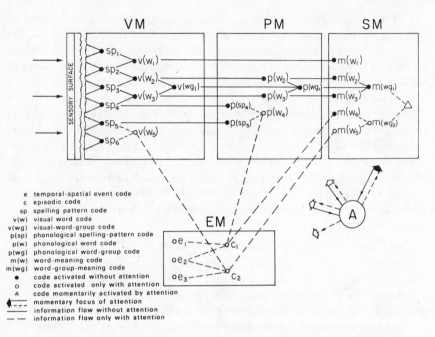

Figure 7. Representation of some of the many possible ways a visually presented word may be processed into meaning. The four major stages of processing shown here are visual memory (VM), phonological memory (PM), episodic memory (EM), and semantic memory (SM). Attention is momentarily focused on comprehension in SM, involving organization of meaning codes of two word-groups.

Option 1: The graphemic stimulus is automatically coded into a visual word code v(w1), which automatically activates the meaning code m (w1). An example is "bear" or "bare" or any very common word which is not processed by Option 2.

Option 2: The graphemic stimulus is automatically coded into a visual word code v(w2), which automatically activates the phonological code p(w2). This code then automatically excites the meaning code m(w2). An example is any very common word which is not processed by Option 1.

Option 3: The graphemic stimulus is automatically coded into the visual word-group code v(wg1). This code automatically activates the phonological word-group code $p(wg_1)$, which in turn activates automatically the meaning code of the word group $m(wg_1)$. An example might be the words "beef stew" or "après ski."

Option 4: The graphemic stimulus is automatically coded into two spelling patterns sp_4 and sp_5. These units activate the phonological codes $p(sp_4)$ and $p(sp_5)$. These two codes are blended with attention into the phonological word code $p(w_4)$, which activates with attention the episodic code c_1. This code is then activated by attention to excite the meaning code $m(w_4)$. An example might be "skylab," for those who have had few experiences with the word.

Option 5: The graphemic stimulus is coded with attention into the visual word code $v(w_5)$. Attention activates this code to excite the episodic code c_2. When attention is shifted to c_2, it generates the meaning code $m(w_5)$. An example is the name of a character in a Russian novel which is too long to pronounce easily.

An act of comprehension is illustrated in Figure 7 by the focusing of attention on the organization of two word groups, one of which, $m(wg_1)$, has been automatically grouped, and the other, $m(wg_2)$, has required attention to be grouped. We assume that $m(w_2)$, $m(w_3)$, $m(w_4)$, and $m(w_5)$ can be organized to make sense to the subject only if he can manage to shift his attention activation quickly among these meaning codes to keep them simultaneously active. We are assuming that the process of organizing is promoted by fast scanning at the semantic level in much the same way that fast scanning of feature detectors promotes unitizing of features into new letter patterns at the usual level.

Options 1 and 2 illustrate what many consider the goal of fluent reading: the reader can maintain his attention continuously on the meaning units of semantic memory, while the decoding from visual to semantic systems proceeds automatically. The rest of the examples serve to emphasize that the reader often has the option of several different ways of processing a given word. When he encounters a word he does not understand, his attention may be shifted to the phonological level to read out the sound for attempts at retrieval from episodic memory. At other times he may shift his attention to the visual level and attempt to associate spelling patterns with phonological units, which are then blended into a word which makes contact with meaning. When the decoding and comprehension processes are automatic, reading appears to be "easy." When they require attention to complete their operations, reading seems to be "difficult."

One could say that every time a word code requires attention we are made aware of that aspect of the reading process. For example, when we encounter a word that does not make sense, we may speak it and thereby are momentarily aware of the sound of the words we are reading. Or if the word does not sound right to us, we may examine its spelling patterns, thereby becoming aware of its visual aspects. However, when reading is flowing at its best, for example in reading a mystery novel in which the vocabulary is very familiar, we can go along for many minutes imagining ourselves with the detective walking the streets of London, and apparently we have not given a bit of attention to any of the decoding processes that have been transforming marks on the page into the deeper systems of comprehension.

Development of Automaticity

Throughout this paper we have stressed the importance of automaticity in performance of fluent reading. Now we turn to a consideration of ways to train reading subskills to automatic levels. Unfortunately, very little systematic research has been directed specifically to this advanced stage of learning. Reviews of studies of automatic activity (Keele, 1968; Welford, 1968; Posner & Keele, 1969) deal mostly with automatic motor tasks and, to our knowledge, there are no studies which systematically compare training methods which facilitate the acquisition of automaticity of verbal skills. Therefore, our remarks here will be speculative, although we are currently putting forth efforts in the laboratory to shed light on this problem.

First of all, we would agree with most practitioners involved in skill learning that practice leads to automaticity. For example, recognizing letters of the alphabet apparently becomes automatic by successive exposures (see Figure 2). Sounding spelling patterns apparently becomes automatic by repetition of the visual and articulatory sequences. Even the meaning of a visual word would seem to achieve automatic retrieval through successive repetitions. Edmond Huey in 1908 emphasized the role of repetitions in the development of automaticity when he wrote, "To perceive an entirely new word or other combination of strokes requires considerable time, close attention and is likely to be imperfectly done, just as when we attempt some new combination of movements, some new trick in the gymnasium, or a new serve at tennis. In either case, repetition progressively frees the mind from attention to details, makes facile the total act, shortens the time, and reduces the extent to which consciousness must concern itself with the process" (Huey, 1908, p. 104).

In the case of perceptual learning, repetitions would seem to provide more than the consolidation of perceptions to the point where they can be run off quite quickly and automatically. Another thing that can happen during these repetitions is that the material can be reorganized into higher-order units even before the lower-order units have achieved a high level of automaticity. For example, when the child reads text in which the same vocabulary is used over and over again, the repetitions will certainly make more automatic the perceptions of each word unit, but if he stays at the word level he will not realize his potential reading speed. If, however, he begins to organize some of the words into short groups or phrases as he reads, then further repetitions can strengthen these units as well as word units. In this way he can break through the upper limit of word-by-word reading and apply the benefits of further repetitions to automatization of larger units. Apparently this sort of higher-order chunking progresses as the child gains more experience in reading. For example, Taylor et al. (1960) found that 1st grade children made as many as two fixations per word whereas 12th graders made one fixation for about every two words.

Reorganization into larger units requires attention, according to the model. We do not know specifically how to train a child to organize codes into higher units although some speed-reading methods make claims that sheer pressure for speed forces the person out of the word-by-word reading into larger units. Nevertheless, we feel reasonably sure that considerable application of attention is necessary if the reorganization into higher-order units is to take place. When a person does not pay attention to what he is practicing, he rules out opportunities for forming higher units because he simply processes through codes that are already laid down.

What may be critical in the determination of upper limits of word-group units is the number of word meanings that the subject can comprehend in one chunk in his semantic memory. Units at the semantic level may determine chunk size at the phonological level which, in turn, may influence how attention is distributed over visual codes. Stated more generally, this hypothesis says that the limiting size of the chunk at early levels is influenced by the existing chunk size at deeper levels. If this hypothesis holds up under experimental test, it would imply that the teaching of higher-order units for the reader should progress from deeper levels to sensory levels, rather than the reverse.

We have suggested that during the development of automaticity the person either may attempt to reorganize smaller units (e.g., words) into larger units (e.g., word phrases) or he may simply stay at the word unit level. It stands to reason that he has more confidence in his performance at the lower unit level where he has had the most practice. Whenever he attempts to reorganize word codes into larger units, he may temporarily slow down and perhaps make more errors. Therefore, to encourage chunking, we may have to relax the demand for accuracy. In general, teachers who stress accuracy too strongly may discourage children from developing sophisticated strategies of word recognition (Archwamety & Samuels, 1973). Thus, a child who has performed successfully at one level of processing may be reluctant to leave it and move to higher levels which could eventually improve reading speed.

In the case of association learning, automaticity presumably develops by the sheer temporal contiguity of the two codes. For example, sounding the word "dog" as it is visually presented with no attention to organization of the stimulus and the response may be sufficient for attainment of automaticity. Presumably, proficient readers continue to increase their speed on word-naming tests by sheer practice without special attention to organizing or reorganizing associations.

However, at the initial stages of association, well before automaticity begins to develop, organizational processes are probably involved during a repetition (Mandler, 1967; Tulving, 1962). While it is possible to form an initial associative link directly (rote learning), most likely the subject organizes the stimulus and response together with an event or with a rule and stores this code in episodic memory, as shown in Figure 3. Later, when the stimulus is presented, attention activates the stimulus code to excite the episodic code. This episodic code now "attracts" attention to activate it further and the code generates its subordinate codes, including the response code. This way of recalling a response requires attention activation and takes a relatively large amount of time. With further repetitions, the stimulus code should begin to short-circuit the episodic code and form a new direct link with the response code. At this point, the stimulus code may require some attention to activate the response code. However, the route through episodic memory remains as an option, and subjects probably use it as a check on the response obtained by the new direct route. With enough practice, of course, activation of the stimulus code excites the response code without attentional assistance.

We expect that the rate of growth of automaticity will depend upon a number of other factors. Two of these, namely distribution of learning and presentation of feedback, have been studied extensively in verbal learning and motor learning experiments. For both motor skill and verbal learning, it has generally been found that distributed practice is better than massed practice, although the optimal interval seems to be a matter of minutes, not days. Massed practice appears to be more favorable when one deals with meaningful material. If we can assume that organizational processing requires massed practice, then we would be inclined to predict that massed practice would be more beneficial for acquiring automatic perceptual processing where organization of codes into larger chunks seems critical. However, automatic associating of sounds or names with these perceptual chunks should involve little if any organization and therefore should profit more from distributed practice.

Since the important growth of automaticity takes place after the subject has achieved accuracy, overt feedback for correct and incorrect responses may be redundant because at this stage of learning the subject knows when he is correct or not (Adams & Bray, 1970). However, there is another type of feedback which may affect the rate of automaticity learning. While learning proceeds toward the automatic level, it might be appropriate to inform the subject of the time it took to execute his response. In fact, the research we have described on acquisition of automaticity routinely informs the subject of his response speed after each trial as well as at the end of a block of trials. Of course, latency feedback for a response to a particular stimulus will not be meaningful by itself, it must be related to some criterion baseline. For example, the time it takes to identify a new word should be compared to the time it takes to identify a word that is already at the automatic level. Thus, the critical metric is the difference between the two latencies. In practice, what we do is present a few old and well-learned patterns along with the new material we wish the subject to learn. At the end of a series of these trials, we show the subject the two latencies. Another way to present feedback is to give it after each response. When his response is faster than the mean on the previous block, he is given a light or sound to indicate a fast response. Aside from the incentive value of knowing how his response speed compares with a criterion, the feedback may influence the way he distributes attention before and immediately after stimulus presentation. This may in turn influence how he organizes the perceptual aspects of reading. As for the purely associative operations, we would suspect that latency feedback would be effective mainly in assuring that the subject continues to respond fast enough to maintain optimal temporal contiguity between stimulus and response codes.

Implications of the Model for Research in Reading Instruction

The model which has been presented here may have several helpful features for the researcher concerned with reading. It provides explanatory power by clarifying a number of phenomena which have puzzled educators for some time, and it suggests directions for pedagogical improvement.

One of the current questions in reading is whether it should be considered as a wholistic process or as a cluster of subskills. In support of the subskill view, Guthrie (1973) found that correlations among subskills were high for a group of good readers but low for poor readers, suggesting that they differ in the way they organize component skills. Jeffrey and Samuels (1966) found that children who were taught all of the subskills necessary for decoding words were able to do so without any guidance from a teacher, whereas children who were not taught a particular component were unable to decode.

From the point of view of a mature reader, however, the process appears to be a unitary one. In fact, it is customarily referred to by one label, namely "reading." When a teacher observes a bright child learning to read, he may see the child slowly attaining one skill. However, when the same teacher is confronted with a slow learner, he may observe the child slowly learning many skills. This comes about because the child often must be given extensive training on each of a variety of tasks, such as letter discrimination, letter-sound training, blending, etc. In this manner, a teacher becomes aware of the fact that letter recognition can be considered a skill itself, to be taught like we teach object-naming, for example, naming birds.

The fluent reader has presumably mastered each of the subskills at the automatic level. Even more important, he has made their integration automatic as well. What this implies is that he no longer clearly sees the dividing lines separating these skills under the demands of his day-to-day reading. In effect, this means that he is no longer aware of the component nature of the subskills as he was required to be when he was a beginning reader, learning skills one-by-one. Therefore, if you should ask a typically fluent reader how he perceives his reading process, he is likely to tell you that he views it as a wholistic one.

It seems from our consideration of this model that all readers must go through similar stages of learning to read but do so at different rates. The slower the rate of learning to read, the more the person becomes aware of these component stages. One of the hallmarks of the reader who learned the subskills rapidly is that he was least aware of them at the time, and therefore now has little memory of them as separable subskills. On the basis of this model, therefore, we view reading acquisition as a series of skills, regardless of how it appears to the fluent reader. Pedagogically, we favor the approach which singles out these skills for testing and training and then attempts to sequence them in appropriate ways.

In consideration of each stage, for example, learning to sound letter patterns, it would appear that there are two criteria of achievement: accuracy and automaticity. During the achievement of accuracy, we assume the student should have his attention focused on the task at hand to code the association between the visual letters and their sounds in episodic memory, or to establish direct associations (cf. Figure 6). Once he has learned letter-sound correspondences, he may or may not be ready to attack the next stage, namely to "blend" these sounds into syllables or words. To ascertain his readiness to move ahead, we must consider a further criterion, namely automaticity. If a good deal of attention is required for him to be accurate in sounding letter patterns, then "blending" will be more difficult to perform owing to the total number of things he must attend to and hold in short-term memory.

In practice, the letter-sound processing need not be fully automatic for him to make progress towards blending, since even the slowest learner has sufficient short-term memory capacity to store a few sounds while he works at blending them. Of course, the less time that his attention must be allocated to the letter-sound processing, the more time he can devote to the blending operation and the faster the progress in learning to blend. We could say that the child who either has a small short-term memory capacity or who has not yet developed the letter-sound skill to the automatic level has too many things to which he must switch his attention in order to carry out the operation of blending. This means that he will forget information crucial to the blending process, and therefore he is more likely to suffer unsuccessful experiences with this task. In short, accuracy is not a sufficient criterion for readiness to advance to skills which build on the subskills at hand. One should take into account the amount of attention required by these subskills as part of the readiness criterion.

Comprehension

We turn now to consider the way the model can be used to clarify some of the comprehension processes and to point to certain pedagogical consequences. In its present simple form, the model does not spell out higher-order linguistic operations such as parsing, predictive processing, and contextual effects on comprehension. If initial tests of the model are successful, it is hoped that it can be elaborated to represent more complex semantic operations such as these. For present purposes, we find it convenient to separate comprehension from word meaning. By word meaning we refer to the semantic referent of a spoken or written word, morpheme, or groups of words that denote a meaningful unit. By comprehension, on the other hand, we refer to the organization of these word meanings. To do this, the meaning units presumably are scanned one-by-one by attention and organized as a coherent whole. The momentary act of comprehension is represented in Figure 7 by the focus of attention on the coding of m(wg₁) with m(wg₂). If a subject maintains attention solely on single-meaning codes, this would constitute a rather low form of comprehension, much like viewing characters in a play one-by-one and ignoring their interactions. On the other hand, for high-level comprehension of passages, attention must be directed to organizing these meaning codes, and presumably this is where effort enters into reading just as it does in understanding difficult spoken sentences.

So long as word meanings are automatically processed, the focus of attention remains at the semantic level and does not need to be switched to the visual system for decoding, nor to the phonological level for retrieving the semantic meanings. On the other hand, attention could be focused on the decoding of visual words into their phonological form and spoken aloud without any attention to comprehension. In fact, this has been frequently observed with some beginning readers, and goes by the label of "word calling."

Another phenomenon which the model may clarify is reading for meaning, but without recall for what has just been read. The model indicates that meanings of familiar words and word groups may be activated automatically, leaving attention free to wander to other matters, perhaps to recent personal episodes. If the reader gives little attention to organizing meanings into new codes for storage, it is not surprising that he later finds he cannot recall what he has been reading.

The complexity of the comprehension operation appears to be as enormous as that of thinking in general. When a person is comprehending a sentence, he quite often adds his own associations to the particular organized pattern of meanings. In addition, the ways in which he might organize the meaning units from semantic memory may be influenced by strategies whose programs of operation are themselves stored in semantic memory. We assume that the act of adding material from one's own experiences to what one is reading is represented by switching to other codes in semantic and episodic memory. When this occurs, the item in semantic memory is used as a retrieval cue to access an association or strategy. The finished organizational product presumably is then stored in episodic or semantic memory. When this is successfully done, we say the person can remember what he has read.

REFERENCES

Adams, J. A., & Bray, N. W. A closed-loop theory of paired-associate verbal learning. *Psychological Review,* 1970, **77,** 385-405.

Archwamety, T., & Samuels, S. J. A mastery based experimental program for teaching mentally retarded children word recognition and reading comprehension skills through use of hypothesis/test procedures. Research Report #50, Research, Development and Demonstration Center in Education of Handicapped Children, Minneapolis, Minnesota, 1973.

Bower, G. H. A selective review of organizational factors in memory. In E. Tulving & W. Donaldson (Eds.), *Organization of memory.* London: Academic Press, 1972.

Bower, T. G. R. Reading by eye. In H. Levin & J. Williams (Eds.), *Basic studies in reading.* New York: Basic Books, 1970.

Broadbent, D. E. *Perception and communication.* London: Pergamon Press, 1958.

Clark, H. H., & Chase, W. G. On the process of comparing sentences against pictures. *Cognitive Psychology,* 1972, **3,** 472-517.

Deutsch, J. A., & Deutsch, D. Attention: Some theoretical considerations. *Psychological Review,* 1963, **70,** 80-90.

Egeth, H., Jonides, J., & Wall, S. Parallel processing of multielement displays. *Cognitive Psychology,* 1972, **3,** 674-698.

Eriksen, C. W., & Spencer, T. Rate of information processing in visual perception: Some results and methodological considerations. *Journal of Experimental Psychology Monographs,* 1969, **72** (2Pt.2), 1-16.

Estes, W. K. *Learning theory and mental development.* New York: Academic Press, 1970.

Estes, W. K. An associative basis for coding and organization in memory. In A. W. Melton & E. Martin (Eds.), *Coding processes in human memory.* New York: Wiley, 1972. Pp. 161-190.

Gibson, E. J. *Principles of perceptual learning and development.* New York: Appleton-Century-Crofts, 1969.

Gibson, E. J. Perceptual learning and the theory of word perception. *Cognitive Psychology,* 1971, **2,** 351-368.

Gough, P. B. One second of reading. In J. F. Kavanaugh and I. G. Mattingly (Eds.), *Language by ear and by eye.* Cambridge: M.I.T. Press, 1972.

Guthrie, J. T. Models of reading and reading disability. *The Journal of Educational Psychology,* 1973, **65,** No. 1, 9-18.

Hall, R. F., & Wenderoth, P. M. Effects of number of responses and recall strategies on parameter values of a paired-associate learning model. *Journal of Verbal Learning and Verbal Behavior,* 1972, **11,** 29-37.

Huey, E. B. *The psychology and pedagogy of reading.* New York: Macmillan, 1908.

Jeffrey, W. E., & Samuels, S. J. The effect of method of reading training on initial learning and transfer. *Journal of Verbal Learning and Verbal Behavior,* 1966, **57,** 159-163.

Johnson, N. F. Organizations and the concept of a memory code. In A. W. Melton & E. Martin (Eds.), *Coding processes in human memory.* New York: Wiley, 1972.

Judd, W. A., & Glaser, R. Response latency as a function of training method, information level, acquisition, and overlearning. *Journal of Educational Psychology Monograph,* 1969, **60,** No. 4, Part 2.

Keele, S. W. Movement control in skilled motor performance. *Psychological Bulletin,* 1968, **70,** 387-403.

Kolers, P. A. Three stages of reading. In H. Levin and J. Williams, (Eds.), *Basic studies in reading.* New York: Basic Books, 1970. Pp. 90-118.

LaBerge, D. Identification of the time to switch attention: A test of a serial and parallel model of attention. In S. Kornblum (Ed.), *Attention and performance* IV. New York: Academic Press, 1973a.

LaBerge, D. Attention and the measurement of perceptual learning. *Memory and Cognition*, 1973b, **1**, 268-276.

LaBerge, D., & Samuels, S. J. On the automaticity of naming artificial letters. Technical Report #7, Minnesota Reading Research Project, University of Minnesota, 1973.

LaBerge, D., Samuels, S. J., & Petersen, R. Perceptual learning of artificial letters. Technical Report #6, Minnesota Reading Research Project, University of Minnesota, 1973.

LaBerge, D., Van Gelder, P., & Yellott, J. I. A cueing technique in choice reaction time. *Perception and Psychophysics*, 1970, **7**, 57-62.

Mandler, G. Organization and memory. In K. W. Spence and J. T. Spence (Eds.), *The psychology of learning and motivation*. Vol. 1. New York: Academic Press, 1967.

Meyer, D. F. On the representation and retrieval of stored semantic information. *Cognitive Psychology*, 1970, **1**, 242-300.

Miller, G. A. The magical number seven plus or minus two: Some limits on our capacity for processing information. *Psychological Review*, 1956, **63**, 81-97.

Millward, R. Latency in a modified paired-associate learning experiment. *Journal of Verbal Learning and Verbal Behavior*, 1964, **3**, 309-316.

Moray, N. Attention in dichotic listening: Affective cues and the influence of instructions. *Quarterly Journal of Experimental Psychology*, 1959, **11**, 56-60.

Norman, D. A. Toward a theory of memory and attention. *Psychological Review*, 1968, **75**, 522-536.

Posner, M. I., & Boies, S. J. Components of Attention. *Psychological Review*, 1971, **78**, 5, 391-405.

Posner, M. I., Boies, S. J. Eichelman, W. H., & Taylor, R. L. Retention of visual and name codes of single letters. *Journal of Experimental Psychology Monograph*, 1969, **79**, No. 1, Part 2.

Posner, M. I., Lewis, J. L., & Conrad, C. Component processes in reading: A performance analysis. In J. F. Kavanaugh & I. G. Mattingly (Eds.), *Language by ear and by eye*. Cambridge: M.I.T. Press, 1972.

Posner, M. I., & Mitchell, R. A chronometric analysis of classification. *Psychological Review*, 1967, **74**, 392-409.

Posner, M. I., & Keele, S. W. Attention demands of movements. *Proceedings of the seventeenth congress of applied psychology*, Amsterdam: Zeitlinger, 1969.

Rubenstein, H., Lewis, S. S., & Rubenstein, M. A. Evidence for phonemic recoding in visual word recognition. *Journal of Verbal Learning and Verbal Behavior*, 1971, **10**, 645-647.

Rumelhart, D. E. A multicomponent theory of the perception of brie/fly exposed visual displays. *Journal of Mathematical Psychology*, 1970, **7**, 191-218.

Shiffrin, R. M., & Gardner, G. T. Visual processing capacity and attentional control. *Journal of Experimental Psychology*, 1972, **93**, 72-82.

Shiffrin, R. M., & Geisler, W. S. Visual recognition in a theory of information processing. In R. L. Solso (Ed.), *Contemporary issues in cognitive psychology:* The Loyola Symposium. New York: Wiley, 1973.

Smith, F. *Understanding reading*. New York: Holt, Reinhart & Winston, 1971.

Sternberg, S. The discovery of processing stages: Extensions of Donder's methods. In Koster (Ed.), *Attention and performance*, Vol. 2. Amsterdam: North Holland Publishing Co., 1969.

Suppes, P., Groen, G., & Schlag-Ray, M. A model for response latency in paired-associate learning. *Journal of Mathematical Psychology*, 1966, **3**, 99-128.

Taylor, S. E., Frackenpohl, H., & Pattee, J. L. Grade level norms for the components of the fundamental reading skill. Bulletin #3, New York: Huntington, Educational Development Laboratories, 1960.

Trabasso, T. R., & Bower, G. H. *Attention in learning: Theory and research.* New York: Wiley, 1968.

Treisman, A. Selective attention in man. *British Medical Bulletin,* 1964, **20,** 12-16.

Tulving, E. Subjective organization in free recall of "unrelated words." *Psychological Review,* 1962, **69,** 344-354.

Tulving, E. Episodic and semantic memory. In E. Tulving & W. Donaldson (Eds.), *Organization of memory.* New York: Academic Press, 1972.

Welford, A. I. *Fundamentals of skill.* London: Methuen, 1968.

Wicklund, D. A., & Katz, L. Short term retention and recognition of words by children aged seven and ten. Visual Information Processing, Progress Report No. 2, University of Connecticut, 1970.

Meaningful Processing of Sentences[*]

RICHARD C. ANDERSON, SHEILA R. GOLDBERG, AND JANET L. HIDDE
University of Illinois

There is reason to believe that there are several stages or levels of process-ing that must occur if a person is to learn from written verbal materials. Two of these stages are auditory encoding and semantic encoding (Anderson, 1970). Auditory encoding consists of rendering words into implicit (or explicit) speech. Semantic encoding is the bringing to mind of meaningful representations of words. It is impossible at the present time to be precise about the nature of semantic encoding, but there is no doubt that it often entails the "mental image" of the things and events named by the words (cf. Bower, 1972; Paivio, 1969).

Evidence for auditory and semantic encoding stages comes from research on memory. Most errors in short-term memory arise from con-fusions between sounds (cf. Wickelgren, 1965, 1966) whereas errors in short-term memory due to confusions in meaning are relatively rare (Baddeley, 1964). In long-term memory, on the other hand, semantic confusion is a more important source of interference than acoustical confusion (Baddeley, 1966; Baddeley & Dale, 1966).

Semantic encoding does not inevitably follow auditory encoding. In simple terms, it is argued that people often "read" without bringing to mind the meaning of the words they are speaking. Our working assump-tion is that people tend to do no more processing than the task requires (Anderson, 1970). If this analysis is correct, procedures that induce the reader to comprehend words rather than merely say them will facilitate learning.

Bobrow and Bower (1969) have completed several experiments which suggest that procedures which cause subjects to comprehend the meaning of sentences strongly facilitate learning. In one experiment, the

[*]Reprinted from *Journal of Educational Psychology, 62,* 5, 1971, 395-399. Copyright 1971 by the American Psychological Association. Reprinted by permission. The research reported in this paper was supported in part by the Advanced Research Projects Agency through the Office of Naval Research under Contract ONR Nonr 3985(08).

subject was instructed to compose a sentence which was a sensible continuation of each sentence he saw. For example, if he saw the sentence "The farmer discovered a diamond," a sensible continuing sentence might be "He sold it to a jeweler and used the money to buy a tractor." Despite the fact that they were vulnerable to interference from the sentences they had created themselves, the subjects in the continuation condition recalled twice as many predicate nouns, given the subject nouns as retrieval cues, than control subjects required to read each sentence aloud three times.

Under some conditions, questions to be answered or blanks to be completed, as in a self-instructional program, may get the reader to process with understanding the material which accompanies the question or blank. Consider the incomplete statement, "Elevators stop at every _____." To complete the sentence with the word "floor" requires a person to bring to mind, in however fleeting a form, a meaningful representation of the rest of the sentence. Simply translating the printed words into speech will not suffice, because the mere sound of the other words can not evoke floor. Floor is semantically rather than acoustically related to the rest of the sentence.

Anderson, Royer, Kulhavy, Thornburg, and Klemt (1971) obtained some indirect evidence that blanks in sentences facilitate learning. In their first experiment, paired associates were learned as readily from simple, unprompted sentences (e.g., "SIG are yellow") and unadorned pairs (e.g., "SIG yellow") as from "thematically prompted" sentences (e.g., "Before turning red, traffic SIG are yellow") displayed as a whole. In two subsequent experiments, the prompted sentences were initially exposed with blanks in place of the response terms in order to induce complete processing of the sentences. Thematic prompts enhanced learning under these conditions. However, this result did not prove that the blank in place of the response term was a critical part of the procedure since none of the experiments directly compared learning from otherwise identical sentences with and without blanks. Herein lies the purpose of the present studies.

Experiment I

Method

Subjects. The subjects were 43 undergraduate women who participated to fulfill a requirement in an introductory educational psychology course. They were randomly assigned to conditions upon appearance for the experiment.

Sentences. Fifty-five sentences were prepared such that the last word of each sentence seemed to be determined by the other words in the sentence. These sentences, with a blank in place of the final word in each sentence, were presented on mimeographed sheets to 75 subjects following their participation in a free recall experiment. They were instructed to fill each blank with the word that most obviously fit the meaning of the sentence. Selected for use in the experiment were 24 sentences which 99% to 100% of the subjects in the norming group completed with the words intended by experimenters. Figure 1 contains several examples of the sentences.

Procedure. The Blank group received each of 24 sentences with a blank in place of the last word. The sentences were displayed as a whole for the No Blank group. The subjects in both groups read each sentence aloud during the 4-second presentation interval. Those in the Blank group were asked to supply the word which most obviously fit the blank as they read.

Study and test trials alternated until three of each had been completed. Within both types of trials, items were presented at a 4-second rate on a Lafayette Model 303A memory drum. On test trials each subject noun was presented as a retrieval cue; the subject responded orally with the last word in the sentence, which, of course, subjects in the Blank group had never seen. There were three randomizations of the sentences and three randomizations of the subject nouns. One third of the subjects began with each randomization.

Results

A strict scoring system was employed in which only words which completed sentences in the No Blank condition were counted correct. Also tried was a lenient scoring procedure in which a word was counted correct if it matched the word given during the preceding study trial. The lenient scores of the Blank group were 1% higher per trial than the strict scores.

Figure 2 shows mean percent recall (strict scoring). The analysis of variance indicated no significant effect for treatment ($F = 3.80$, $df = 1/41$, $p > .05$). However, there were significant effects due to trials ($F = 313.32$, $df = 2/82$, $p < .01$) and the Treatment $\times$ Trials interaction ($F = 12.10$, $df = 2/82$, $p < .01$). Trial by trial comparisons indicated that the Blank and No Blank groups differed significantly on the first trial ($t = 3.61$, $df = 41$, $p < .01$), but not on the second or the third.

A circle has neither a beginning nor _____ .

Diamonds are a girl's best _____ .

Mother bakes delicious apple _____ .

The astronauts were received at the White _____ .

Dictionaries list words in alphabetical _____ .

The physician noted the time on his wrist _____ .

Figure 1.   Examples of incomplete sentences in which the last word is determined by the rest of the sentence.

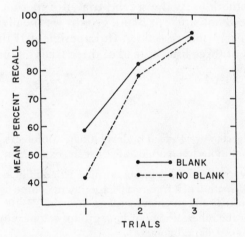

Figure 2.   Mean percentage of recall in Experiment I.

Experiment II

In Experiment I, a group that read sentences with blanks in place of the response terms outperformed, at least on the first trial, a group which read entire sentences. The argument is that a blank forces semantic encoding of the other words in a sentence, and that semantic encoding is the precursor to learning. There is, however, at least one alternative interpretation. It could be that the advantage of the Blank group was due to the fact that there was a greater similarity between conditions of learning and conditions of testing for the Blank group than the No Blank group. During learning, the subjects in the Blank group were required to *produce* the final word of each sentence, while subjects in the No Blank group *read* the final word. On the test, both groups were required to *produce* the final word. Thus, the apparent facilitation from requiring blanks to be filled may have been nothing more than transfer. Experiment II investigated the transfer explanation. A backward association test was included in which the subject was required to produce the subject noun of each sentence given the last word of the sentence as a retrieval cue. During study both groups *read* the subject nouns. Furthermore, since subjects in the Blank group did not see the last word of any sentence during study, on the backward test there was greater dissimilarity between the training and test stimuli in the Blank than the No Blank group. Hence, an advantage accruing to the Blank group could not be attributed to specific transfer. Experiment II was also designed to provide a more sensitive test of the effects of the Blank condition. By the second trial of Experiment I the difference between the Blank and No Blank groups was negligible, apparently because of a performance ceiling. In Experiment II there was one study trial on each of three lists, instead of three trials on one list, in order to raise the ceiling.

Method

Subjects. The subjects were 48 paid undergraduate volunteers, randomly assigned to conditions upon appearance for the experiment.

Sentences. A new group of 30 subjects normed 99 additional sentences following participation in a free-recall experiment. Three lists of 23 sentences were constructed containing sentences which 97%-100% of the subjects in one or the other of the norming groups completed with the words intended by the experimenters.

Design and procedure. Half the subjects received the Blank treatment and half received the No Blank treatment. As in the first experiment subjects in both groups read each sentence aloud as it appeared, with those in the Blank group giving the word that went in the blank. All subjects received three lists; one third began with each list. There was one study trial on each list at a 4-second rate, followed by two test trials, also at a 4-second rate. On the forward test trial, each subject noun was presented and the last word of the sentence was required as the response. On the backward test trial, the last word of the sentence was presented and the subject noun was required as the response. Half the subjects received the forward test before the backward test. The order was reversed for the remainder. In all other respects the procedure was the same as in Experiment I.

Results

Reported here are analyses of strictly scored recall in which only words that completed sentences in the No Blank condition were counted correct. As in Experiment I, the lenient scores of the Blank group averaged 1% higher than the strict scores.

The Blank group (73.8%) performed significantly better than the No Blank group (61.7%), ($F = 10.60, df = 1/44, p < .01$). Treatment entered into two significant interactions. The first was Treatment × Test Sequence ($F = 4.80, df = 1/44, p < .05$) which appeared because the Blank group showed a greater overall advantage over the No Blank group when the backward test was given first than when the forward test was given first. The Treatment × Type of Test × Test Order interaction was significant ($F = 4.96, df = 1/44, p < .05$). As can be seen in Table 1, the Blank group had the greatest relative advantage on the backward test when it was given first but on the forward test when it was given second.

Table 1.   Mean percentage of recall in Experiment II

Group	First test		Second test	
	Forward	Backward	Forward	Backward
Blank	70.8	68.7	82.2	73.6
No Blank	64.7	47.6	62.9	71.7

Performance was higher on the forward test (70.2%) than on the backward test (65.4%), ($F = 50.80, df = 1/44, p < .01$) and on the second test (72.6%) following a list rather than the first (63.0%), ($F = 203.83, df = 1/44, p < .01$). Otherwise, the only significant terms were List (*not* List Order, which was not significant itself and did not enter into any significant interactions), List × Test Sequence, and List × Type of Test. These effects will not be discussed since they are of no interest.

Discussion

The purpose of the present research was to show that a procedure that forces meaningful processing of sentences facilitates learning. In both experiments people who filled blanks as they read learned more than people who read whole sentences. The explanation for this result is that to fill a blank requires semantic encoding of the other words in a sentence whereas a person can "read"—that is, render into speech—a complete sentence without semantic encoding.

A possible alternative explanation is that there was greater similarity between the conditions of learning and testing under the Blank than under the No Blank condition. Therefore, the advantage for the blank condition might be explained as an uninteresting transfer effect. The second experiment ruled out this explanation. The Blank group performed better than the No Blank group on a backward association test as well as the usual forward association test. The stimulus terms in the backward association test were the last words in the sentences, which the Blank group had not even seen during the study trial. Thus, the facilitation from reading sentences containing blanks cannot be attributed to transfer.

People learn pairs of words more quickly if they are required to generate sentences linking the pairs rather then to read sentences that others have prepared (cf. Bobrow & Bower, 1969). This could be interpreted to mean that as they generate sentences people select or create mediators that have idiosyncratically high associative strength. However, the fact that reading incomplete sentences enhanced learning in the present studies cannot be interpreted in terms of idiosyncratic associative strength (idiosyncratic vividness, idiosyncratic elaboration, etc.) because everyone completed the sentences in the same way. The implication is that the important aspect of constructing a sentence is not so much the personalized sentence that results as it is the process of giving meaningful representation to the words. The further implication is that people can learn as readily from sentences written by others as they can from ones they have had a part in constructing, provided techniques can be found to get them to process the sentences fully.

A sentence missing a word highly determined by the rest of the sentence bears a strong resemblance to a frame from a self-instructional program. In the light of the results of the present research, it is surprising, therefore, that many studies have found that students who write answers to frames in a program learn no more than students who "think" the answers or read the frames with the blanks filled in (e.g., Alter & Silverman, 1962; Stolurow & Walker, 1962; Tobias & Weiner, 1963). However, Kemp and Holland (1966) were able to show that the requirement to write answers is facilitative if, and only if, correct answers are contingent upon the material in the program. They developed a measure of this contingency called the "blackout ratio," which is the percentage of words in a program that can be lined through with a black crayon without increasing the frequency of errors. Kemp and Holland (1966) computed blackout ratios for 12 programs. The requirement to make written responses facilitated learning from the four programs with the lowest blackout ratios but made no difference with the remaining eight programs.

Previous discussions have stressed that correct responding in a verbal self-instructional program should require "careful reading" (Holland & Kemp, 1968, p. 92) and "attention" to the critical material (Anderson, Faust, & Roderick, 1968). The present research gives additional perspective: Carefulness and attention probably are not enough; it seems likely that if the requirement to fill blanks in a program is to be beneficial, a correct response must be contingent upon *understanding* the critical material.

REFERENCES

Alter, M., & Silverman, R. E. The response in programed instruction. *Journal of Programed Instruction,* 1962, *1,* 55-78.

Anderson, R. C. Control of student mediating processes during verbal learning and instruction. *Review of Educational Research,* 1970, *40,* 349-369.

Anderson, R. C. Faust, G. W., & Roderick, M. C. "Overprompting" in programmed instruction. *Journal of Educational Psychology,* 1968, *59,* 88-93.

Anderson, R. C., Royer, J. M., Kulhavy, R. W., Thornburg, S. D., & Klemt, L. L. Thematic prompting in paired-associate learning. *Journal of Educational Psychology,* 1971, *62,* 315-321.

Baddeley, A. D. Semantic and acoustic similarity in short-term memory. *Nature,* 1964, *204,* 1116-1117.

Baddeley, A. D. The influence of acoustic and semantic similarity on long-term memory for word sequences. *Quarterly Journal of Experimental Psychology,* 1966, *18,* 302-309.

Baddeley, A. D., & Dale, H. C. A. The effect of semantic similarity on retroactive interference in long- and short-term memory. *Journal of Verbal Learning and Verbal Behavior,* 1965, *5,* 417-420.

Bobrow, S. A., & Bower, G. H. Comprehension and recall of sentences. *Journal of Experimental Psychology,* 1969, *80,* 455-461.

Bower, G. H. Mental imagery and associative learning. In L. Gregg (Ed.), *Cognition in learning and memory.* New York: Wiley, 1972.

Holland, J. G., & Kemp, F. D. A measure of programing in teaching-machine material. *Journal of Educational Psychology,* 1965, *56,* 264-269.

Kemp, F. D., & Holland, J. G. Blackout ratio and overt responses in programed instruction: Resolution of disparate results. *Journal of Educational Psychology,* 1966, *57,* 109-114.

Paivio, A. Mental imagery in associative learning and memory. *Psychological Review,* 1969, *76,* 241-263.

Stolurow, L. M., & Walker, C. C. A comparison of overt and covert response in programmed learning. *Journal of Educational Research,* 1962, *55,* 421-429.

Tobias, S., & Weiner, M. Effect of response mode on immediate and delayed recall from programed materials. *Journal of Programed Instruction,* 1963, *2,* 9-13.

Wickelgren, W. A. Acoustic similarity and retroactive interference in short-term memory. *Journal of Verbal Learning and Verbal Behavior,* 1965, *70,* 102-108.

Wickelgren, W. A. Phonetic similarity and interference in short-term memory for single letters. *Journal of Experimental Psychology,* 1966, *71,* 396-404.

Concretization and Sentence Learning*

RICHARD C. ANDERSON[1]
University of Illinois

A striking fact is that the information embodied in concrete words is two or three times easier to learn than the information conveyed by abstract words (Paivio, 1969). Indeed, concreteness-abstractness, or "image evoking value," is the most potent determiner of the learnability of words that has yet been studied. The practical implications of this knowledge are not readily apparent, however. The teacher whose task is teaching about zebras can be encouraged to believe that his/her students will easily learn because "zebra" is a concrete term of high image-evoking value. But suppose he/she has the more difficult job of, for instance, teaching about regulations? What technique will increase the learnability of information to be acquired in connection with abstract terms such as "regulations?"

A plausible answer is to try to increase the concreteness of the abstract term by modifying it with concrete words. Consider this sentence:

The regulations annoyed the salesman.

Would it be learned more readily if modified as follows?

The strict parking regulations annoyed the salesman.

Answering the general form of this question was the main purpose of the experiments reported in this article.

Previous research on concretization has had mixed results. On the positive side, Yuille and Paivio (1969) and Montague and Carter (1973) have reported that vivid, concrete language facilitates learning from connected discourse. The present studies differed from these in one important respect: In the previous research, the concrete words with which the text was augmented became part of the to-be-recalled material, whereas in the experiments described in this report, the response was the

*Reprinted from *Journal of Educational Psychology, 66,* 2, 1974, 179-183. Copyright 1974 by the American Psychological Association. Reprinted by permission.

[1] The author gratefully acknowledges the assistance of Valerie Koester, Claire Lieberman, Debra Sweet, Steven Sweet, and Peter Zych.

same whether or not a concrete modifier was included. In other words, the present research aimed to show an indirect effect instead of a direct one.

On the negative side, Levin (1972) found that children learned somewhat fewer concretely modified nouns (e.g., spotted turtle) than unmodified nouns (e.g., turtle). However, Levin's experiments differed in many respects from the present ones. In the first place, his nouns were already denotatively specific; that is, they were specific enough so that the referent of each word could be pictured in a line drawing. No more than one or two of the (subject) nouns employed in the present studies could be represented unambiguously in pictures. In the second place, Levin employed the technique of free recall. Concreteness-abstractness does affect free recall, but the strongest effects are obtained when the concrete element serves as the cue in a cued-recall task, which was the arrangement in the studies reported herein. Furthermore, because free recall was required, subjects in Levin's study who received the concretized list had twice as many words to recall. This fact could explain his negative result.

A subsidiary purpose of Experiment 1 was to investigate the effects of variations in recall instructions. Recent research has indicated that people frequently substitute semantically related words for the verbatim language of the sentences they are trying to recall (Anderson, 1974). The question is whether recall instructions given *after* the sentences have been presented alter the frequency of substitutions. If the probability of a semantically related substitute word were to go down following verbatim recall instructions and go up following substance instructions, this would imply that some sentences or sentence constituents are coded in memory in both surface and semantic form. No difference in proportion of semantically related substitutions as a function of recall instructions would imply that there is a single memorial code for each verbal element.

Experiment 1

Method

Subjects. Involved in the experiment were 47 undergraduates, mostly women, for whom participation was a requirement in an introductory educational psychology course. Subjects were randomly assigned to conditions when they appeared for the experiment.

Materials. Sixteen simple declarative sentences in the past tense were constructed. Each had a concrete object noun and a general term for a subject noun. For each sentence, one- to three-word modifiers were prepared which were judged to have the effect of making the subject noun phrase more denotatively specific, that is, more concrete. Some examples of this were as follows:

The (ivory chess) set fell off the table.
The (huge earth-moving) vehicle missed the dog.
The (remote television) control pinched his hand.

Design. The two factors in the experiment were (*a*) type of sentence and retrieval cue and (*b*) type of recall instructions. One third of the subjects received both elaborated sentences and elaborated cues, one third received elaborated sentences but unelaborated cues, and the remaining third received both unelaborated sentences and unelaborated cues. "Elaborated" sentences and cues included the words modifying the subject, noun, whereas "unelaborated" sentences and cues did not. Within each of the groups described thus far, half of the subjects received verbatim recall instructions and half received substance recall instructions. Verbatim instructions stressed literal reproduction of the sentences, whereas substance instructions indicated an answer would be counted correct if it contained the idea, or gist, of the sentence, whether or not identical words were used.

Procedure. Subjects were run individually in a small, sound-deadened cubicle. Learning instructions mentioned that a test was to follow but gave no details. The sentences, which were typed on 5 × 8 inch white unlined file cards, were presented at an eight-second rate paced by beeps from a tape recorder. Prior to each presentation, the cards were shuffled. After one exposure of the sentences, the subject solved addition, subtraction, and multiplication problems for 48 seconds to prevent recall from short-term and, probably, nonsemantic memory. Next came the recall instructions, either verbatim or substance. Finally, the test was presented. The subject noun or the subject noun phrase from each sentence served as the retrieval cue. The cues were typed on 4 × 6 inch white unlined file cards, which were shuffled before each use. The test was subject paced. The subject was instructed to give orally the entire sentence if possible but was also encouraged to give fragments when the rest of the sentence could not be remembered.

Scoring. The recall protocols were scored for numbers of verbs and objects recalled verbatim, discounting changes in number, tense, determiners, and auxiliaries. Also scored were the numbers of semantically related words substituted in place of the verbs and objects in the original sentences. A word was counted as semantically related if it was a synonym, close superordinate, close cohyponym, or hyponym of the word it replaced. These categories have been defined and illustrated elsewhere (Anderson, 1972, 1974). Several people scored the protocols. Disagreements were resolved in conference. Previous research has shown very high interrater agreement with respect to whether a word is semantically related or unrelated (Anderson, 1974).

Results

Table 1 contains mean proportions of verbatim, semantically related and total words recalled under the various conditions that prevailed in the experiment. The data were analyzed in a 3 × 2 (Type of Sentence-Cue Combination × Type of Recall Instruction) unweighted means analysis of variance. (Unweighted means were used because one cell was missing a case.) Type of sentence-cue combination had a significant effect when the dependent variable was number of words recalled verbatim ($F = 7.17$, $df = 2/41$, $p = .002$), number of semantically related substitutes recalled ($F = 9.76$, $df = 2/41$, $p = .000$), and total number of words recalled ($F = 12.40$, $df = 2/41$, $p = .000$). Neither type of recall instructions nor the Type of Recall × Sentence-Cue Combination interaction was significant in any analysis. An analysis in which the dependent variable was the arcsin transform of proportion of semantically related to total words recalled revealed no significant effects.

Newman-Keuls tests showed that the elaborated-sentence—elaborated-cue condition was significantly ($\alpha = .05$) better on all three measures than the elaborated-sentence-unelaborated-cue condition and significantly better on the semantically related words and total words measures than the unelaborated-sentence—unelaborated-cue condition. The elaborated-sentence—unelaborated-cue and unelaborated-sentence—elaborated-cue conditions did not differ significantly on any measure. The detail of the data was generally consistent with the overall results. For instance, there were more total words recalled under the elaborated-sentence—elaborated-cue condition than under the unelaborated-sentence—unelaborated-cue condition for 15 out of the 16 sentences.

Table 1. Mean proportions of words recalled

Sentence cue	Words		
	Verbatim	Semantically related	Total
Elaborated-elaborated	.48	.21	.69
Elaborated-unelaborated	.26	.08	.34
Unelaborated-unelaborated	.38	.08	.46

Note. The total possible score was 32.

Of the 187 responses scored as semantically related substitutes for verbs or objects in the original sentences, 56% were scored as synonyms, 17% as superordinates, 15% as cohyponyms, and 12% as hyponyms.

Discussion

Experiment 1 gave rather clear evidence that concrete modifiers facilitate the learning of sentences whose subject nouns are general terms. Thus, the results were consistent with the original notions about concreteness and image-evoking value. But there is at least one other explanation of the data. Maybe *any* subject noun modifier would facilitate learning, perhaps by increasing orthographic or phonological distinctiveness. The purpose of Experiment 2 was to determine whether the functional attribute of the modifier was its effect on the denotative specificity of the subject noun phrase.

Subjects presented with elaborated sentences did poorly when they received unelaborated cues. Apparently, a vague cue was inadequate for the person to retrieve the representation which had been stored when the sentence was learned. Probably what happened was that the person tended to give a different interpretation to the general term alone than when it was concretely modified. This was unfortunate from a practical perspective for, to stretch a point beyond the data, the implication was that the concrete case employed to illuminate a generalization has to be reinstated if a person is to have access to his memory for that generalization.

It is quite interesting that people who received verbatim and substance recall instructions performed similarly on all measures including, especially, the proportion of semantically related to total words recalled ($F < 1.0$). This must mean that people do *not* have both a coding for the literal surface form of a sentence and a coding for its meaning. Otherwise, they would edit their production when given verbatim recall instructions so as to conform more closely to the original, whereas in all likelihood they would edit their output away from the original when given substance recall instructions so as to employ wording that seemed apt and tasteful. The data are consistent with the view that every sentence (which is learned at all) is represented in memory in semantic form, though this theory is somewhat strained to explain why such a high proportion of words are recalled verbatim (see also Anderson, 1974). In this view, it has to be assumed that verbatim words appear in recall only when a person just happens to select the same lexical items when decoding the semantic representation into language. Another view consistent with the data is that some sentences or sentence constituents are coded literally, whereas the rest are coded semantically.

Experiment 2

Method

Subjects. The subjects were 28 undergraduates, mostly women, who participated to fulfill a requirement in an introductory educational psychology course.

Materials. Sixteen pairs of sentences were constructed. Within each pair, the sentences were identical except for one to three words which modified the subject noun. One of the sentences contained a concrete modifier of the same type employed in Experiment 1. The other entailed a redundant modifier, so called because it was judged to have little or no impact on the denotative specificity of the subject noun phrase. Consider the sentence,

The official regulations annoyed the salesman.

Most regulations are official. The class of official regulations is not much narrower than the class of all regulations. Other illustrations are as follows:

The oil-pressure gauge was covered with dust *versus* The measuring gauge was covered with dust.

The obscene exclamation embarrassed the nun *versus* The excited exclamation embarrassed the nun.

The sports periodical provided the information *versus* The regular periodical provided the information.

Design. The two factors in this experiment were (a) sentence list and (b) type of modifier. The same sentences, except for the modifiers, appeared in each list. Half of the sentences within each list contained concrete modifiers, half contained redundant modifiers. If a sentence included a concrete modifier in the first list, the parallel sentence in the second list included a redundant modifier. In other words, with respect to the factor of principal interest—type of modifier—this was a within-subjects, or mixed-list, design.

Procedure. Subjects were run individually in a small, sound-deadened cubicle. The sentences, which were typed on 5×8 inch white unlined file cards and randomized by shuffling before each use, were presented at an eight-second rate paced by beeps from a tape recorder. After one exposure to one of the two lists of sentences, the subject solved addition, subtraction, and multiplication problems for 48 seconds to prevent recall from short-term memory. Finally, the subject received the test. On each page of a 2¾ × 8½ inch answer booklet was mimeographed the subject noun phrase (always the entire phrase) of one of the sentences. The subject was instructed to write the rest of the sentence, all of it if possible, but any word or phrase he could recall if the whole sentence could not be remembered. Everyone received substance recall instructions. To reduce the likelihood of systematic position or sequence effects, the test booklets were collated in four different random orders and were assigned to subjects about equally often at random. The test was subject paced.

Scoring. The protocols were scored the same way as in Experiment 1.

Results

In Table 2 appear the mean proportions of words recalled. Analyses of variance showed that type of modifier had a significant effect on number of words recalled verbatim ($F = 15.81$, $df = 1/26$, $p = .001$), number of semantically related substitute words ($F = 14.36$, $df = 1/26$, $p = .001$), and total words recalled ($F = 27.87$, $df = 1/26$, $p = .000$).

Table 2.   Mean proportions of words recalled

	Words		
Modifier	Verbatim	Semantically related	Total
Concrete	.34	.21	.55
Redundant	.22	.11	.33

Note. The total possible score was 16.

List was nowhere a main effect (all *F*s < 1.0), but in every analysis except the one involving total words, the List × Type of Modifier interaction was significant. These interactions occurred simply because the substitution of semantically related words was more likely in one list than in the other. Previous work has suggested that the probability of substitution is a function of the aptness of the wording of the original sentences and the availability of semantically equivalent alternative wordings (Anderson, 1974). Apparently the two lists differed in these or other relevant respects.

Concrete modifiers led to better performance than redundant modifiers in 12 of the 16 sentences. There was little difference with the remaining 4 sentences. Of the 144 semantically related substitute words, 44% were scored as synonyms, 26% as superordinates, 17% as hyponyms, and 14% as cohyponyms.

General Discussion

The data show that concrete modifiers strongly facilitate the learning of sentences. The general educational implication for the teacher, author, and curriculum developer is to be as specific and concrete as possible. The results were positive enough to encourage research on other, more elaborate concretization techniques such as the use of metaphor, analogy, and physical models to represent systems of abstract concepts.

There was facilitation only when the entire, concretely modified subject-noun phrase served as the retrieval cue but not when the subject noun alone was the cue. Under the latter condition, it is quite likely that the subject noun was encoded differently at the time of original exposure and at the time of testing (cf. Martin, 1968; Wicker, 1970). It was clearly shown in Experiment 2 that the effective variable was concretization and not merely the presence of modifying words. Bower (1972) has mentioned, in passing, an unpublished experiment which also found no facilitation from redundant words on the stimulus side in a paired-associate task.

Throughout this paper the terms *concrete, specific,* and *vivid* have been used interchangeably. It should be noted that there is some indication that concreteness-abstractness and specificity-generality may be separate, though of course correlated, dimensions (Paivio, 1971, p. 83). Possibly vividness is also a distinct factor, though it appears to affect learning in the same way as concreteness/specificity. Kirchner (1969) inserted "vivid" or "dull" adjectives into appropriate and identical slots in a narrative. She found that people who heard the vivid narrative recalled more nouns than those who heard the dull narrative but, surprisingly, there was no difference in the recall of the adjectives themselves.

REFERENCES

Anderson, R. C. Semantic organization and retrieval of information from sentences. *Journal of Verbal Learning and Verbal Behavior,* 1972, **11,** 794-800.

Anderson, R. C. Substance recall of sentences. *Quarterly Journal of Experimental Psychology,* 1974, *26,* 530-541.

Bower, G. H. Mental imagery and associative learning. In L. Gregg (Ed.), *Cognition in learning and memory.* New York: Wiley, 1972.

Kirchner, E. P. Vividness of adjectives and the recall of meaningful verbal material. *Psychonomic Science,* 1969, **15,** 71-72.

Levin, J. R. *Verbal and visual processes in children's learning: IV. An attempt to reduce picture-word differences in free recall learning through concretization.* (Working paper 106) Madison: University of Wisconsin, Wisconsin Research and Development Center in Cognitive Learning, November 1972.

Martin, E. Stimulus meaningfulness and paired-associate transfer. *Psychological Review,* 1968, **75,** 421-441.

Montague, W. E., & Carter, J. F. Vividness of imagery in recalling connected discourse. *Journal of Educational Psychology,* 1973, **64,** 72-75.

Paivio, A. Mental imagery in associative learning and memory. *Psychological Review,* 1969, **76,** 241-263.

Paivio, A. *Imagery and verbal processes.* New York: Holt, Rinehart & Winston, 1971.

Wicker, F. W. On the locus of picture-word differences in paired associate learning. *Journal of Verbal Learning and Verbal Behavior,* 1970, **9,** 52-57.

Yuille, J. C., & Paivio, A. Abstractness and the recall of connected discourse. *Journal of Educational Psychology,* 1969, **82,** 467-471.

Developmental Models

Basic Assumptions Underlying
the Substrata-Factor Theory*

JACK A. HOLMES
University of California at Berkeley

Introduction

After reviewing over 500 experimental studies, the writer, in 1947, gar-
nered a list of some 80 variables, each of which had some scientific basis
for being *a*) "the" cause, or *b*) one of the causes of success or failure in
reading. As early as 1942, Lazar had objected to the single cause
hypothesis, but she lamented that from the many lists compiled by the
various writers in the field of reading there was no method for successfully
isolating the most significant causal variables from the combination of
many.

　　Armed with factor analytic techniques, the writer addressed himself
to the problem of isolating the most significant causal variables for reading success from his list of 80. However, he soon ran into trouble, not only
because of the many mathematical and methodological difficulties which
plagued the factor analyst at that time, but especially because, as a former
physiologist, he could not make some of the basic assumptions agree with
what he knew or surmised about the neurological dynamics of the brain.
In short, the crux of these difficulties arose because of the several ways in
which factor analysts chose to interpret, or refused to interpret, the cause
and effect relationship underlying a coefficient of correlation.

　　Historical background. Spearman (1904), reasoning from his criterion
of proportionality and tetrad difference ratios, reduced the important
part of the mind to such a highly structured organ of *equipotential cognitive
energy, g,* that it was hypothesized to function with an undifferentiated

*Reprinted from *Reading Research Quarterly, 1,* 1, Fall 1965, 5-27. This paper draws heavily
upon an address delivered by the writer before a joint meeting of the IRA and AERA in
Philadelphia, May, 1964.

mass-action.[1] This interpretation was in line with the later teachings of Karl Lashley (1929) and his experimental findings on the ability of rats, after cortical ablations, to relearn mazes up to habit perfection. True, Spearman conceded that a test could contain a small and inconsequential specific factor, s, but when such a factor appeared by virtue of a particular test, he maintained the test was inappropriate, was not tapping cognitive ability, and should be deleted from the battery. Of course, one wonders, if g represents general cognitive energy, then would Spearman postulate as many different specific *energies* as he found specific factors?

As illustrated in Figure 1, Spearman explained the correlation between tests as arising from the amount of cognitive energy which each drew from the larger general factor g, which he called general intelligence.

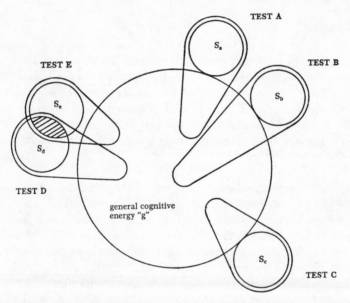

Figure 1.   The correlation between tests as explained by Spearman, arose from the supposed fact that a certain amount of general intelligence, "g", was embedded in each test. After Guilford (1936, p. 463). Note that tests E and D share a "group factor" as well as "g."

Thomson (1919) rejected Spearman's model and proposed one of his own based upon his *sampling theory*. He conceived of the mind as made up

---

[1] Of course, Spearman (1904, Ch. 13) admitted to "group factors," but except for possibly logical, mechanical, psychological, arithmetical abilities and musical appreciation, he declared them to be "astonishingly rare" and acquired (1927, p. 241, 242).

of a very large number of completely independent elements or bonds. Each of these elements, like spot-patterns on dice, was additive on an "all or none" principle (Thomson, 1919, pp. 341-44). As illustrated in *Figure 2,* Thomson made the assumption that when two tests correlated it was because they held a finite number of these independent elements in common. His strict adherence to the independence of each associational bond is indicated by the fact that he specifically defined correlation as the number of independent elements held in common, e_{12}, by two abilities, divided by the square root of the product of *all* the elements, e_1 and e_2, in each of the separate activities. The equation (Thomson, 1919, p. 342) took the form:

$$r_{12} = \frac{\text{Common e's}}{\sqrt{e_1 \times e_2}}$$

This elegantly simple assumption of Thomson's model may be visualized as follows:

Tests	Independent Elements of the Mind a b c d e f g h i j k l m . . .
1	a b c d e f
2	d e f g h i
3	f g h l
4	i j k

Tests	Correlations			
	1	*2*	*3*	*4*
1	—	$\dfrac{3}{\sqrt{6 \times 6}}$	$\dfrac{1}{\sqrt{6 \times 4}}$	$\dfrac{0}{\sqrt{6 \times 3}}$
2	.50	—	$\dfrac{4}{\sqrt{6 \times 4}}$	$\dfrac{1}{\sqrt{6 \times 3}}$
3	.20	.82	—	$\dfrac{1}{\sqrt{4 \times 3}}$
4	.00	.24	.29	—

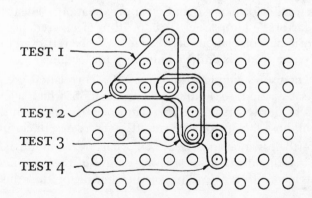

Figure 2.   Thomson explained correlation between tests as arising from the overlapping of independent elements. After Guilford (1936, p. 463).

In short, Thomson (1939, p. 304, 306) denied that the mind had any structure whatsoever; that is, he assumed that there were no fixed or strong linkages between the elements. For him, the mind was an unstructured continuum. Notwithstanding his basic tenet, however, Thomson was forced to concede that education might possibly impose some structure upon the mind by the time a person was an adult. In summary: Spearman considered tests with large loadings on specific factors as nuisance variables, but Thomson felt that any structure education might bestow upon the mind was also a nuisance variable.

As simple as Thomson's model appears, it will be quickly realized that neither he nor anyone else could ever know either the number of independent elements (assuming that such exist) in any one test or the number that might be held in common by two or more tests; hence, its elegance cannot be taken as proof.

Thurstone (1932, 1935) was soon able to show that Spearman's g was only the outcome of a special case of his own model which he called *centroid* factor analysis.[2] Thurstone postulated a limited number of common factors as well as some specific ones. As indicated in Figure 3, any particular test was expected to draw upon one or more of these common factors plus perhaps a specific factor, s. In direct opposition to Spearman's reasoning which led to the deletion of any test that loaded high on a specific factor, Thurstone suggested that one should not only retain that test, but add more tests assessing the same domain; and now, since these would all load on the "specific" factor, it would by definition become a common factor. Factors were assumed to be mutually orthogonal and were rotated as a reference frame about the test vectors until a plausible psychological interpretation could be given to the factors. The "underlying assumption that each test performance is, in first approximation, a linear function of primary factors," (Thurstone, 1938, p. 72) is given credence by the fact that the original correlations between tests can be retrieved by summing over the cross-products of the common factor loadings.

As Thomson's simple explanation of a correlation gives a certain sense of satisfaction, so Thurstone's explanation, which allows a set of factors to be derived from the correlation matrix and then the correlations from those factors to be retrieved, gives a sense of closure.

Nevertheless, one must ask, "Of what are common factors composed?" If elements, then what is the nature of these elements? When three tests have different loadings on the same factor, does this mean that

---

[2] Thompson (1919, p. 341) also included the "possibility of a General Ability as a special case" of his own theory.

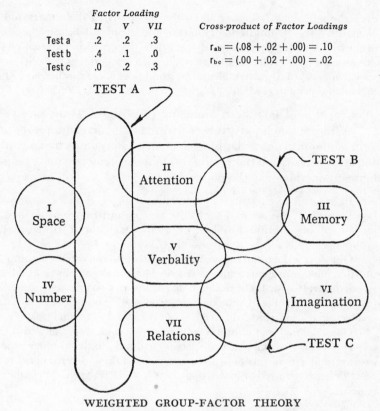

	Factor Loading		
	II	V	VII
Test a	.2	.2	.3
Test b	.4	.1	.0
Test c	.0	.2	.3

Cross-product of Factor Loadings

$$r_{ab} = (.08 + .02 + .00) = .10$$
$$r_{bc} = (.00 + .02 + .00) = .02$$

WEIGHTED GROUP-FACTOR THEORY

Figure 3.   Thurstone's explanation of correlation. After Guilford (1936, p. 463).

the test with the greatest loading simply has more of the identical elements in it than are present in the structures of the other two? Or, is each factor made up of a finite number of elements which are uncorrelated; i.e., is each element unique and independent of all other elements in the same or other factors? Thurstone (1935) does not answer these questions, but devotes some space to the discussion of the problem. Although he conceded that the search for such elements is genetically oriented, he evidently thought it more useful to deal in larger categories. He writes that while the search for:

> . . . unitary elements may be acknowledged to be a worthy objective, it must not be assumed that the larger and cruder categories will then vanish in significance. It is still useful to speak of a man's arms and legs

even though much is known about the hierarchy of their parts and elements. Even if hundreds of unitary and elemental factors should eventually be discovered to be primary determiners of intellectual endowment, it might still be useful to retain such categories as verbality or visual imagery if they demonstrably simplify our comprehension of mental endowment (1935, p. 212).

As a matter of fact, both Hotelling (1933) and Thurstone (1935, 1938, 1947) were much too astute to assume that correlation is merely a measure of identical or overlapping elements. Thurstone's first postulate, in contradistinction with the notion of identical elements, makes a point further examined later in the paper. He says:

> In factorial investigations of mentality, we proceed on the assumption that mind is structured somehow, that mind is not a patternless mosaic of an infinite number of elements without functional groupings . . . .
>
> Our work in factorial study of the human mind rests on the assumption that mind represents a *dynamic system* which can eventually be understood in terms of a finite number of parameters. We have assumed further that all these parameters, or groups of parameters, are not involved in the individual differences of every kind of mental task.
>
> Observational and educational experience lend plausibility to the conception that mental abilities [such as reading] are determined by a great multiplicity of causes or determiners, and these determiners are more or less structured or linked in groups . . . . (1947, pp. 57-58; [italics added]).

Definitions: Correlation and causal relationships. In keeping with Thurstone's above statement, but in direct contrast with Thomson's notion of the overlapping of identical elements, the Pearson product moment coefficient of correlation between two variables is mathematically defined in the *International Dictionary of Applied Mathematics* (1960, p. 181) as the covariance of the cross-products divided by the square root of the product of their separate variances according to the formula:

$$p = \frac{\text{Cov. (xy)}}{\sqrt{(\text{Var. x})\,(\text{Var. y})}}$$

This definition makes no assumptions about the need for overlapping elements, bonds, common factors, or a general reservoir g of cognitive energy. Likewise, James and James (1959, p. 88) define correlation simply as "the interdependence between two sets of numbers; a relation between two sets of quantities, such that when one changes the other does . . . . Hence, correlation under this general definition is mutual."

The reason for referring to the above mathematical definitions is to stress the point that correlations express a *mutual* relationship between variables and nothing need be assumed regarding the nature or mechanism, interplay, or interaction of one variable upon the other.

Although it is the prerogative of each theory builder to make assumptions in accordance with what is known about his field at the time of his activity, one theorist must not be bound by the assumptions of others if science is to progress. Specifically, then, there is nothing inherently sacred in the cause to effect explanations of a coefficient of correlation offered by Spearman, Thomson, Thurstone, the present writer, or anyone else for that matter.

In summary, causal interpretations are imposed on the coefficients of correlation by the basic assumptions which underlie the theoretical model utilizing such correlations. Hammond and Householder put it well:

> . . . The correlation coefficient merely quantifies the degree of association. The correlation coefficient can do no more—assertions of causal connections must rest on other evidence. The reason we must emphasize this point is that most of us jump too quickly to the conclusion that "correlation means causation."
>
> In order to drive this point home, it has become commonplace for instructors to describe situations in which there is a high degree of association but in which it would be absurd to assert a causal connection. One such absurdity often cited is that of the correlation between the number of cases of infant diarrhea per month and the viscosity of the tar roads in southern states. Obviously neither of these phenomena is the cause of the other. *But such illustrations go too far.* To assert a causal relation here would be absurd only because we *already know* what causes diarrhea and what changes the viscosity of the roads. Behavioral scientists, on the other hand, are using the correlation method to explore the unknown.
>
> It is precisely because we do *not* know what kinds of behavior are related to other kinds of behavior that we are investigating the degree of association between two variables in the first place. "What leads to what?" is the very question we wish to answer. And it is for that reason that the behavioral scientist will frequently stumble over the causality question. There is no way of knowing *in advance* that the correlation between two variables may really be due to a third variable which is related to both (as is the case in the example of the roads and diarrhea). This is exactly the kind of thing that has to be discovered.
>
> While it is important to understand that the correlation coefficient merely provides a quantitative measure of the degree of association between two variables, we must also understand that the scientist must interpret the correlation coefficient—he must say what it means. In

doing so, it is inevitable that he will now and then make mistakes. Causation *will* be mistakenly asserted on the basis of correlation. But these mistakes are corrected by further research. True, correlation does not prove causation. On the other hand, nothing ventured, nothing gained (1962, p. 226).

Correlation, Causation, and Assumptions in the Substrata-Factor Theory

In what follows the foregoing distinctions are amplified by discussing the issue in terms of the assumptions which underlie the substrata-factor theory. The topics to be covered are the statistical technique known as a substrata-factor analysis, the basic assumptions underlying the substrata-factor theory, and the psychometric and neurological evidence underlying the assumptions.

The statistical technique known as the substrata-factor analysis. In 1947 Holmes formulated the substrata-factor theory and also made public in his doctoral dissertation (1948) a statistical technique designed to yield a *first approximation* to his statistical model. The technique consists of a derivative analysis achieved through the iterative use of the Wherry-Doolittle multiple correlation test selection method (Garrett, 1947). This technique produces a hierarchy of substrata-factors at successive levels from a large pool of tests (representing varied abilities) that previous research has indicated are related to a criterion. Such a hierarchy is shown in Figure 4.

The analysis begins by selecting, in accordance with the correlations in the matrix, that particular test A which is the *most valid* predictor of the criterion O. Next, the method partials out from the correlation matrix that part of the variance in the criterion thus accounted for, and then systematically analyzes the remaining partial r's for that variable B which will account for the greatest amount of residual variance left in the criterion. Again, that portion of the variance in the criterion O thus explained by the first *and* second selected tests A+B is partialed out, and the remaining variables are searched in order that the test C, making the next greatest contribution to the criterion's variance, can be added to the team of tests already selected at Level I. This process of selecting continues until the F-test indicates at about the one percent level of confidence, that no remaining test in the battery will make a significant contribution to the variance of the criterion *over and above* that already "explained" by the previously selected "preferential predictors."

Level o   Level I   Level II

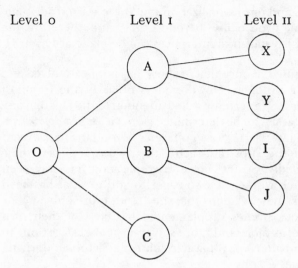

Figure 4.   The substrata-factor model

At Level II substrata sets of variables are selected in the same way, except that now each of the preferential predictor variables at Level I becomes, each in its own right, a subcriterion to be predicted from the variables left in the matrix.

Finally, using Level II predictors as subcriteria, the process is continued so as to produce sets of preferential predictors at Level III (not shown in Figure 4).[3]

Further, the Wherry-Doolittle-Holmes technique, as the substrata analysis is called, yields the *direct* and *joint*[4] contributions which each of the selected variables, now called *substrata-factors,* makes to its immediate criterion.

Basic to the technique is the standard assumption in all multiple correlation solutions; that is, that some *portion* of the variance in the criterion can be "explained" by each of the preferential predictors selected at Level I. However, for two principal reasons, this is where previous multiple correlational analyses halted: *a*) a preconceived notion that correlation had to be explained in terms of identical elements held in

---

[3] If the N is large and the pool of tests sufficiently great, then the substrata analysis may proceed to several levels—at least until the successively more and more fundamental variables in the battery have been exhausted.

[4] In most of these studies, for the sake of ease in reporting, the "joint" variance being shared by two variables is evenly divided by a mathematical identity formula and the equal halves are added to the "direct" contribution made by each of the pair of variables.

common by two tests, and/or *b*) a realization that there was no adequate method of determining probabilities beyond Level I and, therefore, the confidence level at which statistical inferences can be made at Levels II, III, etc., is not certain.

It should be admitted at once that *b*) above has not been solved and still presents a vexing problem. However, this is *one* of the foremost reasons that the writer has repeatedly called attention to the fact that any substrata analysis, so far as can be determined now, yields *first approximations* only. In lieu of a statistical test of significance beyond the first level of analysis, students of the substrata-factor theory have placed their confidence in replicability. So far, however, replication has only been partial because research workers are so eager to add to what has been done and to "discover" new relations that they tend to use only anchor variables from previous studies supplemented by those of their own choosing.[5] At any rate, as more and more substrata analyses are done in the field of reading, a pattern of replicable substrata factors underlying reading should emerge.

Returning to the major problem, *a*) above, the point is stressed that some *portion* of the variance in the criterion can be "explained" by each of the preferential predictors selected at Level I. By virtue of the same type of reasoning, a *portion* of the variance of each of these Level I predictors-turned-subcriterion can be explained in terms of its preferential set of predictors at Level II. Likewise, sets of Level III variables (not shown in Figure 4) can be used to "explain" *portions* of the variance in the Level II subcriteria. On the basis of the above rationale, then, a substrata analysis sequentially *prorates some portion* of the "explained" variance in the criterion, initially allocated to Level I, to the undergirding substrata factors at Levels II, III, etc.

The basic equation used at each level of analysis is as follows:

$$R^2 = \beta_{01}r_{01} + \beta_{02}r_{02} + \beta_{03}r_{03} + \ldots + \beta_{0n}r_{0n}$$

where:

R^2 is the "accounted for" or predicted variance,

β is the beta weight, that is, the partial regression coefficient. For the first variable, β_{01} in its generalized form is $\beta_{01 \cdot 23 \cdots n}$,

r   is the zero-order correlation of the selected variable with the criterion,

βr is equivalent to Wright's (1921) *coefficient of separate determination.*[6]

---

[5] Dr. Frederick B. Davis and the writer are at present engaged in a replication study using the substrata analytic technique and some 400,000 cases from Project TALENT, U.S.A. This study should throw a great deal of light on the decay rate of level of confidence as one goes from Level I to Level V using .01 as P at each level.

[6] See Ezekiel's (1941) proof.

The beta weights are found by solving a set of simultaneous linear equations, the numerical values of which are selected from the "c" row in the Wherry-Doolittle format. Actually, the IBM 7094 digital computer program accomplishes the same end by inverting the correlation matrix of the selected variables and substituting the elements of the matrix in the following general formula:

$$\beta_{ij} = \frac{-r^{ij}}{r^{jj}}$$

where:

β_{ij} is the beta weight for the ith variable for the jth criterion,

r^{ij} is the inverse element of the ith variable for the jth criterion,

r^{jj} is the inverse element of the jth variable for the jth criterion.

When substituted in the above R^2 formula, these beta weights, together with their appropriate zero-order r's, sum up to the raw, or unadjusted multiple correlation, R^2. However, what is really sought is the percent contribution to the variance of the criterion or subcriterion, as the case may be, which each selected variable makes after it has been corrected for any bias due to the fact that it was selected. To accomplish this correction or adjustment each percent contribution is multiplied by $\bar{R}^2/R^2$ when, according to Wherry (1947), the unbiased estimate of R is given by the following formula:

$$\bar{R}^2 = 1 - \left[(1 - R^2) \left(\frac{N - 1}{N - m - 1} \right) \right]$$

where:

$\bar{R}$ is the "shrunken R" or adjusted multiple correlation,

R is the biased estimate of the multiple correlation,

N is the sample size,

m is the number of predictors selected.

As was indicated earlier, the selection of predictors in any set is stopped when the F-test indicates that the null hypothesis ($R_1 - R_2 = 0$) cannot be rejected at the one percent level of confidence. As used here, the F-test enables one to determine whether or not a next-best test, added to the team of tests already selected, makes a statistically significant contribution to the criterion under consideration. McNemar's (1955) formula is used in the present program:

$$F = \frac{R_1^2 - R_2^2/(m_1 - m_2)}{(1 - R_1^2)/(N - m_1 - 1)}$$

where:

R₁ is the multiple correlation based on the selected m₁ variables. (In this program, m₁ is taken as the R computed from the selection of just one more variable and inverting the matrix. Therefore, in each F-test, $m_1 - m_2 = 1$. This modification appears to be the most conservative estimate for a random selection.)

R₂ is the multiple correlation based on m₂ variables, selected from among m₁ variables,

N is sample size,

m₁ is the number of predictors previously selected,

F is the resulting ratio which is determined to be, or not to be, significant by entering a table (stored in the computer) in which n₁ degrees of freedom equals $m_1 - m_2$, and n₂ degrees of freedom equals $N - m_1 - 1$.

Thus, by prorating the values calculated from the R^2 formula the contributions to variance of the criterion made by the selected tests after they have been adjusted for that bias which is inherent in the original test selection method are attained. The adjusted expression takes the following form:

$$\overline{R}^2 = \overline{\beta}_{01}\overline{r}_{01} + \overline{\beta}_{02}\overline{r}_{02} + \overline{\beta}_{03}\overline{r}_{03} + \ldots + \overline{\beta}_{0n}\overline{r}_{0n},$$

and each of these terms is converted into percent contribution to variance of the criterion simply by multiplying through by 100.

It should be understood that the statistical procedure just described is applicable to the selection of the preferential predictors at Level I, and also for the selection of the substrata-factor sets at Levels II and III which underlie the subcriteria in Levels I and II, respectively. But before the technique can be applied, the question, "Is the substrata analysis appropriate?" must be answered in the affirmative.

According to the substrata-factor theory, a substrata analysis is appropriate when, and only when, outside evidence beyond the correlations themselves deems it logical to assume: *a*) that the criterion is complex, *b*) that the "working system" of the processing-skill (measured by the criterion test) can be assumed to be composed of an integral hierarchy of subsystems, and c) that the independent variables have been chosen on the basis of some prior evidence as to their likelihood of having an effect on the criterion. Under these conditions each set of substrata-factors, and each substrata-factor, is *assumed* to reflect in its contribution to the variance of the criterion or subcriteria a partial effect of the integral function of its composite and conjoined constituents. To put it still another way, before the experiment begins, the independent variables must be selected since in the experimenter's judgment they may separately or collectively, somehow directly or indirectly contribute to the individual differences found within a population on the performance of the criterion test.

As an example, suppose through a substrata analysis of a pool of 40 tests only three preferential predictors, A, B, and C, were selected at Level I, and that these three accounted for 40, 20, and 10 percent of the reading criterion, O, respectively. Together these three explain some 70 percent of the variance of the criterion, and the remaining 30 percent is left as an unaccounted for residual. As has been noted in the procedure, the amount of explained variance in the criterion cannot be increased by adding any of the unselected tests in the pool, because there is no remaining test that could account for a statistically significant amount of variance in O at the chosen level of confidence after the variance accounted for by A + B + C had been partialed out. Likewise, a straight multiple correlation using all 39 of the "independent" variables in the pool would not significantly increase the total accounted for variance in the criterion, above that explained by the three preferential predictors. The latter procedure would only spread the total variance accounted for over 39 variables rather than over the three selected ones.

Assuming that a substrata analysis is appropriate for the example followed, the preferential predictor A, as shown in Figure 4, as the subcriterion might be used. A substrata analysis at Level II might precipitate the substrata-factors X and Y to account for 30 and 20 percent, respectively, of the variance of A.

If the above conditions are fulfilled, it would seem reasonable to assume that a substrata analysis would afford an evaluation of the degree of transfer of the effect of a variable or subsystem of variables from a lower to a higher level in the hierarchy. The calculation of what might be called the *partial coefficients of separate determination* will explain how to redistribute the criterion variance accounted for at Level I over the entire working system. Obviously, no matter how many variables may be precipitated at Levels II, III, etc., more of the criterion's variance cannot be accounted for than that which was explained at Level I by A, B, and C, in our example.

The logic of the computation of the partial coefficients of separate determination is straightforward:

Let the following equations represent the state of affairs shown in the first sequence in Figure 4.

$$\bar{R}^2_{0(ABC)} = \bar{\beta}_{0A \cdot BC}\bar{r}_{0A} + \bar{\beta}_{0B \cdot AC}\bar{r}_{0B} + \bar{\beta}_{0C \cdot AB}\bar{r}_{0C}$$
$$(70\%) = (40\%) + (20\%) + (10\%)$$

and

$$\bar{R}^2_{A(XY)} = \bar{\beta}_{AX \cdot Y}\bar{r}_{AX} + \bar{\beta}_{AY \cdot X}\bar{r}_{AY}$$
$$(50\%) = (30\%) + (20\%)$$

From Level I the preferential predictor A "explains" as a *coefficient of separate determination* 40 percent of the variance of the major criterion O, and, from Level II, the substrata-factor X "explains" 30 percent of A. Now that portion of A prorated to X *can be* thought of as the amount which X contributes to O through A. The prorating process for calculating the *partial* coefficient of separate determination then merely requires that, in this case, 30 percent of 40 percent be taken to learn that X exercises some control over 12 percent of the variance of O. Likewise, Y accounts for 8 percent (.20 × .40) of O. Together then, X and Y "explain" 20 percent (.12 + .08) of the criterion O, and A is left explaining A − (X + Y) or 20 percent (.40 − .12 − .08) of the variance of O.

As straightforward as the above explanation seems to be, the rationale for sequentially prorating variance from Level I to subsequent levels has been questioned. The crux of the criticism is that since there is to date no way of knowing that the variance being accounted for in A by X and Y contains the identical elements which A holds in common with the criterion O, it cannot be said for sure that X and Y are really contributing to the explanation of the variance of O through A. To this criticism the author replies that *if* the substrata-factor theory rested upon the Thomson (1919) assumption of "isolated and independent elements" the theory would be in trouble, but fortunately, it is not dependent upon such an explanation of correlation. The author, as did Thurstone many years ago, categorically rejects the Thomson model and its assumption as both statistically outmoded and untenable in the light of modern neurology.

Basic postulates. The logic of a substrata analysis and the sequential prorating of the variance accounted for at the first level to the entire working system rests on two basic postulates.

The *first*, and perhaps most fundamental, assumption of the substrata-factor theory is that a substrata-factor, or any ability for that matter, is composed of an organized system of subsystems. Each subsystem is a composite of yet smaller and smaller systems; in fact, it is hypothesized that the very micro-systems constitute tiny engram-assemblies of the cortical cells themselves. That is, coded bits of information must be stored in the cells, but it is the way in which these cells are organized that gives internal meaningfulness to isolated bits of information. Within the limits of the genetic endowment of the brain of each individual, environmental experiences (internal as well as external) determine what bits of information will be encoded and how they will be organized. Therefore, to some extent, reorganization is always possible.

The total cognitive-conative complex of the brain is thought of as constituting a cosmos of ability-subsystems which, under the guidance of an individual's long-term value system, immediate purposes, and requirements of the task at hand, become dynamically mobilized into a working system.

Each of the substrata-factors within the total working system contains a rich nexus of meaningful associations, and the nature of the special type of information assembled bestows a certain functional integrity on the system. Logical relations, timing, and sequence are important in forming the psychological structure of a system. More fundamental physical and chemical considerations come into play in determining the potential of the genetic nature of the brain itself. But it is important to understand that even at this level the substrata-factor theory posits a mutual and reciprocal relationship between the psycho-educational and neuro-physiological components of the mind-brain contraplex.

The *second* assumption of the substrata-factor theory is that a correlation, to have psycho-educational meaning, must reflect the mean mutual interaction of two sets of test scores which, in turn, represents the dynamic interplay of two working systems, a system with one of its subsystems, or between two subsystems. In the substrata-factor model, variance, σ^2, is an expression which indicates how people differ in an assessed ability, and correlation simply reflects the interdependence of two such cortical systems. It is an expression of a mutual and reciprocal relationship that does not need to be equal in both directions. The concept which the model introduces or calls attention to in psychometrics is this: When a standardized test is designed to assess varying degrees of excellence in an ability, its items are generally selected in such a way as to represent, as far as possible, a total but limited domain of finite dimensions. Therefore, a test score cannot be used legitimately to represent different clusters of independent elements within an ability. Large or small, a test score must remain an integral function of the conjoined constituents producing that score.

Evidently both of the above assumptions are consonant with the mathematical definitions of correlation given earlier in this paper. Variance is an expression reflecting how people differ in the output of some working system, and, if correlation means anything, it must be taken as the average mutual impact which two systems have on each other. One can give examples of correlations which are meaningless, but which are without meaning precisely because the variables co-vary without having any real impact on each other. (See example quoted earlier.)

Explaining the variance of one system in terms of another in accordance with the X on Y and Y on X regression equations may well indicate the relative support which each draws from the other if, and only if, the mutual and reciprocal cause and effect relations can be justified on other grounds. The substrata-factor theory justifies these two basic assumptions not only on the above mathematical, psychometric, and psycho-educational reasoning, but, even more fundamentally, on the neurological evidence as well (Holmes, 1954, 1957, 1958, 1960; Holmes and Singer, 1961, 1965; Holmes and Hyman, 1957; Davis, 1963).

Neurological evidence. The mind here is defined as the sum of the psycho-neurological processes of the brain, which, of course, reflect the quantity and quality of the inherent and logical structure of the information that has been imposed on the basic cell engrams of the brain. Therefore, it is the *structural* relationships of the various complex ability-systems that command our attention in the Theory. The neurological foundation for this point of view is well stated by Kety:

> . . . the brain, more than anything else in the universe perhaps, is far greater than the sum of its parts. Most of its special function stems not *only* from its component cells and cell masses but from the connections and interrelationships among them. [i.e.,] . . . its magnificent organization (1961, p. 100).

But one may ask, "What gets organized, and how?" As indicated in the first assumption, the substrata-factor theory visualizes a test score as representing a sample of the functional processes from *a*) the interaction of systems built up from tightly associated subsystems of cell-assemblies containing *different* but highly related bits of information, plus *b*) the supporting interactions from other subsumed systems organized in similar ways. Each ability-system, or substrata-factor, functions as a dynamic and integral set of subsets of organized associations. The organization of the total, and the subfunctions it subsumes, reflect the cultural pattern of instruction and the internal influence of mediation in reflection.[7] That is, the "mobilizing-values of the mind" (Holmes, 1960; Athey, 1965) may do much to influence the organization of information, and, to some extent, the mind determines its own mental structure. Upon what neurological evidence is this differentiation of mental structure assumed?

Ranson says:

> The cerebral cortex does not have a uniform structure throughout all parts of the hemisphere. Due to the work of Campbell (1915), Brodmann (1909), and von Economo (1929), we have learned to recognize many different cortical areas, each of which has its individual characteristics. These areas differ from one another in the thickness and composition of the cellular layers, in the thickness of the cortex as a whole, in the number of afferent and efferent fibers, and in the number, distinctness, and position of the white striae. The existence and general boundaries of these areas are well established; and, as a result of experimental and pathological research, it is known that specific differences in *function are* correlated with these differences in structure (1943, p. 295).

The greater the complexity of the ability called upon (Power in Reading), the greater the number of such functional cortical-areas that will need to be mobilized into the dynamic working system. John C. Money (1962) has vividly described the neurological possibilities for such dynamic working systems. He recognizes the importance of cortical areas as being correlated with functional differences, but he is more concerned that we understand that the cerebral processes, as they function in language tasks, involve multiple relationships going on within and among such areas. He writes:

> . . . the localization of language functions and sub-functions is no simple matter of areas. One must think rather in three-dimensions as an edifice composed of many different pavillions and built adjacent to, on top of, and inside of one another, each of them webbed to the other in an interconnection of looped circuits, up and down, side to side, front to back, and across the surface. In so ramified a system, it is possible for a lesion to be highly specific in its effect, blocking, say, the visual language recognition roots [reading], but sparing enough compensatory detour roots so as to not even intefere with writing, with object recognition, naming, and with spoken and heard language (1962, p. 15).

While complex and complicated, the brain must not be thought of as a bird's nest of tangled commissures, any more than it should be thought of as a "bowl of mush." These multiple and reciprocal connections of

---

[7] See Penfield (1964).

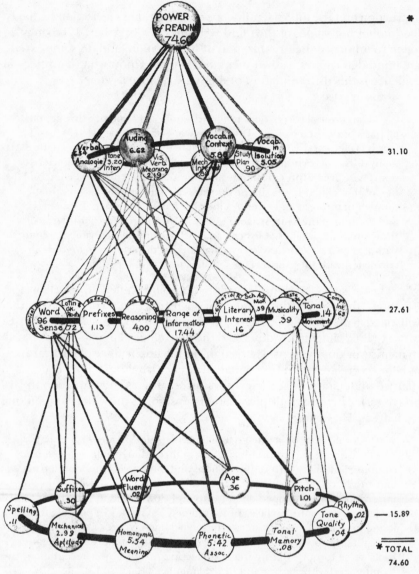

Figure 5. Model illustrates umbellating nature of lines-of-support for substrata-factors underlying Power of Reading at the high school level. The 74.60 percent of the variance accounted for in Power of Reading has been appropriately prorated to the underlying factors as indicated. Note that range of information or breadth of knowledge is the single most important factor. (From Holmes and Singer, 1961, 1965)

which Money speaks have a fixed and definite neurological structure which may be traced out. The substrata-factor theory envisions that, if one could carefully sort out these meaningful structural connections which differentially connect each of these richly endowed cortical area-complexes of coded information (substrata-factors), an ordered cosmos of subabilities in a three-dimensional space would be produced.

Further, if one were to focus his attention on any one of these areas of rich psycho-educational associations of highly related concepts as a criterion, say reading, then a *hypothetical* solid angle might be constructed in a three-dimensional space within which the supporting substrata-factor subsystems would statistically behave *as if* they were ordered in a well-defined hierarchy or working system not unlike that shown in Figure 5. Penfield and Robert (1959, p. 6) write, "The business of the brain is carried out by the passage of nervous impulses from ganglion cell to ganglion cell in an orderly and controlled manner."

Figure 5 illustrates such a model. The ping pong balls represent the high density complexes of circumscribed associations, and the straws indicate lines of support. Actually, the balls and the straws should be of different sizes to indicate differences in magnitude of accrued information and associational impact of the lower upon the higher substrata-factors and therein to the criterion, Power of Reading.

The neurological evidence for the hierarchical conception of mental structure is common knowledge in neurology, but its recognition has been most forcefully expressed in one of the opening paragraphs of Nielsen and Thompson's book, *The Engrammes of Psychiatry* (1947, p. 9). Thus, in essence they say: Anatomically and physiologically not only a longitudinal concept of hierarchies of functional control is essential for all psychiatric thinking about the brain, but there are even differential hierarchies of function and subfunction within the cortical level itself.

In sum, the substrata-factor theory assumes that, once a meaningful psycho-educational association is learned or established within the mind-brain contraplex, the neurological structure retains the memory traces in cell assemblies and supra-assemblies as relatively *permanent* ability-systems. Unlike Thomson's (1939, p. 306) model which finally did admit to structure, albeit, a *momentary* and fleeting structure in which the appropriate independent elements were assembled for the "activity called for by a 'test,'" the substrata-factor theory assumes the various working systems call for an assembling and reassembling of relatively fixed organized bodies of knowledge (substrata factors) in order to cope with the task at hand.

Summary and Conclusions

As Thurstone rejected Spearman's and Thomson's explanations of causation in correlation, so does the present writer.

It was shown that causal interpretations must rest upon grounds other than the correlation, *per se*. In fact, the explanation of the cause of a correlation must follow naturally from the basic assumptions of the theoretical model wherein it is used.

A resumé of the statistics of substrata analysis has been given as a *first approximation* for quantifying the relations delineated in the substrata-factor theory.

The substrata analysis, starting with the most valid predictor in a matrix of inter-test correlations, produces an ordered hierarchy of substrata-factors which together constitute the successive "levels" of the working system of the criterion itself. By using a statistic equivalent to the coefficient of separate determination and then the *partial* coefficient of separate determination, the criterion variance accounted for at Level I can be redistributed over the entire working system.

The basic assumptions of the substrata-factor theory are turned to in order to justify this latter procedure. The *first* postulate holds that the mind-brain contraplex is composed of a cosmos of ability-systems. A substrata-factor is composed of an organized system of subsystems. Each subsystem is a composite of smaller and smaller systems until the very micro-systems which are composed of tiny engram-assemblies of the cortical cells themselves are reached. It is important to note, however, that the *same* information with *different* associations may be deposited in many cells in many *different* areas of the cortex. Therefore, there is no need to posit the overlapping of identical and independent elements to account for correlation.

On the contrary, it is assumed that the over-all working system (and each of the subsystems) has a functional integrity of its own. Large or small, each system acts as an organized body of knowledge. The information of a particular subject is integrated into a cortical subsystem by virtue of its internal logic and certain arbitrary associations. Arbitrary associations are made meaningful by definitions and by the fact that the author agrees that certain symbols are to be associated with other symbols or objects. Thus, the information in a subsystem is given a cohesion allowing it to be tested as a separate entity, i.e., reading, spelling, phonetics, Latin, and Greek roots, etc.

The *second* postulate is that correlation can be interpreted as the mean mutual impact which two systems have on each other. Ordinarily, in analyses interest is centered primarily on the impact of X on Y, but the substrata-factor theory also takes the effect of Y on X into account.[8]

The assumptions underlying the substrata-factor theory, the substrata analysis, and the causal explanation of a meaningful coefficient of correlation in psycho-education are justified on mathematical, psychometric, and neurological grounds.

REFERENCES

Athey, Irene. Reading-personality patterns at the high school level. Unpublished doctoral dissertation, University of California, Berkeley, 1965.

Davis, F. R., Jr. Speed of reading and rate of recovery in certain physiological subsystems. Unpublished doctoral dissertation, University of California, Berkeley, 1963.

Ezekiel, M. *Methods of correlation analysis.* New York: John Wiley and Sons, 1941.

Garrett, H. E. *Statistics in psychology and education.* New York: Longmans, Green and Co., 1958.

Guilford, J. P. *Psychometric methods.* New York: McGraw-Hill, 1936.

Hammond, K. R., & Householder, J. E. *Introduction to the statistical method.* New York: Alfred A. Knopf, 1962.

Holmes, J. A. Factors underlying major reading disabilities at the college level. Unpublished doctoral dissertation, University of California, Berkeley, 1948.

Holmes, J. A. *The substrata-factor theory of reading.* Berkeley: California Book Co., Ltd., 1953.

Holmes, J. A. Factors underlying major reading disabilites at the college level. *Genetic Psychology Monograph,* 1954, *49*, 3-95.

Holmes, J. A. The brain and the reading process. In *22nd Yearbook Claremont College Reading Conference.* Claremont, California: Claremont Graduate School Curriculum Laboratory, 1957. Pp. 49-67.

Holmes, J. A. Equipotentiality versus cortical localization. *Science,* 1958, *127*, 241.

Holmes, J. A. The substrata-factor theory of reading: some experimental evidence. In J. A. Figurel (Ed.), *New frontiers in reading.* Newark, Delaware: International Reading Association, 1960. Pp. i-8.

Holmes, J. A., & Singer, H. *The substrata-factor theory: substrata factor differences underlying reading ability in known-groups at the high school level.* (Final report covering contracts No. 538, SAE-8176 and 538A, SAE-8660.) Washington, D.C.: Office of Education, 1961.

Holmes, J. A., & Singer, H. *Speed and power of reading in high school.* (Office of Education Cooperative Research Project) Washington, D.C.: United States Government Printing Office, 1966.

Holmes, J. A., & Hyman, W. Spelling disability and asyntaxia in a case involving injury to the language formulation area of the brain. *Journal of Educational Psychology,* 1957, *48*, 542-550.

Hotelling, H. Analysis of a complex of statistical variables into principal components. *Journal of Educational Psychology,* 1933, *24*, 417-441, 498-520.

The international dictionary of applied mathematics. Princeton: D. Van Nostrand Co., Inc., 1960.

James, G., & James, R. C. *Mathematics dictionary.* New York: D. Van Nostrand Co., Inc., 1959.

---

[8] See Kling's (1965) elaboration on this point.

Kety, S. S. Regional neurochemistry and its application to brain function. In J. D. French, *Frontiers in brain research*. New York: Columbia University Press, 1962. Pp. 97-120.

Kling, M. The generalization of the substrata-factor theory to general open systems theory. Unpublished doctoral dissertation, University of California, Berkeley, 1965.

Lashley, S. *Brain mechanism and intelligence*. Chicago: University of Chicago Press, 1929.

Lazar, May. A diagnostic approach to the reading program. *Educational Research Bulletin*, 1942, *3*, 1-28.

McNemar, Q. *Psychological statistics*. New York: John Wiley and Sons, 1955.

Money, J. Dyslexia: a post-conference review. In J. Money, *Reading disability: progress and research needs in dyslexia*. Baltimore: Johns Hopkins Press, 1962. Pp. 9-33.

Nielsen, J. M., & Thompson, G. N. *The engrammes of psychiatry*. Springfield, Illinois: Charles C. Thomas, Pub., 1947.

Penfield, W. The uncommitted cortex. *The Atlantic Monthly*, 1964, *7*, 77-81.

Penfield, W., & Roberts, L. *Speech and brain mechanisms*. Princeton: Princeton University Press, 1959.

Ranson, S. W. *The anatomy of the nervous system*. Philadelphia: W. B. Saunders Co., 1943.

Spearman, C. General intelligence objectively determined and measured. *American Journal of Psychology*, 1904, *15*, 201-293.

Spearman, C. *The abilities of man*. New York: The Macmillan Co., 1927.

Thomson, G. H. *The factorial analysis of human ability* (4th ed.). London: University of London Press, 1950.

Thomson, G. H. The hierarchy of abilities. *British Journal of Psychology*, 1919, *9*, 337-44.

Thurstone, L. L. *The theory of multiple factors*. Chicago: University of Chicago Press, 1932.

Thurstone, L. L. *The vectors of mind*. Chicago: University of Chicago Press, 1935.

Thurstone, L. L. *Primary mental abilities*. Chicago: University of Chicago Press, 1938.

Thurstone, L. L. *Multiple factor analysis*. Chicago: University of Chicago Press, 1947.

Wherry, R. J. A new formula for predicting the shrinkage of the coefficient of multiple correlation. *Annual Mathematical Statistics*, 1931, *2*, 440-457.

Wherry, R. J. The Wherry-Doolittle test selection method. In H. E. Garrett, *Statistics in psychology and education*. New York: Longmans, Green and Co., 1958. Pp. 426-444.

Wright, S. Correlation and causation. *Journal of Agricultural Research*, 1921, *20*, 557-585.

Substrata-Factor Patterns Accompanying Development in Power of Reading, Elementary through College Level*

HARRY SINGER
University of California at Riverside

The purpose of this paper is to a) integrate the substrata-factor patterns underlying power of reading at the elementary (Singer, 24, 26), high school (Holmes and Singer, 13), and college levels (Holmes, 9) and b) relate these changing patterns in reading to the development of general intelligence. The first part of the paper is a summary of the substrata-factor theory of reading, from which hypotheses were deduced and tested in each of the reading investigations. The second part is a report of my current research in reading and an explanation of the resulting theoretical model of the development of Power of Reading in grades 3 through 6. The results at the elementary level will then be integrated with those at the high school and college levels. In the last part of the paper I will point out relationships between these findings on development of power of reading and some research on development of intelligence.

Substrata-Factor Theory of Reading

The substrata-factor theory of reading is an explanation of the mental structure and dynamics involved in reading (Holmes, 8, 9, 10; Singer, 22; Holmes and Singer, 13). The theory asserts that as an individual learns

*Reprinted from E. Thurston and L. Hafner (Eds.), *Philosophical and Sociological Bases of Reading.* Fourteenth Yearbook of the National Reading Conference, 1964, 41-56. Reprinted by permission of the National Reading Conference, Inc. The research reported herein was supported through the Cooperative Research Program of the Office of Education, U.S. Department of Health, Education, and Welfare, Cooperative Research Project No. 2011.

to read, he sequentially develops a mental structure that is complexly interwoven and functionally organized in at least three hierarchical levels. Each level contains information stored in cell assemblies, which has been acquired from instruction and learning in such broadly defined areas as word recognition, word meaning, and reasoning-in-context (Singer, 23). As a result of maturation, instruction, and practice in reading, these cell assemblies are organized into substrata-factors or neurological subsystems which may be categorized as interrelated input (sensation and perception of stimuli), mediational (interpreting, inferring, and integrating ideas), and output (response formulation) systems. These systems, coupled by short and long term memory processes, are then available for mobilization into a working system for attaining speed and/or power of reading according to the purposes of the reader and the demands of the reading task (Holmes and Singer, 14). The operation of each working system is influenced by the individual's attitudes, emotions, values, and biological support systems (Davis, 3).

The mobilization process selects the components of the subsystems and orders them into a functional neural communication network or working system of different substrata levels for solving a particular reading task. At one moment the reader may organize a working system to recognize a word, at another instant to associate meaning to the word, and at still another time to integrate, transform, or to encode ideas for an overt response. Hence, working systems are constantly being organized and reorganized according to the reader's changing purposes and the shifting demands of the perceived task.

But, in the initial stages of learning to read, an individual's attempts to mobilize his developing subsystems into a working system for responding to the printed page are characterized by hesitancy, rigidity, and frequent lack of success because he does not yet have adequately developed subsystems nor the necessary mental structures and flexibility for changing appropriately from one working system to another (Inhelder and Piaget, 17; Laycock, 21). Gradually, however, his subsystems improve in variety, magnitude, and intercommunicability because of maturation, learning, and experience in mobilizing subsystems into a multitude of working systems; consequently, he becomes more capable of shifting from one mental organization to another. Also, the individual becomes better able to mobilize conceptual systems that are appropriate for responding to various stimulus categories and for selecting and organizing word meanings applicable to the context because of his growing capability to conceptualize stimuli in his input and mediational processing systems (Singer, 22; Bruner and Olver, 2).

With continued development, instruction, and practice in reading progressively more challenging material, the individual forms his subsystems into a hierarchical organization of word-recognition, word-meaning, and reasoning-in-context substrata (Singer, 23). When the necessary subsystems have been developed and can be mobilized in proper order and magnitude, the individual attains working systems for speed and power of reading that function fluently and harmoniously. However, increased speed and power of reading are not only related to changes in magnitude and variety of available substrata-factors but also to their integration and consequent interfacilitation. At reading maturity, therefore, an individual is able to mobilize rapidly and flexibly a hierarchical organization of subsystems in which a minimum of mental energy is devoted to the input system and a maximum is expended upon mediational and output systems.

Many kinds of working systems or conceptual strategies for attaining speed and power of reading result from individual differences in a) rate of maturation and degree of capacities, b) method, sequence, and degree of learning, c) background experiences and range of resulting ideas, and d) temperament and motivation, as well as values. These differences are manifested in the kinds and relative amounts of subskills which each individual mobilizes into a working system to solve a particular task. Hence, the degree of achievement attained and the processes underlying the solution of a task may vary from person to person, not only because of quantitative differences in substrata factors but also because of qualitative differences in organization of working systems. However, there is more than one route to successful reading; that is, two individuals may attain the same level of achievement but by means of different working systems.

In essence, the substrata-factor theory of reading is an explanation of the development and dynamic functioning of an intellect that is increasingly able to transform symbolic stimuli into meaningful mental processes, and then purposefully interrelate these processes by various mediational systems in order to efficiently and effectively comprehend and react to the thoughts of another person as expressed in his writing.

Problem

The following hypothesis, drawn from the substrata factor theory of reading, was tested at the elementary school level: As an individual, in general, learns to read he sequentially develops a mental structure of complexly interwoven subsystems which he can mobilize or functionally organize into various working systems according to his purposes and the demands of the task. However, at least at the high school level, if the individual is to read at all, he must call upon certain necessary subsystems, whether these subsystems are strengths or weaknesses in his substrata factor repertoire (Holmes and Singer, 13, 15). This finding suggests the hypothesis that there is a necessary, developmental working system for attaining speed and power of reading around which individuals vary according to their unique pattern of strengths and weaknesses. Furthermore, developmental improvements in speed and power of reading would seem, in some degree, to be related to a) quantitative and qualitative developments in the substrata elements and substrata factors which make up these systems and b) the interfacilitation resulting from the integration of these factors and from their subsequent organization into a hierarchical structure. Therefore, the purposes of this study was to test the following developmental hypothesis: As an individual, in general, improves in reading ability his underlying substrata elements and substrata factors have concomitant changes in magnitude and/or organizational position in his mental structure for attaining speed and power of reading. Hence, the specific problem was to discover a) what elements and substrata factors change and in what degree and b) whether the general working system undergoes a reorganization in substrata-factors mobilized for reading ability in grades 3 through 6.

A previous report (Singer, 25) confirmed the first part of the hypothesis: For the average reader, all the substrata elements improve in more or less quantitatively uniform increments concomitantly with development of speed and power of reading in grades 3 through 6. Consequently, the present study will be concerned primarily with the remainder of the hypothesis, specifically with identifying the factors which account for individual differences in speed and power of reading at each grade level and with changes in the organization of these factors as individuals improve in speed and power of reading in grades 3 to 6.

The problem may be restated in terms that are more meaningful to the classroom teacher. The average scores of a class of pupils in speed and power of reading typically increase each year when measured on such a test battery as the *Gates Reading Survey*.[1] Pupils within these grades, however, vary widely not only in speed and power of reading, but also in a multitude of subabilities, such as phonics, knowledge of affixes, vocabulary, interpretation of paragraphs, and many other skills which teachers emphasize in the belief that development of these skills will effect an

---

[1] In this study, *Speed of Reading* was assessed at all grade levels by a seven minute subtest of the Gates Reading Survey (5). *Power of Reading* was measured by the Level of Comprehension subtest of the Gates Reading Survey (6).

improvement in general reading ability. Although teachers know what and when they teach a particular subskill, they do not know what factors pupils may be learning, integrating, and mobilizing for attaining improvement in speed and power of reading. In other words, teachers need to know the particular constellation of factors which, in fact, do account for variability in speed and power of reading at each grade level. Also, they need to know the specific quantitative, qualitative, and organizational changes that occur in the constellation of factors associated with the development of speed and power of reading. Consequently, this study was designed to give teachers and curriculum makers a better understanding of reading development and provide them with a statistically-determined model to use as a guide in planning instruction for improving speed and power of reading in grades 3 through 6.

Experimental Design

The developmental hypothesis was tested by means of a selected battery of scales which had precipitated as predictors in previous investigations at the college (Holmes, 9), high school (Holmes and Singer, 13), or elementary level (Singer, 23). These tests encompassed measures of mental abilities, listening comprehension, linguistic meaning, word recognition, and visual and auditory perception.[2] Personality, interest, and motivation variables were not included because factors representing these domains either had not precipitated from the substrata analysis in previous studies or tests from these domains were not psychometrically suitable for administration at the elementary school level.

The scales were administered to samples of about 250 pupils each in grades 3 through 6.[3,4] From comparison of the means of the sample data with standardized test norms on age, IQ, Speed and Power of Reading, the sample appears to be representative of the general population. Morever, the cumulative records of the subjects revealed that they had been taught by a wide variety of teachers, used a heterogeneous set of basal and supplementary readers, and had been registered in many school systems

---

[2] Tests were selected from the following batteries: Durrell and Sullivan (4), Gates (5; 6), Holmes (11), Kwalwasser and Dykema (19), Singer (24), Thurstone and Thurstone (28), and Van Wagenen (29).

[3] In Grades 3, 4, 5, and 6, there were 122, 128, 149, and 76 boys and 101, 155, 122, and 83 girls, respectively.

[4] The writer wishes to express his appreciation to the Alvord Unified School District, to the Riverside County Superintendent of Schools Office, and to his research staff at the University of California, Riverside for participating and cooperating in this research project.

throughout the country. Therefore, the results of the investigation cannot be related to any particular set of materials nor to any particular methodological emphasis.

Preliminary analysis of the data revealed that all the tests have substantially high reliabilities. Bivariate distributions of each variable with Speed and Power of Reading, respectively, satisfactorily passed the chi-square test for rectilinear regression.[5]

Analysis of the Data

Substrata analysis (Holmes, 7; Holmes and Singer, 13), an extension and modification of the Wherry-Doolittle Multiple Selection Technique (Wherry, 30), was used to analyze the data.[6] Essentially the Wherry-Doolittle is a multiple correlation technique in which a minimum number of first level predictors are selected from a correlation matrix that tend to yield the maximum prediction of a criterion, which in this study was Speed or Power of Reading. The technique is extended to identify lower levels of the hierarchy by next eliminating the major criterion variable and then utilizing each of the first level predictors as a subcriterion and finding which of the remaining variables in the correlation matrix are substrata factors for each subcriterion. The substrata analysis was thus carried out to several levels to obtain a best estimate of the pattern of abilities underlying Speed and Power of Reading for the *average* individual. The first level predictors from each grade were then utilized in the construction of the models in order to emphasize the developmental scope and sequence of substrata factors that accompany improvement in Speed and Power of Reading for the average reader. However, this interim report will present only the model for Power of Reading and attempt to integrate it with models for Power of Reading at the high school and college levels.[7,8]

---

[5] Computations were performed on the IBM 7090 Computer at the University of California, Berkeley by means of RSCAT program written by M. Maruyama.

[6] Price Stiffler modified the substrata analysis program for the IBM 7090 Computer at the University of California, Berkely, and assisted in all statistical analyses for this investigation.

[7] A paper on the model for Speed of Reading was read at the Annual Convention of the National Council of Teachers of English, Cleveland, November 27, 1964, and published: Harry Singer. A developmental model for speed of reading in grades three through six. *Reading Research Quarterly, 1,* 1, Fall 1965, 29-49.

[8] A final report on the complete project was made: Harry Singer. *Substrata-Factor Reorganization Accompanying Development in Speed and Power of Reading at the Elementary School Level,* Final Report on Contract No. 2011, Cooperative Research Program, U.S. Office of Education, 1965.

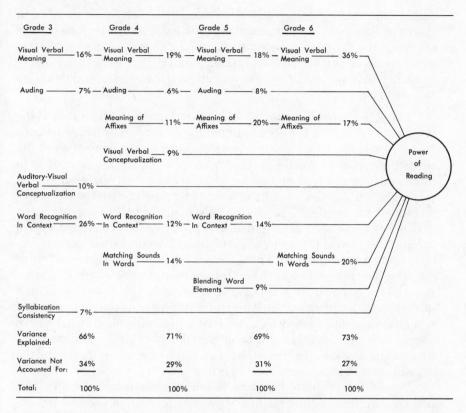

Figure 1. Diagrammatic model of the substrata-factors accompanying development of power of reading in grades 3 to 6. The model shows for each grade the first level substrata factors and their percent contributions to variance in power of reading. The variance *not* accounted for is probably attributable to attitudinal factors, verbal flexibility, and mobilizers.

Results

The diagrammatic model for development of Power of Reading in grades 3 through 6 is shown in Figure 1. The model reveals a) the factors which accounted for variance in Power of Reading at each grade level and b) the developmental changes in substrata factors that accompany improvement in Power of Reading from grades 3 to 6. In the left hand column of each figure are the substrata factors or predictors for grade 3, followed in successive columns by the predictors for grades 4, 5, and 6.

Adjacent to each predictor is its percent contribution to the variance in Power of Reading for the particular grade level. At the bottom of each column is the variance in Power of Reading that was not accounted for, which must be attributable to variables other than those used in the construction of the model, such as mobilizers (Holmes, 10), and flexibility (Laycock, 20; 21).

Developmental model for power of reading. Figure 1 reveals that at the third grade level, five factors accounted for 66 percent of the variance in Power of Reading. Two word recognition factors contributed half of the predicted variance: Word Recognition in Context, the use of context to infer a missing word, accounted for 26 percent, and Syllabication Consistency, the application of syllabication rules to the division of words, accounted for another 7 percent. The remaining half of the predicted variance is distributed among the following three factors: Visual Verbal Meaning, 16 percent; Auding, 7 percent; and Audio-Visual Verbal Conceptualization, 10 percent. These factors consist of knowledge of word meaning, listening comprehension for words and stories, and the formation and use of concepts, respectively. Thus, at the third grade level, half of the predicted variance in Power of Reading is attributable to word recognition abilities or factors involved in transforming visual verbal stimuli into meaningful mental processes; the other half is accounted for by association of meaning through the auditory of visual modality and the organization of these word meanings into ideas.

At the fourth grade level, the following quantitative changes have occurred in the substrata factors: Word Recognition in Context has declined to only 12 percent in contribution to variance in Power of Reading. Visual Verbal Meaning, however, has increased to 19 percent and Meaning of Affixes has emerged with 11 percent contribution to variance. But, Auding is approximately the same at 6 percent. Two other factors also precipitated from the analysis: Matching Sounds in Words, the ability to recognize homonyms or whole word sounds, accounts for 14 percent and Visual Verbal Conceptualization, the ability to conceptualize printed words, contributes another 9 percent to the variance in Power of Reading. Thus, at the fourth grade level, variation in Power of Reading is more attributable to word meaning than to word recognition factors.

The trend discernible in the fourth grade continues at the fifth grade with another quantitative decrease in word recognition factors (Word Recognition in Context, 14 percent and Blending Word Elements, 9 percent) and another increment in word meaning factors (Visual Verbal Meaning, 18 percent, Auding, 8 percent and Meaning of Affixes, 20 percent).

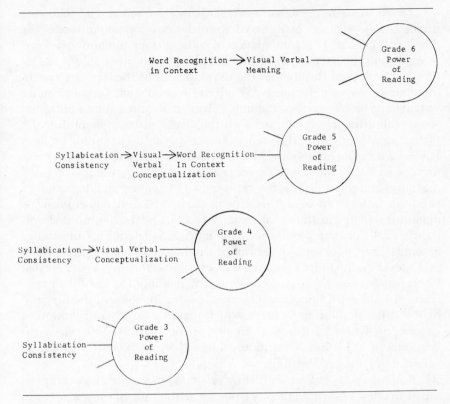

Figure 2. A developmental integration of one subsystem for power of reading in Grades 3 through 6. The figure shows that syllabication consistency makes a *direct* contribution to variance in Power of Reading in Grade 3 but an *indirect* contribution through other factors at Grade 4, 5, and 6. Harry Singer, 1964.

Only three factors accounted for 73 percent of the variance in Power of Reading at the sixth grade level: Visual Verbal Meaning, 36 percent, Meaning of Affixes, 17 percent, and Matching Sounds in Words, 20 percent. Again, word meaning and ability to reason out word meanings that are not directly known through the visual or auditory modalities account for more variance in Power of Reading than they did at previous grade levels. Success in intra-group competition in Power of Reading at the sixth grade level, therefore, depends upon skillfully transforming stimuli through the visual or auditory modalities into mental processes which can then be associated with meaning, either directly or through an analytical and synthesizing mediational system.

Trends in the developmental model for power of reading. The following trends can be gleaned or inferred from the developmental model for Power of Reading: 1) A combination of context clues and auditory word recognition processes are gradually integrated with other substrata factors and mobilized throughout the development of the working system for attaining Power of Reading. 2) Both auding and visual verbal meaning systems are mobilized for attaining Power of Reading, but auding becomes subordinately integrated with the visual verbal system after the fifth grade. 3) Individual differences at successively higher grade levels in Power of Reading are less attributable to word recognition processes and more associated with word meaning analysis and knowledge of word meanings and the concepts they represent. 4) A sequential integration of substrata-factors can be inferred from the model and was empirically demonstrated by substrata analysis at the second and third substrata levels (Singer, 26). For example, as shown in Figure 2, Syllabication Consistency accounts directly for some of the variance in Power of Reading at the third grade level. At the fourth grade level it contributes through Visual Verbal Conceptualization to variance in Power of Reading. At the fifth grade level, Visual Verbal Conceptualization accounts for some of the variance in Word Recognition in Context, which makes a direct contribution to variance in Power of Reading. Finally, at the sixth grade level, Word Recognition in Context contributes through Visual Verbal Meaning to variance in Power of Reading.

Elementary, high school, and college substrata-factor patterns. A comparison of first level substrata factors from the sixth grade of the above study and from previous investigations at the high school (Holmes and Singer, 13) and college levels (Holmes, 9), as shown in Figure 3, can at best only suggest hypotheses for a longitudinal investigation, since neither the test batteries nor the subjects in these grades were identical.[9] With this necessary qualification in mind, Figure 3 reveals the following similarities and differences in substrata-factor patterns from grade 6 through the college level:

1. Although some variance in Power of Reading may be distributed over several vocabulary measures as shown in the substrata-factors at the high school level, the fact that the total variance attributed to vocabulary abilities increases significantly after the fifth grade and then remains approximately the same from the sixth grade through the college level suggests that the vocabulary domain has consequently attained a stage of

---

[9] If factor analytic data at these school levels had been based upon identical tests or subjects, then Kaiser and Bianchini's (18) program for relating factors could have been utilized for a quantitative comparison of the results.

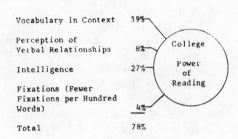

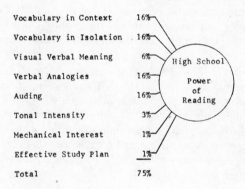

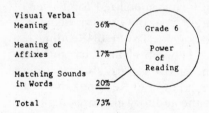

Figure 3.   First level substrata factors and their percent contributions to variance in power of reading at the sixth grade, high school, and college levels. Harry Singer, 1964.

development at the sixth grade that quantitatively approximates its contribution to variance in mature organization for Power of Reading.

2. Auding was included in the test batteries at all except the college levels. However, Auding did not precipitate at the sixth grade, but does so at the lower grades and again at the high school level. This discrepancy may be partly due to differences in the response systems of the two auding measures and partly to developmental changes in mental organization for reading. At the elementary level, the auding test consists of listening comprehension with responses to printed pictures and consequently seems to tap auditory-visual factors at a concrete or associational level (Singer, 27); at the high school level, the auding test measures listening comprehension with responses to verbally stated multiple choices. Therefore, the resulting hypothesis from these observations is that reading remains an "audiovisual verbal processing skill of symbolic reasoning" (Holmes and Singer, 13), but the auding contribution to variance shifts at the sixth grade to auding ability at a more abstract level of organization.

3. Meaning of Affixes and Matching Sounds in Words precipitated as first level substrata factors only at the sixth grade, even though measures for these factors were in the matrices at each school level. These factors become subordinately integrated with other factors at the higher school levels. Knowledge of affixes becomes integrated with Auding at the high school level and Vocabulary in Context at the college level, while auditory processes become subordinated to auding and visual vocabulary factors at the higher levels.

To summarize: this comparison has suggested the following hypotheses: 1) subordinate integration within factors mobilized for Power of Reading continues throughout the grades; 2) at the sixth grade level, a stage characteristic of mature organization for Power of Reading has occurred in the vocabulary domain; 3) between elementary and high school levels, auding shifts from a concrete to a more abract level of organization in contribution to variance in Power of Reading; and 4) the visual modality becomes dominant over the auditory in processing input stimuli.

Relationship between development of intelligence and power of reading. The following explanations of the development of intelligence are consistent with the substrata-factor theory of reading and may help explain some developmental changes in factor patterns for attaining power of reading: 1) Bruner and Olver (2, p. 133) found that level of conceptualization in elementary school is an inverse function of the difficulty of the concept. For example, an individual could attain generalizability and economy in information processing by using the superordinating concept of "fruit" for integrating the relatively easy elements, "orange" and "banana." But, as elements increasingly more distant on a continuum from concrete to abstract were added until the elements finally exceeded the capability of an individual to integrate them by means of superordination, he would resort to a less mature type of organization, sometimes simply linking the elements of the concept into a story, much as a reader who could not answer a question on the central thought of a passage might reply by merely repeating what he had read. Bruner and Olver then theorized that in the growth of intelligence, strategies develop for encoding information in simpler form, connecting this encoded information with other information already encoded, and maximizing the possibility of combinatorial operations for grouping and regrouping information. In general, therefore, an older individual is less complex than a younger person in the sense that the older individual's information is more organized, interconnected, and capable of reorganization. Likewise in the substrata-factor theory of reading, factors or subsystems of information are hierarchically organized and interrelated with other subsystems, which are mobilized into working systems according to the purposes of the reader and the demands of the task. When the task becomes increasingly difficult, the motivated individual may respond by mobilizing a more complex working system, consisting of some factors which had developed at an earlier stage, for example, an individual might resort to reading difficult material aloud, but for easier material he would use a more mature visual processing subsystem. 2) Piaget (Inhelder and Piaget, 17, and Inhelder 16) has categorized mental development as progressing through three emerging levels of organization which can be accelerated or delayed by environmental factors but is mostly biologically determined: a) The sensori-motor stage consists of operations that require action on objects, but the action is not accompanied by simultaneous mental representation, b) a concrete stage emerges about age 6 that is characterized by simultaneous mental representation, but in this stage the individual is not yet able to carry out more than one simultaneous operation, such as reversibility or conservation or transitivity, and c) a stage of formal operations, beginning about age 12 and reaching a peak at age 15, at which the individual becomes capable of generating all hypothetical combinatorial possibilities in the solution of a problem. Passage from an "inferior" to a "superior" stage is equivalent to an integration in which the inferior serves as a base for the superior and becomes part of the superior. Piaget's theory of developmental stages may explain the changes in factor patterns that emerge about the sixth grade: the average sixth grader may be passing from a concrete to a more abstract, formal stages of development. Closely related to the developmental pattern of changes that accompany development of power of reading is the conclusion on the growth of intelligence reached by Bayley (1, p. 807) in her monumental longitudinal study: "Intelligence . . . appears to be a dynamic succession of developing functions with the more advanced and complex functions in the hierarchy depending on the prior maturing of earlier, simpler ones."

Although the structure of intelligence and power of reading have some degree of communality (Holmes, 12), the factors typically measured by intelligence and reading tests are not identical. In the working system mobilized for attaining power of reading some subsystems, such as word recognition, are tapped which would not necessarily be mobilized for performance on an individual test of intelligence, even though conceptualization abilities may enter into the acquisition of the word recognition system (Singer, 22). Another way of stating the argument is simply to point out that although an individual may be bright, he still has to learn to read. This is tantamount to saying that he must acquire the necessary hierarchy of subsystems and learn to mobilize them into an integrated working system for attaining power of reading.

REFERENCES

1. Bayley, Nancy, "On the Growth of Intelligence," *The American Psychologist,* 10:805-818, December, 1955.

2. Bruner, J. and Rose Olver, "Development of Equivalence Transformations in Children," *Monographs of the Society for Research in Child Development,* 28:125-143, 1963.

3. Davis, F., "The Substrata Factor Theory of Reading: Human Physiology as a Factor in Reading," In J. A. Figurel (Ed.), *International Reading Association Conference Proceedings,* Newark, Delaware: International Reading Association, 9:292-296, 1964.

4. Durrell, D. and Helen Sullivan, *Manual for Durrell-Sullivan Reading Capacity and Reading Achievement Tests,* New York: World Book Company, 1937.

5. Gates, A., *The Manual of Directions for Gates Reading Survey,* New York: Teachers College, Columbia University, Bureau of Publications, 1953.

6. Gates, A., *Manual for the Gates Reading Survey,* New York: Teachers College, Columbia University, Bureau of Publications, 1958.

7. Holmes, J., *Factors Underlying Major Reading Disabilities at the College Level,* Unpublished doctoral dissertation, Berkeley: University of California, 1948.

8. Holmes, J., *The Substrata-Factor Theory of Reading,* Berkeley: California Book, 1953. (Out of Print).

9. Holmes, J., "Factors Underlying Major Reading Disabilities at the College Level," *Genetic Psychology Monographs,* 49:3-95, February, 1954.

10. Holmes, J., "Personality and Spelling Ability," *University of California Publications in Education,* 12:213-292, 1959.

11. Holmes, J., *California Language Perception Tests,* Palo Alto: Educational Development Corporation, Revised, 1962.

12. Holmes, J., "Fundamental Assumptions in a Substrata Factor Analyses of Reading," In J. A. Figurel (Ed.), *International Reading Association Conference Proceedings.* Newark, Delaware: International Reading Association, 9: 1964.

13. Holmes, J., and H. Singer, *The Substrata-Factor Theory: Substrata Factor Differences Underlying Reading Ability in Known-Groups,* Final report covering contracts 538 and 538A, Office of Education, U.S. Department of Health, Education, and Welfare, 1961.

14. Holmes, J. and H. Singer, "Theoretical Models and Trends Toward More Basic Research in Reading," *Review of Educational Research,* 34:127-155, 1964.

15. Holmes, J. and H. Singer, "Speed and Power of Reading at the High School Level," *U.S. Office of Education Monograph Series,* 1966.

16. Inhelder, B., "Criteria of the Stages of Mental Development," In R. Kuhlen and G. J. Thomson (Eds.), *Psychological Studies of Human Development,* New York: Appleton-Century-Crofts, Second Edition, 1963.

17. Inhelder, B. and J. Piaget, *The Growth of Logical Thinking from Childhood to Adolescence,* New York: Basic Books, 1958.

18. Kaiser, H. and J. Bianchini, *Fortran Program for Relating Factors Between Studies Based Upon Different Individuals,* Urbana: University of Illinois, Bureau of Educational Research, 1964.

19. Kwalwasser, J. and P. Dykema, *Kwalwasser-Dykema Music Tests,* New York: Carl Fischer, 1930.

20. Laycock, F., "Flexibility in Reading Rate and *Einstellung,*" *Perceptual and Motor Skills,* 8:123-129, 1958.

21. Laycock, F., "The Flexibility Hypothesis in Reading and the Work of Piaget," In J. A. Figurel (Ed.), *International Reading Association Conference Proceedings,* New York: Scholastic Magazines 7:241-243, 1962.

22. Singer, H., *Conceptual Ability in the Substrata-Factor Theory of Reading,* Unpublished doctoral dissertation, Berkeley: University of California, 1960.

23. Singer, H., "Substrata-Factor Theory of Reading: Theoretical Design for Teaching Reading," In J. A. Figurel (Ed.), *International Reading Association Conference Proceedings.* New York: Scholastic Magazines, 7:226-232, 1962.

24. Singer, H., *Linguistic Test: A Battery for Elementary School,* Riverside: University of California, Revised, 1963.

25. Singer, H., "Substrata-Factor Theory of Reading: Grade and Sex Differences in Reading at the Elementary School Level," In J. A. Figurel (Ed.), *International Reading Association Conference Proceedings,* Newark, Delaware: International Reading Association, 9:313-320, 1964.

26. Singer, H., *An Investigation of Changes Accompanying Development of General Reading Ability at the Elementary School Level,* U.S. Office of Education, Contract 2011, February 1, 1963 to January 31, 1965. Final report in preparation.

27. Singer, H., "The Validity of the Durrell-Sullivan Reading Capacity Test," *Journal of Educational and Psychological Measurements, 125,* Summer 1965, 479-491.

28. Thurstone, L. and Thelma Thurstone, *SRA Primary Mental Abilities, Elementary Form,* Chicago: Science Research Associates, 1954.

29. Van Wagenen, M., *Diagnostic Examination of Silent Reading Abilities,* Minneapolis: Van Wagenen, 1953.

30. Wherry, R., "The Wherry-Doolittle Test Selection Method, in H. E. Garrett, *Statistics in Psychology and Education,* New York: Longmans, Green, 1947, 435-451.

Theoretical Models of Reading[*]

HARRY SINGER

University of California at Riverside

Theoretical models of reading are currently being used implicitly and explicitly in research and in teaching to explain the processes of decoding, comprehending, and encoding of printed messages. Several of these models have been selected for critical review in this paper. In addition to use of such criteria as heuristic value and empirical support, these models will also be evaluated from a developmental point of view. Since these models primarily utilize and depict interrelationships among cognitive and linguistic systems as they function in reading performance, this review will begin with a summary of the development of cognition, language, and reading ability.

Cognitive Development

A major theory of cognitive development has been formulated by Piaget (Piaget, 1937; Inhelder & Piaget, 1958; Inhelder, 1963; Flavell, 1963). He uses two mental processes to explain how information is incorporated into the individual's mental repertoire and how new mental structures are formed. When the individual is confronted by new information derived from his action on objects, he "assimilates" or interprets this information according to "schemas" or mental structures that have been formed out of interactions between him and his environment. When new information departs too much from existing schemas—if the difficulty level of the information is not too great—the individual tends to resolve the discrepancy by the process of accommodation or the formation of a new schema and thus achieves a stage of equilibrium again. These mental processes operate not only in relation to tangible objects, but also in interaction with oral and printed language. However, the level of thought that the child can attain in these interactions is dependent upon his stage of mental development.

[*]Reprinted from *Journal of Communication*, 19, 2, 1969, 134-156. Reprinted with permission of the International Communication Association.

Piaget has posited four cumulative stages of cognitive development. In the first stage, from about birth to age 2, the child adapts to his environment through sensori-motor rather than through symbolic means. The child's mental activity during this stage consists of establishing relationships between sensory experience and action by physically manipulating the world. The child's sensori-motor actions on objects thus results in knowledge of perceptual invariants of his environment. If the appropriate linguistic forms are associated with these perceptual invariants and the child is normal, he begins to use these linguistic forms to identify objects and to represent his actions on them.

From approximately age 2 to 4, the individual goes through the second major stage of development in which he rapidly learns to represent objects by symbolic means. For example, fifty percent of children age 2 can identify common objects, such as a cup and parts of a doll's body, and can repeat two numbers. At age 4, they can repeat a 9 to 10 word sentence, name a variety of objects, and answer some simple questions, such as "why do we have a house." During this stage, the child learns to represent his world symbolically. He has acquired knowledge of spatial, temporal, and causal relationships among the perceptual invariants of his environment, and use of movables appear in his speech at this time.

In the third stage, from about age 4 to 7, the child is going through the initial stages of logical thought. He can group objects into classes by noting similarities and differences. He can also form the superordinate concept of "fruit" for relating "orange" and "apple." Through social reinforcement, he has intuitively learned and uses the grammar of the language spoken in his environment. He has also acquired a vocabulary of about 2,500 to 7,500 words and has learned the physical relationships of time, space, and has some idea of causality; but his causal reasoning is dependent upon his perceptions and is often erroneous because his attention is attracted by irrelevant or insufficient attributes. For example, he concludes that a tall, thin jar contains more liquid than a broad, shallow container, even though he has seen the liquid poured from one vessel into the other.

Beginning about age 7, the child develops the capability of carrying out logical operations, which means he can internalize actions that represent physical objects and relationships. For example, the child can use his imagination to mentally reverse actions: you break a candy bar in half and he can mentally put the parts together. He can also transform and manipulate sentences. Such operations reflect the freeing of thought and language from dependence upon sensation and perception. But, during this stage the child's mental operations can only be applied to concrete or physical situations.

About age 11 to 15, an individual attains the fourth and mature stage of mental development in which he can imagine possible and potential relationships and think in terms of formal propositions. His thinking is freed from dependence on directly experienced events. Conditional, suppositional, and hypothetical statements are likely to begin to appear in the individual's language. But not all adults reach this ability to soar into the abstract and those who do can regress to more immature modes of thought.

Although the sequence of these stages of cognitive development are presumably the same for all individuals, concepts or basic means of representing experience can vary from individual to individual. In responding to words, either orally or graphically presented, concepts may be evoked.[1] Whether or not an individual comprehends a message then is a function in part of the degree to which the concepts transmitted by the sender are congruent with the concepts elicited in the receiver of the message.

However, as individuals mature, their concepts tend to become more congruent. With increased range of experience, an individual's concepts broaden, become clearer, and hierarchically organized. They also change from egocentric to conventionalized significance. As the concepts of individuals become consistent with the concepts of their culture, they can and do communicate more effectively and efficiently (Russell, 1956; Bruner & Olver, 1963; Singer, 1964).

Children whose experience is more limited and who have less verbal interchange with adults are less likely to attain the information, linguistic forms, and syntax for organizing and communicating new experiences. Because of some gaps in the materials or content of their thinking, they might not be able to communicate effectively in certain content areas, even though they have the requisite general mental capabilities (Gagné, 1966).

Thus, the level of thought and the variety of an individual's ideas are a function of his stage of cognitive development and his interaction with his environment. These interactions operate in oral as well as in written communication and underlie his general language development.

---

[1] The same word, for example, "apple," may be a label for a particular object, or a name for a concept or set of interrelated attributes, such as color, shape, size, etc. (Osgood, 1956; Singer, 1956a).

Language Development

The child's language development is slow at first and then accelerates. At age 12 months, the average child can say two words (Bayley, 1949). The gradient of vocabulary development remains low from age one to two as the child continues to learn the perceptual invariants of his environment. During the next four years, the vocabulary gradient accelerates as the child goes from a vocabulary of approximately 100 to 2500 words. By age 6, he uses all parts of speech and has unconsciously learned and intuitively uses the rules of grammar in expressing his ideas and manipulating his vocabulary into a variety of utterances (Smith, 1926; McCarthy, 1946; Noel, 1953; Ervin & Miller, 1963). He can communicate effectively with his peers and with adults provided that the intended meaning of the communication does not exceed his mental capabilities (Strickland, 1962). Indeed, upon entrance to school, the average child has learned through various processes, such as conditioning, shaping of utterances, echoes of heard speech, unconscious acquisition of the transformation rules of grammar, and through identification with language models to speak whatever sound system, vocabulary, and grammar are characteristics of his home and neighborhood (Noel, 1953). The child is then ready to transfer his oral language system to learning how to read and in responding to printed material.

Oral language continues to develop through the elementary school years. In a longitudinal study of a representative sample of 237 pupils, Loban (1963) analyzed the characteristics of oral language development, using a standardized interview and a set of six pictures to elicit language responses. Loban applied a recently devised method of analysis for recording and quantifying these responses. The method consists of dividing speech into phonological units (utterances between initial and terminal junctures), communication units (usually independent clauses with their modifiers) and mazes ("tangles of language"). Recording these, Loban discovered that linguistic fluency increases each year. After the third grade, there was a general decrease in incidence of mazes and in number of words per maze; consequently, there was improvement in coherence of speech. Improvement in effectiveness and control of language was not attained through changes in pattern of communication unit, but by degree of flexibility, expansion, and elaboration of elements within the pattern. Children who are more proficient in oral language use a greater degree of subordination, are more sensitive to conventions of language, score higher on vocabulary and intelligence tests, and perform better in reading and writing. Although those who are less proficient in language tend to improve throughout the grades, the gap between the most and least proficient tends to widen.

In a study similar to Loban's, but using a cross-sectional rather than a longitudinal design, Strickland (1962) also found significant relationships throughout the grades between structure of oral language and reading ability. At the second grade, the superior readers used greater sentence length. At the sixth grade level, those who were high in oral and silent reading used in their oral language greater sentence length, made more use of movables and subordination, had fewer short utterances, and used more common linguistic patterns. In oral reading, the better readers were freer of errors of substitution, repetitions, hesitations, mispronunciations, insertions, refusals and self-corrections. They were more fluent and used more appropriate phrasing and intonation.

In an interesting linguistic analysis of basal reading textbooks, Strickland (1962) found that language patterns increased from a few common ones in primary grades to many patterns in grade six, but not in a systematic manner. There was some expansion in elaboration from grade to grade and movables (expressions of time, place, manner, purpose, and cause) began to appear from grade 2 on. However, there was no clear arrangement for subordination and the sentence structure patterns appeared to be used randomly with no attempt to gain mastery through repetition. Whether control of sentence structure as vocabulary is controlled in basal readers would help or not, she pointed out, was unknown.

Following up Strickland's research, Ruddell (1965a) tested and confirmed the hypothesis, at the fourth grade level, that greater correspondence between the structure of oral language and reading paragraphs would improve comprehension as assessed by the cloze test. Then, drawing on the theory of transfer of learning that similarity between oral language pattern and reading pattern of instruction would aid in rate of achievement in word recognition and reading comprehension, Ruddell (1965b) undertook a training study at the first grade level, in which he compared the achievement of pupils taught by basal versus programed instructional material. The programed material had a high consistency of correspondence in grapheme-phoneme relationships whereas the basal reader did not. Instruction of half of each of these groups was supplemented by use of materials designed to improve their language development with respect to certain aspects of morphemes and syntax. He found that the supplement to a program of instruction which had a high degree of phoneme-grapheme correspondence as compared with basal reader instruction, whether supplemented or not, tended to result in better achievement in word recognition and reading comprehension. He also discovered that the degree of control over certain aspects of the morphological and syntactical language systems at the beginning of first grade is predictive of reading achievement at the end of grade one. Ruddell concluded that degree and control of language ability are significant components in learning to read, particularly when they reinforce a program that stresses grapheme-phoneme correspondence.

Reading Development

An average child's receptive, mediational, storage, and oral subsystems for processing and responding to spoken language are fairly well developed before he systematically starts to form his subsystems for decoding, comprehending, and encoding responses to printed language. Consequently, the popular strategy in teaching the child to read is to have him learn to reconstruct printed messages into spoken language through use of vocal, subvocal, or even inner speech so that he can then comprehend printed messages with his subsystems for spoken language. In the process, intermodal communication subsystems between auditory and visual systems are developed which are necessary for transfer of meaning from one modality to the other (Holmes, 1957).

Individuals taught through an oral method might continue to subvocalize or use inner speech when reading silently (Edfeldt, 1960), but they can learn on their own or be taught through sensory feedback mechanisms to suppress subvocalization (Hardyck, Petrinovich, & Ellsworth, 1966). Although a non-oral method of instruction could be used to teach children to read silently from the very beginning of reading instruction (Buswell, 1945), formation of oral reconstruction or at least recoding subsystems are necessary for oral reading. However, a reader who has attained maturity in both oral and silent reading has not only developed subsystems for both of these types of reading but can minimize or suppress his oral reconstruction and recoding subsystems when reading silently. He also learns to reorganize his mental organization as he shifts from one reading task or purpose to another (Holmes, 1960; Singer, 1965a, 1965c, 1965f, 1967).

Peripherally and centrally determined changes in eye-movement behavior accompany development in reading (Laycock, 1966). By grade 9, the average individual has attained maturity in functional oculomotor efficiency and accuracy in targeting familiar printed stimuli in reading (Gilbert, 1953). At first grade level, eye-movement behavior on primary grade material consists of two fixations per word, each lasting about seven-tenths of a second, and one regression or backword eye-movement about once for every two words. As children learn to perceive words, associate meaning to them, process information, and formulate appropriate responses, their eye-movement behavior also tends to improve. At the college level, eye-movement behavior is more rhythmic (one regression for every two lines of print), broader in span of perception (one and one-fourth words per fixation), and relatively rapid in pause duration (one quarter second per fixation). The developmental curve of span and pause duration in reading is relatively steep in grades 1-4, tends to level off from grades 5-10, has another upward spurt at grade 10, and then levels off again, but rhythmic growth continues all the way to college (Buswell, 1922).

As individuals progress through the grades, perceptual processes tend to decrease in relative importance while meaning factors tend to increase. Systematic changes also occur in general mental organization of factors underlying speed and power of reading (Holmes, 1954, 1961; Holmes & Singer, 1964, 1966; Singer, 1964, 1965d).

Theoretical Models of Reading

Several models, varying in heuristic value and empirical testing, have been formulated to define, depict, and explain the structure and functioning of subsystems that underlie performance in reading. Four of these models have been selected for presentation.

The first model is simple because it uses extremely broad categories and minimizes the use of hypothetical constructs. This model is implicit in Carroll's (1964) definition of reading:

> We can define reading ultimately as the activity of reconstructing (overtly or covertly) a reasonable spoken message from a printed text and making meaning responses to the reconstructed message that would parallel those that would be made to the spoken message (p. 62).

He defines the responses made by the listener to a spoken sentence in the following way:

> A sentence is a series of discriminative stimuli, learned by the speaker of a language, which in effect "program" the mediating responses of the hearer in such a way that certain constructions are put on the sentence and corresponding responses are evoked in the hearer (p. 61).

Figure 1 systematically depicts his model. The input stimulus is on the left. The individual then internally orally reconstructs the message and to this orally reconstructed message gives whatever meaning responses he would give to the identical spoken message. The meaning responses to the spoken message consist of mediating responses whose sequence is determined by the orally reconstructed message.

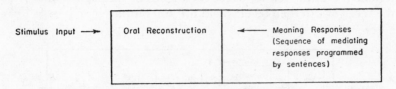

Figure 1. Carroll's Implicit Model of Reading

A more explicit model composed of three simultaneous systems has been postulated by Goodman (1966) for comprehending printed messages. He defines reading in the following way:

> Let's start with the simple statement that through reading the reader acquires meaning from written language. This means that the reader goes from written language, visually perceived, toward a reconstruction of a message which had been encoded in written language by the writer. In a basic sense, the extent to which his reconstructed message agrees with the writer's intended message is the extent to which he has comprehended (p. 188).

> To reconstruct the message, the reader must decode from language. This means that he must know and use the language in pretty much the same way that the writer knows and uses it. It also means that he must have sufficient experience and conceptual development so that the message will be comprehensible to him. The process of reading comprehension differs from the process of listening comprehension only in the form of the perceptual input. The latter works from aural input; the former from visual input (p. 188).

The three decoding systems in his model, shown in Figure 2, are: 1) the graphophonic, 2) syntactic cues, and 3) the semantic system. The graphophonic system refers to the perception of printed cues, such as letters, words, and punctuation marks, and to the utilization of knowledge of spelling sound patterns. The syntactic cues system consists of knowledge of sentence patterns, pattern markers, usually suffixes, that signal information or redundantly confirm the use of a word, function words that point to meaning bearing elements, punctuation marks that partly replace suprasegmental phonemes. The semantic system consists of concepts, information, and other experiences elicited by the message. These three systems work together to reconstruct the message, which leads to tentative meaning choices that are then tested and, if necessary, modified by going back to get more information. The receiver of the message will

understand it to the extent that a) the reconstructed message is in agreement with message of the sender and b) the receiver shares concepts and
experiences with the sender of the message. The message as understood
by the receiver can then be encoded for oral output.

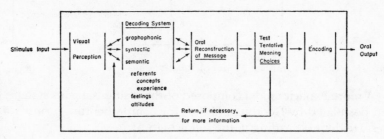

Figure 2.   Goodman's Implicit Model of Reading

A systems of communication model has been constructed by Ruddell
(1967). This model, shown in Figure 3, consists of four dynamically
interacting levels:

1) Auditory and visual input systems; 2) a surface structure level,
containing graphemic, phonemic, morphemic systems, and their interrelationships; 3) a structural and semantic level, incorporating a syntactical system, short term memory, transformational and rewrite rules, and a
mental dictionary; and 4) a deep structure level, consisting of semantic
interpretation, structural and semantic markers, and long term memory.
Structural and semantic markers, generated by the semantic interpretation system which integrates structural and semantic components of a
sentence, operate in feedback lines and are stored in long term memory.
Three other systems complete the model: 1) affective mobilizers, representing individual interests and values, enter into the goal-setting and
evaluating phases of communication, 2) cognitive strategies, interacting
with affective mobilizers, influence the organization and reorganization
of components for decoding, processing, and encoding information, and
3) context feedback lines for verifying decoding and syntax, and for
evaluating discourse.

The operation of the model can be explained by tracing the act of
reading from the surface to the deep structure level through one of many
possible sequences for perceiving, decoding, structural and semantic
processing, interpreting, feeding back, and storing information: stimuli,
input through the visual system, initiate the process of decoding. In
accordance with the individual's objective and cognitive strategy, knowledge of the language code and one or more subsystems are mobilized to

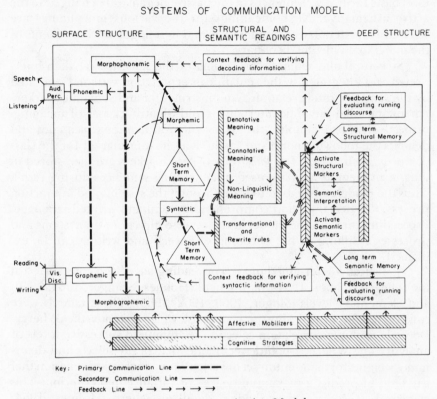

Figure 3. Ruddell's Systems of Communication Model

decode the message. If utilization of phoneme-grapheme relationships does not succeed in decoding the message, sound-spelling clues at the morphographemic and morphophonemic levels may become involved. Also, other systems, such as context feedback from the deep structure level may influence the decoding process. More advanced readers can minimize this surface level of decoding and maximize a more meaningful response by proceeding more directly to a morphemic level.

At the next level, the syntactical system, cued in part by variations in pitch, stress, and juncture within the sentence, is involved in determining the structure of the sentence. For example, different concepts are called forth from the sentence, "They are frying chickens," when the sentence structure is shifted as implied by the questions, "What are they doing," and "What kind of chickens are they?" Information on the structure of the sentence is stored in short-term memory and then transformational and rewrite rules operate on the structure of the sentence to reduce it to its most basic form, e.g., sentences in the passive negative are changed to the active affirmative. Next, meanings for the various morphemes are selected from denotative, connotative, and non-linguistic components of the individual's mental dictionary.

Structural and semantic processing of the sentence are then interpreted and integrated in the semantic interpretation system. Generated by the semantic interpretation system, structural and semantic markers narrow possible semantic alternatives and identify classes of meaning, respectively. For example, "the" is a structural marker which cues and delimits the following noun and "male" is a semantic marker for the class of words, such as *man, boy, father, son.* These markers are then stored in long-term memory and are used in generating sentences during recall. Thus the model can be used to trace through the systems and interacting processes of decoding and comprehending oral and printed language. Proceeding through the model in the reverse direction, the systems and processes resulting in the encoding of speech and writing can be explained.

Statistically-determined models of reading have been constructed at the college (Holmes, 1954), high school (Holmes & Singer, 1961, 1966) and elementary levels (Singer, 1960, 1962, 1965). These models were constructed by use of substrata analysis, which extends the Wherry-Doolittle multiple correlation selection technique to successive levels of analysis. The Wherry-Doolittle technique analytically selects and determines weights for a minimum set of variables in a regression equation that will tend to predict a maximum degree of variance in a criterion. This statistical procedure, described in detail elsewhere (Holmes, 1954; Holmes & Singer, 1966; Singer, 1965e), was applied to a matrix of 36 variables that had been administered to an average sample of fourth graders. Since the variables had been determined by previous research or had been postulated from theoretical formulations to be predictors of speed or power of reading, substrata analysis resulted in the parsimonious structure shown in the model in Figure 4. Adjacent to each predictor is its percent contribution to the variance of a criterion, speed or power of reading, or subcriterion, such as vocabulary in isolation or word recognition in context.

The model reveals that four systems, inferred from predictors selected for the multiple regression equations, accounted for 89 percent of the variance in Power of Reading, and three systems accounted for 77 percent of the variance in Speed of Reading. (Only the Test names of the predictors are shown in the model; system names are given in parentheses in the text.) The remaining variance must be attributable to other variables that were not included in the study, such as personality (Athey,

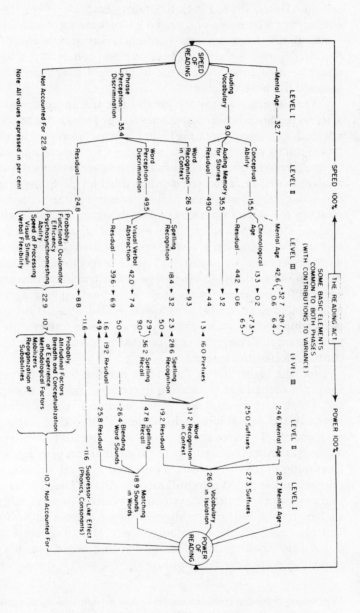

Figure 4. Flow chart to show the results of the substrata analysis of speed and power of reading at the fourth grade level

Note: The level I subsystems for predicting speed and power of reading can be renamed with the following current terminology: Mental Age = Reasoning in Reading; Suffixes = Morphemic Analysis; Vocabulary in Isolation = Semantics; Matching Sounds in Words = Graphophonemics; Reading Vocabulary = Semantics (Concrete level); Phrase Perception Discrimination = Perceptual-Oculomotor System. Syntax which does not precipitate as a predictor may be subsumed by the subsystem of Reasoning in Reading.

1965), attitudes and values (Athey & Holmes, 1967), biological support systems (Davis, 1963, 1964), flexibility (Laycock, 1958, 1966), functional oculomotor efficiency and speed of processing visual stimuli (Gilbert, 1953, 1959). Since general reading ability was assessed by the Gates Reading Survey subtests, "Level of Comprehension" and "Speed," the structure of the model depicted in Figure 4 is delimited to the domains assessed by these variables.

On the left side of the model are the three broadly categorized systems for Speed of Reading: mental age (reasoning in context), auding vocabulary (word meaning), and phrase perception discrimination (visuo-motor perceptual systems). Except for mental age which could not be predicted from other variables in the matrix, these systems are analyzed further at the second and third levels. Subsystems for auding vocabulary are conceptual ability (conceptual subsystem) and auding memory for stories (memory); underlying conceptual ability are mental age and chronological age. The sequence of subsystems for phrase perception discrimination are word recognition in context (word recognition and syntactical subsystems), and word perception discrimination (visual perception); underlying word perception discrimination are spelling recognition (subsystems for spelling, including sequencing and phoneme-grapheme relationships) and visual verbal abstraction (subsystem for perceiving and abstracting recurring groups or letters). "Residual" refers to unaccounted variance, attributable to variables not included in the construction of the model.

On the right side of the model are the four systems for Power of Reading: mental age (reasoning in context), suffixes (morphemic analysis), vocabulary in isolation (word meaning) and matching sounds in words (word recognition, which includes decoding subsystems such as phonemics). The systems for word meaning and word recognition are analyzed further. Subsystems for vocabulary in isolation are mental age (reasoning in context), suffixes (morphemic analysis) and word recognition in context (word recognition and syntax). Underlying word recognition in context are the subsystems of prefixes (morphemic analysis) and spelling recognition and recall (spelling subsystems, including sequencing and phoneme-grapheme relationships). Matching word sounds breaks down into spelling recall and blending word sounds (integrating phoneme-graphemic relationships).[2]

---

[2] The figures in the center columns are estimates of contributions of second and third level subsystems to the variance of speed and power of reading, computed by multiplying percent contributions across a sequence of subsystems in a particular system (Holmes, 1965).

Thus, the model indicates that silent reading ability is divisible into two major interrelated components, speed and power of reading. Underlying each of these components is a complexly interwoven hierarchy of predictors which represent systems and subsystems that can be mobilized for attaining speed and power of reading. It can be inferred from the model that in changing from one task to another in reading, for example, from speed to power of reading, an individual reorganizes his set of systems and subsystems from one that emphasized his visuo-motor perceptual system to one that stressed his morphemic and word recognition systems, in addition to word meaning and reasoning in context.

The model may be read in various other ways to determine how an individual might organize his subskills, ideas, and capacities to solve a problem in reading. For example, spelling recognition together with prefixes and spelling recall (Figure 4, right hand side, Level III), enter into the constellation of subabilities that could be mobilized for solving a problem in Word Recognition in Context. The subsystems of word recognition in context, plus suffixes and mental age, could then be organized for associating meaning to Vocabulary in Isolation. Finally, on the highest level, vocabulary in isolation could be integrated with suffixes, mental age, and matching sounds in words to culminate in a combination of systems for attaining Power of Reading. Again, starting with spelling recognition, a set of systems for achieving Speed of Reading can similarly be worked out. Thus, as an individual reads, he is continuously organizing and reorganizing his systems and subsystems according to his changing purposes and the demands of the reading material.

Discussion of the Models

Two of the four models have been explicitly formulated and therefore only these two models can be compared and critically evaluated. The other two, Carroll's and Goodman's, taken as examples of implicit models, are consequently less detailed and therefore not comparable, but nevertheless have certain general features which can be discussed in relation to Ruddell's and Singer's models.

Both Carroll and Goodman postulate that oral reconstruction of printed material necessarily occurs in the process of reading, presumably in both oral and silent reading. Ruddell (1967) agrees with Edfeldt (1960) that some oral component, subvocalization or inner speech, albeit at a minimal level, accompanies the process of reading. But, Singer, adducing other evidence (Hardyck et al., 1966), takes the position that when an advanced reader is reading familiar material rapidly, he can suppress or not activate at least part of it, if not his entire, oral system. Therefore, the difference among the models in regard to oral reconstruction may be a function of the type of reading. For slow, analytical or study type of reading, oral reconstruction may be a part of the process, but for rapid, skimming type of reading, oral reconstruction may be suppressed or not mobilized. If empirical testing finds that this hypothesis is tenable, then a model of reading would have to depict an oral reconstruction system that is activated or suppressed according to the maturity level of the reader, his purpose in reading, and the difficulty of the material.

Feedback lines from the comprehension stage of the model back to the decoding or surface level are explicit in Goodman's and Ruddell's models. Such lines are implicit in Singer's model. Indeed the central hypothesis of the substrata-factor theory of reading postulates that there is a dynamic interrelation among systems and subsystems. Also, predictors which identify them are, in fact, statistically associated with each other. However, it must also be postulated that if some systems or subsystems are suppressed when others are mobilized or activated for a particular reading task, then feedback lines would be necessary for facilitory and for inhibitory functions.

Different procedures were used in constructing the models. For example, Ruddell reviewed and attempted on a *logical* basis to interrelate psycholinguistic research in defining and organizing his model, while Singer selected his variables from a comprehensive review of research in reading and then used statistical procedures in constructing his model. Nevertheless, there is considerable overlap in the models, which becomes apparent when comparing the models, system by system. Broadly categorized, the four systems for Power of Reading in Singer's model are word recognition, word meaning, morphemic analysis, and reasoning in reading. In addition, a visuo-motor perceptual system, but not morphemic analysis nor word recognition, accounted for individual differences in Speed of Reading. Word recognition and word meaning appear to be similar to Goodman's graphophonic, syntactic, and semantic systems for decoding and to Ruddell's phonemic, graphemic, morphemic and syntactic systems, plus feedback from the deep structure level to the decoding level. Word meaning consists of knowledge of vocabulary and conceptual ability and, in general, what Russell (1956) has labeled as "materials of thinking" (percepts, images, concepts, information, and feeling tone). Morphemic analysis consists of ability to analyze words into their meaning components and through this process arrive at the meaning of words. Word meaning and morphemic analysis appear to be functionally equivalent to Ruddell's mental dictionary and morphemic system and to Goodman's semantic system. Reasoning in context includes cognitive processes and strategies for inferring, interpreting, integrating, and conceptualizing ideas, which seem to be comparable to the semantic interpretations and cognitive strategies of Ruddell's model and might include at least part of the system for transforming and rewriting sentences. At least part of the visuo-motor perceptual system would probably correspond to Ruddell's and Goodman's visual perception system. Both Singer and Ruddell accept evidence and include in their models systems of values, attitudes, and interests which can influence a system or even the entire operation of their models. Singer also includes in his model a biological support system which physiologically affects the functioning of the reading process.

In contrast, Singer's model does not contain certain subsystems found in Ruddell's model. Missing are structural and semantic markers and storage systems for classifying sentences and semantic aspects of words. Nor does Singer's model identify transformational and rewrite rules and syntactical systems as such. While Ruddell's model is intended for all four aspects of communication, Singer's is limited to the particular criterion used, speed or power of reading, and to the particular grade level at which the model was constructed.

From the cursory review above of certain aspects of development, the conclusion can be supported that qualitative and quantitative changes occur in the interrelated areas of cognition, language, and reading performance. Consequently, a series of models is necessary in order to explain and predict reading performance throughout the educational continuum. Indeed, Singer (1964, 1965d) found that qualitative and/or quantitative changes do occur in the organization of systems and subsystems that accompany development in speed and power of reading.

Summary and Conclusion

Four models, representing the structure and functioning of systems in reading performance, were explained, compared, and critically evaluated. The models did not agree on the necessity of oral reconstruction of printed material in silent reading. However, three of the models were similar, particularly in the systems mobilized for decoding purposes.

In an attempt to integrate these models, which are somewhat similar, the following description of the reading act was formulated: Oral reading is a process of utilizing oculomotor and visual processes for perceiving and transforming printed stimuli through a decoding phase, consisting of reasoning, word meaning, morphemic, word recognition and syntactic systems, into mental representations. In the process, the reader mobilizes his knowledge of the language code and syntactic cues to reconstruct and to transform these representatives into simpler sentence structures whenever possible. He then responds to the reconstructed or transformed message with materials of thinking, such as concepts, images, information, and feeling tones retrieved from his memory storage systems, and with appropriate thought processes and cognitive strategies. The structural and semantic aspects of the sentence are then interpreted, tested for meaning, and, if necessary, feedback impulses are sent to systems closer to the surface structure level to modify the processing and output of one or more systems or to reorganize the systems employed for the particular reading task.

Structural and semantic markers, generated by the interpretation system, are stored in long term memory. These markers can be utilized for regenerating and encoding stored meanings into oral output. The mobilization and organization of responses to the message, evaluation of and feelings aroused by the message, and emphases given to encoded messages through choice of words as well as through such suprasegmental phonemes as pitch, stress, and juncture, are a function, in part, of the reader's attitudes, needs, and values. The person's style of reading is also a function of his biological subsystems.

For other types of reading, such as rapid reading, a general reorganization of systems and subsystems mobilized for the reading task occurs. In silent reading, oral reconstruction and encoding systems may be suppressed, particularly as the individual matures in reading to the level where he has formed and gained control over feedback mechanisms for suppressing these components of reading (Singer, 1967). Such suppression is more likely to occur when the individual's purpose is to read rapidly and the demands and difficulty level of the material for the individual are not high.

All of the models need to be put to empirical and statistical tests to determine whether they can explain and predict reading behavior. Evidence from statistically determined models of reading and from a cursory review of development of language, cognition, and reading suggest that a series of models is necessary to account for quantitative and qualitative changes in systems and subsystems associated with improvement in reading achievement as individuals progress through school. Also, the models will, of course, have to be up-dated as new concepts are formulated. Already such concepts as perceptual scanning (Geyer, 1966) and linguistic form (Reed, 1965) may have to be incorporated into the models.

None of the models has yet been used for experimental purposes, but one of them was used for clinical diagnosis and evaluation (Singer, 1965b). However, these as well as other models, such as one that has been designed for developing conceptual responses in the initial stages of reading (Singer, 1966; Singer, Balow, and Dahms, 1968) and one that has been hierarchically structured (Gagné, 1965), need to be experimentally tested and evaluated (Singer, 1968). Through such means, it would be possible to determine empirically the heuristic and explanatory value of models that are currently being used explicitly or implicitly in teaching and in research.

REFERENCES

Athey, Irene J. *Reading-Personality Patterns at the Junior High School Level.* Doctoral dissertation. Berkeley: University of California, 1965.

Athey, Irene J. and Holmes, Jack A. *Reading Success and a Personality Value-Systems Syndrome: A Thirty-year THEN and NOW Study at the Junior High School Level.* Final Report, Contract No. S-248; Bureau of Research No. 5-8027-2-12-1, Washington, D.C.: Office of Education, U.S. Department of Health, Education, and Welfare, 1967.

Bayley, Nancy. "Consistency and Variability in the Growth of Intelligence from Birth to Eighteen Years." *Journal of Genetic Psychology* 75: 165-96, 1949.

Bruner, J. and Olver, Rose. "Development of Equivalence Transformations in Children." *Monographs of the Society for Research in Child Development* 28: 125-43, 1963.

Buswell, Guy T. *Fundamental Reading Habits: A Study of Their Development.* Chicago: University of Chicago Press, 1922.

Buswell, Guy T. *Non-oral Reading–A Study of Its Use in the Chicago Public Schools.* Chicago: University of Chicago Press, 1945.

Carroll, John B. *Language and Thought.* Englewood Cliffs, N.J.: Prentice-Hall, 1964.

Davis, Frank R., Jr. *Speed of Reading and Rate of Recovery in Certain Physiological Subsystems.* Berkeley: University of California, 1963.

Davis, Frank R., Jr. "The Substrata-Factor Theory of Reading: Human Physiology as a Factor in Reading." *Improvement of Reading Through Classroom Practice.* International Reading Association Conference Proceedings, Vol. 9, 1964. (Edited by J. Allen Figurel.) Newark, Del.: International Reading Association, 1964, p. 292-96.

Edfeldt, Ake W. *Silent Speech and Silent Reading.* Chicago: University of Chicago Press, 1960.

Ervin, Susan M. and Miller, W. R. "Language Development." *Sixty-second Yearbook of the National Society for the Study of Education, Part* 1. Chicago: University of Chicago Press, 1963. p. 108-43.

Flavell, John H. *The Developmental Psychology of Jean Piaget.* Princeton, N.J.: Van Nostrand, 1963.

Gagné, Robert. *The Conditions of Learning.* New York: Holt, 1965.

Geyer, John J. *Perceptual Systems in Reading: The Prediction of a Temporal Eye-Voice Span Constant.* Final Report, Contract No. O. E. 5-10-362. Cooperative Research Program, Washington, D.C.: Office of Education, U.S. Dept. of Health, Education, and Welfare, 1966.

Gilbert, L. C. "Functional Motor Efficiency of the Eyes and Its Relation to Reading." *University of California Publications in Education* 2: 159-232, 1953.

Gilbert, L. C. "Speed of Processing Visual Stimuli and Its Relation to Reading." *Journal of Educational Psychology* 55: 8-14, 1959.

Goodman, Kenneth S. "A Psycholinguistic View of Reading Comprehension." *New Frontiers in College-Adult Reading.* (Edited by George B. Schick and Merrill M. May.) Fifteenth Yearbook of the National Reading Conference. Milwaukee, Wisc.: The National Reading Conference, 1966, p. 188-96.

Hardyck, C., Petrinovich, L., and Ellsworth, D. "Feedback of Speech Muscle Activity During Silent Reading: Rapid Extinction." *Science* 154: 1467-68, 1966.

Holmes, Jack A. "Factors Underlying Major Reading Disabilities at the College Level." *Genetic Psychology Monographs* 49: 3-95, 1954.

Holmes, Jack A. "The Brain and the Reading Process." *Reading is Creative Living.* Twenty-second Yearbook of the Claremont Reading Conference, Claremont, Calif.: Curriculum Laboratory, 1957, p. 49-67.

Holmes, Jack A. "The Substrata-Factor Theory of Reading: Some New Experimental Evidence." *New Frontiers in Reading.* International Reading Association Conference Proceedings, Vol. 5, 1960. (Edited by J. Allen Figurel.) New York: Scholastic Magazines, 1960, p. 115-21.

Holmes, Jack A. "Personality Characteristics of the Disabled Reader." *Journal of Developmental Reading* 4: 111-22, 1961.

Holmes, Jack A. "Basic Assumptions Underlying the Substrata-Factor Theory." *Reading Research Quarterly* 1: 5-28, 1965.

Holmes, Jack A., and Singer, Harry. *The Substrata-Factor Theory: The Substrata Factor Differences Underlying Reading Ability in Known Groups.* Final report, Contracts 538 and 538A, Office of Education, U.S. Department of Health, Education, and Welfare, Washington, D.C.: 1961.

Holmes, Jack A. "Theoretical Models and Trends Toward More Basic Research in Reading." *Review of Educational Research* 34: 127-55, 1964.

Holmes, Jack A. *Speed and Power of Reading in High School.* Office of Education, U.S. Department of Health, Education, and Welfare. A publication of the Bureau of Educational Research and Development, Washington, D.C.: U.S. Government Printing Office, 1966.

Inhelder, Bärbel. "Criteria of the Stages of Mental Development." *Psychological Studies of Human Development.* (Edited by R. Kuhlen and G. J. Thomson.) Second Edition, New York: Appleton-Century-Crofts, 1963, p. 28-48.

Inhelder, Bärbel and Piaget, Jean. *The Growth of Logical Thinking from Childhood to Adolescence.* New York: Basic Books, 1958.

Laycock, Frank. "Flexibility in Reading Rate and Einstellung." *Perceptual and Motor Skills* 8: 123-29, 1958.

Laycock, Frank. "Conceptual and Personality Factors Underlying Flexibility in Speed of Reading." *New Frontiers in College-Adult Reading.* (Edited by George B. Schick and Merrill M. May.) Fifteenth Yearbook of the National Reading Conference, Milwaukee, Wisc.: The National Reading Conference, 1966. p. 140-46.

Loban, Walter D. *The Language of Elementary School Children.* Champaign, Ill.: National Council of Teachers of English, 1963.

McCarthy, Dorothea. "Language Development in Children." *Manual of Child Psychology.* (Edited by Leonard Carmichael.) New York: John Wiley, 1964. p. 476-581.

Noel, Doris L. "A Comparative Study of the Relationship Between the Quality of the Child's Language Usage and the Quality and Type of Language Used in the Home." *Journal of Educational Research* 47: 161-67, 1953.

Osgood, Charles E. *Method and Theory in Experimental Psychology.* New York: Oxford University Press, 1956.

Piaget, Jean. "Principal Factors Determining Intellectual Evolution From Childhood to Adult Life." *Factors Determining Human Behavior.* Harvard Tercentenary Conference of Arts and Sciences, Cambridge, Mass.: Harvard University, 1937, p. 32-48.

Reed, David W. "A Theory of Language, Speech and Writing." *Elementary English* 42: 845-51, 1965.

Ruddell, Robert B. "The Effect of the Similarity of Oral and Written Patterns of Language Structure on Reading Comprehension." *Elementary English* 32: 403-10, 1965.

Ruddell, Robert B. *The Effect of Four Programs of Reading Instruction With Varying Emphasis on the Regularity of Grapheme-Phoneme Correspondences and the Relation of Language Structure to Meaning on Achievement in First Grade Reading.* Cooperative Research Project No. 2699, U.S. Office of Education. Berkeley, California: University of California, 1965. (Multilith)

Ruddell, Robert B. *Linguistics and Language Learning.* Redwood City, Calif.: Bay Region Instruction Television for Education, 1967.

Russell, David B. *Children's Thinking.* New York: Ginn, 1956.

Singer, Harry. Conceptual Ability in the Substrata-Factor Theory of Reading. Doctoral dissertation. Berkeley: University of California, 1960.

Singer, Harry. "Substrata-Factor Theory of Reading: Theoretical Design for Teaching Reading." *Challenge and Experiment in Reading.* International Reading Association Proceedings, Vol. 7, 1962. (Edited by J. Allen Figurel.) New York: Scholastic Magazines, 1962, p. 226-32.

Singer, Harry. "Substrata-Factor Patterns Accompanying Development in Power of Reading, Elementary Through College Level." *The Philosophical and Sociological Bases of Reading.* (Edited by Eric Thurston and Lawrence Hafner.) Fourteenth Yearbook of the National Reading Conference, Milwaukee, Wisc.: The National Reading Conference, 1965. p. 41-56.

Singer, Harry. "Conceptualizations in Learning to Read." *New Frontiers in College-Adult Reading.* (Edited by George B. Schick and Merrill M. May.) Fifteenth Yearbook of the National Reading Conference, Milwaukee, Wisc.: The National Reading Conference, 1966. p. 116-32.

Singer, Harry. "Substrata-Factor Evaluation of a Precocious Reader." *The Reading Teacher* 18: 288-96, 1965.

Singer, Harry. "A Theory of Human Learning for Teaching Reading: A Discussion of Professor Arthur Staast's 'Integrated Functional Learning Theory for Reading." *Use of Theoretical Models in Research.* (Edited by Albert J. Kingston.) Newark, Del.: International Reading Association, 1965. p. 68-73.

Singer, Harry. *Substrata-Factor Reorganization Accompanying Development in Speed and Power of Reading.* Final report, Project No. 2011, U.S. Office of Education, Washington, D.C.: 1965.

Singer, Harry. "Symposium on the Substrata-Factor Theory of Reading: Research and Evaluation of Critiques." *Reading and Inquiry.* International Reading Association Proceedings, Vol. 10, 1965. (Edited by J. Allen Figurel.) Newark Del.: International Reading Association, 1965. p. 325-31.

Singer, Harry. "An Instructional Strategy for Developing Conceptual Responses in Reading Readiness." *Vistas in Reading,* II, Part I. International Reading Association Proceedings, Vol. 11, 1966. (Edited by J. Allen Figurel.) Newark, Del.: International Reading Association, 1966. p. 425-31.

Singer, Harry. "Developmental Changes in the Subsystems of Reading and Listening." *Paper Abstracts.* (Edited by Ellis B. Page.) Washington, D.C.: American Educational Research Association, 1967. p. 127.

Singer, Harry. "Stimulus Models for Teaching Reading." *Proceedings of the Fifth Annual Conference of the United Kingdom Reading Association,* Edinburgh, Scotland: 1968.

Singer, Harry; Balow, Irving H.; and Dahms, Patricia. "A Continuum of Teaching
    Strategies for Developing Reading Readiness at the Kindergarten Level." *Forging
    Ahead in Reading.* International Reading Association Proceedings, Vol. 12, 1968.
    (Edited by J. Allen Figurel.) Newark, Del.: International Reading Association, 1968. p.
    463-68.

Smith, Medorah E. "An Investigation of the Development of the Sentence and the Extent of
    Vocabulary in Young Children." *University of Iowa Studies of Child Welfare* 3: No. 5, 1926.

Strickland, Ruth B. *The Language of Elementary School Children: Its Relationship to the Language
    of Reading Textbooks and the Quality of Reading of Selected Children.* Bulletin of the School of
    Education, Indiana University 38: 1-131, 1962.

Affective Model

The Function of Attitude in the Reading Process

GROVER C. MATHEWSON
Florida International University

Athey (1:96) has pointed out that affective factors have, with a few exceptions, been neglected in models of the reading process. This omission may reflect a lack of definition concerning the role of affect. The concepts of attitude, motivation, interest, belief, and value may seem to have a vague quality resisting systematic treatment. Further, relationships between these concepts and the cognitive processes operating during reading may appear to be indeterminable. Ruddell's Systems of Communication model (53:253) approaches this problem by specifying the influence of affective mobilizers upon communication processes, but does so in a way requiring further elaboration before specific effects may be predicted. It therefore appears appropriate to propose a research-based model identifying central substantive units (constructs) and processes describing the role of affect in reading.

By necessity, the attempt to construct a model dealing with affect in the reading process must be limited. There are many approaches to affect, including those of personality psychology, social psychology, and psychiatry. Each of these areas is based upon its own unique body of literature even though some overlap is present. It is apparent, then, that if a model is to be coherent, the model builder may have to choose among the possible underlying points of view. Unless this is done, there might be so much to include in the model that no model at all would be possible.

The present approach to affect and reading therefore is anchored primarily in a single source discipline: experimental social psychology. The choice of social psychology means that much of the literature of personality psychology is set aside for a time. This may be a wise strategy because a general model representing affective processes common to all readers may result. The emphasis on general principles does not mean, of course, that constructs from personality psychology and psychiatry are not important to include. Individual difference must eventually be accounted for within the structure of the model since, as Marlowe and

Gergen (*39:*645) have pointed out, personality plays "an important part in understanding almost all aspects of social processes." Its inclusion at the present stage of model development, however, may be premature.

With the work in personality and individual difference temporarily set aside, the present effort rests on a foundation provided by social psychologists, reading researchers whose bent has been toward social psychology, and other psychologists whose work relates to the present effort. In order to facilitate a clear exposition of the model, its components are developed one by one in terms of the theory and research underlying them. Only then is the model presented in its integrated form. It is hoped that this developmental method of presentation will not only reveal more effectively the functions of the model, but also shed some light on the rationale underlying its structure.

Attitude

To begin, it is necessary to establish a central affective component around which to build the model. The possible candidates are value, belief, interest, attitude, and perhaps some others. Only attitude, however, "has played a central role in the development of American social psychology" (*32:1*). This primacy may have arisen from early attempts to define it and to measure it rigorously. Hundreds of experimental studies have been performed using attitude as the central construct. The primacy may also have come from the flexibility of attitude as opposed to belief and value. Attitude is considered capable of formation and change in a way not usually associated with these other affective constructs. Perhaps, too, the primacy was a result of the ability of attitude to focus on specifiable objects. Whatever the explanation, it would seem reasonable to choose attitude as the central construct in a model of affective influence upon reading.

One difficulty posed by selecting attitude as the kernel component of an affective model of reading is that the concept may not appear to be sufficiently dynamic. Getzels (*21:*98) has pointed out that "we do not ordinarily speak of being driven by an attitude; we are necessarily driven by our interests." Thus it seemed to Getzels that interest had an active, energizing quality lacked by attitude. This observation, however, may be clarified by Jones and Gerard's statement (*30:*163) that an action tendency—or, in their words, an action orientation—is one of the dimensions of attitude. In view of this clarification, it is apparent that a favorable attitude with a strong action orientation may be the same as an interest. More concretely, a child having only a favorable attitude toward books might not necessarily be "driven" to read them. If his favorable attitude had in addition a strong action orientation, it is likely that he would not only seek out books and read them, but also find a place to keep them in his home. This latter constitutes what is ordinarily known as a literary interest.

In view of the apparent synonymity of interest on the one hand and attitude with a positive action orientation on the other, the term *interest* is seldom used in the present attempt at model development. Rather, it is assumed that what is commonly called interest in the educational literature and elsewhere is a favorable attitude with a strong action orientation.

Motivation

The choice of attitude as the central construct of the model does not mean that action orientation is to be neglected. Instead, it means that a special provision must be made in the model to include a component insuring the presence of a strong action orientation. A clue as to what this component might be comes from Cofer and Appley (*12*:805). These investigators have concluded in their extensive review of the literature that "it is largely an assertion of faith that it is useful to conceive of attitudes as motivational variables." In addition, Newcomb, Turner, and Converse (*48*:40) have defined attitude as "a state of readiness for motive arousal." Both of these observations point to the need to introduce a motivational component into the model in order to insure that favorable attitude has a separate, energizing process to accompany it. Thus, if a child is to read, he will need not only a favorable attitude toward reading materials, but also an appropriate motivation.

The addition of the motivational component to the model requires that appropriate motivational processes be identified. These motives should be capable of causing reading behavior in children who already have a favorable attitude toward reading. While motivational psychology is still in a state of flux (*54*:1), it may be wise to select those basic motives for use in the model which seem to have the greatest relevance and support.

One obvious motive for reading is curiosity and exploration (*5, 10, 24*). A child who has favorable attitude concerning books may read when he comes across a book stimulating his curiosity. Another motive capable of stimulating reading is achievement (*2, 3, 37*). A child may read a book because he wants to receive a high mark in a classroom or the knowledge of his own scholastic success. Similarly, the motives of self-actualization (*40, 50*), activity (*12*:271-273; *27; 44; 63*), and anxiety (*43; 46*:20; *62*) may cause reading behavior.

An important thing to notice in this selection is that motivational psychologists appear to have identified only a limited number of basic motives (*12, 54*). Of these, the motives selected here are for the most part "higher" motives: that is, they appear to be related less to the biological than to the cerebral needs. Motives such as hunger and thirst would not ordinarily be used to motivate reading behavior, though behavior modification proponents indicate that they may be used in that way.

The identification of motivational processes as a second component of the model brings up the question of how the motivational and attitudinal processes work together. At first it may seem that both motivation and favorable attitude must be present if reading is to occur, but deeper consideration shows that this may not be true. In a hypothetical case, a young person may have a very unfavorable attitude toward reading *Silas Marner*. However, he may know that if he is to receive an "A" in a course, he will have to read the book and demonstrate his knowledge on a test. Therefore, he reads the book with good comprehension. This is an example of achievement motivation sustaining reading despite unfavorable attitude. It demonstrates that the two factors need not always work together to energize the reading process.

It would appear, however, that a strong, favorable attitude toward reading matter is necessary if the primary motives for reading are to be curiosity and exploration, self-actualization, or activity. Such motives appear to be much more closely tied to the reading materials themselves and are fulfilled only to the degree that a favorable attitude toward the reading remains. In addition, it appears that all reading which is self-sustaining, not the result of external press, must be accompanied by a favorable attitude toward the reading materials. This acceptance model hypothesis needs future testing, of course, in order to validate its claim.

Form, Content, and Format

When analyzing the effects of motivation and attitude toward reading, it is necessary to become more specific concerning the identity of the object of a reading attitude. It may not be proper to talk of attitude toward reading in general because most readers like some books while they dislike others. Saying, "John likes reading" usually means that there are some books that John likes, and that he reads them frequently. It would seem then that one primary attitude object in reading is *content*. The content or meaning of a book is a primary attitude object because it may correspond with the reader's motivations and general background, or it may not correspond. It is much more appropriate to say, "John likes science fiction," specifying a content type, than to say, "John likes reading." In fact, John may not like reading unless he is reading science fiction.

In addition to content, another possible determinant of reading attitude is *format*. This would include the presence or absence of pictures in a literary selection (55, 56), type of book cover (36), and print size and style. Another determinant of attitude may be *form*, including such aspects as dialect (41) or syntax. To specify these three aspects—content, format, and form—as possible factors determining attitude toward reading selections may help considerably in the attempt to differentiate the most potent elements contributing to a favorable reading attitude.

In the course of identifying aspects of text contributing to reading attitude, it is necessary to remember that attitudes toward reading selections may be determined by particular combinations of these aspects. Form, content, and format may, in some cases, have to appear together in precisely the correct way before some effects emerge. Rosenblatt (51:45) emphasized this, stating that it is impossible "to experience 'content' apart from some kind of form" in a literary work. Methods such as those suggested by Brown (9) may be used in studying particular combination effects upon attitude.

In summary, response to reading materials may depend upon motivation and attitude toward specified aspects of reading materials. Reading attitude may be defined as a positive or negative affective response to these aspects, following the lead of Thurstone (64) and Edwards (14). This conceptualization assumes that attitude toward reading is always linked to some particular set of reading materials, and that there is probably no general attitude toward reading. This makes sense in that even the individual who professes to "like reading" may display negative attitudes if the form of the reading materials is wrong (another language) or if the content does not suit him (perhaps advanced theory of relativity). The only reason people speak of "liking reading" at all is that they experience a need for cognitive consistency (38, 68). They feel that if someone likes a part of something, he must like the whole thing. This, of course, is not possible with reading because there is no person who likes *all* types of reading.

Comprehension, Attention, and Acceptance

Up to this point, the model has only two components. The first is an attitudinal component and the second is a motivational component. Clearly, it is also necessary to identify the locus of effect upon which attitude and motivation operate. Three studies in particular provide evidence concerning this locus of effect. These were performed by Bernstein (6), Groff (22), and Shnayer (59). The conclusion of these investigators was that attitude (or interest, as explained earlier) may have a positive, facilitating effect upon comprehension. In each case it was demonstrated that increasing the favorability of attitude toward a reading selection may result in superior comprehension. Though this experimental foundation is far from complete, it would nevertheless appear appropriate to add a comprehension component to the model. This comprehension component may be viewed as being directly facilitated by favorable attitude and appropriate motivation. The component may also be viewed most properly as a process rather than a static entity. Comprehension clearly involves many operations (53) although these are grouped in one component of the model for simplicity's sake.

With the addition of a comprehension component, it is also necessary to consider the inclusion of attention. Attention is by definition prior to comprehension. It must be secured before any reading can take place. Zimbardo and Ebbesen (69:18) have pointed this out, stating that attention is a prerequisite to comprehending and reacting to a message. The attentional component may be viewed as operating separately from the comprehension component because attention does not necessarily guarantee comprehension, though it increases the probability of it. A child who is attracted by a bright book cover with a pretty picture (format) may, when attempting to read, discover that the reading level is far too difficult. This discovery might modify the initial favorable attitude in the negative direction, thus decreasing attention.

The model as it has now been described consists of four components: attitude, motivation, attention, and comprehension. One more component is necessary to complete the model. This component again is suggested by the work of Zimbardo and Ebbesen (69:19). These social psychologists have proposed that acceptance or rejection of the meaning of a communication "is certainly at the core of the attitude-change sequence . . . ." Thus it may be appropriate to add an acceptance process component to the model. In this component, the meaning derived from reading is compared with prior attitudes, beliefs, and values. It is also evaluated in the light of the current motivation for reading. The output of the acceptance component is viewed as a modification of attitude toward the reading selection. If the acceptance is favorable, the attitude toward the selection is modified in a favorable direction, thus stimulating attention and comprehension. If the attitude is modified in a negative direction, attention and comprehension will fail to be sustained. The acceptance processes are thus at the heart of continued reading. An exciting novel may keep a reader attending and comprehending all night long because acceptance maintains a favorable attitude.

The Model

With all the components of the model described, it is appropriate to present the graphic representation of the model. This representation is presented in Figure 1 and, for convenience, is labeled "The Acceptance Model." At the top of the acceptance model are the motivation and attitude components. The attitude component is at the upper right and is labeled "Relevant Attitude Toward Reading" because it is assumed that this component represents a child's attitude at a given instant toward a given set of reading materials. This attitude is conceptualized as being unified, but also as being based on potentially separable evaluational responses to the three aspects of the reading input: content, format, and form. The unity of the resulting attitude is predicted based on the consistency of affect usually existing within the confines of a given attitude (*31:* 444). For instance, if content is viewed very positively, then the relevant attitude toward reading may be very positive in spite of a neutral evaluation of form and format.

The "Motivational Processes" component presented at the upper left acceptance model may be defined as ". . . the process of arousing action, sustaining the activity in progress, and regulating the pattern of activity" (*67:24*). As mentioned earlier, the number of basic motivations experienced by humans are viewed as limited. In contrast, there may be an infinite number of attitudes since these are limited only by the number of possible attitude objects. They, of course, are infinite.

Like attitude, motivation may be expected to differ from time to time. At various times one motivation may surface as dominant, at other times another. Depending upon the particular motivation, the child may have mental energy available for the reading act. It is unlikely a hungry child (hunger motivation dominant) would have his reading behavior energized, but a child whose activity or curiosity and exploration motives were dominant would more likely turn to reading.

The two components at the top of the model—motivation and attitude—thus work together to create the condition in which the child begins to pay attention to books. This is represented by the "Attentional Processes" component at the center of the model. This component directs the attention of the child first to the gross physical characteristics of the book(format), and then to the print inside the book. It therefore may be viewed as operating at levels of successively increasing complexity. First,

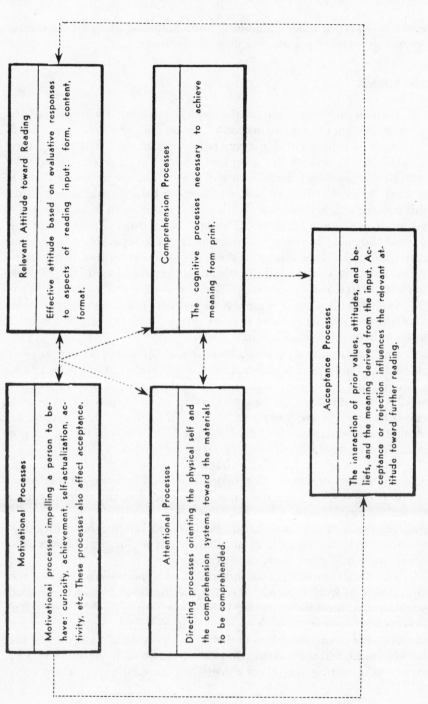

Figure 1.   The Acceptance Model: A Model of Attitude Influence in Reading Comprehension

the mere color of a book may attract attention. Then, attention may move to the pictures in the book, to the print size, or to the book length to determine appropriateness. Then, attention may be directed to the title and, following that, to the first paragraph. This sequence is probably different for each reader. The one presented here is only an example.

As the attentional processes go to levels of increasing complexity, the "Comprehension Processes" component is brought into operation. This component is also influenced directly by motivation and attitude. As attention becomes stabilized on the print, the comprehension component decodes the meaning of the reading selection. If attitude is favorable and the motivations are appropriate, comprehension works at peak efficiency. If, however, attitude is unfavorable or if motivation is inappropriate or not present, comprehension becomes inefficient.

The "Acceptance Processes" component at the bottom of the model begins to function when meaning derived from the reading selection is decoded. This component receives the meaning from the print and compares it with previous attitude, beliefs, values, and motives. If there is a good fit, then the relevant attitude toward reading (upper right component) is modified in a favorable direction. A lack of fit would cause this attitude to become negative. The resulting attitude change would be expected to cause a new modification of attention and comprehension. The model therefore operates in a cyclical fashion. It is similar to the "live circuit set up between reader and text" identified by Rosenblatt (51:25). As long as the acceptance processes maintain a favorable relevant attitude toward reading, and as long as the motivational processes continue to be optimal, the child will continue to read. This explanation presupposes, of course, an ideal reading situation in which there are no distractions.

The acceptance model, then, attempts to explain reading on the basis of motivation and attitude toward aspects of reading materials. Its emphasis upon the affective component of reading is not unique in recent educational writing (4, 6, 7, 8, 9, 11, 13, 15, 16, 17, 18, 19, 20, 21, 22, 23, 25, 26, 29, 33, 34, 36, 41, 42, 45, 47, 49, 51, 52, 53, 55, 56, 57, 58, 59, 60, 61, 65, 70), but a systematic theoretical framework in which to view the various facets of affect has been lacking. For instance, the terms *motivation*, *attitude*, and *interest* have been used loosely and almost interchangeably in much of the literature. This looseness has led to a vagueness concerning what has been happening. It is hoped that the acceptance model will contribute in some way to an understanding of how affective factors influence reading during the reading act. At the very least, it generates testable hypotheses concerning what will happen to comprehension when attitude and motivation are manipulated experimentally.

The Acceptance Model and Reading Achievement

While the acceptance model was designed to predict reading attention and comprehension at any given instant during the reading process,
it may also be used to generate predictions concerning reading achievement. These predictions may be derived from the expected effects of
favorable attitude toward reading coupled with appropriate motivation
when both persist over an extended period of time. Since these effects are
predicted to be an increase in attention to and comprehension of reading
materials, it would be expected that large amounts of reading practice
would result if the duration of the favorable reading attitude and appropriate motivation were, say, several months or more. The consequence of
this extended practice would be expected to be an increase in reading
achievement.

A number of experimental studies tend to support this prediction for
reading achievement. One conducted by Rowell (52) has indicated that
the effect of attitude upon reading achievement may be detected over a
period as short as six weeks. Among other things, Rowell was interested in
the relationship between attitude toward reading and the reading subskills of both the Silent Reading Diagnostic Tests and the Gates Basic
Reading Tests among elementary and junior high aged students. He
investigated this relationship by exposing an experimental group to a six
week program including various interesting reading activities. Following
the program, Rowell correlated the change in attitude during the reading
program with achievement in the various subskills. He found that the
greatest correlation occurred between attitude and syllabication (.477),
followed by the correlations of attitude with letter sounds (.415), level of
comprehension (.398), and recognition of words in isolation (.354). All
other correlations were not statistically significant. Rowell concluded that
"there was some indication that change in attitude was more highly
correlated with achievement in those skills which call for the least number
of operations and were possibly easier for students." This conclusion is
consistent with the view that attitude mediates advanced reading skills
slowly, facilitating the simple skills first with the more complex skills
following.

More than time is necessary, however, for attitude to influence the
development of reading skill. Also necessary are strong motivations relevant to reading, availability of reading materials, and freedom from
distraction. The necessity of all these factors, together with such uncontrolled factors as IQ, suggests that the measured correlation between
attitude toward favored reading content and achievement may not always
be strong in studies failing to establish the appropriate preconditions. In

addition, experiments attempting to investigate the attitude-achievement relationship may measure attitude toward reading as a school course or as a school activity rather than attitude toward preferred reading content. This strategy would insure a low correlation for the child who has sharpened his reading skills on adventure stories. He might not indicate a favorable attitude toward reading since only attitude toward school reading is being measured, not attitude toward his adventure stories. For all these reasons, then, it is not surprising to find studies in the literature showing only a small relationship between attitude and reading achievement.

One such study was performed by Neale, Gill and Tismer (47). These investigators correlated attitude toward various school subjects, including reading, with achievement in those areas. Attitude was measured by use of the semantic differential. One result of the study was correlations between attitude and reading achievement ranging between .20 and .35. These were statistically significant ($p < .01$), but not high. It should be noted, however, that attitude toward reading as a school subject was measured, not attitude toward preferred reading content, and that such factors as availability of reading material and freedom from distraction had not been assured. The failure to take these factors into consideration may have caused the correlations to be spuriously low, though their significance confirms the acceptance model prediction of a relationship between attitude and reading achievement.

A third study also supports the prediction of a positive attitude-achievement relationship. Healy (26) did a follow-up study on an earlier attempt (25) to change fifth grade children's attitudes toward reading. In the earlier attempt, she had used "a combination of small group instruction, flexible grouping, reading partners, and individualized instruction" to change an experimental group's attitudes toward reading. This attempt had been successful. She then measured the children's reading achievement and the number of books they read during the first semester in junior high school. The results showed that the experimental program had resulted in significantly higher reading achievement ($p < .01$) and in a greater number of books read ($p < .01$) than had the control program. Again, this supports the acceptance model's prediction concerning attitude and achievement.

The literature thus supports the acceptance model's prediction of increased achievement based on favorable attitude. While this is true, it is also apparent that future research should assure appropriate motivation, availability for preferred reading materials, and freedom from distraction when testing for the effect of attitude upon long-term achievement.

Changing Attitude toward Reading Materials

The preceding sections have dealt with the effects of attitude upon comprehension and long-term achievement of reading skill. In each case, studies in the literature were found to support the contention of a positive, significant relationship. This support for the general structure of the acceptance model suggests that it may be appropriate to examine how attitudes may be changed in order to improve reading functioning and capacity. This examination is a necessary precursor to experimentation and application of the acceptance model.

The basic prediction of the acceptance model is that attitude determines attention and comprehension. This attitude either may be the result of some preconceived notion concerning reading or may be formed during the process of reading a specific selection. If the relevant attitude is the result of a notion derived from an earlier experience with reading or from the attitudes of others, then the primary difficulty in changing the attitude is to facilitate an initial exposure of the child to reading materials that he may like. If this initial exposure is accomplished, then the child may become, in Fader's words, "hooked on books" (17).

The difficulty in introducing new, appropriate materials as a sort of "pump priming" may be overcome in a number of ways. First, the teacher may resort to external praise or punishment in order to begin reading activity. Of these two alternatives, Skinner has pointed out that punishment is the less effective (28:64). In contrast, praise may be used to increase reading behavior and, eventually, to form favorable attitudes toward the form, content, and format of reading materials.

It is important to notice that praise cannot be used as a long-term support for reading behavior. When the child is no longer under the control of the praising person, whether it be the parent or teacher, the child will have to rely upon his own motivations and attitudes in order to sustain his reading behavior. At the very best, praise only serves a stopgap function.

In addition to praise, there are other ways to begin the formation of favorable attitudes toward reading. Among these is individualization of reading instruction (25, 26, 29). The teacher may present children with a large array of reading materials in the hopes that something may spark a favorable attitude. At first, it would most likely be an aspect of format, such as the cover picture on a book, that would mobilize curiosity and elicit attention. A title might do the same thing. After that point, the process postulated in the acceptance model would take over to create favorable attitudes toward accepted reading form and content. The child would then be on the road to a life of active reading.

A third way to "prime the pump" may be utilization of the achievement motive. Despite a child's neutrality or aversion to what he visualizes reading content to be, he may read for a teacher simply to achieve parental recognition, good academic evaluations, or the knowledge that he has become a better reader. As stated earlier, it is possible that achievement motive alone can sustain reading behavior. This is confirmed by Zimmerman and Allebrand (70), who found that good readers had more favorable attitudes toward achievement than did poor readers. The use of achievement motivation, however, suffers the same limitation that the use of praise suffered: once the motive to achieve is no longer activated, the child no longer reads. Therefore the strategy of the teacher must be to use achievement motivation to build favorable attitudes toward the various aspects of reading materials, but meanwhile to encourage motives such as curiosity and exploration or self-actualization so that reading becomes based on multiple motivation. Once this is done, the achievement motive could wither away as a factor energizing the reading process because the other motives would continue to sustain it.

There is a final way that a favorable attitude toward reading can be established, but it involves so many undesirable factors that extreme caution should be exercised in its use. This is the method of motivating initial reading with anxiety. Anxiety may begin to motivate reading behavior when a child is told, "You had better read your assignment or you will fail the test" or "If you don't read, you will not get a job." These statements and many others like them may activate anxiety and, quite independent of any attitude toward the aspects of reading materials, the child may attend and comprehend reading selections only through the energizing force of this fear-related motivation.

The difficulties involved in using anxiety to motivate reading are twofold. First, it may be inherently bad to use anxiety to motivate anything. There are more positive motivations available if only the teacher can activate them. Second, anxiety is a negative state which may generalize to reading if it is used to motivate. That is, if a child feels bad every time he reads, it is possible that he may eventually form negative attitudes toward all aspects of the reading process.

There is a third possibility, but it is a risky one. It is possible that mild anxiety used to motivate reading may lead to eventual favorable acceptance of reading materials if the child discovers that he likes the content. The anxiety may therefore allow such motivations as curiosity and exploration, activity, and self-actualization to take over in motivating reading behavior. Such a possibility is risky because the attachment of negative feelings to reading may be just as likely if not more so. Therefore, in the absence of further information, it would probably be advisable to ignore anxiety as a possible motive for reading behavior.

As an interesting sidelight, it may be noted that escape reading may be primarily motivated by anxiety and not by the "higher" motivations. When a child reads to escape, it may be at times when the world is pressing too hard on him. He may feel as if he cannot cope, and this feeling may activate anxiety. In order to relieve this anxiety, the child may escape into literature that removes him from the world. The underlying anxiety may still be there providing the energy for reading, but it may be somewhat allayed by the plot and the identification with the major character. This possibility could easily be tested by comparing anxiety test results of two groups of equally skilled readers, one which reports doing much escape reading and one which does not.

In conclusion, the difficulty of a teacher faced with a child who claims to "hate reading" is to discover how to introduce him to reading form, content, and format which he likes. After the initial exposure, the child may become a self-sustaining reader if the appropriate motivations and attitudes are connected to reading materials.

Using Reading to Change Attitudes

If a child accepts the content of a reading selection, the acceptance model predicts that his attitude toward the selection will be modified favorably. Not shown in Figure 1, but a logical extrapolation of acceptance model reasoning, is the possibility that the acceptance of reading content may also lead to a favorable attitude toward attitude objects portrayed in the reading. For instance, if a story about circuses is accepted by a child, it may follow that this acceptance may not only give rise to a favorable attitude toward the story itself, but also result in a more favorable attitude toward actual circuses. Were this possibility represented in the model, there would be an arrow from the acceptance process component leading to a new component labeled "Content-Related Attitudes." These would be defined as those nonliterary attitudes which are formed through the acceptance of the content of reading materials.

An experiment done by Litcher and Johnson (34) illustrates how the acceptance model might be used to explain formation of these content-related attitudes. Litcher and Johnson predicted that the pictures in Scott-Foresman multiethnic readers would change the attitudes of Mid-western white children toward Negroes in a favorable direction. In terms of the acceptance model, this attitude formation would be dependent

upon the acceptance of the meaning communicated by the format (pictures) of the multiethnic readers. Since the pictures all showed the Negroes in a favorable, middle-class setting, there was no reason to believe
that the children would not accept this meaning. The results of the
experiment indeed confirmed that the group exposed to the multiethnic
readers had a significantly more favorable attitude toward Negroes than
did a control group using regular readers. In acceptance model terms, the
acceptance of the meaning derived from the picture format changed
attitude toward Negroes, a content-related attitude.

It must be emphasized that the primary purpose of the acceptance
model is prediction of the factors increasing attention and comprehension. If the model can predict and therefore control content-related
attitudes, it is an extension of its basic framework. As such, there is no
need to add this extension to the schematic diagram in Figure 1. Instead, it
becomes an addition to the more general structure of acceptance theory.
This strategy allows retention of the five component schematic representation while acceptance theory itself may be elaborated to any extent.

Laboratory Use of the Acceptance Model

If it is to be successful, the acceptance model must be capable of
generating predictions which, when tested, clarify the reading process.
These predictions may be tested either under controlled, laboratory-type
conditions or in the open forum of the classroom. Because experimental
rigor is greater in the laboratory-type situation, possible predictions in this
area will be explored first.

The typical laboratory-type reading experiment involves presenting
a child with carefully designed reading materials and observing his comprehension responses under different conditions. This type of study
requires that the researcher isolate a single child and work with him using
standardized procedures. Many children are tested in this way and normative results are tabulated and analyzed. It is in this type of study that the
acceptance model receives its most rigorous test. The procedure begins
with the researcher studying the acceptance model and constructing
hypotheses logically derivable from it. Then an experiment is constructed
in order to test these hypotheses. To date, only one experiment based on
the acceptance model has been attempted. This was reported by Mathewson (41).

Mathewson was interested in the possible effects of attitude toward
form of reading materials upon comprehension. Using the acceptance

model, he predicted that if the form of reading materials, in this case a dialect, were to elicit favorable attitudes from children, stories written in that dialect would be comprehended better than the same stories written in standard English (SE). This direct, obvious acceptance model prediction was tested using Black English (BE) in black folktales. The specific prediction was that black children, who were assumed to have a favorable attitude toward the dialect of their own culture, would comprehend BE folktales better than SE folktales.

To test the prediction, both SE and BE folktales were presented to black children and to children with other ethnic backgrounds. Some children listened to the stories while other children read them. Following exposure to the stories, the children evaluated them using four semantic differential scales and answered six multiple-choice comprehension questions testing literal knowledge. An analysis of the results showed that the black children preferred the BE folktales and comprehended them better than the SE tales when they were heard, but not when they were read. These findings, of course, failed to confirm the acceptance model's predictions with reference to reading.

In retrospect, it is clear why the acceptance model's reading predictions were not supported. Third grade children have been raised to read SE regardless of their ethnicity, and therefore their strategies are geared to decoding only that form of English. In consequence, *all* of the children had difficulty with the print-mediated phonological, lexical, and syntactic dialect forms. Most children in the black English reading condition showed frustration in reading and, when queried at the end of the experiment, indicated that they believed that nobody at all spoke in the way the story had been written.

Though the model appears to have failed in its prediction of elevated comprehension of black English text by black children, it is possible to explain that failure in terms of the acceptance model itself. Referring back to the model, it is apparent that there had been a blockage of output from the comprehension processes when the small children attempted to read dialect. Since the prior intent of the children had been to comprehend the story, the severely degraded meaning output by the comprehension processes met with unfavorable acceptance. The unfavorable acceptance, in turn, caused a decrement in attitude toward the dialect reading materials and thus decreased both attention and whatever comprehension might have been present. This interpretation is consistent with both the obtained data and with the model. It shows that the failure to find the predicted results can be explained by reexamining the model and finding the difficulty.

Thus, while the Mathewson experiment failed with reference to its reading prediction, it gave reason to have continued confidence in the acceptance model. In the light of this, continued testing of predictions drawn from the model appear to be indicated. The fact that the model allowed a post hoc explanation of the failure of the reading hypothesis was encouraging. Without a theoretical model, such an analysis would have been difficult at best. With the model, there was a definite guide for locating the difficulty.

The Acceptance Model in the Classroom

Even as the professional educational researcher may use the acceptance model to test predictions concerning reading, it may also be used by the teacher in the classroom in a less formal way. Of course, teachers have been going on the assumption that motivation and attitude are important in reading for a long time, but the acceptance model provides a structure suggesting selection of reading materials having specific aspects which may facilitate attitude and make provision for measuring the outcomes of using such materials.

First, the teacher is alerted that she cannot intuitively make a decision concerning what reading materials children like best any more than a publisher can do so. Instead, it may be necessary to utilize techniques confirming children's preferences. The semantic differential scale modified for the use of third graders (41), projective measures (35), Likert scales (16), and other instruments and observer rating (65) may all be used for this purpose. The teacher may then try to discover whether it is something about the content, form, or format that makes a difference. Finally, either informally or formally, she may compare the children's comprehension of preferred and nonpreferred reading materials.

The teacher who keeps in mind the possible motivations of children will also have an advantage. The motivations of curiosity and self-actualization may maintain reading behavior in a child whether he is in school or out, whereas motivation based on anxiety (You *must* read this book or you will flunk!) may be effective only as long as the child is in the school situation. Therefore the teacher may try to maintain an open, relaxed classroom atmosphere and try to provide a diversity of reading material in order to stimulate the sometimes elusive "higher" motivations for reading.

Last, the teacher who keeps the acceptance model in mind may be more likely to understand the reading behavior she sees around her. A child who usually likes to read but does not read on some particular day may not be experiencing the motivations which usually energize favorable reading attitudes. Another child who says that he does not like reading may mean that he has not yet found the content type which stimulates him. The teacher's job in this case is to show the child that there is some reading that fits his prior attitudes, beliefs, and values. If such content is found, acceptance processes will operate to increase the favorability of his attitudes toward that content and therefore foster improved attention and comprehension.

The Acceptance Model in
the Design of Reading Materials

While the teacher may keep informal records concerning what reading materials elicit favorable attitudes, those concerned with designing materials for the reading curriculum may wish to be more precise. For them, the identification of reading content congruent with children's attitudes, beliefs, and values is of critical importance if the processes proposed in the acceptance model do in fact mirror reality. If children are provided with reading texts which do not elicit favorable responses, their attention to such materials may dwindle and their comprehension may suffer. If, on the other hand, texts are received favorably, the children may attend, comprehend, and gain greater skill in reading. Considering the nationwide distribution of many reading programs, it would seem best not to leave the attitudinal responses of children to chance.

One way to assure a favorable response from children would be to present many content types to various child populations and to measure their attitudinal responses. This might be done by presenting abridged stories of given content types and measuring children's attitudes either by paper-and-pencil techniques or by behavioral techniques such as those described by Brown (9). The results would indicate the types of content preferable for use in reading texts.

In addition to measuring content types appropriate for various ethnic, geographic, and socioeconomic groups of children within the population, it might be profitable to create tests of attitude toward content types which teachers could administer to individual children prior to any reading assignments. This would only be an advantage if all teachers of reading had access to a library of reading materials keyed to the children's identified attitudes. If, for instance, a teacher were to find that a particular child had a favorable attitude toward the content type "Adventures of Wild Animals," she should be able to provide the child with unlimited reading materials containing this content type. Then the teacher might not have to "assign" any reading to the child, merely bring the appropriate book to his attention.

The efficacy of identifying reading materials favorably accepted by children depends, however, on support for the acceptance model. While the model is supported by prior studies, its full implications have not yet been tested. This must be done before a full-scale application, such as the one outlined above, can be attempted.

The Future of the Model

At its best, the acceptance model can serve three functions. First, it can serve as a summary for the relationship of processes which may otherwise be difficult to visualize. The model is not and does not purport to be a full explanation for the reading process. Rather, it is a map which may simplify the terrain and give direction without taking into consideration many of the difficulties which might be encountered by the actual traveller.

Second, the acceptance model may form the foundation of the theory of attitude in reading. Such a theory would include much that is not included in the model: definition of terms, specification of the operation of processes, and exploration of the many ramifications of the model when more data become available.

Last, the model may provide a framework for the design of reading materials for the schools. If its postulated processes do mirror reality, then the systematic identification and use of reading materials corresponding to children's attitudes, beliefs, and values is indicated.

REFERENCES

1. Athey, I. J. "Language Models and Reading," *Reading Research Quarterly*, 7, (1971), 16-110.
2. Atkinson, J. W. (Ed.) *Motives in Fantasy, Action and Society*. New York: Van Nostrand Reinhold, 1958.
3. Atkinson, J. W., and G. H. Litwin. "Achievement Motive and Test Anxiety Conceived as Motive to Approach Success and Motive to Avoid Failure," *Journal of Abnormal and Social Psychology*, 60 (1960), 52-63.
4. Baker, E. H. "Motivation: for the Disadvantaged, Special Problems," *Grade Teacher*, 85 (1968), 104-107, 116.
5. Berlyne, D. E. "Novelty and Curiosity as Determinants of Exploratory Behavior," *British Journal of Psychology*, 41 (1950), 68-80.
6. Bernstein, M. R. "Relationship Between Interest and Reading Comprehension," *Journal of Educational Research*, 49 (1955), 283-288.
7. Braun, C. "Fostering a Need to Read," *The Elementary School Journal*, 72 (1971), 132-141.

8. Brittain, M. M. "Informal Reading Procedures: Some Motivational Considerations," *Reading Teacher,* 24 (1970), 216-220.

9. Brown, L. T. "A Behavioral Index of the Exploratory Value of Prose Materials," *Journal of Educational Psychology,* 63 (1972), 437-445.

10. Butler, R. A., and H. F. Harlow. "Discrimination Learning and Learning Sets to Visual Exploration Incentives," *Journal of General Psychology,* 57 (1957), 257-264.

11. Clark, P. M. "Psychology, Education, and the Concept of Motivation," *Theory into Practice,* 9 (1970), 16-22.

12. Cofer, C. N., and M. H. Appley. *Motivation: Theory and Research.* New York: John Wiley and Sons, 1964.

13. Damien, Sister M. "A Classroom 'TV' Motivates Reading," *Catholic School Journal,* 65 (1965), 50.

14. Edwards, A. L. *Techniques of Attitude Scale Construction.* New York: Appleton-Century-Crofts, 1957.

15. Eller, W. "Reading Interest: A Function of the Law of Effect," *The Reading Teacher,* 13 (1959), 115-120.

16. Estes, T. H. "A Scale to Measure Attitudes Toward Reading," *Journal of Reading,* 15 (1971), 135-138.

17. Fader, D. N. *Hooked on Books: Program & Proof.* New York: Berkley Publishing Corporation, 1968.

18. Fox, L. K. "Building on Children's Eagerness to Read," *Childhood Education,* 38 (1962), 215-219.

19. Gans, R. "Don't Let Them Become 'Dropout' Readers," *Grade Teacher,* 84 (1966), 119.

20. Gans, R. "Forget the Method—Teach them Desire," *Grade Teacher,* 84 (1966), 84-5, 169.

21. Getzels, J. W. "The Problems of Interests: A Reconsideration," in H. A. Robinson (Ed.), *Reading: Seventy-five Years of Progress.* Chicago: University of Chicago Press, 1966.

22. Groff, P. J. "Children's Attitudes Toward Reading and Their Critical Reading Abilities in Four Content-Type Materials," *Journal of Educational Research,* 55 (1962), 313-317.

23. Gurney, D. "The Effect of an Individual Reading Program on Reading Level and Attitude Toward Reading," *The Reading Teacher,* 19 (1966), 277-280.

24. Harlow, H. F., M. K. Harlow, and D. R. Meyer. "Learning Motivated by a Manipulation Drive," *Journal of Experimental Psychology,* 40 (1950), 228-234.

25. Healy, A. K. "Changing Children's Attitudes Toward Reading," *Elementary English,* 40 (1963), 255-257, 279.

26. Healy, A. K. "Effects of Changing Children's Attitudes Toward Reading," *Elementary English,* 42 (1965), 269-272.

27. Hill, W. F. "Activity as an Autonomous Drive," *Journal of Comparative and Physiological Psychology,"* 49 (1956), 15-19.

28. Hill, W. F. *Learning.* Scranton: Chandler Publishing Company, 1971.

29. Hurley, E. M. "Motivating Reluctant Readers," *Elementary English,* 38 (1961), 328-329.

30. Jones, E. E., and H. B. Gerard. *Foundations of Social Psychology.* New York: John Wiley and Sons, 1967.

31. Katz, D., and E. Stotland. "A Preliminary Statement To a Theory of Attitude Structure and Change," in S. Koch (Ed.), *Psychology: A Study of a Science,* 3. New York: McGraw-Hill, 1959.

32. Kiesler, C. A., B. E. Collins, and N. Miller. *Attitude Change.* New York: John Wiley and Sons, 1969.

33. Lane, P., C. Pollack, and N. Sher. "Remotivation of Disruptive Adolescents," *Journal of Reading,* 15 (1972), 351-354.

34. Litcher, J. H., and D. W. Johnson. "Changes in Attitudes Toward Negroes of White Elementary School Students After Use of Multiethnic Readers," *Journal of Educational Psychology*, 60 (1969), 148-152.

35. Lowery, L. F. "Development of an Attitude Measuring Instrument for Science Education," paper read at the AAS meeting held at the University of California, Berkeley, December 30, 1965.

36. Lowery, L. F., and W. Grafft. "Paperback Books and Reading Attitudes," *Reading Teacher*, 21 (1968), 618-623.

37. McClelland, D. C., J. W. Atkinson, R. A. Clark, and E. L. Lowell, *The Achievement Motive*. New York: Appleton-Century-Crofts, 1953.

38. McGuire, W. J. "A Syllogistic Analysis of Cognitive Relationships," in M. J. Rosenberg, C. I. Hovland, W. J. McGuire, R. P. Ableson, and J. W. Brehm (Eds.), *Attitude Organization and Change*. New Haven, Conn.: Yale University Press, 1960.

39. Marlowe, D., and K. J. Gergen. "Personality and Social Interaction," in G. Lindzey and E. Aronson (Eds.), *The Handbook of Social Psychology*, 3. Reading, Massachusetts: Addison-Wesley, 1969, 645.

40. Maslow, A. H. *Motivation and Personality*. New York: Harper and Row, 1970.

41. Mathewson, G. C. "Relationship Between Ethnic Group Attitudes Toward Dialect and Comprehension of Dialect Folktales," *Journal of Educational Research*, 68 (1974), 15-18, 35.

42. Miller, N. L. "Out of the Classroom," *Exceptional Children*, 31 (1964), 91-92.

43. Miller, N. E. "Studies of Fear as an Acquirable Drive," in W. A. Russell (Ed.), *Milestones in Motivation: Contributions to the Psychology of Drive and Purpose*. New York: Appleton-Century-Crofts, 1970.

44. Montgomery, K. C. "The Effect of Activity Deprivation upon Exploratory Behavior," *Journal of Comparative Physiological Psychology*, 46 (1953), 438-441.

45. Moore, W. J. "About Reading in the Content Fields?" *English Journal*, 58 (1969), 707-718.

46. Mowrer, O. H. *Learning Theory and Personality Dynamics: Selected Papers*. New York: Ronald Press, 1950.

47. Neale, D. C., N. Gill, and W. Tismer. "Relationship Between Attitudes Toward School Subjects and School Achievement," *Journal of Educational Research*, 63 (1970), 232-237.

48. Newcomb, T. M., R. H. Turner, and P. E. Converse. *Social Psychology*. New York: Holt, Rinehart, and Winston, 1965.

49. Robinson, H. A. "Developing Lifetime Readers," *Journal of Reading*, 11 (1968), 261-267.

50. Rogers, C. R. *Freedom to Learn: A View of What Education Might Become*. Columbus, Ohio: Merill, 1969.

51. Rosenblatt, L. M. *Literature as Exploration*. New York: Noble and Noble, 1968.

52. Rowell, C. G. "An Investigation of Factors Related to Change in Attitude Toward Reading," *Journal of Reading Behavior*, 5 (1972), 266-272.

53. Ruddell, R. B. "Psycholinguistic Implications for a Systems of Communication Model," in H. Singer and R. B. Ruddell (Eds.), *Theoretical Models and Processes of Reading*. Newark, Delaware: International Reading Association, 1970.

54. Russell, W. A. (Ed.) *Milestones in Motivation: Contributions to the Psychology of Drive and Purpose*. New York: Appleton-Century-Crofts, 1970.

55. Samuels, S. J. "Effects of Pictures on Learning to Read, Comprehension and Attitudes," *Review of Educational Research*, 40 (1970), 397-407.

56. Samuels, S. J., E. Biesbrock, and P. R. Terry. "The Effect of Pictures on Children's Attitudes Toward Presented Stories," *The Journal of Educational Research*, 67 (1974), 243-246.

57. Schab, F. "Motivation in Remedial Reading," *Reading Teacher,* 20 (1967), 626-627, 631.

58. Shankman, F. V. "Developing Permanent Reading Interests in Children," *Elementary English,* 40 (1963), 411-414.

59. Shnayer, S. W. "Relationships Between Reading Interest and Reading Comprehension," in J. A. Figurel (Ed.), *Reading and Realism.* Newark, Delaware: International Reading Association, 1969.

60. Squire, J. R. "About Attitudes Toward Reading?" *English Journal,* 58 (1969), 523-533.

61. Taff, T. G. "Motivation: Batman to the Rescue," *Grade Teacher,* 85 (1968), 112-117.

62. Taylor, J. A. "The Relationship of Anxiety to the Conditioned Eyelid Response," in W. A. Russell (Ed.), *Milestones in Motivation: Contributions to the Psychology of Drive and Purpose.* New York: Appleton-Century-Crofts, 1970.

63. Thompson, W. R., and W. Heron. "The Effects of Early Restriction on Activity in Dogs," *Journal of Comparative Physiological Psychology,* 47 (1954), 77-82.

64. Thurstone, L. L. Comment. *American Journal of Sociology,* 52 (1946), 39-50.

65. West, S., and D. Uhlenberg. "Measuring Motivation," *Theory into Practice,* 9 (1970), 17-22.

66. White, R. W. "Motivation Reconsidered: The Concept of Competence," *Psychological Review,* 66 (1959), 297-333.

67. Young, P. T. *Motivation and Emotion. A Survey of the Determinants of Human and Animal Activity.* New York: John Wiley and Sons, 1961.

68. Zajonc, R. B. "The Concepts of Balance, Congruity, and Dissonance," *Public Opinion Quarterly,* 24 (1960), 280-296.

69. Zimbardo, P., and E. B. Ebbesen. *Influencing Attitudes and Changing Behavior.* Reading, Massachusetts: Addison-Wesley, 1970.

70. Zimmerman, I. L., and G. N. Allebrand. "Personality Characteristics and Attitudes Toward Achievement of Good and Poor Readers," *The Journal of Educational Research,* 59 (1965), 28-30.

Section Four

TEACHING
AND
RESEARCH ISSUES

Introduction to Teaching and Research Issues

In this section, we have sought to answer the following questions:

1. What implications does a theoretical model of reading have for classroom reading instruction?
2. What problems in the process of reading need to be investigated?
3. Do developmental theories have valid implications for processes of reading?

We attempted to answer these questions by selecting four papers. We shall briefly introduce each of them.

Drawing upon the substrata-factor theory of reading and a statistically-determined model based upon the assumptions of the theory, Singer explicates the usefulness of his model for classroom instruction in reading. He explains his model can be used to depict individual differences in conceptual, morphemic, semantic, graphophonemic, perceptual-oculomotor and motivational subsystems underlying attainment of speed and power of reading. Also, the model can guide teachers in determining curriculum objectives, grouping students for instruction, and in diagnosing and evaluating performance in general reading ability.

Other models also have implications for classroom instruction in reading. Ruddell[1] has written a professional preservice and inservice methods text for teaching systems of communication based on his model. Yetta Goodman and Carolyn Burke[2] have constructed their *Miscue Reading Inventory* upon the rationale of Kenneth Goodman's theory and model of reading. The LaBerge-Samuels model has been applied to classroom experimental research.[3,4] Although Gough's model has implications for diagnosis and improvement of reading, no one has yet attempted to use it for such applied purposes.

Models do have implications for classroom reading instruction, but further research is necessary to answer a host of questions on the reading

---

[1] Robert B. Ruddell. *Reading-Language Instruction: Innovative Practices.* Englewood-Cliffs, New Jersey: Prentice-Hall, 1974.

[2] Yetta M. Goodman and Carolyn L. Burke. *Reading Miscue Inventory.* New York: Macmillan, 1972.

[3] Patricia R. Dahl. A Mastery Based Experimental Program for Teaching High Speed Word Recognition Skills. Unpublished doctoral dissertation, University of Minnesota, 1973.

[4] Patricia Dahl, S. Jay Samuels, and Teara Archwamety. A Mastery-Based Program for Teaching High Speed Word Recognition. Technical Report, Research and Development Center for Handicapped Children, University of Minnesota, 1973.

process. Venezky, Massaro, and Weber provide a list of needed research in their National Institute of Education Panel Report on "Recommendations for Research on Models for Reading Processes." Only the last part of Miller's lengthy panel report, dealing with "Text Comprehension Skills and Process Models of Text Comprehension," could be included in this volume. These papers were two of 10 panel reports commissioned by the National Institute of Education. The purpose of the panels was to help NIE determine research directions, establish priorities, formulate guidelines, and stimulate research in reading. The reports, all written in a numbered, outline style according to NIE's specifications, consist of lists of recommendations. The intent is to have the recommendations discussed, analyzed, and formulated into research proposals, one recommendation at a time, hopefully in graduate courses in education and psychology. Because of space limitations, we could include only two of the 10 panel reports. The 10 panel reports and chairpersons of each panel are listed below:

National Institute of Education
Panel Papers on Reading[5]

Chairperson	Topic
George Miller	Semantics, Concepts, and Culture
Thomas Trabasso	Structure and Use of Language
Sheldon White	Attention and Motivation
Richard Venezky	Modeling the Reading Process
Ernest Rothkopf	Assessment of Reading Comprehension
Lauren Resnick	Applications of Existing Reading Comprehension Research
Mina Shaughnessy	Reading Comprehension and the High School Graduate
Richard Hodges	Learning and Motivation in Early Reading
Manuel Ramirez	Reading Strategies for Different Cultural and Linguistic Groups
Irene Athey	Essential Skills and Skills Hierarchies in Reading Comprehension and Decoding Instruction

We also had to drastically limit our selection of research papers to only one for each process area. Among excellent papers we could not include were the following:

Chapman, Carita A. A test of hierarchical theory of reading comprehension. *Reading Research Quarterly*, 9, 2, 1973-1974, 232-234.

Davis, Frank R. Environmental influences on substrates of achievement leading to learning disability. *Journal of Learning Disabilities*, 2, 3, March 1969, 39-43.

Fisher, Dennis. Reading and visual search. *Memory and Cognition*, 1974 (in press).

---

[5] Panel Paper on Reading, National Institute of Education, Learning Division, 1200 19th St., NW, Washington 20208. Papers available upon request.

Gilbert, Luther C. Saccadic movements as a factor in visual perception in reading. *Journal of Educational Psychology,* 50, 1959, 15-19.

Gillooly, William B. The influence of writing system characteristics on learning to read. *Reading Research Quarterly,* 8, 2, Winter 1973, 167-199.

Gleitman, Lila R. and Paul Rozin. Teaching reading by use of a syllabary. *Reading Research Quarterly,* 8, 4, Summer 1973, 447-483.

Kintsch, Walter. Comprehension and recall of text as a function of content variables. *Journal of Verbal Learning and Behavior,* 1975 (in press).

Kolers, Paul A. Two kinds of recognition. *Canadian Journal of Psychology,* 28, 1, 1974, 51-61.

Kolers, Paul A. and David J. Ostry. Time course of loss of information regarding pattern analyzing operations. *Journal of Verbal Learning and Verbal Behavior,* 13, 1974, 599-612.

Liberman, Isabelle Y., Donald Shankweiler, Alvin M. Liberman, Carol Fowler, and F. William Fischer. Phonetic segmentation and recoding in the beginning reader. In A. S. Reber and D. Scarborough (Editors). *The CUNY Conference* (tentative title). New York: Erlbaum Associates, 1975 (in press).

Posner, Michael I., Joe E. Lewis and Carol Conrad. Component processes in reading: a performance analysis. In James F. Kavanagh and Ignatius Mattingly (Editors), *Language by Ear and by Eye.* Cambridge, Massachusetts: M. I. T. Press, 1972. Pp. 158-204.

Ryan, Ellen B. and Melvyn I. Semmel. Reading as constructive language process. *Reading Research Quarterly,* 5, 1, Fall 1969, 59-83.

Venezky, Richard L. Theoretical and experimental bases for teaching reading. In Thomas A. Sebeok (Editor), *Linguistic and Adjacent Arts and Sciences.* Hague, Netherlands: Mouton, 1974. Pp. 2057-2100.

Readers might want to consider the issues raised by Athey in the final paper in this section. Under what conditions can a developmental theory have useful implications for reading instruction? What steps or procedures have to be followed for a theory or basic research study to be put into a form appropriate for classroom instruction in reading? Some procedures along these lines can be found elsewhere.[6,7]

Although theories, models, and basic research have roles to play in education, they must be put into a form appropriate for instruction in reading, then field tested and evaluated. Important in this evaluation is use of measurement and observations relevant to teacher, curriculum, students, and to interactions among these factors in the classroom.

If theory and basic research are to make a difference in classroom instruction in reading, questions on their appropriateness, relevancy, and usefulness will need to be answered. As they are answered, we shall find classroom instruction more adequately based on theory and research evidence.

---

[6] Ernest R. Hilgard and Gordon H. Bower. *Theories of Learning* (Fourth Edition). New York: Appleton-Century-Crofts, 1975.

[7] Harry Singer. Research that should have made a difference. *Elementary English,* 45, 1970, 27-34.

Teaching

Substrata-Factor Theory of Reading: Theoretical Design for Teaching Reading[*]

HARRY SINGER
University of California at Riverside

Implicit in the substrata-factor theory of reading (*11, 12, 14, 17, 18, 29*) is a theoretical design for teaching reading. This design is visually represented by a statistically-determined model of substrata-factors that an individual might mobilize for attaining power and speed of reading. Because substrata-factors mobilized in a general working-system undergo qualitative and/or quantitative changes with maturity in reading, several models are necessary in order to cover the developmental range of general reading ability. Each model, however, is only *a momentary* organization of the structure of the general working-system that underlies power and speed of reading. To explain the dynamics of the model, and to show how it can be used as a theoretical design for teaching reading, I shall draw upon the substrata-factor theory of reading. The model at the fourth grade level will serve as an example.

Substrata-Factor Model: Grade 4

After a comprehensive review of the literature, 36 variables were selected (*4, 7, 13, 15, 21*) or constructed (*28*), and administered to an apparently representative sample of 60 fourth graders. Substrata analyses of the matrix resulted in the model (*29*). This model, Figure 1, shows the levels and positions of the selected variables, and their direct and indirect

---

[*]Reprinted from J. A. Figurel (Ed.), *Challenge and Experiment in Reading,* Proceedings of the International Reading Association Annual Convention, 7, 1962, 226-232. The research reported herein was supported through the Cooperative Research Program of the Office of Education, U.S. Department of Health, Education, and Welfare.

contributions to the variance of the subcriteria and to the major criteria, Speed and Power of Reading. The number adjacent to each variable gives its percent contribution to the variance of the predicted subcriterion or criterion. Because three variables are common, the total number is only 17. Altogether these variables account for 77.1 and 89.3 percent of the variance in Speed and Power of Reading, respectively. Variances not accounted for must, of course, be attributable to variables other than those used in the construction of the model, such as: functional oculomotor efficiency (9), speed of processing visual stimuli (10), mobilizers (17), and flexibility (22).

The model may be read in various ways to determine how the mind might organize its subskills, ideas, and capabilities to solve a problem in reading. For example, the use of spelling recognition together with prefixes, and spelling recall (right-hand side, Level III) enter into the constellation of subabilities that make up Word Recognition in Context. Word recognition in context, plus suffixes, and mental age contribute to the variance in Vocabulary in Isolation. Finally, on the highest level, vocabulary in isolation becomes integrated with suffixes, mental age, and matching sounds in words to culminate in Power of Reading.[1] Again, starting with spelling recognition, Speed of Reading can similarly be worked out.

The dynamic processes may be visualized as a sequence of constantly changing sub-models, each a representation of a working-system, momentarily mobilized to satisfy the purposes of the reader and the demands of the task. For example, an individual at one time may organize a substrata-factor sequence for the purpose of transforming symbolic stimuli into mental processes for the association of meaning; at another moment, for solving a word-meaning problem; and, at the next instant, for conceptualizing, relating ideas, making inferences, or, in short, for reasoning-in-context.

To summarize the model: at least three substrata-factor sequences constitute the general working-systems for Speed and Power of Reading; these may be broadly categorized as word-recognition, word-meaning, and reasoning-in-context. Differences within the general working-systems for Speed and Power of Reading appear to be related to the difficulty of the reading material and the varied purposes of the reader. In both Speed and Power of Reading, a reader brings a complex of ideational processes to bear upon the reading task. When reading for speed, a fourth grader tends to mobilize a working-system undergirded by the processes of *visual* word recognition, concrete and functional

---

[1] The predictors at this highest level are purified by a suppressor-like effect (16, 23), contributed by consonant phonics.

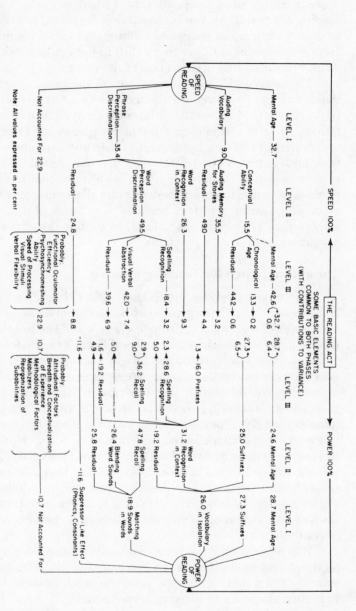

Figure 1.

Flow chart to show the results of the substrata analysis of speed and power of reading at the fourth grade level

Note: The level I subsystems for predicting speed and power of reading can be renamed with the following current terminology: Mental Age = Reasoning in Reading; Suffixes = Morphemic Analysis; Vocabulary in Isolation = Semantics; Matching Sounds in Words = Graphophonemics; Reading Vocabulary = Semantics (Concrete level); Phrase Perception Discrimination = Perceptual-Oculomotor System. Syntax which does not precipitate as a predictor may be subsumed by the subsystem of Reasoning in Reading.

concepts rather than abstract levels of word meaning. However, when reading for power, his working-system is organized to utilize more *auditory* word recognition processes, auding, and visual vocabulary abilities. Hence, the model indicates that a shift in the reading task necessitates a change in the mental organization of the reader.

The degree of achievement attained, the processes employed, and the subabilities mobilized for the solution of a task vary from person to person because of individual differences in: a) capacities, rate of maturation, and level of subabilities; b) method, sequence, and scope of learning; c) experiences and range of resulting ideas; and d) temperament, motivation, and values. These differences are manifested in the kinds and relative amounts of subskills which each individual mobilizes into his working system. However, there is more than one route to the goal of success in reading; two individuals may attain the same degree of achievement by means of qualitatively and/or quantitatively different organizations of working-systems.

Theoretical Design for Teaching Reading

The model provides the teacher with a "cognitive map" of "what-leads-to-what" (*30*) in the general working-system for attainment of speed and power of reading at the fourth grade level. The insight gained from this cognitive map enables the teacher to formulate the following design:

Objectives. The instructional program should at least encompass the educationally modifiable elements represented in the model. Moreover, instruction should aim to give the reader the necessary versatility to reorganize his working-system according to his purposes and the demands of the task. For example, an unfamiliar word constitutes a barrier to a working-system mobilized for whole word recognition. To eliminate this barrier, a more analytical working-system is necessary. This versatility may be attained by instruction which: a) develops a broad structure of subskills and processes, b) provides practice in switching from one working-system to another, and c) creates an emotional atmosphere conducive to the utilization of different routes to the goal of power and speed in reading.

Whenever possible, subskills for power and speed of reading should be developed in alternation. In agreement with the meaning theory of learning (*2*), understanding or power of reading should be developed first, then efficiency or speed of response next.

Diagnosis. Substrata diagnosis starts with a symptom at the criterion level and proceeds through the relevant substrata levels to discover whether there are causal deficiencies in the underlying elements.

For general evaluation, an individual's profile of substrata elements may be compared with psychographs for most powerful vs. least powerful and fastest vs. slowest readers, Figures 2 and 3, respectively. These psychographs indicate that, in general, subabilities tend to be evenly developed. Therefore, a significant departure from the generality may be attributed to a differential in methodological emphasis or intra-individual variation in a learner's capabilities, or some interaction of these causal factors.

Processes in reading should also be evaluated because two individuals may attain the same level of accomplishment, but one individual may do so by a more mature process than the other (1). In general, readers develop through a gradient-shift in modal dominance from kinesthetic to auditory to visual perception (12). To progress through this sequence, an individual has to acquire the necessary response repertoire and learn to reorganize his "habit-family-hierarchy" (19) of working-systems so that the visual modality may, in fact, become dominant. Speeded practice in formulating and reading to answer questions (8) may not only effect this reorganization, but also enhance reasoning-in-context.

Subgrouping. Subgrouping should be based not only on degree of achievement in the major criteria, Speed and Power of Reading, but also on level of performance in each of the subcriteria and their specific underlying elements. Some individuals, however, may deviate so markedly from the group that models at other grade levels would be more suitable for their instructional designs.

Development of word recognition ability. Although basal readers implicitly instruct beginning readers to rely upon memorization for word recognition, students apparently learn to utilize higher mental processes because cognitive factors do enter into word recognition abilities (20, 29). To facilitate such use of higher mental processes, materials could be organized for teaching pupils to conceptualize word recognition responses. For example, after teaching some sight words, the teacher could group these words according to a common kinesthetic, auditory, or visual perceptual element, and instruct children to perceive, abstract, and generalize this common element. Words which do not contain this element could serve to limit the generalization, and, perhaps, help the child develop necessary versatility in word attack. Under similar conditions, transfer of training has been successful for spelling (6), and may be even more effective for word recognition. Thus, instead of learning a separate response for each stimulus word, students would gradually develop an adequate repertoire of "mediated responses" (24) to mobilize in varying combinations for recognizing any unknown word.

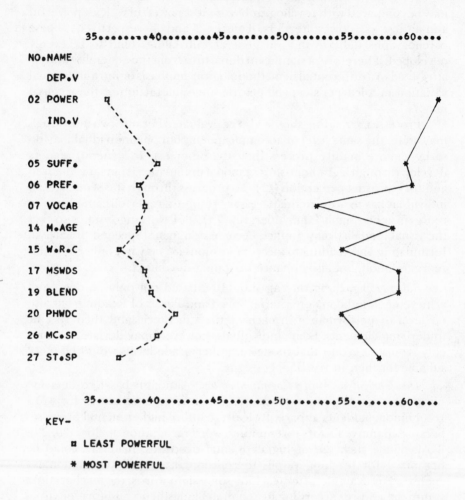

Figure 2.   Psychograph of selected substrata elements for Power of Reading. The psychograph compares the average standard scores of the upper and lower 27 percent of 60 fourth graders, separated on the dependent variable, Power of Reading. The groups are compared on variables that underlie Power of Reading at the fourth grade level, as shown in the model, Figure 1. These variables, in the order listed in the figure, are: Power of Reading, Suffixes, Prefixes, Vocabulary in Isolation, Mental Age, Word Recognition in Context, Matching Sounds in Words, Blending Sounds, Consonant Phonics, Multiple Choice Spelling Recognition, and Stanford Spelling Recall.

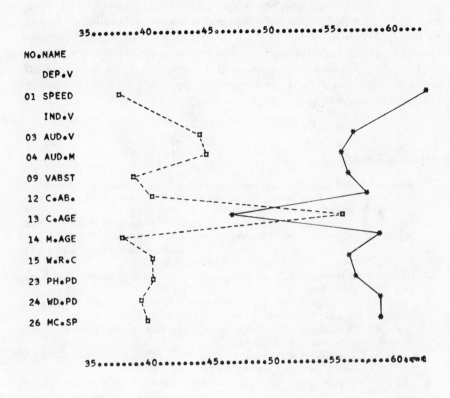

STANDARD SCORE SCALE

35•••••••••40•••••••••45•••••••••50•••••••••55•••••••••60••••

NO•NAME

   DEP•V

01 SPEED

   IND•V

03 AUD•V

04 AUD•M

09 VABST

12 C•AB•

13 C•AGE

14 M•AGE

15 W•R•C

23 PH•PD

24 WD•PD

26 MC•SP

35•••••••••40•••••••••45•••••••••50•••••••••55•••••••••60••••

KEY-

   ◻ SLOWEST READERS

   ✳ FASTEST READERS

Figure 3.   Psychograph of selected substrata elements for Speed of Reading. The psychograph compares the average standard scores of the upper and lower 27 percent of 60 fourth graders, separated on the dependent variable, Speed of Reading. The groups are compared on variables that underlie Speed of Reading at the fourth grade level, as shown in the model, Figure 1. These variables, in the order listed in the figure, are: Speed of Reading, Auding Vocabulary, Auding Memory for Stories, Visual Verbal Abstraction, Conceptual Ability, Chronological Age, Mental Age, Word Recognition in Context, Phrase Perception Discrimination, Word Perception Discrimination, Multiple Choice Spelling Recognition.

Development of word meaning. Both the formation of, and the appropriate response to concrete, functional, and abstract levels of word meanings (*5, 25*) may be developed by instruction in material graded according to these conceptual levels (*3, 27*). A variety of instructional material should also be devised for teaching other dimensions of a concept, such as span, clarity, richness, organization, and communicability (*26, 31*). Conceptual ability, however, is also dependent upon mental and chronological age, and upon organic and personality factors (*31*).

REFERENCES

1. Brownell, W. A. "Rate, Accuracy, and Process in Learning," Abridged by Theodore L. Harris and Wilson E. Schwahn, *Selected Readings on the Learning Process.* New York: Oxford University Press, 1961, pp. 388-400.

2. Brownell, W. A., and Moser, H. E. "Meaningful versus Mechanical Learning: A Study in Grade 3 Subtraction." *Duke University Research Studies in Education,* No. 8 (1949).

3. Carner, R. L., and Sheldon, W. D. "Problems in the Development of Concepts Through Reading." *Elementary School Journal,* 55 (1954), pp. 226-229.

4. Durrell, D. D., and Sullivan, Helen B. *Manual for Durrell-Sullivan Reading Capacity Test.* New York: World Book, 1937.

5. Feifel, H., and Lorge, I. "Qualitative Differences in the Vocabulary Responses of Children." *Journal of Educational Psychology,* 41 (1950), pp. 1-18.

6. Gates, A. I. *Generalization and Transfer in Spelling.* New York: Teachers College, Columbia University, Bureau of Publications, 1935.

7. Gates, A. I. *The Manual of Directions for Gates Reading Survey.* New York: Teachers College, Columbia University, Bureau of Publications, 1953.

8. Gilbert, Doris W. *Power and Speed in Reading.* Englewood Cliffs, New Jersey: Prentice-Hall, 1954.

9. Gilbert, L. C. "Functional Motor Efficiency of the Eyes and Its Relation to Reading." *University of California Publications in Education,* 2, No. 3 (1953), pp. 159-232.

10. Gilbert, L. C. "Speed of Processing Visual Stimuli and Its Relation to Reading." *Journal of Educational Psychology,* 55 (1959), pp. 8-14.

11. Holmes, J. A. *Factors Underlying Major Reading Disabilities at the College Level.* Unpublished Doctoral Dissertation, University of California, Berkeley, 1948.

12. Holmes, J. A. *The Substrata-Factor Theory of Reading.* Berkeley: California Book, 1953. (Out of Print)

13. Holmes, J. A. *California Language Perception Tests.* Palo Alto: Educational Development Corporation, Revised, 1962.

14. Holmes, J. A. "Factors Underlying Major Reading Disabilities at the College Level." *Genetic Psychology Monographs,* 49 (1954), pp. 3-95.

15. Holmes, J. A. "A Substrata Analysis of Spelling Ability for Elements of Auditory Images." *Journal of Experimental Education,* 22 (1954), pp. 329-349.

16. Holmes, J. A. "Personality and Spelling Ability." *University of California Publications in Education,* 12, No. 4 (1959), pp. 213-292.

17. Holmes, J. A. "Personality Characteristics of the Disabled Reader." *Journal of Developmental Reading,* 4 (1961), pp. 111-122.

18. Holmes, J. A., and Singer, H. *Substrata Factor Differences Underlying Reading Ability in Known-Groups.* Final Report Covering Contracts No. 538, SAE-8176, and No. 538A, SAE-8660, U. S. Office of Education, 1961.

19. Hull, C. L. *A Behavior System.* New Haven: Yale University, 1952.

20. Kress, R. A. *An Investigation of the Relationship Between Concept Formation and Achievement in Reading.* Unpublished Doctoral Dissertation, Temple University, 1955.

21. Kuhlmann, F., and Anderson, Rose. *Manual for Kuhlmann-Anderson Test,* 6th Ed., Form E. Princeton: Personnel Press, 1952.

22. Laycock, F. "Flexibility in Reading Rate and *Einstellung.*" *Perceptual and Motor Skills,* 8 (1958), pp. 123-129.

23. Lubin, A. "Some Formulae for Use with Suppressor Variables." *Educational and Psychological Measurement,* 17, (1957), pp. 286-291.

24. Osgood, C. *Method and Theory in Experimental Psychology.* New York: Oxford University, 1956.

25. Piaget, J. "Principal Factors Determining Intellectual Evolution from Childhood to Adult Life." In *Factors Determining Human Behavior.* Cambridge: Harvard University, 1937, pp. 32-48.

26. Russell, D. H. *Children's Thinking.* New York: Ginn, 1956.

27. Serra, Mary C. "How to Develop Concepts and Their Verbal Representations." *Elementary School Journal,* 53 (1953), pp. 275-285.

28. Singer, H. *Linguistic Tests: A Battery for Elementary School.* Berkeley: University of California, 1956. (Mimeo.)

29. Singer, H. *Conceptual Ability in the Substrata-Factor Theory of Reading.* Unpublished Doctoral Dissertation. University of California, Berkeley, 1960.

30. Tolman, E. C. "Cognitive Maps in Rats and Men." *Psychological Review,* 55 (1948), pp. 189-208.

31. Zaslow, R. W. *Study of Concept Formation in Brain Damaged Adults, Mental Defectives and Normals of Different Age Levels.* Unpublished Doctoral Dissertation, University of California, Berkeley, 1957.

Research

Modeling the Reading Process[*]

RICHARD L. VENEZKY AND DOMINIC W. MASSARO
University of Wisconsin

ROSE-MARIE WEBER
McGill University

The goal of this report is to suggest studies that will lead to a better understanding of the processes involved in reading. Although the organizing principle of our recommendations is an information-processing model, we have included in the scope of our concern a broad range of experimental studies that could produce information for a variety of different approaches to modeling. Our primary goal is to prepare a programmatically related set of suggestions which could lead cumulatively to a clearer account of reading, or at least to an ability to pose successively better research questions.

Models

A good model is one which organizes complex and seemingly unrelated data in an interesting manner, and which generates testable hypotheses. In this sense, a good model for a reading process is one that reveals its limitations in a hurry; that is, it leads to experiments which themselves produce data for building an improved model. In this regard we are following the opinions of Kleene (1952), Popper (1959), and Kaplan (1964).

The types of models we endorse are those positing component processes or stages (but not necessarily discrete stages) and attempting to

---

[*]Richard Venezky was chairperson of the National Institute of Education Panel No. 4, Conference on Studies in Reading, Washington, D.C., 1975. Dominic Massaro and Rose-Marie Weber were members of the Panel. In addition, there were 11 field consultants and over 100 other researchers and educators who were consulted by the Panel.

describe the forms of information involved with each stage. Models that are so general in their descriptions or so vague in their inner workings that no interesting hypotheses can be generated from them for experimental testing, while they may have pedagogical or other applications, are of no value for the experimental work proposed here.

The absence here of any discussion of the complete models for the reading process published in the last 10 years is intentional. After extensive analysis of such models, we believe that we know too little about the various components of the reading process to justify attention to complete models. Advances in understanding of reading processes have come primarily from narrowly delimited areas in which models are easily constructed and tested.

On Relevance

The recommendations of this panel are an attempt to gain through systematic and precise means an understanding of fundamental processes and relationships. This goal is justified on two grounds. First, an understanding of the fundamental processes in reading is essential for evaluating current teaching and testing practices. Second, such understanding can also lead to the construction of improved strategies for diagnosis and intervention. Our present ability to isolate causes of reading failure is limited to the assessment of differences in behavior—blending, word recognition, getting the main idea, and so on. In spite of some suggestive notions from developmental psychologists, we have been able neither to isolate fundamental processes distinguishing good from poor readers, nor to explain the abnormal rate of learning of some children. A processing model, in its attempt to define operations and relationships between components in testable terms, allows the definition of potential points for diagnosis. Whereas methods of diagnosis and instructional intervention would remain to be determined experimentally, the study of component processes in reading can serve as a foundation for such practical research.

Reading—Undefined

Because the goal of the work we propose is to define component processes in reading, we find little use for any of the conventional definitions of reading which presuppose particular reading processes, e.g., translation from writing to meaning or translation from writing to inner speech. Instead, we propose to start with observed behaviors of the skilled reader, and to continue from there by experimental means in an attempt to infer component psychological processes. The resulting model or models for these processes become their definitional mechanisms. The problem of defining types of reading behavior is addressed specifically in Approach 4.5.

Issues and Priorities

The recommendations that follow are aimed at resolving fundamental issues in the understanding of reading processes and, as such, should receive a high priority in the funding of basic research. With respect to funding priorities across issues, the Panel suggests that all research proposals attending to these issues be considered on the basis of quality and imagination. However, two approaches deserve special attention: Approach 4.1, Development of a Model for Word Recognition During Reading, could show major results in a short time with a minimal allocation of new funding. This area has already attracted the interests of a large number of competent psychologists. Approach 4.3, Characterization of the Development of Reading Ability in Children, is a crucial concern for the design and evaluation of both instruction and diagnosis, but as yet has received little systematic attention from psychologists or educators. Proposals attending to basic methodological issues in this latter area should be encouraged.

Approach 4.1
Development of a Model for Word
Recognition During Reading

Studies on word recognition comprise the major portion of the experimental literature related to reading. Controversies over the features and processes by which readers recognize words attest to the continuing vitality of the reading issue in experimental psychology. The history and current status of these controversies can be gleaned from Huey (1908), Woodworth (1938), Smith and Spoehr (1974), Massaro (1975), and Gibson and Levin (1975).

From this literature the following questions emerge:

(a) Under what conditions do tachistoscopic studies speak to the issue of word recognition in reading?

(b) What visual information in the letter string does the reader use for word recognition (e.g., word shape, feature sets of letters, feature sets of words)?

(c) How does orthographic structure contribute to recognition?

(d) How does syntactic or semantic context contribute to recognition?

(e) Is phonological mediation required for word recognition?

(f) What kind of long-term memory storage units are necessary in word and letter recognition?

Program 4.1.1 *Determination of the Relevance of Tachistoscopic Studies of Letter and Word Recognition to Reading.*

The majority of the recent work on word recognition has involved brief exposures of isolated words in foveal vision. However, in reading, individuals move their eyes to words generally first encountered in peripheral vision. Furthermore, once these words are fixated, they remain available for as long as the reader wants them in view. These differences raise several issues concerning tachistoscopic presentations. One is: Does the presence of the word in peripheral vision facilitate its recognition when the eye jumps to it? The following study addresses this question. Subjects first fixate on a point while a word is presented in peripheral vision. Subjects are then instructed to fixate on the word itself. When they do so, it is masked, as in tachistoscopic experiments. This case is compared with the case in which subjects are presented with a point rather than a word in the periphery. Subjects are then instructed to fixate on the point itself. The test word is presented at this point while the subjects are moving their eyes. When they have fixated on the word, it is then masked as in the first case. Since subjects in the second case have not had the test words in their periphery, while subjects in the first case have, the study should give information about the importance of peripheral vision to word recognition. Other studies are needed to explore fully the relationship of recognition strategies for briefly exposed words to recognition strategies for continually exposed words.

Program 4.1.2 *Determination of What Visual Information in the Letter String the Reader Uses in Word Recognition.*

We need research to determine which visual features contribute to word recognition in continuous, natural reading. For example, given a typical type-font of beginning reading texts, confusion errors, similarity ratings, and multidimensional scaling procedures can be used to isolate these features. Bouma (1971) has had considerable success in isolating the visual features in IBM Courier 10 type-font. We should explore new approaches to this particular problem. See, for example, Rumelhart's study (1971) with an artificial type-font for a promising approach.

Program 4.1.3 *Determination of How Orthographic Structure Facilitates Word Recognition.*

Two mechanisms have been proposed to account for the use of orthographic structure in reading. The first assumes that readers store specific information about spelling units, that is to say, each spelling pattern is represented in long-term memory. The second mechanism assumes that readers use rules dynamically for combining letters. A central concern should be with innovative work that not only distinguishes between these two theories, but draws its hypotheses from a thorough analysis of the orthographic structure of English words and their occurrences in texts.

Program 4.1.4 *Determination of How Syntactic and Semantic Context Contribute to Word Recognition.*

An information-processing approach to reading requires that various stages of processing be isolated and that the forms of information coming in and going out of each be specified. For the most part, the experiments that have demonstrated the effect of semantic and syntactic context in reading have not been precise enough to identify which processing stage is facilitated, e.g., word recognition or immediate memory. A promising approach for further research is the additive-factor method which could be used to isolate the processing stages affected by context.

Program 4.1.5 *Determination of Whether Phonological Mediation is Necessary for Word Recognition.*

A number of investigators have proposed that phonological mediation is necessary for word recognition and experimental tests of this hypothesis are being carried out. However, we need experiments to determine whether phonological mediation is necessary in natural reading situations, not just whether it might occur in a particular experimental task. We must know the conditions, if any, which lead the reader to use phonological mediation in deriving meaning from text.

Program 4.1.6 *Determination of What Kind of Long-Term Memory Storage Units are Necessary in Letter and Word Recognition.*

Consider the well-known findings, since the time of Cattell, that a reader can recognize a word as easily as a single letter. To explain this finding, models have proposed hierarchically structured storage units corresponding to letter features, spelling patterns, and words (e.g., Estes, 1975; LaBerge and Samuels, 1974). We need experiments to define more explicitly the nature of these structures.

Approach 4.2
Investigation of the Integration of Word
Meanings into Higher Order Structures

In the information-processing approach that we have proposed, reading involves the successive recognition of larger and more abstract meanings. How does the reader go from the recognition of word meaning to the recognition of the meaning of phrases, sentences, and stories? Panels 1 and 2 are concerned with this problem, so we refer the reader to those reports for detailed research proposals. Here we delineate some critical issues as they relate to an information-processing approach. However, we are far less confident in our ability to posit relevant questions in this area than we are in the area of eye movements and word recognition, where the procedures and knowledge base are sufficiently well-developed to allow a clearer definition of issues. Readers have available for comprehending a text, a complete store of knowledge and experience built up over a lifetime. They also appear to have a variety of strategies to apply in obtaining and retaining meaning. We are only now beginning to find promising models for the information content of texts or conversations, and for the ways in which people store information in long-term memory.

The temporary storage structures available in reading provide a critical limitation on the processing of sentence and paragraph meaning. Clearly, we need research aimed at defining these limitations in adult and child readers. How soon does the integration of word meaning occur after word recognition and to what extent do syntactic structures contribute to the integration of meaning? What representation of sentence and text meaning is most appropriate for the on-line processing of phrase, sentence, and text meaning? How does subvocalization or phonological translation contribute to the integration of word meaning across sentence and storage units?

Program 4.2.1 *Determination of How the Reader Integrates Word Meanings into High Order Semantic Structures.*

Smith (1971), influenced by the work of Miller (1962), proposed that higher order meaning units are recognized as wholes in a direct, non-mediated feature-to-meaning correspondence. However, it seems unlikely that higher order meaning units such as sentences can be recognized in this way. Speech perception work by Bever and his colleagues (Bever, Lackner, and Kirk, 1969) has shown that higher order syntactic and semantic processing must occur after word recognition, that is, after word meaning is derived. Similar work should be carried out using written language.

Program 4.2.2 *Determination of the Temporal Course of Comprehension in Reading.*

A variety of different paradigms have been used in recent years to explore the temporal course of sentence comprehension. Aaronson's and Scarborough's (1976) subjects, for example, control the presentation rate of successive words in a printed sentence. The recorded exposure times related to higher level grammatical units when the subjects were reading for verbatim recall, but did not vary with grammatical structure when they were reading only for comprehension. Isakson (1974) employed a task in which subjects had to detect an auditory signal while reading a sentence. He found that reaction times increased at points where a case structure model would predict the termination of a semantic unit. Phoneme monitoring tasks (Fodor, Bever, and Garrett, 1974) have been used successfully in exploring semantic and syntactic processing in listening. Parallel tasks for reading comprehension may be equally profitable (Corcoran, 1966; Cohen, 1970). Continued investigation and integration of work in these areas seems necessary both for the development of a valid model of reading and for the eventual understanding of how to develop more readable materials.

Program 4.2.3 *Determination of What Role Inner Speech Plays in Reading.*

Studies by Hardyck and Petrinovich (1970) and by McGuigan and Rodier (1968) have shown that subvocalization increases when the perceptual or cognitive load in reading increases. Cleland (1971) suggests that subvocalization is tied to reading speed and has demonstrated such an effect in one experiment. Erickson, Mattingly, and Turvey (1973) showed that phonological translation influenced immediate memory for characters in Japanese Kanji. Before we can interpret fully any of these results, we must resolve two basic questions: Do subvocalizations which occur during reading consist of inner pronunciations of the words being read, or are they noise? At what stage of information processing does subvocalization occur?

Approach 4.3
Characterization of the Development of Reading Ability in Children

From the time children begin to demonstrate rudimentary reading skills to the time they may be considered proficient, adultlike readers, they may go through a number of stages characterized by processes which differ from those postulated for adult readers. On the other hand, children may function, according to the same processes, with variation in performance ascribable to differences in degree of competence, e.g., reading speed, or size of vocabulary. Conceptualizations of children's reading must resolve by empirical means the question of the degree to which these alternatives come into play. This is one major requirement of developmental studies.

A second and equally provocative requirement is to characterize the dynamics of transition: How do changes occur? This issue is relevant to whether children's reading processes vary in kind or degree. If different processing stages occur in development, one must account for how children proceed from one processing stage to another. We understand that these issues constitute the crux of developmental psychology and as such are not amenable to easy answers. It is imperative, nevertheless, that reading research address these questions systematically.

There have been few attempts to construct models that would account for the development of eye movements, word recognition, and integration skills that fluent readers evidence. One notable exception is the work of Gibson and her colleagues who relate the acquisition of reading skills to a theory of perceptual learning (Gibson and Levin, 1975). To construct a model for a child who has had 4 years of reading experience would require knowledge not yet available on the cognition, memory, and language processing of children. In fact, the literature sorely neglects these topics, particularly for the ages from 8 to 12. How these capacities might be marshaled by children in learning and refining reading skills remains elusive. Adults' progress in learning to read is not suggestive, since here the observations have been only anecdotal.

Given these reservations, we have concentrated our recommendations on studies of the reading processes of skilled readers. A set of recommendations related to developmental models follows, but these recommendations concern for the most part the gathering of basic information from which developmental questions could be derived.

Program 4.3.1 *Empirical Verification of Which of the Methods Used in Determining Reading Processes in Adults Are Valid for Children.*

Such an effort would be useful not only for characterizing reading development but also for comparing groups with respect to instructional methods and success in learning.

Program 4.3.2 *Determination of Which of the Components of the Reading Process Postulated for Skilled Adult Readers Are Operative in Children.*

Of particular interest are the accuracy of regressive eye movements, the use of orthographic and syntactic or semantic context in word recognition, and the temporal course of integration of word meanings into higher semantic units. Studies by Marcel (1974) and by Golinkoff (1974) have already addressed some of these issues.

Program 4.3.3 *Examination of the Role of Instructional Histories in the Development of Children's Reading Skills.*

It is worth considering whether or not we can regard learning to read as independent of instruction. The developmental view that emphasizes cognitive and linguistic growth depending on internal maturation and rule construction (Moore, 1973) would suggest that specific sorts of instruction influence learning to read in only a remote way. The fact that some children learn the basics of reading with no formal instruction at all would support this view, but the fact that other healthy children avoid or postpone learning to read makes it clear that any such development may not be inevitable. The research background is equivocal and limited on this issue. Comparisons of the effectiveness of reading methods discriminate among groups of children in minor ways which tend to wash out after the first several years of reading experience. Similarly, the method of comparing errors that children make in reading texts has not always brought sufficient refinement or perspective to the issue. For example, Weber (1970) shows essentially no differences between two first-grade classes which received different reading instruction on measures of the graphic similarity and syntactic acceptability of their errors, whereas Barr (1972) shows differences in graphic similarity when children are taught sets of words through two different training procedures. One potentially powerful approach would be to study word recognition and the use of orthographic and syntactic or semantic context as a function of the type of reading instruction. Promising developmental work showing that children are aware of letter strings that conform to English orthographic patterns by second or third grade has been done by Rosinski and Wheeler (1972). Now it is necessary to show that children at these same grade levels use this information in reading. One strategy is to match readers who have received different initial reading instruction on the basis of proficiency in word recognition, and test these subjects in the word recognition paradigms discussed in Approach 4.1.

Program 4.3.4 *Identification of the Differences between Good and Poor Readers with Respect to Processing Components.*

The development of poor readers needs examination, not only for applying findings to assist in diagnosis and remediation, but also as a test of the generalizability of the model of the successful learner. We should systematically study differences in the use of information by poor and good readers under controlled conditions. The evidence from extensive studies of reading errors (Goodman, 1973) shows that children who are poor readers do not exploit the various sources of contextual and visual information in optimal proportions. In the middle grades, for instance, they seem to be grappling with word identification with only moderate success and at the expense of attention to syntactic and semantic constraints, especially when passages become difficult for them.

Program 4.3.5 *Examination of Those Behaviors Observed in the Learner, But Not Generally Observed in Skilled Readers.*

Decoding, which involves letter-sound generalizations and blending, occupies a major part of initial reading instruction and is acquired to some degree by all readers, regardless of their instructional programs (Venezky, 1974). Studies by Venezky and Johnson (1973) and by Venezky, Chapman, and Calfee (1972) have shown interesting developmental

trends for certain letter-sound patterns, but have not attempted to uncover specific processes or structures to account for these data. We should
examine the acquisition of letter-sound patterns, and in particular those
which change over time, from an information-processing viewpoint.

Approach 4.4
Development of a Model for Eye-Movement
Guidance During Reading

The movement of the eyes has been studied extensively since the
latter part of the nineteenth century. Javal (1879) established that the eyes
move in jerks or saccades, the information coming in only during the
fixation pauses. Studies by Judd and Buswell (1922), Ballantine (1951),
and Gilbert (1959) concerned the eye movements of readers of all ages
reading material of different complexities. More recently computer-
controlled eye-movement monitoring has led to renewed interest in
measuring eye movements and in analyzing the ability of the reader to
process information from different points in the visual array (McConkie
and Rayner, 1974; Abrams and Zuber, 1972; Stern, 1974).

Models of reading must be concerned with the nature of the
mechanism which guides the eye's movements in reading. To what extent
are eye movements dependent upon visual information in the periphery
and upon preceding semantic or syntactic information, and to what extent
are they dependent on the physiological properties of the optical system?

Models of eye-movement control may be classified according to the
extent current processing determines where the eyes move next
(Hochberg, 1970; Bouma and de Voogd, 1974). Models that posit strict
control of eye movements view reading as analogous to picture or scene
scanning. As in picture processing, these models assume that the reader
moves his eyes on the basis of what he has already seen and what looks
interesting in peripheral vision. Another class of models, however, sees
eye movements serving to place each word of the text in foveal vision for a
brief period so that it may be seen clearly. Woodworth (1938) compared
these eye movements to shoveling coal into a furnace at a relatively
constant and fixed rate.

Models that assume that the eyes are guided voluntarily from fixation
to fixation require experimental support for the following assumptions:
(1) the eyes can be guided accurately to a particular location, (2) the
information obtained in one eye fixation can be resolved soon enough to
be used in determining the location of the next fixation, (3) the reader can
resolve sufficient information from the periphery to locate succeeding

fixation points, (4) the reader retains sufficient information about the visual properties of the text in order to guide regressive eye movements, and (5) the reader can both guide the eyes on the basis of what he has just read (or on the basis of what information is available in peripheral vision) and simultaneously integrate the meaning of a word.

The issue of eye-movement control in reading is a good example of the consequences of lack of knowledge of a skill basic to reading. There have been attempts to teach readers to move their eyes in a rhythmic manner, since work on eye movements seemed to indicate that skilled readers move their eyes at a fairly fixed rate. The failure of such programs led investigators to question the contribution of an understanding of eye movements to understanding reading (Tinker, 1958). However, viewing reading as a sequence of psychological processes demands a knowledge of how the reader guides his eyes in reading. The success of Bouma and de Voogd (1974) in testing whether strict control over eye guidance is a necessary component of normal reading illuminates the payoff potential on this issue. This approach should incorporate a number of experimental approaches and not be limited to the prototypical eye-movement paradigm. One can appreciate the advantages of converging operations here, especially because this area is a complex one, in which paradigmatic artifacts frequently occur. Although many of these studies require the monitoring of eye movements in reading, they also require analysis of effects in isolation to assess processing limitations. For example, tachistoscopic studies employing partial report can define how much visual information can be resolved in a single eye-fixation.

Program 4.4.1 *Determination of How Accurately the Eyes Can Be Moved in a Saccade.*

The guided eye-movement model assumes that readers can select a particular point in peripheral vision, such as the first letters of an as yet unidentified word, to fixate on. Similarly, in regressing to a misperceived word, the model assumes that readers can fixate their eyes accurately at that location. The central concern of this program is to determine how accurately readers move their eyes in a single saccade to a designated point. Accuracy should be determined over the entire vertical and horizontal range within a page of text. This project will establish an upper limit on eye-movement accuracy. Later programs will attempt to determine the degree to which readers utilize this capacity under different reading conditions.

Program 4.4.2 *Determination of How Long Subjects Need to Integrate Visually Presented Information and Move Their Eyes on the Basis of that Information.*

A typical experiment would present subjects with a visual field containing maximally discriminable forms offset from a fixation point. Then the researcher would present a directional signal at the fixation point and measure the accuracy and latency of the eye movement to the designated form.

Program 4.4.3 *Determination of What Types of Information Can Be Resolved at Different Points in the Periphery.*

The traditional approach to this problem has been the assessment of acuity as a function of retinal location, using isolated letters (Ruediger, 1907; Bouma, 1970) or letter strings (Woodworth, 1938; Bouma, 1973). Interference effects from adjacent letters have been studied by Korte (1923) and Bouma (1973). McConkie and Rayner (1974) have attempted to determine how well words, parts of words, and word shape can be resolved at different locations to the right of the fixation point. As in the previous program, experimental techniques should be used to establish recognition limits, employing the most direct methods possible. Then procedures should be devised to determine the degree to which readers utilize this capacity in reading. One experiment could use a partial report task for letter strings printed on a horizontal line (Sperling, 1970; Smith and Ramunas, 1971). In this task the visual display is followed by a report cue designating which letter to report. The research should determine accuracy of report as a function of the spatial location of the letter. Further studies should include manipulation of orthographic, syntactic, and semantic constraints in the letter strings. The results would delimit a functional visual field during an eye fixation.

Program 4.4.4 *Determination of How Much Visual Information Can Be Resolved in the Periphery with Unlimited Processing Time.*

In the typical study in this area subjects maintain their fixation and report everything they can from the periphery. Estes, Allmeyer, and Reder (1976) have employed this paradigm to study the use of spatial information about letters in the periphery, and have shown that orthographic structure can help resolve letter position.

Program 4.4.5 *Determination of How Much Information about the Spatial Properties of the Text Is Available to Readers for Guiding Regressive Movements.*

This research question has been virtually ignored, yet guidance models assume that sufficient spatial information is available for guiding regressive movements not only on the same line but also on immediately preceding lines. A variety of methods of the nature described above should be attempted in this area, e.g., partial report.

Program 4.4.6 *Determination of Whether Readers Can Resolve Meaning and Simultaneously Decide Where to Go Next.*

Consider the task of readers who guide their eyes on the basis of what they have just read or what they see in peripheral vision. In the period of roughly ¼ of a second, they must make the eye-movement decision and initiate the movement. We need experiments to test whether, in fact, the skilled reader and the beginning reader have the capacity to read in this manner. Other experiments are necessary to determine how long it takes readers to notice something in peripheral vision and initiate an eye movement to that position. One possible paradigm might present subjects with the name of a figure, e.g., a square, in foveal vision with simultaneous exposure of two different figures at different places on the horizontal to the right. Their task would be to fixate on the shape designated by the name as quickly and as accurately as possible. Measures of eye movement latency and accuracy should establish boundaries on this ability.

Approach 4.5
Measurement of the Information-Processing Habits of Competent Readers when They are Confronted with Complex Reading Tasks

For light information loads, or for tasks in which readers are not concerned with complete or nearly complete processing of ideas or facts, reading may be composed of predominantly forward-going eye movements. However, the form of reading that appears to place the greatest processing demands upon readers is called, for lack of an agreed-upon label, careful reading. It is the process by which competent readers gain recallable information from a text. For the present, we assume that this process does not involve overt articulation, but may involve subvocalizations. As integration and recall demands increase, readers move backward and forward, taking in new materials and returning to previously scanned parts as they discover that they need to reexamine them. This form of reading probably predominates for almost all subject matter children encounter in their schooling and is especially true for materials presenting a high conceptual load to readers of any age.

Forward-going (single pass) reading, with only occasional regressions is characteristic of the popular notion of reading, and is also the type of reading that most instructional programs strive for. Timed comprehension tests, for example, implicitly demand regressionless reading, yet it may be that the amount of information gained in this manner is far below that presented to children by most school books or to adults in more complex texts. It is interesting to note that most eye-movement research, due in part to difficulties in tracking vertical movements, ignores careful reading. We do not even have an adequate term for the rereading of words or phrases when the rereading is not due to immediate recognition-integration problems (i.e., is not a regression).

Careful reading is probably atypical; most adults probably do not read for high recall and therefore can afford the luxury of a predominantly forward-going process.

Skimming, directed search, and of course the predominantly forward-going reading which characterizes the reading of light novels and news articles are directly related to careful reading, but how they differ from it remains to be explored. One hypothesis is that rapid skimming, careful reading, and most other observed forms of reading behavior differ only in quantitative ways, that is, in the relative amounts or types of information utilized at each processing stage. For example, skimming might use more syntactic or semantic information for word recognition than does deliberate reading, while the latter might rely predominantly upon visual cues (e.g., letter shape, word shape) for the same process. The opposing hypothesis is that the processes differ in qualitative ways.

Program 4.5.1 *Development of a Measure of Information Load for Short Texts.*

To carry out studies which vary information load we need to develop procedures and a metric for scaling texts on this dimension. Much previous work on the readability of text exists and might be useful here. We should also consider approaches to assessing the redundancy of text, the ratio of familiar to unfamiliar words in the text, and the importance of syntactical and semantic cues in the development of the measure.

Program 4.5.2 *Development of Eye-Movement Tracking Procedures for Careful Reading.*

The study of the underlying processes and strategies employed in careful reading will be hindered until we develop procedures for tracking eye movements in multipass reading behavior. These procedures should be applicable for a variety of text conditions and for varying recall criteria.

Program 4.5.3 *Collection of Baseline Data on Silent Reading Rates for Careful Reading under Varying Information Load and Recall Conditions and for Extent of Recall for Single Pass Reading under Conditions of Varying Information Load.*

Such data would be very informative for interpreting studies of differences between the processes involved in careful and single pass reading.

Program 4.5.4 *Measurement of Reading Behavior for Texts of Varying Information Load and for Varying Required Recall Criteria.*

Descriptive studies of careful reading using the information load measure (Program 4.5.1) and the eye-movement tracking procedures developed in Program 4.5.2 are necessary before we may determine how careful reading behavior differs from single pass reading. Once we gather this information we may contrast it with new or existing data on single pass reading. Such a comparison might help to resolve the issue of whether the differences are quantitative or qualitative. Another strategy for getting at the same issue might be to vary recall requirements for careful reading until the demands on the reader reduce to those ordinarily satisfied by single pass reading. The changes in reading behavior in response to the gradual reduction in recall requirements should indicate the nature of changes in the processes. Still another procedure might entail starting out with recall demands which may be met by single pass reading, and gradually increasing the recall demands until multiple passes are required.

Program 4.5.5 *Determination of the Accuracy with Which Readers Can Return to Previously Read Materials in the Immediate Reading Task.*

Skilled reading requires a reader to identify the physical location of a fact or idea within a short text, given prior information for such location recall (Rothkopf, 1971). Yet little information exists about the accuracy with which readers can carry out this task or how accuracy varies with the complexity of the material and the degree to which readers recall the particular item (e.g., is location recall for "forgotten" items any better or worse than location recall for remembered items?). Beyond simply assessing accuracy, knowledge of the strategies careful readers employ for relocating facts or ideas within text seems important both for understanding reading and for instructional purposes. Studies directed at these issues will require tracking eye movements of careful readers in controlled conditions.

Program 4.5.6 *Determination of the Effect on Accuracy of Recalling Nonverbal Information in a Text.*

A companion set of studies to Program 4.5.5 which could aid the development of readable text would involve the measurement of accuracy of recall for textual variations in graphical information (e.g., whether or not numbers were present verbally or as numerals; which word was in italics) and in page configuration, especially when tables, figures, pictures, and varying column formats are used.

REFERENCES

Aaronson, D., and Scarborough, H. S. Performance theories for sentence coding: some quantitative evidence. *Journal of Experimental Psychology, Human Perception and Performance,* 1976, 2, 56-70.

Abrams, S. G., and Zuber, B. L. Some temporal characteristics of information processing during reading. *Reading Research Quarterly,* 1972, 8, 40-51.

Ballantine, Francis A. Age changes in measures of eye movements in silent reading. *Studies in the Psychology of Reading,* Monographs in Education, No. 4. Ann Arbor: University of Michigan Press, 1951.

Barr, Rebecca C. The influence of instructional conditions on word recognition errors. *Reading Research Quarterly,* 1972, 7, 509-529.

Bever, T. G., Lackner, J. R., and Kirk, R. The underlying structures of sentences are the primary units of immediate speech processing. *Perception and Psychophysics,* 1969, 5, 227-233.

Bouma, H. Interaction effects in parafoveal letter recognition. *Nature,* 1970 (April 11), 177-178.

Bouma, H. Visual recognition of isolated lower-case letters. *Vision Research,* 1971, 11, 459-474.

Bouma, H. Visual interference in the parafoveal recognition of initial and final letters of words. *Vision Research,* 1973, 13, 767-782.

Bouma, H., and de Voogd, A. H. On the control of eye saccades in reading. *Vision Research,* 1974, 14, 273-284.

Cleland, D. L. Vocalism in silent reading. *Visible Language,* 1971, 2, 145-157.

Cohen, G. Search times for combinations of visual, phonemic, and semantic targets in reading prose. *Perception and Psychophysics,* 1970, 8, (5B), 370-372.

Corcoran, D. W. J. An acoustic factor in letter cancellation. *Nature,* 1966, 210, 658.

Erickson, D., Mattingly, I. G., and Turvey, M. T. Phonetic activity in reading: an experiment with Kanji. *Status Report on Speech Research SR-33,* Haskins Laboratories, New Haven, Conn., 1973.

Estes, W. K. Memory, perception, and decision in letter identification. R. L. Selso (Ed.). *Information Processing and Cognition: The Loyola Symposium.* New Jersey: Erlbaum Associates, 1975.

Estes, W. K., Allmeyer, D. H., and Reder, S. M. Serial position functions for letter identification at brief and extended exposure durations. *Perception and Psychophysics,* 1976, 19, 1-15.

Fodor, J., Bever, T., and Garrett, M. *The Psychology of Language.* New York: McGraw-Hill, 1974.

Gibson, E. J. and Levin, H. *The Psychology of Reading.* Cambridge: MIT Press, 1975.

Gilbert, Luther C. Speed of processing visual stimuli and its relation to reading. *Journal of Educational Psychology,* 1959, 50, 8-14.

Golinkoff, R. M. Children's discrimination of English spelling patterns with redundant auditory information. AERA Paper, Chicago, Ill., 1974.

Goodman, K. S. Theoretically based studies of patterns of miscues in oral reading performance. Final Report, USOE Project No. 9-0375, Detroit, Mich.: Wayne State University, 1973.

Hardyck, C. D., and Petrinovich, L. F. Sub-vocal speech and comprehension as a function of difficulty level of reading material. *Journal of Verbal Learning and Verbal Behavior,* 1970, 9, 647-652.

Hochberg, J. Components of literacy: speculations and exploration research. H. Levin and J. P. Williams (Eds.). *Basic Studies in Reading.* New York: Basic Books, 1970.

Huey, Edmund B. *The Psychology and Pedagogy of Reading.* New York: The Macmillan Co., 1908. (Reprinted, with an introduction by Paul A. Kolers, Cambridge: MIT Press, 1968)

Isakson, R. L. *Case role identification and sentence meaning.* Unpublished doctoral dissertation, Ithaca, N.Y.: Cornell University, 1974.

Javal, Emile. Essai sur la physiologie de la lecture. *Annales d'Oculistique,* 1879, 82, 242-253.

Judd, C. H., and Buswell, G. T. Silent reading: a study of the various types. *Supplementary Educational Monographs,* No. 23, Chicago, Ill.: University of Chicago Press, 1922.

Kaplan, A. *The Conduct of Inquiry.* San Francisco, Cal.: Chandler Publishing Co., 1964.

Kleene, S. C. Representation of events in nerve nets and finite automata. C. E. Shannon and J. M. McCarthy (Eds.). *Automata Studies.* Princeton, N.J.: Princeton University Press, 1952.

Korte, Wilhelm. Uber die gestaltauffassung im indirekten sehen. *Zeitschrift für Psychologie,* 1923, XCII, 17-82.

LaBerge, D., and Samuels, S. J. Toward a theory of automatic information processing in reading. *Cognitive Psychology,* 1974, 6, 293-323.

Marcel, T. The effective visual field. *British Journal of Psychology,* (in press).

Massaro, D. W. (Ed.). *Understanding Language: An Information Processing Analysis of Speech Perception, Reading, and Psycholinguistics.* New York: Academic Press, 1975.

McConkie, G. W., and Rayner, K. An on-line computer technique for studying reading: identifying the perceptual span. NRC 22nd, 1974, 119-130.

McGuigan, F. J., and Rodier, W. I. Effects of auditory stimulation on covert oral behavior during silent reading. *Journal of Experimental Psychology,* 1968, 76, 649-655.

Miller, G. Decision units in the perception of speech. *IRE Transactions on Information Theory,* 1962, 81-83.

Moore, T. E. (Ed.). *Cognitive Development and the Acquisition of Language.* New York: Academic Press, 1973.

Popper, K. *The Logic of Scientific Discovery.* New York: Basic Books, 1959.

Rosinski, Richard R., and Wheeler, Kirk E. Children's use of orthographic structure in word discrimination. *Psychonomic Science,* 1972, 26, 97-98.

Rothkopf, Ernst Z. Incidental memory for location of information in text. *Journal of Verbal Learning and Verbal Behavior,* 1971, 10, 608-613.

Ruediger, W. C. The field of distance vision. *Archives of Psychology,* 1907, 1.

Rumelhart, D. E. A multicomponent theory of confusion among briefly exposed alphabetic characters. Center for Human Information Processing. San Diego, Cal.: University of California, 1971.

Smith, E. E., and Spoehr, K. T. The perception of printed English: a theoretical perspective. B. H. Kantowitz, (Ed.), *Human Information Processing: Tutorials in Performance and Cognition.* Potomac, Md.: Erlbaum Press, 1974.

Smith, Frank. *Understanding Reading.* New York: Holt, Rinehart and Winston, 1971.

Smith, M. C., and Ramunas, S. Elimination of visual field effects by use of a single report technique: evidence for order of report artifact. *Journal of Experimental Psychology,* 1971, 87, 23-28.

Sperling, G. Short-term memory, long-term memory, and scanning in processing visual information. F. A. Young and D. B. Lindsley (Eds.), *Early Experience and Visual Information Processing in Perceptual and Reading Disorders.* Washington, D.C.: National Academy of Sciences, 1970.

Stern, J. Computer-assisted biofeedback techniques utilized in the development of reading skills. NSF Project EC-41504, St. Louis, Mo.: Washington University, 1974.

Tinker, M. A. Recent studies of eye movements in reading. *Psychological Bulletin,* 1958, 55, 215-231.

Venezky, R. L. Language and cognition in reading. B. Spolsky (Ed.), *Current Trends in Educational Linguistics,* The Hague: Mouton & Co., 1974.

Venezky, R. L., and Johnson, D. Development of two letter-sound patterns in grades one through three. *Journal of Educational Psychology,* 1973, 64, 109-115.

Venezky, R., Chapman, R., and Calfee, R. The development of letter-sound patterns from second through sixth grade. Technical Report No. 231, Madison, Wisconsin Research and Development Center for Cognitive Learning, September 1972.

Weber, R. M. First graders use of grammatical context in reading. H. Levin and J. Williams (Eds.), *Basic Studies in Reading.* New York: Harper and Row, 1970.

Woodworth, R. S. *Experimental Psychology.* New York: Holt, Rinehart and Winston, 1938.

Text Comprehension Skills and Process Models of Text Comprehension

GEORGE A. MILLER*
The Rockefeller University

Approach Statement

The goal of this approach is to identify those skills that are important for text comprehension, as distinguished from word or sentence comprehension, and to determine how these skills can be taught.

Approach Potential

An understanding of what readers do when they comprehend text is critically important to design instruction that strengthens comprehension skills.

Approach Rationale

We intend to focus on those factors which are unique, or especially important, to text comprehension and which are not treated in discussion of word, concept, or sentence comprehension. Thus, while word comprehension skills are clearly essential to text comprehension, they will not be discussed here.

Work on text comprehension is not yet far-advanced. There are major gaps in our understanding of the anatomy of the text comprehension process, and in our knowledge of the skills that make comprehension

---

*Chairman of the National Institute of Education Conference on Studies in Reading, Panel 1. Other panel members were Susan C. Block, John Bormuth, John R. Hayes, Claudia Mitchell-Kernan, and Herbert A. Simon. The Panel also had 12 field consultants. Because of space limitations, only the last third of the Panel's 54 page report could be reprinted here. The full report, entitled "Semantics, Concepts, and Culture: Conference on Studies in Reading, Panel Report 1," was published in 1975 by the National Institute of Education, U.S. Department of Health, Education, and Welfare, Washington, D.C.

possible. The task will be to draw on imperfect empirical knowledge and on hints contained in a few simulation studies to arrive at reasonable guesses as to what this process is and what these skills may be.

The following model, while very incomplete, appears consistent with available data and ideas, and provides a framework in which to place our guesses about comprehension skills. The model starts with raw text as input and ends with information coded in a format acceptable to some special processor as output. For example, if the text is a problem statement, then the comprehension process must generate an output that is acceptable as input for some problem-solving process.

We assume that the raw text is processed by a parser and that anaphoric reference is handled by another processor. Neither of these processors will be discussed here. The model then has three general steps.

First, we need to identify important elements of the text. The output of the above processes is passed to an attention program that makes preliminary judgments about what is important in the text. These judgments include identifying major themes, judging which elements of the text are relevant to the major themes, etc. It seems essential that the attention process be responsive to context. Thus, in a history text, the attention process might tag dates as important and interpersonal relationships as not, but do the opposite in a novel.

Second, we need to construct internal representations of the important information in the text. Once the important aspects of the text have been identified, a representation that incorporates these aspects must be constructed. The construction of representations seems to involve many subprocesses:

(a) *Retrieval of information from long term memory.* To understand a story about a vicious dog, for example, it is essential to know that dogs bite and that they are more than a centimeter tall, even if the story does not mention these facts. Presumably, construction of internal representation depends heavily on retrieval of this kind of knowledge from long term memory. This, in turn, clearly depends on the existence of a large store of well-indexed information in long term memory.

(b) *Elaborating and abstracting.* In forming representations, people display at different times quite contrary tendencies. In some cases, they elaborate on the information in the text by adding details of appearance, spatial and temporal settings, etc. It is possible that this elaboration enhances retention. In other cases, the subject may strip the representation to its bare essentials. It is not uncommon in problem-solving situations to observe a subject construct an elaborate representation of the problem situation and then, late in the solution process, generate a new, more abstract representation with all unessential detail removed.

(c) *Integrating the representation*. This includes drawing inferences implied by the representation (see Bransford and Franks' article, pages 103-107) and detecting and correcting inconsistencies between two parts of a representation or between the representation and new text elements. For example, at one point in a text, readers may interpret the words "perform for x" to mean "perform for the benefit of x," while at another point they may interpret that same phrase to mean "perform instead of x." Later in the comprehension process, they should correct this inconsistency and successfully resolve the ambiguity.

(d) *Naming*. The assignment of unique names to the elements of the representation appears to be an important part of the comprehension process. This fact becomes more evident in situations that interfere with the naming process. For example, if we hear a narrative about a family upstairs and a family downstairs, we have little trouble comprehending as long as the families do not move. However, if the family upstairs moves downstairs from the family downstairs, we may find that comprehension is aided by calling them Family A and Family B. Simple naming, of course, is trivial; the real skill here is to recognize when, and what, to name.

Third, we need to match the representation to an appropriate special processor. We view the comprehension process as being complete when the representation has been constructed and mapped onto the appropriate special processor. (By "appropriate processor" we do not necessarily mean a processor that will solve the problem.) This step, of course, requires both that a large and well-indexed set of special processors be available, and that the mapping onto the appropriate processor be accomplished. This last requirement is by no means trivial, as experience in problem-solving shows. Often, superficial changes in the form of a problem will make its solution either much more difficult or in some cases impossible. For example, in one situation a subject who was working on an isomorph of the Tower-of-Hanoi problem constructed a representation that resembled the Tower of Hanoi except that it was upside down. This simple difference in orientation prevented the subject from recognizing that he already knew how to solve the problem. In some cases, the mapping is facilitated by the use of multiple representations. The puzzle literature is full of situations in which comprehension is very difficult indeed until one hits on the right representation, at which point the problem becomes trivial.

Divisions of the Approach

The division into programs parallels the division of Approaches 1.1, Word Recognition Skills, and 1.2, Sentence Comprehension Skills.

Program 1.3.1 *Process Models of Text Comprehension.*

Program Statement

The aim of this program is to develop models for the text comprehension process and for subprocesses of the total process.

Program Potential

Work has proceeded on question-answering and natural-language understanding systems for a number of years now. This work has met with considerable success, particularly with respect to the solution of parsing problems. With this work as background and with several new developments in text comprehending systems, it seems likely that models of text comprehension can now be developed more rapidly.

Program Research Considerations

In this program we should emphasize computer simulation studies which can be closely checked against observation of human performance. Artificial intelligence studies, while potentially of great value, seem less likely than simulation studies to generate ideas useful in practical reading contexts. Similarly, mathematical models or other less formal models seem less appropriate than simulation models for *handling* complex processes such as text comprehension.

Divisions of the Program

The program is divided into a global project and a number of specific projects. The specific projects were chosen because they seem to be highly isolatable and "doable" parts of the total process. The global project was included because we believe that if all the parts were built separately, there would still be much to learn by putting them together in a total text comprehension system.

Project 1.3.1.1 *Simulation of the Text Comprehension Process.*

Project Statement

The goal of this project is to conduct psychological studies of text comprehension and construct computer simulation models of the observed behavior.

Project Potential

See Program 1.3.1

Project Research Considerations

Because of the complexity of the text comprehension process, there are many parameters which seem likely to influence human behavior in this task, e.g., the organization of the text, the relation of the text to information in long term memory, special training procedures, etc. Generating sufficient data to exercise a simulation model should not be difficult.

Project 1.3.1.2 *Models of Relevance Judgments.*

Project Statement

The goal of this project is to conduct psychological studies of relevance judgments in text comprehension and to develop models of the judgmental process.

Project Potential

Although relevance judgments constitute only a small part of the text comprehension process, they are likely to play a critical role in determining the efficiency of the total process. This area of investigation is quite narrowly defined, and it may be relatively easy to progress with it.

Project Research Considerations

A number of heuristics suggest themselves as possible candidates for use by readers in identifying relevant elements in a text. For example, the reader might judge relevant: (1) those elements most frequently mentioned; (2) those elements most frequently connected by logical or grammatical relationships to other elements in the passage; (3) those elements entering into important logical relationships, such as set relationships or negotiation; or (4) all of the above.

It might be interesting to focus this research on the identification of the heuristics which subjects in fact use.

Project 1.3.1.3   *Models of Isomorph Recognition.*

Project Statement

The goal of this project is to conduct psychological studies of the conditions under which humans can identify the isomorphism of two text structures (e.g., two narratives, two problems) and construct models of the identification process.

Project Potential

It seems likely that human use of information from long term memory in text comprehension is severely limited by failure to recognize the isomorphism of complex structures. Success of this project could contribute much to our understanding of memory-use limitations.

Project Research Considerations

One possible line of research in this area is the exploration of the role superficial features play in hiding the identity of isomorphs of problems or narratives. The Tower-of-Hanoi problem can be coded in a great many forms that differ superficially, e.g., as a problem in which a set of people exchange tasks on the basis of their route or as a problem in which tribes exchange villages depending on their birthplaces, etc. Some of these codings are much easier to recognize as the original Tower-of-Hanoi problem than others. Finding those factors that interfere most with isomorph identification may shed light on the identification process.

Program 1.3.2 *Procedures for Facilitating Comprehension.*

Program Statement

The aim of this program is to develop procedures for facilitating comprehension of text, and test the procedures with human subjects.

Program Potential

While there is relatively little work in this area, and what there is, is scattered, the practical importance of advances in this area is great.

Program Research Considerations

The lack of theoretical integration, which has characterized this area in the past, suggests that work on this program should be coordinated with work on Program 1.3.1 in order to give it theoretical focus.

Divisions of Program

Six strategies for approaching this problem appear promising.

Project 1.3.2.1 *The Role of the Readers' Knowledge Base.*

Project Statement

The goal of this project is (1) to explore the relationship between the size and nature of readers' knowledge base and their ability to comprehend (a) general text passages (passages for which nearly all readers have the relevant information), (b) text passages on topics that are especially familiar to readers, and (c) text passages on topics with which readers are not familiar; and (2) to explore the effects on text comprehension of increasing the subjects' knowledge base (a) over the shortrun in specific subject matters and (b) by an intensive and long term push in a broad range of topics.

Project Potential

Semantic memory is currently an active research area; thus, this project should be able to profit by borrowing from the rich pool of theoretical ideas which has recently become available.

Project 1.3.2.2 *Questioning Skills.*

Project Statement

The goal of this project is to determine ways to provide subjects with skills for detecting gaps in their own knowledge bases and for increasing these knowledge bases over an extended period of time.

Project Potential

If successful, this project could be of great practical value, for the same reason that all self-instructional material is valuable—it could provide knowledge at low cost. Similarly, it would have the disadvantages of self-instructional material in that it would depend on individual interest and effort in the target population.

Project Research Considerations

Skills that subjects would need to acquire include: (1) skills for detecting gaps in the knowledge base. These might include the use of systematic checking procedures such as checklists of standard knowledge and the use of "failure to understand" as a cue to self-questioning; and (2) skills for retrieving information from information sources, e.g., teachers and librarians.

To succeed, it seems likely that this project would need to make a long term change in the fine grain of subject behaviors. This suggests that it would involve intensive training—perhaps for short periods of time, repeated at intervals.

Project 1.3.2.3 *Knowledge Integration.*

Project Statement

The goal of this project is to develop procedures for improving readers' ability to integrate knowledge acquired from a passage of connected text.

Project Potential

Because it has been reported that poor readers are deficient in the ability to integrate information, this project may be concerned with a skill of central importance to reading comprehension.

Project Research Considerations

Bransford and Franks' procedures may provide a valuable technique for conducting research in this area. Detection of inconsistencies in the text might provide another useful dependent measure. Techniques developed in connection with Project 1.3.2.4 might suggest useful training techniques.

Project 1.3.2.4 *Elaboration Skills.*

Project Statement

The goal of this project is to develop training procedures to increase subjects' ability to elaborate on relevant text elements, and conduct psychological tests to determine if such elaborations increase memory for, or comprehension of, the text.

Project Potential

It may be that when one says that individuals are taking an "active attitude toward a text," what is meant is that they are employing elaboration skills. If so, training in such skills may aid text comprehension.

Project 1.3.2.5 *Using Pictures as Aids.*

Project Statement

The goal of this project is to determine under what circumstances pictures aid text comprehension, and under what circumstances they hinder text comprehension.

Project Potential

A great deal of effort and expense goes into illustrating school texts and other educational materials; but there is some evidence that illustrations can actually hinder comprehension of the text. This project is, thus, of considerable importance.

Project Research Considerations

The research on the effects of pictures on learning to read and on comprehension of text has been reviewed by Samuels (*Review of Educational Research*, 1970, 40, No. 3, 397-407). He concludes that "There was almost unanimous agreement that pictures, when used as adjuncts to the printed text, do not facilitate comprehension." This evaluation comes as a surprise to most educators and publishers when they first encounter it. It is widely assumed that interesting pictures help children infer meanings of unfamiliar words and interpret difficult constructions in the text, motivate them to read, and instill positive attitudes toward reading. Those unwilling to abandon their intuitive beliefs find the research results difficult to accept.

An important word to note in Samuels' conclusion is "adjuncts." An adjunct picture is redundant—it repeats in visual form information that is given by the text in linguistic form. An adjunct picture may divert children's attention from the text. At best, they acquire the information without having to puzzle over the text; at worst, they pay attention to irrelevant aspects of the picture and, so, acquire the wrong information.

It is not necessary, however, for a picture to be a mere adjunct to the text. Bransford and Johnson (*Journal of Verbal Learning and Verbal Behavior*, 1972, 11, 717-726) have studied comprehension of passages that presuppose information given in a picture—pictures are used as advance organizers. For such texts, comprehension and recall are poor if the picture has not been seen in advance; readers feel they have come in at the middle of something. References are made to things, relationships, or situations which they do not recognize; and they are unable to guess about them intelligently. Thus, it is possible for pictures to play an important role in total communication if the pictures provide a representation necessary for processing textual information. In most basal readers, however, pictures are not used in this manner. Whether they should be, or whether they should be eliminated entirely from instructional materials designed to teach reading, cannot be answered without further research.

Project 1.3.2.6 *Identifying Relevant Information In Text.*

Project Statement

The aim of this project is to develop procedures for improving readers' ability to identify relevant information in text, and to conduct psychological tests to measure the effectiveness of the procedures. The goal is to promote educational applications of work performed under Project 1.3.1.2.

Project Potential

It has been observed in some text comprehension tasks that half of the text material is irrelevant to the completion of the task. The ability to make accurate judgments of relevance, then, may be very important in insuring efficiency in processing text information.

Project Research Considerations

Good dependent measures for this project might include (1) direct relevance judgments, (2) identification of major themes, (3) construction of an outline for the text, and many others.

Program 1.3.3 *Development of Text Comprehending Skills.*

Program Statement

The goal of this program is to conduct psychological studies of developmental changes in text comprehending skills.

Program Potential

Study of the development of text comprehending skills is important, both for clarification of theoretical issues and for practical applications. Developmental observations should help in understanding how the integrated package of skills which underlies adult competence in text comprehension was put together, and, hence, should provide insights into its functioning. Such observations should also be directly applicable in the classroom to help define teaching goals and to determine performance expectations. If children at a given developmental stage cannot make relevance judgments, for example, then it is unreasonable to expect them to outline paragraphs well or to write sensible book reports.

Although developmental norms have been established for vocabulary and grammatical skills and for text comprehension as a whole, there is a lack of such norms for the component skills which make up text comprehension. Research would help to fill this important gap.

Program Research Considerations

A theoretical orientation for research in this area could be obtained by integrating this research with other work in Approach 1.3, and/or by employing a Piagetian framework. Within the latter framework, the developing abilities for basic metalinguistic and metaconceptual judgments seem particularly relevant.

For some comprehension skills, it may be important to extend the range of developmental stages studied below the age of reading by exploring the child's developing comprehension of spoken passages.

Division of the Program

The division of this program reflects the rationale outlined above for Approach 1.3.

Project 1.3.3.1 *Development of Relevance Judgments.*

Project Statement

The goal of this project is to conduct psychological studies of the development of children's ability to make judgments about the relevance of text elements.

Project Potential

Relating the temporal course of development of this skill to the course of development of comprehension as a whole can help to define the role of this skill in the total process.

Project Research Considerations

Experiments in this area need to be designed so that the preliminary relevance judgments readers make prior to full comprehension are studied, rather than judgments of relevance made after the text is comprehended. Thus, it may be important to present the text one sentence at a time, and to obtain relevance judgments of each sentence before the next is given.

Project 1.3.3.2   *Development of Text Integration.*

Project Statement

The goal of this project is to conduct developmental studies of children's ability to draw appropriate inferences relating the elements of a text.

Project Potential

This project parallels that of Project 1.3.3.1.

Project Research Considerations

Potentially valuable dependent measures include discrimination of new and old text elements (in the manner of Bransford and Franks) and detection of inconsistencies in the text. Independent measures might include the number of text elements required to make an inference, and the distance separating them in the text.

Project 1.3.3.3   *Development of Retrieval Processes.*

Project Statement

The aim of this project is to conduct psychological studies of developmental changes in the processes by which information is retrieved from long term memory.

Project Potential

This project parallels that of Project 1.3.3.1.

Project Research Considerations

Of particular interest for understanding reading comprehension would be evidence concerning developmental changes (1) in the probability that a cue will lead to retrieval, and (2) in the nature of effective retrieval cues.

Project 1.3.3.4   *Basic Metalinguistic and Metaconceptual Skills.*

Project Statement

The goal of this project is to relate developmental changes in text comprehending skills (Projects 1.3.3.1, 1.3.3.2, and 1.3.3.3) to basic cognitive development, especially in the realm of metalinguistic and metaconceptual abilities.

Project Potential

Learning to decode text requires basic metalinguistic skills. Children must be able to segment speech into words and phonemes if they are to learn the conventions of writing. Recent work has shown that most children under 5 lack these metalinguistic skills, that many poor readers in the early elementary grades lack these skills, that these skills can be taught, and that teaching them improves reading at the decoding level. Analogously, higher level text comprehending skills require that children be able to make their thoughts the objects of their thinking. It is plausible that this is a general ability which develops during the elementary school years, and that lags in developing higher order comprehension skills follow directly from lags in this ability.

Project Research Considerations

There are several paradigms, scattered in the developmental literature, which potentially relate to the ability to think about one's own thinking. Piaget's stage of concrete operations can be seen in this light. In determining children's developmental stages, Piaget emphasizes children's justifications for their judgments. The apparently different concepts of life which Piaget finds characteristic of children under 12 may reflect the requirement of consciously defining "life," rather than a truly different conceptual structure. That is, once children have committed themselves in a Piagetian interview to the definition "life = movement," they say that clouds are alive, the sun is alive, etc., even though in ordinary circumstances they might not make that confusion. Similarly, the lack of clustering in free recall tasks is often taken as evidence that children do not "have" some abstract conceptual distinction. It is equally likely that children simply fail to recruit a distinction they make in other contexts as a strategy for this task. That is, adults characteristically adopt strategies for dealing as efficiently as possible with any task they are set; children do not have comparable flexibility. This difference may reflect an inability to represent and manipulate the demands of the task. If there are basic developmental changes in these abilities during the elementary school years, they would underlie the higher order comprehension skills we have isolated. If this can be demonstrated, effort should be put into direct attempts to foster these basic cognitive skills.

Program 1.3.4 *Cultural Differences in Text Comprehension.*

Program Statement

The goal of this program is to determine whether there are subcultural differences in the development of text comprehending skills.

Program Potential

Research in this area is extremely important, for the percentage of children failing to attain full literacy is especially great among some cultural subpopulations. Programs 1.1.4 and 1.2.4 seek reasons for this difference at the level of processing individual words and sentences; in this program, we look directly at the text comprehending skills we isolated in Approach 1.3. The work of Michael Cole and his associates suggests that a large proportion of the variance among subpopulations might be found at this level. They have found that apparent differences in knowledge are often differences in *deployment* of knowledge, especially as it relates to strategies for particular tasks.

Program Research Considerations

This work must follow the work in Program 1.3.3. We cannot look for subcultural differences in the development of text comprehending skills without some idea of the general course of development of these skills. Therefore, we cannot guess at present *which*, if any, of the text comprehension abilities we have isolated will be most sensitive to such differences.

Various lines of cross-cultural research are currently converging on the idea that cultural differences in cognitive tasks are attributable to factors that call particular operations into play and regulate their role in the performance of a task. It is important, therefore, to study not only cultural differences in the acquisition of cognitive skills, but also cultural differences in the way those skills are employed in particular situations.

Division of the Program

The program has been divided into three projects. The first concerns basic metalinguistic and metaconceptual skills and the second the particular text comprehension skills we have isolated. The third is more basic, and even more ambitious. We seek relevant descriptions of communication practices among different cultural subgroups which account for any subcultural differences found in the first two projects.

Project 1.3.4.1 *Subcultural Differences in Metalinguistic and Metaconceptual Skills.*

Project Statement

The goal of this project is to determine if cultural variations exist in the nature of, and in the rate of attainment of, various metalinguistic and metaconceptual strategies and abilities.

Project Potential

Just as there is evidence for the development of abilities to "think about thinking" in the elementary school ages (Project 1.3.3.4), there is also evidence for cultural differences in this development. This situation might be expected if cultural subgroups differ in the degree to which they play metalinguistic games with their children, or if they differ in more basic aspects of the use of language (Project 1.3.4.3).

Project Research Considerations

The tasks devised to obtain an overall picture of the development of metaconceptual skills (Project 1.3.3.4) should be given to children with varying subcultural backgrounds. The aim of this research is to discover if there are differences in the development of abilities for constructing strategies appropriate to some particular cognitive task, for rationalizing one's thinking, etc. More important, if there are such differences, there should be work on discovering what kinds of experience foster the matalinguistic or metaconceptual attitude.

Project 1.3.4.2 *Subcultural Differences in Text Comprehending Skills.*

Project Statement

The goal of this project is to determine the extent to which differences among subgroups in their attainment of full literacy depend upon differences in text comprehension skills.

Project Potential

Although it seems likely that many of the differences in ultimate reading skills depend on text comprehension skills, this dependence cannot be tested until work under Programs 1.3.1, 1.3.2, and 1.3.3 has a firm beginning.

Project Research Considerations

See Project Potential.

Project 1.3.4.3 *Communicative Resources of Cultural Subgroups.*

Project Statement

The goal of this project is to conduct a series of anthropological-sociological studies to determine if cultural subgroups differ in their communication resources and communication practices.

Project Potential

Differences in the size of vocabularies and meanings of words seem unlikely to explain fully the differences observed in comprehension abilities of cultural subgroups. Even if differences in vocabulary sizes do occur, they will require further explanation. This explanation is very likely to point to factors in the socialization milieu which promote strategies for conveying semantic information other than the rules of lexical selection and syntactic concatenation. It appears that, in bilingual and bidialectal speech communities, code switching can convey information of considerable social and expressive (and perhaps even referential) importance. It would seem important to understand better the relationship between the type of linguistic responses available in different speech communities and such factors as vocabulary size, development, and elaboration. The availability of alternate communication strategies may be relevant to understanding the sources of differences in vocabulary development among children who belong to different social groups.

Project Research Considerations

The object of this research is to obtain a better understanding of the impingement of social and cultural factors on the way language functions in the social life of a speech community and of the relationship between this functioning and the kind of linguistic skills acquired by developing children in the community. Basic ethnographic information on the functions of language among social groups can yield insight into the kind of communication settings which may be useful in promoting the development of new language skills.

In particular, subcultural differences in the role assigned to reading should be studied. Students whose culture teaches them the pragmatic and economic value of reading may approach the learning task quite differently from students who believe that reading is an activity useful for learning something new about the world. Two readers differing in this way might also differ considerably in the level of information processing they would bring to the task of reading a text dealing with unfamiliar subjects. The information extracted from a text is highly sensitive to the task demands placed on the reader, yet we know little about the task demands that beginning readers place on themselves or the factors, situational or cultural, that lead them to such interpretations of their task. Students' conceptions of what reading is all about probably differ in different social strata; we need to know whether their conceptions significantly affect how they go about the activity of reading. The problem may not be that students do not know how to perform the various cognitive processes involved in reading comprehension, but that they simply do not recognize that those processes are relevant to the task they think they have been given.

We have argued that reading a text can be regarded as a problem-solving task. It is a well-established fact that the difficulty of a problem varies according to context, even when the logical structure of the problem is the same. This variation should be studied in cultural terms. Subcultures differ in their knowledge of and interest in different domains of knowledge. It should be possible to estimate the importance of the content domain for reading by varying the content of text according to these cultural variations in knowledge while keeping the texts equivalent in terms of syntactic, logical, and rhetorical structure. Such processes as elaboration or representation may be spontaneously practiced in one domain but not in another—in relation to social life, say, as opposed to physical phenomena. In that case, the problem would become one of determining how operations well-developed for one domain may be generalized to other domains.

Priorities and Recommendations

General Discussion

The organizing idea behind this report was an attempt to characterize different strata of language skills at which reading comprehension can be frustrated: (1) decoding; (2) word recognition; (3) sentence interpretation; and (4) textual analysis. In proficient readers, information processing at levels (1), (2), and possibly (3) should occur automatically, so their conscious efforts can be directed totally to level (4). Poor readers, on the other hand, may be deficient at any level, with the most noticeable and disruptive deficiencies being ordered first. (We do *not* assume, however, that this order dictates a corresponding order of acquisition of skills, or that success at a higher level does not interact with performance of lower level skills.)

Incompetent, inaccurate, or slow decoding, attributable either to pathological causes or to lack of practice, can cause serious difficulties for all processing at higher levels. It is possible that some failures to learn to comprehend text easily result from insufficient automaticity of decoding.

How frequently this occurs is not known, although it would seem to be important information for allocating priorities. The panel, however, accepted the popular consensus that the majority of poor readers in the upper grades are both accurate and proficient decoders; their problems arise from other, more complex sources.

The panel concentrated, therefore, on difficulties in word recognition, sentence interpretation, and textual analysis. Attention was further limited to the scientific aspects of these processes, and to the basic information required for intelligent educational applications and development; how these applications should be realized was little explored. Even with these limitations, however, the plan of the report is quite ambitious, so that in the short time available to prepare it the panel could not go as deeply into many questions as the questions deserved.

For each of the three levels considered, the division into programs followed the same plan. First, we called for a better theory of adult competence at that level. Second, we asked how that competence develops in children. Third, we wanted studies based on this knowledge of children's developing linguistic skills that would enable educators to facilitate reading comprehension, or to ameliorate difficulties at each level. And, finally, we pointed to subcultural variations whose effects at each level are poorly understood, but which seem to provide valuable opportunities for testing and extending theories of cognitive competence and their developmental course.

Priorities could be assigned to the various programs that resulted from this scheme either (1) in terms of the seriousness of the difficulties at each level or (2) in terms of the scientific of intellectual merits of the programs. For the former rating, it would be important to know how frequently each type of difficulty occurs in different populations of students. Lacking such studies, the panel was forced to rely on the impressions and intuitions of its members, which are of doubtful validity. For the latter rating, judgment is easily prejudiced by one's personal interests and intellectual history. Weighing objectively the host of relevant factors—expense, time required, probability of success, dependence on outcomes of related research, utility of the results, relevance to existing or developing psychological or linguistic theories, number of established facts to which new facts can be related, difficulty of execution, general level of interest among workers in the field, excellence of personnel willing and able to do the work, and so on—would have been difficult, even if we had been able to make valid judgments of each program or each factor in isolation.

Criteria and Priorities

All panelists determined their own criteria, but there was some consensus (1) that a survey of poor readers would probably reveal more students deficient in text comprehension than in lower level skills, so Approach 1.3 was of greater social importance; and (2) that practical applications are not feasible lacking valid theories to apply, so that the more basic studies deserve priority at the present time. Together, the panel selected Program 1.3.1 as of highest priority based on these criteria.

The general picture that emerges from the panelist's rating is that priority should go to modeling the comprehension process (at all three levels: word, sentence, and text comprehension levels), then to collecting information on the development of those processes in children (at all three levels), and finally to application of this information to practical educational problems. This ordering presumably reflects an opinion that this is the sensible order in which to work toward fruitful applications, not a judgment that applied research and development is of secondary or tertiary importance. In particular, it is not a judgment that the reading problems of children from various American subcultures are uninteresting or unimportant. Rather, it follows from the panel's interpretation of the task it was assigned, namely, to propose approaches to establishing a knowledge base on which more successful teaching of reading comprehension skills might rest.[1]

---

[1] *Editor's note.* For recent models on processing text and on discourse analysis, see: Carroll, John B., and Roy O. Freedle (Eds.), *Language Comprehension and the Acquisition of Knowledge.* Washington, D.C.: V. H. Winston and Sons, 1972.

Frederiksen, Carl H. Discourse comprehension and early reading. Pittsburgh Conference on Reading, May 12-14, 1976. Proceedings to be published in 1977, Lauren Resnick and Phyllis Weaver, Editors.

Mandler, Jean M., Nancy S. Johnson, and Marsha DeForest. *A Structural Analysis of Stories and Their Recall. From "Once Upon a Time" to "Happily Ever After."* Center for Human Information Processing, University of California, San Diego, La Jolla, California 92093, 1976.

Rothkopf, Ernest L. Writing to teach and reading to learn: A perspective on the psychology of written instruction. In N. L. Gage (Ed.), *The Psychology of Teaching Methods:* The Seventy-Fifth Yearbook of the National Society for the Study of Education, Part I. Chicago: University of Chicago Press, 1976, 91-129.

Rumelhart, David E. *Toward an Interactive Model of Reading.* Center for Human Information Processing, University of California, San Diego, 1976.

Developmental Processes and Reading Processes—Invalid Inferences from the Former to the Latter*

IRENE ATHEY

The University of Rochester

Most educators believe that, while teaching is an art, there is a body of established knowledge which constitutes a science of education. The basic content of this science, however, seems to be somewhat difficult to define. One can, of course, make analyses of teacher behavior, or conduct field studies comparing the consequences of organizational, or curricular intervention. Such enterprises constitute the bulk of doctoral dissertations and faculty research emanating from our graduate schools of education. Some sciences, especially those which employ so-called hard data, tend to look down on these kinds of activities as imprecise, lacking objectivity and, in general, barely meriting the label scientific.

People in education have another function or responsibility, which is perhaps no more objective, but certainly just as difficult as the task of instilling rigor into educational research. I am referring to the task of keeping abreast with developments in the sciences (not to mention social and political events which may also have profound effects on education but are not under consideration here) in order to determine how these developments impinge, or should impinge, on our educational beliefs and practices. Having determined the relevancy of a particular field to education, the educational expert has the following tasks: a) He must assess the validity and relevance of findings from a particular scientific discipline. Since he is unlikely to be an expert in the field (and is certainly not going to be an expert in all of them), and since experts in the field frequently disagree about these matters, the educator finds himself in a role rather like that of a congressman in committee. He must weigh the various

*Reprinted from Frank P. Greene (Ed.), *Investigations Relating to Mature Reading*, Twenty-First Yearbook of the National Reading Conference, 1972, 171-182. Reprinted by permission of the author and the National Reading Conference, Inc.

730

testimonies, and draw his own conclusions. b) Then he must attempt to synthesize, or at least balance the inputs from the different disciplines, to discover whether they are at best congruent, at worst contradictory, but more likely incomplete, piecemeal, and limited in perspective, so that they appear unrelated and incapable of synthesis. c) Next, from the above information he must draw valid interpretations concerning the implications of these findings for educational theory. d) Finally, he must consider the most effective ways to implement the conclusions he has drawn in the practical setting of the schools. The educator's task has been compared to that of the juggler who must keep many balls in the air at the same time, but for the juggler all balls are equal in appearance, weight, and value. The educator has the additional problem of determining which balls to use, and the relative worth of those he chooses.

I believe that the processes of weighing, synthesizing, and interpreting the many and varied inputs we in education receive from the sciences (again, I am omitting, without discounting, the inputs from social and political sources to which education must constantly lend a listening ear), are extraordinarily difficult, and that the recurring phenomenon known as the bandwagon effect may be attributable, at least in part, to this difficulty. Hence we find a tendency among educators to latch on to the findings of some biologist, psychiatrist, or sociologist, and to elevate his pronouncements to the status of a cult, especially if they happen to be in line with their own educational philosophy. A psychologist speaks, and programmed instruction is hailed as an innovation which will change the face of education. A sociologist speaks, and we may well find ourselves deschooling society and issuing educredit cards in the maternity ward.

It is important, of course, that education remain an open system capable of receiving and using data from the sciences, but as the discipline where synthesis and evaluation of the input must also take place, education has the responsibility of maintaining perspective and of having the strength to withstand scientific incursions which are excessive or unduly limited in their perspective. This may sound conservative, and many educators are afraid of being thought reactionary, out-of-date, or apathetic. We should indeed be open, flexible, and innovative, we should welcome an interdisciplinary approach to the problems of education, but we should be on guard against being subject to every wind that blows from every quarter of the academic globe.

My introductory remarks have been couched in terms of education in general but they apply with equal force to reading. For many years, reading has been the exclusive province of the education profession, and its career both in research and practice, has followed the ups-and-downs of education. For example, during an era of progressive education, the tendency was to delay the teaching of reading, and to use introductory methods which placed emphasis on units of meaning, such as the whole word or phrase, whereas the no-nonsense, back-to-basics philosophy (e.g. the Rafferty "Education in Depth" approach) called for early and specific training which would give children the tools—usually phonics training; the research of this era is concerned largely with the efficacy of Method X versus Method Y. Similarly a period which emphasized the education of the "whole child" saw the ascendancy of the maturation hypothesis linking reading age with such physiological measures as skeletal age, dental age, etc. as well as psychological measures such as mental age (Olson, 1949).

Like education itself, reading is today the focus of interdisciplinary interest and effort. Personally, I welcome this expansion, this opening of windows to let more sunshine in. Just let us be careful that, if our position happens to be near one window, we are not blinded by the light from that particular window, so that we cannot see the view from other windows. In this paper, I have attempted to take some of the most recent knowledge from other disciplines notably psychology and linguistics, and to use them, not to put the whole child together again, since I feel this may be premature, but to achieve in some measure the kind of balance I have alluded to above. I will discuss briefly some findings in perception, cognition, psycholinguistics, and finally motivation. In each case, the development of these processes in the non-reading child, rather than the mature processes of the skilled reader, will be the focus of consideration.

Perception

We may accept at the outset Haber's (1969) view, which is shared by many other researchers, that "sensation, perception, memory, and thought must be considered on a continuum of cognitive activity. They are mutually interdependent and cannot be separated except by arbitrary rules of momentary expediency [p. 1]." It appears that all processes on the continuum are geared to the single objective of reducing the uncertainty experienced by the organism in confronting both his inner and outer world. While recognizing the continuum, psychologists still find the terms perception, cognition, etc. useful.

There are many exciting developments in the field of perception, and we can refer to only a few of them. Infant perception has been studied intensively, and we now have evidence that the infant's world is not the booming, buzzing confusion hypothesized by William James, but is characterized even as early as 16 weeks, by pattern discrimination, object permanence, size constancy, and depth perception. Fantz (1970) and Miranda (1969) at Case Western Reserve University's Perceptual Development Laboratory have found that infants show visual preference for complex, brightly patterned or colored, moving stimuli. In 1961, Walk and Gibson developed the simulation of a "visual cliff" by means of a divided patterned surface. Subsequent research on a variety of species has shown that all except flying and swimming animals avoid the "cliff edge" at a very young age, e.g. at three days of age for monkeys (Rosenblum & Cross, 1963). Infants cannot be tested on this situation until they begin to crawl, but Walk (1966) found that 90% of infants between 6 and 16 months make avoidance responses.

Other areas of study with infants are the perception of size constancy over distance, linking of visual and tactual cues in perception of objects, and the relationship between the position of a stationary object and its movement from place to place. All confirm the presence of stability and coherence in the infant's perceptual world. In fact, Denis-Prinzhorn (1961) found that after infancy, there is even a trend toward over-constancy in size judgments.

Bower (1966, 1971) has conducted some ingenious experiments which show that the very young child is capable of more and finer discriminations than previously suspected, and can register most of the visual information adults can, though they are able to process and use lesser amounts.

If we now consider the data on early infant perception in conjunction with Gibson's (1969) work on perception of letters by means of their distinctive features, the conclusion might be irresistible that teachers could take advantage of this early development to begin teaching recognition of letters, word shapes etc. at a much younger age than is usually the case. Proponents of the academic preschool, for example, might see these studies as presenting yet further evidence that we are failing to capitalize on the young child's abilities and are wasting valuable years of potential learning in 'meaningless play.' Such a conclusion however would represent an inference from a limited segment of data. For one thing, we do not know precisely the operations of the perceptual mechanisms in the adult reader, much less how well such operations are matched in the perception of the young child. Most theorists in this area see the organism as inhabiting a world of 'noise' from which he needs to extract such information as will reduce his uncertainty about present and future events, but they disagree as to the mechanisms which are used to this end. Moray (1969) includes the following elements: mental concentration, vigilance (paying attention in the hope the event will occur), selective attention (selection of one of several messages to receive attention), search, activation (getting ready to deal with the event), and set (preparation to respond in a certain way) [p. 6]. Gibson (1970) isolates three attentional processes involved in extracting invariant information from the variable flux: perceptual abstraction of information from the context, filtering irrelevant aspects of stimulation, and active exploratory search. Filtering as a perceptive mechanism for reducing noise is the object of some dispute. First proposed by Broadbent (1958) and subsequently revised by him (1967, 1970) and by Triesman (1964) to account for the fact that information supposedly filtered out may reach the subject's attention under certain circumstances, the concept has been opposed by Deutsch and Deutsch (1963) who maintain that all stimuli reaching the senses are analyzed for meaning. Other writers view selective attention as testing and remembering one set of anticipations over another (Hochberg, 1970), or as the allocation of cognitive resources to a limited segment of the stimulus field (Neisser, 1967). Complementing his account of selective attention, Neisser presents a "fragment theory" to explain veridical perception from incomplete stimulus information; he suggests that set, familiarity, and context predispose the organism to perceive one stimulus configuration over another.

All these variables have implications for reading, and have indeed been discussed in relation to the perceptual mechanisms of the adult reader. Much of the work on perception cited in this section is relatively new and refers to the perceptual processes of adult subjects, but we do not know how well these descriptions fit the perception of the young child. Bower's work suggests that the infant's perception begins to approximate that of the adult in some respects at quite an early age, but we cannot be certain that this is true in all respects. The variables of set, familiarity, and context advanced by Neisser are likely to change with the child's developing cognitive and linguistic competencies. Further studies of both visual and auditory perception as it functions through the preschool and elementary school years are needed.

Piaget takes a different view of the early perceptual processes we have been discussing. For him they are not truly developmental, because they do not show sequential changes with age. They are "field effects," or basic organizing forces, part of the infant's initial equipment which have survival value for the individual and persist without appreciable change throughout life. By contrast, "perceptual regulations" begin to emerge around the age of three. During the preoperational period, when decentering of both perception and thought occur, the child becomes increasingly able to reverse figure and ground, to integrate parts and wholes and to scan configurations in systematic and novel ways. Perception is centered on the dominant aspects of the visual field, which tend to be overestimated, while the remaining elements are underestimated. Perceptual strategies such as exploration, reorganization, and schematization can compensate in part for the primary deformations, especially as these activities come more and more under the control of operational thought. From Piaget's theory of perception, it would follow then, that training in the above-mentioned perceptual activities after age 3 would be more valuable than early attention to reading *per se*. Elkind (1970) found that black second-grade children made more progress as a result of such training than a control group which received equal time in regular reading instruction.

Piaget's theory and research thus provide a counterbalance to the premature conclusion that the young child's perception is similar to the adult's, enabling him to accomplish the same tasks albeit at a more primitive level. Work by Vurpillot (1968), and some Soviet psychologists (Zaporozhets, 1969) support the developmental aspects of perception.

Cognition

At the other end of the sensation-cognition continuum we find that the most comprehensive framework for investigation has been provided by Piaget's theory. The genetic evolution of intelligence has been studied in the development of the child's concepts of conservation, causality, reality, and morality. Unlike his theory of perception, Piaget's theory of intelligence has not as yet been applied directly to reading, the probable reason being that in general, the visual decoding aspects of reading have received much greater attention than the processes of comprehension. One may speculate that the application of Piagetian cognitive theory to reading may open up a highly fruitful field of inquiry. Even at the practical level it seems reasonable to suppose that an understanding of the child's cognitive development in terms of Piaget's concepts would have implications for the kinds of reading materials suitable for different age groups. It would be premature to suggest what these might be, however, until a more complete rapprochement between cognitive psychology and the psychology of reading occurs.

Furth (1970) has made a broader application of Piaget's theory to reading and to education. The school, he believes, has failed in its primary mission, which is to produce citizens who are adept at solving problems. It goes without saying that our society is in desperate need of people who can solve scientific, technological, and social problems. Traditional education, with its emphasis on information gathering and respect for authority seems to be ill-equipped to fulfil this mission. Its task should be to give children opportunities for solving problems, to show them how to find alternative paths to the same goal, and to provide them with the tools for problem-solving. Reading would be such a tool—one of an entire arsenal. Unfortunately, as Furth sees it, the school has chosen to elevate the tools, especially reading, to the status of a major objective. It has lost sight of the end, and has substituted a means to the goal for the goal itself. Furth maintains that a school cannot gear its resources to the teaching of reading and at the same time expect to do an adequate job of teaching problem solving. This may seem an extreme statement to some teachers, but if one sees reading instruction as inexorably tied in with the lock-step curriculum, it becomes more acceptable. Furth expands on his major thesis to suggest a variety of ways in which the teacher may institute a curriculum which emphasizes problem solving by the children.

Thus, two authors, both working within a Piagetian framework, reach different conclusions about the teaching of reading. Elkind proposes perceptual training for some (perhaps all) children as a precursor to reading instruction in the early grades, while Furth seems to view reading as a skill which might well be acquired over the elementary years as an incidental tool for problem-solving.

Interestingly enough, Rohwer (1971), who specifically rejects the Piagetian notion of critical periods, has come to a similar conclusion based on different premises. In a recent article in the *Harvard Educational Review* entitled "Prime time for education—early childhood or adolescence?" Rohwer cites cognitively oriented preschool programs as the only kind which have produced demonstrable long-standing gains in achievement. However, his conclusion is not, as one might expect, that more programs of this kind are needed. On the contrary he maintains that very little of present-day elementary education is relevant to life outside the school, and should be radically changed to incorporate skills of discrimination, classification, communication, and problem-solving. All these skills, including the "sacred cow" of reading, should be learned not at a particular age laid down by society, but at the time the child can acquire the skills (and the prerequisite subskills) readily and successfully, a conclusion not too far removed from the general position assumed by Furth.

A consideration of some recent thinking in children's congnitive development thus presents us with a situation in which the reading teacher may derive two different conclusions from the same theory, or a similar conclusion from two different theoretical standpoints.

Language

A preoccupation with the child's perceptual and cognitive development may well lead to our placing primary emphasis on the decoding and word recognition aspects of reading. But the work of Chomsky and others on the generative nature of language has drawn attention to the role of linguistic and information-processing skills in reading. Kolers (1970), in an article entitled "Reading is only incidentally visual," cites evidence from several studies to show that good readers are faithful not to the words they see printed but to the substance of the message the words convey. Words are not neutral graphic stimuli awaiting translation into associated phonemes, for in order to identify them, one has to know something about them, e.g. that they belong to a certain language. Moreover, there is no necessary serial sequence in the rapid reader's scanning of text. He has mastered the art of selecting clues which enable him to process and assimilate the information directly into his own cognitive structures. In Smith's (1971) terms, the skilled reader goes directly to "immediate meaning," whereas the less fluent reader resorts to the "lower route" of "mediated meaning identification," which interposes a step of word-by-word identification. The implication is that reading instruction should move away somewhat from emphasis on visual recognition, and concentrate on search for clues and information-extracting skills, a suggestion which is congruent with Rohwer's idea of postponing reading until it is relevant to life tasks.

On the other hand, theories of language acquistion which were developed in the 1950s and 60s tended to emphasize the early formation of a complete grammar. Thus as late as 1966, McNeill (1966) was writing: "The fundamental problem to which we adress ourselves is the simple fact that language acquisition occurs in a surprisingly short time. Grammatical speech does not begin before 1½ years of age; yet as far as we can tell, the basic process is complete by 3½ years [p. 15]." Lenneberg (1967) also sees the period from 2-4 years as critical for language learning (although he does see primary language acquisition continuing until adolescence). From this fact one might be tempted to draw either of two conclusions. The first would be that the process of language acquisition is largely irrelevant to reading, since it is virtually complete before reading begins (Wardhaugh, 1971). The second would again emphasize the importance of early reading activity to capitalize on the rapid growth of language.

More recent work, while not discounting the importance of the early period, has restored some emphasis to the continued learning of grammar throughout the elementary school years. Numerous investigations have shown that significant language development occurs after age six. C. Chomsky (1969), for example, points out that several grammatical developments occur after age 6, a most striking example being growth in the use of pronouns. O'Donnell, Griffin, and Norris (1967) found acquisition of new transformations between grades 3 to 5 and 5 to 7, while Menyuk (1964) found examples of more complicated structures as age increased.

Hence inferences about reading based on the earlier position of the linguists are no longer tenable in the light of this more recent research.

Another aspect of language development which has current salience for reading practice is the issue of dialect. Many linguists appear to be discarding the notion of language deficit which was in vogue about five years ago. Rather they see the inner-city child as having a language system which is well developed both syntactically and semantically, which has some overlap with standard English, but also many differences. Since most school texts and other reading materials are in standard English, the issue becomes that of finding the most effective ways of introducing the dialect speaker to these standard materials. The various alternatives have been discussed by Wolfram (1970). If extant materials are retained, one may teach standard English, prior to reading, and the child may be asked to render these materials in standard English or in dialect form. The latter requires that the teacher be thoroughly familiar with the dialect in order to distinguish between the dialect rendition and genuine reading errors. If materials are revised, one may eliminate all features which may cause problems for the lower-class speaker (e.g. the possessive's), or one may construct beginning materials in dialect form with gradual transition to standard text. Wolfram concludes that, in spite of the outspoken rejection of dialect readers by some member of the black community, "the magnitude of the reading problem suggests that experiments must be made, with alternatives which may involve the potential changing of materials and curricula [p.22]." Another possible approach is to mix standard- and dialect-speaking children in the preschool to permit the latter to gain an understanding of standard English even though they do not use it in speech. While this may be a preferable alternative, it is probably not feasible on a large scale at this time.

On this particular issue, the educator may find that, however well-grounded in linguistic theory his inferences may be, he cannot translate them into practice without taking cognizance of the social and political context in which the school operates.

Motivation

Unfortunately there is no technical sense of "affection" corresponding to use of the term, "cognition": If there were, it would more accurately describe the complex of factors which might be considered under the present rubric.

The study of affective factors and their relationship to cognitive development has undergone considerable change in the last decade. In one sense with the current disillusionment with formal education, motivational aspects have come into prominence in such forms as humanistic education, sensitivity training, alternate universities, etc. On the other hand, the boom in cognitive psychology has deflected much research energy from the study of nonintellectual factors. If one wanted to trace the development of this movement away from the effective toward the cognitive, no doubt White's (1959) classic paper in which he elevated competence to the status of a primary drive would stand as a landmark. But the major source of the change is probably to be found in the current absorption with Piaget's cognitive theory. Piaget does not disregard the motivational aspects of thought; on the contrary he seems to consider motivation as an inherent and inseparable dimension of thought, in the sense that it is part of the ongoing process of intellectual activity. Perhaps the perennial difficulty of measurement in the affective domain is also partly responsible. Whatever the reasons, the fact remains that research on nonintellectual factors in learning seems to have suffered a relative decline. It is interesting to note that the 600-page report of the Literature Search project (Davis, 1971) which addressed itself to every facet of reading made only passing reference to the entire affective domain—a gross omission in my estimation. (The one exception being the paper by Entwisle, referred to below.)

I believe that there is a dimension here which is perhaps more difficult to take hold of, and therefore less rewarding in immediate payoff, but which nonetheless demands continuing attention. I have reviewed the literature on affective factors and reading elsewhere (Athey, 1970). Although it is plentiful, one misses the connecting thread of a good theory to make sense of the plethora of inconclusive and contradictory data. Perhaps such a theory, when we find it, will address itself to the changing motivations and how they affect learning at each age of the lifespan. Meanwhile, it is to be hoped that we will not lose sight of this important domain of inquiry.

Such a theory would need to explain the effects on learning of cultural and social class differences. These have been well-documented in relation to language and reading by Entwisle (1971), and include such variables as control beliefs (knowledge of one's ability to manipulate the environment to meet one's needs), self-confidence, inflexible family role learnings, and the like. Entwisle concludes from her review that "we can only meaningfully teach reading to lower class children when it begins to make sense of their lives [p. VI, 145]."

Conclusion

In this paper, I have discussed some recent literature in perception, cognition, language, and motivation as they pertain to reading. Such a review must of necessity be highly restricted in each area, but I chose to touch on all four areas deliberately, to make the point that the reading teacher, as well as the professor of education, needs not only to be cognizant of what is happening in these (and other) fields, but to keep some perspective among them. If we fail to keep this balance, we are at the mercy of temporary fads which offer panaceas on the basis of limited data.

If education is to be a science, it must progress in the same way other sciences do, by acquiring a systematic body of knowledge, rather than by chasing every fad which claims to have some scientific basis. Education is particularly vulnerable to faddism, because its sources of input are more numerous, but at the same time disparate. Consequently, educators need to be in one sense more open to new developments, and yet more defensive. They must scrutinize each innovation for its scientific underpinnings, and determine whether these conflict with what is known in other fields.

We lost the "whole child" in the 1950's, and are rebuilding him scientifically from our accumulated wisdom. Putting him together again promises to be a long and arduous, but rewarding, process.

REFERENCES

Athey, I. J. Affective factors in reading. In H. Singer & R. B. Ruddell (Eds.), *Theoretical models and processes of reading.* Newark, Del.: International Reading Association, 1970. Pp. 98-119.

Bower, T. G. R. The visual world of infants. *Scientific American,* 1966, *215* (6), 80-92.

Bower, T. G. R. The object in the world of the infant. *Scientific American,* 1971, *225* (4), 30-38.

Broadbent, D. E. *Perception and communication.* London: Pergamon Press, 1958.

Broadbent, D. E. Word frequency effect and response bias. *Psychological Review,* 1967, *74,* 1-15.

Broadbent, D. E. Stimulus set and response set: two kinds of selective attention. In D. I. Mostofsky (Ed.), Attention: contemporary theory and analysis. New York: Appleton-Century-Crofts, 1970.

Chomsky, C. S. *The acquisition of syntax in children from 5 to 10.* Cambridge, Mass.: M. I. T. Press, 1969.

Davis, F. B. *The literature on research in reading with emphasis on models.* New Brunswick, N.J.: Rutgers University, 1971.

Denis-Prinzhorn, M. Perception des distances et constance de grandeur (etude genetique). *Archives Psychol Geneve,* 1961.

Deutsch, J. A., & Deutsch, D. Attention: some theoretical considerations. *Psychological Review,* 1963, *70,* 80-90.

Elkind, D. Reading, logic, and perception. In D. Elkind (Ed.), *Children and adolescents.* New York: Oxford University Press, 1970.

Entwisle, D. Implications of language socialization for reading models and for learning to read. In F. B. Davis (Ed.), *The literature of research in reading with emphasis on models.* New Brunswick, N. J.: Rutgers University, 1971. Pp. 6/101-158.

Fantz, R. L. Visual perception and experience in infancy: issues and approaches. In F. A. Young & D. B. Lindsley (Eds.), *Early experience in visual information processing in perceptual and reading disorders.* Washington, D. C.: National Academy of Sciences, 1970. Pp. 351-381.

Furth, H. J. *Piaget for teachers.* Englewood Cliffs: Prentice-Hall, 1970.

Gibson, E. J. *Principles of perceptual learning and development.* New York: Meredith Corp., 1969.

Gibson, E. J. The development of perception as an adaptive process. *American Scientist,* 1970, *58,* 98-107.

Haber, R. N. *Information-processing approaches to visual perception.* New York: Holt, Rinehart and Winston, 1969.

Hochberg, J. Attention, organization, and consciousness. In D. I. Mostofsky (Ed.), *Attention: contemporary theory and analysis.* New York: Appleton-Century-Crofts, 1970.

Kolers, P. A. Reading is only incidentally visual. In K. Goodman & J. T. Fleming (Eds.), *Psycholinguistics and the teaching of reading.* Newark, Del.: International Reading Association, 1970. Pp. 8-16.

Lenneberg, E. H. *Biological foundations of language.* New York: Wiley, 1967.

McNeill, D. Developmental psycholinguistics. In F. Smith & G. A. Miller (Eds.), *The genesis of language: a psycholinguistic approach.* Cambridge, Mass.: M. I. T. Press, 1966. Pp. 15-84.

Menyuk, P. Alteration od rules in children's grammar. *Journal of Verbal Learning and Verbal Behavior,* 1964, *3,* 480-488.

Miranda, S. B. Visual abilities and pattern preferences of premature infants and full-term neonates. Unpublished manuscript, Case Western Reserve University, 1969.

Moray, N. *Attention: selective processes in vision and hearing.* New York: Academic Press, 1969.

Neisser, U. *Cognitive psychology.* New York: Appleton-Century-Crofts, 1967.

O'Donnell, R. C., Griffin, W. J., & Norris, R. C. A transformational analysis of written and oral grammatical structure in the language of children in grades 3, 5, and 7. *Journal of Educational Research,* 1967, *61,* 35-39.

Olson, W. C. *Child Development.* Boston: D. C. Heath, 1949.

Rohwer, W. D., Jr. Prime time for education—early childhood or adolescence? *Harvard Educational Review,* 1971, *42,* 316-341.

Rosenblum, L. A., & Cross, H. A. Performance of neonatal monkeys on the visual cliff situation. *American Journal of Psychology,* 1963, *76,* 318-320.

Smith, F. *Understanding reading.* New York: Holt, Rinehart and Winston, 1971.

Triesman, A. M. Selective attention in man. *British Medical Bulletin,* 1964, *20,* 12-16.

Vurpillot, E. The development of scanning strategies and their relation to visual differentation. *Journal of Experimental Child Psychology,* 1968, *6,* 632-650.

Walk, R. D. The development of depth perception in animals and human infants. In H. W. Stevenson (Ed.), *Concept of development.* Society for Research in Child Development Monograph No. 107, 1966, *31*, 82-108.

Walk, R. D., & Gibson, E. J. A comparative and analytic study of visual depth perception. *Psychological Monographs,* 1961, *75*(15).

Wardhaugh, R. Theories of language acquisition in relation to beginning reading instruction. *Reading Research Quarterly,* 1961, *7*, 168-194.

White, R. W. Motivation reconsidered: the concept of competence. *Psychological Review,* 1959, *66*, 297-333.

Wolfram, W. Sociolinguistic alternatives in teaching reading to nonstandard speakers. *Reading Research Quarterly,* 1970, *6*, 9-33.

Zaporozhets, A. V. Some of the psychological problems of sensory training in early childhood and the preschool period. In M. Cole & I. Maltzman (Eds.), *A handbook of contemporary Soviet psychology.* New York: Basic Books, 1969. Pp. 86-120.

Author Index

743

AUTHOR INDEX

Content Index*

*This Content Index has been developed on the basis of major categories related to various aspects of the reading process. Note that subcategories are cross referenced and listed alphabetically for the reader's convenience.